INTERMEDIATE

The IDEA MAGAZINE FOR TEACHERS® MAILBOX®

2010–2011 YEARBOOK

The Education Center, Inc.
Greensboro, North Carolina

The Mailbox® *2010–2011 Intermediate Yearbook*

ISBN 978-1-61276-141-1
ISSN 1088-5552

Printed in the United States of America.

The Mailbox® Yearbook
PO Box 6189
Harlan, IA 51593-1689

HPS 232521

Contents

Reading and Language Arts

Reading and Language Arts TIPS & TOOLS

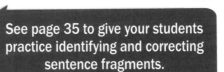

Reading Reactions

Literary response

Want your students to write meaningful reading responses? Try this! Have each child tape a copy of page 18 inside her journal. When it's time for the student to write about her reading, she chooses a prompt from the column for that day of the week. Then she lists the prompt's number in her journal and writes a thoughtful response.

Angelique Kwabenah, Potomac Landing Elementary
Fort Washington, MD

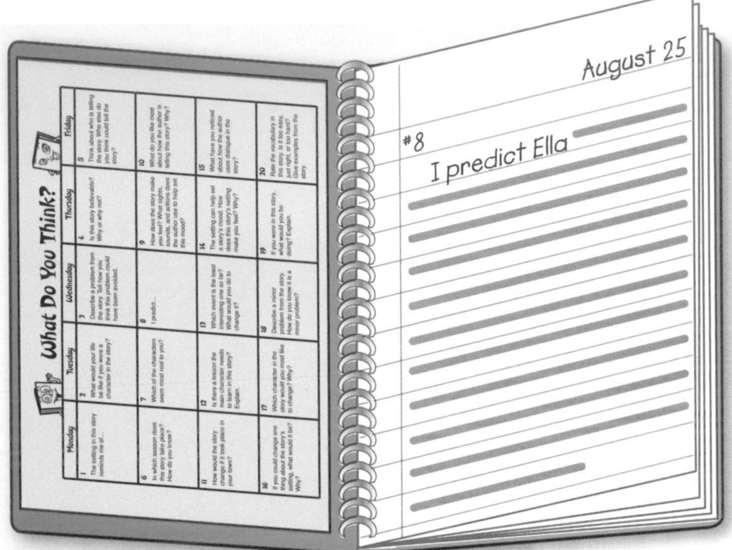

See page 35 to give your students practice identifying and correcting sentence fragments.

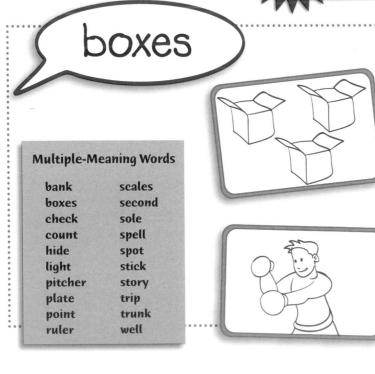

boxes

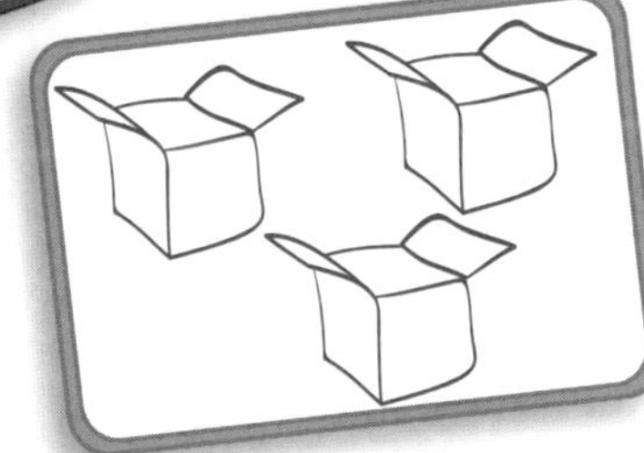

Multiple-Meaning Words

bank	scales
boxes	second
check	sole
count	spell
hide	spot
light	stick
pitcher	story
plate	trip
point	trunk
ruler	well

Quick Draw

Multiple-meaning words

To set up this activity, give each student a dry-erase board, a wipe-off marker, and an eraser. Next, announce a multiple-meaning word. Then set a timer for 30 seconds and have each student draw a sketch that shows what the word means. At the end of the time, have students display their sketches, and observe how they show the word's different meanings. If all the sketches show the same meaning, have students look up the word in the dictionary to discover and then quickly sketch the word's other definition(s). Then have students wipe their boards clean and repeat as time allows.

Stella Loveland, Russell Cave Elementary, Lexington, KY

Brick by Brick

Plural nouns

Just copy and cut apart the cards on page 19 to set up this easy-to-use center. A student reads each noun card and places it next to the brick that tells how to spell the word's plural form. To record his work, the child draws a four-column chart, labels it as shown, and writes the plural form of each noun in its appropriate column.

Linda Briggs, Oak Grove East, Bartonville, IL

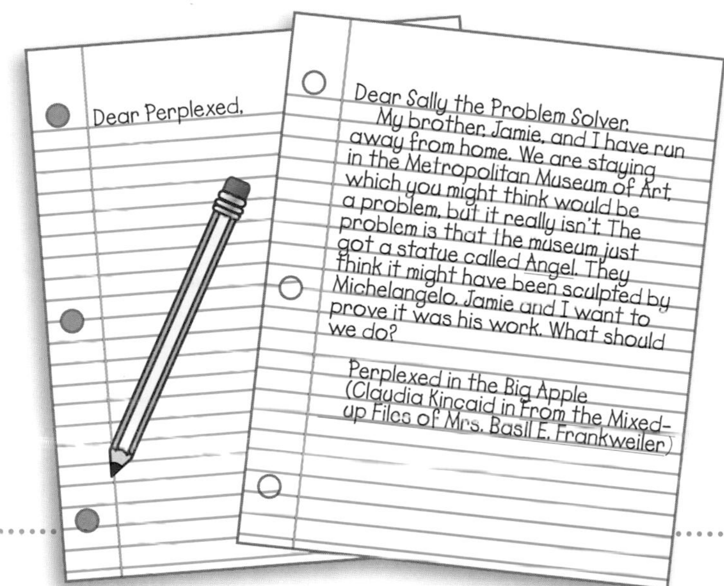

Dear Perplexed,

Dear Sally the Problem Solver,
My brother, Jamie, and I have run away from home. We are staying in the Metropolitan Museum of Art, which you might think would be a problem, but it really isn't. The problem is that the museum just got a statue called Angel. They think it might have been sculpted by Michelangelo. Jamie and I want to prove it was his work. What should we do?

Perplexed in the Big Apple
(Claudia Kincaid in From the Mixed-up Files of Mrs. Basil E. Frankweiler)

In a Quandary

Problem and solution

For this idea, share with students the letters and responses from a children's magazine advice column, such as "Ask Arizona" in *Highlights* magazine. Next, guide students to identify the main problem in a current reading. Then have each child write a letter asking for help with the problem from the main character to an imaginary advice columnist named Sally the Problem Solver. After the student finishes her letter, she trades papers with a partner, assumes the role of Sally, and writes a response describing her ideas for solving the problem.

Courtney English, Southeast Middle School, Salisbury, NC

Spelling by Committee

Spelling

Make weekly spelling words unforgettable by having your students introduce them! Assign each small group of students several of the words from the week's list and give them a few minutes to plan a presentation that highlights the words' spelling patterns. The group might lead a cheer, give a dramatic reading, chant spelling hints, sing a song, or do a dance. Then have each group introduce its words while the remaining students take notes.

Isobel L. Livingstone, Rahway, NJ

EY! EY!
We've got hockey: h-o-c-k-e-y.
We've got valley: v-a-l-l-e-y.
We've got money: m-o-n-e-y.
EY! EY!

Reading and Language Arts TIPS & TOOLS

"Ad-onyms"

Synonyms, antonyms

Stock a center with advertising inserts from a newspaper along with a thesaurus, small sticky notes, crayons, and unlined paper. A pair of students chooses an ad and then looks up the ad's main words in the thesaurus. If a word has synonyms, the partners choose one that fits the ad. Next, they write the synonym on a sticky note and place the note over the word. Then the duo re-creates the ad using the synonyms in place of the original words. If time allows, the partners remove the sticky notes and repeat the exercise using antonyms instead of synonyms. For a fun display, post students' work along with the original ads on a board titled "'Ad-onyms.'"

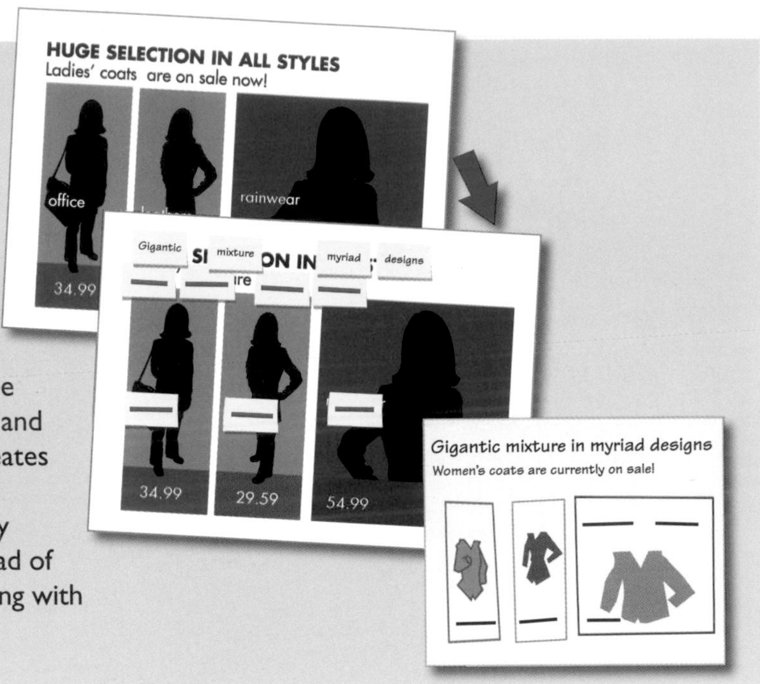

The Inside Story

Literature response, plot

For this no-hassle book project, have each student fold a sheet of legal-size paper as shown. Next, guide the child to illustrate on the folded paper his book's most interesting or exciting event *(the climax)*. Then have him open the paper and summarize the story's plot inside.

adapted from an idea by Terry Healy
Marlatt Elementary, Manhattan, KS

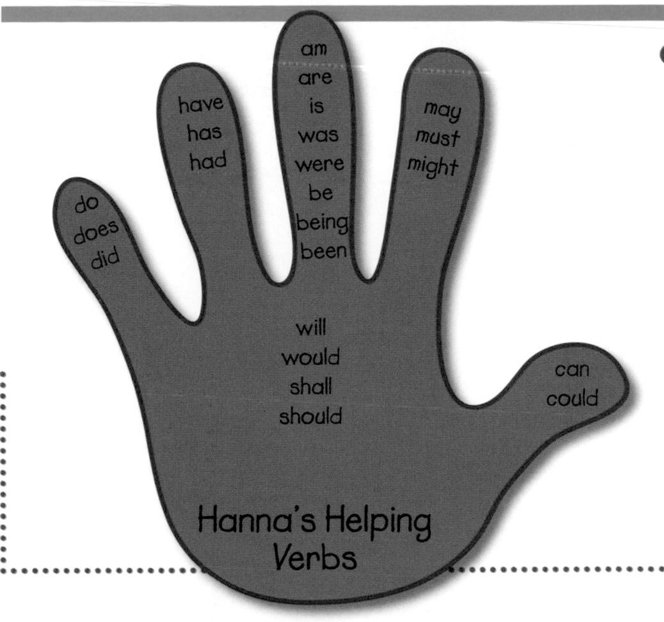

Keep 'em Handy!

Helping verbs

Give students a hand when it comes to identifying helping verbs! First, review the verbs with students. Then have each student trace her hand on construction paper and cut out the shape. Next, have the child title the shape, add her name, and record the helping verbs to make a handy reference!

Gina Carter
St. Augustine School
Lebanon, KY

Editor's Tip:
To make a class poster, project a tracing of your hand onto bulletin board paper. Trace and cut out the outline. Then list the helping verbs and display the poster!

A Very-Long-Word Contest

Building vocabulary

With this activity, students learn to appreciate long words rather than avoid them. To begin, have students predict what the adjective sesquipedalian (ses-kwə-pə-dāl-yən) might describe. Explain that the word can be used to describe very long words or someone who uses them. Next, guide each child to look for very long words when he reads, recording and describing the words on a copy of page 20 as directed. At the end of the day, or after several days, have students share and compare their words. Then award a small prize to the child who found the longest word. Repeat periodically to encourage your sesquipedalian-word hunters!

Juanita Winner, Wrightsville Beach Elementary, Wrightsville Beach, NC

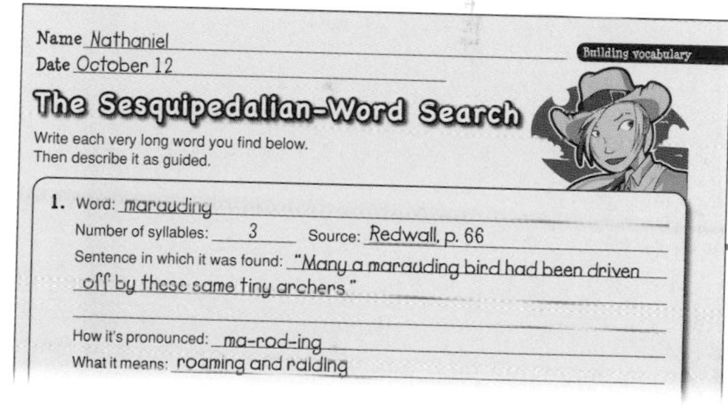
Name Nathaniel
Date October 12
Building vocabulary
The Sesquipedalian-Word Search
Write each very long word you find below.
Then describe it as guided.
1. Word: marauding
Number of syllables: 3 Source: Redwall, p. 66
Sentence in which it was found: "Many a marauding bird had been driven off by these same tiny archers."
How it's pronounced: ma-rod-ing
What it means: roaming and raiding

Candy-Coated Connections

Making text connections

Here's an idea perfect for motivating students in small groups to make meaningful reading connections. Before the session, purchase a bag of small, individually wrapped candies. Next, display a code that matches the candies' colors, such as the one shown. During the small-group session, pause periodically and have each student take a candy (without seeing its color) from the bag. Then guide the child to check the code and describe a matching connection she can make about the reading. Follow up by having students write about their connections as they enjoy their candy.

Kelly Shock, Clinton Valley Elementary, Mount Clemens, MI

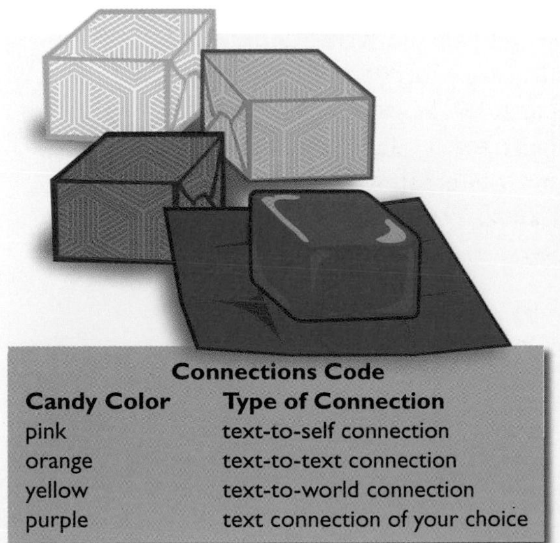

Connections Code

Candy Color	Type of Connection
pink	text-to-self connection
orange	text-to-text connection
yellow	text-to-world connection
purple	text connection of your choice

Reading and Language Arts TIPS & TOOLS

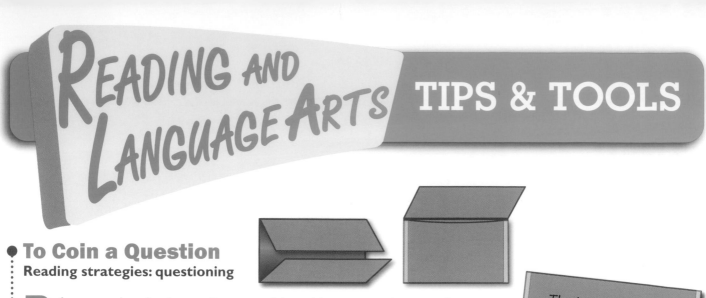

To Coin a Question
Reading strategies: questioning

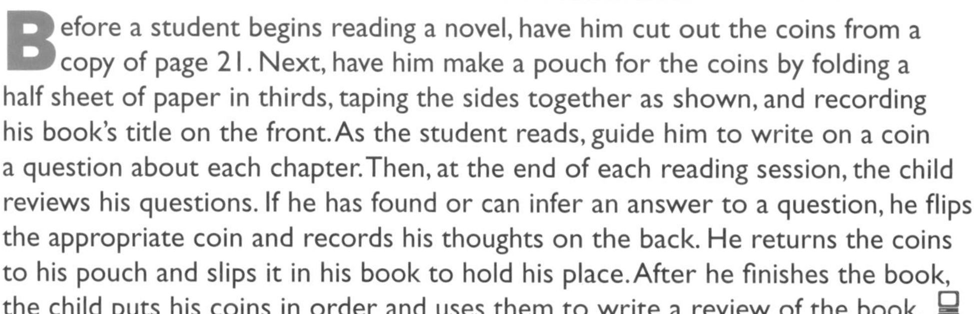

Before a student begins reading a novel, have him cut out the coins from a copy of page 21. Next, have him make a pouch for the coins by folding a half sheet of paper in thirds, taping the sides together as shown, and recording his book's title on the front. As the student reads, guide him to write on a coin a question about each chapter. Then, at the end of each reading session, the child reviews his questions. If he has found or can infer an answer to a question, he flips the appropriate coin and records his thoughts on the back. He returns the coins to his pouch and slips it in his book to hold his place. After he finishes the book, the child puts his coins in order and uses them to write a review of the book.

inspired by an idea from Kathleen Bulter, Meadows Elementary, Millbrae, CA

Amizarwazwer B. Beingbin
Verbs

Want to help your students remember the forms of the verb *be?* Start by listing the verbs in a rush so that "am, is, are, was, were, be, being, been" sounds like the name Amizarwazwer B. Beingbin. Next, ask each student to sketch this mystery person as you repeat the name. After several repetitions, begin saying the name a little slower until students realize you are actually listing the verbs. Then have students repeat after you, saying the name in a rush and then clearly naming each verb. What a fun way to remember the forms of *be!*

Maria Bickel, Myerstown, PA

Off the Top of My Head
Prepositional phrases

Take the struggle out of teaching prepositional phrases with this whole-class game. To play, have each student secretly choose an object in the classroom and record its name on an index card. Next, guide the child to write three or more prepositional phrases that give clues about the object's location and underline each preposition. Then have a volunteer read her clues aloud, emphasizing the prepositions, and challenge the class to name the object. Repeat as time allows.

Joseph Lemmo, Chapman Intermediate, Woodstock, GA

our clock
inside the classroom
on the wall
below the ceiling
at the front
between two posters
above the board

Read, Flag, Write

Summarizing

Use sticky notes to help your students figure out what belongs in their summaries. To begin, have each student read a multiparagraph selection. Next, have the child cut small sticky notes into strips so that he has a strip for each of the article's paragraphs. Then have the student follow the directions below.

Steps:

1. Stick one flag next to the first sentence in each paragraph. Read each sentence you flagged.
2. If the sentence gives the paragraph's main idea, leave the flag.
3. If the sentence does not give the paragraph's main idea, move the flag to the next sentence. Read the sentence and decide whether it is the main idea.
4. Repeat until you have flagged each paragraph's main idea.
5. Use the flagged sentences and your own words to summarize the selection.

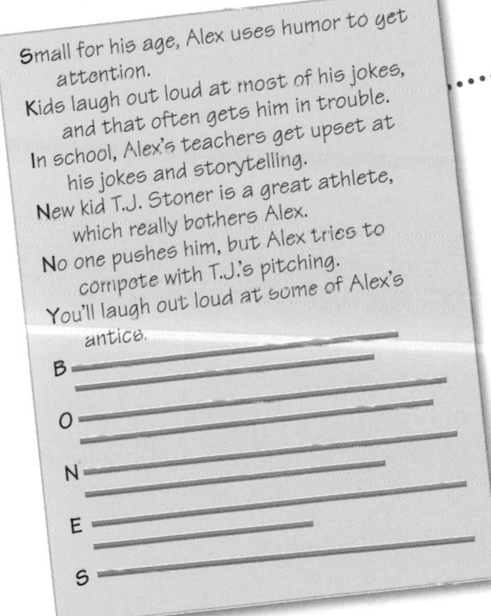

Small for his age, Alex uses humor to get attention.
Kids laugh out loud at most of his jokes, and that often gets him in trouble.
In school, Alex's teachers get upset at his jokes and storytelling.
New kid T.J. Stoner is a great athlete, which really bothers Alex.
No one pushes him, but Alex tries to compete with T.J.'s pitching.
You'll laugh out loud at some of Alex's antics.

B
O
N
E
S

A Poetic Reaction

Literary response

Looking for a unique yet simple book report idea? Try these acrostic reports! Have each student list the title of her book vertically and then write a sentence about the book that begins with each letter of the title. To extend the exercise, challenge the student to jot the author's name vertically and then write a sentence beginning with each letter that describes the author's style or purpose.

Danika Ripley, Frank M. Sokolowski School, Chelsea, MA

And the Next Letter Is...

Spelling practice

For this variation on the Sparkle game, students spell the words from your weekly spelling list letter by letter. Before playing, tell each student that he will be called on to name the next letter of the word. If the letter he needs to say is e, he says *buzz* instead. To begin playing, announce a word and then direct individual students to spell it.

Michael Foster, Heartland Elementary, Overland Park, KS

For a great practice grid on Greek and Latin roots, flip to page 42!

Reading and Language Arts TIPS & TOOLS

Tell and Retell
Fiction analysis

For this partner activity, have each pair of students cut out and fold a copy of page 22 as guided to make a storyteller. Then have the partners take turns manipulating the storyteller to select four questions or prompts about a current class reading. After reading each one, the students discuss and then record their answers.

Tracy Baggott, Little River Elementary, Orlando, FL

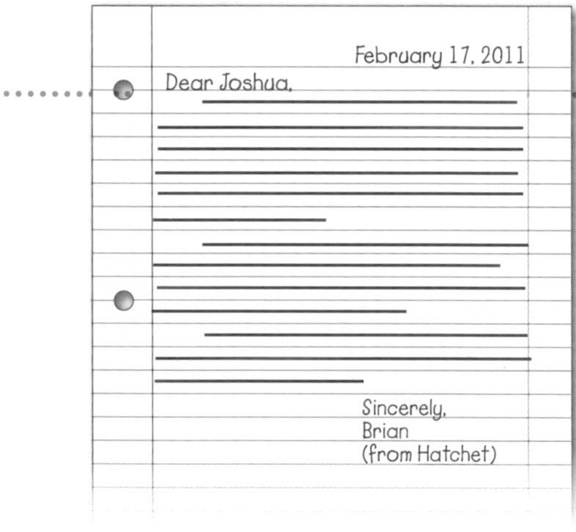

Dear Reader
Character analysis

Count on this letter-writing idea to engage students in analyzing a character's point of view. Guide each child to choose a character from a current reading and then imagine what he or she feels during the story. Next, have the student write a friendly letter to himself, pretending that the character is the letter writer. As time allows, have each child share his letter with students who have read the same story.

Kathleen Scavone, Coyote Valley Elementary, Middletown, CA

How Does It Feel?
Mood

Help students identify the pieces that create a story's mood. Begin by having each student cut out four same-size heart shapes. Next, guide the child to label each shape as shown and staple the hearts together to make a booklet. Then, as the child reads, she jots notes about the story's setting, the author's style, and her own feelings. After reading, each student reviews her notes and determines the story's mood, recording it on the last page of the booklet.

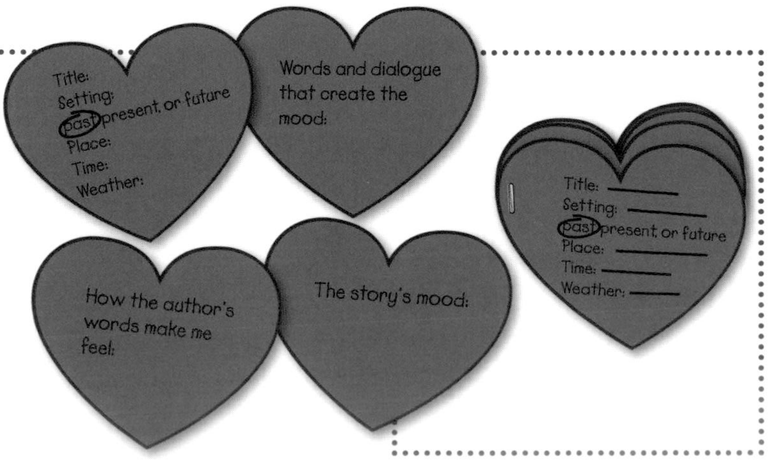

Lift and Learn

Building vocabulary

For this easy-to-maintain center, cut five sheets of construction paper in half and fold each piece in half to make a card. Then glue a copy of a vocabulary activity card from page 23 inside each card as shown. Staple the cards onto a bulletin board along with a current list of spelling or vocabulary words. At the board, each student lifts a flap, records the activity number on his paper, and completes the task as guided. When students learn the posted words, simply replace the list.

adapted from an idea by Mary Beth Smith, Davidson Elementary
Water Valley, MS

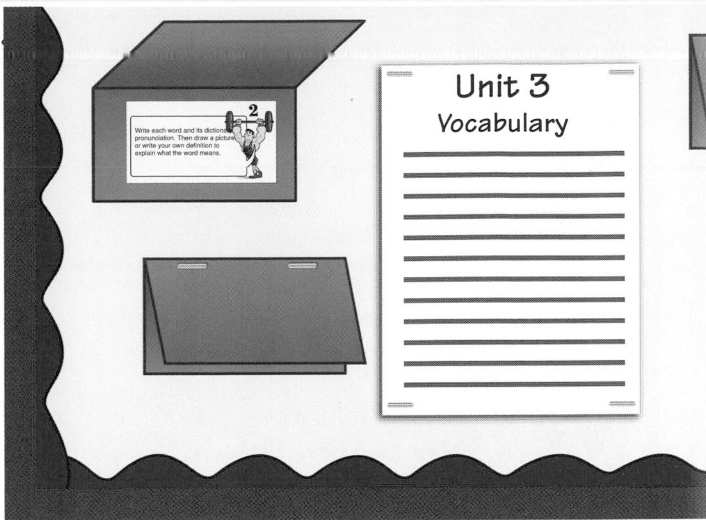

Stand Up!

Parts of speech

Here's an active review you can use anytime! Announce two parts of speech categories, such as past and present tense verbs. Then direct students to stand when you name a word from one category and sit when you say a word from the other. If a student sits or stands incorrectly, he sits out the rest of the round. (To keep everyone involved, start the next round as soon as a few students are sitting down.)

Angela Williams, Atoka Elementary, Atoka, OK

PARTS OF SPEECH CATEGORIES

nouns or verbs
singular or plural nouns
pronouns or common nouns
proper or common nouns
concrete or abstract nouns
regular or irregular verbs
past or present tense verbs
comparative or superlative adjectives

Just-the-Facts Jigsaw

Outlining, main idea

Use the jigsaw strategy to give students firsthand practice with outlining. Before reading a nonfiction selection, divide it into six parts. Have each student label small sticky notes with roman numerals I through VI and put one note on the selection at the beginning of each section. Then divide the class into groups of six and have each member read a different section.

Next, have each child meet with the other students who read the same section. The new group identifies its section's main idea and supporting details. Each student writes her roman numeral on an index card and records the main idea. Then she lists each supporting detail beside a capital letter. After that, all students return to their original groups. In the groups, the students share their outline sections, in turn, while the other group members record the outlined sections on their own cards. When students finish, each one has six cards that outline the selection!

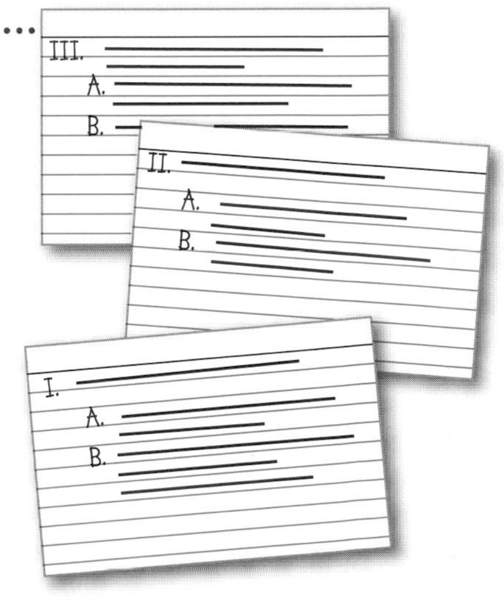

Susan Hass, Shields Elementary, Saginaw, MI

Reading and Language Arts TIPS & TOOLS

In Between
Making inferences

Want to make sure your students are thinking between the lines? Try this! Give each child a copy of the organizer on page 24 when you make a reading assignment. As students read, have them stop every five minutes to recognize and record the inferences they are making. At the end of the session, have each child share his inferences in a small group.

adapted from an idea by Colleen Dabney, Williamsburg, VA

Word-Watching Week
Vocabulary

Here's a fun idea for building students' vocabulary. Each day for a week, have each student list the alphabet on a sheet of paper, leaving space beside each letter for writing. Then announce a category for the day (see the list). Challenge students to write items from the category that begin with each letter of the alphabet, filling in as many lines on their papers as possible.

Day 1: Homophone Hullabaloo
Students list homophone pairs *(awl/all, bear/bare, carat/carrot, deer/dear,…)*.

Day 2: Palindrome Party
Students list words spelled the same forward and backward *(Anna, bob, civic, dad,…)*.

Day 3: In the "Sport-light"
Students list words about sports and games *(athlete, basketball, coach, dribble,…)*.

Day 4: Short-Stuff Day
Students list acronyms or abbreviations and the words for which they stand *(AWOL, Absent Without Leave; blvd., boulevard; cm, centimeter; DC, District of Columbia;…)*.

Day 5: Salad Day
Students list fruits and vegetables *(avocado, banana, carrot, date,…)*.

Extra! Extra!
Responding to literature

With this book report idea, students create newspapers that tell all about the books they've read. For each project, have a child fold a large sheet of construction paper in half and then follow the directions on a copy of page 25. When she's finished, have her read one article from her newspaper aloud. Then post students' work on a board titled "Read All About It!"

Editor's Tip:
To grade students' work, use each student's copy of page 25 as a checklist and award up to ten points for each item.

Got Five Minutes?

Vocabulary, spelling

Use a set of alphabet, Bananagram, or Scrabble tiles for this anytime activity. First, draw a tile and write its letter on the board. Add a squiggle line and then draw another tile. Write this letter at the end of the squiggle line and challenge each pair of students to list words that begin and end with the letters. Then have students share their lists and record the words on the board. Award a point for each correctly spelled word and repeat as time allows. When time's up, declare the partners with the most points the day's Word Wizards.

Cynthia Mosley, Durham, NC

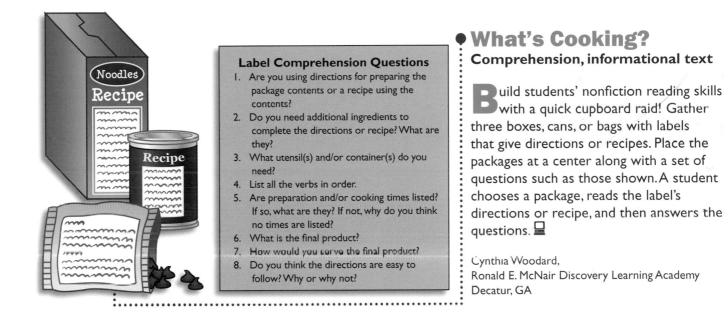

Label Comprehension Questions

1. Are you using directions for preparing the package contents or a recipe using the contents?
2. Do you need additional ingredients to complete the directions or recipe? What are they?
3. What utensil(s) and/or container(s) do you need?
4. List all the verbs in order.
5. Are preparation and/or cooking times listed? If so, what are they? If not, why do you think no times are listed?
6. What is the final product?
7. How would you serve the final product?
8. Do you think the directions are easy to follow? Why or why not?

What's Cooking?

Comprehension, informational text

Build students' nonfiction reading skills with a quick cupboard raid! Gather three boxes, cans, or bags with labels that give directions or recipes. Place the packages at a center along with a set of questions such as those shown. A student chooses a package, reads the label's directions or recipe, and then answers the questions.

Cynthia Woodard,
Ronald E. McNair Discovery Learning Academy
Decatur, GA

Carefully Sorted

Adverbs

To help students understand adverbs, post a list of verbs such as those shown. Next, have each child fold a sheet of paper in thirds and label the columns as shown. Then have the student cut apart the adverb strips from a copy of page 26. Guide the child to read each adverb with a verb and then glue the strip in the column that shows which question the adverb answers. When the child finishes, have him choose four adverbs from each column and use each one in a different sentence.

Alice Derrick, Eastside Elementary, Clinton, MS

Verbs

rush
scramble
shuffle
cheer
stretch
tug
watch
convince
think
trudge
bump
stroll
dribble
speak
draw
whisper

When?	Where?	How?
never	down	too
early	above	skillfully
now	outside	quietly

Reading and Language Arts TIPS & TOOLS

Teeny, Tiny Tongue Twisters
Alliteration

For this fun figurative language idea, display the chart shown. For each column, lead students to brainstorm words that begin with a specific letter. Next, use the words to write a class tongue twister. Then have each student draw the chart, choose a letter, fill in her chart, and write five tongue twisters of her own. As time allows, have each student choose her favorite tongue twister, read it aloud, and challenge the class to repeat it three times.

Natalie Hughes-Tanner, Ermel Elementary, Houston, TX

Who?	Does What?	How?	Where?	When?
Susie	swims	slowly	swamp	sometime
Santa	sleeps	sadly	sandbox	soon
Sid the snake	sings	silently	Sahara Desert	Saturday
Sir Smith	slides	swiftly	San Antonio	Sunday

Sid the snake swims swiftly through San Antonio every Saturday.

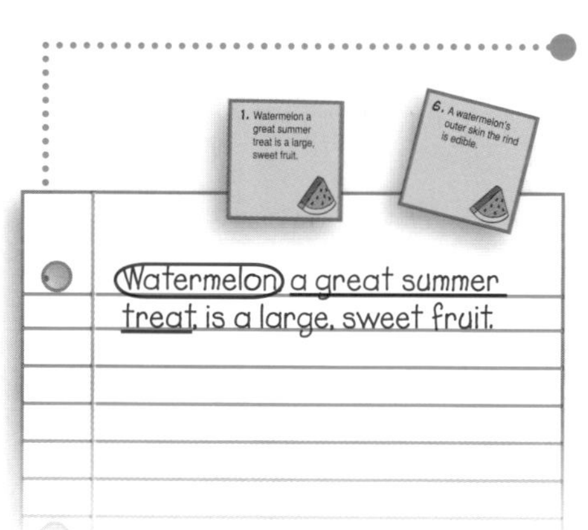

Watermelon a great summer treat is a large, sweet fruit.

Positive Practice
Identifying, punctuating appositives

This easy-to-prepare partner game helps students learn to spot and punctuate appositives. Have each pair of students cut apart the cards and answer key on a copy of page 27 and then follow the directions below.

Directions:
1. Stack the cards facedown and set the key aside.
2. When it is your turn, draw a card. Copy the sentence on your paper.
3. Circle the sentence's simple subject. Find the appositive word or phrase that renames the subject. Underline the appositive. Then add commas to set off the appositive.
4. Have your partner check the key. If your answer is correct, keep the card. If your answer is incorrect, put the card at the bottom of the stack. Your turn is over.
5. Continue until all the cards have been played. The player with more cards wins.

Shop Talk
Drawing conclusions

To give students real-world practice drawing conclusions, try this. From a catalog, choose ten different items that have detailed descriptions. Next, read aloud one object's description without naming the object. Then challenge each child to name the item as specifically as she can and record her conclusion. After that, read the description again and guide each student to explain her reasoning and cite the details that support her deduction. Reveal the item and then repeat the activity with the remaining catalog descriptions.

Your favorite youngster will love this charming analog with its amusing and lively theme. The round gold-tone case includes three-hand movement, dot markers, and numbers at twelve, three, six, and nine. Coordinating colorful daisy and gold-tone link bracelet.

Spell and Tell

Spelling

For this anytime review, divide students into two groups: spellers and tellers. Then announce a word from a current spelling list. Have the spellers agree on the word's spelling and announce it; then the tellers decide whether it's correct. If the tellers think the spelling is correct, they give thumbs-up signals. If the word was spelled correctly, award each group a point. If the groups aren't correct, don't award any points. When the tellers think the spellers are incorrect, they give thumbs-down signals and then spell the word. Award a point to the group that spells the word correctly. If both groups are wrong, announce the correct spelling and repeat the word later in the game. When time's up, declare the group with more points spelling champs for the day.

Joyce Hovanec, Glassport Elementary, Glassport, PA

Wherever.

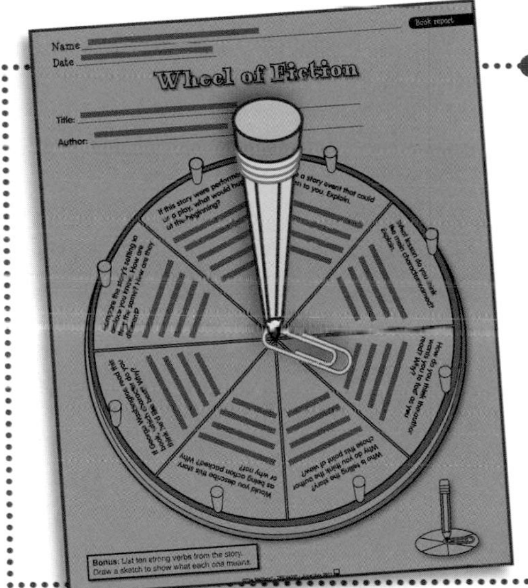

Wheel of Fiction

Literary response

Take this book report idea for a spin! Have each child write about his reading as guided on a copy of page 28. When it's time to share students' work, have each child spin a paper clip on his page and then read aloud his response in the section on which the clip lands.

Colleen Dabney, Williamsburg, VA

Editor's Tip:
Use copies of page 28 to help students prepare for discussions on class readings. Then just spin to get the conversation started!

The Story's the Same...

Using a thesaurus

Want to give students practice using a thesaurus? Give each small group of students a familiar picture book and a thesaurus. Then guide the group to rewrite the book, replacing its nouns, verbs, adjectives, and adverbs with synonyms. Have the students write their revised text on large sticky notes and put each note on the appropriate page. Next, have the students in each group practice reading their version of the story and then share it with the rest of the class. **For a technological twist,** show students how to use the thesaurus feature in your word processing program. Then have the students in each group type their book's text in the program, highlight the words they want to replace, choose synonyms, and replace them.

Flip to page 57 for fun practice on idioms!

What Do You Think?

Monday	Tuesday	Wednesday	Thursday	Friday
1 The setting in this story reminds me of…	2 What would your life be like if you were a character in the story?	3 Describe a problem from the story. Tell how you think this problem could have been avoided.	4 Is this story believable? Why or why not?	5 Think about who is telling the story. Who else do you think could tell the story?
6 In which season does this story take place? How do you know?	7 Which of the characters seem most real to you?	8 I predict…	9 How does the story make you feel? What sights, sounds, and actions does the author use to help set this mood?	10 What do you like most about how the author is telling this story? Why?
11 How would the story change if it took place in your town?	12 Is there a lesson the main character needs to learn in this story? Explain.	13 Which event is the least interesting one so far? What would you do to change it?	14 The setting can help set a story's mood. How does this story's setting make you feel? Why?	15 What have you noticed about how the author uses dialogue in the story?
16 If you could change one thing about the story's setting, what would it be? Why?	17 Which character in the story would you most like to change? Why?	18 Describe a minor problem from the story. How do you know it is a minor problem?	19 If you were in this story, what would you be doing? Explain.	20 Rate the vocabulary in this story. Is it too easy, just right, or too hard? Give examples from the story.

Note to the teacher: Use with "Reading Reactions" on page 6.

Brick and Wall Cards

Use with "Brick by Brick" on page 7.

journey	brush	company	lunch	woman
century	toolbox	birthday	bus	battery
fax	holiday	mouse	property	equinox
recess	alley	goose	activity	wrench
highway	buzz	valley	tooth	strategy

The plural forms of some nouns are irregular.

If the noun ends in a consonant and then y, change the y to *i* and add *es*.

If the noun ends in a vowel and then y, add *s*.

If the noun ends in *sh*, *ch*, *x*, *s*, or *z*, add *es*.

Only 3,236,401 bricks to go!

Name ______________________________

Date ______________________________

The Sesquipedalian-Word Search

Write each very long word you find below.
Then describe it as guided.

1. Word: ______________________________

Number of syllables: __________ Source: ______________________________

Sentence in which it was found: ______________________________

____

____

How it's pronounced: ______________________________

What it means: ______________________________

____

2. Word: ______________________________

Number of syllables: __________ Source: ______________________________

Sentence in which it was found: ______________________________

____

____

How it's pronounced: ______________________________

What it means: ______________________________

____

3. Word: ______________________________

Number of syllables: __________ Source: ______________________________

Sentence in which it was found: ______________________________

____

____

How it's pronounced: ______________________________

What it means: ______________________________

____

Note to the teacher: Use with "A Very-Long-Word Contest" on page 9.

Coin Patterns

Use with "To Coin a Question" on page 10.

Chapter

TEC44052

Chapter

TEC44052

Chapter

TEC44052

Chapter

TEC44052

Chapter

TEC44052

Chapter

TEC44052

Chapter

TEC44052

Chapter

TEC44052

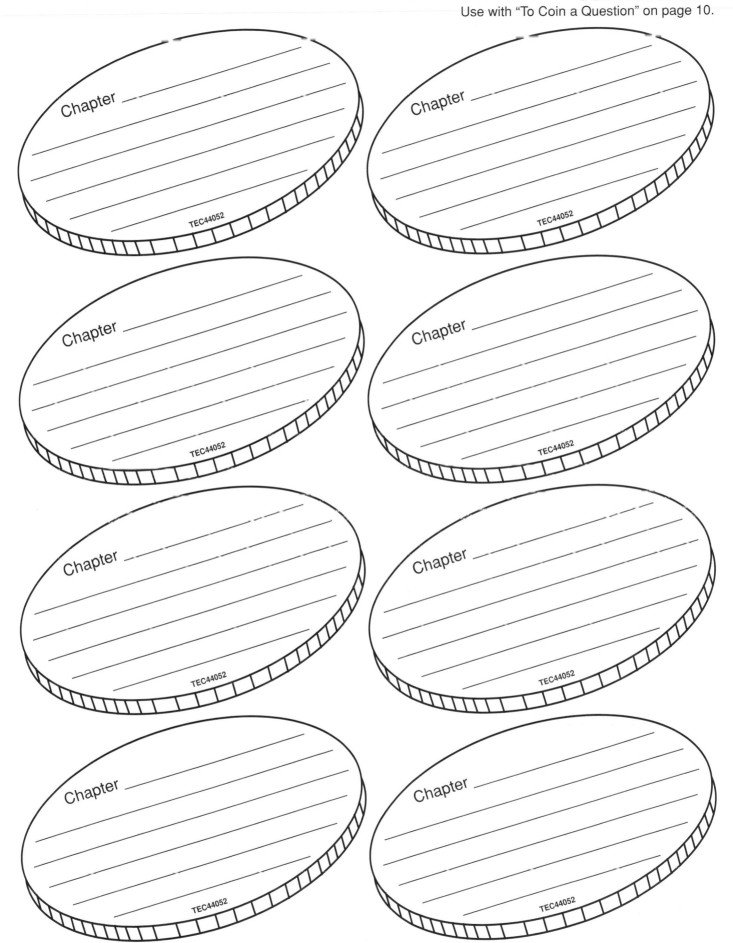

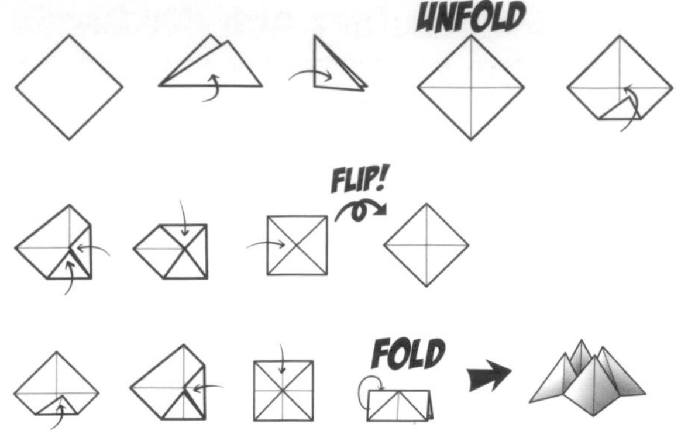

Fiction Storyteller

Folding directions:

1. Cut out the pattern. With the print side facedown, fold the bottom corner to the top corner, making a triangle. Fold the triangle in half. Then unfold the cutout.
2. Fold the bottom corner to the center fold line. Repeat with each corner to make a small square. Then flip the square.
3. Fold the bottom corner to the center fold line. Repeat with each corner to make a smaller square.
4. Fold the square in half. Open the square, rotate it, and fold it in half again. Then pull the corners out to make spaces for your fingers as shown.

1 2 3 4 5 6 7 8

A B C D E F G H

A. Is the main character very much like you or very different from you? Explain.

B. Think about who is telling the story. Who else do you think could tell the story? Explain.

C. Describe a problem from the story. Tell how you think this problem could have been avoided.

D. Would you describe the author's tone as serious or humorous? Explain.

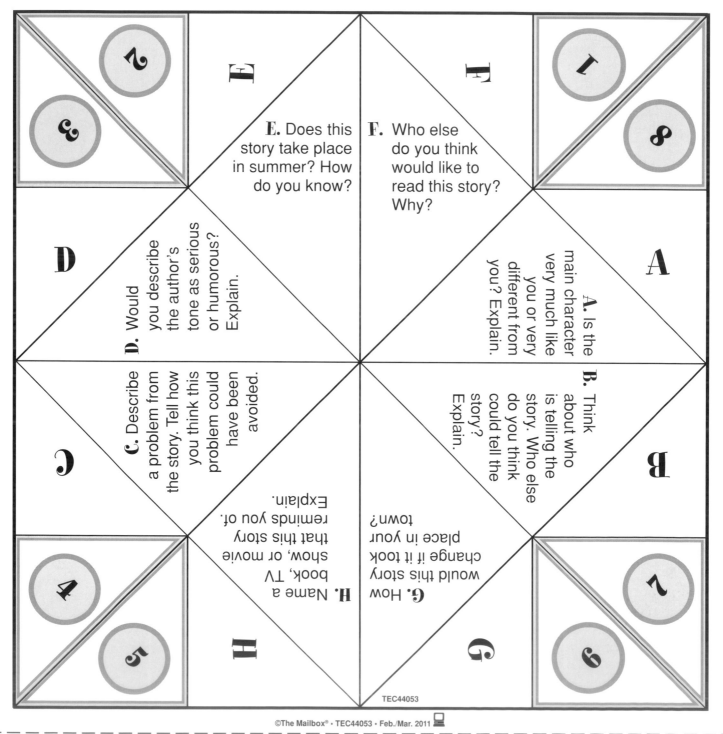

E. Does this story take place in summer? How do you know?

F. Who else do you think would like to read this story? Why?

G. How would this story change if it took place in your town?

H. Name a book, TV show, or movie that this story reminds you of. Explain.

TEC44053

Note to the teacher: Use with "Tell and Retell" on page 12.

Vocabulary Activity Cards

Use with "Lift and Learn" on page 13.

1

Write a true or false statement using each word. Underline the word. Then tell whether the statement is true or false.

Examples: I heard a frog <u>croak</u> when I walked by the pond. (true) The frog's <u>croak</u> is a soft, sweet sound. (false)

TEC44053

2

Write each word and its dictionary pronunciation. Then draw a picture or write your own definition to explain what the word means.

TEC44053

3

Write each word on a paper strip. Next, look up the words in a thesaurus. If a word is listed, write three of its synonyms on different paper strips. Then staple all the strips together to form a paper chain.

TEC44053

4

For each word, draw a flower. Write the word on the flower. Next, draw a stem and then add a leaf for each of the word's syllables. Write one syllable on each leaf. Then draw a flowerpot and record the word's meaning on it.

TEC44053

5

Write a story using all the words. Circle each word in your story as you use it.

TEC44053

6

Find each word in a dictionary. Write the word, its dictionary page number, and the guide words on the page. Then record the number of definitions listed and the word's other forms.

TEC44053

7

Write a riddle about each word. Then write the answer in parentheses.

Example: I am a verb that means "to think something is probable." What word am I? *(suppose)*

TEC44053

8

Sort the words into the following three categories: words with Latin origins, words with Greek origins, and words without Greek or Latin origins.

TEC44053

9

Write each word. Then underline each word's prefixes and suffixes. Make a list of the prefixes and suffixes and tell what each one means.

TEC44053

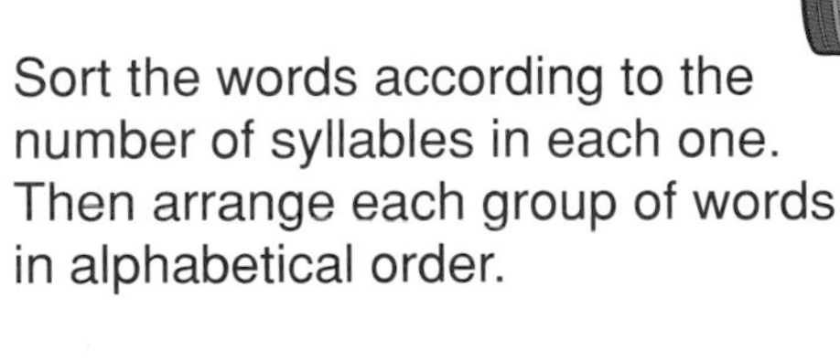

10

Sort the words according to the number of syllables in each one. Then arrange each group of words in alphabetical order.

TEC44053

Name ____________________

Date ____________________

READING BETWEEN THE LINES

Make an inference about
- what the author is really trying to say
- what a character is feeling
- why a character acts, feels, or thinks a certain way
- why an event is or isn't important
- the story's setting
- the possible cause or effect of an action

____
selection

What I read:	What I think the author meant:	Hints and details that help me make this inference:

 Note to the teacher: Use with "In Between" on page 14.

Name ______________________________

Date ______________________

Write All About It!

Create a four-page newspaper about the book you read. When you finish each item, check the box. Each item is worth ten points.

Front page:

- ☐ Create the newspaper's masthead. Choose a name for your newspaper that relates to the book. Choose a date that tells when the story takes place. Add the publisher's name (you) and the newspaper's price.
- ☐ Write a news article that describes the story's rising action. Add a catchy headline and an illustration.
- ☐ Write a news article about the story's main character. Add a catchy headline and an illustration of the character from the end of the story.

Editorial page:

- ☐ Write an editorial column that tells your opinion about the book's main character. Add an illustration of the main character.
- ☐ Write a letter to the editor that tells your opinion about the main problem in the story.
- ☐ Write a letter to the editor that tells a different opinion on the main problem in the story.

Feature page:

Choose and complete two.

- ☐ Create an advertisement that encourages people to visit the story's main setting.
- ☐ Create a four-panel comic that shows the story's climax.
- ☐ Write a news article that summarizes the story's plot. Add a catchy title.

Back page:

Choose and complete two.

- ☐ Make a classified ads section. Write three ads for important items from the story.
- ☐ Make a word search with 15 key words from the story.
- ☐ Create an advertisement for a brand-new movie version of the story.

Note to the teacher: Use with "Extra! Extra!" on page 14.

Adverb Strips

Use with "Carefully Sorted" on page 15.

first TEC44054	loudly TEC44054	clumsily TEC44054
above TEC44054	hard TEC44054	early TEC44054
quietly TEC44054	away TEC44054	tomorrow TEC44054
soon TEC44054	before TEC44054	outside TEC44054
well TEC44054	down TEC44054	always TEC44054
now TEC44054	gracefully TEC44054	backward TEC44054
everywhere TEC44054	finally TEC44054	usually TEC44054
here TEC44054	too TEC44054	quickly TEC44054
near TEC44054	eventually TEC44054	shyly TEC44054
anywhere TEC44054	often TEC44054	slowly TEC44054
never TEC44054	happily TEC44054	sometimes TEC44054
yesterday TEC44054	perfectly TEC44054	late TEC44054
there TEC44054	together TEC44054	forever TEC44054
tonight TEC44054	skillfully TEC44054	underneath TEC44054
fast TEC44054	inside TEC44054	then TEC44054

Sentence Cards and Answer Key

Use with "Positive Practice" on page 16.

1. Watermelon a great summer treat is a large, sweet fruit. TEC44055

2. The center of a watermelon the flesh may be orange. TEC44055

3. Watermelon rind the outer skin can be striped or solid. TEC44055

4. Watermelon a great thirst quencher is about 93 percent water. TEC44055

5. Watermelon a fun-to-eat fruit is packed with vitamins. TEC44055

6. A watermelon's outer skin the rind is edible. TEC44055

7. Watermelon a round or oval fruit can be grown in cube form. TEC44055

8. Watermelon runners the plant's vines might be 40 feet long. TEC44055

9. China the top watermelon-producing country has grown the melons for 1,000 years. TEC44055

10. The watermelon plant's scientific name *Citrullus lanatus* is hard to say. TEC44055

11. A long growing season 75 to 100 days is vital to watermelon farming. TEC44055

12. In a seed-spitting contest, each contestant a spitter tries to spit a watermelon seed the farthest. TEC44055

13. The record seed-spitting distance 68 feet 9 $\frac{1}{8}$ inches was set in 1989. TEC44055

14. Each watermelon kind or variety is unique. TEC44055

15. A Sugar Baby one of 1,200 kinds of watermelons is a small melon. TEC44055

16. The Honey-Heart watermelon a yellow-fleshed fruit has no seeds. TEC44055

17. One of the largest watermelons the Crimson Sweet can weigh 25 pounds. TEC44055

18. The watermelon thump an old test for ripeness doesn't really work. TEC44055

19. A Tennessee gardner Bill Carson grew a 262-pound watermelon. TEC44055

20. Pumpkin, squash, and cucumbers watermelon cousins all grow on vines. TEC44055

Answer Key for "Positive Practice"

1. Watermelon, a great summer treat, is a large, sweet fruit.
2. The center of a watermelon, the flesh, may be orange.
3. Watermelon rind, the outer skin, can be striped or solid.
4. Watermelon, a great thirst quencher, is about 93 percent water.
5. Watermelon, a fun-to-eat fruit, is packed with vitamins.
6. A watermelon's outer skin, the rind, is edible.
7. Watermelon, a round or oval fruit, can be grown in cube form.
8. Watermelon runners, the plant's vines, might be 40 feet long.
9. China, the top watermelon-producing country, has grown the melons for 1,000 years.
10. The watermelon plant's scientific name, *Citrullus lanatus*, is hard to say.
11. A long growing season, 75 to 100 days, is vital to watermelon farming.
12. In a seed-spitting contest, each contestant, a spitter, tries to spit a watermelon seed the farthest.
13. The record seed-spitting distance, 68 feet 9 1/8 inches, was set in 1989.
14. Each watermelon kind, or variety, is unique.
15. A Sugar Baby, one of 1,200 kinds of watermelons, is a small melon.
16. The Honey-Heart watermelon, a yellow-fleshed fruit, has no seeds.
17. One of the largest watermelons, the Crimson Sweet, can weigh 25 pounds.
18. The watermelon thump, an old test for ripeness, doesn't really work.
19. A Tennessee gardener, Bill Carson, grew a 262-pound watermelon.
20. Pumpkin, squash, and cucumbers, watermelon cousins, all grow on vines.

TEC44055

Name ____________________

Date ____________________

Wheel of Fiction

Title: ____________________

Author: ____________________

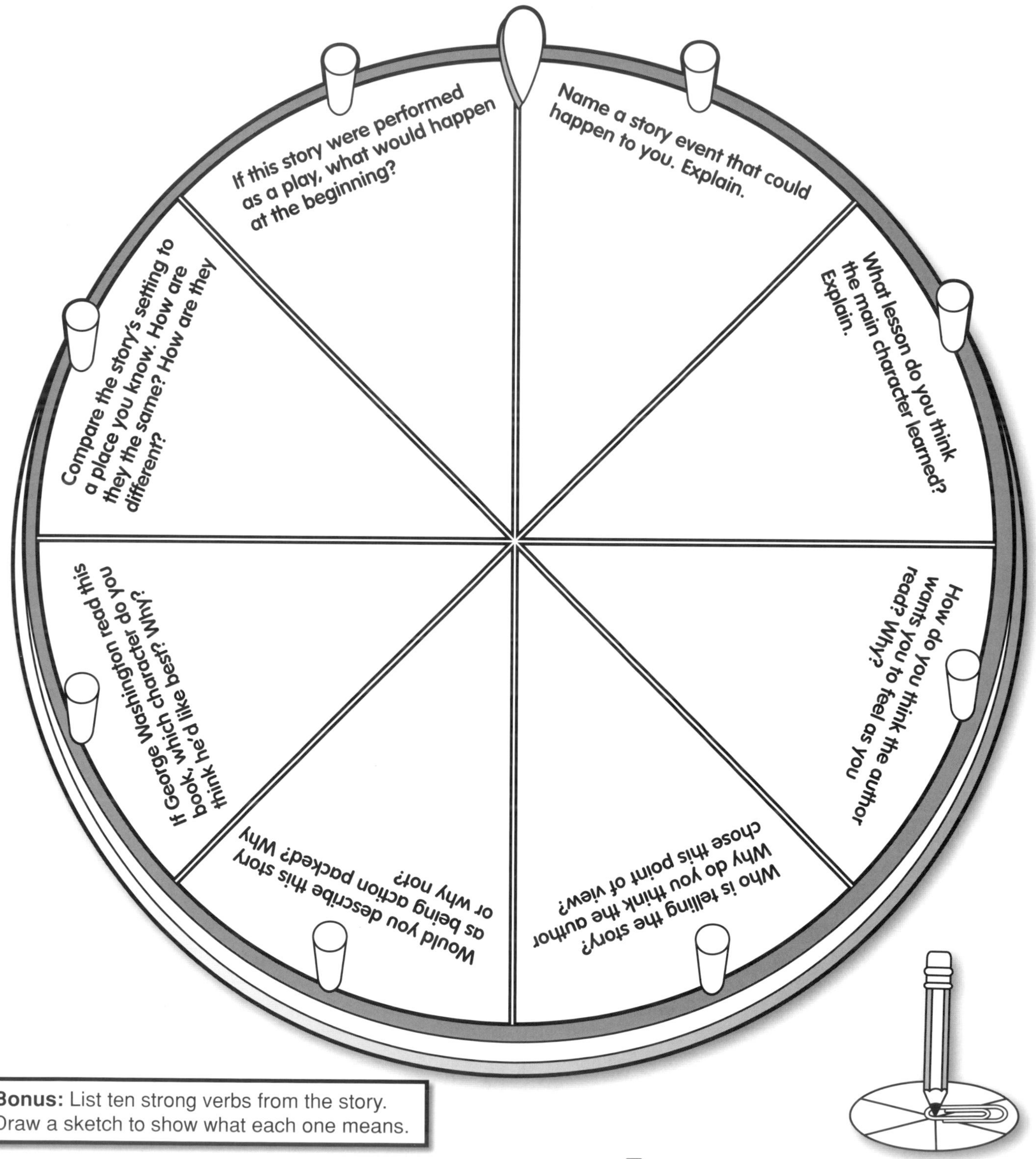

If this story were performed as a play, what would happen at the beginning?
Name a story event that could happen to you. Explain.
What lesson do you think the main character learned? Explain.
How do you think the author wants you to feel as you read? Why?
Who is telling the story? Why do you think the author chose this point of view?
Would you describe this story as being action packed? Why or why not?
If George Washington read this book, which character do you think he'd like best? Why?
Compare the story's setting to a place you know. How are they the same? How are they different?

Bonus: List ten strong verbs from the story. Draw a sketch to show what each one means.

 Note to the teacher: Use with "Wheel of Fiction" on page 17.

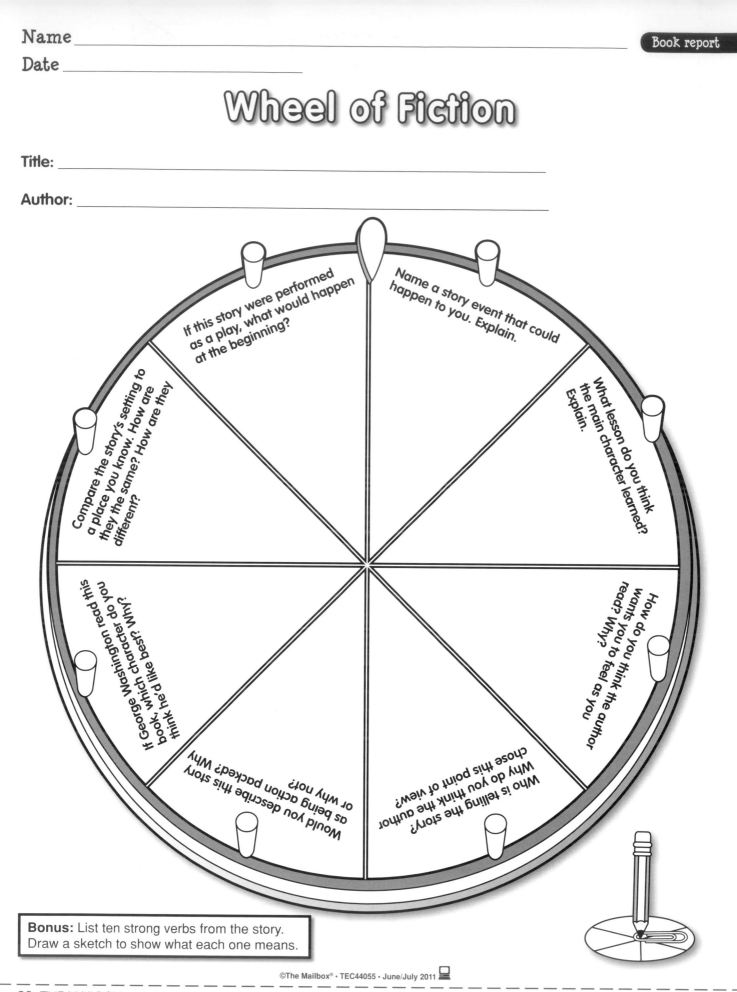

Name____________________

Date____________

ON TARGET!

1 List important points from the selection.

IMPORTANT POINTS:

-
-
-
-
-
-
-
-

5 **SUMMARY:**

2 Circle the most important point above.

3 Underline three points above that are more important than the rest.

4 Use the circled and underlined points to summarize the selection on the target.

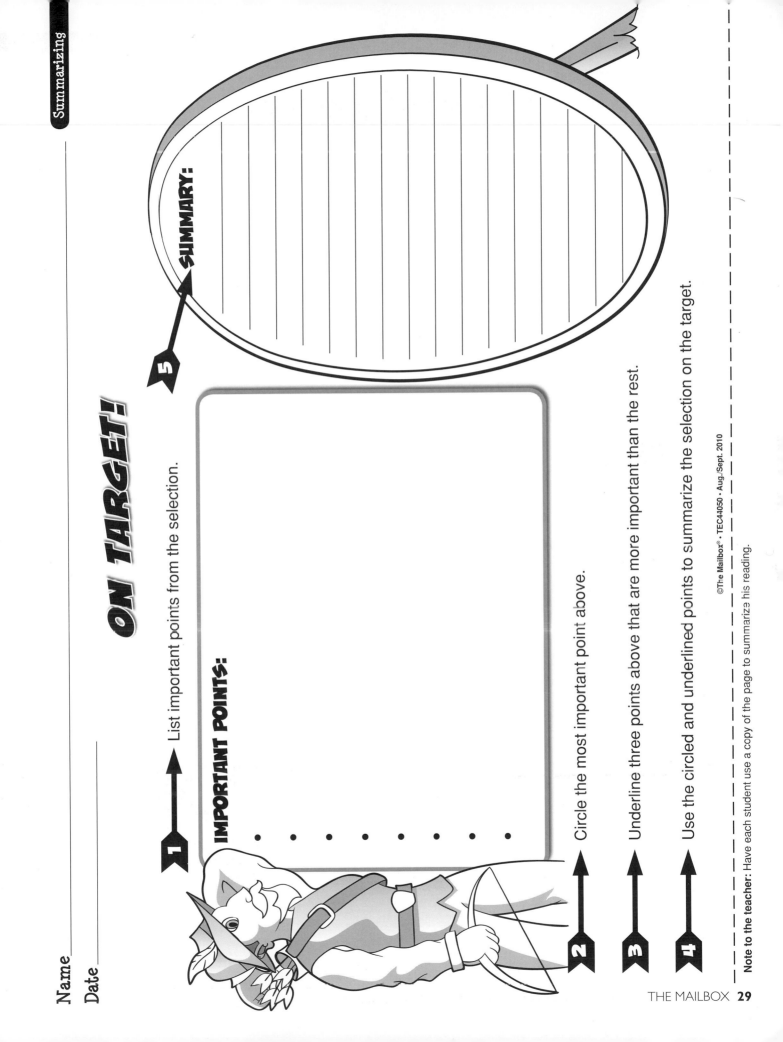

Note to the teacher: Have each student use a copy of the page to summarize his reading.

Name ________________________
Date ____________

GO FOR A SPIN!

____
title

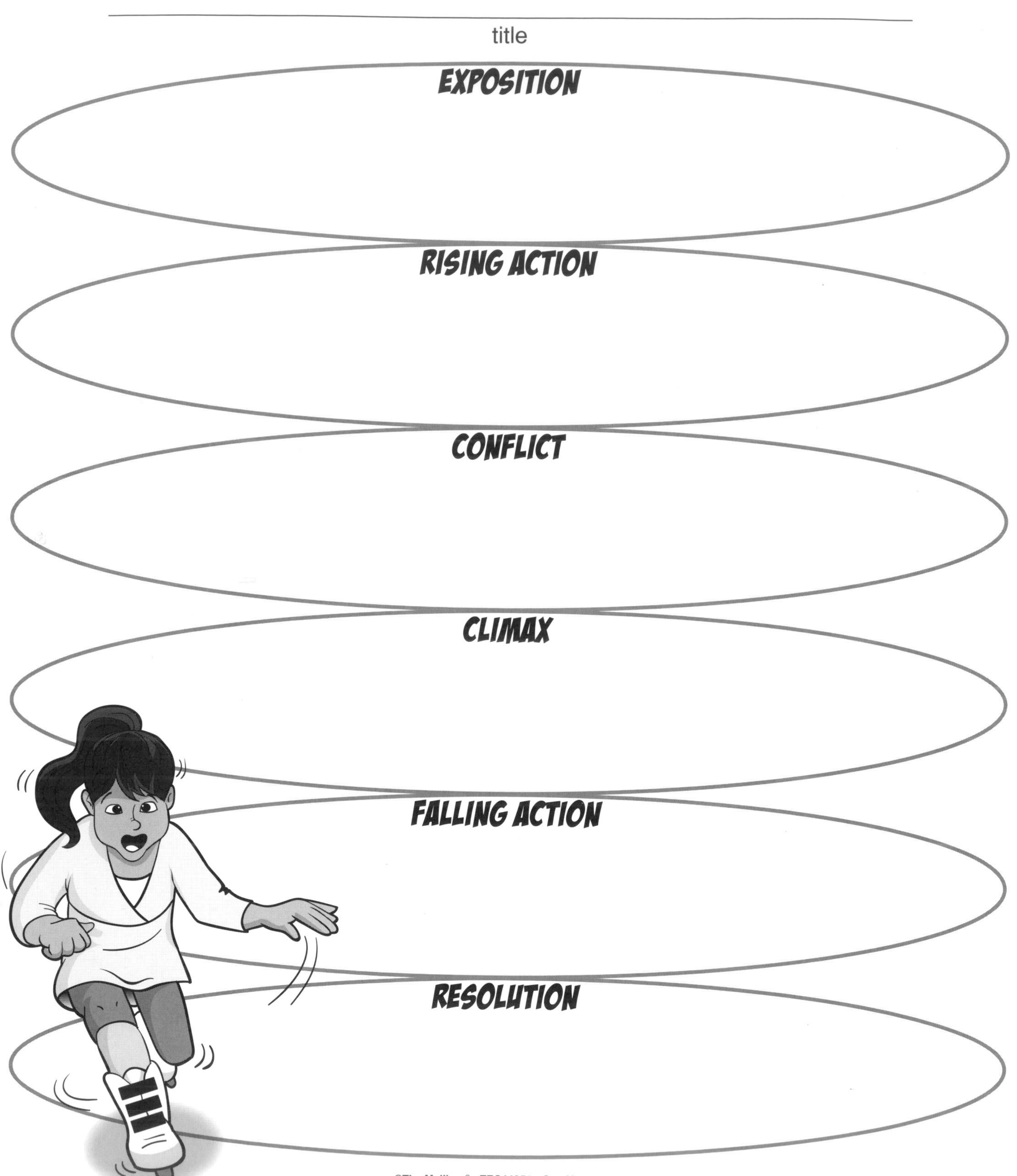

 How to use: Have each student use a copy of the page to analyze the plot of a story.

Name ______________________

Date ______________________

DOORS TO UNDERSTANDING

Write questions you have before, during, and after you read.
Then color each box according to the code.

COLOR CODE

red = I found the answer.
blue = I figured out the answer.
green = I'm still wondering.

____
title

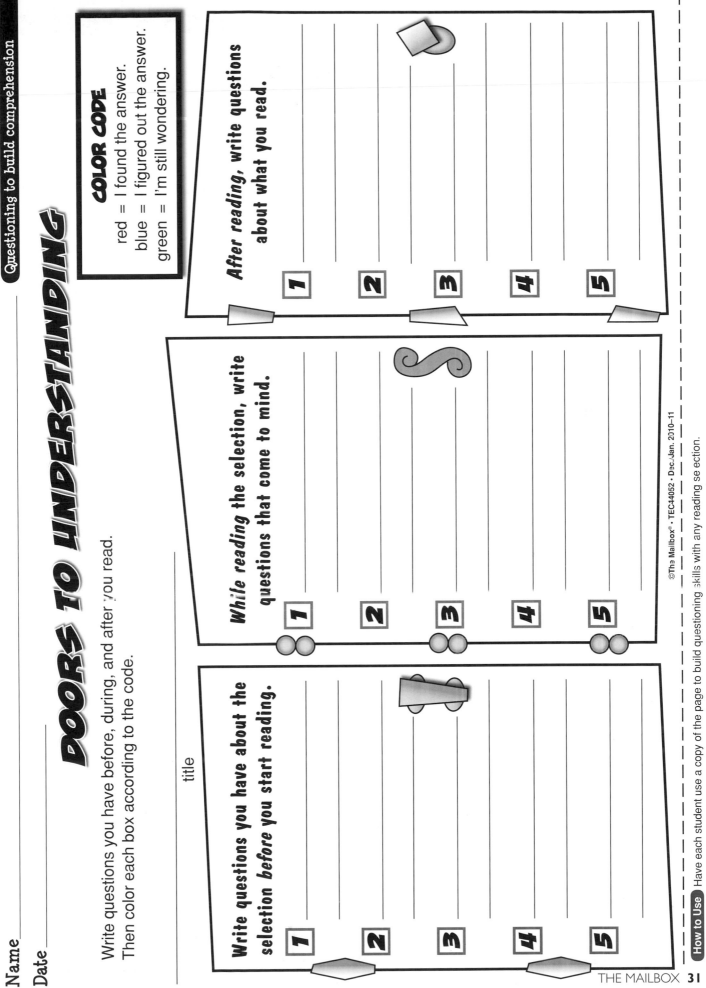

Write questions you have about the selection *before* you start reading.

1 ______________________

2 ______________________

3 ______________________

4 ______________________

5 ______________________

***While reading* the selection, write questions that come to mind.**

1 ______________________

2 ______________________

3 ______________________

4 ______________________

5 ______________________

***After reading*, write questions about what you read.**

1 ______________________

2 ______________________

3 ______________________

4 ______________________

5 ______________________

How to Use Have each student use a copy of the page to build questioning skills with any reading selection.

Name ______________________________ Graphic organizer

Date ____________________

All About the Main Character

This is how ______________ looks.
main character

These are some things ______________ does.
main character

These are some things ______________ says.
main character

These are some things ______________ wonders or worries about.
main character

This is the main problem ______________ faces.
main character

This is what ______________ does about the problem.
main character

This is the main concept or lesson ______________ learns in the story.
main character

This is how ______________ changes in the story.
main character

____
main character

____

____

____
selection title

 How to use: Have each student use a copy of this page to analyze a story's main character.

Name ______________________________

Date ____________________

Dig Deeper!

Answer each question.
Then write the theme of the story in the space provided.

____
selection

____
author

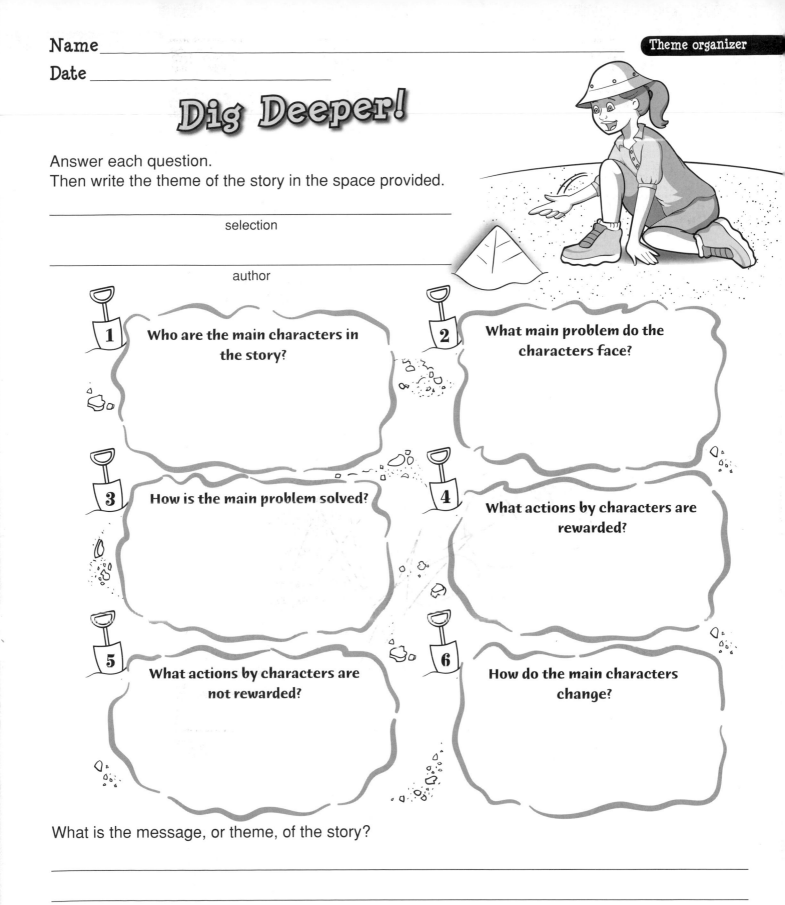

1 Who are the main characters in the story?

2 What main problem do the characters face?

3 How is the main problem solved?

4 What actions by characters are rewarded?

5 What actions by characters are not rewarded?

6 How do the main characters change?

What is the message, or theme, of the story?

____

____

____

____

How to use: Have a student use a copy of the page to analyze a fiction selection's theme.

Name ____________________

Date ____________________

So That's the Big Idea!

Pick _____ activities to do.
When you finish an activity, color its number.

1 Copy and complete this topic sentence. Add three details that support the topic sentence.

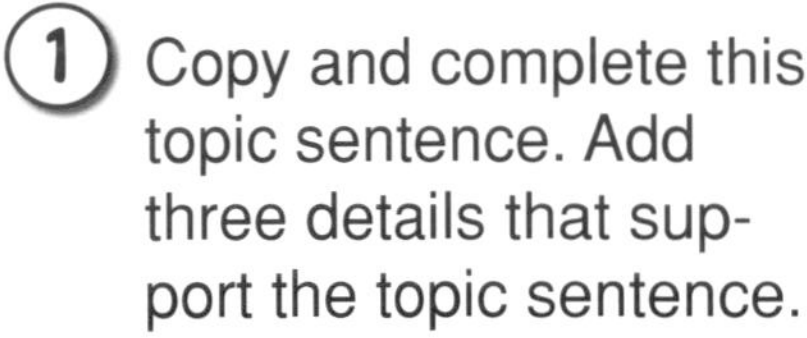

My favorite thing to do after school is...

2 Write a topic sentence for this paragraph.

JAY PUTS AIR IN HIS TIRES. HE BUCKLES ON HIS HELMET AND CHECKS HIS BRAKES. JAY CHECKS FOR ONCOMING TRAFFIC BEFORE PULLING OUT ONTO THE STREET.

3 Draw the organizer and then fill it out about the story you are reading.

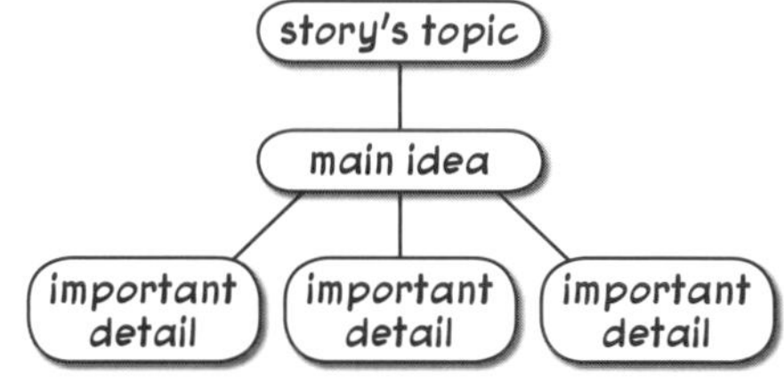

4 Complete the formula to describe the main idea of your current reading.

topic + author's message about the topic = main idea

5 Draw a circle with five spokes. On each spoke, write an important detail from your reading. Then reread the details and write the main idea in the circle.

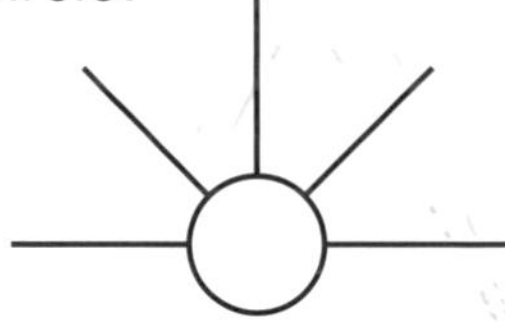

6 For each title below, write the first sentence of the first paragraph that might go with it.

Dena's Dilemma
Don't Fence Me In!
That's What Friends Are For!

7 Draw the organizer below. Then use it to describe the main idea of the last story you read.

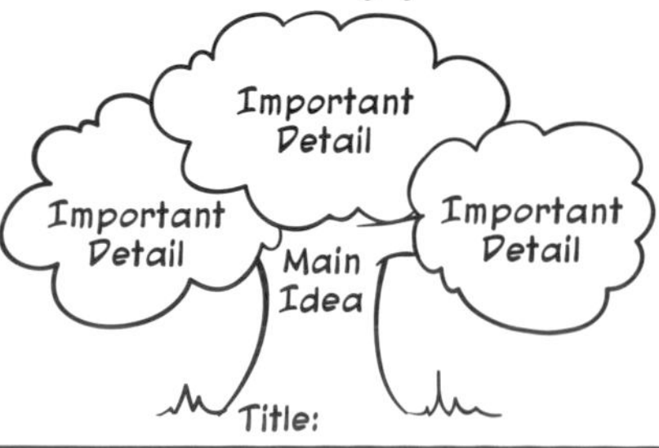

8 Write a different topic sentence about each topic below.

- **riding a school bus**
- **heavy backpacks**
- **texting**
- **video games**

9 Read a chapter from a current reading. As you read, make a note about the main idea of each paragraph. Then use your notes to name the chapter's main idea.

Independent Practice Grid: Program the student directions with the number of activities to be completed. Then copy the page for each student.

Name ______________________________

Date ______________________________

Mega Mart Promotions

If the ad is a sentence fragment, color the ad yellow.
If the ad is a complete sentence, color the ad green.

1. Get everything you need at one store—*Mega Mart!* (A)

2. **50% off all rings at the jewelry counter!** (R)

3. **Clearance sale in the shoe department!** (E)

4. All luggage is marked down. (D)

5. **10% discount on all cameras** (T)

6. **Buy now!** (M)

7. **Sign up for our newsletter.** (F)

8. **Now through Friday** (A)

9. Just one week until the tax-free weekend! (I)

10. *Sidewalk sale Saturday: too many bargains to miss!* (L)

11. **All DVDs are 5% off!** (B)

12. Free food samples on Monday. (S)

13. *Stop in and shop seven days a week!* (O)

14. **GIGANTIC** *sale on running shoes!* (T)

What should a dog do if it loses its tail?

To find out, write each letter from the yellow-colored ads in order on the lines below.

It should go to a "___ ___ - ___ ___ ___ ___" ___ ___ **O R E!**

Bonus Box: On another sheet of paper, revise each ad that is a fragment so it will be a complete sentence.

Name ______________________________

Date ______________________________

To Be Continued...

Pick ___ activities to complete. Use your spelling list. When you finish an activity, color its number.

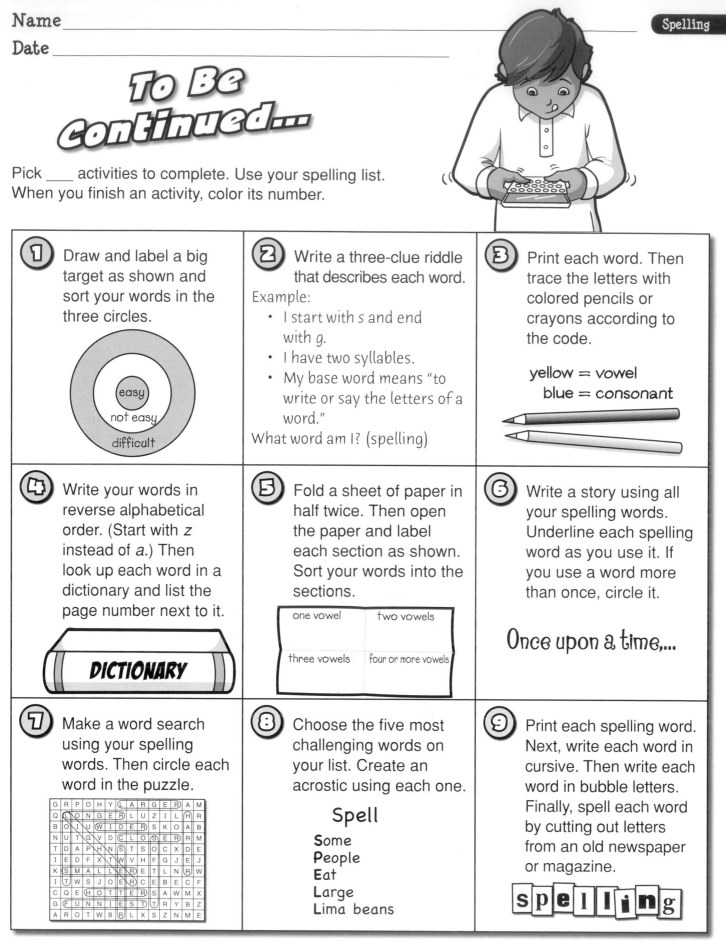

1 Draw and label a big target as shown and sort your words in the three circles.

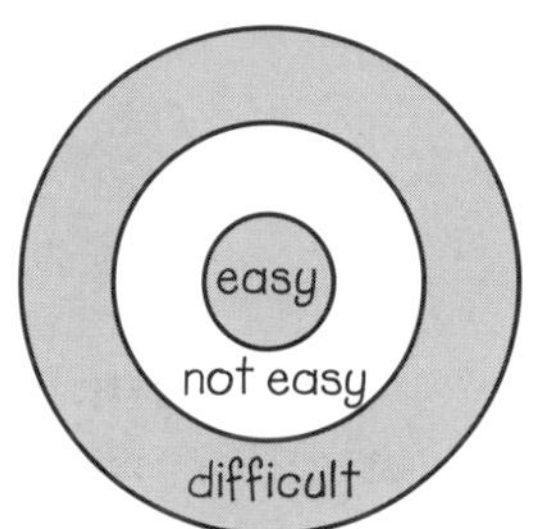

2 Write a three-clue riddle that describes each word.

Example:

- I start with *s* and end with *g*.
- I have two syllables.
- My base word means "to write or say the letters of a word."

What word am I? (spelling)

3 Print each word. Then trace the letters with colored pencils or crayons according to the code.

yellow = vowel
blue = consonant

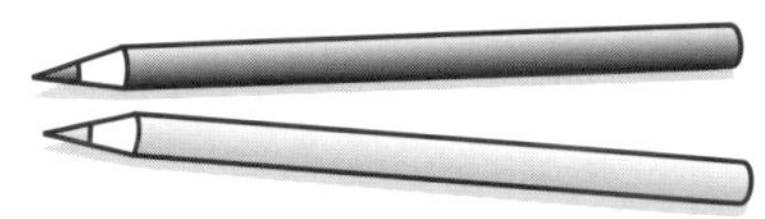

4 Write your words in reverse alphabetical order. (Start with *z* instead of *a*.) Then look up each word in a dictionary and list the page number next to it.

5 Fold a sheet of paper in half twice. Then open the paper and label each section as shown. Sort your words into the sections.

one vowel	two vowels
three vowels	four or more vowels

6 Write a story using all your spelling words. Underline each spelling word as you use it. If you use a word more than once, circle it.

Once upon a time,...

7 Make a word search using your spelling words. Then circle each word in the puzzle.

G	R	P	O	H	Y	L	A	R	G	E	R	A	M
Q	L	O	N	G	E	R	L	U	Z	I	L	H	R
B	O	I	U	W	I	D	E	R	S	K	O	A	B
N	U	T	G	V	D	C	L	O	S	E	R	R	M
T	D	A	P	H	N	S	T	S	O	C	X	D	E
I	E	D	F	X	T	W	V	H	F	G	J	E	J
K	S	M	A	L	L	E	R	E	T	L	N	R	W
I	T	W	S	J	O	E	R	C	E	B	E	C	F
C	Q	E	H	O	T	T	E	R	S	A	W	M	X
G	F	U	N	N	I	E	S	T	T	R	Y	B	Z
A	R	O	T	W	B	R	L	X	S	Z	N	M	E

8 Choose the five most challenging words on your list. Create an acrostic using each one.

Spell

Some
People
Eat
Large
Lima beans

9 Print each spelling word. Next, write each word in cursive. Then write each word in bubble letters. Finally, spell each word by cutting out letters from an old newspaper or magazine.

Independent practice grid to use with any spelling list: Program the student directions with the number of activities to be completed. Then copy the page for each student.

Names ____________________

Date ____________________

Tit-Tac-"Toe"?

A Game for Two Players

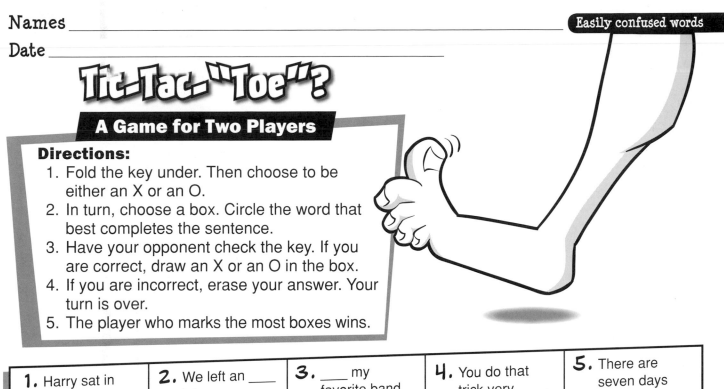

Directions:

1. Fold the key under. Then choose to be either an X or an O.
2. In turn, choose a box. Circle the word that best completes the sentence.
3. Have your opponent check the key. If you are correct, draw an X or an O in the box.
4. If you are incorrect, erase your answer. Your turn is over.
5. The player who marks the most boxes wins.

1. Harry sat in row ____. a. for b. four	2. We left an ____ late. a. hour b. our	3. ____ my favorite band. a. They're b. There	4. You do that trick very ____. a. well b. good	5. There are seven days in one ____. a. weak b. week
6. Her dress isn't fancy; it's ____. a. plain b. plane	7. He ____ his bike to school. a. road b. rode	8. Is this ____ hat or mine? a. your b. you're	9. Her front tooth is ____. a. lose b. loose	10. The boys are ____ for the game. a. already b. all ready
11. Please be ____; the baby is sleeping. a. quite b. quiet	12. I like all colors ____ yellow. a. accept b. except	13. I want a ____ of pizza. a. piece b. peace	14. The ____ is leaving the airport. a. plain b. plane	15. I want to go ____! a. too b. to
16. Max ate the ____ pizza! a. whole b. hole	17. What will you ____ at the store? a. by b. buy	18. I like chocolate better ____ vanilla. a. then b. than	19. Last week we had rainy ____. a. whether b. weather	20. My house is on the ____. a. right b. write

Answer Key

1. b
2. a
3. a
4. a
5. b
6. a
7. b
8. a
9. b
10. b
11. b
12. b
13. a
14. b
15. a
16. a
17. b
18. b
19. b
20. a

TEC44051

Name ______________________

Date ______________

SHE SHOOTS!

Not an air ball...not an air ball!

Write the possessive form of each word on the line. Then circle the word in the maze. Connect the circles to get to the basket.

START

players' referees' referee's mascots' player's ball's balls' coach's trainer's trainers' clock's clocks' coaches' fans' shoe's mascot's teams' shoes' team's cushion's seats' seat's courts fan's courts' court's goals' backboard's backboards' goal's

FINISH

1. players ______________
2. referee ______________
3. ball ______________
4. fans ______________
5. seats ______________
6. court ______________
7. goal ______________
8. backboard ______________
9. teams ______________
10. shoe ______________
11. clock ______________
12. coach ______________
13. trainer ______________
14. mascots ______________

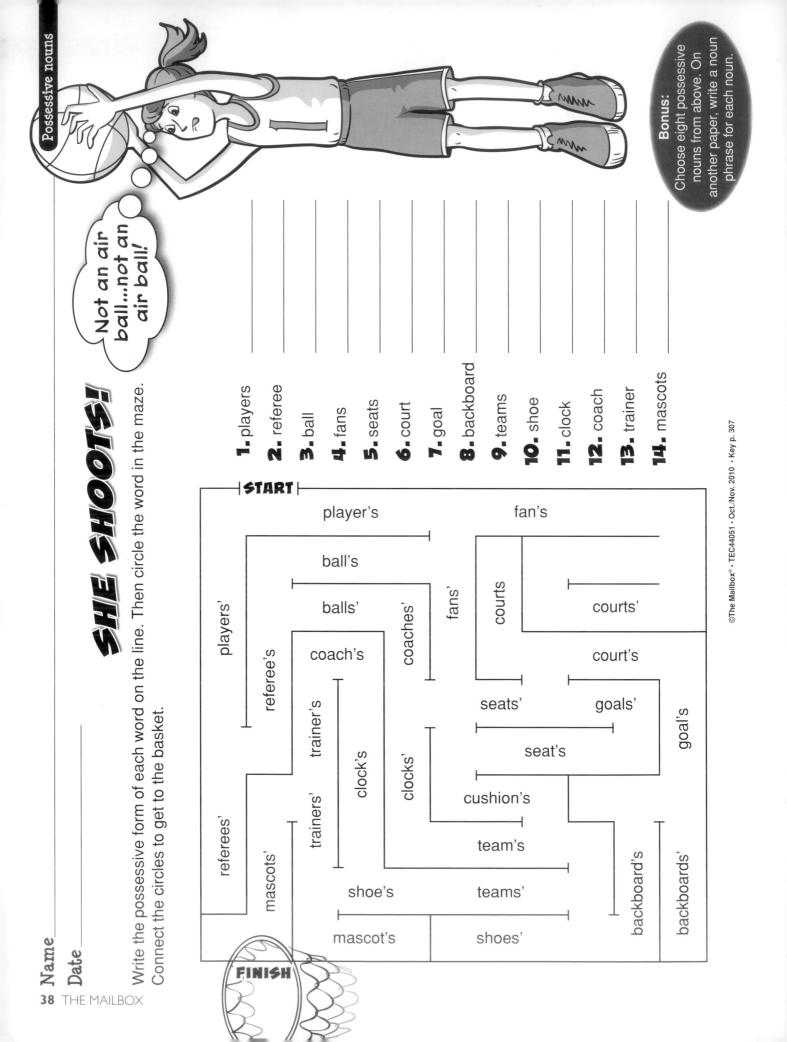

Bonus: Choose eight possessive nouns from above. On another paper, write a noun phrase for each noun.

 • Key p. 307

Name ______________________________
Date ______________________________

That's the Way the Cookie Crumbles!

Read each sentence below. Underline the cause and circle the effect. Then draw a box around the clue word or words in each sentence.

1. The cookie jar was empty, **s**o Mom decided to make cookies.
2. Due **t**o an interruption, Mom burned the first batch.
3. She left the next batch of cookies on the table **b**ecause they were hot.
4. Maddy grabbed a cookie right from the pan; consequentl**y**, she burned her fingers.
5. Then a mouse got a snack beca**u**se Maddy dropped her cookie on the floor.
6. The cat almost caught the mouse sinc**e** it stopped to nibble the cookie.
7. The mouse scurried past the dog, which caus**e**d the dog to jump onto the kitchen table.
8. The cookies flew onto the floor as a **r**esult of the dog's jump.
9. Since the cat slid through the cookies, there were crumbs all over the floor.
10. The dog got blamed for the mess bec**a**use it was eating a cookie when Mom came in.
11. Mom was furious about the mess; there**f**ore, the dog was sent outside.
12. As a resu**l**t of the disaster, the cookie jar was still empty.
13. Since we didn't get any of the cookies, our stomachs started growling.
14. To solve the proble**m** of the growling stomachs, Mom started mixing a fresh batch of cookies.

Cause and Effect Clues

as a result
because
caused
consequently
due to
for that reason
problem
since
so
therefore

Bonus: On another page, write five more cause and effect statements.

Why did the cookie go to the doctor?

To find out, write the boldfaced letter from each boxed word or words on its matching numbered line or lines below.

The cookie went to the doctor

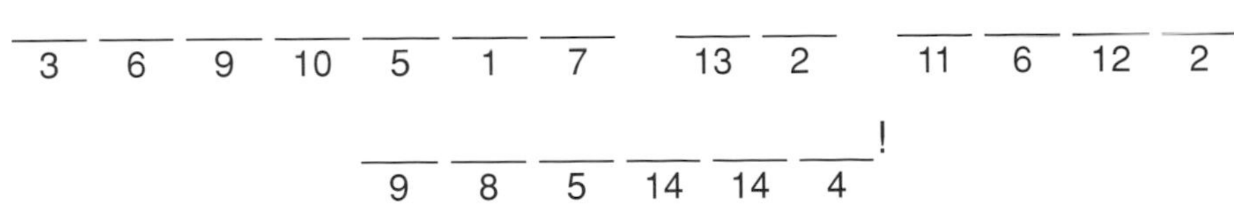

___ ___ ___ ___ ___ ___ ___   ___ ___   ___ ___ ___ ___
3 6 9 10 5 1 7   13 2   11 6 12 2

___ ___ ___ ___ ___ ___!
9 8 5 14 14 4

Name ______________________

Date ______________

"PEN-SATIONAL" DESCRIPTIONS

Circle the subject of each sentence below. Then, on another sheet of paper, rewrite each sentence using a simile to describe the subject. After that, rewrite each sentence using a metaphor to describe the subject.

example: My (kite) soars into the sky.
simile: My kite soars like a hawk into the air.
metaphor: My kite is a hawk soaring through the sky.

1. I'll wear the shirt that is bright red.
2. The bus's engine is really loud.
3. Before school, the playground is crowded with children.
4. Our goldfish looks lonely swimming around in its little bowl.
5. Our class hamster escapes and dashes across the floor.
6. Everyone in our class is reading quietly.
7. Hannah, the fastest girl in our class, won the race.
8. After P.E., I am very thirsty.
9. My sandwich tastes terrible.
10. Today's milk is especially cold.
11. In the lunchroom, we get really noisy.
12. Ms. Jones is really busy answering questions.
13. Trying to get Ms. Jones's attention, I wave my arm in the air.
14. The last hour of the day goes by quickly.
15. I hurry to stuff all my homework in my backpack.
16. My backpack is really heavy.
17. I run, trying to be the first one on the bus.
18. The bus is more crowded than usual.
19. After school, I'm so hungry that I'll eat anything.
20. My puppy goes wild when I get home.

Bonus: Choose the simile or metaphor you like best. Circle it and then tell why it's your favorite.

Name ______________________________

Date ______________________________

Bear and Skunk

A trickster is a clever character who outsmarts another bigger or stronger character.

One spring day long ago, Bear was badly stung by bees. He'd been digging honey out of a beehive. Skunk, who loved to eat bees as well as honey, heard the news. It wasn't long before Skunk had an idea.

"Bear," Skunk said sweetly, "I want to help you. Let me eat the bees and give you all the honey. In return, you can keep me safe from my enemies." Bear had been afraid to face the bees, but he hated missing out on the honey. So he agreed.

For many weeks, Skunk stayed awake into the day. Each day, Skunk used her strong claws to break the honeycombs apart. She ate the bees, brought the honeycombs to Bear, and enjoyed protection from all her enemies. Although staying up late was hard for Skunk, she had a plan. Now, remember, skunks are nocturnal animals. Skunk waited until Bear fell asleep each night and then slurped all the honey she wanted.

One night, a noise woke Bear. He opened his sleepy eyes to see Skunk sneaking away with a honeycomb. Bear realized he had been tricked!

In anger, Bear searched the forest for putrid flowers. He knew that Skunk liked to curl up in a hollow log and sleep all day. So Bear pushed the stinky flowers into the log and waited. Sure enough, Skunk crawled in and fell fast asleep. That evening, when Skunk woke up, she was coated with the terrible smell. To this day, the critters in the forest know Skunk by her sneaky deeds and awful smell.

Shade the best answer. Then answer questions 6–10 on another sheet of paper.

1. Which character in this story is the trickster?
   - (A) Bear
   - (B) Skunk
2. According to the selection, which event happens first?
   - (A) Bear looks for putrid flowers.
   - (B) Bear catches Skunk eating honey.
   - (C) Bear gets stung by bees.
3. Which sentence explains why Bear got mad?
   - (A) Bear realized he had been tricked!
   - (B) One spring day long ago, Bear was badly stung by bees.
   - (C) In anger, Bear searched the forest for putrid flowers.
4. Which word best describes how Bear felt about Skunk at the end of the story?
   - (A) annoyed
   - (B) furious
   - (C) relaxed
5. In the fifth paragraph, what does the word *putrid* mean?
   - (A) ugly
   - (B) sticky
   - (C) stinky
6. Why do you think Skunk ate the honey?
7. Which character in this story is more likeable? Why?
8. Which action in the story is punished? How is it punished?
9. Was the outcome of the story fair? Why or why not?
10. Does this trickster tale teach a lesson or tell how something natural came to be? Explain.

Bonus: In your own words, write a one paragraph summary of the story.

Name ______________________________

Date ______________________________

I think I can, I think I can...

Break It Apart!

Pick ______ activities to do.
For each activity, use the list of Greek and/or Latin Roots in box 5.
When you finish an activity, color its number.

1 Make your paper look like the one shown. In each box, write a different Greek root and its meaning. Then write a word that contains the root and draw a sketch to show the word's meaning.

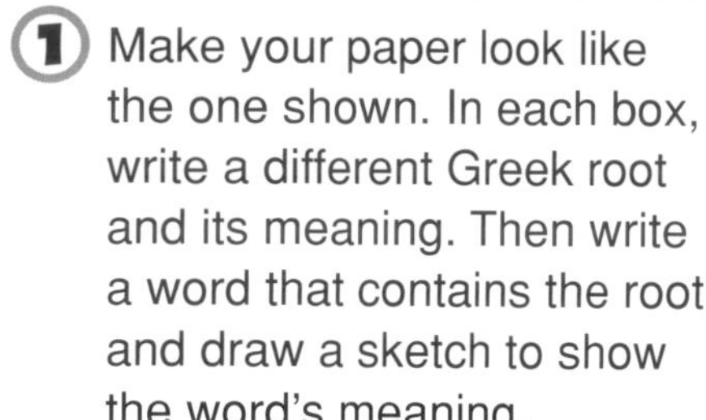

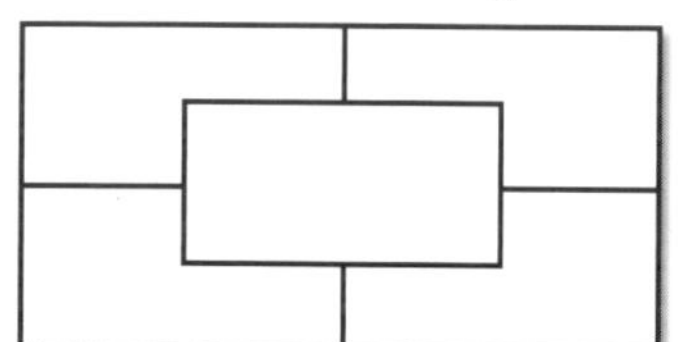

2 Copy the chart. Then list the Latin roots. Write each root's meaning and two words that contain the root.

Latin Root	Meaning	Word	Word

3 Copy the words shown. Circle each Greek root. Then use the root or roots to predict each word's meaning.

A. biologist
B. altimeter
C. synchronize
D. asteroid
E. geography
F. diameter
G. asterisk
H. autobiography
I. chronological
J. geochemistry

4 Draw six circles. Write a Latin root or set of Latin roots in each circle. Then sort the words below according to their roots and write each one under the appropriate circle.

vacuum
aquarium
invisible
export
remove
portable
extraterrestrial
evacuate
promote
territory
evidence
aquifer

5

Greek Roots

ast (star)
bio (life)
chron (time)
geo (earth)
graph (write)
meter (measure)

Latin Roots

aqua (water)
mob, mot, mov (move)
port (carry)
terr (land)
vac (empty)
vid, vis (see)

6 Copy the meanings shown. Then draw an arrow from each one and write the correct Greek or Latin root next to each arrow.

see
water
time
move
measure
star
empty
earth
carry
life
write
land

7 Unscramble the words shown. (Each one contains a Greek or Latin root.) Then underline the root and tell what you think the word means.

A. aquamnraie
B. astdireo
C. biolgyo
D. chronciel
E. geogyol
F. graphtei
G. kloimeter
H. mobzilei
I. stranport
J. terrina
K. vactaoin
L. videnpohoe

8 Make your paper look like the one shown. Then create a colorful brochure that advertises the Latin or Greek roots from box 5.

9 Draw ten boxes on your paper. In each box, write a Greek or Latin root. Then draw a sketch that shows what each root means.

Independent Practice Grid Program the student directions with the number of activities to be completed. Then copy the page for each student.

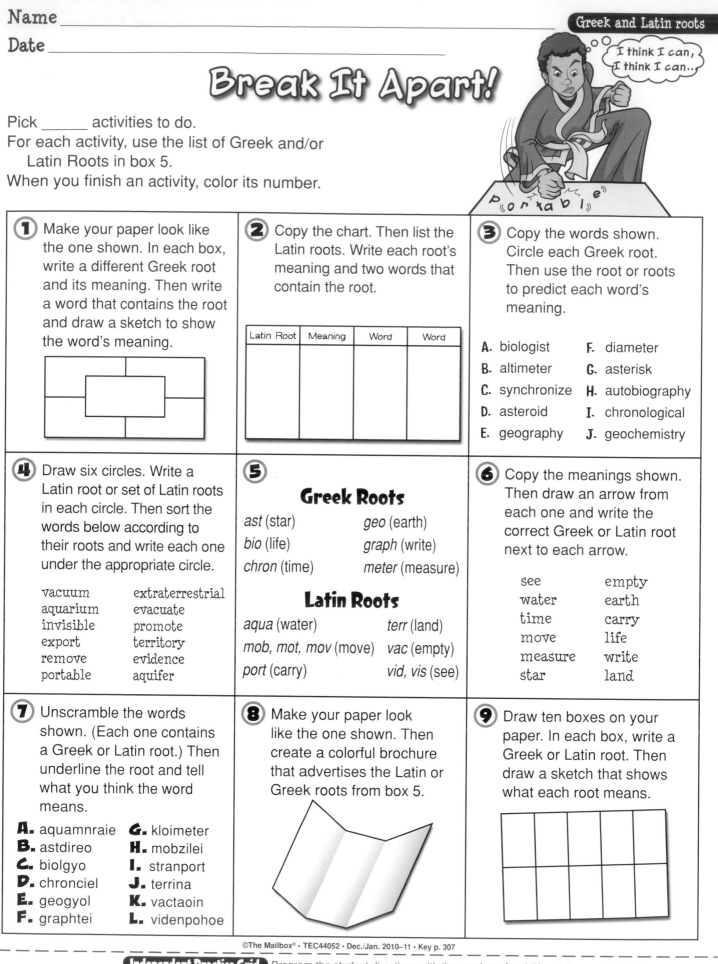

1 What is another word for *excited?* TEC44052	**2** Where is the syllable break in the word *slalom?* TEC44052	**3** Does the word *mogul* have a Latin root? TEC44052	**4** Can the word *slope* be used as an adjective? TEC44052	**5** What is an antonym of *descend?* TEC44052
6 From which language does the word *schuss* come? TEC44052	**7** How many definitions are listed for the verb *slush?* TEC44052	**8** What is the plural form of *ski?* TEC44052	**9** Is *happy* an antonym for *nervous?* TEC44052	**10** Is *bracing* a synonym of *cold?* TEC44052
11 Can the word *ticket* be a noun? TEC44052	**12** What is the correct spelling for the past tense form of *ski?* TEC44052	**13** Is *dull* an antonym for *fun?* TEC44052	**14** How do you pronounce *aerial?* TEC44052	**15** Is there more than one definition for the word *resort?* TEC44052
16 Can the word *soak* be replaced with *damp?* TEC44052	**17** What is a synonym for *cautious?* TEC44052	**18** How many syllables are in the word *avalanche?* TEC44052	**19** Does *Alpine* always have to be capitalized? TEC44052	**20** What is the opposite of *calm?* TEC44052
21 Is this how to spell *gondola?* TEC44052	**22** Is there a synonym for the noun *snow?* TEC44052	**23** Is *lift* another way of saying *ride?* TEC44052	**24** From which country does the word *ski* come? TEC44052	**25** What is the best antonym of *warm?* TEC44052

ANSWER KEY FOR "SCHUSS!"

1. thesaurus
2. dictionary
3. dictionary
4. dictionary
5. thesaurus
6. dictionary
7. dictionary
8. dictionary
9. thesaurus
10. thesaurus
11. dictionary
12. dictionary
13. thesaurus
14. dictionary
15. dictionary
16. thesaurus
17. thesaurus
18. dictionary
19. dictionary
20. thesaurus
21. dictionary
22. thesaurus
23. thesaurus
24. dictionary
25. thesaurus

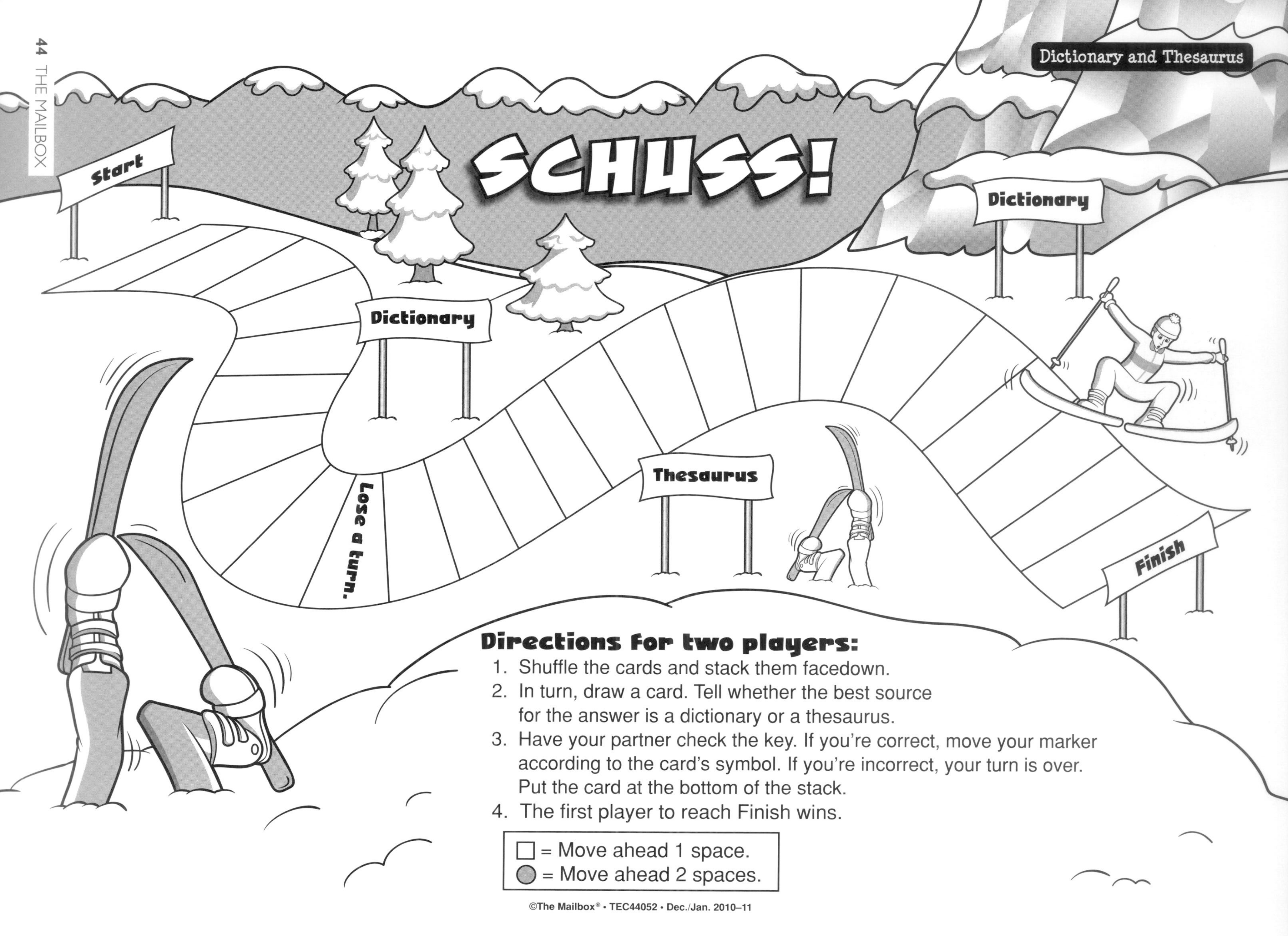

Directions for two players:

1. Shuffle the cards and stack them facedown.
2. In turn, draw a card. Tell whether the best source for the answer is a dictionary or a thesaurus.
3. Have your partner check the key. If you're correct, move your marker according to the card's symbol. If you're incorrect, your turn is over. Put the card at the bottom of the stack.
4. The first player to reach Finish wins.

□ = Move ahead 1 space.
● = Move ahead 2 spaces.

Names ______________________________

Riding the Rapids!

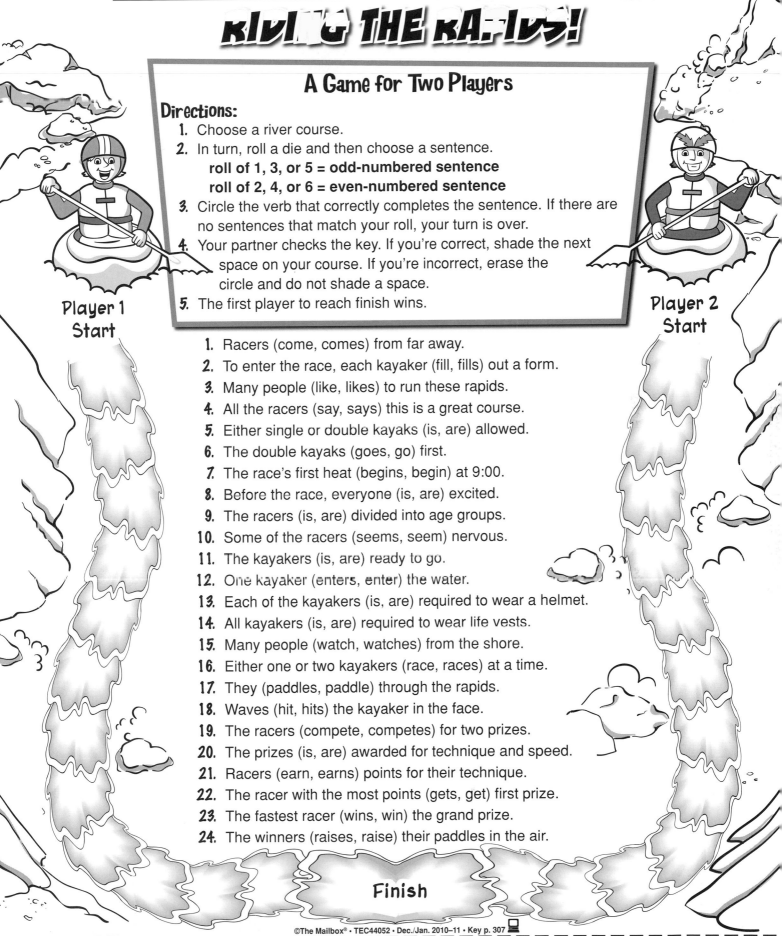

A Game for Two Players

Directions:

1. Choose a river course.
2. In turn, roll a die and then choose a sentence.
   roll of 1, 3, or 5 = odd-numbered sentence
   roll of 2, 4, or 6 = even-numbered sentence
3. Circle the verb that correctly completes the sentence. If there are no sentences that match your roll, your turn is over.
4. Your partner checks the key. If you're correct, shade the next space on your course. If you're incorrect, erase the circle and do not shade a space.
5. The first player to reach finish wins.

Player 1 Start

Player 2 Start

1. Racers (come, comes) from far away.
2. To enter the race, each kayaker (fill, fills) out a form.
3. Many people (like, likes) to run these rapids.
4. All the racers (say, says) this is a great course.
5. Either single or double kayaks (is, are) allowed.
6. The double kayaks (goes, go) first.
7. The race's first heat (begins, begin) at 9:00.
8. Before the race, everyone (is, are) excited.
9. The racers (is, are) divided into age groups.
10. Some of the racers (seems, seem) nervous.
11. The kayakers (is, are) ready to go.
12. One kayaker (enters, enter) the water.
13. Each of the kayakers (is, are) required to wear a helmet.
14. All kayakers (is, are) required to wear life vests.
15. Many people (watch, watches) from the shore.
16. Either one or two kayakers (race, races) at a time.
17. They (paddles, paddle) through the rapids.
18. Waves (hit, hits) the kayaker in the face.
19. The racers (compete, competes) for two prizes.
20. The prizes (is, are) awarded for technique and speed.
21. Racers (earn, earns) points for their technique.
22. The racer with the most points (gets, get) first prize.
23. The fastest racer (wins, win) the grand prize.
24. The winners (raises, raise) their paddles in the air.

Finish

How to use: Each pair needs a copy of the page, a copy of the key from page 307, a die, and two pencils.

Name ____________________

Date ____________________

Editing practice

FROM SPY TO SPY

Add punctuation where needed. Circle each misspelled word.
For each punctuation mark you add, cross out a matching editing mark on the letter's border.

December 7 2010

1234 Mystery Lane
Somewhere NY 56789

Dear Ms Watson

I hear that youve enrolled in my old supersecret spy academy Wat wonderful news I woud like to offer my support and best wishes. If you happin to meet Samantha Spade please give her my best. We tooke beginning code-breaking together. Ms Spade used to be a supersecret agent but now she might soon be one of youre teachers. She teaches advanced code-breaking at your scool.

I still remember my first day at the academy I took a nine-hour buse ride to get there. It was a long trip from my hoem. During the first day the chief of polic came to welcome us Woulde you believe I was one of only 20 students There must be hundreds of students there now

Have you learned how to makke invisible ink yet I think that was my favorite lesson Old Professor Hardy had each of us brind a lemon to class. Then we used the lemon juice to write secret messages. After we heated the lemon juice we could read each others messages and then write badk. This reminds me; theres a secret message in this letter. I wish you good luck finding the message and even better luck at the supersecret spy academy

Sincerely

Herlock Sholmes

Bonus: Write a letter to Herlock Sholmes from Ms. Watson about her first day at the supersecret spy academy.

To find Herlock Sholmes's secret message, rewrite the circled words (spelling them correctly!) in order on the lines below.

________ ________ ________ if you ________

________ ________ ________ ________?

The ________ ________ ________ you ________

it ________.

Name ______________________________

Date ______________________

The Ants Went Marching...

Write the present tense form of each verb. Then find each word in the puzzle.

1. went ____________
2. bought ____________
3. torn ____________
4. brought ____________
5. heard ____________
6. taken ____________
7. wrote ____________
8. thought ____________
9. grew ____________
10. caught ____________
11. begun ____________
12. broken ____________
13. chose ____________
14. drawn ____________
15. drove ____________
16. frozen ____________
17. slid ____________
18. stung ____________
19. swum ____________
20. taught ____________
21. told ____________
22. burst ____________
23. clung ____________
24. drank ____________
25. worn ____________
26. beat ____________
27. forgiven ____________
28. hid ____________
29. kept ____________
30. bitten ____________

F	O	R	G	I	V	E	B
R	C	H	O	O	S	E	R
E	A	E	B	I	T	E	I
E	T	A	B	E	G	I	N
Z	C	R	S	T	I	N	G
E	H	B	L	E	D	T	R
B	O	R	I	A	R	E	O
U	D	E	D	C	A	A	W
R	R	A	E	H	W	R	E
S	I	K	E	E	P	F	A
T	V	S	A	B	U	Y	R
E	E	W	R	I	T	E	N
L	H	I	D	E	H	T	I
L	B	M	D	R	I	N	K
O	D	C	L	I	N	G	I
B	E	A	T	A	K	E	E

Bonus: Circle each verb that can only be used as a verb with a helping verb, such as *have*, *had*, or *will have*.

Why didn't the anteater ever get sick?

To find out, write the letters that aren't circled in order, from left to right.

It never got sick because it was full

__ __ "__ __ __ - __ __ __ __ __ __ __ s!"

Name ____________________

Date ____________________

PICK AND PRACTICE!

Pick _____ activities to do.
When you finish an activity, color its number.

1 Draw sketches to show two different meanings for each word below.

trip check tear batter bark

2 Write a sentence using each word below as a noun.

bend pound look play order sink

3 Write a sentence using each word below as a verb.

permit sign project present paint produce

4 Draw four columns and write each word below in the first one. In the other three columns, write different meanings for each word.

A. bill
B. note
C. seal
D. bow
E. range
F. roll

5 Use each word below in two sentences to show two different meanings.

A. trick
B. watch
C. stick
D. light
E. round
F. grade

6 Make a poster that shows six different meanings of the word *break*.

7 Which of the words below have more than one meaning? Write them in alphabetical order.

fast tape almost patch sightseeing ship mind skirt koala draft judge meant quarter guitar shake

8 Write a paragraph using two meanings of each word below.

land park school space odd

9 Write a riddle for each word below.

spot root time model mine will point case

Example: I am a group of animals who hunt together or something you do before you go on a trip. (pack)

Independent Practice Grid Program the student directions with the number of activities to be completed. Then copy the page for each student.

Names ____________________

Date ____________________

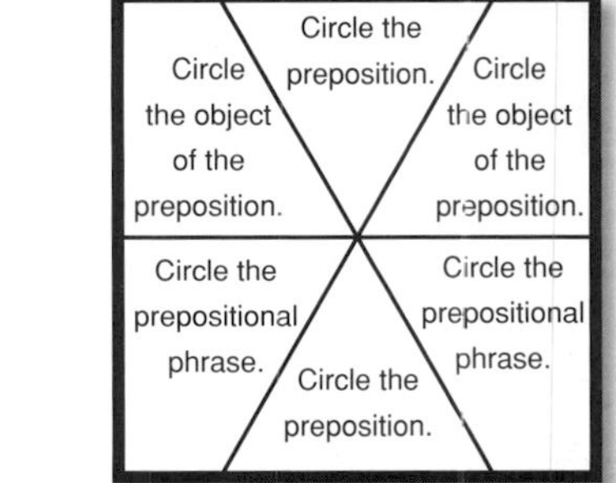

A LITTLE TO THE LEFT

A Game for Two Players

Directions:

1. Choose a pencil that is a different color than your partner's.
2. In turn, choose a box. Then spin the spinner to find out which word or words to circle.
3. After you draw your circle, have your partner check the key. If you are correct, color the square. If you are incorrect, erase your circle.
4. Play for a set amount of time or until all the squares are colored. The player with more colored squares wins.

Example: Don't walk under the crane, Cal!

Prepositional Phrase	Preposition	Object of the Preposition
under the crane	under	crane

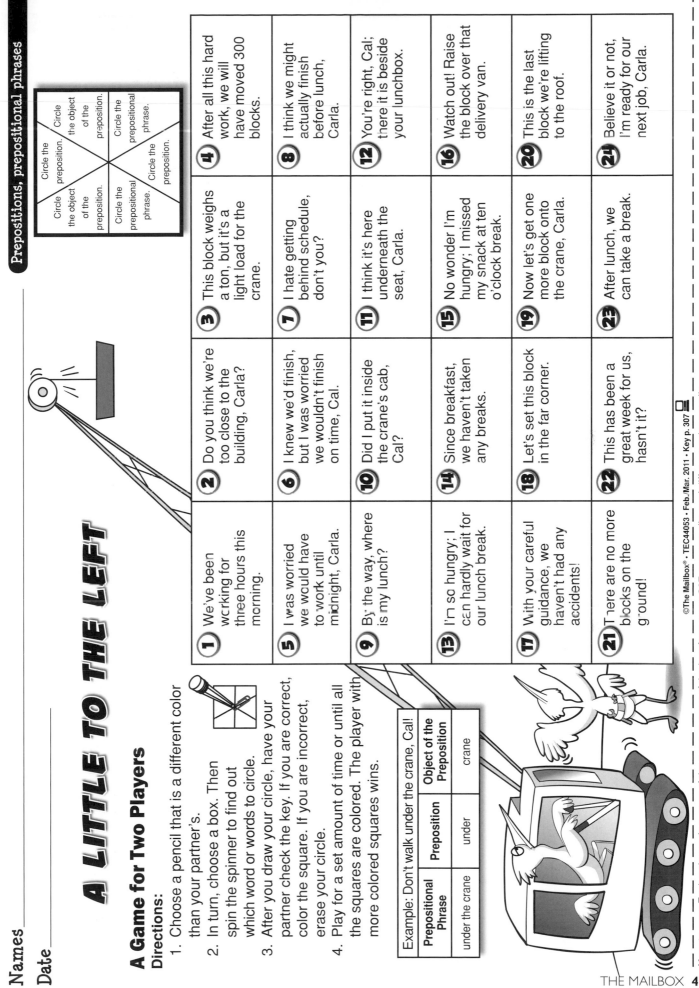

1 We've been working for three hours this morning.	2 Do you think we're too close to the building, Carla?	3 This block weighs a ton, but it's a light load for the crane.	4 After all this hard work, we will have moved 300 blocks.
5 I was worried we would have to work until midnight, Carla.	6 I knew we'd finish, but I was worried we wouldn't finish on time, Cal.	7 I hate getting behind schedule, don't you?	8 I think we might actually finish before lunch, Carla.
9 By the way, where is my lunch?	10 Did I put it inside the crane's cab, Cal?	11 I think it's here underneath the seat, Carla.	12 You're right, Cal; there it is beside your lunchbox.
13 I'm so hungry; I can hardly wait for our lunch break.	14 Since breakfast, we haven't taken any breaks.	15 No wonder I'm hungry; I missed my snack at ten o'clock break.	16 Watch out! Raise the block over that delivery van.
17 With your careful guidance, we haven't had any accidents!	18 Let's set this block in the far corner.	19 Now let's get one more block onto the crane, Carla.	20 This is the last block we're lifting to the roof.
21 There are no more blocks on the ground!	22 This has been a great week for us, hasn't it?	23 After lunch, we can take a break.	24 Believe it or not, I'm ready for our next job, Carla.

How to use: Each pair needs a copy of the page, a copy of the key from page 307, a paper clip, and different-color pencils.

Name ____________________ Comparative, superlative adjectives and adverbs

Date ____________________

A Better Angler?

Circle the word or words that correctly complete each sentence.

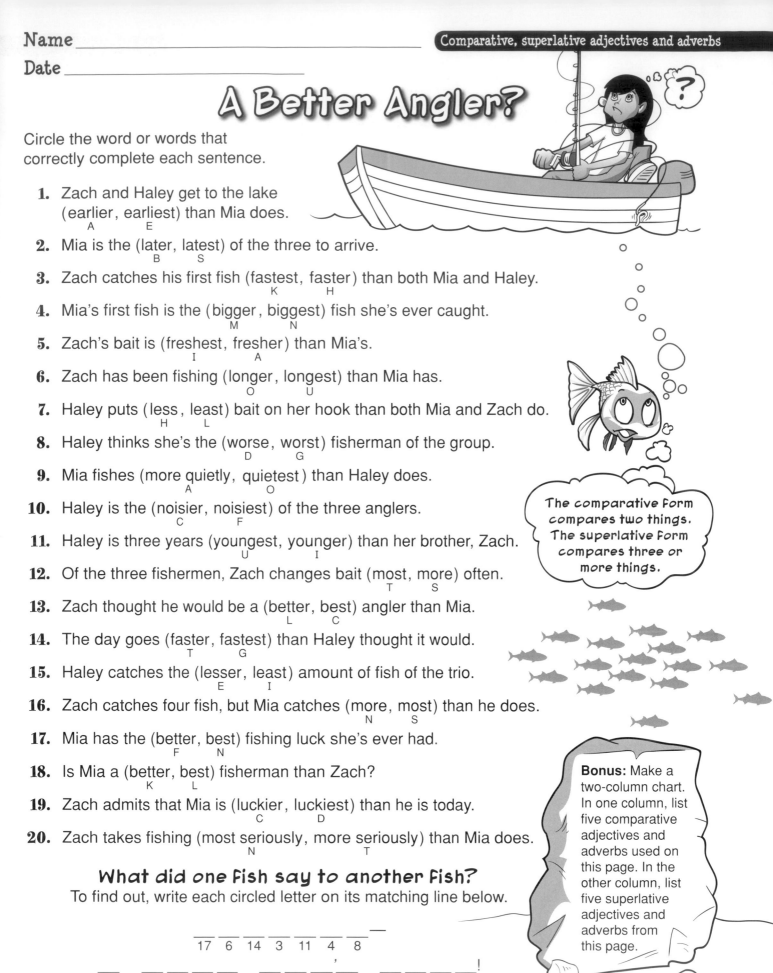

1. Zach and Haley get to the lake (earlier, earliest) than Mia does.
   A E

2. Mia is the (later, latest) of the three to arrive.
   B S
3. Zach catches his first fish (fastest, faster) than both Mia and Haley.
   K H
4. Mia's first fish is the (bigger, biggest) fish she's ever caught.
   M N
5. Zach's bait is (freshest, fresher) than Mia's.
   I A
6. Zach has been fishing (longer, longest) than Mia has.
   O U
7. Haley puts (less, least) bait on her hook than both Mia and Zach do.
   H L
8. Haley thinks she's the (worse, worst) fisherman of the group.
   D G
9. Mia fishes (more quietly, quietest) than Haley does.
   A O
10. Haley is the (noisier, noisiest) of the three anglers.
    C F
11. Haley is three years (youngest, younger) than her brother, Zach.
    U I
12. Of the three fishermen, Zach changes bait (most, more) often.
    T S
13. Zach thought he would be a (better, best) angler than Mia.
    L C
14. The day goes (faster, fastest) than Haley thought it would.
    T G
15. Haley catches the (lesser, least) amount of fish of the trio.
    E I
16. Zach catches four fish, but Mia catches (more, most) than he does.
    N S
17. Mia has the (better, best) fishing luck she's ever had.
    F N
18. Is Mia a (better, best) fisherman than Zach?
    K L
19. Zach admits that Mia is (luckier, luckiest) than he is today.
    C D
20. Zach takes fishing (most seriously, more seriously) than Mia does.
    N T

The comparative form compares two things. The superlative form compares three or more things.

Bonus: Make a two-column chart. In one column, list five comparative adjectives and adverbs used on this page. In the other column, list five superlative adjectives and adverbs from this page.

What did one fish say to another fish?

To find out, write each circled letter on its matching line below.

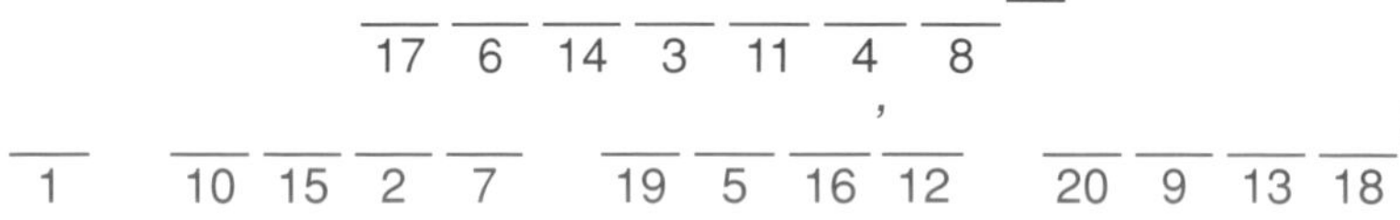

___ ___ ___ ___ ___ ___ ___ —
17 6 14 3 11 4 8

___ ___ ___ ___ ___ ___ ___ ___ ' ___ ___ ___ ___ ___ !
1 10 15 2 7 19 5 16 12 20 9 13 18

Name ______________________________

Date ____________________

Now We're Rollin'

Read the poems.

Precious Girl

A Poem for Two Voices

Voice One	Voice Two
Grandpa's girl–	My ole girl–
Will soon be mine.	
	I bought her back in sixty-nine.
Roll-down windows, no AC.	
	There was no cooler ride for me.
No GPS, no MP3s.	
	We hadn't even heard of DVDs.
Faded paint and leather seats.	
	I always kept her nice and neat.
My friends' cars are showroom new.	
	You'll never have a payment due.
My grandpa's girl will have to do.	
	And I'm proud to give her to you!

Finally!

Walked dogs, mowed leaves, babysat,
Did the dishes, fed the cat,
Saved my pennies, added sums—
Now the day has really come!
The owner's gone to get the keys.
Hope I can drive with wobbly knees!

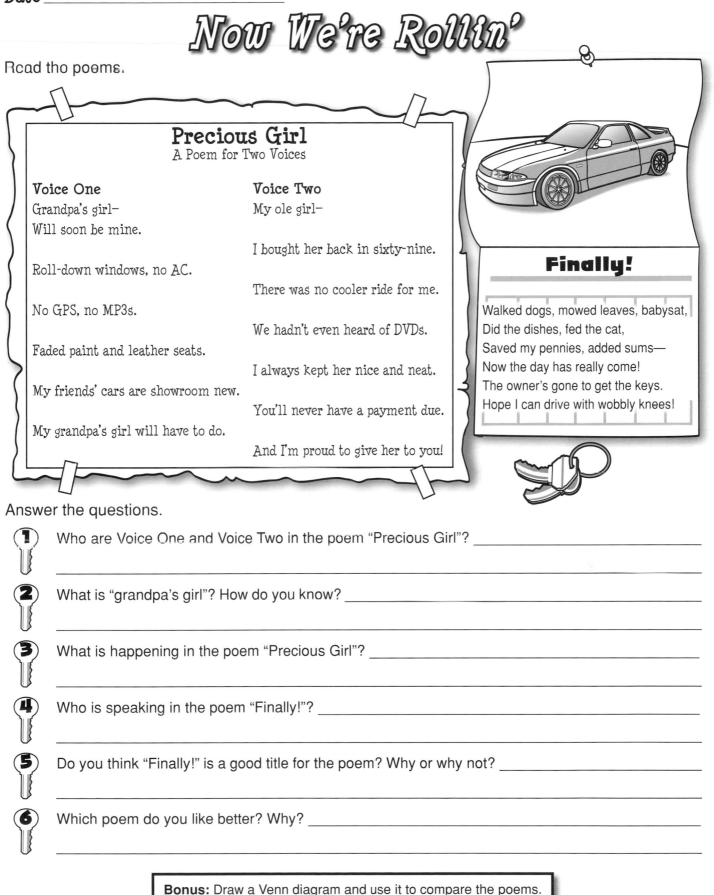

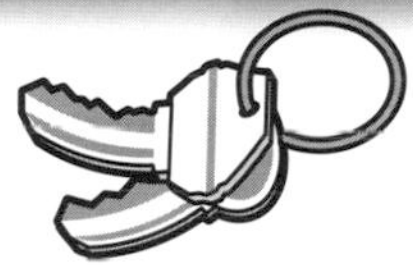

Answer the questions.

1. Who are Voice One and Voice Two in the poem "Precious Girl"? ______________________

2. What is "grandpa's girl"? How do you know? ______________________

3. What is happening in the poem "Precious Girl"? ______________________

4. Who is speaking in the poem "Finally!"? ______________________

5. Do you think "Finally!" is a good title for the poem? Why or why not? ______________________

6. Which poem do you like better? Why? ______________________

Bonus: Draw a Venn diagram and use it to compare the poems.

Name ____________________

Date ____________________

It's a Toss Up!

This is a fluffy flamingo.

It's a sinister snake.

That's a slimy snail.

That's a rambunctious raccoon.

See the persistent panda?

Is that a hectic hippo?

Is this a timid tiger?

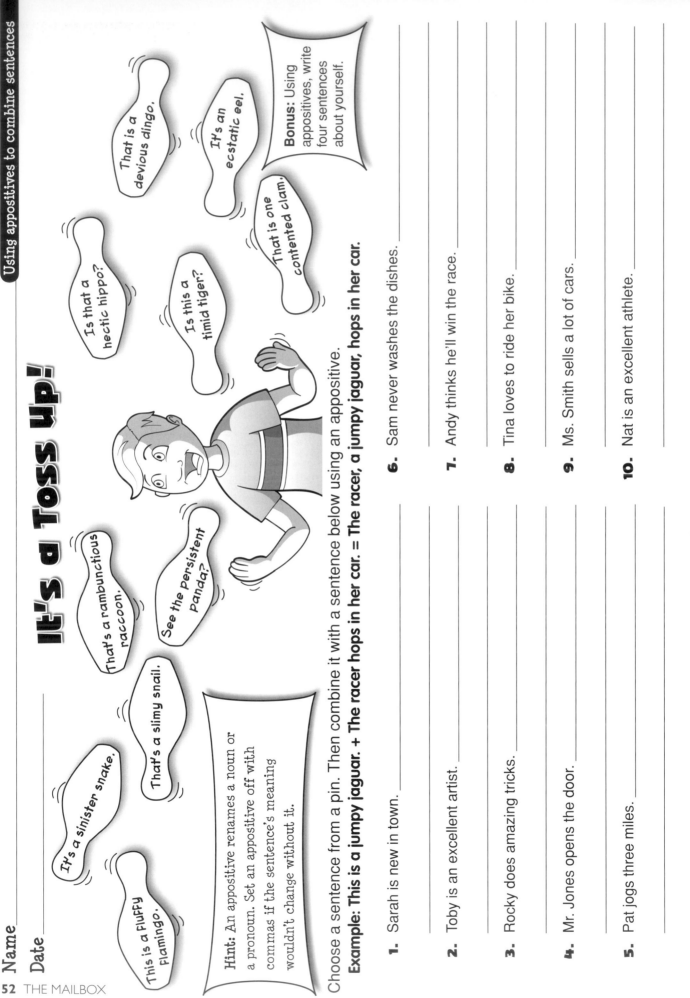

That is a devious dingo.

It's an ecstatic eel.

That is one contented clam.

Hint: An appositive renames a noun or a pronoun. Set an appositive off with commas if the sentence's meaning wouldn't change without it.

Bonus: Using appositives, write four sentences about yourself.

Choose a sentence from a pin. Then combine it with a sentence below using an appositive.

Example: This is a jumpy jaguar. + The racer hops in her car. = The racer, a jumpy jaguar, hops in her car.

1. Sarah is new in town. ____________________
2. Toby is an excellent artist. ____________________
3. Rocky does amazing tricks. ____________________
4. Mr. Jones opens the door. ____________________
5. Pat jogs three miles. ____________________
6. Sam never washes the dishes. ____________________
7. Andy thinks he'll win the race. ____________________
8. Tina loves to ride her bike. ____________________
9. Ms. Smith sells a lot of cars. ____________________
10. Nat is an excellent athlete. ____________________

Names ______________________________

Date ______________________

Zipping Through the Jungle

A Game for Two Players

Directions:

1. Choose a path. In turn, flip the coin. Choose a sentence according to the code. If all the sentences for your coin flip have been used, your turn is over.
2. Read the sentence. If it is a compound sentence, check the box. If the sentence is a complex sentence, underline the dependent clause and draw an X in the box.
3. Have your partner check your answer. If you are correct, shade the number of spaces on your path that are shown in parentheses. If you are incorrect, erase your answer. Your turn is over.
4. The player who reaches Finish first wins.

Start

Coin Code

heads = even-numbered sentence   tails = odd-numbered sentence

Start

- ☐ **1.** Jungle birds are beautiful, and they make many different sounds. **(1)**
- ☐ **2.** Gorillas seem scary because they can make loud noises slapping their chests. **(2)**
- ☐ **3.** A hippopotamus's vision is not very good, but it has a great sense of smell. **(3)**
- ☐ **4.** Although zebras mainly eat grass, you may see them eating bark, leaves, and fruit too. **(1)**
- ☐ **5.** You should study the habits of jungle animals before you plan a safari. **(2)**
- ☐ **6.** A jungle may seem frightening, but it is a very interesting place. **(3)**
- ☐ **7.** If you want to go to a jungle, you should find an experienced guide. **(2)**
- ☐ **8.** Elephants fill their trunks with water, and then they carry the water to their mouths. **(2)**
- ☐ **9.** Chimpanzees are intelligent animals, they are known to be very playful and curious. **(2)**
- ☐ **10.** When it stands up, a male gorilla can be six feet tall. **(2)**
- ☐ **11.** Before you sleep in a jungle, you should put up a mosquito net. **(2)**
- ☐ **12.** A zebra can run fast, but it is not faster than a cheetah. **(2)**
- ☐ **13.** Because elephants have no sweat glands, they cool off by rolling in mud. **(1)**
- ☐ **14.** There are different kinds of snakes in the jungle, and some of them are vividly colored. **(3)**
- ☐ **15.** The hippopotamus is considered a land animal although it spends most of its time in the water. **(3)**
- ☐ **16.** Chimpanzees walk on all fours, but they can also walk upright. **(3)**
- ☐ **17.** A zebra can swivel its ears to find a sound, and its night vision is as good as an owl's. **(2)**
- ☐ **18.** Because cheetahs run so fast, it is exciting to watch them. **(1)**
- ☐ **19.** A cheetah can run up to 70 miles per hour, but it can only run that fast for a short time. **(3)**
- ☐ **20.** Since cheetah populations have rapidly declined, the cheetah is now listed as an endangered species. **(2)**
- ☐ **21.** Even though they are fascinating, you must be careful around wild animals. **(3)**
- ☐ **22.** A jungle is filled with interesting animals, and it is a wonderful place to visit. **(3)**
- ☐ **23.** Elephants have very strong trunks, and they can carry objects that weigh as much as 600 pounds. **(2)**
- ☐ **24.** If you are afraid of snakes, it is probably not a good idea to go on a jungle safari. **(2)**

Finish

Finish

How to use: Each student pair needs a coin, a copy of the page, and a copy of the key on page 308.

Center Cards and Answer Key

Use with "You Crack Me Up!" on page 55.

(1) How can you tel whether a snake is a baby? It has a ratle! TEC44054	(2) Which birds' like to work construction? Cranes do of course? TEC44054
(3) Which card game do Alligators love to play? Their favorite Game is Snap. TEC44054	(4) What has 18 legs and catchs flies? A baseball teem does. TEC44054
(5) Which of a birds' sides has more feathers? It's outside has more feathers, than its inside. TEC44054	(6) What could you call snake carpenter? You could call it a boa constructor! TEC44054
(7) Why are geese terible drivers? Thay honk all the time! TEC44054	(8) Why did the duck crossed the road? The chicken needed a day off. TEC44054
(9) Why did the goose fly North for Summer? It was way too far to walk. TEC44054	(10) Whats orange, and sounds like a parrot? *A carrot* sounds a lot like *a parrot.* TEC44054
(11) Why does the Flamingo stand on one leg? if it lifts both legs, it will Fall over! TEC44054	(12) Which bird does you always need when you eat? You need a swallow! TEC44054
(13) What would be the worse kind of tile to find in your bathroom? A reptile would be the worse kind. TEC44054	(14) How are Birds and flies different? Birds can fly, but flies can't Bird. TEC44054
(15) What wold hapen if a duck flew upside down? It woluld quack up! TEC44054	(16) If a rooster laid an egg on a slanted roof which way would the egg roll? There would not be an egg Rooster's cant lay eggs. TEC44054
(17) What, did the chicken, say to the bully? It said Why dont you peck on someone your own size. TEC44054	(18) Why does a Hummingbird always hum? It's a Bird, Silly; it doesn't know the Words! TEC44054
(19) Why did the turkey crosses the road? It wanted to prove it weren't chicken. TEC44054	(20) Why did the hen lay so meny eggs? If she had just droped them, they wuould have brocken! TEC44054

Answer Key for "You Crack Me Up!"

Usage or Grammar	Spelling	Punctuation	Capitalization
6, 8, 12, 13, 19	1, 4, 7, 15, 20	2, 5, 10, 16, 17	3, 9, 11, 14, 18

TEC44054

YOU CRACK ME UP!

Proofreading

Directions:

1. Shuffle the cards and then draw one.
2. Read the joke and identify its error or errors. Place the card on the matching egg.
3. After you sort all the cards, use the key to check your work.
4. Then write each joke on another sheet of paper, correcting its error or errors.

Usage or Grammar

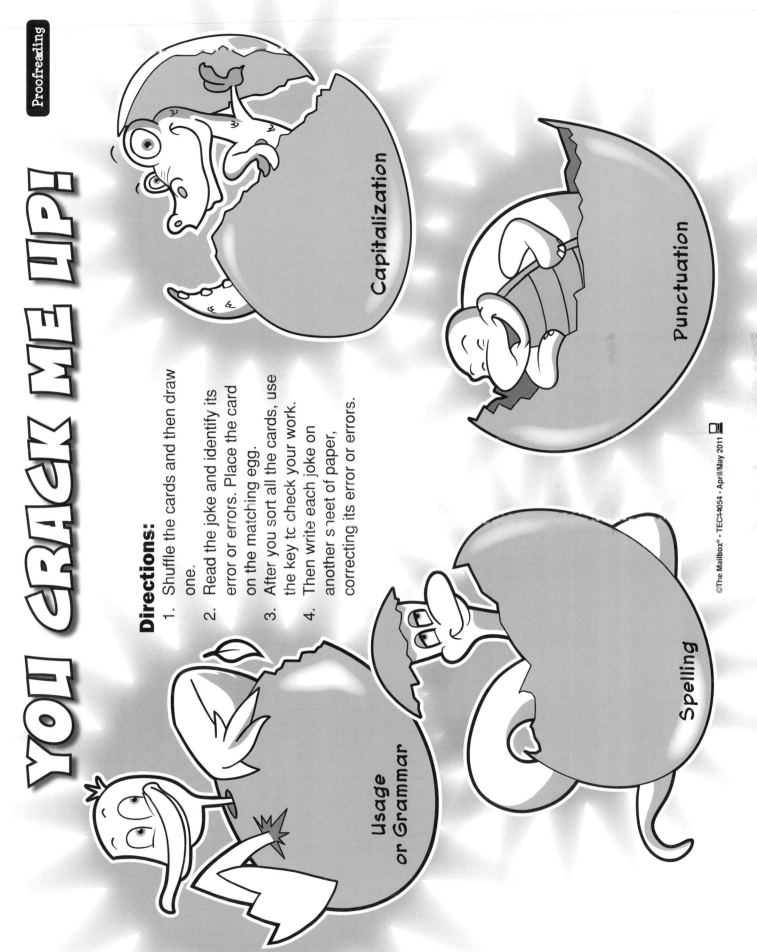

Capitalization

Name ______________________________ **Comprehension, informational text**

Date ____________________

Manta Ray Memos

There are nearly 550 species of rays, such as guitarfish, manta rays, sawfish, skates, stingrays, and electric rays. A ray is a fish that, like a shark, has a skeleton made of cartilage. Most rays have flat bodies. The manta ray is the largest of the rays, weighing up to 3,000 pounds. Its *pectoral*, or side, fins are so big they look like wings. The average manta ray is 22 feet wide. That's about as wide as a two-story house is tall!

To swim, the manta ray flaps its pectoral fins like wings. A manta ray can seem to fly through the water. The manta ray is one of the strongest rays. In fact, mantas are such strong swimmers that they can jump out of the water. Manta rays have been spotted soaring out of the water and landing headfirst, landing tail first, or somersaulting. These behaviors may be forms of manta ray play, or they may be manta ways of attracting mates.

Most rays' mouths are on their undersides. The manta ray's mouth is at the front of its head. A manta ray has 12 to 18 rows of teeth on its lower jaw but no teeth on its top. Like most rays, mantas are filter feeders. These gentle giants sometimes eat small fish, but they survive on tiny plankton. As a manta ray swims, it filters plankton from the water through its huge, open mouth.

Complete each sentence using facts from the selection. Underline the facts you use. Then number the facts to match the sentences.

1. Like a shark, a manta ray ______________________________.
2. The average manta ray ______________________________.
3. Surprisingly, a manta ray ______________________________.
4. Like most rays, a manta ray ______________________________.
5. When a manta ray eats, ______________________________.
6. A swimming manta ray can be compared to ______________________________.
7. Unlike most rays, a manta ray ______________________________.
8. A manta ray's main diet ______________________________.
9. A better title for this selection would be ______________________________.
10. The author's purpose for writing this selection is ______________________________.

Bonus: Draw a picture showing one thing you learned about the manta ray. Add a caption that explains your drawing.

Name ____

Date ______________________

Singing Up a Storm

Use an idiom to complete each sentence.

1. Rock E. Starr ______________________________ (listens carefully) when his favorite rocker, Cari Oakey, steps up to the mike.
2. One day, ______________________________ (unexpectedly), Cari calls Rock.
3. When Rock figures out that Cari Oakey is on the phone, he gets ______________________________ (nervous feelings).
4. Cari thinks Rock can be a big star, so she ______________________________ (helps or guides him).
5. Cari ______________________________ (teaches all she knows about the business) of being a rock star.
6. When Cari invites Rock to perform with her, he starts to panic, but he ______________________________ (acts bravely) and joins her on stage.
7. Rock is ______________________________ (thrilled) when he hears that his first solo concert is sold out.
8. For Rock, working with Cari Oakey is unbelievably cool; getting his own show is just ______________________________ (one more good thing).
9. Rock's concert is fabulous, and news about Rock spreads ______________________________ (quickly).
10. After five more shows, Rock will ______________________________ (begin a journey) on his own concert tour.
11. Soon, performing a solo concert is ______________________________ (easy) for Rock.
12. When Rock thinks of his future, it seems like ______________________________ (anything is possible).

Idioms

a walk in the park	bites the bullet	butterflies in his stomach
hit the road	icing on the cake	is all ears
like wildfire	out of the blue	shows him the ropes
takes him under her wing	the sky's the limit	walking on air

Bonus: Use each of the following idioms in a sentence.
- just along for the ride (just a passenger, not a helper)
- walk on eggshells (to be very careful)
- a stroke of genius (a great idea)

Name ______________________

Date ______________________

Mystery Groceries

Use what you know and what you read to identify the product that belongs with each label. Write the type of product on the line. Circle the clue or clues in each label that helped you name the product.

1. Mix with one can of water or milk. Heat for two minutes. Serve with crackers.
   canned soup

2. Real Fresh Fruit in every jar. Picked Fresh from the vine! It's peanut butter's best partner.
   ____

3. Squeeze out a small amount. Use after each meal to keep your smile bright!
   ____

4. **Works on tough stains—even grass and mud! Safe for all fabrics!**
   ____

5. Hold the bottle ten inches from surface and spray. Wipe with a paper towel for a streak-free shine.
   ____

6. **More real cheese! Premium pepperoni! Rising crust! Ready to eat in 20 minutes!**
   ____

7. Spoon the batter onto a hot griddle. Cook 2 minutes on each side. Serve warm with maple syrup.
   ____

8. **Smart choice for breakfast! Just add milk! Whole-grain oats fortified with vitamins and minerals!**
   ____

9. **For Clean and Tangle-Free Hair Conditioning for Extra Softness**
   ____

10. **Made from ripe tomatoes at the peak of the season. Great on hamburgers, hot dogs, and french fries!**
    ____

11. Excellent Source of Calcium and Vitamins A & D Drink it every day!
    ____

12. *Ready to Pop!* Movie Theater Butter Microwave 3-Pack
    ____

13. **100% Natural No Pulp! 100% Vitamin C Pour a glass today!**
    ____

14. Farm Fresh Grade A Large One Dozen Perishable–Keep Refrigerated
    ____

15. **20 Sterile Assorted Sizes Adhesive Flexible Fabric We help you heal!**
    ____

16. **Baked With Real Cheese No Artificial Flavors Fun-Shaped Crispy Snack**
    ____

Bonus: Create a new package for your favorite snack without naming or showing the snack. Include clues that will help others figure out what's inside.

Think or Sink

Use the letters on the fish to write a four-letter word down the side of your paper. (Use each letter only once.) Then write a response to each of the four matching prompts.

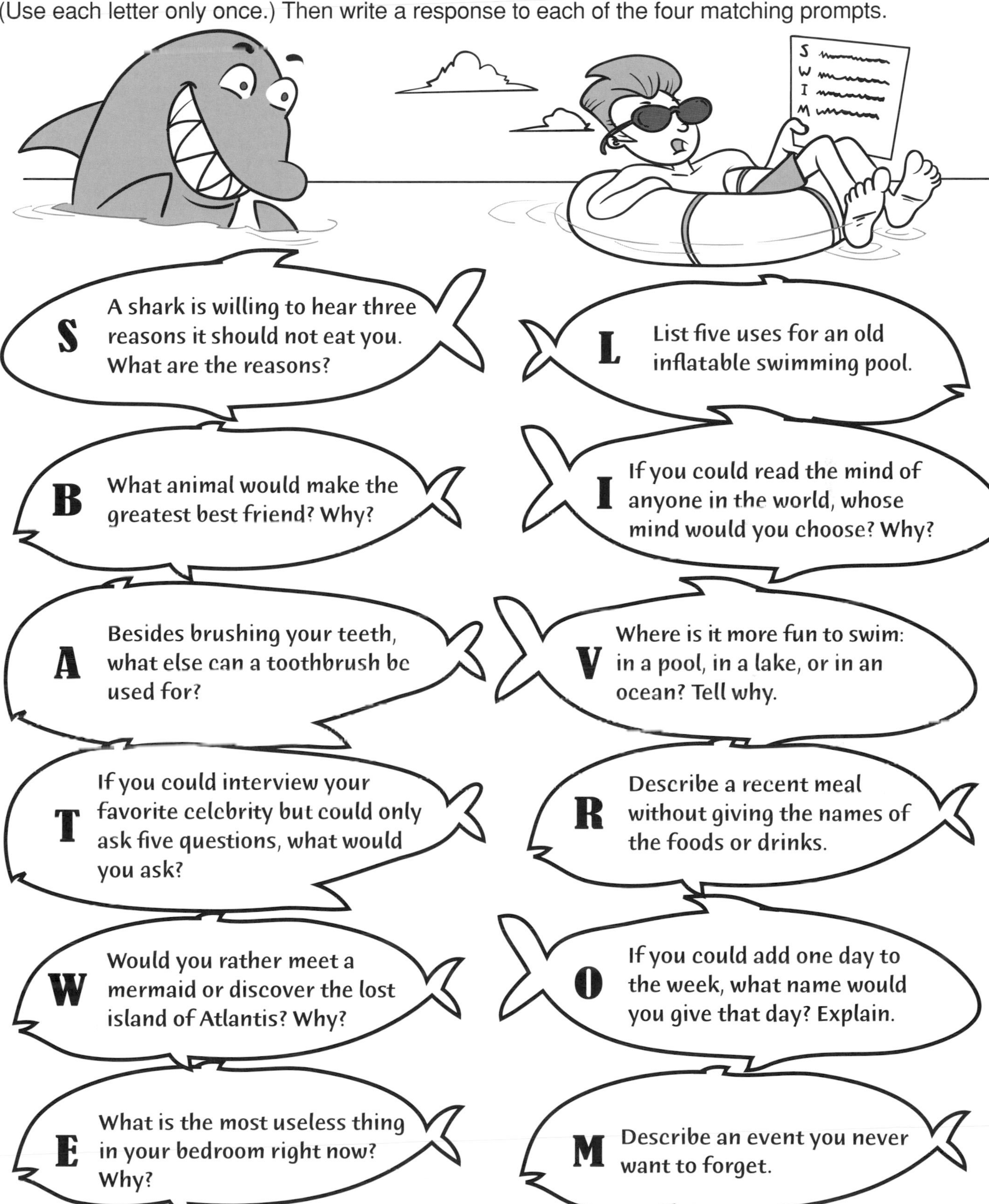

S
W
I
M
S A shark is willing to hear three reasons it should not eat you. What are the reasons?
L List five uses for an old inflatable swimming pool.
B What animal would make the greatest best friend? Why?
I If you could read the mind of anyone in the world, whose mind would you choose? Why?
A Besides brushing your teeth, what else can a toothbrush be used for?
V Where is it more fun to swim: in a pool, in a lake, or in an ocean? Tell why.
T If you could interview your favorite celebrity but could only ask five questions, what would you ask?
R Describe a recent meal without giving the names of the foods or drinks.
W Would you rather meet a mermaid or discover the lost island of Atlantis? Why?
O If you could add one day to the week, what name would you give that day? Explain.
E What is the most useless thing in your bedroom right now? Why?
M Describe an event you never want to forget.

How to use: Display this page. Then guide each student to write thoughtful responses.

Names ____________________

Date ____________________

THE WINNING WORD

A Game for Two Contestants

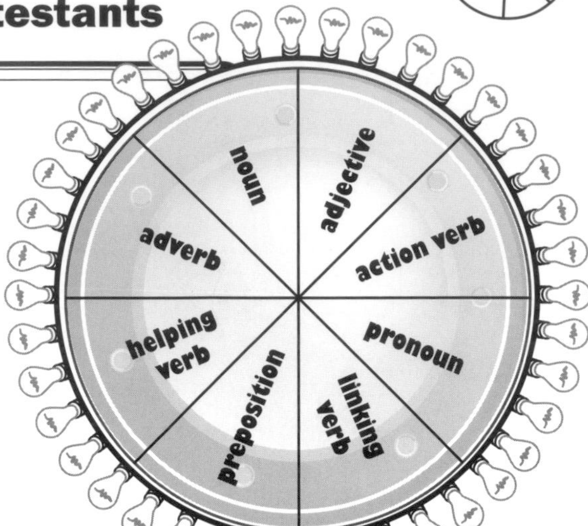

DIRECTIONS:

1. Choose a grid.
2. In turn, spin to determine the part of speech you will look for. Then circle a word in the paragraphs below that is that part of speech. Have your opponent use the answer key to check your answer.
3. If you are correct, write the word in a matching box on your grid. If you are not correct, erase your circle. Your turn is over.
4. If you have already filled the box or boxes for the part of speech, your turn is over.
5. Fill all the boxes on your grid first to win.

Otto Winn is the youngest contestant on this game show. He has already won five times. If Otto wins today, he will have won over ten thousand dollars. Otto says he does not get nervous, but he seems jumpy. Otto hopes he will win today.

Anita Wynn is Otto's opponent today. This is Anita's first game show. She says she is nervous, but she seems very calm. If Anita wins the game, she will buy a new laptop. Anita has been practicing for two years. She reads a different encyclopedia every day.

Otto answers the first ten questions correctly. Then Anita gives the next ten correct responses. Otto and Anita are tied. No one knows who will win. It comes to the final question. Otto buzzes right before Anita, and his response is right! Otto wins! Anita gets the consolation prize. To her surprise, it is a new laptop!

Player 1

noun	adjective
action verb	pronoun
linking verb	helping verb
preposition	adverb
adjective	action verb
linking verb	helping verb
preposition	adverb

Player 2

noun	adjective
action verb	pronoun
linking verb	helping verb
preposition	adverb
adjective	action verb
linking verb	helping verb
preposition	adverb

 How to use: Each pair of students needs a copy of the page, a copy of the answer key on page 308, and a paper clip.

BRAIN BOOSTERS

Brain Booster 1

A. There are _____ *e*'s in this complete sentence.

B. The word _____ tells how many *r*'s are in this complete sentence.

TEC44050

Brain Booster 2

Rearrange the blocks of letters to spell a common 10-letter word.

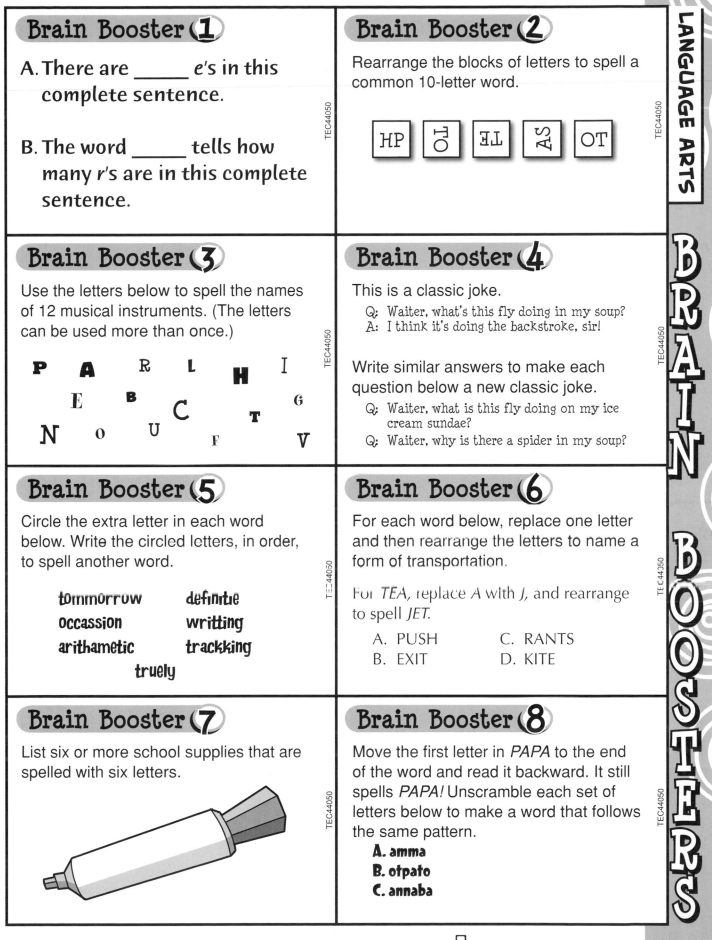

HP | TO | TE | AS | OT

TEC44050

Brain Booster 3

Use the letters below to spell the names of 12 musical instruments. (The letters can be used more than once.)

P A R L H I E B C G T N O U F V

TEC44050

Brain Booster 4

This is a classic joke.

Q: Waiter, what's this fly doing in my soup?
A: I think it's doing the backstroke, sir!

Write similar answers to make each question below a new classic joke.

Q: Waiter, what is this fly doing on my ice cream sundae?
Q: Waiter, why is there a spider in my soup?

TEC44050

Brain Booster 5

Circle the extra letter in each word below. Write the circled letters, in order, to spell another word.

tommorrow
occassion
arithametic
definitie
writting
trackking
truely

TEC44050

Brain Booster 6

For each word below, replace one letter and then rearrange the letters to name a form of transportation.

For *TEA*, replace *A* with *J*, and rearrange to spell *JET*.

A. PUSH
B. EXIT
C. RANTS
D. KITE

TEC44050

Brain Booster 7

List six or more school supplies that are spelled with six letters.

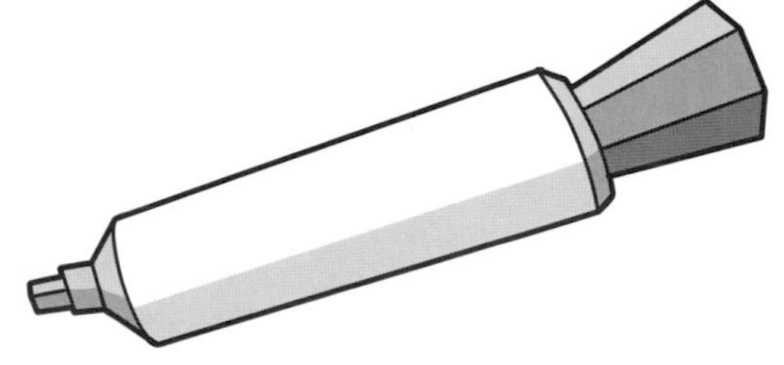

TEC44050

Brain Booster 8

Move the first letter in *PAPA* to the end of the word and read it backward. It still spells *PAPA!* Unscramble each set of letters below to make a word that follows the same pattern.

A. amma
B. otpato
C. annaba

TEC44050

Note to the teacher: Give each student a copy of this page (or one card at a time) to work on during free time.

LANGUAGE ARTS

BRAIN BOOSTERS

Brain Booster 1

Spell at least ten nouns using only the letters in *October*.

O C O T E R B

TEC44051

Brain Booster 2

Find the name of an animal hidden in each city name below.

Example: find *lion* in **Li**nc**o**l**n**, NE.

A. Dexter, KS
B. Buena Park, CA
C. Colorado City, AZ
D. Chicken, AK
E. Harvey, LA

TEC44051

Brain Booster 3

For which profession might a person use each pair of tools?

A. metronome and baton
B. anemometer and barometer
C. level and chisel

TEC44051

Brain Booster 4

At her party, Patti only wants to serve snacks that begin with the letter *P.* Name eight or more snacks she can serve. (Be sure to include some healthy fruits!)

TEC44051

Brain Booster 5

One of the boldfaced words in each proverb is in the wrong saying. Correct each statement.

a. It is easier to make **money** than to **well** it.
b. If you don't scale the **keep**, you can't view the **plain**.
c. Dig a **mountain** before you are **thirsty**.

TEC44051

Brain Booster 6

Write these holidays in the order they appear on a calendar.

Columbus Day
Memorial Day
Thanksgiving Day
Labor Day
Veterans Day
Presidents' Day
Independence Day

TEC44051

Brain Booster 7

What is the longest sentence you can write using words that start with consecutive letters of the alphabet? (You can start with any letter.)

Example: **A**lex **b**rought **C**arla **d**elightful **e**arrings **F**riday.

TEC44051

Brain Booster 8

Write the word that means "a roadside place for overnight lodging." Then remove the *o* and rearrange the letters to write a word that means "to change from a solid to a liquid."

TEC44051

How to use: Give each student a copy of this page (or one card at a time) to work on during free time.

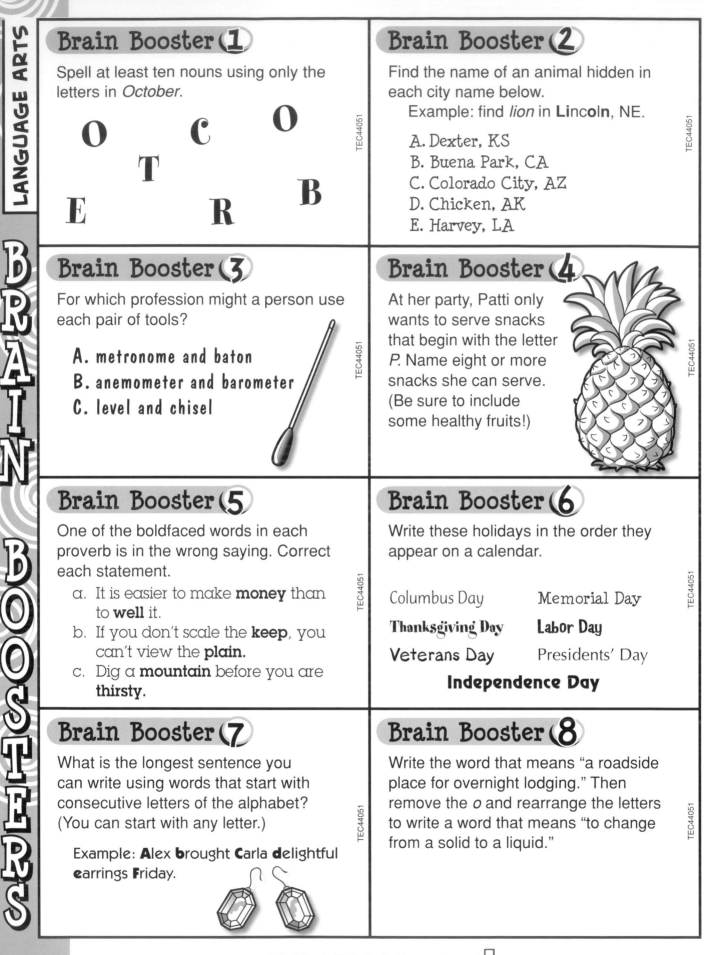

BRAIN BOOSTERS

Brain Booster 1

List at least five sets of three homonyms.

Example: pear, pair, pare

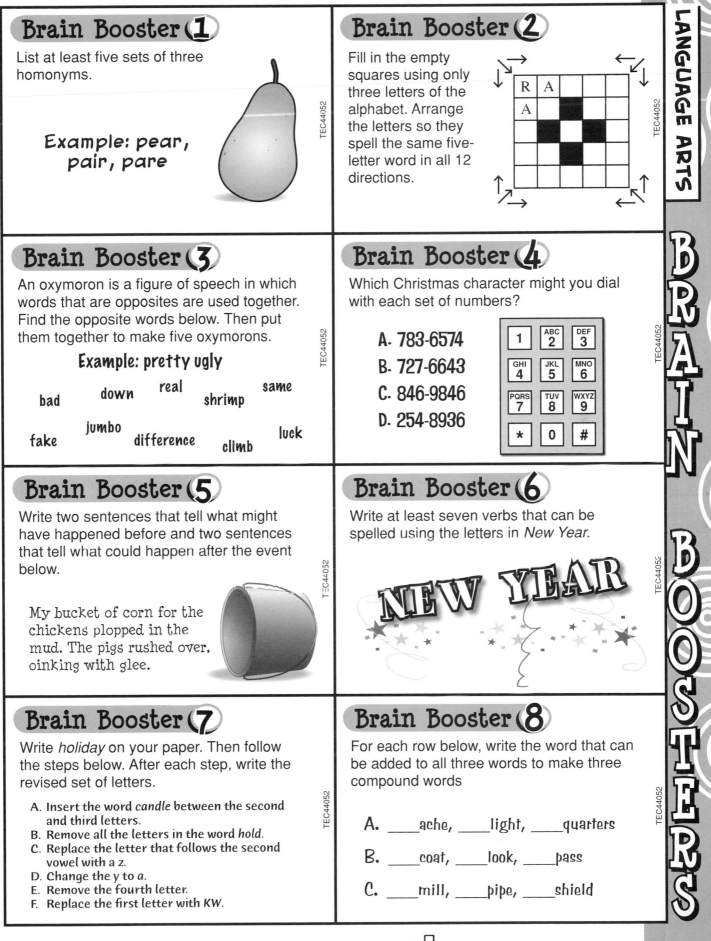

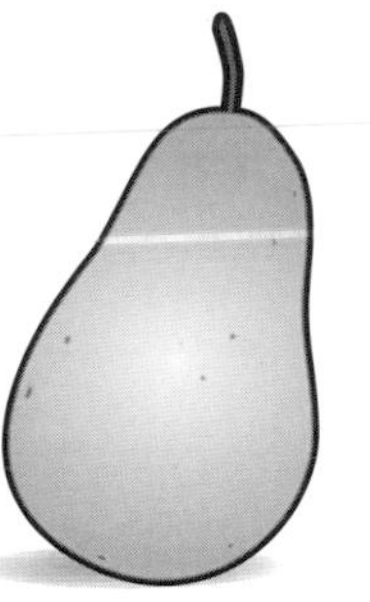

TEC44052

Brain Booster 2

Fill in the empty squares using only three letters of the alphabet. Arrange the letters so they spell the same five-letter word in all 12 directions.

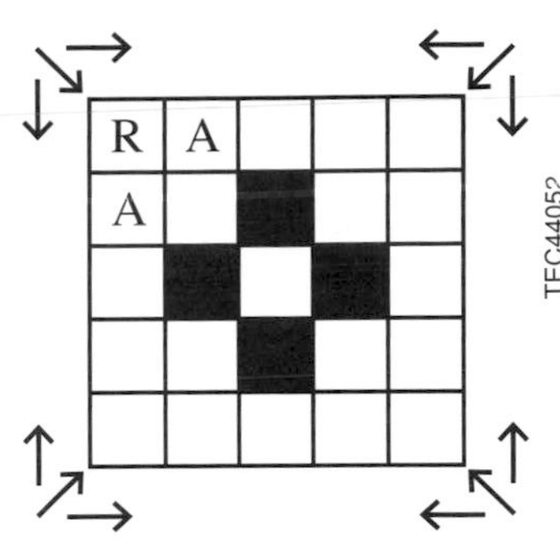

TEC44052

Brain Booster 3

An oxymoron is a figure of speech in which words that are opposites are used together. Find the opposite words below. Then put them together to make five oxymorons.

Example: pretty ugly

bad down real shrimp same

fake jumbo difference climb luck

TEC44052

Brain Booster 4

Which Christmas character might you dial with each set of numbers?

A. 783-6574
B. 727-6643
C. 846-9846
D. 254-8936

1	ABC 2	DEF 3
GHI 4	JKL 5	MNO 6
PQRS 7	TUV 8	WXYZ 9
*	0	#

TEC44052

Brain Booster 5

Write two sentences that tell what might have happened before and two sentences that tell what could happen after the event below.

My bucket of corn for the chickens plopped in the mud. The pigs rushed over, oinking with glee.

TEC44052

Brain Booster 6

Write at least seven verbs that can be spelled using the letters in *New Year.*

TEC44052

Brain Booster 7

Write *holiday* on your paper. Then follow the steps below. After each step, write the revised set of letters.

A. Insert the word *candle* between the second and third letters.
B. Remove all the letters in the word *hold*.
C. Replace the letter that follows the second vowel with a z.
D. Change the y to *a*.
E. Remove the fourth letter.
F. Replace the first letter with *KW*.

TEC44052

Brain Booster 8

For each row below, write the word that can be added to all three words to make three compound words

A. ____ache, ____light, ____quarters

B. ____coat, ____look, ____pass

C. ____mill, ____pipe, ____shield

TEC44052

How to use: Give each student a copy of this page (or one card at a time) to work on during free time.

LANGUAGE ARTS

BRAIN BOOSTERS

Brain Booster (1)

Write the word in each line that does not belong. Then tell why it doesn't belong.

A. them, him, we, us
B. was, went, are, were
C. right, well, came, done

TEC44053

Brain Booster (2)

For each category, list one word that *ends* with the letters in *LAST*.

	State Capital	Animal
L		
A		
S		
T		

TEC44053

Brain Booster (3)

Complete each analogy.

A. words : dictionary :: maps : ____
B. allowed : aloud :: bored : ____
C. ton : ounce :: boulder : ____
D. left : right :: ____ : horizontal

TEC44053

Brain Booster (4)

Write ten or more words using only the letters in *valentine.*

TEC44053

Brain Booster (5)

The early bird catches the worm.

This well-known proverb reminds us to be prompt. Write three original proverbs about a whale, a mouse, and a bee. Then tell what each one means.

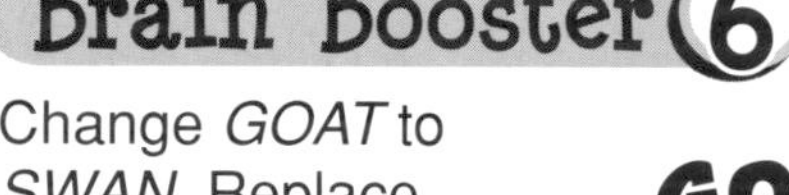

TEC44053

Brain Booster (6)

Change *GOAT* to *SWAN.* Replace only one letter to make a different word on each line.

GOAT
__ __ __ __
__ __ __ __
__ __ __ __
__ __ __ __
SWAN

TEC44053

Brain Booster (7)

A *kangaroo word* has a synonym hiding inside it. Find the synonym in each kangaroo word below. (Hint: Don't rearrange the letters to find the synonym.)

Example: illuminated→**lit**

A. observe
B. deceased
C. precipitation

TEC44053

Brain Booster (8)

Make a silly sentence by removing all extra letters.

TALHISLISAEXTSILRLALYSEENTTTEENRCES.

TEC44053

How to use: Give each student a copy of this page (or one card at a time) to work on during free time.

BRAIN BOOSTERS

Brain Booster 1

In a seven-letter word,

- letters 1, 3, 4, 5, and 6 spell a word meaning "strong and sturdy"
- letters 2, 4, and 7 spell a word meaning "a simple shelter"
- letters 1, 4, and 5 spell a word meaning "to pull with effort"
- letters 1, 3, and 7 spell a word meaning "a small child"

What is the seven-letter word?

___ ___ ___ ___ ___ ___ ___
1 2 3 4 5 6 7

TEC44054

Brain Booster 2

A business's phone number can often spell something related to its business. Decode each business phone number below.

Example: An auto mechanic's number might be 349-2277 (*FIX CARS*).

A. medical office: 362-8677
B. school supply shop: 736-2457
C. airline ticket sales: 247-3273
D. hair salon: 742-6766

TEC44054

Brain Booster 3

Invent four or more new words by combining two words, such as those shown, that share some letters. Then write the definition of the new word.

Example: laptop + operation = laptoperation: a procedure for fixing a laptop

early, near, clear, disappear, hear, BEAR, earring, eardrum, earth, earthquake, earning, year

TEC44054

Brain Booster 4

Add one letter to each underlined word to help this paragraph make sense.

Tom sad the rakes on hi tuck need to be repaced before he dries it to wok. Otherwise, it may be had for him to top on tim. Tat's why Tom is gong to he repar hop.

TEC44054

Brain Booster 5

A child gets taller as time passes. Name five or more things that get smaller as time passes.

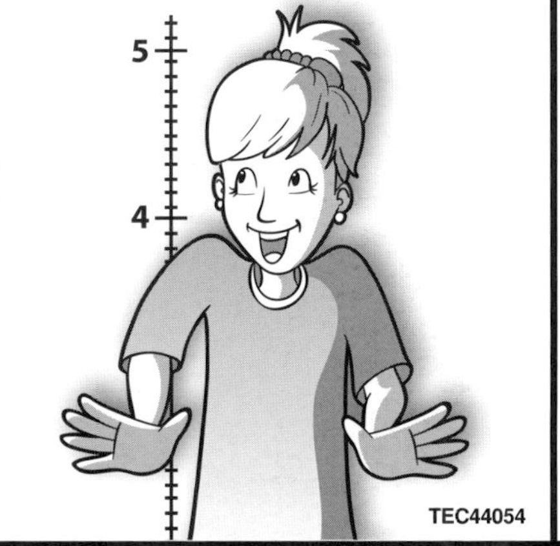

TEC44054

Brain Booster 6

Replace each word with a synonym to make rhyming pairs.

Example: chef, creek: cook, brook

A. brag, seashore: b_____, c_____
B. beneath, awe: u_____, w_____
C. danger, aircraft: t_____, j_____
D. rock, file: b_____, f_____
E. concise, sorrow: b_____, g_____

TEC44054

Brain Booster 7

The number words *ten* and *five* have been hidden in the sentence below. Write two more sentences, hiding at least two number words in each one.

I of**ten** take a nap after lunch, especially i**f I've** missed some sleep the night before.

TEC44054

Brain Booster 8

List eight or more words that rhyme with *shield.*

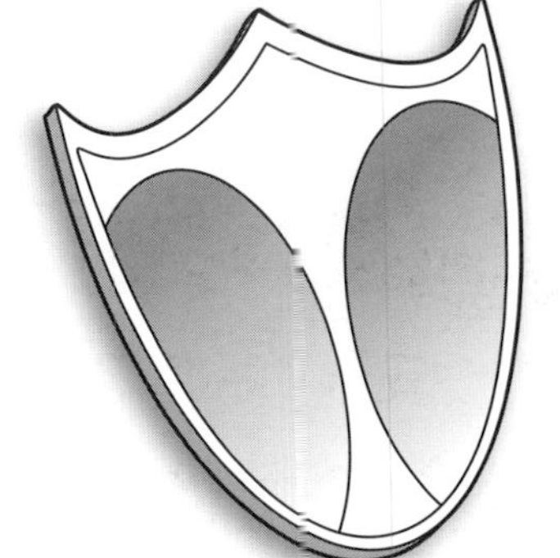

TEC44054

How to use: Display this page or give each student a copy of the page (or one card at a time) to work on during free time.

BRAIN BOOSTERS

LANGUAGE ARTS

Brain Booster 1

Use the clues below to identify the mystery word.

A. It has eleven letters and four syllables.
B. Some of its synonyms are *atmosphere*, *surroundings*, and *climate*.
C. Its last letter is *t*.

TEC44055

Brain Booster 2

Remove each letter of the alphabet in order from *A* to *Z*. Then add spaces where they are needed to uncover a Dutch proverb.

AABHCADNEDFFULOFPAG
THIIENCEJISKWOLRTHM
MONOREPTHAQRNSATUB
UVSHEWLOXFBRAYINZS.

TEC44055

Brain Booster 3

How many words that end with *-ful* can you name? List them.

-ful

TEC44055

Brain Booster 4

The answer is "belly flop." What are all the questions you can think of that have this answer?

TEC44055

Brain Booster 5

Complete each analogy. Then write four more analogies of your own.

a. steam : gas :: water : ________
b. sofa : noun :: happy : ________
c. dog : bark :: snake : ________
d. ride : ridden :: eat : ________

TEC44055

Brain Booster 6

Write at least 20 five-letter words using the letters in *Massachusetts*.

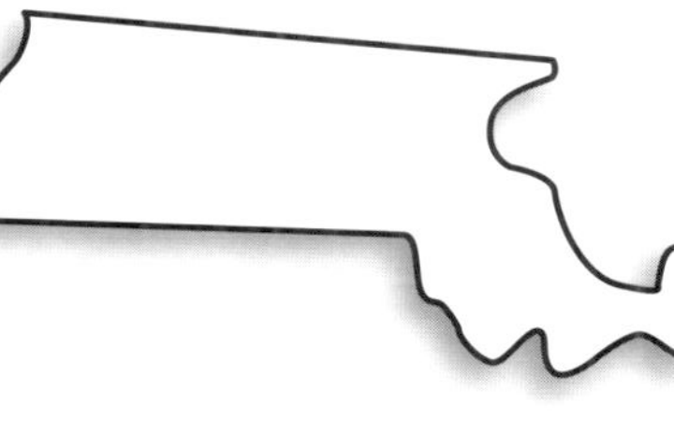

TEC44055

Brain Booster 7

Add the letters *st* to the letters of each word below. Then rearrange the letters to spell a new word that begins with *st*.

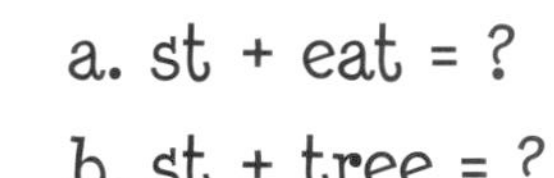

a. st + eat = ?
b. st + tree = ?
c. st + anger = ?
d. st + pier = ?
e. st + sock = ?

TEC44055

Brain Booster 8

Which month comes next in this sequence?

September, October,
November, May, ________

TEC44055

How to use: Display this page or give each student a copy of this page (or one card at a time) to work on during free time.

Writing

WRITE NOW!

It's in the Cards!

Prewriting, narrative writing

For this idea, copy and cut apart the story element cards on page 79. Then label four envelopes as shown and sort the cards into the matching envelopes. Next, have each pair of students choose two envelopes and draw one card from each one. Guide the partners to read the cards and then work together to write the rest of the story. As time allows, have each duo share its story. Then collect students' cards, put them back in the envelopes, and keep them handy for anytime writing inspiration.

MaryLouise Curto, Newgrange School
Hamilton, NJ

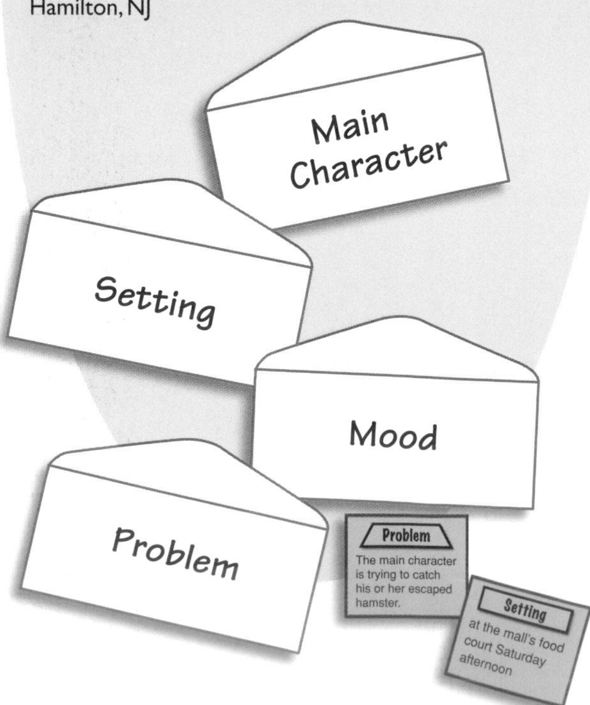

Fly the Flag

Writing process

Here's a simple tip for keeping track of students' writing progress! Give each child five sticky notes and have her label each one with a step in the writing process. Have the student keep the sticky notes inside her writing folder. Then, at the end of each writing session, have her stick the note that describes the stage of her writing on her paper so it shows at the top of her folder like a flag. With just a glance, you can tell the status of each student's writing.

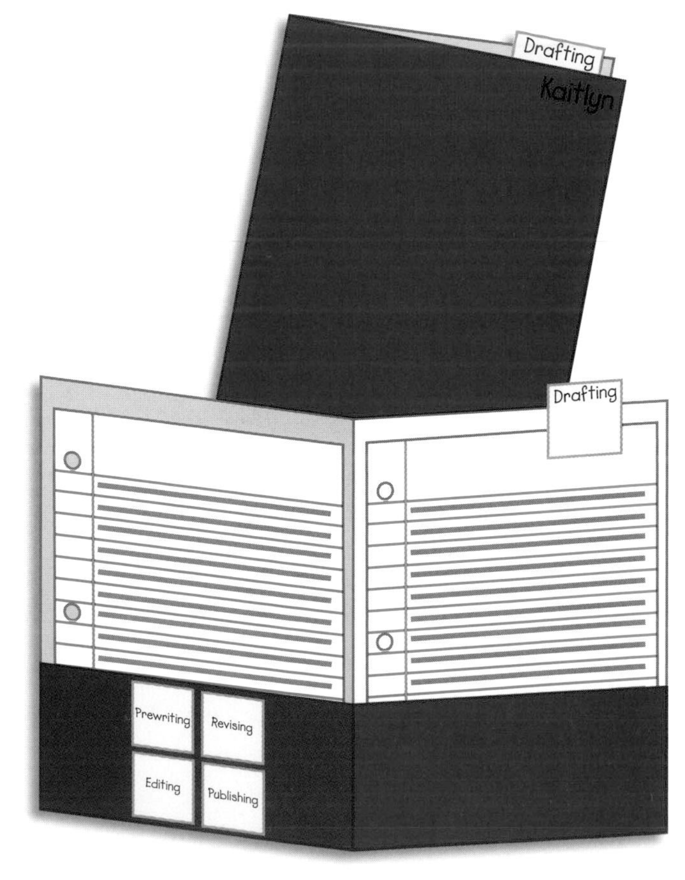

Name Dropper
Descriptive writing

This whole-class game, a twist on the Name That Tune game show, helps students write better descriptions! Before playing, choose a mystery person, place, or thing and make a list of ten phrases that describe it. Then, keeping the item secret, read aloud one phrase at a time. Have students record the phrases as they try to guess what you are describing. If someone guesses correctly before you read the tenth phrase, share the rest of the phrases and guide the class to write a descriptive paragraph about the person, place, or thing. If students do not guess the answer, tell them what it is. Then have each student use his list of phrases to write a paragraph that describes the person, place, or thing.

adapted from an idea by Colleen Dabney, Williamsburg, VA

(tiger)
lives in the Asian rain forest
sharp vision and keen hearing
powerful neck, shoulders, and forelegs
good swimmer
nocturnal hunter
whitish throat and belly fur
black stripes in fur
300- to 420-pound feline
largest cat
brownish-yellow or orange-red fur

It's a good swimmer.

Is it a crocodile?

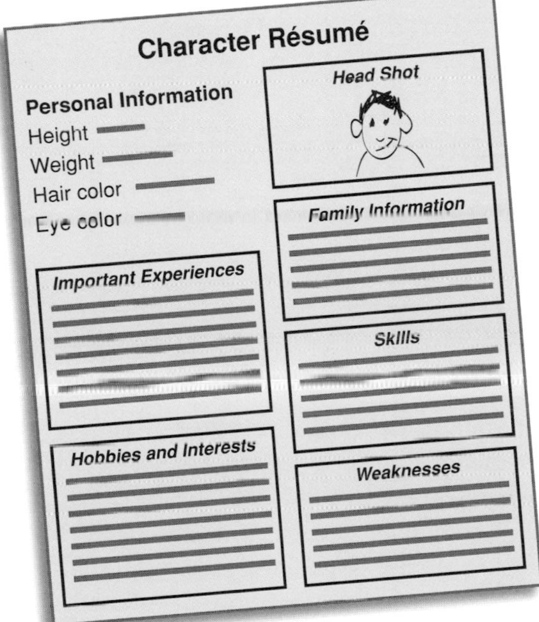

Character Résumé
Personal Information
Height
Weight
Hair color
Eye color
Head Shot
Family Information
Important Experiences
Skills
Hobbies and Interests
Weaknesses

Characters Wanted
Narrative writing

Help students develop rich characters for their stories by creating character résumés. First, have each child make a résumé about himself and use it to include rich details in a short personal narrative about getting ready for the first day of school. Then, when it's time to write a fictional narrative, have each child create a résumé about his main character and use it to make the fictional character come alive in his story!

Katie Jensen, St. Timothy's School, Los Angeles, CA

Proofreading Panels
Editing

Use the team approach to help students edit their rough drafts! Divide students into groups of four and name each group member the spelling, capitalization, punctuation, or grammar editor. Next, have each student edit her own rough draft for her assigned category and then pass the paper to a teammate who edits it for the category he was assigned. Once every group member has edited all the papers, each writer reviews the corrections to her writing and gets to work on her final copy.

Isobel Livingstone, Rahway, NJ

PUNCTUATION EDITOR

Write Now!

Double Draw

Descriptive details

For this partner activity, have each student draw a detailed robot, dragon, or butterfly. Next, have the child write three paragraphs that describe her drawing and then fold her drawing in half. After that, have each student read her paragraph aloud to a partner who draws the figure being described. Then have the partners switch roles. When both partners finish drawing, each student compares her original with her partner's reproduction. Then the child revises her description as necessary to include missing details.

adapted from an idea by Sharon Schlup
Mann Elementary, St. Louis, MO

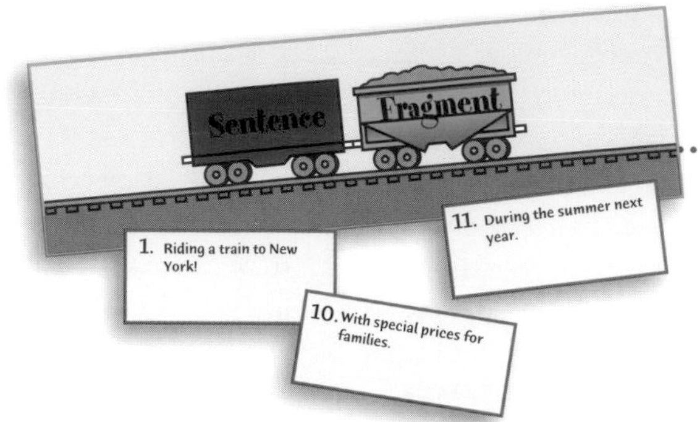

All Aboard!

Sentence fragments and run-on sentences

Want your students to eliminate sentence fragments and run-on sentences in their writing? Try using these clever analogies! Point out that a sentence fragment is like a group of train cars that has no engine: it doesn't go anywhere. Each sentence must have a subject, have a predicate, and express a complete thought to get the reader moving. Then focus on run-on sentences by having students describe how it feels to wait at a railroad crossing while a very long train passes. Explain that a run-on sentence is like a very long train: it can leave a reader bored and frustrated. For a follow-up center activity, copy and cut apart the labels and cards from page 80. A student sorts the cards and then, on a sheet of paper, writes a corrected version of each run-on sentence or fragment.

Michelle Malchuk, Evans, CO

Directors' Cuts
Writing a script

Help students turn a class novel into readers' theater. To begin, have each small group choose a chapter with dialogue between two or more characters. Next, guide the group to write a narrator's introduction to the chapter, describing the setting and giving background information about the story and characters. Then have the group write a script that tells the chapter's story through the characters' dialogue. Remind students to use parenthetical directions as necessary to describe a character's movements, expressions, or emotions. As time allows, have each group practice and then perform its readers' theater for the rest of the class.

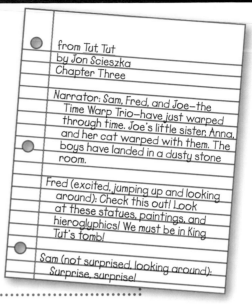

from Tut, Tut
by Jon Scieszka
Chapter Three

Narrator: Sam, Fred, and Joe—the Time Warp Trio—have just warped through time. Joe's little sister, Anna, and her cat warped with them. The boys have landed in a dusty stone room.

Fred (excited, jumping up and looking around): Check this out! Look at these statues, paintings, and hieroglyphics! We must be in King Tut's tomb!

Sam (not surprised, looking around): Surprise, surprise!

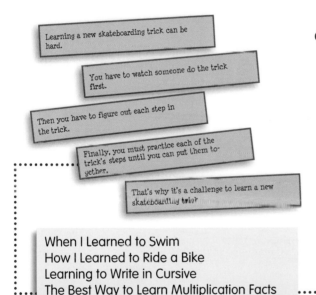

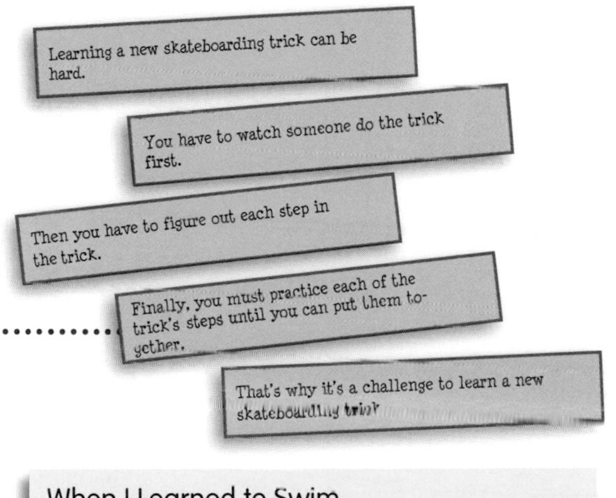

Learning a new skateboarding trick can be hard.
You have to watch someone do the trick first.
Then you have to figure out each step in the trick.
Finally, you must practice each of the trick's steps until you can put them together.
That's why it's a challenge to learn a new skateboarding trick.

When I Learned to Swim
How I Learned to Ride a Bike
Learning to Write in Cursive
The Best Way to Learn Multiplication Facts

A Model Activity
How-to paragraph

To get this activity started, give each student one sentence strip from a copy of page 81. Next, guide the child to determine her sentence's topic and silently find four other students whose sentences are on the same topic. When each group of five students has found all its members, have the group silently arrange its sentences to create a paragraph. Then have each group read its paragraph aloud. Follow up by having each student write her own how-to paragraph on one of the topics shown.

Lauren Cox, Princeton Elementary, Princeton, NC

A Writing Resource
Generating writing ideas

Create a class writing journal that's sure to help your young authors help themselves! In advance, record in a notebook several ideas, observations, or questions about familiar topics. Next, read aloud a few of the entries. Then lead students to choose one entry and help you develop it into a story, descriptive essay, or letter. Follow up by putting the journal at your writing center. Encourage students to look inside for writing inspiration and remind them to jot their own ideas, observations, and questions inside as well.

Kim Minafo, Apex, NC

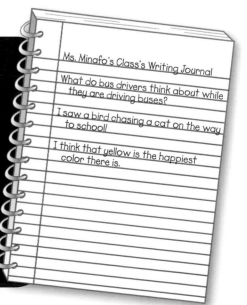

Ms. Minafo's Class's Writing Journal

What do bus drivers think about while they are driving buses?

I saw a bird chasing a cat on the way to school!

I think that yellow is the happiest color there is.

WRITE NOW!

Creative Conversations
Writing dialogue

Use puppets to encourage your students to write and punctuate interesting dialogue! Provide an assortment of puppets and several situation prompts such as those shown. Next, have each pair of students choose two puppets and a prompt. Then have the pair act out the situation using their puppets and record the characters' conversation. After a set amount of time, guide the partners to revise and edit their written chat, making sure each quotation is correctly capitalized and punctuated.

Christine Cooley, C. C. Meneley Elementary, Gardnerville, NV

Situation Prompts

- One character is teaching the other how to ride a bike.
- The characters are best friends, but this is the first time they've seen each other in two weeks.
- One character is trying to convince the other that he or she saw a famous actor or actress.
- One character is trying to convince the other to try the cookies he or she just baked. (The cookies look and smell terrible!)
- The characters have just taken a very hard spelling test.

Watch out for grammar mistakes.
Recheck spelling.
Ask whether each sentence makes sense.
Proofread punctuation.

It's a Wrap!
Editing

Here's an easy-to-remember tip with a focus on editing! Post the acronym shown and review each step with students. Then, after a child finishes writing, remind him to "WRAP" it up with careful editing!

Barclay Marcell, Chicago, IL

Before, During, and After
Imaginative narrative writing

For this idea, copy and cut apart a class supply of the picture cards on page 82, or cut out interesting pictures from old calendars or magazines. Next, challenge each child to describe what is happening on her card and then write a story that tells what happened before, during, and after the picture was taken. If desired, challenge each student to write a story of 500 or more words. Then post students' final copies along with the pictures on a board titled "Pictures Worth 500 Words!"

Whitney Fisher, North Elementary, Morgantown, WV

Writer to Writer

Writing fluency

Want to hold students accountable for their journal responses without lugging home a pile of notebooks every night? Try this! Post an open-ended prompt (such as one of those on pages 91–96) and guide each child to write a thoughtful response. Next, assign each student a journal buddy and have the buddies trade journals. Then have each child read his partner's writing and jot a sentence or two in the margin about her response. Repeat every few days, periodically setting aside time for the buddies to meet and talk about their journal responses.

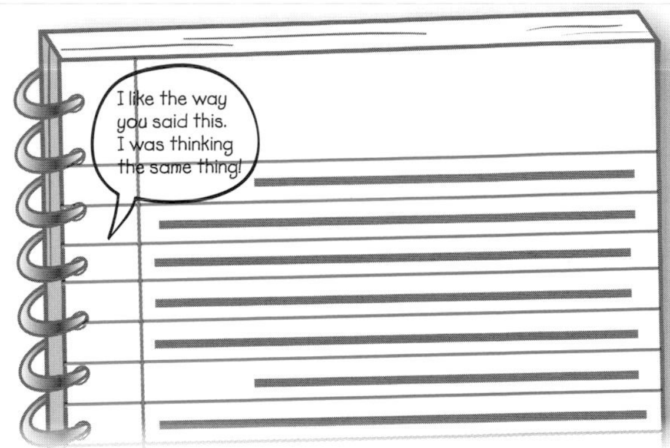

I like the way
you said this.
I was thinking
the same thing!

Jean Ricotta, Signal Hill Elementary, Dix Hills, NY

Game Time!

How-to writing, writing process

For this idea, have each student name her favorite sport and brainstorm details about it on a web labeled as shown. Next, have the child use the paragraph starters shown to plan an essay that explains how to play her favorite sport. Then have each child draft, edit, and revise her essay. If desired, have the student glue her final copy to a cutout shape that reflects her essay's topic.

Virginia Zeletzki, Banyan Creek Elementary, Delray Beach, FL

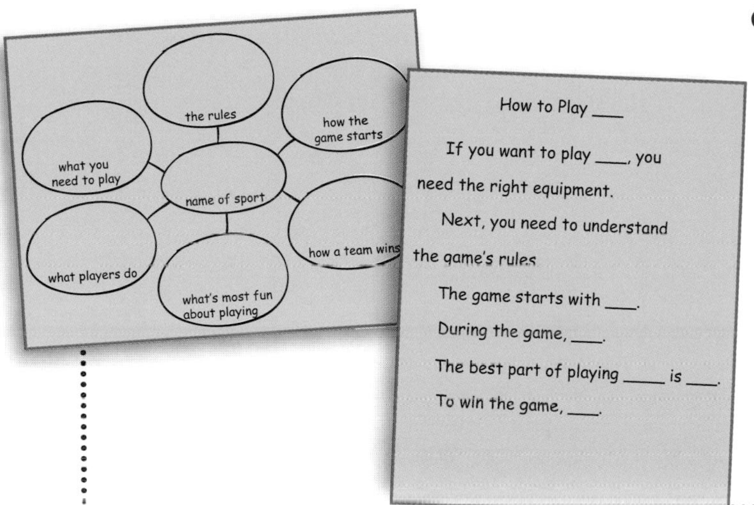

how the game starts
what you need to play
name of sport
what players do
how a team wins
what's most fun about playing

If you want to play ___, you need the right equipment.
Next, you need to understand the game's rules.
The game starts with ___.
During the game, ___.
The best part of playing ___ is ___.
To win the game, ___.

In the Bag

Using concrete sensory details

To begin, secretly put a small object inside a paper bag and close it. Next, display the bag, vaguely describe the item inside, and ask students to guess what the object is. When they can't guess, give a vivid description and have them guess again. Elaborate on your description as necessary until students name the item. Then write your final description on the board and discuss with students the details that best described the object. After that, have each student secretly choose an item from his desk and describe it using concrete sensory details. As time allows, have students take turns hiding their objects in the bag and reading their descriptions aloud. Award a point toward a class reward for every object that is identified on the first guess!

Amanda Holland and Mindy Adamonis, Longdale Elementary, Glen Allen, VA

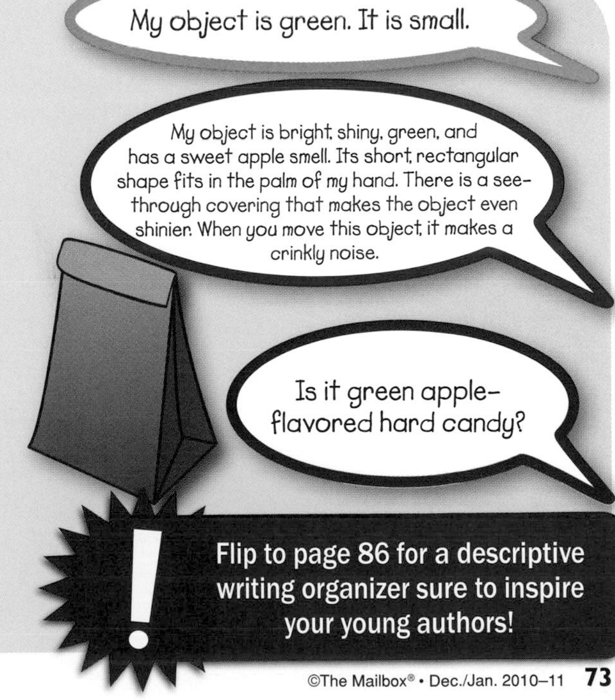

My object is green. It is small.
My object is bright, shiny, green, and has a sweet apple smell. Its short, rectangular shape fits in the palm of my hand. There is a see-through covering that makes the object even shinier. When you move this object, it makes a crinkly noise.
Is it green apple-flavored hard candy?

Flip to page 86 for a descriptive writing organizer sure to inspire your young authors!

WRITE NOW!

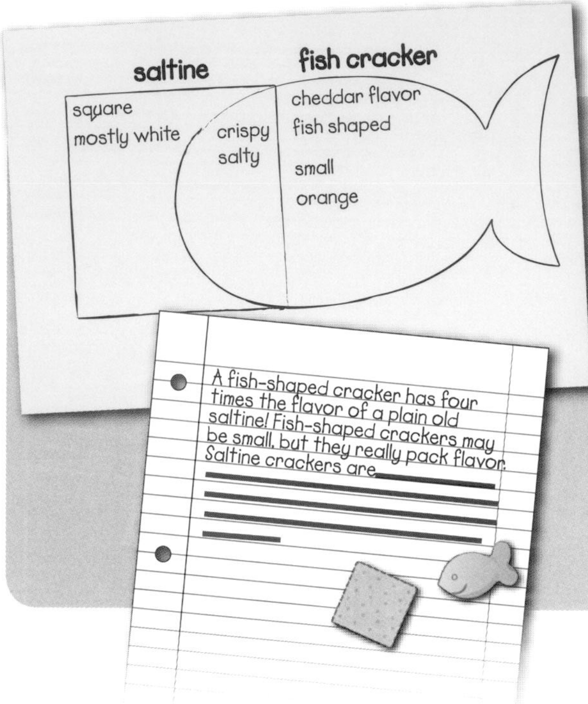

saltine
fish cracker
square
mostly white
crispy
salty
cheddar flavor
fish shaped
small
orange
A fish-shaped cracker has four times the flavor of a plain old saltine! Fish-shaped crackers may be small, but they really pack flavor. Saltine crackers are

Polly Wants a Cracker!

Persuasive writing

For this idea, give each student two different crackers and have her draw a Venn diagram using the crackers' shapes. Next, guide the child to taste the crackers and compare and contrast their qualities on the diagram. When she finishes, have the student choose her favorite cracker. Then guide her to use her diagram to write an article in which she persuades readers to buy her favorite cracker instead of the other kind.

Marie E. Cecchini, West Dundee, IL

For Stupendous Writing

Revising

Use this catchy checklist to remind your young authors of what it means to revise. Simply copy and cut apart a supply of the cards on page 83 to keep at your writing center. When a student finishes his first draft, he takes a card and checks the boxes as he reviews and revises his writing. Then the child staples the card to his rough draft to document his work.

Barclay Marcell, Chicago, IL

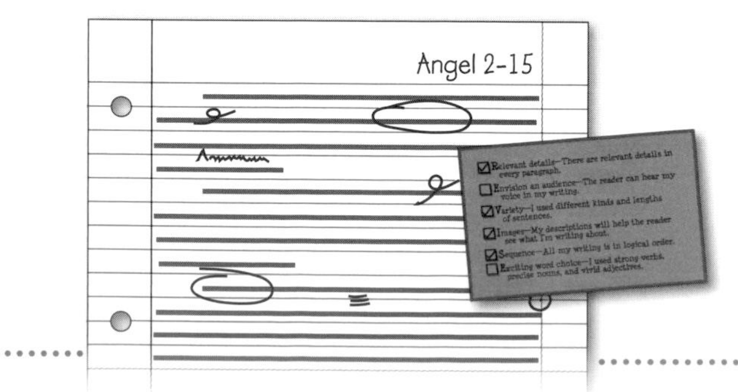

Paragraph Puttering

Organizing writing into paragraphs

If a student's draft includes too many ideas in one big paragraph, try this. Guide the child to use different-color markers to highlight each of his main ideas. Next, have the child use corresponding colors to highlight each idea's supporting details. Then have the child reorganize each main idea and its supporting details into a new paragraph. If the child can't find any supporting details, guide him to delete the idea or write a new paragraph that includes supporting details.

Statuesque Statements
Narrative writing

Challenge each student to imagine that, in the future, she becomes so well-known that her city decides to erect a statue of her in front of city hall. Next, guide each student to draw her statue and write a narrative from third-person point of view that describes the contributions that have made her statue-worthy!

Marie E. Cecchini, West Dundee, IL

Savannah Johnson, native of West Dundee, invented the artificial bee. She says her interest in science was sparked by her fifth-grade teacher, Ms. Cecchini.

"Punctu-actions"

- STAND UP when you indent a paragraph.
- CLAP when you use a capital letter.
- SNAP YOUR FINGERS when you use a period.
- WHISTLE when you use a comma.
- STOMP YOUR FEET when you use a question mark.
- RAISE YOUR LEFT ARM when you use an opening quotation mark.
- RAISE YOUR RIGHT ARM when you use the closing quotation mark.
- SAY, "WOW!" when you use an exclamation mark.

"Punctu-action!"
Mechanics

Looking to energize students' awareness of writing mechanics? Have them act out each paragraph indention or punctuation mark they use! Simply post the directions shown. Then have students perform the actions as they write.

There's a great how-to writing prompt and organizer on page 87!

Watch and Write
Writing dialogue

Here's a fun challenge! Play the first few minutes of a short video version of a fairy tale or children's book. Guide students to identify the story's characters and record their names. Then mute the sound and continue the video, guiding each student to write the dialogue he imagines as he watches. Every few minutes, pause the video so each student can make sure he's caught up. When the video ends, have each child edit his dialogue and write a final copy. Before students turn in their work, have each student read his dialogue aloud to a partner.

Isobel L. Livingstone, Rahway, NJ

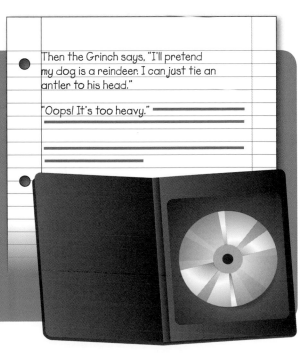

Then the Grinch says, "I'll pretend my dog is a reindeer. I can just tie an antler to his head."
"Oops! It's too heavy."

WRITE NOW!

Get Specific!

Using vivid adjectives

For this descriptive idea, place two objects in a bag for every four students. Next, challenge each group of students to list ten or more vivid adjectives that describe each object. Then collect students' lists and display the objects. Read a list aloud. Ask students to name the adjectives that are most vivid and then guess which object is being described. For a fun display, put a rubber band around each object. Then tack the object and its list of adjectives to a board titled "Detailed Descriptors."

Terry Healy, Marlatt Elementary, Manhattan, KS

clear
glossy
crinkly
empty
recyclable
flimsy
partially ribbed
partially smooth
curved
skinny

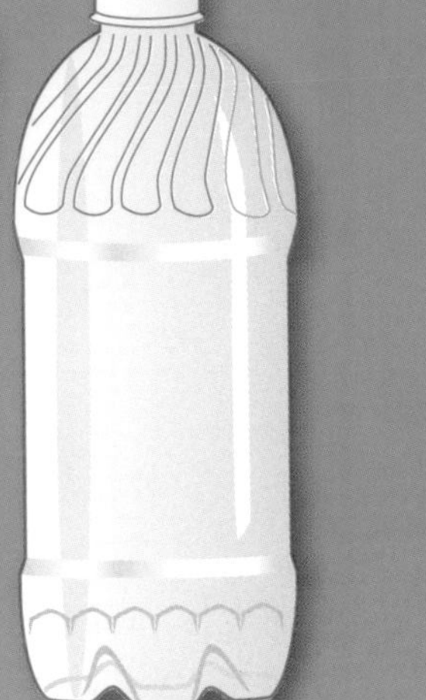

State your opinion.
Give reasons for your opinion.
List facts or details that support your opinion. (Use words and phrases such as *for instance*, *in order to*, or *in addition*.)
In your conclusion, restate your opinion.

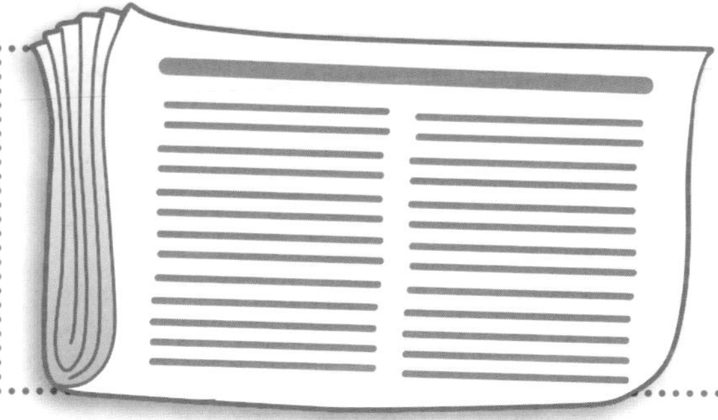

The Power of the Pen

Writing to express an opinion

Use the editorial page of your local newspaper to give students real-world writing practice. To begin, explain that citizens of a community can respectfully share their opinions in letters to the editor. Next, read aloud a letter that addresses an issue with which your students can relate. Discuss the letter with students, leading each child to form her own opinion on the issue. Then post reminders such as those shown and have each student pretend she is the newspaper's editor. Guide the child to draft a letter back to the writer, expressing and supporting her own opinion. As time allows, have student volunteers read their letters aloud.

Michelle Cobb, New Lebanon, OH

Make It Manageable!

Editing

Since editing an essay can be an overwhelming task, try this creative tip. Have each child cut out the window on a copy of an editing strip from page 77. Then guide the student to place the strip on a page of his work so its beginning shows through the window. Have the child study the writing in the window, make corrections as necessary, and then slide the strip over the rest of his page to edit his work. When the student finishes editing, have him clip the strip inside his writing folder and keep it handy for the next editing task!

Karen Young Aita, Belle Haven, VA

Flip to pages 85–90 for fun writing organizers!

Today's Forecast: A Brainstorm

Prewriting

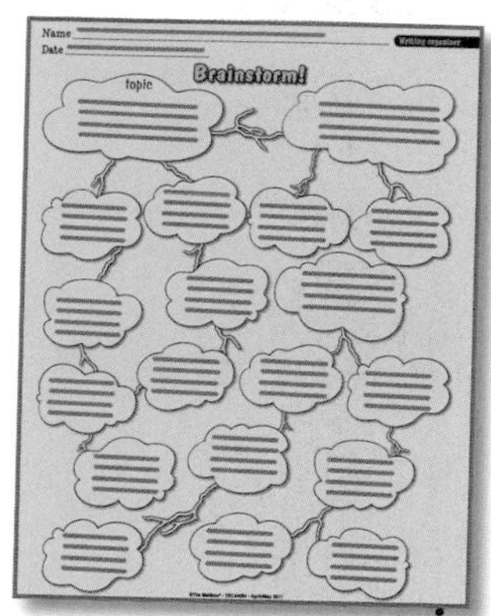

Want to help your young authors get more out of prewriting? Try this! Read aloud a prompt such as one from page 95. Then display a copy of page 88 and record the writing topic. Next, challenge students to share ideas, details, and facts on the topic, filling each space on the page. Then lead students to review the organizer. Use different-color markers to highlight similar, interesting, or inspiring ideas. After that, have each student write on the topic for five minutes. Then guide the child to share his writing with a partner, determine his focus, and draft a thoughtful response to the prompt.

adapted from an idea by Bonnie Pettifor, Urbana, IL

Our Time Capsule to the Past
2011
Ms. Cox's Class

Back in Time

Explanatory writing

Here's a fun twist on having students create a time capsule. Instead of filling a capsule with items for a future generation, have students choose items to put in a capsule that could be sent back in time 250 years! Have each child draw the item he chooses. Then guide the student to write an essay that describes the item and explains how it's used in the modern world. Remind students to write for people living in the 18th century, who wouldn't know anything about our modern world. Bind students' work in a class book titled "Our Time Capsule to the Past."

Editing Strip

Use with "Make It Manageable!" on page 76.

≡ = capitalize / = lowercase ℘ = delete ◯ = check spelling ^ = insert

TEC44054

⊙ = add period ∿ = transpose ¶ = start new paragraph ◯→ = move

≡ = capitalize / = lowercase ℘ = delete ◯ = check spelling ^ = insert

TEC44054

⊙ = add period ∿ = transpose ¶ = start new paragraph ◯→ = move

WRITE NOW!

Grab a Bag and Write!

Narrative writing

For this idea, bring in a small paper bag for each group of three students. Then collect a variety of objects from around your classroom. Put three different items in each bag and close the bag. Next, divide your class into groups of three and have each group choose a bag. Then challenge the group to write a story in which each object plays an important role. For a fun follow-up, have the students in each group take turns reading their story aloud, elaborately showing each object every time it's mentioned.

Chele Weiglein, Lawton, OK

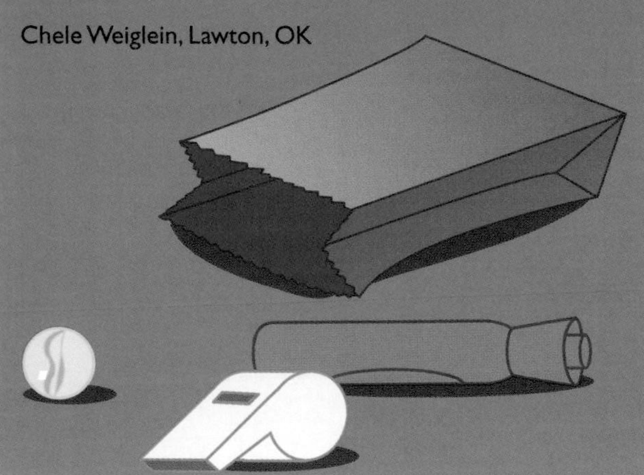

On the Go

Writing a poem, prepositional phrases

To begin this lyrical activity, lead students to brainstorm a list of prepositions and then make each one a prepositional phrase by adding an object. Next, have each student choose a favorite activity and write five prepositional phrases that tell about the activity. Have the child arrange his phrases to create a prepositional poem. Then have him title his work and write it on a construction paper cutout that represents the activity. Post students' work along with the title "On the Go—Prepositional Poetry!"

Skating
On a board
Along a rail
Up a ramp
In the air
Off the board

Flip to page 90 for a fun outline organizer!

Stress Busters

Drafting

Help your students meet writer's block head on! First, point out that even professional writers sometimes struggle to write, but that they develop strategies for getting their writing done. Next, discuss the tips on page 84. Then brainstorm with students tactics that can help them get back on the "write" track. Have each student record the brainstormed strategies on her copy of page 84 and then staple the page inside her writing journal or folder.

Kim Minafo, Cary, NC

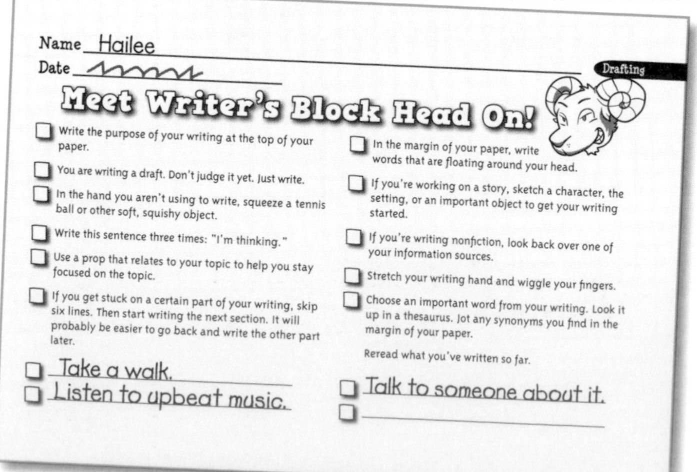

Name Hailee
Date

Drafting

Meet Writer's Block Head On!

- ☐ Write the purpose of your writing at the top of your paper.
- ☐ You are writing a draft. Don't judge it yet. Just write.
- ☐ In the hand you aren't using to write, squeeze a tennis ball or other soft, squishy object.
- ☐ Write this sentence three times: "I'm thinking."
- ☐ Use a prop that relates to your topic to help you stay focused on the topic.
- ☐ If you get stuck on a certain part of your writing, skip six lines. Then start writing the next section. It will probably be easier to go back and write the other part later.
- ☐ Take a walk.
- ☐ Listen to upbeat music.
- ☐ In the margin of your paper, write words that are floating around your head.
- ☐ If you're working on a story, sketch a character, the setting, or an important object to get your writing started.
- ☐ If you're writing nonfiction, look back over one of your information sources.
- ☐ Stretch your writing hand and wiggle your fingers.
- ☐ Choose an important word from your writing. Look it up in a thesaurus. Jot any synonyms you find in the margin of your paper.

Reread what you've written so far.

- ☐ Talk to someone about it.
- ☐

Story Element Cards

Use with "It's in the Cards!" on page 68.

Setting at the mall's food court Saturday afternoon TEC44050	**Setting** first thing in the morning at a doctor's office TEC44050	**Setting** on the school playground during recess TEC44050	**Setting** in the public library after school TEC44050	**Setting** in the school cafeteria on pizza day TEC44050
Setting at the mall the day before Christmas TEC44050	**Setting** during a soccer game TEC44050	**Setting** afternoon in the classroom TEC44050	**Setting** on the school bus going to school TEC44050	**Setting** on a field trip to the zoo TEC44050
Main Character a school principal TEC44050	**Main Character** a famous author TEC44050	**Main Character** a famous athlete TEC44050	**Main Character** a famous actor TEC44050	**Main Character** a superhero TEC44050
Main Character a wacky scientist TEC44050	**Main Character** a magician TEC44050	**Main Character** a fifth grader TEC44050	**Main Character** a fourth grader TEC44050	**Main Character** a cat that can talk TEC44050
Problem The main character is trying to catch his or her escaped hamster. TEC44050	**Problem** The main character loses an important object. TEC44050	**Problem** The main character's best friend is missing. TEC44050	**Problem** The main character is trying to get to an important event. TEC44050	**Problem** A priceless object is stolen, and the main character is on the case. TEC44050
Problem The main character breaks an important object. TEC44050	**Problem** The main character gets amnesia. TEC44050	**Problem** The main character and his or her best friend enter the same contest. TEC44050	**Problem** The main character wants something that's impossible to get. TEC44050	**Problem** The main character is trying to find a hidden treasure. TEC44050
Mood bouncy TEC44050	**Mood** exaggerated TEC44050	**Mood** funny TEC44050	**Mood** happy TEC44050	**Mood** hopeful TEC44050
Mood joyous TEC44050	**Mood** mysterious TEC44050	**Mood** peaceful TEC44050	**Mood** serious TEC44050	**Mood** silly TEC44050

Sentence Fragment and Run-on Sentence Labels and Cards

Use with "All Aboard!" on page 70.

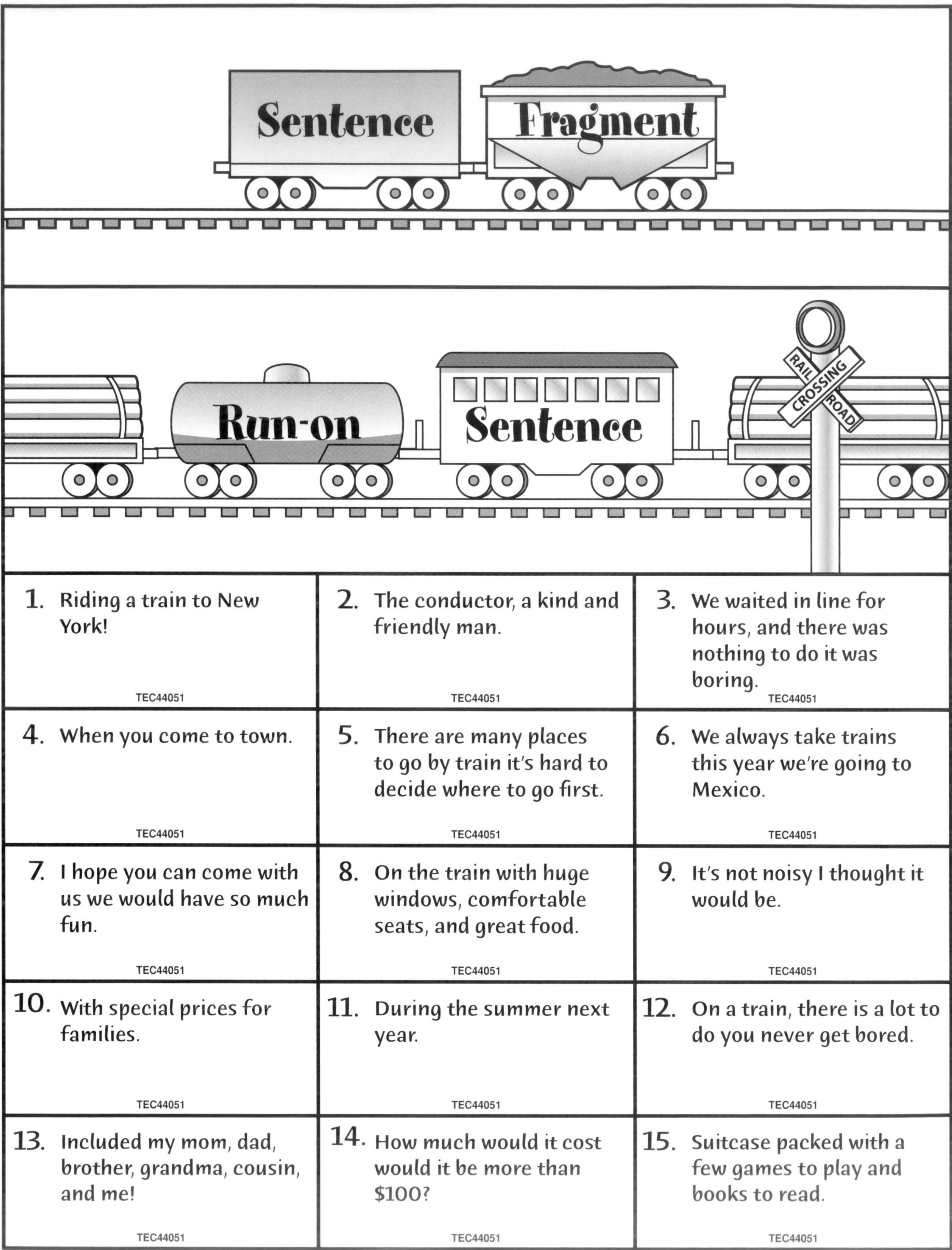

1. Riding a train to New York! TEC44051	2. The conductor, a kind and friendly man. TEC44051	3. We waited in line for hours, and there was nothing to do it was boring. TEC44051
4. When you come to town. TEC44051	5. There are many places to go by train it's hard to decide where to go first. TEC44051	6. We always take trains this year we're going to Mexico. TEC44051
7. I hope you can come with us we would have so much fun. TEC44051	8. On the train with huge windows, comfortable seats, and great food. TEC44051	9. It's not noisy I thought it would be. TEC44051
10. With special prices for families. TEC44051	11. During the summer next year. TEC44051	12. On a train, there is a lot to do you never get bored. TEC44051
13. Included my mom, dad, brother, grandma, cousin, and me! TEC44051	14. How much would it cost would it be more than $100? TEC44051	15. Suitcase packed with a few games to play and books to read. TEC44051

Use with "A Model Activity" on page 71.

Learning a new skateboarding trick can be hard. TEC44051	Learning to skate isn't always easy. TEC44051
You have to watch someone do the trick first. TEC44051	I started skating when I was five. TEC44051
Then you have to figure out each step in the trick. TEC44051	Getting on skates the first time was scary. TEC44051
Finally, you must practice each of the trick's steps until you can put them together. TEC44051	I fell a lot, but I got back up and kept skating. TEC44051
That's why it's a challenge to learn a new skateboarding trick. TEC44051	After practicing every day for a week, I learned to skate well. TEC44051
I still remember learning to write in kindergarten. TEC44051	Believe it or not, I had to learn to ride the school bus! TEC44051
At first, I could only write the letters in my name. TEC44051	I was afraid and wouldn't ride the bus for the first month of school. TEC44051
So I had to learn all the letters first. TEC44051	Then I started getting on the bus, but I would get right back off. TEC44051
Then I learned to make all my letters the same size. TEC44051	Next, I would ride the bus if my mom drove our car behind it. TEC44051
It took all year to learn to write my letters on the line, but I did it. TEC44051	Finally, I learned to get on the bus and ride it without being afraid at all. TEC44051
I love warm flour tortillas so much that I learned to make them. TEC44051	Do you know how to fly a kite? It's easy to learn! TEC44051
First, I mix flour, salt, water, and oil to make the dough. TEC44051	First, hold your kite up in the air. TEC44051
Next, I make little balls of dough and roll each one into a circle. TEC44051	Next, start running until you feel the wind catch the kite. TEC44051
Then I cook each circle of dough on a hot griddle. TEC44051	Then, holding onto the kite's string, let go of your kite and stop running. TEC44051
Finally, I spread butter on a warm tortilla and eat it! TEC44051	Let out the kite string a little at a time until your kite is high in the air. TEC44051

Picture Cards

Use with "Before, During, and After" on page 72.

Revising Cards

Use with "For Stupendous Writing" on page 74.

- [ ] **R**elevant details—There are relevant details in every paragraph.
- [ ] **E**nvision an audience—The reader can hear my voice in my writing.
- [ ] **V**ariety—I used different kinds and lengths of sentences.
- [ ] **I**mages—My descriptions will help the reader see what I'm writing about.
- [ ] **S**equence—All my writing is in logical order.
- [ ] **E**xciting word choice—I used strong verbs, precise nouns, and vivid adjectives.

name ____________ date ____________

TEC44053

- [ ] **R**elevant details—There are relevant details in every paragraph.
- [ ] **E**nvision an audience—The reader can hear my voice in my writing.
- [ ] **V**ariety—I used different kinds and lengths of sentences.
- [ ] **I**mages—My descriptions will help the reader see what I'm writing about.
- [ ] **S**equence—All my writing is in logical order.
- [ ] **E**xciting word choice—I used strong verbs, precise nouns, and vivid adjectives.

name ____________ date ____________

TEC44053

- [ ] **R**elevant details—There are relevant details in every paragraph.
- [ ] **E**nvision an audience—The reader can hear my voice in my writing.
- [ ] **V**ariety—I used different kinds and lengths of sentences.
- [ ] **I**mages—My descriptions will help the reader see what I'm writing about.
- [ ] **S**equence—All my writing is in logical order.
- [ ] **E**xciting word choice—I used strong verbs, precise nouns, and vivid adjectives.

name ____________ date ____________

TEC44053

- [ ] **R**elevant details—There are relevant details in every paragraph.
- [ ] **E**nvision an audience—The reader can hear my voice in my writing.
- [ ] **V**ariety—I used different kinds and lengths of sentences.
- [ ] **I**mages—My descriptions will help the reader see what I'm writing about.
- [ ] **S**equence—All my writing is in logical order.
- [ ] **E**xciting word choice—I used strong verbs, precise nouns, and vivid adjectives.

name ____________ date ____________

TEC44053

- [ ] **R**elevant details—There are relevant details in every paragraph.
- [ ] **E**nvision an audience—The reader can hear my voice in my writing.
- [ ] **V**ariety—I used different kinds and lengths of sentences.
- [ ] **I**mages—My descriptions will help the reader see what I'm writing about.
- [ ] **S**equence—All my writing is in logical order.
- [ ] **E**xciting word choice—I used strong verbs, precise nouns, and vivid adjectives.

name ____________ date ____________

TEC44053

- [ ] **R**elevant details—There are relevant details in every paragraph.
- [ ] **E**nvision an audience—The reader can hear my voice in my writing.
- [ ] **V**ariety—I used different kinds and lengths of sentences.
- [ ] **I**mages—My descriptions will help the reader see what I'm writing about.
- [ ] **S**equence—All my writing is in logical order.
- [ ] **E**xciting word choice—I used strong verbs, precise nouns, and vivid adjectives.

name ____________ date ____________

TEC44053

- [ ] **R**elevant details—There are relevant details in every paragraph.
- [ ] **E**nvision an audience—The reader can hear my voice in my writing.
- [ ] **V**ariety—I used different kinds and lengths of sentences.
- [ ] **I**mages—My descriptions will help the reader see what I'm writing about.
- [ ] **S**equence—All my writing is in logical order.
- [ ] **E**xciting word choice—I used strong verbs, precise nouns, and vivid adjectives.

name ____________ date ____________

TEC44053

- [ ] **R**elevant details—There are relevant details in every paragraph.
- [ ] **E**nvision an audience—The reader can hear my voice in my writing.
- [ ] **V**ariety—I used different kinds and lengths of sentences.
- [ ] **I**mages—My descriptions will help the reader see what I'm writing about.
- [ ] **S**equence—All my writing is in logical order.
- [ ] **E**xciting word choice—I used strong verbs, precise nouns, and vivid adjectives.

name ____________ date ____________

TEC44053

- [ ] **R**elevant details—There are relevant details in every paragraph.
- [ ] **E**nvision an audience—The reader can hear my voice in my writing.
- [ ] **V**ariety—I used different kinds and lengths of sentences.
- [ ] **I**mages—My descriptions will help the reader see what I'm writing about.
- [ ] **S**equence—All my writing is in logical order.
- [ ] **E**xciting word choice—I used strong verbs, precise nouns, and vivid adjectives.

name ____________ date ____________

TEC44053

Name ______________________________ Drafting

Date ____________________

Meet Writer's Block Head On!

- [ ] Write the purpose of your writing at the top of your paper.
- [ ] You are writing a draft. Don't judge it yet. Just write.
- [ ] In the hand you aren't using to write, squeeze a tennis ball or other soft, squishy object.
- [ ] Write this sentence three times: "I'm thinking."
- [ ] Use a prop that relates to your topic to help you stay focused on the topic.
- [ ] If you get stuck on a certain part of your writing, skip six lines. Then start writing the next section. It will probably be easier to go back and write the other part later.
- [ ] ______________________________
- [ ] ______________________________
- [ ] In the margin of your paper, write words that are floating around your head.
- [ ] If you're working on a story, sketch a character, the setting, or an important object to get your writing started.
- [ ] If you're writing nonfiction, look back over one of your information sources.
- [ ] Stretch your writing hand and wiggle your fingers.
- [ ] Choose an important word from your writing. Look it up in a thesaurus. Jot any synonyms you find in the margin of your paper.
- [ ] Reread what you've written so far.
- [ ] ______________________________
- [ ] ______________________________

Name ______________________________ Drafting

Date ____________________

Meet Writer's Block Head On!

- [ ] Write the purpose of your writing at the top of your paper.
- [ ] You are writing a draft. Don't judge it yet. Just write.
- [ ] In the hand you aren't using to write, squeeze a tennis ball or other soft, squishy object.
- [ ] Write this sentence three times: "I'm thinking."
- [ ] Use a prop that relates to your topic to help you stay focused on the topic.
- [ ] If you get stuck on a certain part of your writing, skip six lines. Then start writing the next section. It will probably be easier to go back and write the other part later.
- [ ] ______________________________
- [ ] ______________________________
- [ ] In the margin of your paper, write words that are floating around your head.
- [ ] If you're working on a story, sketch a character, the setting, or an important object to get your writing started.
- [ ] If you're writing nonfiction, look back over one of your information sources.
- [ ] Stretch your writing hand and wiggle your fingers.
- [ ] Choose an important word from your writing. Look it up in a thesaurus. Jot any synonyms you find in the margin of your paper.
- [ ] Reread what you've written so far.
- [ ] ______________________________
- [ ] ______________________________

©The Mailbox® • TEC44052 • June/July 2011

 Note to the teacher: Use with "Stress Busters" on page 78.

Name ______________________________

Date ______________________________

Caught by Surprise

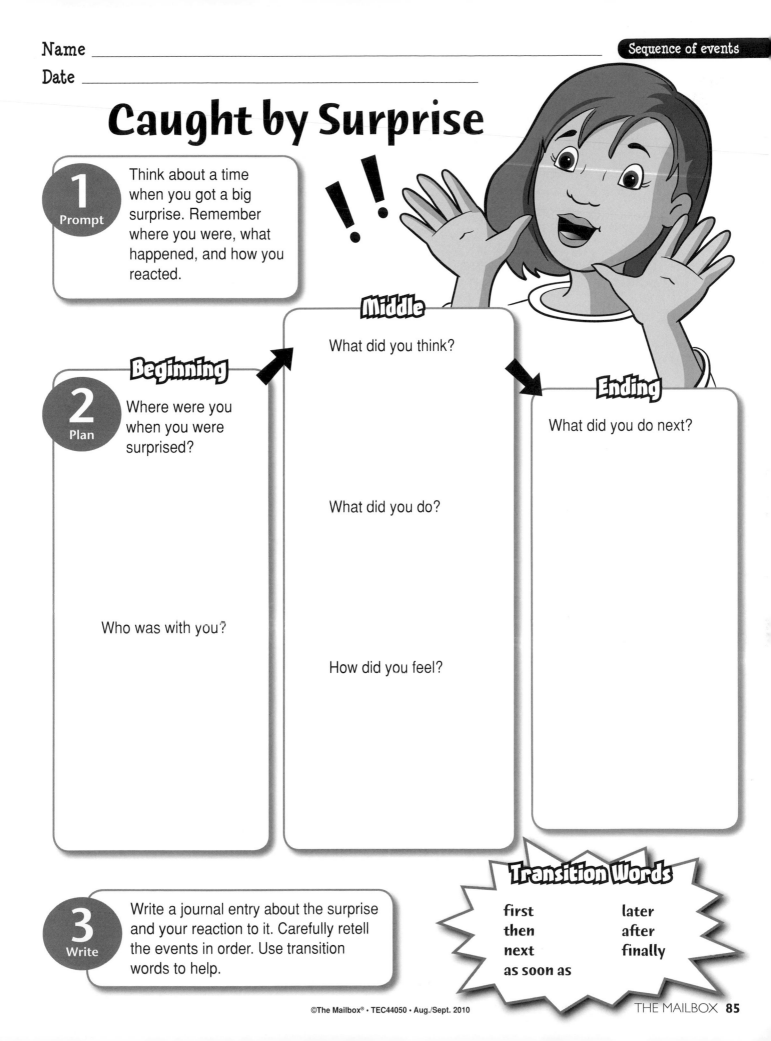

Think about a time when you got a big surprise. Remember where you were, what happened, and how you reacted.

What did you think?

What did you do?

How did you feel?

Beginning

Where were you when you were surprised?

Who was with you?

Ending

What did you do next?

3 Write

Write a journal entry about the surprise and your reaction to it. Carefully retell the events in order. Use transition words to help.

Transition Words

first
then
next
as soon as
later
after
finally

Name ______________________________

Date ______________________________ Adding details

Surprise Sighting

1 Prompt

On your way home from school, you see something big out of the corner of your eye. You look again and see a huge furry creature. You freeze and then watch as it disappears around the corner. What did you see?

2 Plan

Sketch the creature.

Describe it.

size

fur

face

body

arms

legs

feet

How did it move?

3 Write

Write a letter to Dr. Missy Terious. (She's a cryptozoologist and researches mythical creatures.) Tell Dr. Terious there is a strange creature living in your town. Make your description of it vivid. (Maybe Dr. Terious will come to your town and ask you to help search for the creature!)

Name

Date

Loop the Loop!

1 Prompt — You have just been asked to help your four-year-old cousin learn how to tie his shoes.

2 Plan — Break the process into six easy steps.

First:	Second:	Third:
Fourth:	Fifth:	Sixth:

Learning how to tie your shoelaces can be frustrating. What are two things you might say that will encourage your young cousin to keep practicing?

-
-

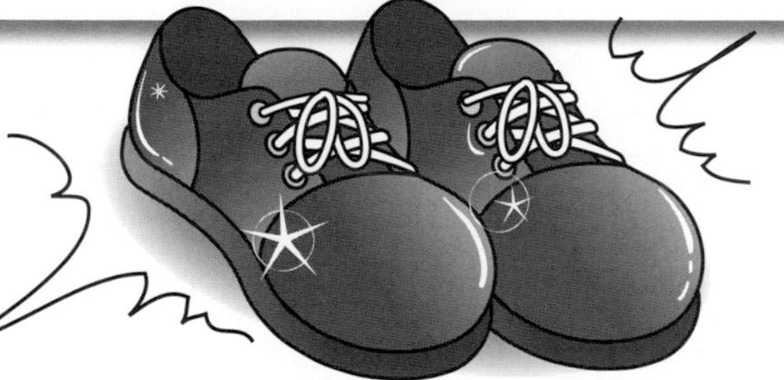

3 Write — Write directions to teach children how to tie their shoes. Be sure to encourage your young students so they don't get frustrated.

Name ______________________________

Date ________________

Brainstorm!

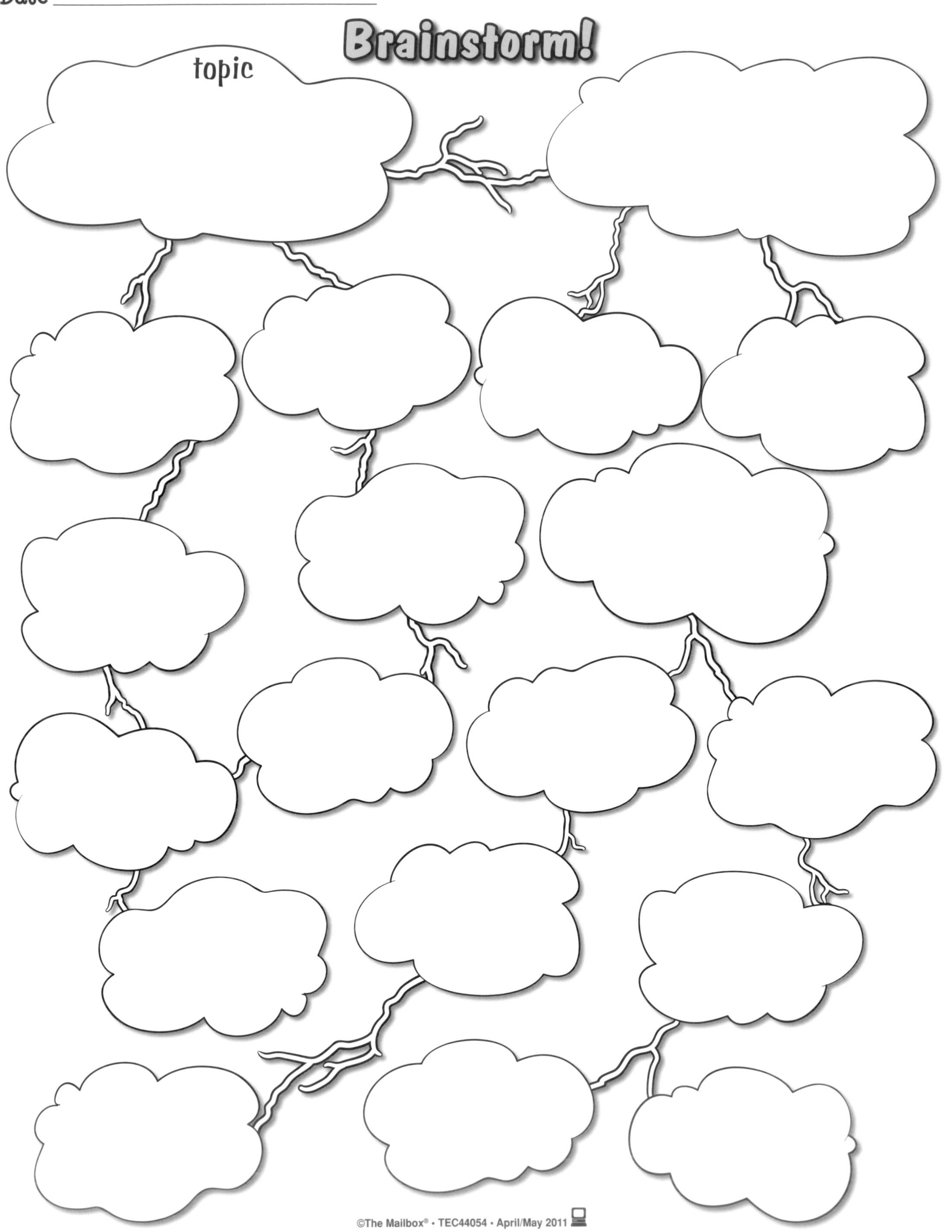

 Note to the teacher: Use with "Today's Forecast: A Brainstorm" on page 77.

Name ______________________________

Date ______________________________

Take a Spin!

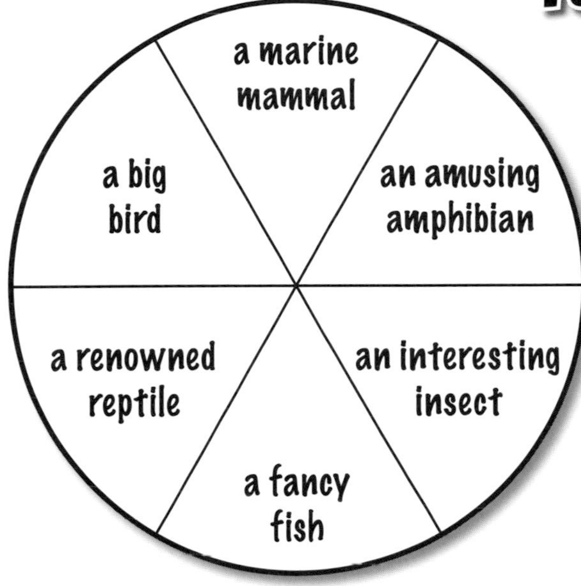

Spin to find a research category.

My category: ______________________________

Choose an animal within that category.

My animal: ______________________________

Research your animal. Choose the three **most important points** (MIP) about it. For each MIP, list three **supporting facts** (SF) or **supporting details** (SD).

MIP 1: ______________________________

SF or SD: ______________________________

SF or SD: ______________________________

SF or SD: ______________________________

MIP 2: ______________________________

SF or SD: ______________________________

SF or SD: ______________________________

SF or SD: ______________________________

MIP 3: ______________________________

SF or SD: ______________________________

SF or SD: ______________________________

SF or SD: ______________________________

Write a five-paragraph article about the animal. In the first paragraph, introduce the most important points. Then write a detailed paragraph about each important point. In the last paragraph, summarize all the important points about the animal.

Name ______________________________

Date ______________________________

Carve It Out!

I. Main idea and three main points: ______________________________

II. First main point: ______________________________

A. Detail about first point: ______________________________

B. Detail about first point: ______________________________

C. Detail about first point: ______________________________

III. Second main point: ______________________________

A. Detail about second point: ______________________________

B. Detail about second point: ______________________________

C. Detail about second point: ______________________________

IV. Third main point: ______________________________

A. Detail about third point: ______________________________

B. Detail about third point: ______________________________

C. Detail about third point: ______________________________

V. Main idea restated: ______________________________

How to use: Have each student use a copy of the page to plan an essay.

Name

August Writing Prompts

- [ ] Write a short tale that explains why the phrase "the dog days of summer" is used to describe summer's hottest days.
- [ ] Describe the perfect back-to-school outfit. What makes it special?
- [ ] Tell about a time when a vacation or outing didn't go quite as you had planned.
- [ ] List five rules you follow during summer that don't apply to school. List five rules you follow at school that don't apply during summer. How are the lists alike? How are they different?
- [ ] August is Happiness Happens Month. Write a free-verse poem that describes one thing that makes you very happy.
- [ ] How would you complete this sentence? My life would be a lot easier if my parents bought me... Explain.
- [ ] August is National Inventors' Month. Think about one object you have used today. Write a humorous story about how it might have been invented.
- [ ] Write a letter to a child who is nervous about starting kindergarten. Give the youngster advice about how to have a great year.
- [ ] Imagine you are an explorer who has just discovered your town. Write a journal entry describing the adventure.
- [ ] Your mom bought you something unusual at a flea market. Describe it and tell what you plan to do with it.

Name

September Writing Prompts

- [ ] Write a letter to convince your principal to add driver's education as a special subject this year. Tell why you think this topic is important to learn.
- [ ] Everyone should learn to repair a car, and everyone should learn to cook. Do you agree with this statement? Why or why not?
- [ ] September is National Chicken Month. Why do you think people who don't seem brave are called chickens? Do you think this label makes sense? Why or why not?
- [ ] Imagine you have a robot for a substitute teacher. Write a story about what happens in class.
- [ ] September is Library Card Sign-Up Month. Write a commercial to encourage everyone to use your town's public library.
- [ ] You've been asked to plan your class's next field trip. Where will you go? Write your plan. Include details about transportation, lunch, and what you will do.
- [ ] In honor of International People Skills Month, write a paragraph that explains how to get along with grumpy people.
- [ ] If you didn't have a calendar, how you would know it is September? Explain.
- [ ] September is National Coupon Month. Imagine you find a magical coupon on the playground. Tell what it is for and describe how you will use it.
- [ ] List five different ways a person can eat an apple. Then describe your favorite way to eat one.

Note to the teacher: Have each student staple a copy of this page in his writing journal. Or cut copies in half and distribute only one month's prompts at a time to students. When a student uses a prompt, he checks its box.

Name

October Writing Prompts

- ☐ Imagine the perfect autumn day. What would the weather be like? Where would you go? What would you do?
- ☐ It's Adopt-a-Shelter-Dog month. Write a speech to convince your teacher that your class should adopt a dog.
- ☐ What will Halloween be like in the year 2510? Describe it.
- ☐ Create a new topping for popcorn. Then write an article that tells popcorn lovers everywhere about the new flavor.
- ☐ You sneezed when your school picture was taken. Then you were absent for retakes. Write a letter to convince the photographer to come back to your school and retake your picture.
- ☐ How can having a positive attitude affect your school day? List five situations in which it can help.
- ☐ Which would you rather do: roller-skate or ice-skate? Why?
- ☐ Everyone loves cooked spinach, right? Write a commercial that will convince people to eat this super healthy but slimy green vegetable!
- ☐ Write a play about being a sailor on Columbus's ship when it finally reaches land.
- ☐ It's National Dental Hygiene Month. Write ten steps that tell how to brush and floss your teeth.

Name

November Writing Prompts

- ☐ Imagine you are one of the Wright brothers, Orville or Wilbur, when he was 12. Write a journal entry about your dream of flying.
- ☐ Write a speech to convince the citizens of your city to vote for you to be the next mayor.
- ☐ When do you feel more patriotic: when you see a U.S. flag waving or when you hear the national anthem? Explain.
- ☐ Think about the best and worst meals you've ever eaten. How were they different? How were they the same?
- ☐ Imagine you find a lost baby dragon on the playground. What happens? Write a story about it.
- ☐ It's about time for some animals to hibernate. List ten items you would make sure to take if you were going to snuggle in and sleep all winter.
- ☐ The week of November 21–27 is National Game and Puzzle Week. Which board game do you most like to play? Why?
- ☐ Imagine you and your best friend were at the first Thanksgiving dinner. Write the dialogue that might have taken place between you.
- ☐ Write a couplet (two lines of rhyming verse) that tells what you are most thankful for.
- ☐ You have just been asked to choose the next children's book that will be made into a 3-D movie. Which book will you choose? Why?

How to use the prompts: Have each student staple a copy of this page in his writing journal. Or cut copies in half and distribute one month's prompts at a time. When a student uses a prompt, he checks its box.

Name # December Writing Prompts	Name # January Writing Prompts
☐ Basketball was created on December 1, 1891. Which would you rather do: watch an exciting professional basketball game or play an exciting basketball game with children your age? Why?	☐ Describe the most awesome gift a person your age could possibly receive.
☐ Rewrite the lyrics of "Jingle Bells" so that it is a song about your best friend and you playing in the snow.	☐ Make a list of five things you hope you'll never do again. For each one, tell why you don't want to repeat it.
☐ Write directions for making your favorite winter snack.	☐ To some people, January is a cold, dreary month. Do you agree? Why or why not?
☐ Pretend you have a silly Aunt Zelda who gives you odd gifts. This year's present is weirder than ever. Write a thank-you letter to Aunt Zelda.	☐ The state zoo just adopted a polar bear that has an amazing rescue story. Write that story.
☐ School should be closed during the entire month of December instead of July. Do you agree or disagree with that statement? Explain.	☐ Which would be the best for your family and you: a home gym or a family membership at a nearby gym? Explain.
☐ It's Safe Toys and Gifts Month. Describe the safest toy or gift you have received during the past year.	☐ Imagine you put on your winter coat from last year for the first time this season. When you put your hand in your pocket, you find something you forgot you had. What is it? How do you feel about finding it? What do you do with it?
☐ If you had a store of your very own, what would you sell? Why?	☐ It's National Skating Month. Would you rather spend an afternoon roller-skating, ice-skating, or in-line skating? Why?
☐ Imagine that you open a present and find a gift card inside. The minute you pick up the card, it starts talking to you. Write a story about what happens next.	☐ January is Oatmeal Month. Describe the look, smell, texture, and taste of a bowl of hot oatmeal or another breakfast cereal.
☐ List ten things you plan to do during winter vacation. Write complete sentences. Then star the three things you are looking forward to most.	☐ Are you most tempted to peek out the classroom window when it's snowing, raining, or sunny? Why? How do you resist the temptation?
☐ Compare the last day of school before winter vacation to the last day of school before summer vacation. How are they the same? How are they different?	☐ Make up a game you could play to celebrate National Handwriting Day on January 23. Write the game's rules.

How to use the prompts: Have each student staple a copy of this page in his writing journal. Or cut copies in half and distribute one month's prompts at a time. When a student uses a prompt, he checks its box.

Name

February Writing Prompts

- [ ] The poet Langston Hughes was born on February 1, 1902. His poetry is known for its short, rhythmic lines. Using this same style, write a poem about school.
- [ ] Create a four-panel comic strip about Groundhog Day.
- [ ] *February* is often misspelled. Make a list of ten other words you think are often misspelled. Then use a dictionary to check your spelling of each word.
- [ ] February 12–15 is the Great Backyard Bird Count. Write a letter to persuade your neighbors to help count the number and types of birds that live in your neighborhood.
- [ ] Describe the world's best Valentine's Day party.
- [ ] Write a one-act play titled "One Lousy Valentine's Day."
- [ ] Harriet Tubman helped hundreds of people escape from slavery. Two of the people she led to freedom were her parents. How do you think Harriet felt about helping her parents become free?
- [ ] Describe one way you have changed since January 1 of this year.
- [ ] With which of these proverbs do you most agree? Tell why.
  - Better late than never.
  - A little too late is much too late.
- [ ] The U.S. Postal Service releases a special love-themed stamp every year. Would you buy a love stamp? Why or why not?

Name

March Writing Prompts

- [ ] Every child in America is encouraged to read a book on March 2, Dr. Seuss's birthday. Do you think Dr. Seuss would be happy his birthday is being celebrated with reading? Why or why not?
- [ ] The Peace Corps started in 1961. Since then, over 170,000 people have volunteered to help people learn to help themselves. What would you like to help other people learn? How would you teach it?
- [ ] Describe your favorite way to eat peanut butter. Then create and describe a new, wacky way to eat this nutritious snack.
- [ ] Dr. Elizabeth Blackwell, the first woman in the United States to get a medical degree, applied to 30 schools. Of those schools, 29 rejected her application because she was a woman. How do you think she felt?
- [ ] Write five questions you would ask a leprechaun if you were lucky enough to meet one.
- [ ] Which subject is easiest for you: math, social studies, science, or language arts (English)? Is it your favorite subject? Why or why not?
- [ ] March 26 is Make Up Your Own Holiday Day. Write a letter to the editor of your local newspaper. Describe the holiday you would invent and persuade readers to celebrate it.
- [ ] What is the weirdest thing you have ever eaten for breakfast? Describe it.
- [ ] Write an email that explains why the students in your class and you deserve a free pizza party. Use this greeting:

  To Whom It May Concern:
- [ ] Sally Ride was the first female astronaut to travel in space. Her first flight was on the space shuttle *Challenger.* Astronaut Ride was in space for six days. Imagine you are Sally. Write a journal entry about your first day in space.

How to use the prompts: Have each student staple a copy of this page in his writing journal. Or cut copies in half and distribute one month's prompts at a time. When a student uses a prompt, he checks its box.

April Writing Prompts

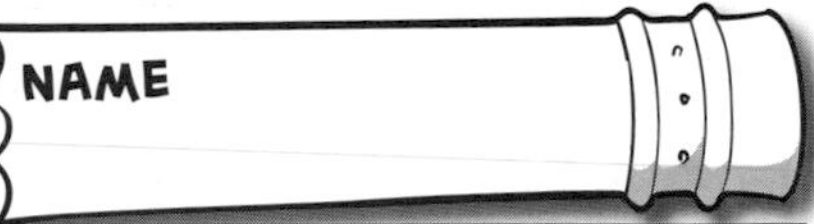

Write a short story about the very first April Fools' Day. How do you think the custom got started?	What would someone who tries to see the sunny side of life be like? Do you try to see the sunny side of life? Why or why not?
How can you tell when spring arrives? List ten or more signs of spring.	Think of one thing you do to help protect the planet. Write a radio commercial that will convince listeners to do the same thing.
Imagine that you have just built the perfect tree house. Describe it.	If you were to make a time capsule to remember this school year, name five items you would include. Describe one of the items and explain why you would put it in the time capsule.
Pretend you are an astronaut on an outer space adventure. Write a journal entry about it.	April is National Humor Month. What is the funniest book you've ever read? Why is it so funny?
April is a Car Care Month. Write five steps to tell how to wash a car.	Write a story about the day you met your principal.

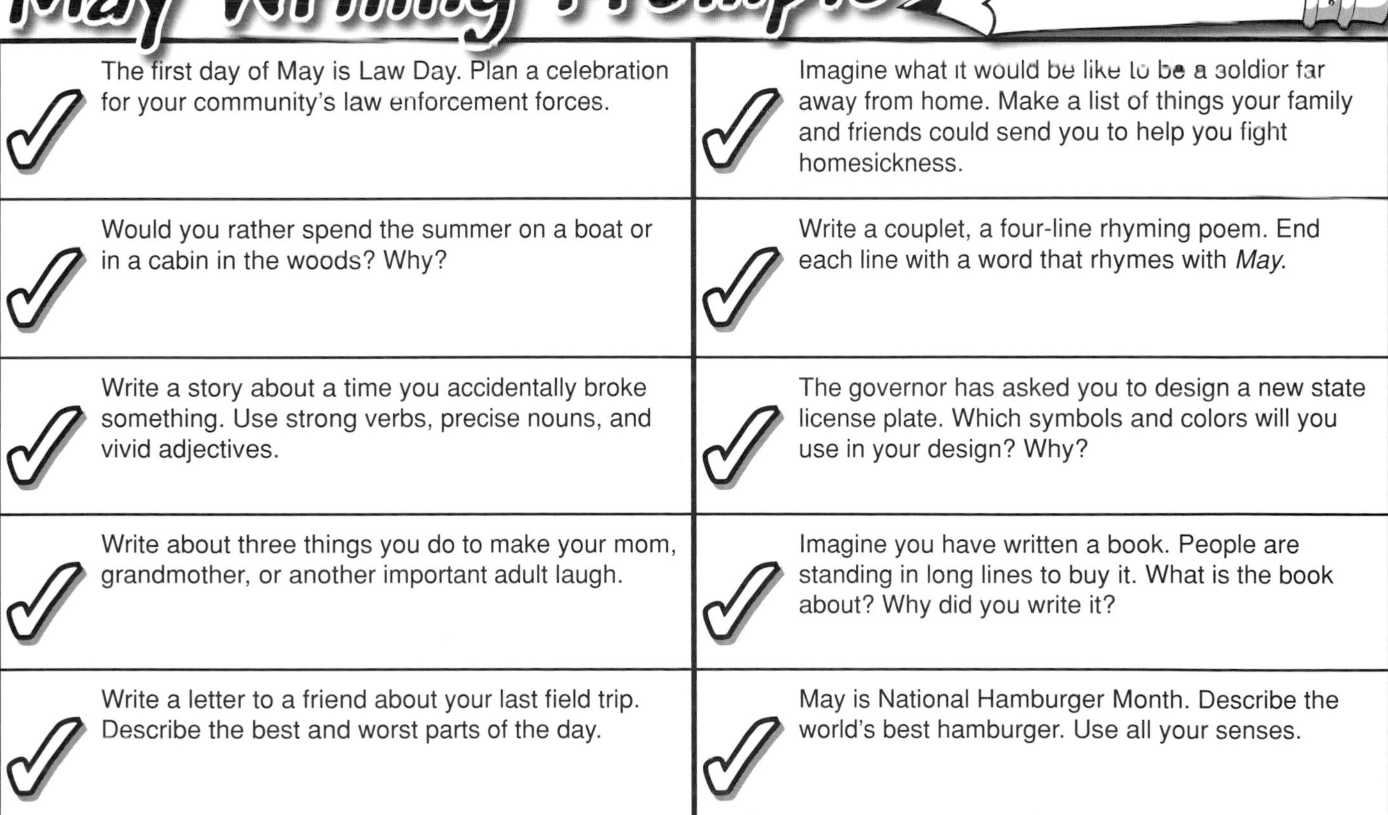

May Writing Prompts

NAME

The first day of May is Law Day. Plan a celebration for your community's law enforcement forces.	Imagine what it would be like to be a soldier far away from home. Make a list of things your family and friends could send you to help you fight homesickness.
Would you rather spend the summer on a boat or in a cabin in the woods? Why?	Write a couplet, a four-line rhyming poem. End each line with a word that rhymes with *May.*
Write a story about a time you accidentally broke something. Use strong verbs, precise nouns, and vivid adjectives.	The governor has asked you to design a new state license plate. Which symbols and colors will you use in your design? Why?
Write about three things you do to make your mom, grandmother, or another important adult laugh.	Imagine you have written a book. People are standing in long lines to buy it. What is the book about? Why did you write it?
Write a letter to a friend about your last field trip. Describe the best and worst parts of the day.	May is National Hamburger Month. Describe the world's best hamburger. Use all your senses.

How to use: Have each student staple a copy of this page in his writing journal. Or cut copies in half and distribute one month's prompts at a time. When a student uses a prompt, he shades the checkmark.

June Writing Prompts

NAME

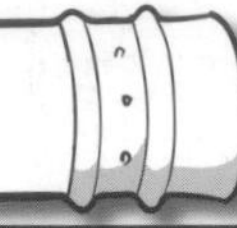

Who do you think would enjoy National Dairy Month (June) more: a dairy farmer or an ice cream truck driver? Explain.	Imagine that you are walking along a riverbank and you see something bobbing in the water. You look closer. It's a very old bottle with a cork stopper, and there's something inside. What happens next?
Write a story about a crabby crab that washes onto the beach from deep in the ocean.	June is National Safety Month. Write a letter to the nearest fire station to thank the firefighters for helping keep your town safe.
Write a haiku (five-, seven-, five-syllable pattern) about summer vacation.	What would you do if one of the trees near your home started growing money?
On June 16, 1884, the first roller coaster in America opened. What would it be like to ride a roller coaster if you kept your eyes closed for the whole ride? Describe it.	It's Skyscraper Month (June). Would you like to help build a skyscraper? Why or why not?
Write an email to your best friend about building a tree house. In the email, convince your friend to help you build one.	Where would you rather spend an afternoon—at a swimming pool, lake, water park, or beach? Explain.

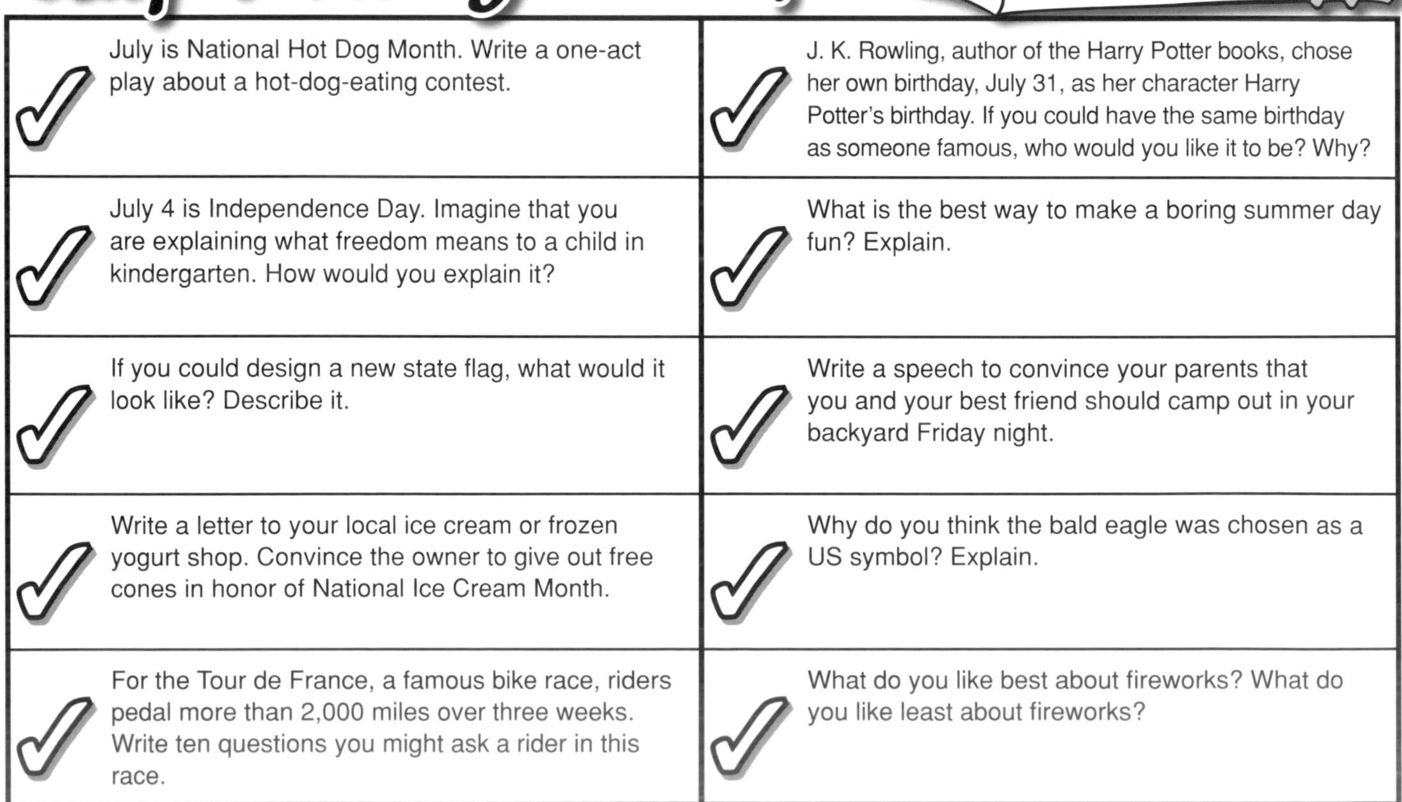

July Writing Prompts

NAME

July is National Hot Dog Month. Write a one-act play about a hot-dog-eating contest.	J. K. Rowling, author of the Harry Potter books, chose her own birthday, July 31, as her character Harry Potter's birthday. If you could have the same birthday as someone famous, who would you like it to be? Why?
July 4 is Independence Day. Imagine that you are explaining what freedom means to a child in kindergarten. How would you explain it?	What is the best way to make a boring summer day fun? Explain.
If you could design a new state flag, what would it look like? Describe it.	Write a speech to convince your parents that you and your best friend should camp out in your backyard Friday night.
Write a letter to your local ice cream or frozen yogurt shop. Convince the owner to give out free cones in honor of National Ice Cream Month.	Why do you think the bald eagle was chosen as a US symbol? Explain.
For the Tour de France, a famous bike race, riders pedal more than 2,000 miles over three weeks. Write ten questions you might ask a rider in this race.	What do you like best about fireworks? What do you like least about fireworks?

How to use: Have each student staple a copy of this page in his writing journal. Or cut copies in half and distribute one month's prompts at a time. When a student uses a prompt, he shades the checkmark.

Math

MATH TIPS + TOOLS

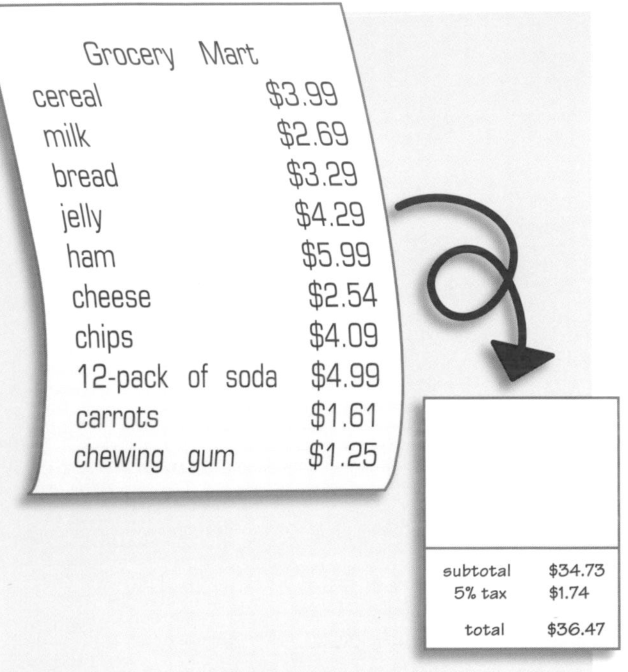

Grocery Mart
cereal $3.99
milk $2.69
bread $3.29
jelly $4.29
ham $5.99
cheese $2.54
chips $4.09
12-pack of soda $4.99
carrots $1.61
chewing gum $1.25
subtotal $34.73
5% tax $1.74
total $36.47

Shop 'til You Drop
Adding and subtracting decimals

Here's a partner activity that gives students real-world practice working with decimals! In advance, collect several itemized receipts that each total less than $100. Cut off each receipt's subtotal, tax, and total. Then glue the subtotal, tax, and total on the flip side. Next, give each partner a receipt and have him calculate the subtotal. After he checks his work against the back of the strip, he calculates his change as if he paid with a $100.00 bill. Then the partners trade receipts and repeat the steps to check each other's work. For a more challenging activity, have each student multiply the subtotal by the local tax percentage and add the product to find the total.

Vickie Robertson, Meadow Green Elementary, Whittier, CA

Step-by-Step
Order of operations

Remind students to solve problems one step at a time with this simple idea! To begin, have each child write a multistep problem on a construction paper strip. Next, have the student write and solve the first step on another strip. Then have the child complete each remaining step on a different strip until she solves the problem. After checking her work, have the child link and then staple the strips, in order, to create a paper chain. If desired, display students' chains as a reminder to solve problems one step at a time.

Julie Nolan, Little Falls, NJ

Turn to page 123 for a partner game that helps students build strong mental math skills!

Let's Roll!
Area

For this engaging measurement review, give each pair of students a copy of page 110, two dice, and two colored pencils. Then guide the duo to follow the directions on the page as the students practice calculating area using the assortment of rectangles.

Jennifer Otter, Oak Ridge, NC

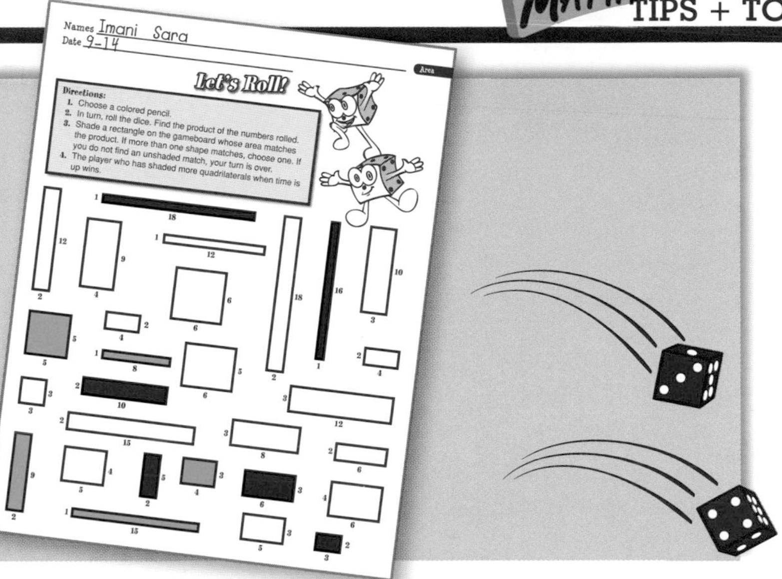

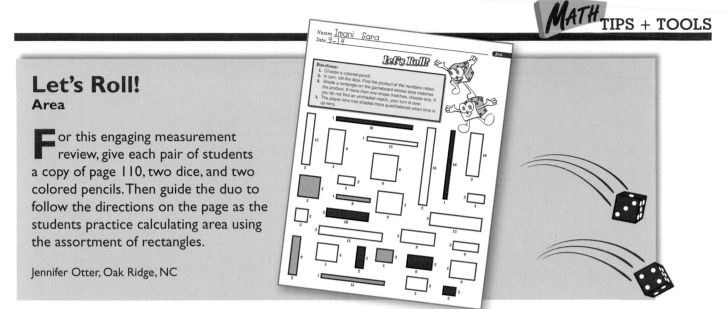

Multiplication Made Easy
Multiplication facts

Show students that remembering multiplication facts can be a breeze when they narrow down the facts they actually have to memorize. To begin, display a copy of the mini poster from page 111 and give each student a multiplication table, marker, and highlighter. Next, read the poster's first tip and guide the child to mark out the products she knows. Repeat with each tip and then have each student highlight the remaining products on her table. Finally, guide the child to count the facts she still needs to memorize (the highlighted ones) and compare them with the number of facts she actually knows (the marked-out ones). If desired, have students make flash cards for the highlighted facts.

Carol Mobley, Oakland, CA

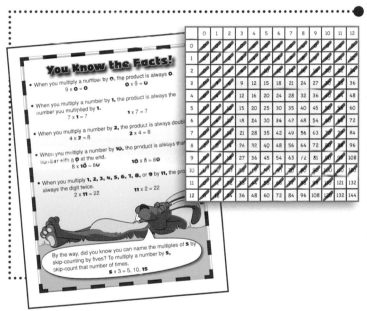

Outsmart Your Teacher
Place value

What student doesn't want to try to outsmart his teacher? For this whole-class challenge, draw place value lines on the board, as shown, and have each student draw matching lines on his paper. Next, roll a die and write the number on a line. Then challenge each student to record the number so he creates a number larger than the one you are building. Continue rolling until you've named a number for each place. Then read your number aloud and invite students to share any numbers they built that have greater values. After congratulating each student who creates a number larger than yours, repeat as time allows. If desired, add decimals to increase the level of challenge.

Leigh Newsom, Cedar Road Elementary, Chesapeake, VA

Statistics Superstars

Data analysis

Want your students to really learn the steps required to identify range, mean, median, and mode? Try this! Give each pair of students a copy of page 112, two dice, and scissors. Have the partners cut apart the number cards, shuffle them, choose a game card, and then follow the directions to get started. Guide the students to shuffle and reuse their number cards to play each round. When the partners finish one game, they choose another game and keep on learning!

Angel David, Paradise Elementary, Ball, LA

☆ In the Range ☆

1. Each player rolls a die. Add the numbers. You each take that number of cards.
2. Arrange your cards in order and then record the numbers.
3. Remove all your cards except those with the lowest and highest numbers.
4. Subtract the lowest number from the highest to find the range and record it.
5. Trade papers with your partner to check each other's work. The player with the greater range scores a point. The player with more points after ten rounds wins.

The Button Slide

Two-digit multiplication

1. 38 × 26 = 228 + 760 = 988

2. 43 × 8 = 344

To help students focus on multiplying by one number at a time, give each child a small button! Have the student place the button over the digit in the tens place as shown. Then guide her to multiply each digit in the top row by the digit in the ones place. When she finishes with the top row, the child slides the button to cover the digit in the ones place and multiplies by the tens digit. No more confusion!

Christine Cooley, C. C. Meneley Elementary
Gardnerville, NV

It All Stacks Up!
Decimal computation

Set up this hands-on practice center by labeling the edges of six small foam cups with different decimals. Then add a die and a code similar to the one shown. At the center, a student rolls the die and checks the code. He stacks the guided number of cups, rotates the cups to align the decimals, and completes the named function. The child records his work on his own paper and repeats the steps as time allows, building computation skills as he goes!

adapted from an idea by Jennifer Otter, Oak Ridge, NC

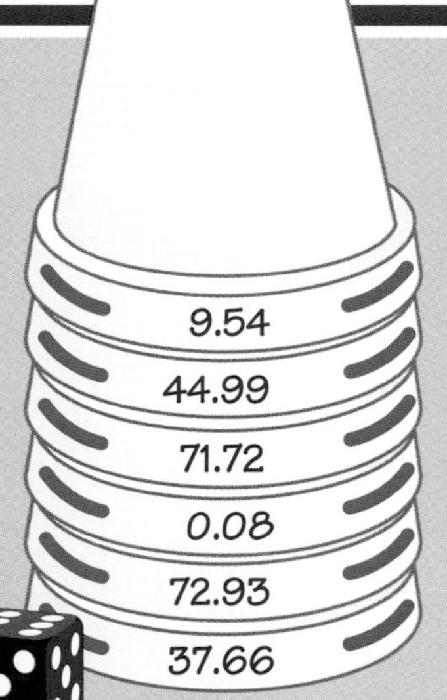

Cup Code

1 = Take two cups. Multiply.
2 = Take two cups. Subtract.
3 = Take three cups. Add.
4 = Take four cups. Add.
5 = Take five cups. Add.
6 = Take six cups. Add.

Memory and the Missing Number
Solving algebraic equations

Here's a game that gives students practice identifying variables. To play, each pair of students cuts apart the cards on a copy of page 113 and turns the cards facedown. The partners take turns flipping two cards at a time. If a student turns over an equation card and its matching answer, he keeps the cards. Students continue playing until all the matches have been made. The partner with more cards wins the game.

Flipbook Facts
Capacity

For this helpful flipbook, have each child stack three sheets of paper one inch apart, fold them down, and then staple the pages together as shown. Next, have the student label the top flap *capacity* and define the term. Then have the child label each remaining flap with a unit of capacity and its equivalencies. Once students have their booklets ready, lead them to brainstorm examples of containers that are measured by each unit. As students share their ideas, have each child jot the containers' names on the matching flaps. Then have each student keep her flipbook handy for regular review.

Marisa Martinez, Shaw Elementary, Mesquite, TX

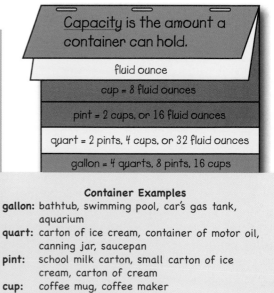

Capacity is the amount a container can hold.

fluid ounce

cup = 8 fluid ounces

pint = 2 cups, or 16 fluid ounces

quart = 2 pints, 4 cups, or 32 fluid ounces

gallon = 4 quarts, 8 pints, 16 cups

Container Examples

gallon: bathtub, swimming pool, car's gas tank, aquarium
quart: carton of ice cream, container of motor oil, canning jar, saucepan
pint: school milk carton, small carton of ice cream, carton of cream
cup: coffee mug, coffee maker
ounce: bottle of cough syrup, can of soda, baby bottle, bottled water

MATH TIPS + TOOLS

It All Adds Up!

Adding, subtracting, and ordering fractions

This no-fuss game gives students lots of fraction practice! Have each group of three students cut apart the cards and answer key from a copy of page 114. Next, each student draws a card and solves its equation. Then the players check the key. The student with the largest correct answer earns three points. The player with the next-largest correct answer earns two points, and the player with the smallest correct answer earns one point. The students continue until all the cards have been played. The child with the highest score wins.

Corrie Brubaker, Providence School, Chambersburg, PA

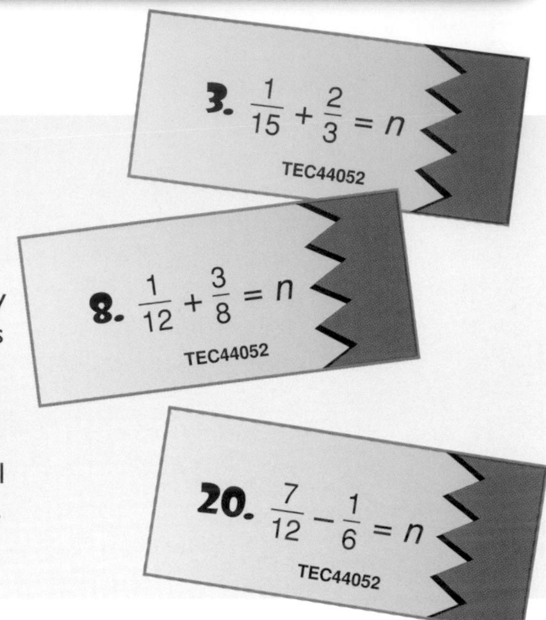

Middle
Element
Displayed
In
A set of
Numbers

Most
Often
Displayed
Element

Mean
Expresses the
Average
Number

M, M, & M Clues

Data analysis

Post these clever acrostics to help students remember the differences between finding the mean, median, and mode! Then review each process with students and have them jot the reminders in their math journals.

Amanda Stimpson, Dillard Drive Elementary, Raleigh, NC

Slide, Flip, and Turn Tango

Transformations

Get students moving with this memorable review! After studying transformations, direct each small group of students to create a 30-second chant and march or song and dance to show translations, rotations, and reflections. Give students time to practice and then set aside time for each group to put on its show!

Rachel Proctor, Mt. Hope/Nanjemoy Elementary, Nanjemoy, MD

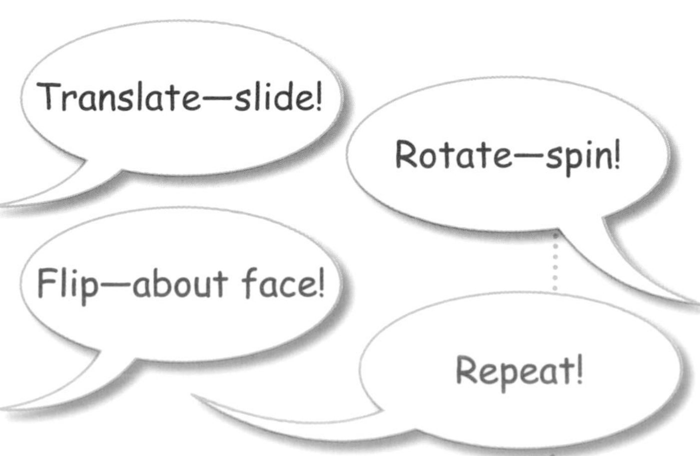

Translate—slide!
Rotate—spin!
Flip—about face!
Repeat!

Load 'em Up!
Finding volume

To give students practice calculating volume, have each child cut apart the cards and forklift labels from a copy of page 115. Next, guide the student to fold another sheet of paper into four columns and glue each forklift on one section of the page as shown. Then have the student calculate and record the volume of each box. To check his work, the child sorts the cards into the appropriate sections. (There should be four boxes in each section.) Then he glues the boxes in stacks on each forklift.

Jennifer Otter, Oak Ridge, NC

22.04

23.01

23.03

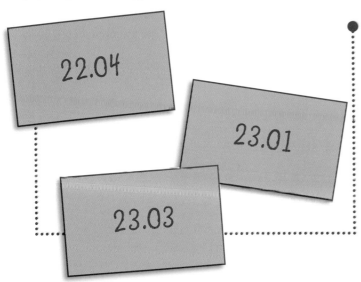

Filling in the Gaps
Ordering decimals

For this small-group activity, program ten index cards with decimals. Next, guide the students in the group to arrange the cards from least to greatest. Have each child copy the numbers onto his paper, leaving space between them. Then, in each space, he writes a decimal that comes between the numbers immediately above and below the space. Follow up by having students compare and discuss their answers.

Shoptalk
Writing fractions

For this double-duty idea, place several used catalogs and a supply of sticky notes at a center. Next, have each pair of students cut out a catalog page that shows several items. Guide the duo to think of a fraction question about items on the page. Have the pair write its question on the front of a sticky note and jot the answer on the back. Then have the partners write nine more questions and answers and stick their notes around the page. After approving students' work, return the pages to the center for independent practice. Each student chooses a page, answers the questions, and then flips the notes to check his work.

What fraction of the shoes has polka dots?
$\frac{2}{3}$ of the shoes have polka dots.
Shoe Sale!

Colleen Dabney, Williamsburg, VA

Don't miss the problem-solving practice page on page 135!

MATH-O!

Vocabulary review

When it's time to review important math terms, try this whole-class game! Have each student draw a five-by-six grid and title it across the first row as shown. Then post 25 math terms and have each child write them on her grid. To play, randomly pick a term and define it without naming it. Have each student find the matching term on her grid and put a marker on it. When a child gets five in a row, she calls out, "MATH-O!" If she correctly identified the terms you defined, give her a small treat, have students clear their boards, and play again.

Abigail Green, McIntire-Munson Elementary
Zanesville, OH

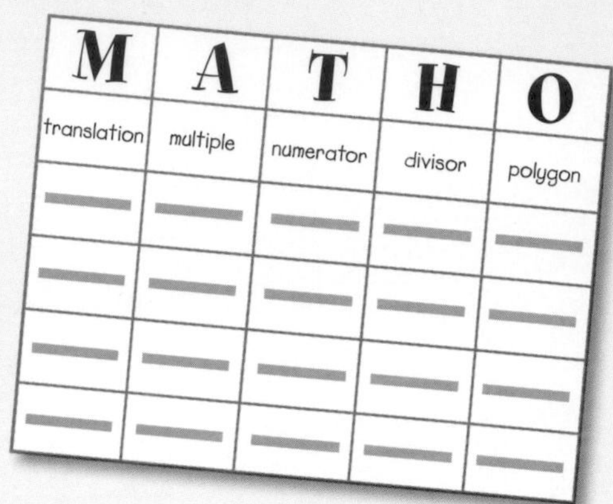

Elizabeth
I compared the weights of classroom items with the weight of a one-pound bag of dried beans.
Classroom Item
Lighter
Heavier
About the Same
Dried
BEANS
16 Ounces (1 Pound)
DOG
FOOD
2 kilograms (4.4 pounds)
3 pounds

Guess My Weight!

Estimating weight and mass

Stock this hands-on center with an object that has a clearly marked weight or mass. Then add a tub of classroom items with assorted weights. A student draws a chart similar to the one shown. Next, she lifts and holds the marked object, getting a feel for its weight. Then she picks up each classroom item, deciding whether it is heavier than, lighter than, or about the same weight or mass as the primary object. She records each item and notes her estimate. After all students rotate through the center, have them discuss and compare their estimates.

Traveling Story Problems

Problem solving

For this group activity, assign each student a math equation. Then guide him to write the first sentence of a story problem for the equation. Next, have each child pass his paper to another student. Guide each child to read the problem's first sentence and write the next one. Then have the student pass this paper, read the problem he gets, and write its question. Finally, have each student pass his paper again and then solve the problem he's handed. For a fun follow-up, collect students' work and use the problems later to keep students thinking during transitions.

Look ahead to pages 139 and 140 for fun practice sheets on mean, median, mode, and range and on division!

Practice Plus!

Graphing data

Here's an idea for giving students graphing practice with all kinds of data! To get students started, display the sugar-content table shown. Then guide each pair of students to graph the data on a copy of page 116. Once the partners finish their graph, have them analyze it as guided at the bottom of the page. After that, put copies of page 116 at a center along with weather reports, attendance charts, and other sets of data to give students independent graphing practice!

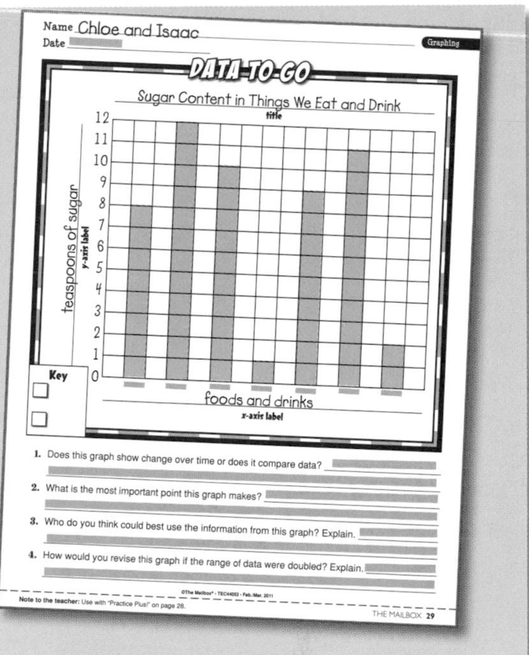

Sugar Content Table		
Food or Drink	Serving Size	Sugar Content in One Serving
punch made from a sweetened drink mix	12 ounces	8½ teaspoons
orange soda	12 ounces	12 teaspoons
cola	12 ounces	10 teaspoons
graham crackers	2 crackers	1 teaspoon
candy bar	1 bar	9 teaspoons
fruit-flavored low-fat yogurt	1 cup	11 teaspoons
bubble gum	1 piece	2 teaspoons

In the Bank

Elapsed time

Want to help students master elapsed-time calculations? Copy the mini poster on page 117! Then display the poster and guide students to follow its commonsense steps.

Melissa Bodnar, Zephyr Elementary, Whitehall, PA

A Bird's-Eye View

Three-dimensional figures

Begin this challenge by displaying the diagrams shown. Then explain that they represent the front, overhead, and side views of a structure built with five blocks. Next, challenge each student to build the structure. Once a student builds the matching structure, challenge him to build a different structure using five cubes and then to draw its overhead, front, and side views. Repeat with six and seven cubes as time allows.

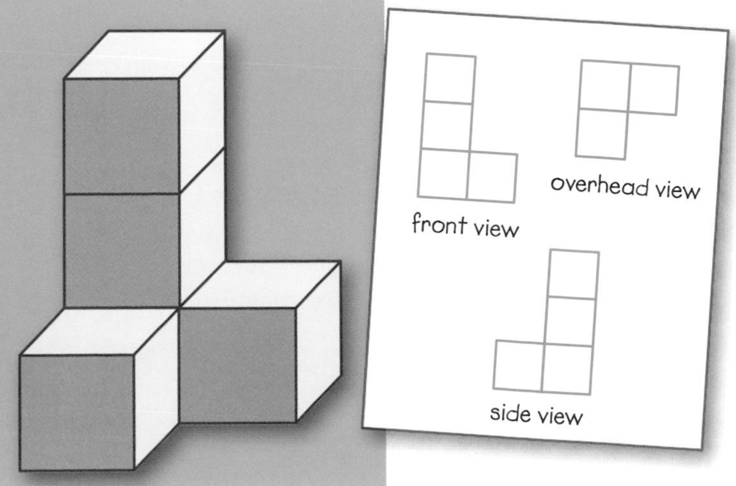

What a Series!

Multiplication, number patterns

Here's a multiplication review that's sure to get your students thinking! First, write on the board the number shown and have each student multiply the number by 2. Then guide students to compare the product with the posted number. *(When this* cyclic number *is multiplied by 2, 3, 4, 5, or 6, the product includes the same digits in a different order.)* Next, challenge students to multiply the posted number by 3, 4, 5, and 6 to explore and then describe the pattern.

142,857 x 2 = 285,714
142,857 x 3 = 428,571
142,857 x 4 = 571,428
142,857 x 5 = 714,285
142,857 x 6 = 857,142

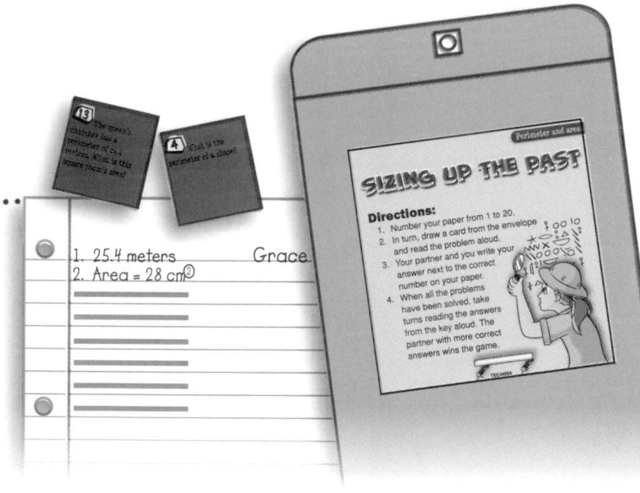

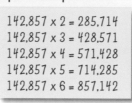

Sizing Up the Past

Perimeter, area

Use this simple-to-prepare center to give students practice with tested measurement concepts. Cut apart a copy of the direction card, question cards, and answer key on page 118. Glue the direction card on the front of an envelope and the key on the back. Then slip the question cards inside, and the center's ready to use!

adapted from an idea by Teresa Vilfer-Snyder, Fredericktown Elementary, Fredericktown, OH

Numbers in the News

Decimals, place value, ordering

For this activity, have each student make a chart labeled as shown. Next, guide the child to find and cut out of old newspapers and magazines ten or more numbers that include decimals. Then have the student glue one number at the left of each row and write the digits in the appropriate columns. Finally, have students write the numbers from least to greatest at the bottom of the page.

Suzette Westhoff, Fredericksburg, VA

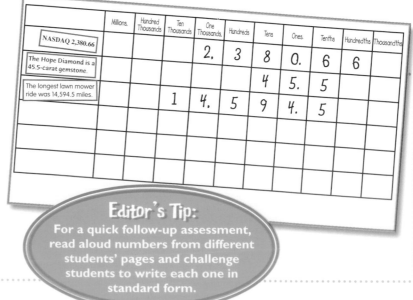

	Millions,	Hundred Thousands	Ten Thousands	One Thousands,	Hundreds	Tens	Ones.	Tenths	Hundredths	Thousandths
NASDAQ 2,380.66				2,	3	8	0.	6	6	
The Hope Diamond is a 45.5-carat gemstone.						4	5.	5		
The longest lawn mower ride was 14,594.5 miles.			1	4,	5	9	4.	5		

Editor's Tip: For a quick follow-up assessment, read aloud numbers from different students' pages and challenge students to write each one in standard form.

All in a Day's Practice
Fraction operations

Grab a couple of ten-, 12-, or 20-sided dice to give students daily practice working with fractions. Start each math lesson by having a volunteer roll the dice to name the numerator and denominator for one fraction. Have another child roll the dice to name a second fraction. Then guide each student to add the fractions, subtract the lesser fraction from the greater fraction, multiply the fractions, and change each fraction to a decimal. If desired, post a number line from zero to one. Then add each day's fractions to the number line to help students compare and order the fractions too!

Matt Lehtonen, Framingham, MA

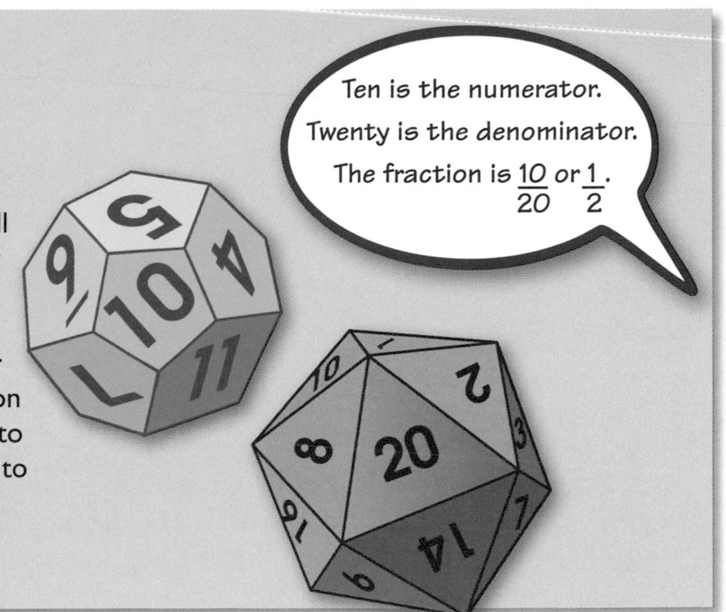

Round and Round
Adding time

Want to give your students practice adding time? Try this! Bring in a stack of music CDs. Then give each small group of students three CDs. Have the students use the song list in each CD's insert to find and then add the CD's total minutes and seconds of music. Next, have the group order the CDs from the least music to the most. To extend the activity, have each group of students determine the range of song times and the median song time. **For an additional challenge**, name each CD's price and guide students to figure out which CD provides the most music for the money.

Kim Minafo, Cary, NC

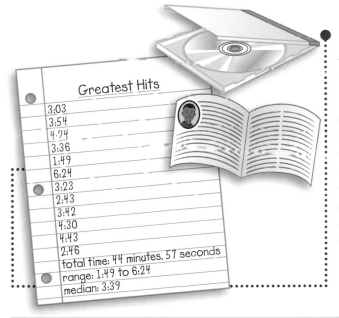

Greatest Hits
3:03
3:54
4:24
3:36
1:49
6:24
3:23
2:43
3:42
4:30
4:43
2:46
total time: 44 minutes, 57 seconds
range: 1:49 to 6:24
median: 3:39

Oops-a-Daisy!
Mixed review

For this anytime review, make a copy of page 119. Write equations with which your students need practice on the flowers' petals, making mistakes on half the equations. Then copy the page for students and challenge them to find and fix the incorrect equations.

Colleen Dabney, Williamsburg, VA

A Big Deal

Comparing decimals

For this center activity, remove the tens and face cards from a deck of cards. Also stock the center with twelve buttons. At the center, the student shuffles the cards and then draws three. She arranges the cards to the right of a button (decimal point) to make the largest decimal she can. Then she records the number. Next, the child draws three more cards and repeats the steps using another button. After she has written two decimals, she compares the numbers and draws the appropriate symbol (<, >, or =) between them. She continues until she uses all the cards in the pile. Then she circles the largest decimal overall and draws a star next to the smallest decimal overall.

Shawna Miller, Wellington Elementary, Flower Mound, TX

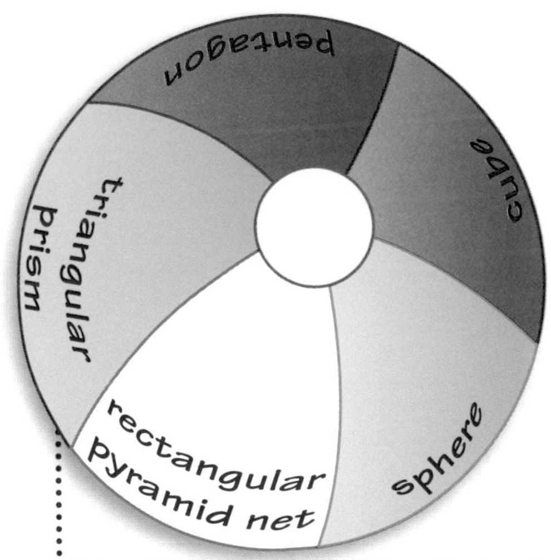

Overhauled Beach Ball

Plane figures, solid figures, nets

To prepare this lively review, copy page 120 for each student and use a permanent marker to list the page's terms on an inflated beach ball. Then toss the ball to a student. When he catches the ball, have him announce the term nearest his right index finger. Next, guide each child to label the matching figure on his copy of the page. After that, have the student toss the ball to someone else and repeat as time allows or until students have labeled every term on the page.

Colleen Dabney, Williamsburg, VA

On a Roll

Probability

Here's a quick activity that gives students plenty of probability practice! Give each pair of students two dice. Guide the duo to complete a tree diagram that shows all the possible combinations of rolls. Then lead a class discussion about the results with questions such as those shown.

How many combinations result in a sum of 7? *(6)*
How many combinations result in doubles? *(6)*
Which sum occurs more often: 6 or 9? *(6)*
What is the probability of rolling two 1s? *($\frac{1}{36}$)* Doubles? *($\frac{6}{36}$ or $\frac{1}{6}$)*
What is the probability of getting a sum of 7? *($\frac{6}{36}$ or $\frac{1}{6}$)*
What is the probability of getting a sum of 10 or higher? *($\frac{6}{36}$ or $\frac{1}{6}$)*
What is the probability of getting a sum of 7 or 11? *($\frac{8}{36}$ or $\frac{2}{9}$)*

Measure Up

Metric measurement, data analysis

Use this activity to give students real-world data analysis practice. Have each small group of students use a meter stick or a meter tape to measure each other's height, head length, arm length, and leg length. Guide the students in each group to record their measurements in a chart and determine the range, mean, median, and mode for their data. Then guide each student to draw a double-bar graph that compares her data with her group's mean statistics. As time allows, compile each group's numbers, lead students to analyze the class's data, and have each student add the class's mean statistics to her bar graph.

Name	Height	Head Length	Arm Length	Leg Length
Range				
Mean				
Median				
Mode				

Line 'em Up

Fraction concepts

Build students' fraction skills with this whole-class game. First, give each student a different fraction card and then divide the class into small groups. Next, give the groups 30 seconds to silently arrange their cards from least to greatest. As each group finishes, its members stand and show their cards in order. When time's up, check each team's work. Award a point to each correct team. Then announce a different instruction, such as one of those shown, and play again. After three rounds, collect students' cards, redistribute them, and keep playing. When time's up, declare the group with the most points the fraction champions.

Colleen Dabney, Williamsburg, VA

- Arrange the fractions from least to greatest.
- Arrange the fractions from greatest to least.
- Show fractions that are greater than ¼.
- Show fractions that are smaller than ⅓.
- Show fractions that are greater than ½.
- Show fractions that are smaller than ¾.
- Show two fractions with a sum that is greater than one.
- Show the fractions that are in simplest form.
- Show fractions that are equal to ½.
- Show three fractions with a sum that is less than one.

A Cup of Comparisons

Capacity

For this center activity, collect disposable cups that hold 8, 9, 12, 16, 32, and 44 ounces. Next, cut apart a copy of the capacity labels and cards on page 121. Tape the matching label to each cup and tape each card onto a plastic straw. Then place the cups and straws at a center. A student folds a sheet of paper in half and then in thirds to make six sections; she labels each section as shown. Then she sorts each straw into the appropriate cup and records her work.

Jennifer Otter, Oak Ridge, NC

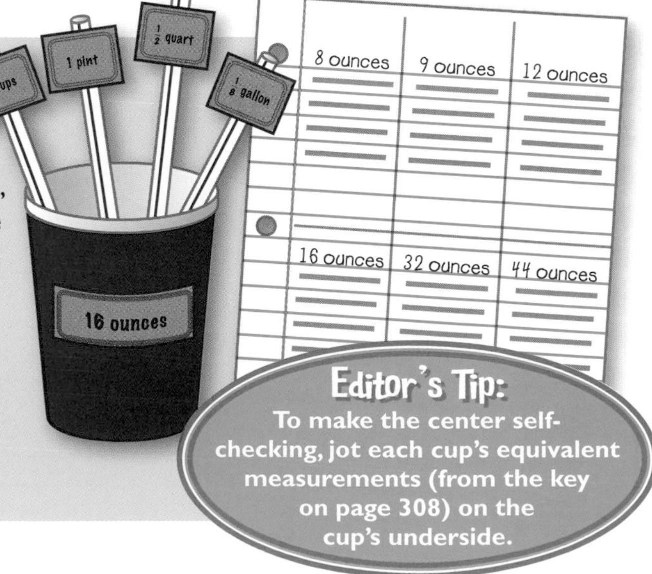

Editor's Tip:
To make the center self-checking, jot each cup's equivalent measurements (from the key on page 308) on the cup's underside.

Names ______________________________

Date ______________________________

Let's Roll!

Directions:

1. Choose a colored pencil.
2. In turn, roll the dice. Find the product of the numbers rolled.
3. Shade a rectangle on the gameboard whose area matches the product. If more than one shape matches, choose one. If you do not find an unshaded match, your turn is over.
4. The player who has shaded more rectangles when time is up wins.

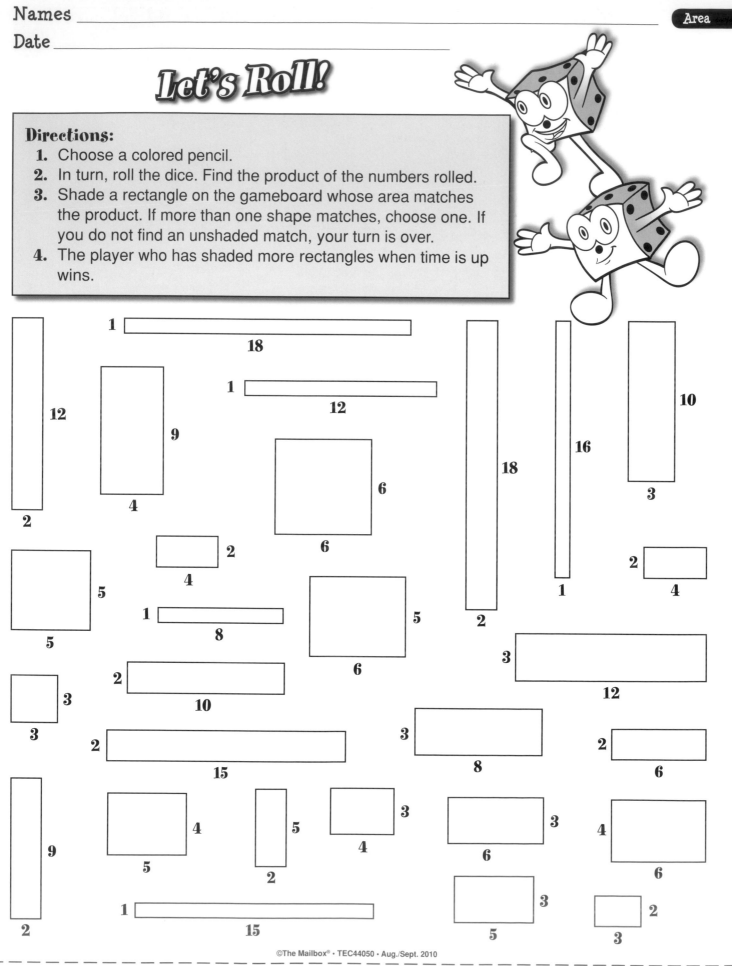

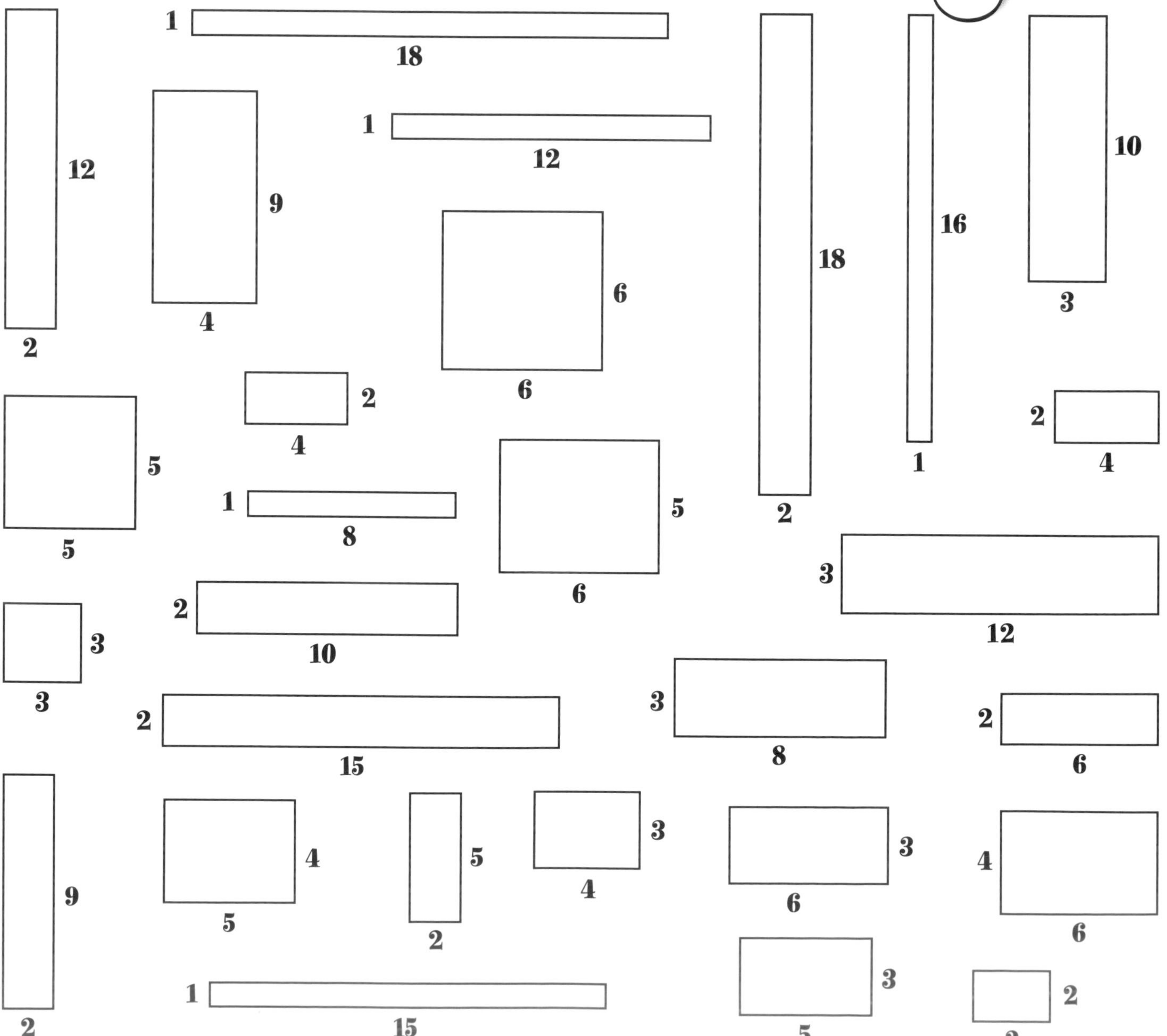

Note to the teacher: Use with "Let's Roll!" on page 99.

You Know the Facts!

- When you multiply a number by **0,** the product is always **0**.

  9 x **0** = **0** 0 x 9 = **0**

- When you multiply a number by **1,** the product is always the number you multiplied by **1.**

  7 x **1** = 7 **1** x 7 = 7

- When you multiply a number by **2,** the product is always doubled.

  4 x **2** = 8 **2** x 4 = 8

- When you multiply a number by **10,** the product is always that number with a **0** at the end.

  8 x **10** = 8**0** **10** x 8 = 8**0**

- When you multiply **1, 2, 3, 4, 5, 6, 7, 8,** or **9** by **11,** the product is always the digit twice.

  2 x **11** = 22 **11** x 2 = 22

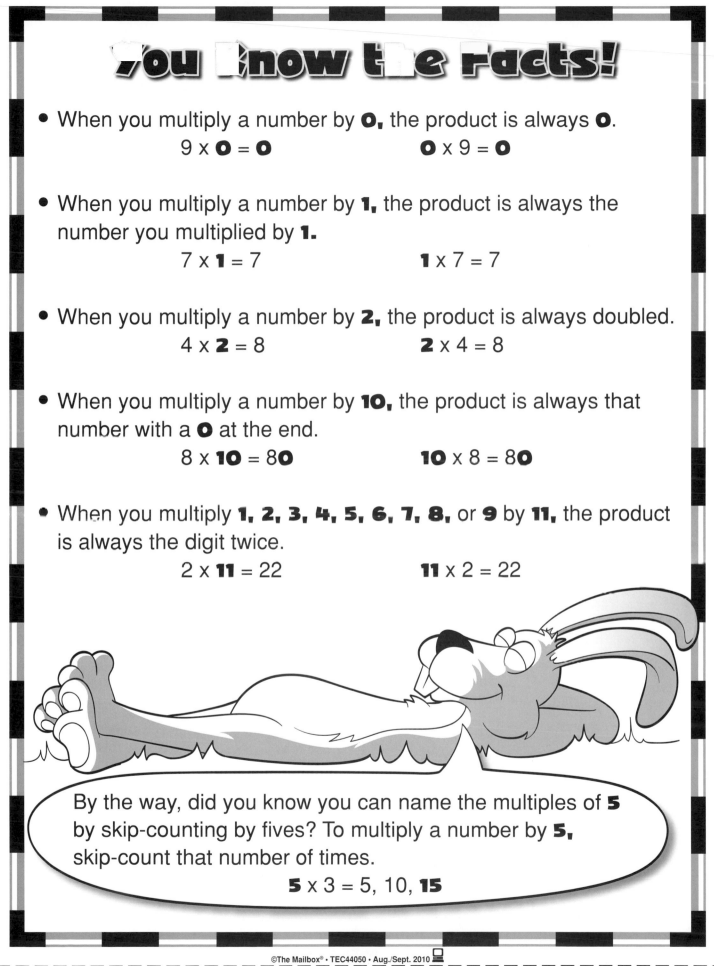

By the way, did you know you can name the multiples of **5** by skip-counting by fives? To multiply a number by **5,** skip-count that number of times.

5 x 3 = 5, 10, **15**

Note to the teacher: Use with "Multiplication Made Easy" on page 99.

Number and Direction Cards

Use with "Statistics Superstars" on page 100.

☆ In the Range ☆

1. Each player rolls a die. Add the numbers. You each take that number of cards.
2. Arrange your cards in order and then record the numbers.
3. Remove all your cards except those with the lowest and highest numbers.
4. Subtract the lowest number from the highest to find the range and record it.
5. Trade papers with your partner to check each other's work. The player with the greater range scores a point. The player with more points after ten rounds wins.

TEC44051

☆ We Mean Business ☆

1. Each player rolls a die. Add the numbers. You each take that number of cards.
2. Record your cards' numbers.
3. Add the numbers. Divide that sum by the number of cards to find the mean, and record it.
4. Trade papers with your partner to check each other's work. Each player who is correct earns a point.
5. The player with more points after ten rounds wins.

TEC44051

☆ Make Way for the Median! ☆

1. Each player rolls a die. Add the numbers. You each take that number of cards.
2. Arrange your cards in order and record the numbers.
3. Remove the lowest and highest number cards in pairs until there are only one or two cards left.
4. If there is one card left, the number on the card is the median. If there are two cards left, add the numbers and divide the sum by two to find the median. Record the median.
5. The player with the higher median earns a point. If you both have the same median, you each earn a point. The player with more points after ten rounds wins.

TEC44051

☆ The Mode With the Most ☆

1. Each player takes ten cards.
2. Arrange your cards in order and record the numbers.
3. Circle the mode or modes (the number or numbers repeated most often).
4. The partner with the highest mode overall earns a point. If you both have the same mode, you each earn a point.
5. The player with more points after ten rounds wins.

TEC44051

Game Cards

Use with “Memory and the Missing Number” on page 101.

1	$n + 12 = 38$	TEC44051
2	$n - 7 = 6$	TEC44051
3	$56 \div n = 7$	TEC44051
4	$n + 17 = 20$	TEC44051
5	$14 + n = 49$	TEC44051
6	$54 - n = 45$	TEC44051
7	$n + 8 = 37$	TEC44051
8	$16 + n = 33$	TEC44051
9	$n - 8 = 16$	TEC44051
10	$8 \times n = 40$	TEC44051
11	$n \div 12 = 6$	TEC44051
12	$8 \times n = 56$	TEC44051
13	$n + 8 = 64$	TEC44051
14	$n - 9 = 24$	TEC44051
15	$18 + n = 45$	TEC44051
16	$n \times 11 = 132$	TEC44051
17	$29 - n = 14$	TEC44051
18	$n + 46 = 65$	TEC44051
19	$75 - n = 28$	TEC44051
20	$n \times 12 = 48$	TEC44051
21	$11 \times n = 121$	TEC44051
22	$63 \div n = 3$	TEC44051
23	$n \div 3 = 27$	TEC44051
24	$n - 19 = 32$	TEC44051

$n = 8$	TEC44051
$n = 35$	TEC44051
$n = 13$	TEC44051
$n = 72$	TEC44051
$n = 29$	TEC44051
$n = 27$	TEC44051
$n = 26$	TEC44051
$n = 24$	TEC44051
$n = 5$	TEC44051
$n = 21$	TEC44051
$n = 4$	TEC44051
$n = 33$	TEC44051
$n = 17$	TEC44051
$n = 81$	TEC44051
$n = 9$	TEC44051
$n = 3$	TEC44051
$n = 15$	TEC44051
$n = 19$	TEC44051
$n = 56$	TEC44051
$n = 47$	TEC44051
$n = 11$	TEC44051
$n = 51$	TEC44051
$n = 12$	TEC44051
$n = 7$	TEC44051

Cards and Answer Key

Use with "It All Adds Up!" on page 102.

1. $\frac{1}{3} + \frac{3}{8} = n$ TEC44052	**2.** $\frac{7}{10} - \frac{1}{4} = n$ TEC44052	**3.** $\frac{1}{15} + \frac{2}{3} = n$ TEC44052	**4.** $\frac{1}{6} + \frac{3}{10} = n$ TEC44052
5. $\frac{4}{5} - \frac{1}{2} = n$ TEC44052	**6.** $\frac{1}{4} + \frac{1}{8} = n$ TEC44052	**7.** $\frac{8}{9} - \frac{2}{3} = n$ TEC44052	**8.** $\frac{1}{12} + \frac{3}{8} = n$ TEC44052
9. $\frac{5}{7} - \frac{1}{21} = n$ TEC44052	**10.** $\frac{7}{8} - \frac{2}{3} = n$ TEC44052	**11.** $\frac{3}{7} + \frac{1}{3} = n$ TEC44052	**12.** $\frac{1}{2} - \frac{1}{3} = n$ TEC44052
13. $\frac{2}{5} + \frac{1}{4} = n$ TEC44052	**14.** $\frac{6}{7} - \frac{1}{2} = n$ TEC44052	**15.** $\frac{7}{10} + \frac{1}{8} = n$ TEC44052	**16.** $\frac{11}{12} - \frac{3}{4} = n$ TEC44052
17. $\frac{4}{5} + \frac{1}{9} = n$ TEC44052	**18.** $\frac{4}{7} - \frac{1}{14} = n$ TEC44052	**19.** $\frac{1}{2} + \frac{5}{11} = n$ TEC44052	**20.** $\frac{7}{12} - \frac{1}{6} = n$ TEC44052
21. $\frac{3}{4} + \frac{1}{6} = n$ TEC44052	**22.** $\frac{4}{5} - \frac{1}{4} = n$ TEC44052	**23.** $\frac{1}{7} + \frac{5}{6} = n$ TEC44052	**24.** $\frac{5}{9} - \frac{1}{3} = n$ TEC44052
25. $\frac{6}{7} + \frac{1}{9} = n$ TEC44052	**26.** $\frac{23}{24} - \frac{4}{12} = n$ TEC44052	**27.** $\frac{3}{8} - \frac{1}{3} = n$ TEC44052	**28.** $\frac{1}{3} + \frac{3}{5} = n$ TEC44052
29. $\frac{9}{10} - \frac{1}{2} = n$ TEC44052	**30.** $\frac{7}{8} + \frac{1}{9} = n$ TEC44052	**31.** $\frac{2}{7} + \frac{1}{5} = n$ TEC44052	**32.** $\frac{11}{12} - \frac{1}{6} = n$ TEC44052
33. $\frac{4}{5} - \frac{3}{15} = n$ TEC44052	**34.** $\frac{1}{2} + \frac{1}{3} = n$ TEC44052	**35.** $\frac{5}{6} - \frac{5}{12} = n$ TEC44052	**36.** $\frac{2}{3} + \frac{1}{8} = n$ TEC44052

Answer Key for "It All Adds Up!"

1. $n = \frac{17}{24}$	**7.** $n = \frac{2}{9}$	**13.** $n = \frac{13}{20}$	**19.** $n = \frac{21}{22}$	**25.** $n = \frac{61}{63}$	**31.** $n = \frac{17}{35}$
2. $n = \frac{9}{20}$	**8.** $n = \frac{11}{24}$	**14.** $n = \frac{5}{14}$	**20.** $n = \frac{5}{12}$	**26.** $n = \frac{5}{8}$	**32.** $n = \frac{3}{4}$
3. $n = \frac{11}{15}$	**9.** $n = \frac{2}{3}$	**15.** $n = \frac{33}{40}$	**21.** $n = \frac{11}{12}$	**27.** $n = \frac{1}{24}$	**33.** $n = \frac{3}{5}$
4. $n = \frac{7}{15}$	**10.** $n = \frac{5}{24}$	**16.** $n = \frac{1}{6}$	**22.** $n = \frac{11}{20}$	**28.** $n = \frac{14}{15}$	**34.** $n = \frac{5}{6}$
5. $n = \frac{3}{10}$	**11.** $n = \frac{16}{21}$	**17.** $n = \frac{41}{45}$	**23.** $n = \frac{41}{42}$	**29.** $n = \frac{2}{5}$	**35.** $n = \frac{5}{12}$
6. $n = \frac{3}{8}$	**12.** $n = \frac{1}{6}$	**18.** $n = \frac{1}{2}$	**24.** $n = \frac{2}{9}$	**30.** $n = \frac{71}{72}$	**36.** $n = \frac{19}{24}$

TEC44052

Volume Cards and Labels

Use with "Load 'em Up!" on page 103.

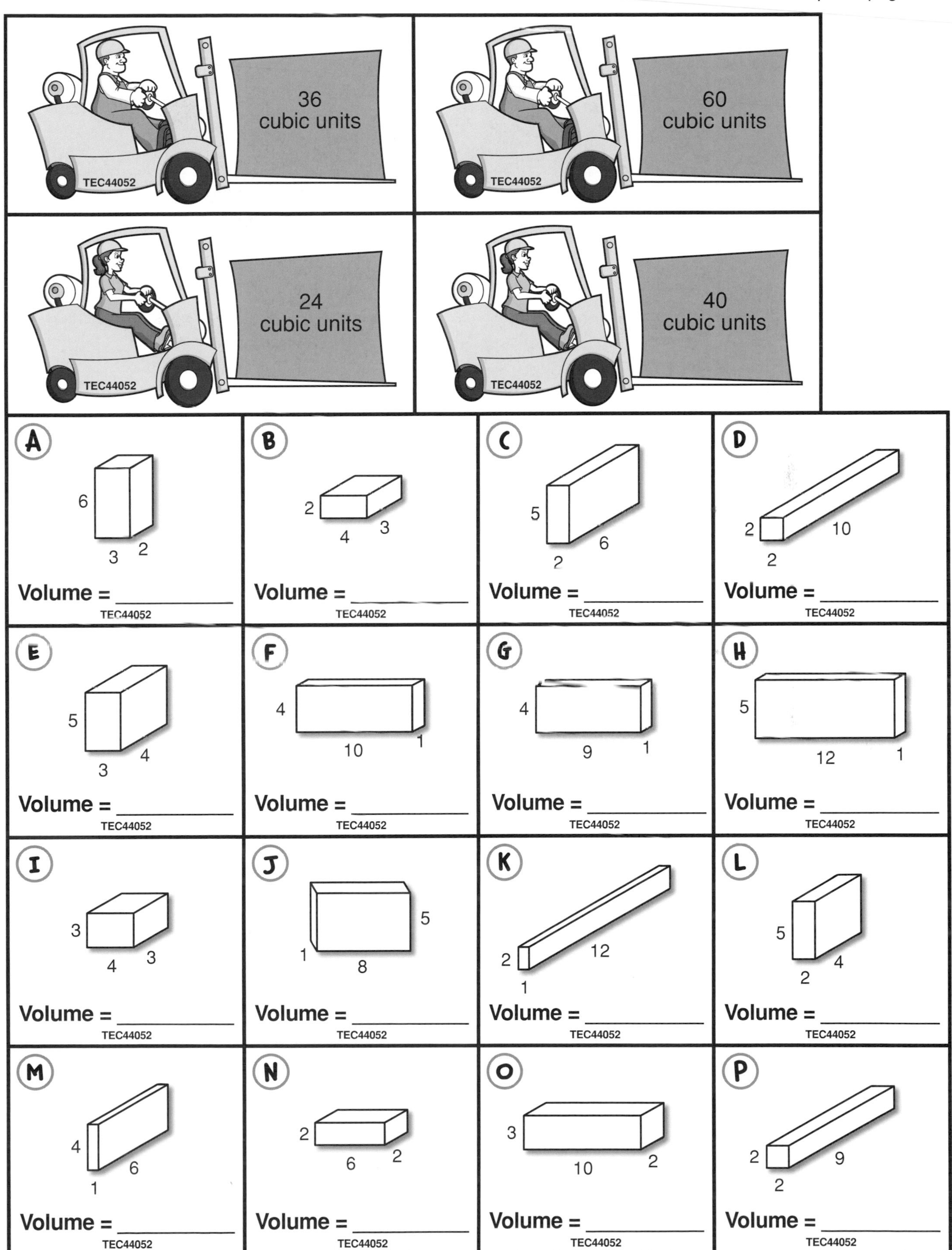

Name ______________________________

Date ______________________

DATA TO GO

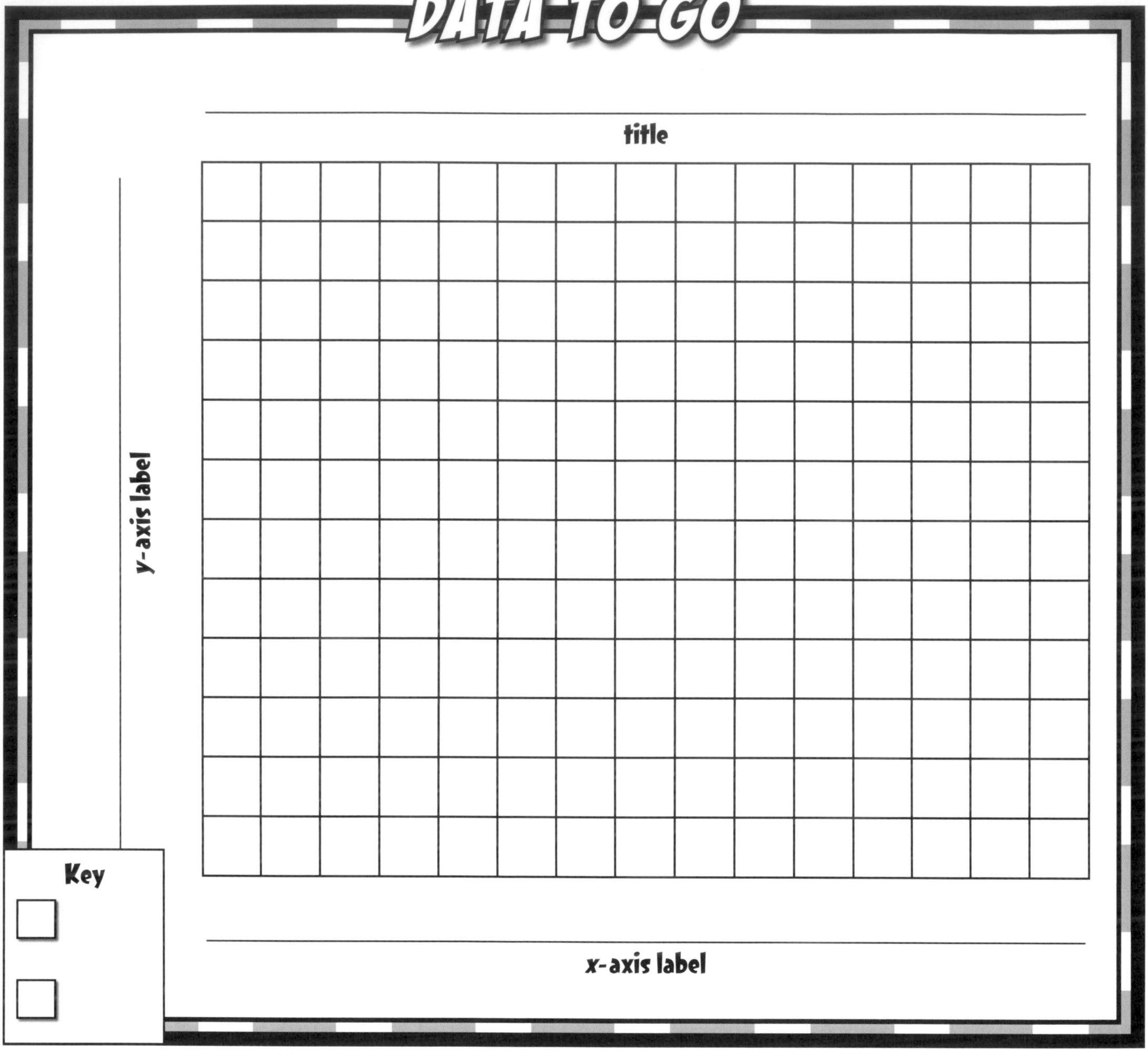

____

title

y-axis label

____

x-axis label

Key

1. Does this graph show change over time or does it compare data? ______________________________
2. What is the most important point this graph makes? ______________________________
3. Who do you think could best use the information from this graph? Explain. ______________________________
4. How would you revise this graph if the range of data were doubled? Explain. ______________________________

 Note to the teacher: Use with "Practice Plus!" on page 105.

Time in the Bank

What is the elapsed time between 4:38 PM and 7:16 PM?

1. What is the next whole hour after the first time in the problem?

2. How many minutes are there until that next hour? Bank 'em!

There are 22 minutes from 4:38 PM to 5:00 PM.

5:00 PM

3. How many hours and minutes are there from that whole hour until the second time? Bank 'em!

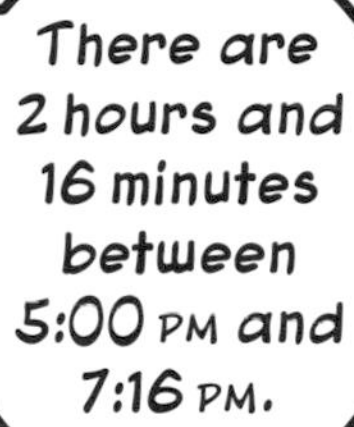

There are 2 hours and 16 minutes between 5:00 PM and 7:16 PM.

5:00 PM

4. How many total minutes are in the bank? (If there are 60 or more total minutes, regroup.)

5. How many total hours are in the bank?

There are 38 minutes in the bank—22 minutes + 16 minutes = 38 minutes.
There are 2 hours in the bank.

6. Add the banked hours and minutes to find the elapsed time!

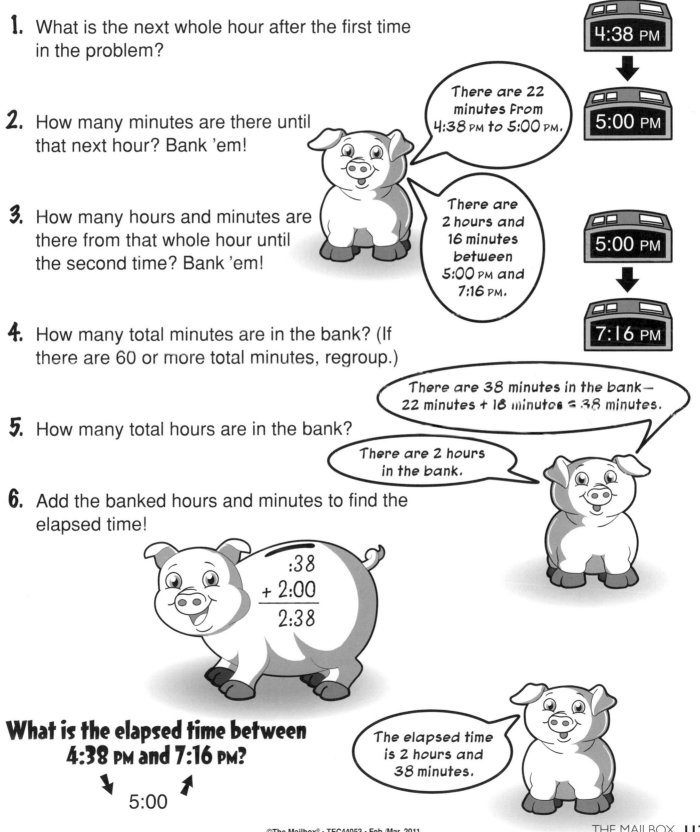

+ 2:00
2:38

What is the elapsed time between 4:38 PM and 7:16 PM?

5:00

The elapsed time is 2 hours and 38 minutes.

Cards, Direction Card, and Answer Key

Use with "Sizing Up the Past" on page 106.

1 An Egyptologist's dig site is 3.5 meters wide by 9.2 meters long. How much rope will she need to rope off the site?

TEC44054

2 What is missing from the area measurement shown?

A = 28 cm

TEC44054

3 To find out how much stone covers the floor of the king's chamber, would you figure the perimeter or area?

TEC44054

4 What is the perimeter of a shape?

TEC44054

5 The king's chamber measures 5.1 meters wide and 5.3 meters long. How much stone covers the floor?

TEC44054

6 What is the formula for finding the area of a rectangle?

TEC44054

7 What is the formula for finding a rectangle's perimeter?

TEC44054

8 A box-shaped artifact is 10 cm wide by 15 cm long. What is its perimeter?

TEC44054

9 The area of a square chamber is 36 square meters. What is the length of each side?

TEC44054

10 What is the formula for finding a square's perimeter?

TEC44054

11 The area of one rectangular burial chamber is 54 square meters. Two walls are each 6 meters long. How long is each of the other walls?

TEC44054

12 One of the pyramid's passageways is 105 meters long and 3.5 meters wide. What is the passageway's perimeter?

TEC44054

13 The queen's chamber has a perimeter of 24.4 meters. What is this square room's area?

TEC44054

14 Two sides of a pentagon artifact are 12 cm long. Two sides are 8 cm long. The artifact's perimeter is 50 cm. What is the missing measurement?

TEC44054

15 One large artifact is 1.5 meters wide and 2.9 meters long. What is its perimeter?

TEC44054

16 The area of the pyramid's square base is 6,400 square meters. How long is each side?

TEC44054

17 The area of the pyramid's square base is 6,400 square meters. What is its perimeter?

TEC44054

18 The floor of the rectangular underground chamber has a perimeter of 14 meters. One wall is 5 meters long. Is the room a square?

TEC44054

19 One wall of the rectangular underground chamber is 5 m long. The perimeter of the room is 14 m. What is the room's area?

TEC44054

20 What is the area of a tarp that would cover the 3.5 m x 9.2 m dig site?

TEC44054

Perimeter and area

SIZING UP THE PAST

Directions:

1. Number your paper from 1 to 20.
2. In turn, draw a card from the envelope and read the problem aloud.
3. Your partner and you write your answer next to the correct number on your paper.
4. When all the problems have been solved, take turns reading the answers from the key aloud. The partner with more correct answers wins the game.

TEC44054

ANSWER KEY FOR "SIZING UP THE PAST"

1. 25.4 m
2. $A = 28$ cm②
3. area
4. the distance around the shape
5. 27.03 m^2
6. $A = s \times s$, or $l \times w$
7. $P = 2l + 2w$
8. 50 cm
9. 6 m
10. $P = 4s$
11. 9 m
12. 217 m
13. 37.21 m^2
14. 10 cm
15. 8.8 m
16. 80 m
17. 320 m
18. no
19. 10 m^2
20. 32.2 m^2

TEC44054

Name ______________________

Date ______________

OOPS-A-DAISY!

Some of these answers are crazy!
Find and correct the mistakes.

Note to the teacher: Use with "Oops-a-Daisy!" on page 107.

Name ____________________

Date ____________________

Vocabulary Toss

Label each figure.

A. ____________ B. ____________ C. ____________

  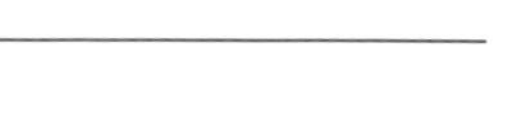  

D. ____________ E. ____________ F. ____________

G. ____________ H. ____________ I. ____________

J. ____________ K. ____________ L. ____________

 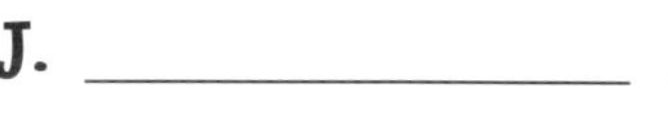 

M. ____________ N. ____________ O. ____________

P. ____________ Q. ____________ R. ____________

S. ____________ T. ____________ U. ____________

V. ____________ W. ____________ X. ____________

Word Bank

- cone
- cone net
- cube
- cube net
- cylinder
- cylinder net
- hexagon
- octagon
- parallelogram
- pentagon
- rectangle
- rectangular prism
- rectangular prism net
- rectangular pyramid
- rectangular pyramid net
- rhombus
- sphere
- square pyramid
- square pyramid net
- trapezoid
- triangular prism
- triangular prism net
- triangular pyramid
- triangular pyramid net

Note to the teacher: Use with "Overhauled Beach Ball" on page 108.

Capacity Labels and Cards

Use with “A Cup of Comparisons” on page 109.

8 ounces TEC44055	9 ounces TEC44055	12 ounces TEC44055
16 ounces TEC44055	32 ounces TEC44055	44 ounces TEC44055

1 cup TEC44055	$\frac{1}{2}$ pint TEC44055	$\frac{1}{4}$ quart TEC44055	$\frac{1}{16}$ gallon TEC44055	$1\frac{1}{8}$ cup TEC44055	$\frac{9}{16}$ pint TEC44055
$\frac{9}{32}$ quart TEC44055	$\frac{9}{128}$ gallon TEC44055	$1\frac{1}{2}$ cups TEC44055	$\frac{3}{4}$ pint TEC44055	$\frac{3}{8}$ quart TEC44055	$\frac{3}{32}$ gallon TEC44055
2 cups TEC44055	1 pint TEC44055	$\frac{1}{2}$ quart TEC44055	$\frac{1}{8}$ gallon TEC44055	4 cups TEC44055	2 pints TEC44055
1 quart TEC44055	$\frac{1}{4}$ gallon TEC44055	$5\frac{1}{2}$ cups TEC44055	$2\frac{3}{4}$ pints TEC44055	$1\frac{3}{8}$ quarts TEC44055	$\frac{11}{32}$ gallon TEC44055

Name ____

Date ____________________________________

Time for a Treat

Well, I was really in the mood for chocolate-covered termites.

Pick ____ activities to do.
When you finish an activity, color its number.

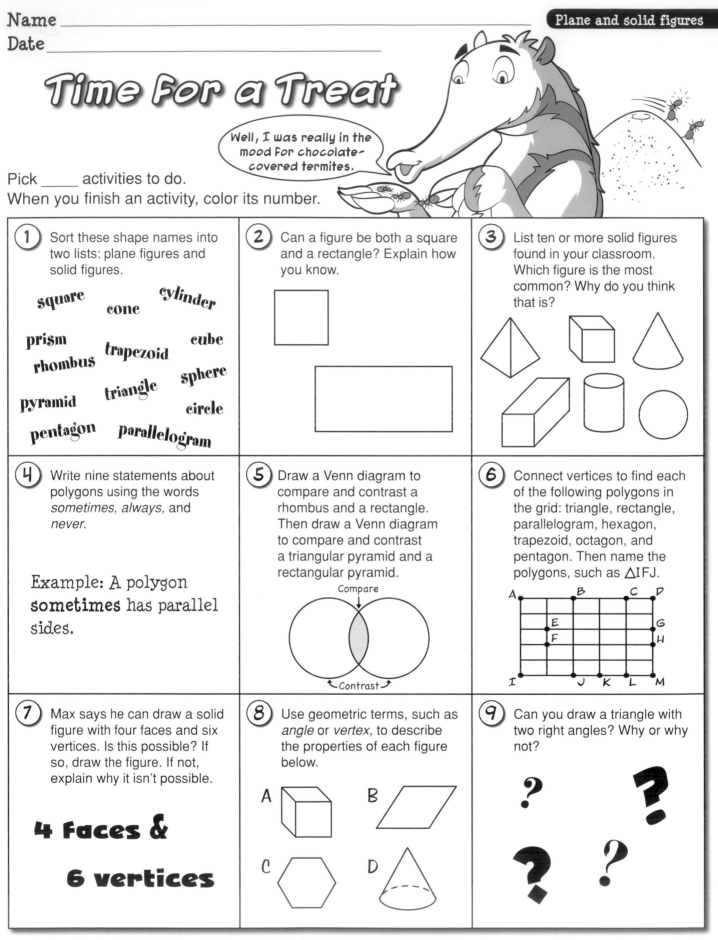

1 Sort these shape names into two lists: plane figures and solid figures.

square cone cylinder
prism trapezoid cube
rhombus sphere
pyramid triangle circle
pentagon parallelogram

2 Can a figure be both a square and a rectangle? Explain how you know.

3 List ten or more solid figures found in your classroom. Which figure is the most common? Why do you think that is?

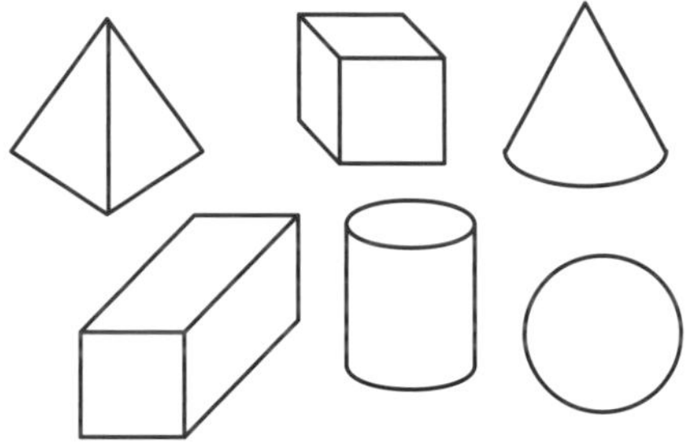

4 Write nine statements about polygons using the words *sometimes, always,* and *never.*

Example: A polygon **sometimes** has parallel sides.

5 Draw a Venn diagram to compare and contrast a rhombus and a rectangle. Then draw a Venn diagram to compare and contrast a triangular pyramid and a rectangular pyramid.

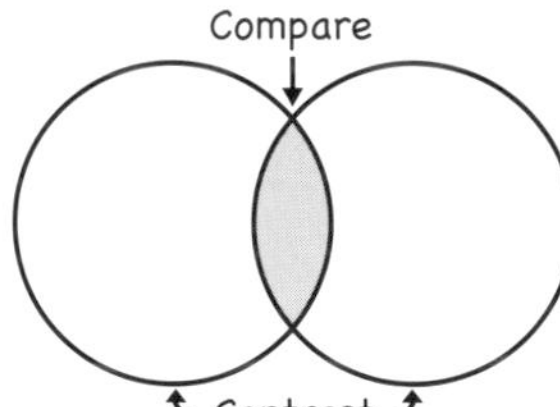

6 Connect vertices to find each of the following polygons in the grid: triangle, rectangle, parallelogram, hexagon, trapezoid, octagon, and pentagon. Then name the polygons, such as △IFJ.

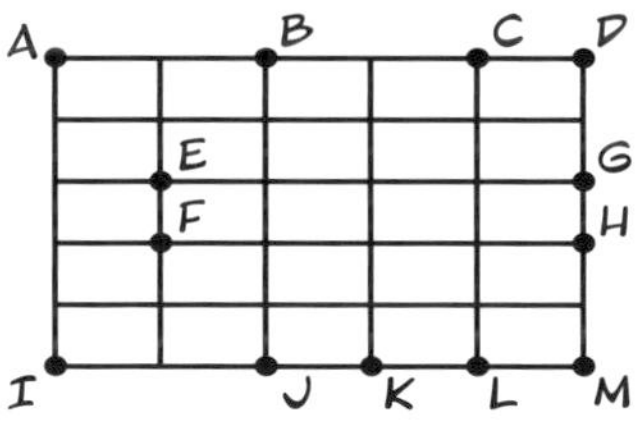

7 Max says he can draw a solid figure with four faces and six vertices. Is this possible? If so, draw the figure. If not, explain why it isn't possible.

4 Faces &

6 vertices

8 Use geometric terms, such as *angle* or *vertex,* to describe the properties of each figure below.

A

B

C
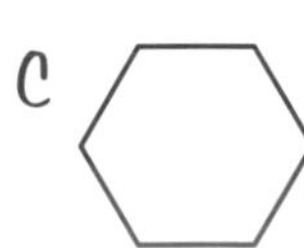

D

9 Can you draw a triangle with two right angles? Why or why not?

Independent Practice Grid: Program the student directions on a copy of this page with the number of activities to be completed. Then copy the page for each student.

Names ____

Date ______________________________

Player 2

Finish

Score!

A Game for Two Players

Directions:

1. Choose a path.
2. Cut the player lists from the gameboard. Then take the list that matches your path.
3. When it's your turn, have your partner read aloud the first problem on his or her list without giving the solution.
4. Solve the problem mentally and write your answer in the next blank space on your path. Have your partner check the solution. If you are correct, leave your answer. If you are incorrect, erase your answer; try this problem again on your next turn.
5. The first player to reach his or her goal wins.

Finish

Player 1

List for Player 1 to Ask

1. 33 + 28 = 61
2. 83 – 49 = 34
3. 71 + 19 = 90
4. 70 – 31 = 39
5. 14 + 17 = 31
6. 75 – 16 = 59
7. 45 + 37 = 82
8. 71 – 42 = 29
9. 32 + 29 = 61
10. 57 – 39 = 18
11. 69 + 26 = 95
12. 37 – 29 = 8

List for Player 2 to Ask

1. 26 + 15 = 41
2. 63 – 47 = 16
3. 52 + 18 = 70
4. 92 – 74 = 18
5. 24 + 28 = 52
6. 82 – 57 = 25
7. 77 + 14 = 91
8. 31 – 14 = 17
9. 59 + 26 = 85
10. 95 – 86 = 9
11. 49 + 33 = 82
12. 72 – 66 = 6

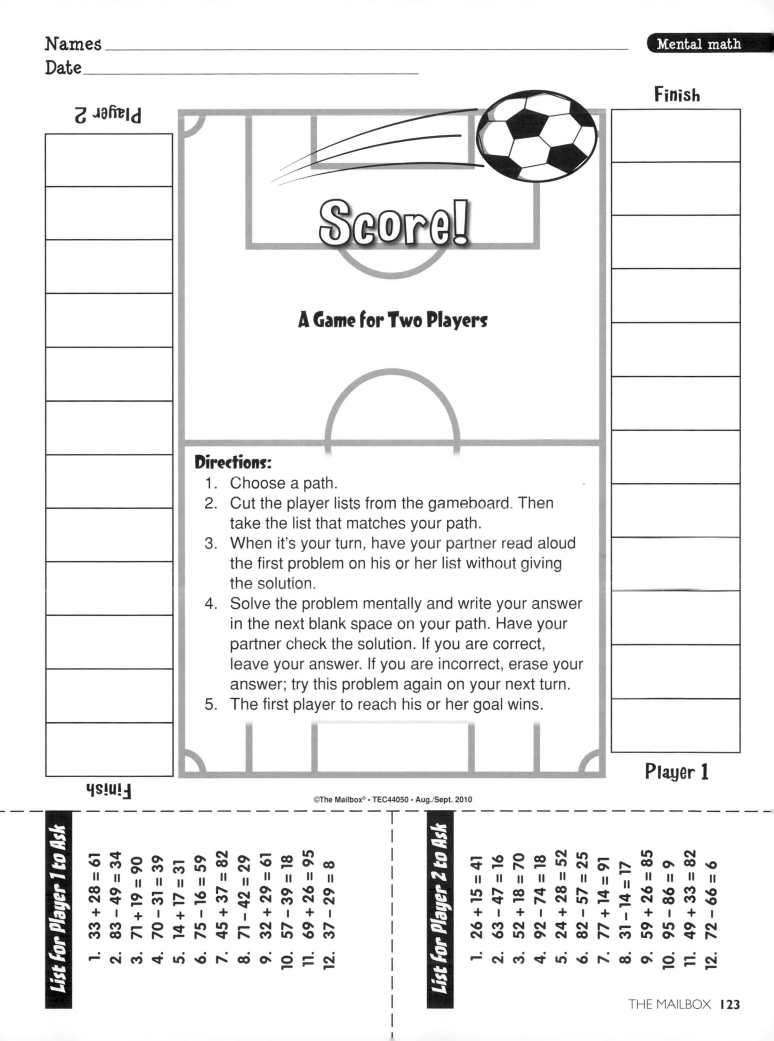

Name ______________________________

Date ______________________________

Treasure Troubles

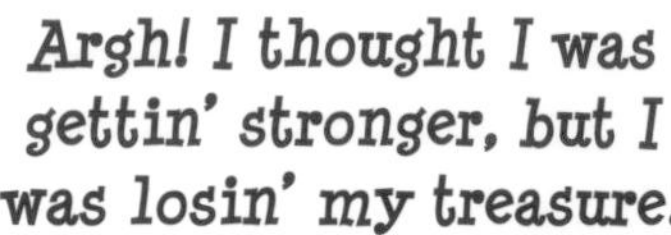
Argh! I thought I was gettin' stronger, but I was losin' my treasure!

I. Shade the symbol that belongs in each circle.

1.	22,605 ◯ 22,650	<	>	=
2.	37,050 ◯ 37,005	<	>	=
3.	9,950 ◯ 9,905	<	>	=
4.	7,146 ◯ 7,429	<	>	=
5.	6,000,148 ◯ 600,148	<	>	=
6.	345,812 ◯ 345,812	<	>	=
7.	49,212 ◯ 49,202	<	>	=
8.	5,926 ◯ 5,926	<	>	=
9.	1,987,234 ◯ 1,978,243	<	>	=
10.	307,806 ◯ 370,608	<	>	=
11.	2,989 ◯ 2,998	<	>	=
12.	735 ◯ 1,230	<	>	=
13.	82,640 ◯ 82,466	<	>	=
14.	421,210 ◯ 421,210	<	>	=
15.	6,957,349 ◯ 6,643,932	<	>	=
16.	126,400 ◯ 126,404	<	>	=

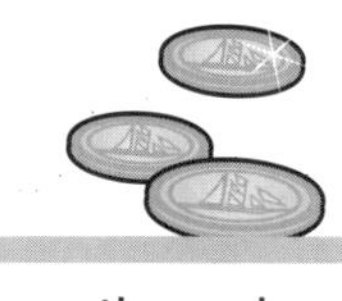

II. On another sheet of paper, arrange the numbers from least to greatest.

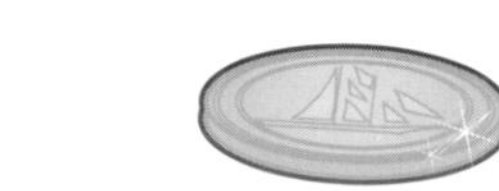

Name____________________

Date____________________

A Problematic Pit Stop

Estimate each product. Then shade the estimate on a wrench.

1. 35 x 11 = __________
2. 97 x 24 = __________
3. 86 x 36 = __________
4. 271 x 19 = __________
5. 185 x 46 = __________
6. 289 x 77 = __________
7. 125 x 18 = __________
8. 236 x 26 = __________
9. 691 x 74 = __________
10. 325 x 164 = __________
11. 189 x 376 = __________
12. 574 x 310 = __________
13. 441 x 785 = __________
14. 649 x 193 = __________
15. 782 x 674 = __________
16. 216 x 785 = __________
17. 441 x 862 = __________
18. 312 x 507 = __________
19. 138 x 632 = __________
20. 865 x 754 = __________

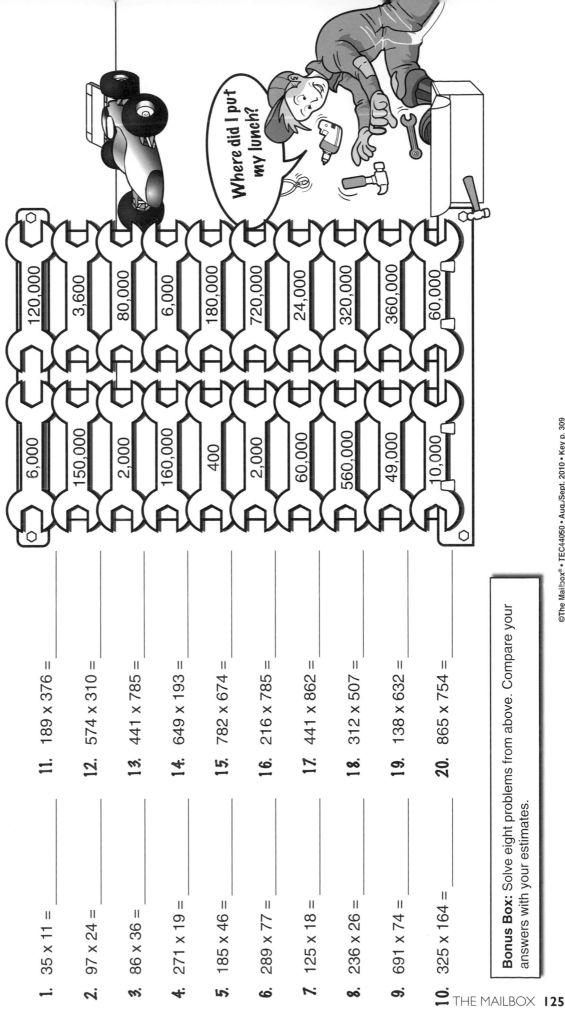

6,000 | 120,000
150,000 | 3,600
2,000 | 80,000
160,000 | 6,000
400 | 180,000
2,000 | 720,000
60,000 | 24,000
560,000 | 320,000
49,000 | 360,000
10,000 | 60,000

Where did I put my lunch?

Bonus Box: Solve eight problems from above. Compare your answers with your estimates.

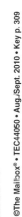

Name ______________________________

Date ______________________________

A Starry Night

Use properties of addition and multiplication to complete each problem. Then color each star according to the code.

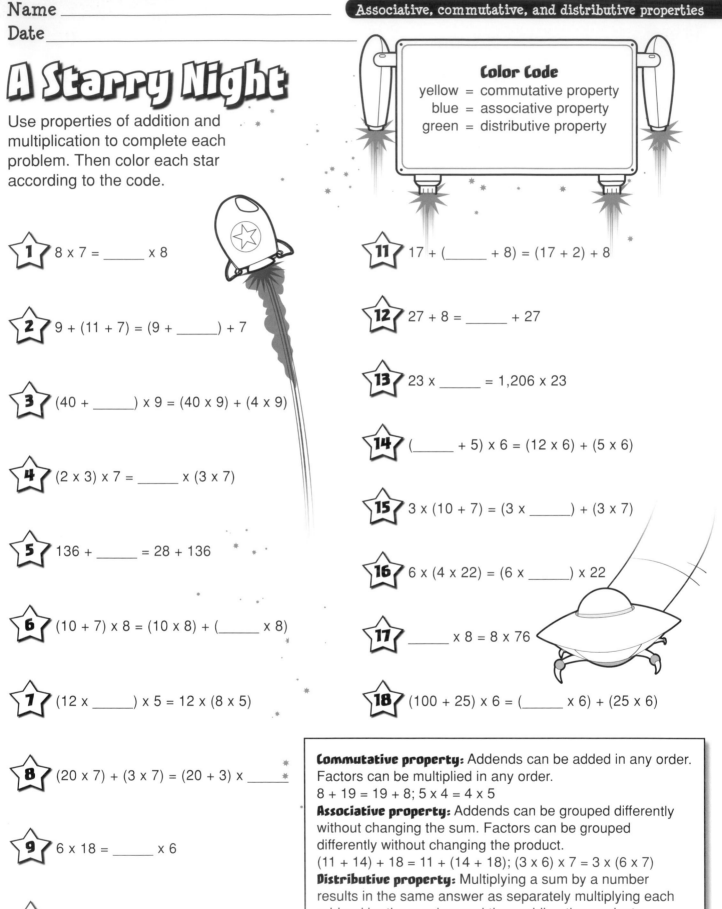

Color Code

yellow = commutative property

blue = associative property

green = distributive property

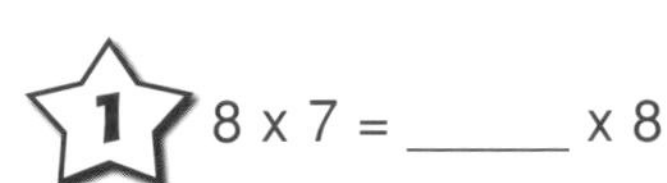

1. 8 x 7 = ______ x 8

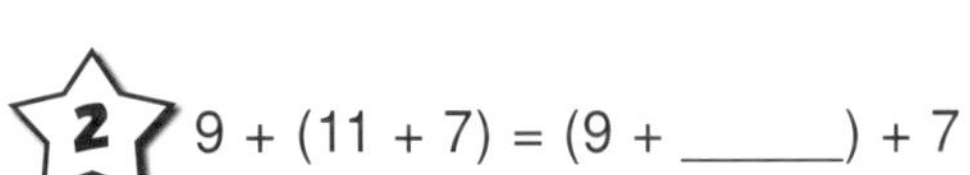

2. 9 + (11 + 7) = (9 + ______) + 7

3. (40 + ______) x 9 = (40 x 9) + (4 x 9)

4. (2 x 3) x 7 = ______ x (3 x 7)

5. 136 + ______ = 28 + 136

6. (10 + 7) x 8 = (10 x 8) + (______ x 8)

7. (12 x ______) x 5 = 12 x (8 x 5)

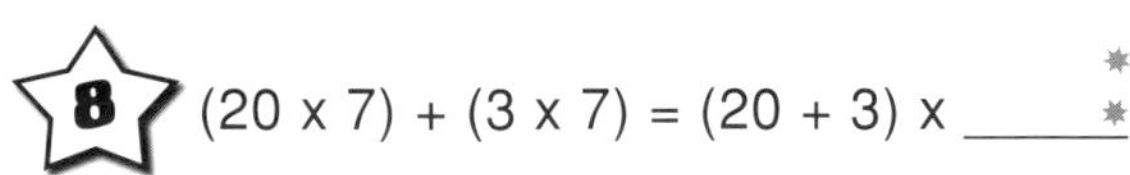

8. (20 x 7) + (3 x 7) = (20 + 3) x ______

9. 6 x 18 = ______ x 6

10. (10 x ______) + (3 x 9) = (10 + 3) x 9

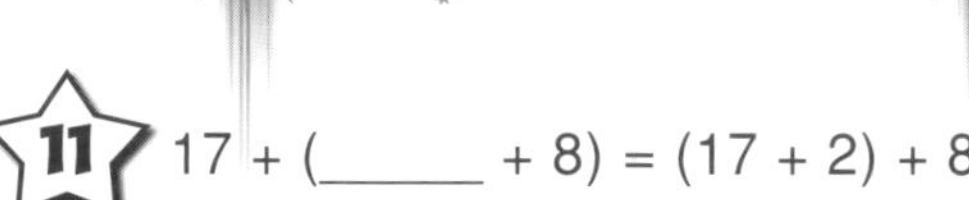

11. 17 + (______ + 8) = (17 + 2) + 8

12. 27 + 8 = ______ + 27

13. 23 x ______ = 1,206 x 23

14. (______ + 5) x 6 = (12 x 6) + (5 x 6)

15. 3 x (10 + 7) = (3 x ______) + (3 x 7)

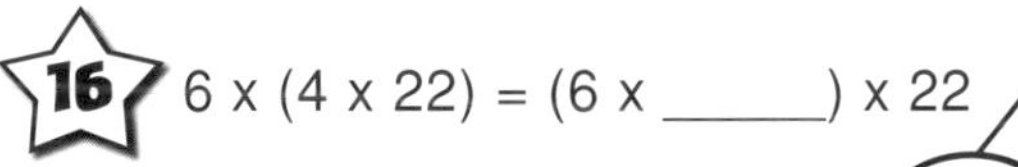

16. 6 x (4 x 22) = (6 x ______) x 22

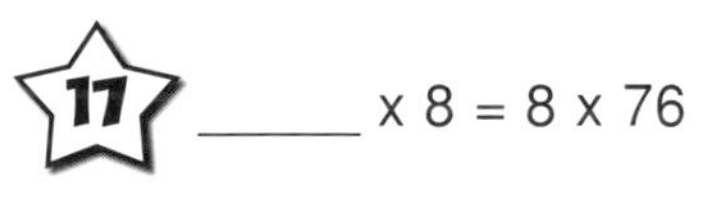

17. ______ x 8 = 8 x 76

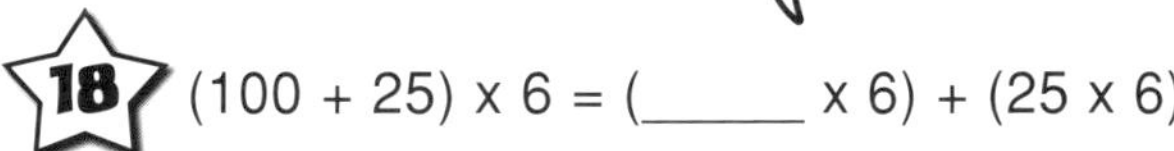

18. (100 + 25) x 6 = (______ x 6) + (25 x 6)

Commutative property: Addends can be added in any order. Factors can be multiplied in any order.
8 + 19 = 19 + 8; 5 x 4 = 4 x 5

Associative property: Addends can be grouped differently without changing the sum. Factors can be grouped differently without changing the product.
(11 + 14) + 18 = 11 + (14 + 18); (3 x 6) x 7 = 3 x (6 x 7)

Distributive property: Multiplying a sum by a number results in the same answer as separately multiplying each addend by the number and then adding the products.
3 x (2 + 7) = (3 x 2) + (3 x 7); 5 x (9 + 7) = (5 x 9) + (5 x 7)

Name ____________________

Date ____________________

3-D EXPERIENCE!

Cool!

Pick _____ activities to do.
When you finish an activity, color its number.

1 Use the numbers shown to write and solve ten multiplication problems.

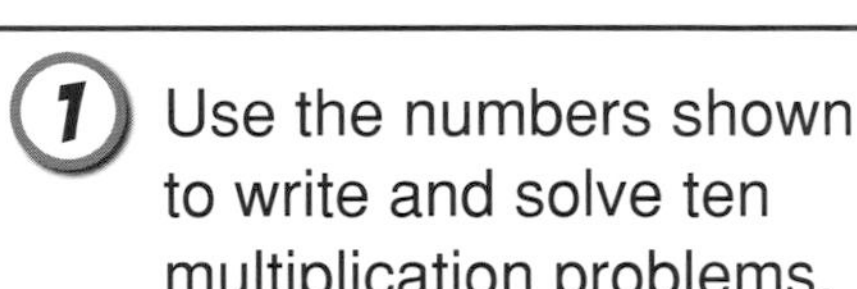

23 14 31
13 22 21

2 Find ten two-digit numbers that, when multiplied by themselves, have products between 300 and 800.

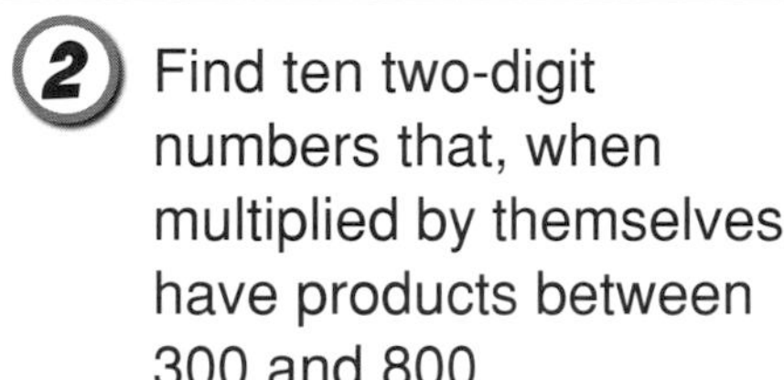

Example:
25 x 25 = 625

3 Explain how the steps for solving these two problems are different.

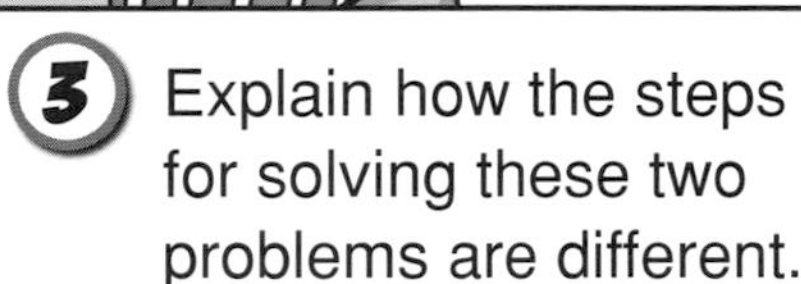

A. 56 x 34 **B.** 43 x 21

4 Write five two-digit multiplication problems with estimated products of 2,000. Then solve each one.

Example:
36 ⟶ 40
x 54 ⟶ x 50
2,000

5 Write each number shown. Then reverse its digits and multiply the two numbers.

78 96 84 62 39 56

Example: 78 x 87

6 Write three two-digit multiplication problems with products that are less than 1,000. Then write three two-digit multiplication problems with products that are greater than 1,000.

A. product $< 1,000$
B. product $> 1,000$

7 For each inequality shown, write a two-digit multiplication problem whose product can replace the question mark.

- $2,000 < ? < 2,400$
- $3,300 < ? < 3,700$
- $4,500 < ? < 5,200$

8 Find the missing digit in each problem.

A. ☐4 x 28 = 2,352
B. 54 x 4☐ = 2,484
C. 32 x ☐5 = 1,440

9 Write and solve a two-digit multiplication problem for each region of the Venn diagram.

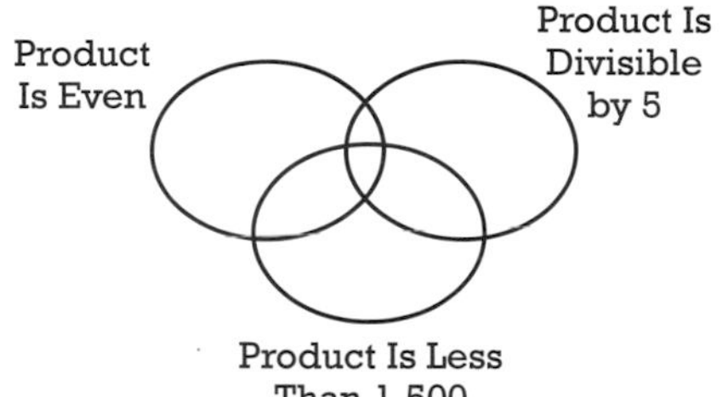

Independent practice grid: Program the student directions on a copy of this page with the number of activities to be completed. Then copy the page for each student.

Name____________________

Date____________________

On a Roll!

I. Complete each factor tree.

II. Color by the code.

blue = prime number
orange = composite number

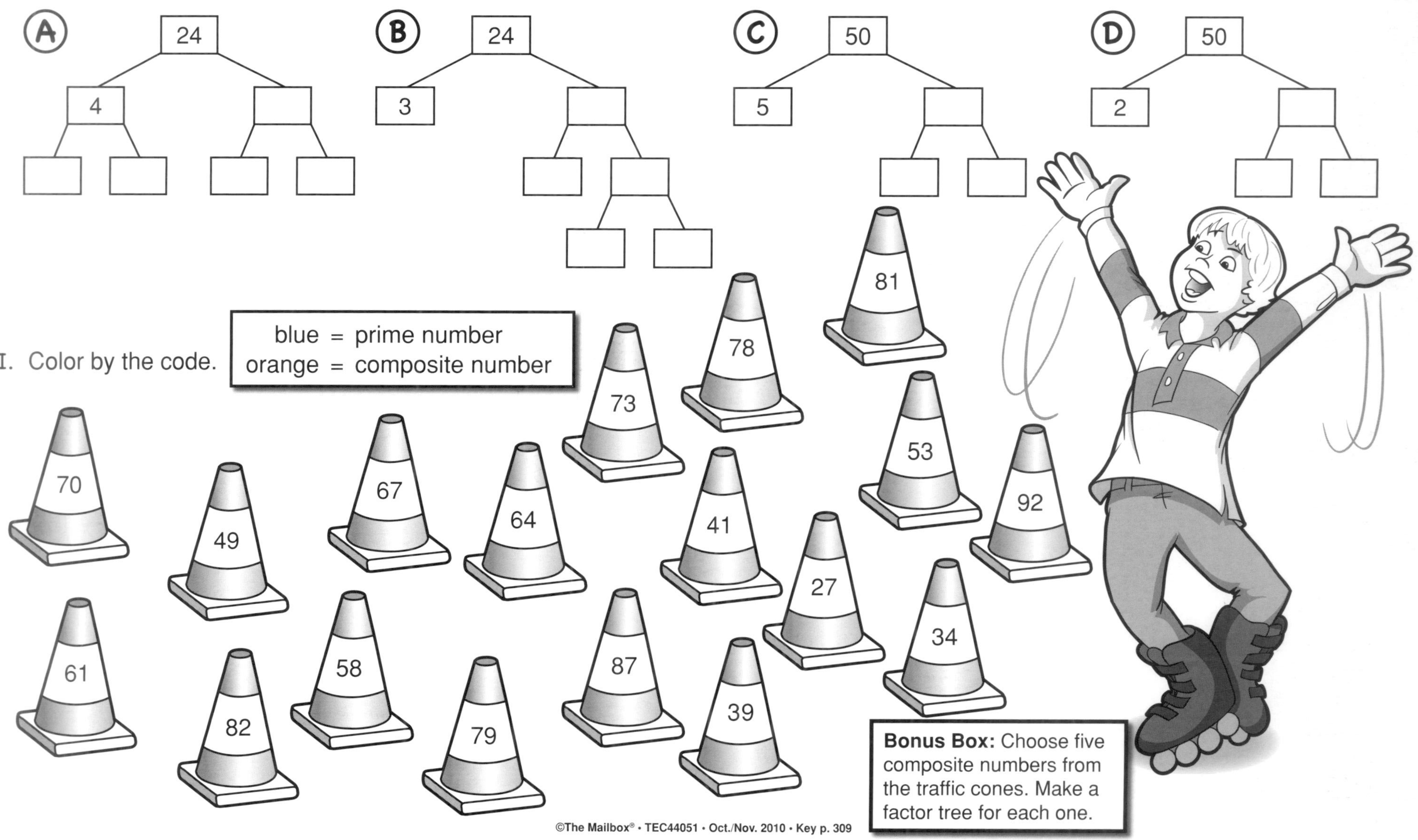

Bonus Box: Choose five composite numbers from the traffic cones. Make a factor tree for each one.

Name ______________________________

Date ______________________

Write the missing measurements on the rectangles below. Then find each shape's perimeter and area.

	(A)	(E) 42' x 6'			
		(H)	(N)	(B)	(L) 8' x 12'
		(D) 6' x 24'		(I) 18' x 6'	
	(A) 6' x 48'		(Y)		
			(R)		(G) 12' x 18'
		(S)			

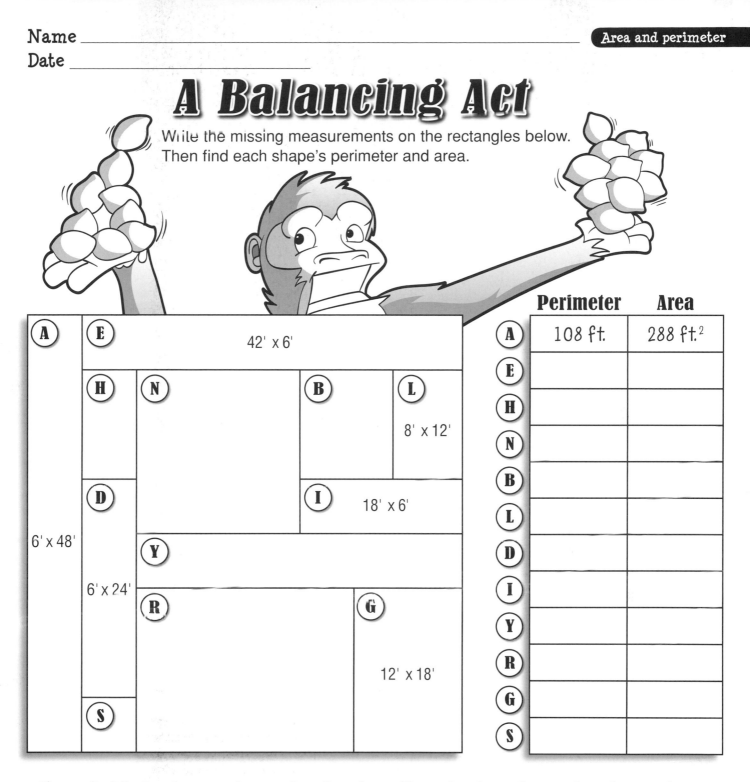

	Perimeter	Area
A	108 ft.	288 ft.^{2}
E		
H		
N		
B		
L		
D		
I		
Y		
R		
G		
S		

If you hold nine lemons in one hand and ten limes in the other, what do you have?

To find out, write each letter next to the matching description.

___ A = 432 ft.^{2} ___ A = 252 ft.^{2} ___ P = 108 ft. ___ A = 96 ft.^{2} ___ P = 40 ft. ___ A = 216 ft.^{2}

___ A = 120 ft.^{2} ___ A = 108 ft.^{2} ___ A = 216 ft.^{2} ___ P = 36 ft. ___ A = 288 ft.^{2} ___ A = 324 ft.^{2} ___ A = 144 ft.^{2} ___ P = 24 ft.

Bonus Box: Find the perimeter and area of the rectangle-filled square above.

Name ____________________
Date ____________________

Snapshot Safari

Draw a bar graph to display the data shown. Use the key to make each bar look different. Then answer questions 1–5.

Number of Pictures Taken

Animal	Day 1	Day 2	Day 3
giraffe	III	卌 卌 卌 III	卌 卌 II
lion	卌 III	卌 II	III
zebra	卌 卌 卌 II	卌 卌 III	卌 卌 卌 I

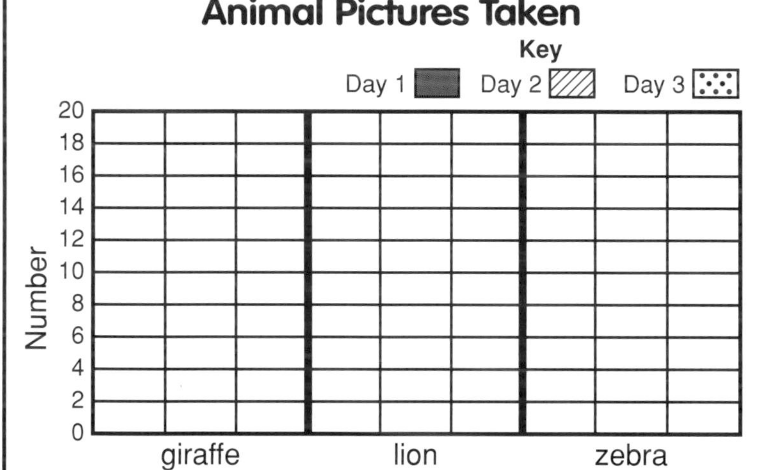

1. On which day were the most pictures taken?
____
2. Which animal was photographed most often?
____
3. For which animal is **5** the range of the number of pictures taken?
____
4. For which animal is **12** the median number of pictures?
____
5. For which animal is **6** the mean number of pictures?
____

Make a stem-and-leaf plot of the data shown. Then answer questions 6–10.

Number of Animal Pictures

Day 1	Day 2	Day 3	Day 4	Day 5	Day 6	Day 7
28	38	31	43	39	30	36
Day 8	**Day 9**	**Day 10**	**Day 11**	**Day 12**	**Day 13**	**Day 14**
35	38	42	47	47	47	45

Number of Animal Pictures

Stem	Leaf
2	
3	
4	

6. On which day were the fewest animals photographed?
____
7. What is the range of this data?
____
8. What is the mode of this data?
____
9. On average, how many pictures were taken each day?
____
10. What is the median number of pictures taken?
____

Cards and Answer Key

Use with "Hanging Around" on page 132.

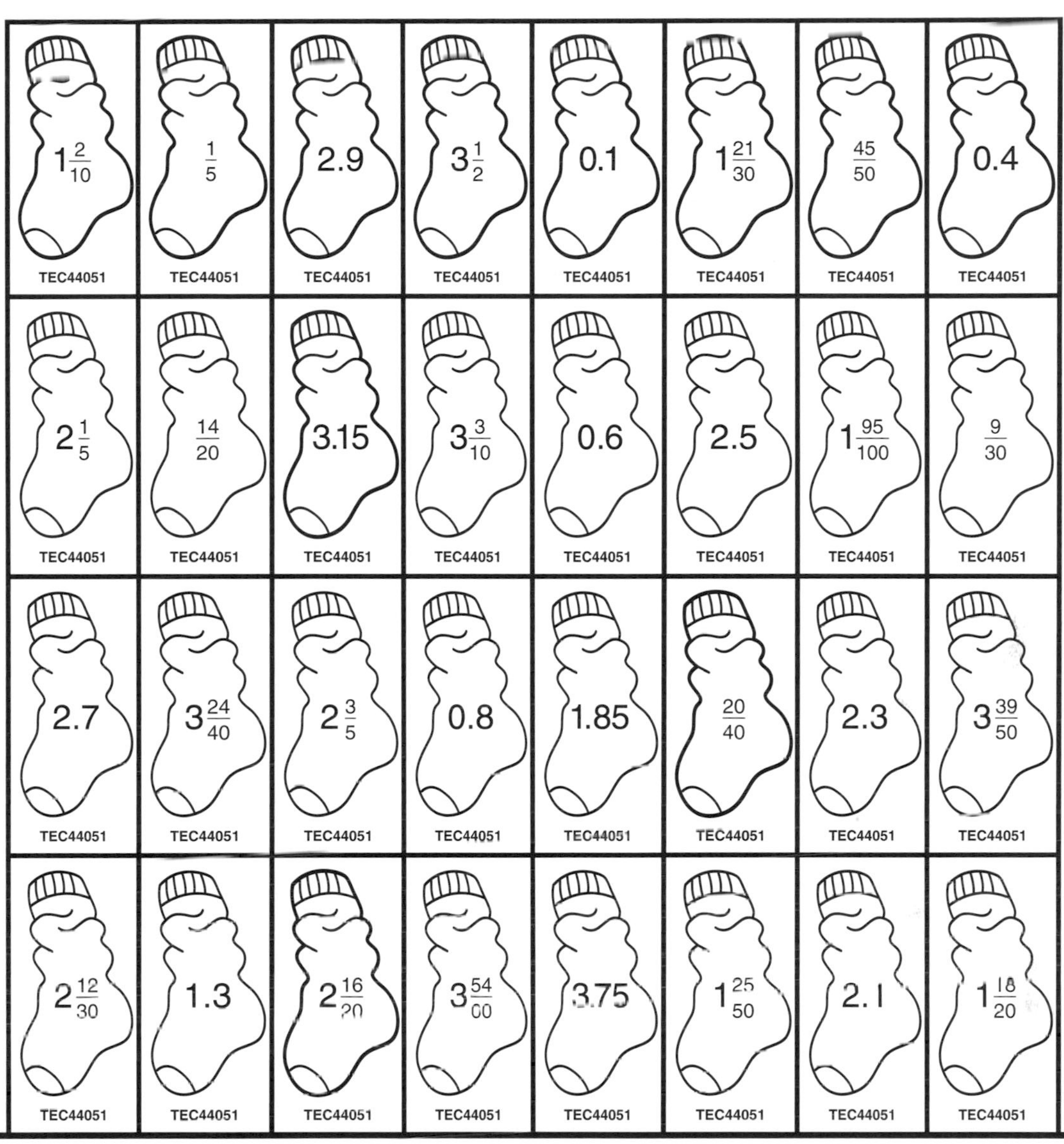

ANSWER KEY FOR "HANGING AROUND"

Numbers used on the laundry lines:

$0.1, \frac{1}{5}, \frac{9}{30}, 0.4, \frac{20}{40}, 0.6, \frac{14}{20}, 0.8, \frac{45}{50}$

$2.1, 2\frac{1}{5}, 2.3, 2\frac{12}{30}, 2.5, 2\frac{3}{5}, 2.7, 2\frac{16}{20}, 2.9$

Numbers not used on the laundry lines:

$1\frac{2}{10}, 1.3, 1\frac{25}{50}, 1\frac{21}{30}, 1.85, 1\frac{18}{20}, 1\frac{95}{100}, 3.15, 3\frac{3}{10}, 3\frac{1}{2}, 3\frac{24}{40}, 3.75, 3\frac{39}{50}, 3\frac{54}{60}$

All the numbers in order:

$0.1, \frac{1}{5}, \frac{9}{30}, 0.4, \frac{20}{40}, 0.6, \frac{14}{20}, 0.8, \frac{45}{50}, 1\frac{2}{10}, 1.3, 1\frac{25}{50}, 1\frac{21}{30}, 1.85, 1\frac{18}{20}, 1\frac{95}{100}, 2.1, 2\frac{1}{5}, 2.3, 2\frac{12}{30}, 2.5, 2\frac{3}{5}, 2.7,$
$2\frac{16}{20}, 2.9, 3.15, 3\frac{3}{10}, 3\frac{1}{2}, 3\frac{24}{40}, 3.75, 3\frac{39}{50}, 3\frac{54}{60}$

TEC44051

HANGING AROUND

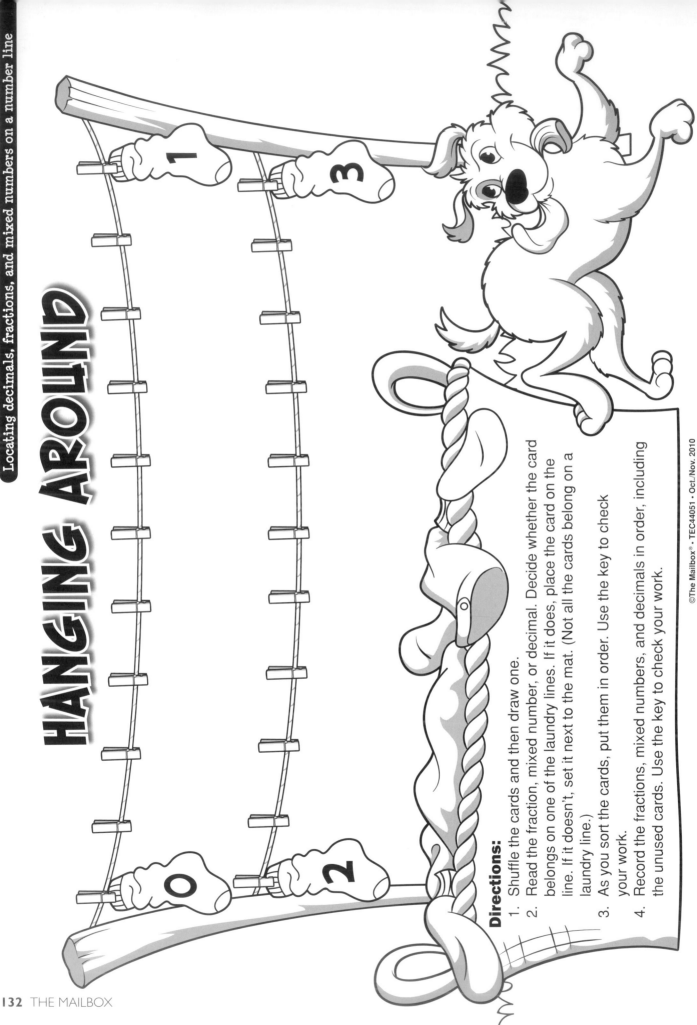

Directions:

1. Shuffle the cards and then draw one.
2. Read the fraction, mixed number, or decimal. Decide whether the card belongs on one of the laundry lines. If it does, place the card on the line. If it doesn't, set it next to the mat. (Not all the cards belong on a laundry line.)
3. As you sort the cards, put them in order. Use the key to check your work.
4. Record the fractions, mixed numbers, and decimals in order, including the unused cards. Use the key to check your work.

Names ____

Date ______________________

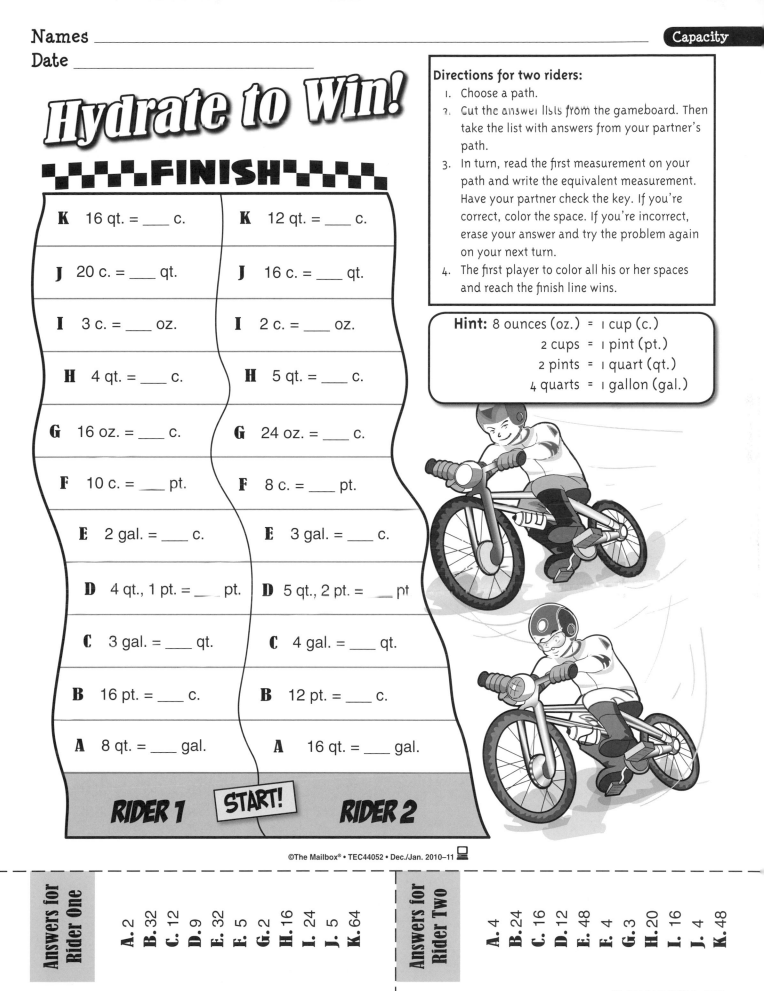

Hydrate to Win!

Directions for two riders:

1. Choose a path.
2. Cut the answer lists from the gameboard. Then take the list with answers from your partner's path.
3. In turn, read the first measurement on your path and write the equivalent measurement. Have your partner check the key. If you're correct, color the space. If you're incorrect, erase your answer and try the problem again on your next turn.
4. The first player to color all his or her spaces and reach the finish line wins.

Hint: 8 ounces (oz.) = 1 cup (c.)
2 cups = 1 pint (pt.)
2 pints = 1 quart (qt.)
4 quarts = 1 gallon (gal.)

FINISH

Rider 1	Rider 2
K 16 qt. = ___ c.	**K** 12 qt. = ___ c.
J 20 c. = ___ qt.	**J** 16 c. = ___ qt.
I 3 c. = ___ oz.	**I** 2 c. = ___ oz.
H 4 qt. = ___ c.	**H** 5 qt. = ___ c.
G 16 oz. = ___ c.	**G** 24 oz. = ___ c.
F 10 c. = ___ pt.	**F** 8 c. = ___ pt.
E 2 gal. = ___ c.	**E** 3 gal. = ___ c.
D 4 qt., 1 pt. = ___ pt.	**D** 5 qt., 2 pt. = ___ pt.
C 3 gal. = ___ qt.	**C** 4 gal. = ___ qt.
B 16 pt. = ___ c.	**B** 12 pt. = ___ c.
A 8 qt. = ___ gal.	**A** 16 qt. = ___ gal.

RIDER 1

RIDER 2

Answers for Rider One

A. 2
B. 32
C. 12
D. 9
E. 32
F. 5
G. 2
H. 16
I. 24
J. 5
K. 64

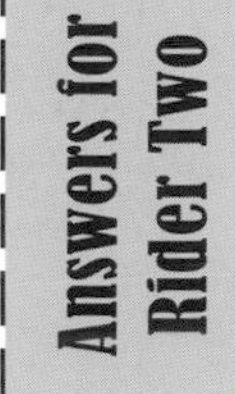

A. 4
B. 24
C. 16
D. 12
E. 48
F. 4
G. 3
H. 20
I. 16
J. 4
K. 48

Name ____________________

Date ____________________

Bit by Bit

Pick ______ activities to do.
When you finish an activity, color its number.

(1) Replace the circled digits so each problem has a remainder of one. 6)9⑥ 7)8④ 8)42④ 9)61②	(2) Fill each box with a different digit between 0 and 9. Then solve each problem. □)□□ □)□□ □)□□□	(3) Use these digits to write and solve four division problems. 6 7 8 9
(4) Fill in the missing digits so the quotient will be a number that is greater than 65 but less than 66. 5)□2□	(5) Tell whether each problem will have a remainder. Then solve to check your prediction. A. 4)896 B. 3)245 C. 2)714 D. 6)482	(6) Replace the missing digits with the numerals 0–9. Use each numeral one time. 1□ R□ over 8)9□ □ over 7)□3 □□ R□ over 9)4□□
(7) How many cows are in the field if the farmer counts ___ hooves? Solve for each number. A. 388 B. 152 C. 296 D. 864 	(8) Write and solve four animal problems similar to activity 7. 	(9) Write and solve six division problems. Use the vertical numbers as divisors and the horizontal numbers as dividends. 1 | 2 | 3 4 | 5 | 6 Example: 14)123

Independent Practice Grid Program the student directions on a copy of this page with the number of activities to be completed. Then copy the page for each student.

Name ______________________________

Date ______________________

Power Play

Solve each problem. Do your work on another sheet of paper. Then shade the pucks according to the codes on the jerseys.

B	W	Problem	Answer
B	W	1. Each hockey puck weighs six ounces. How much do 13 pucks weigh?	______
B	W	2. Black-Eyed Bart scores four goals during each of 11 games. How many total goals does he score?	______
B	W	3. The Beavers' manager orders jerseys for the 16 players. He orders each player six jerseys. How many jerseys does he order in all?	______
B	W	4. During the season, the Woodchucks travel 88 miles to play the Beavers. They play the Beavers four times. How many miles do they travel altogether?	______
B	W	5. The Eager Beaver Fan Club buys 29 tickets for each game. There are 19 total games. How many tickets does the fan club purchase altogether?	______
B	W	6. The Woodchucks reserve the rink for 75 minutes for 27 days in a row. How many minutes are they planning to practice?	______
B	W	7. Thirty-seven fans ask Woody Woodchuck for autographs. Each fan gets three autographs. How many autographs does Woody sign?	______
B	W	8. Gavin the goalie receives 23 stitches after each of five games. How many stitches does Gavin have in all?	______
B	W	9. The Beavers' trainer orders 27 boxes of bandages. Each box contains 16 bandages. How many bandages does the trainer order?	______
B	W	10. During each game, the trainer uses 33 bandages. How many total bandages does he use in 46 games?	______
B	W	11. Boris spends 15 minutes in the penalty box during each of 18 games. How much game time does he spend in the box?	______
B	W	12. Every day, the Beavers' goalie practices for 95 minutes. How many minutes does he practice in five weeks?	______

Which team scores the most goals? ______________

To find out, count the number of shaded pucks for each team.

Bonus: During 24 games, the Beavers score four goals each game. The Woodchucks score six goals each game. How many more goals do the Woodchucks score in all than the Beavers?

Name ______________________________

Date ______________________

Star Light, Star Bright

Estimate the sum, difference, product, or quotient of each problem.
Color by the code.

Code
estimate < 1,000 = blue
estimate > 1,000 = yellow

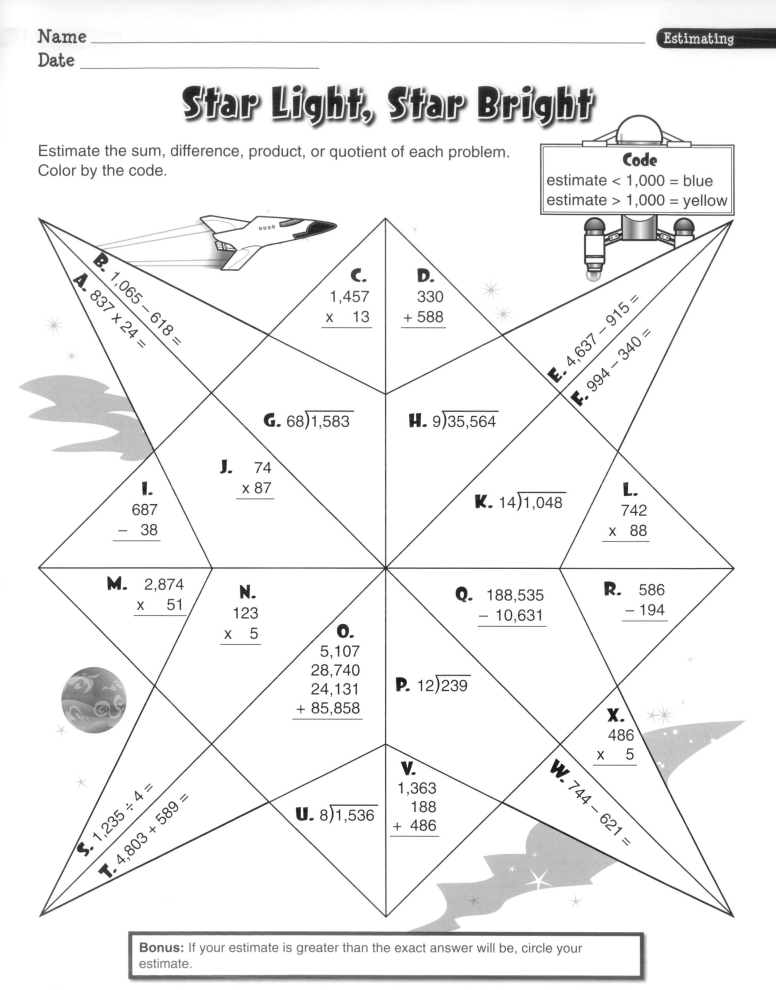

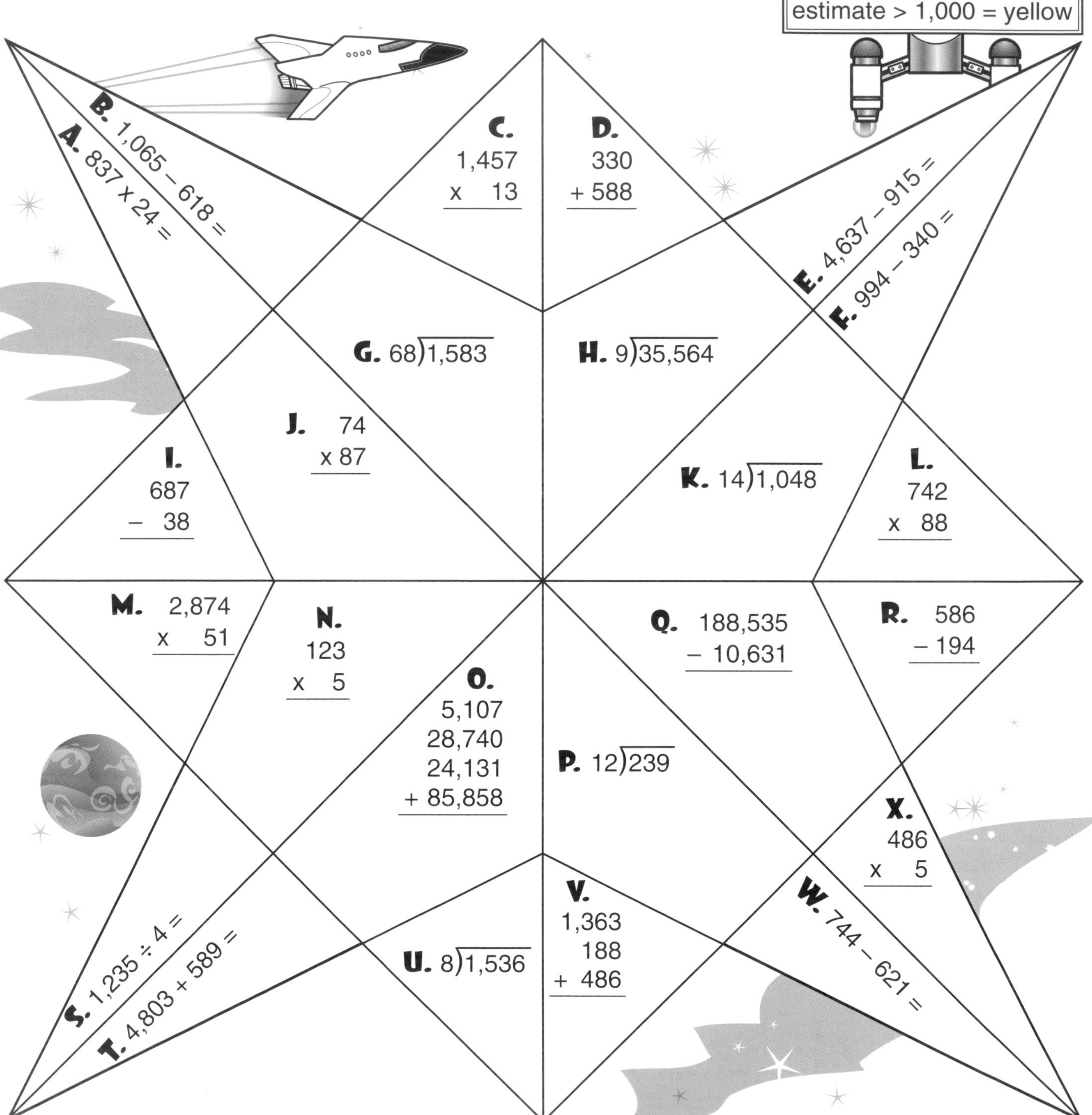

Bonus: If your estimate is greater than the exact answer will be, circle your estimate.

Name ______________________________
Date ____________________

Slurp It Up!

The least common multiple of a pair of numbers is the smallest multiple both numbers have in common.

Shade the least common multiple. To find out which kind of smoothie Bryce is trying to drink, circle the column with the most shaded boxes.

A. 2 and 12	6	4	12	8
B. 7 and 3	14	6	21	28
C. 6 and 2	16	6	3	12
D. 4 and 5	30	15	40	20
E. 3 and 4	3	12	6	8
F. 10 and 4	40	20	4	2
G. 15 and 6	30	3	15	5
H. 5 and 3	3	10	5	15
I. 5 and 20	15	20	4	5
J. 6 and 4	2	24	12	16
K. 3 and 2	6	12	24	18
L. 10 and 2	5	20	10	2
M. 2 and 4	8	4	6	2
N. 8 and 12	24	8	4	12
O. 2 and 7	21	7	14	24
P. 3 and 9	18	9	3	27
Q. 5 and 7	12	30	45	35
R. 6 and 8	36	24	48	32
S. 9 and 4	40	13	24	36
T. 6 and 9	18	54	3	12

BONUS: Which pair of numbers has a least common multiple of 12? Explain.

A. 3 and 9 B. 2 and 6
C. 3 and 6 D. 3 and 4

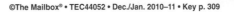

Names ______________________________

Date ______________________

GOIN' HOME

A Game for Two Players

Directions:

1. Choose a path.
2. In turn, read a statement on your path. Circle *true* or *false.*
3. Your partner checks the key. If you're correct, shade the space. If you're not correct, erase your answer.
4. The first player to shade all the spaces on his or her path wins.

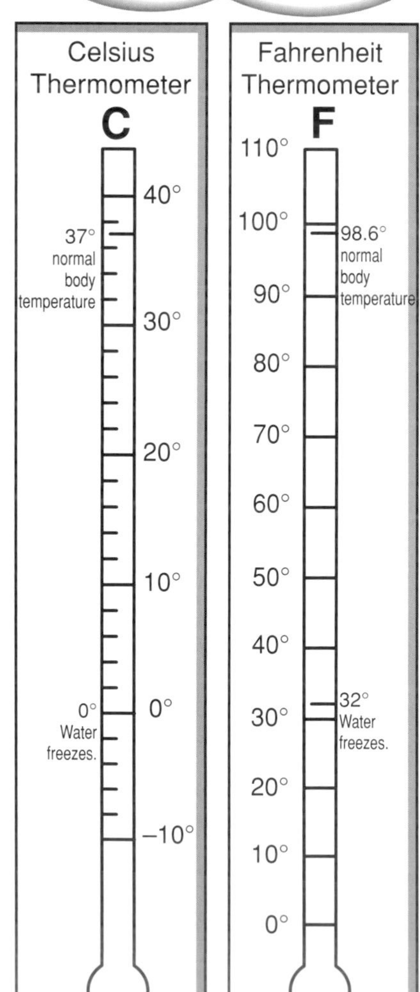

PLAYER 1

1. At 32°F, water will freeze. True False
2. My sister has a terrible cold. Her temperature is 40°C. True False
3. When it's 26°F, snow will melt. True False
4. When the temperature is over 37°C, it's nice and cool. True False
5. Food that is still 150°F is too hot to eat. True False
6. The temperature was 30°F when we were skiing. True False
7. Enough snow could fall so you could easily build a snowman when it's 42°F outside. True False
8. A snowman will melt if the temperature is 21°C. True False
9. If the temperature drops from 81°F to 56°F, it is 25 degrees cooler. True False
10. If the temperature rose from 13°C to 26°C, it would be 8 degrees hotter. True False
11. The temperature last night was 73°F, and now it's 38°F, or 35 degrees warmer. True False
12. At 2:00 PM, the temperature will be 57°F. Then it will drop 19 degrees to 38°F. True False

PLAYER 2

1. Water will not freeze at 0°C. True False
2. A normal body temperature is about 37°C. True False
3. You should wear a warm coat when it's 15°F. True False
4. A summer temperature of 35°F is no surprise. True False
5. A 37°C winter day is normal. True False
6. The water started to boil when it reached 50°F. True False
7. A snowman will stay frozen if the temperature is 5°C. True False
8. My temperature is 100.5°F, so I'm not running a fever. True False
9. If the temperature rises from 78°F to 102°F, it is 24 degrees hotter. True False
10. If the temperature drops from 51°C to 37°C, it drops 14 degrees. True False
11. The temperature this morning was 15°C, and now it's 23°C, or 8 degrees cooler. True False
12. At 7:00 AM, the temperature will be 63°F. Then it will increase 18 degrees to 81°F. True False

How to use: Each student needs a copy of the other player's answer key on page 309.

Name ______________________________

Date ____________________

Hey, Batter, Batter, Swing!

Pick ___ activities to do.
When you finish an activity, color its number.

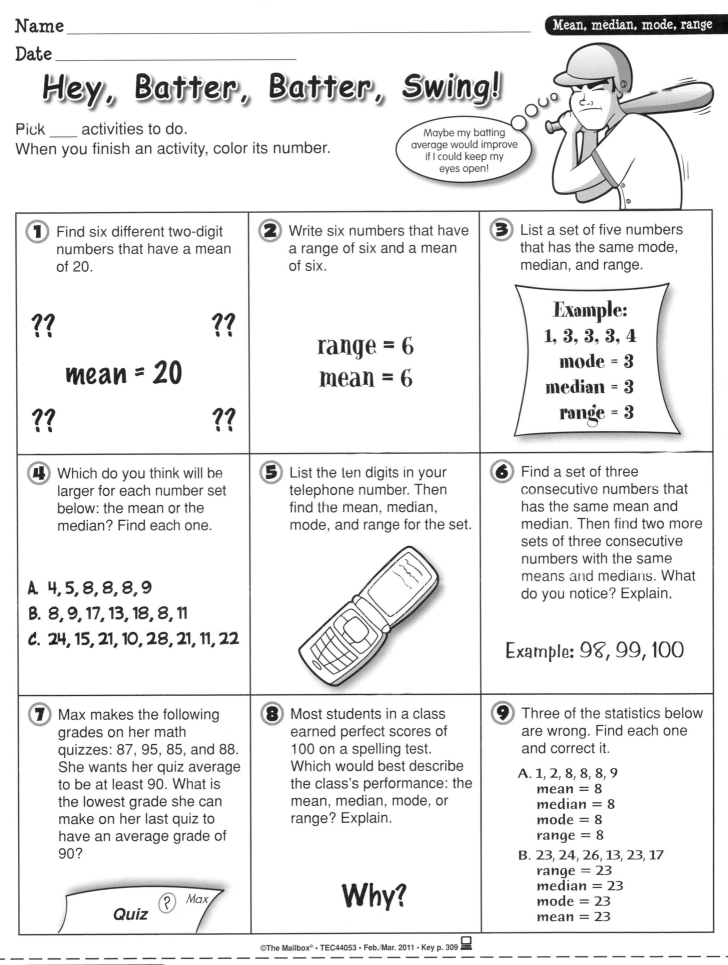

1 Find six different two-digit numbers that have a mean of 20. ?? ?? mean = 20 ?? ??	**2** Write six numbers that have a range of six and a mean of six. range = 6 mean = 6	**3** List a set of five numbers that has the same mode, median, and range. **Example:** **1, 3, 3, 3, 4** **mode = 3** **median = 3** **range = 3**
4 Which do you think will be larger for each number set below: the mean or the median? Find each one. A. 4, 5, 8, 8, 8, 9 B. 8, 9, 17, 13, 18, 8, 11 C. 24, 15, 21, 10, 28, 21, 11, 22	**5** List the ten digits in your telephone number. Then find the mean, median, mode, and range for the set. 	**6** Find a set of three consecutive numbers that has the same mean and median. Then find two more sets of three consecutive numbers with the same means and medians. What do you notice? Explain. Example: 98, 99, 100
7 Max makes the following grades on her math quizzes: 87, 95, 85, and 88. She wants her quiz average to be at least 90. What is the lowest grade she can make on her last quiz to have an average grade of 90?  	**8** Most students in a class earned perfect scores of 100 on a spelling test. Which would best describe the class's performance: the mean, median, mode, or range? Explain. Why?	**9** Three of the statistics below are wrong. Find each one and correct it. A. 1, 2, 8, 8, 8, 9 mean = 8 median = 8 mode = 8 range = 8 B. 23, 24, 26, 13, 23, 17 range = 23 median = 23 mode = 23 mean = 23

Independent Practice Grid Program the student directions with the number of activities to be completed. Then copy the page for each student.

Name ______________________________ **Division**

Date ____________________

MORE, PLEASE!

Solve. Then write each problem number on the pizza with the matching remainder description.

1. 74)3,451 (46 R47; −296; 491; −444; 47)

2. 33)7,459

3. 16)4,336

4. 31)9,796

5. 12)5,304

6. 92)4,253

7. 23)4,567

8. 18)9,486

9. 11)6,413

10. 47)6,824

11. 16)1,459

12. 38)3,149

13. 54)3,327

14. 65)4,345

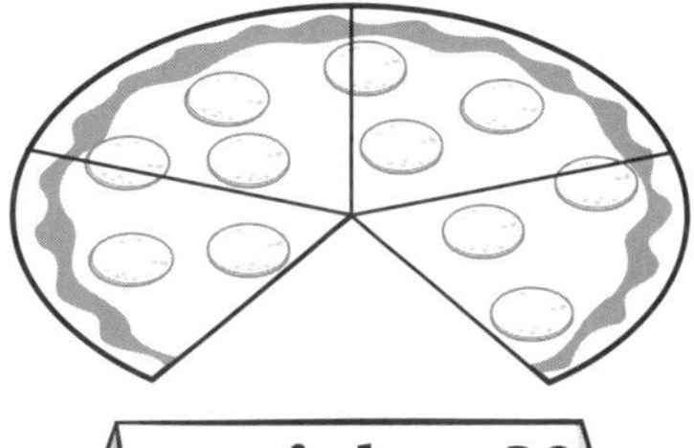

remainder < 20

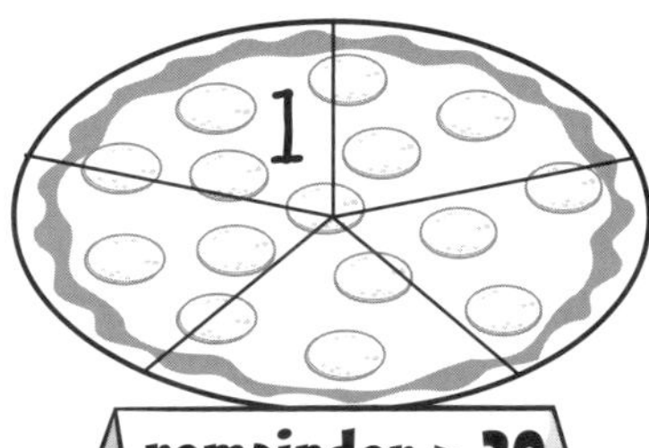

remainder > 20

no remainder

Bonus: Penny, the pizza-eating champ, solved this division problem. Is her quotient correct? If not, explain where she made a mistake.

59 R59
43)2,576
−215
426
−307
59

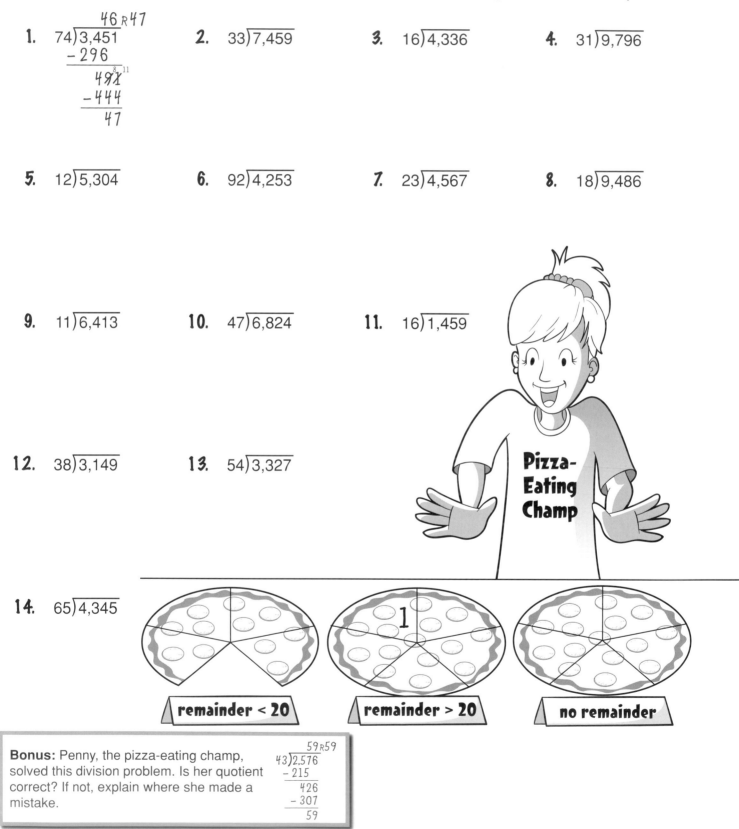

Name ____________________

Date ____________________

Pampered Pooches

Write the elapsed time for each dog's spa treatment.

Dog Client	Spa Service	Start Time	Finish Time	Elapsed Time
1. Emma	Doggie-Delight Walk	8:05 AM	8:48 AM	
2. Sasha	standard bath and groom	8:50 AM	9:40 AM	
3. Tito	standard groom, no bath	9:45 AM	10:05 AM	
4. Longfellow	standard walk	10:10 AM	11:03 AM	
5. Sebastian	luxury bath, groom, and nails	10:53 AM	12:22 AM	
6. Olivia	Doggie-Delight Walk	11:25 AM	12:30 PM	
7. Skippy	Doggie-Delight Walk	11:38 AM	2:13 PM	
8. Lexi	standard walk	3:35 PM	4:05 PM	
9. Max	standard walk	4:21 PM	4:40 PM	
10. Jack	Extrafluff Bath	4:43 PM	5:53 PM	

Answer each question.

11. At 11:20 AM, Carleigh goes on a 20-minute walk. Then she gets a 35-minute luxury bath. What time is her bath finished? ________

12. Toby's owner drops him off for a 90-minute Doggie-Delight Walk. His walk is over at 1:15 PM. What time did Toby's walk begin?

____

13. Milli goes on a 40-minute standard walk and then gets a 25-minute deluxe bath. Her walk starts at 11:30 AM. What time is she finished?

____

14. Zeus's owner wants his dog to have the 90-minute Ultrawalk and the 70-minute Extrafluff Bath. The salon has a 2½-hour appointment available. Is there enough time for Zeus's services? ________

Bonus: Lulu's owner drops her off at 10:15 AM. She goes for a 120-minute Doggie-Delight Walk and then gets a 70-minute Extrafluff Bath. If her owner comes back at 2:00 PM, will Lulu be ready? Explain.

Name ____________________

Date ____________________

Swish!

Solve. Find the basketball with the matching sum or difference.
Then color the item number as guided.

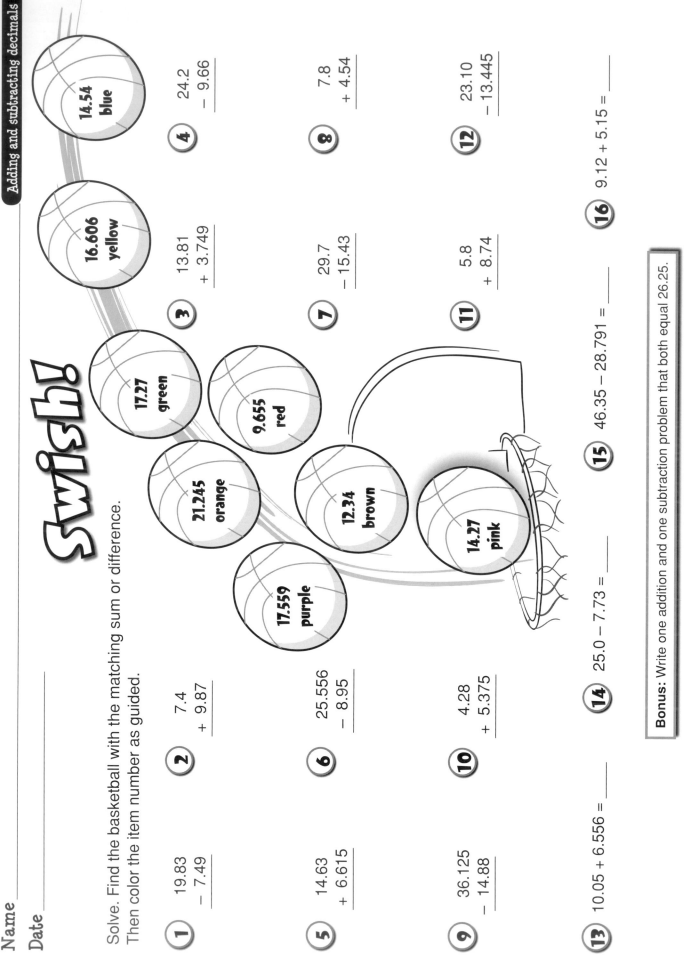

16.606 yellow

14.54 blue

17.27 green

21.245 orange

9.655 red

17.559 purple

12.34 brown

14.27 pink

1. 19.83 − 7.49

2. 7.4 + 9.87

3. 13.81 + 3.749

4. 24.2 − 9.66

5. 14.63 + 6.615

6. 25.556 − 8.95

7. 29.7 − 15.43

8. 7.8 + 4.54

9. 36.125 − 14.88

10. 4.28 + 5.375

11. 5.8 + 8.74

12. 23.10 − 13.445

13. 10.05 + 6.556 = ____

14. 25.0 − 7.73 = ____

15. 46.35 − 28.791 = ____

16. 9.12 + 5.15 = ____

Bonus: Write one addition and one subtraction problem that both equal 26.25.

Game Cards and Answer Key

Use with "'Bot Builder" on page 144. Students will need protractors and paper to record their answers.

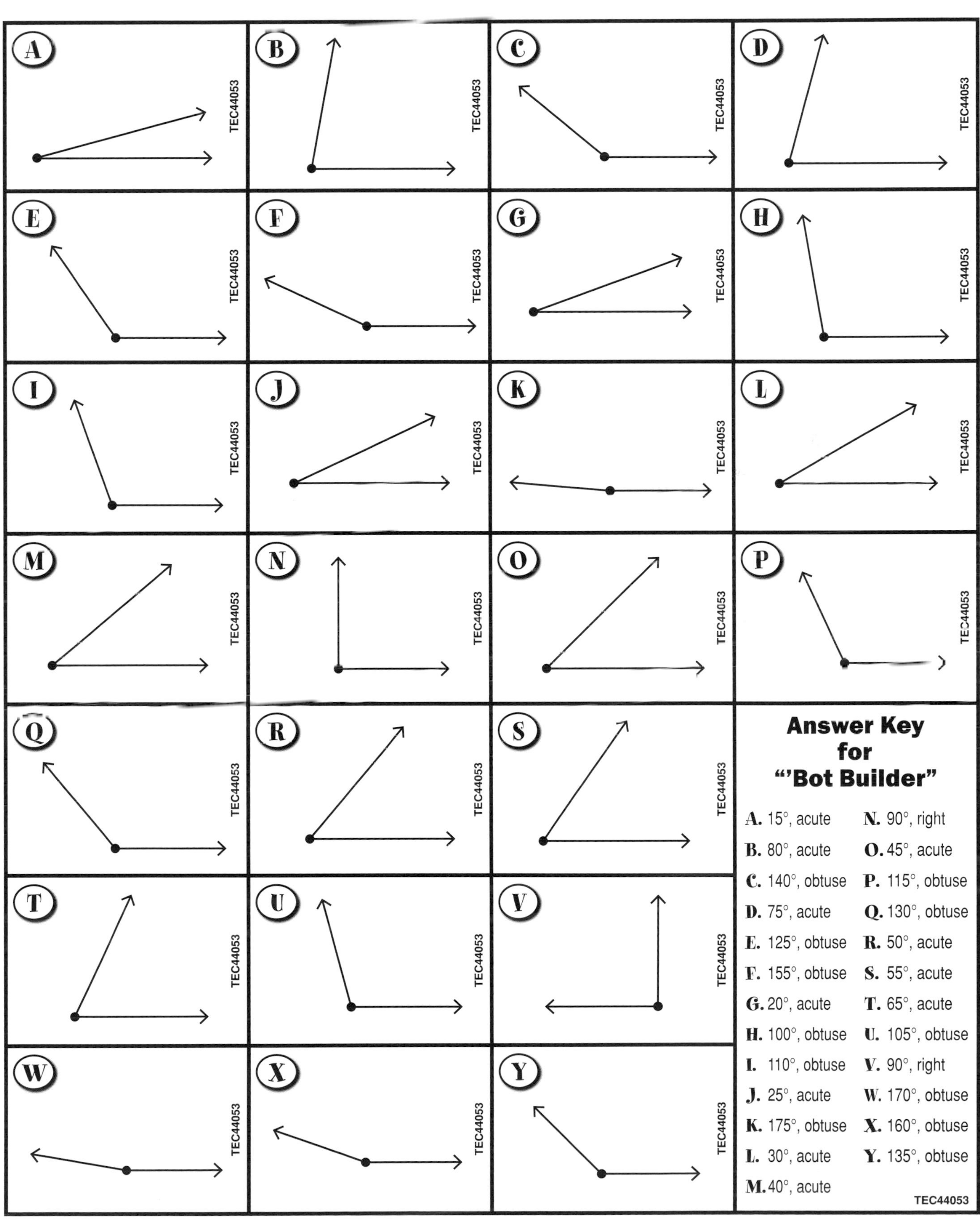

A
B
C
D
E
F
G
H
I
J
K
L
M
N
O
P
Q
R
S
T
U
V
W
X
Y
TEC44053
Answer Key for "'Bot Builder"
A. 15°, acute
B. 80°, acute
C. 140°, obtuse
D. 75°, acute
E. 125°, obtuse
F. 155°, obtuse
G. 20°, acute
H. 100°, obtuse
I. 110°, obtuse
J. 25°, acute
K. 175°, obtuse
L. 30°, acute
M. 40°, acute
N. 90°, right
O. 45°, acute
P. 115°, obtuse
Q. 130°, obtuse
R. 50°, acute
S. 55°, acute
T. 65°, acute
U. 105°, obtuse
V. 90°, right
W. 170°, obtuse
X. 160°, obtuse
Y. 135°, obtuse
TEC44053

'BOT BUILDER

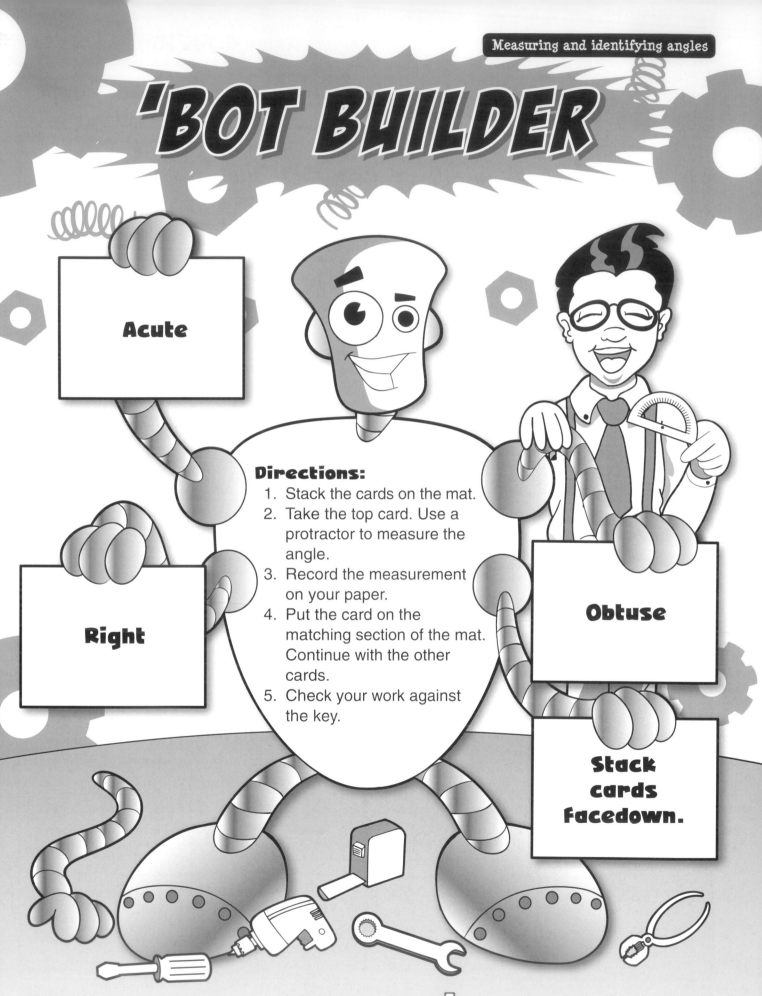

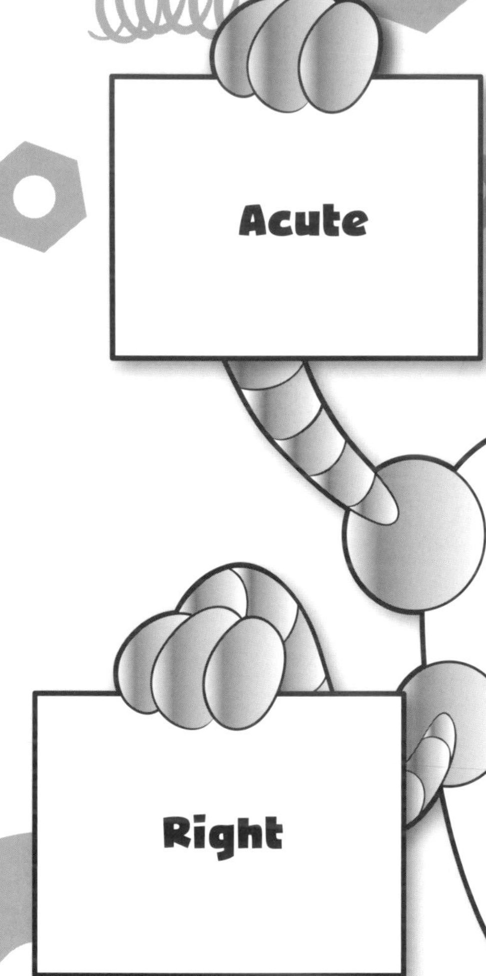

Directions:

1. Stack the cards on the mat.
2. Take the top card. Use a protractor to measure the angle.
3. Record the measurement on your paper.
4. Put the card on the matching section of the mat. Continue with the other cards.
5. Check your work against the key.

Obtuse

Stack cards Facedown.

Name ____________________

Date ____________________

Three in a Row

Follow the directions below. Circle each answer on the grid next to it. Then draw a line through three circled answers in a row.

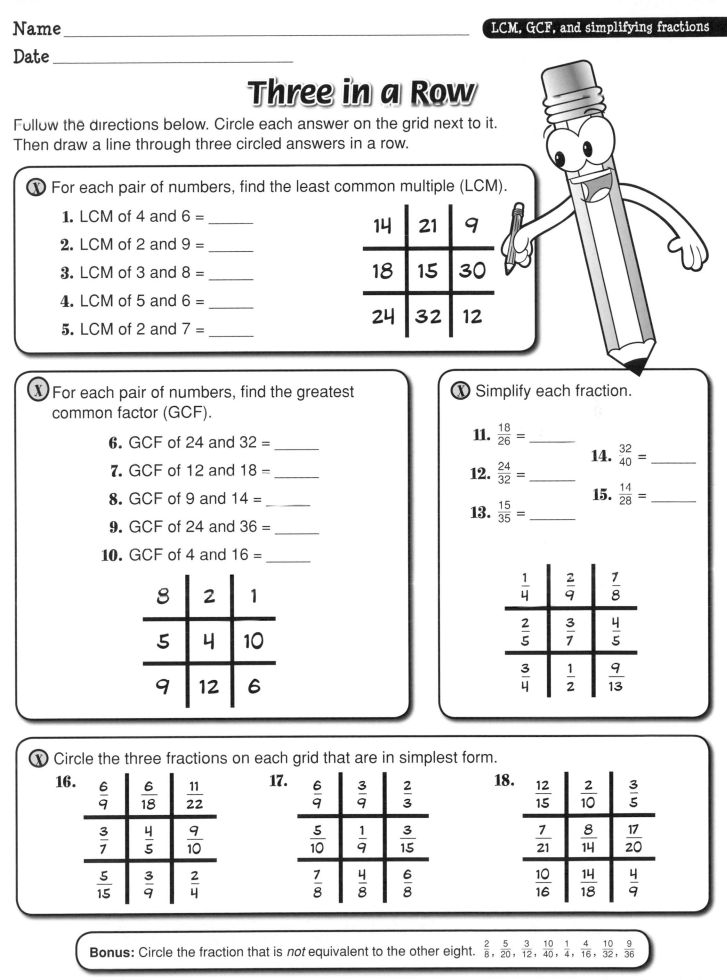

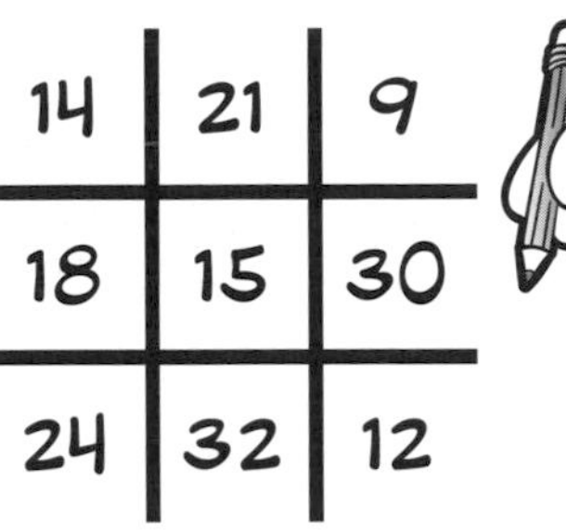

Ⓧ For each pair of numbers, find the least common multiple (LCM).

1. LCM of 4 and 6 = ______
2. LCM of 2 and 9 = ______
3. LCM of 3 and 8 = ______
4. LCM of 5 and 6 = ______
5. LCM of 2 and 7 = ______

14	21	9
18	15	30
24	32	12

Ⓧ For each pair of numbers, find the greatest common factor (GCF).

6. GCF of 24 and 32 = ______
7. GCF of 12 and 18 = ______
8. GCF of 9 and 14 = ______
9. GCF of 24 and 36 = ______
10. GCF of 4 and 16 = ______

8	2	1
5	4	10
9	12	6

Ⓧ Simplify each fraction.

11. $\frac{18}{26}$ = ______
12. $\frac{24}{32}$ = ______
13. $\frac{15}{35}$ = ______
14. $\frac{32}{40}$ = ______
15. $\frac{14}{28}$ = ______

$\frac{1}{4}$	$\frac{2}{9}$	$\frac{7}{8}$
$\frac{2}{5}$	$\frac{3}{7}$	$\frac{4}{5}$
$\frac{3}{4}$	$\frac{1}{2}$	$\frac{9}{13}$

Ⓧ Circle the three fractions on each grid that are in simplest form.

16.

$\frac{6}{9}$	$\frac{6}{18}$	$\frac{11}{22}$
$\frac{3}{7}$	$\frac{4}{5}$	$\frac{9}{10}$
$\frac{5}{15}$	$\frac{3}{9}$	$\frac{2}{4}$

17.

$\frac{6}{9}$	$\frac{3}{9}$	$\frac{2}{3}$
$\frac{5}{10}$	$\frac{1}{9}$	$\frac{3}{15}$
$\frac{7}{8}$	$\frac{4}{8}$	$\frac{6}{8}$

18.

$\frac{12}{15}$	$\frac{2}{10}$	$\frac{3}{5}$
$\frac{7}{21}$	$\frac{8}{14}$	$\frac{17}{20}$
$\frac{10}{16}$	$\frac{14}{18}$	$\frac{4}{9}$

Bonus: Circle the fraction that is *not* equivalent to the other eight. $\frac{2}{8}$, $\frac{5}{20}$, $\frac{3}{12}$, $\frac{10}{40}$, $\frac{1}{4}$, $\frac{4}{16}$, $\frac{10}{32}$, $\frac{9}{36}$

Name ____________________ **Interpreting data from graphs**

Date ____________________

It's Movie Time!

ADMIT ONE

Study each graph. Then answer the questions.

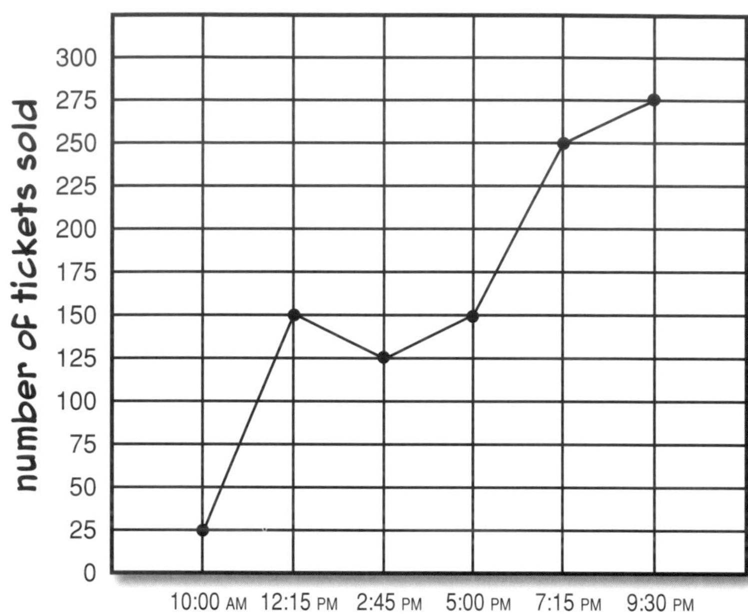

1. At which time were the most tickets sold?

   ____

2. How many more tickets were sold at 7:15 PM than at 2:45 PM? ____________________

3. At which times were ticket sales the same?

   ____

4. Between which two consecutive times did ticket sales change the most?

   ____

5. A movie ticket costs $9.00. How much did the theater take in for ticket sales at 12:15 PM?

   ____

6. Why do you think ticket sales are higher at 7:15 PM than at 2:45 PM?

   ____

   ____

7. Which two snacks are the most popular?

   ____

8. Which snack is the least popular?

   ____

9. Which snacks are more popular: sweet snacks or snacks that aren't sweet?

   ____

10. If 100 snacks were sold, how many of the snacks were nachos? ____________________

11. If 100 snacks were sold, how many were popcorn or candy? ____________________

12. Write a fraction to describe each of the following snack sales:

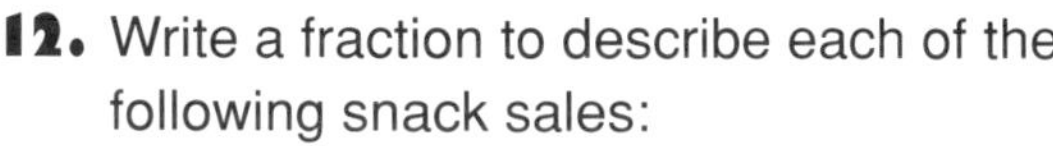

popcorn ________ candy ________

nachos ________

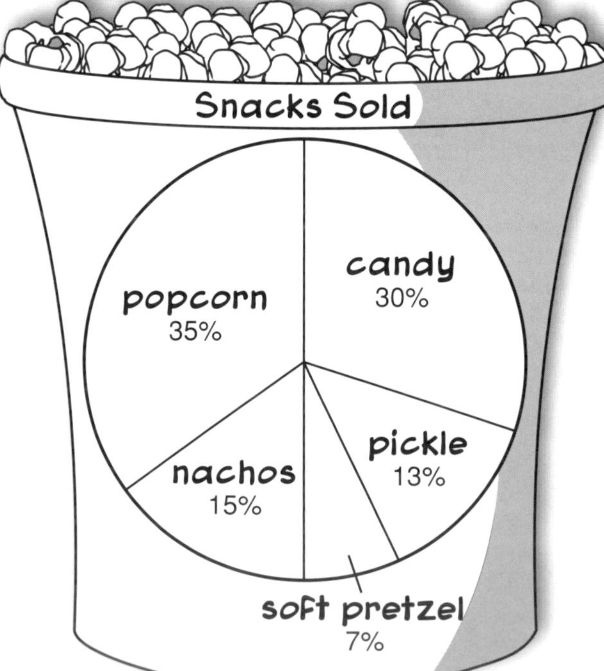

Bonus: Why do you think popcorn is the most popular snack? When do you think the theater sells the most popcorn?

Name ______________________________

Date ______________________________

Pick and Practice!

Pick ______ activities to do.
When you finish an activity, color its number.

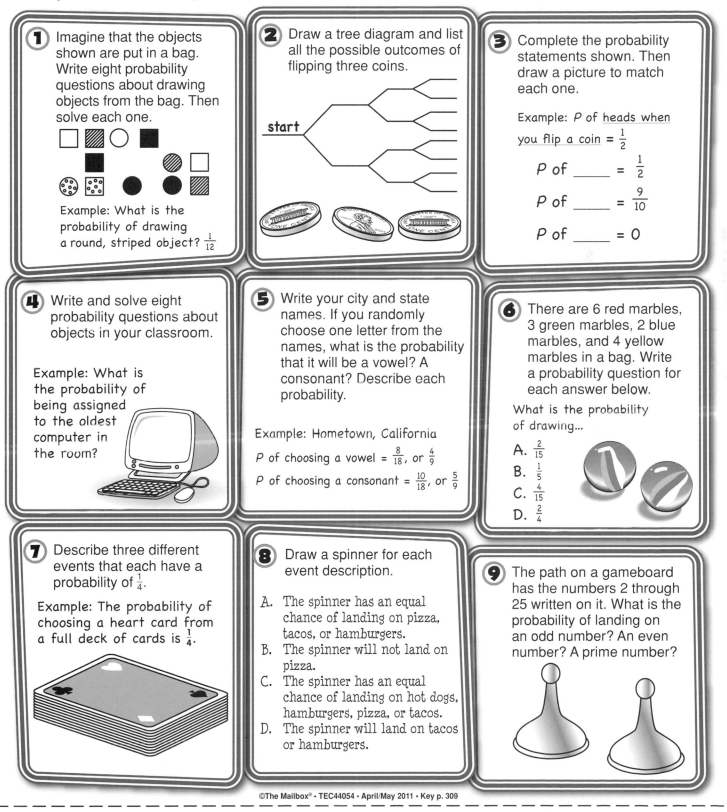

1 Imagine that the objects shown are put in a bag. Write eight probability questions about drawing objects from the bag. Then solve each one.

Example: What is the probability of drawing a round, striped object? $\frac{1}{12}$

2 Draw a tree diagram and list all the possible outcomes of flipping three coins.

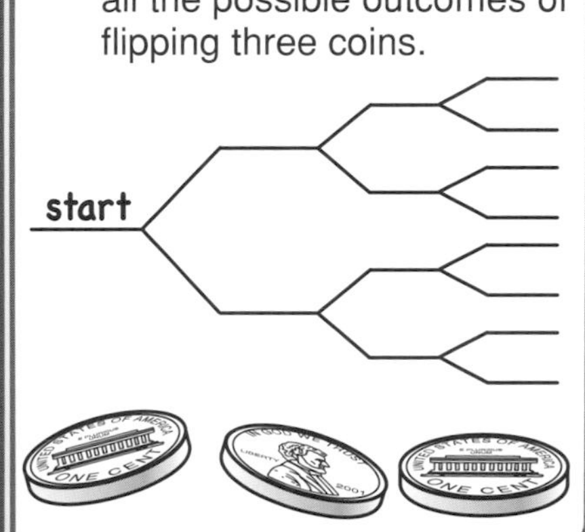

3 Complete the probability statements shown. Then draw a picture to match each one.

Example: P of heads when you flip a coin = $\frac{1}{2}$

P of _____ = $\frac{1}{2}$

P of _____ = $\frac{9}{10}$

P of _____ = 0

4 Write and solve eight probability questions about objects in your classroom.

Example: What is the probability of being assigned to the oldest computer in the room?

5 Write your city and state names. If you randomly choose one letter from the names, what is the probability that it will be a vowel? A consonant? Describe each probability.

Example: Hometown, California

P of choosing a vowel = $\frac{8}{18}$, or $\frac{4}{9}$

P of choosing a consonant = $\frac{10}{18}$, or $\frac{5}{9}$

6 There are 6 red marbles, 3 green marbles, 2 blue marbles, and 4 yellow marbles in a bag. Write a probability question for each answer below.

What is the probability of drawing...

A. $\frac{2}{15}$
B. $\frac{1}{5}$
C. $\frac{4}{15}$
D. $\frac{2}{4}$

7 Describe three different events that each have a probability of $\frac{1}{4}$.

Example: The probability of choosing a heart card from a full deck of cards is $\frac{1}{4}$.

8 Draw a spinner for each event description.

A. The spinner has an equal chance of landing on pizza, tacos, or hamburgers.
B. The spinner will not land on pizza.
C. The spinner has an equal chance of landing on hot dogs, hamburgers, pizza, or tacos.
D. The spinner will land on tacos or hamburgers.

9 The path on a gameboard has the numbers 2 through 25 written on it. What is the probability of landing on an odd number? An even number? A prime number?

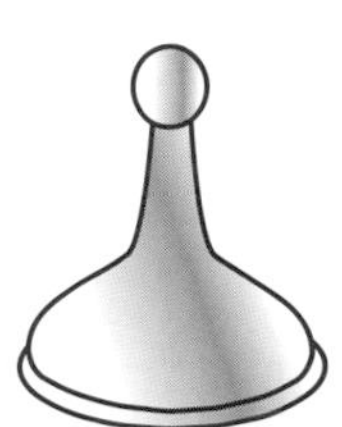

How to use: Program the student directions on a copy of this page with the number of activities to be completed. Then copy the page for each student.

Names ____

Date ______________________

Gumballs Galore!

A Game for Two Players

Directions:

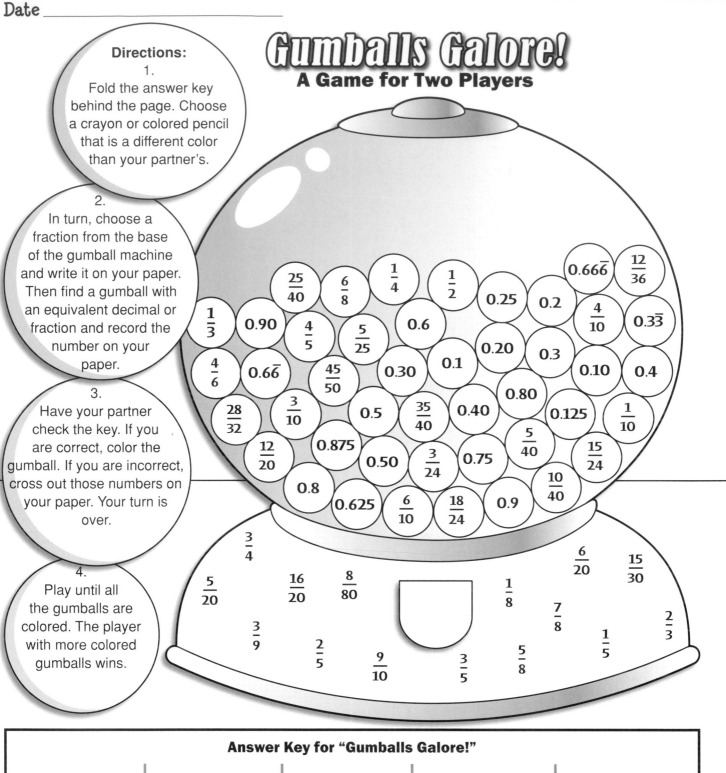

1. Fold the answer key behind the page. Choose a crayon or colored pencil that is a different color than your partner's.

2. In turn, choose a fraction from the base of the gumball machine and write it on your paper. Then find a gumball with an equivalent decimal or fraction and record the number on your paper.

3. Have your partner check the key. If you are correct, color the gumball. If you are incorrect, cross out those numbers on your paper. Your turn is over.

4. Play until all the gumballs are colored. The player with more colored gumballs wins.

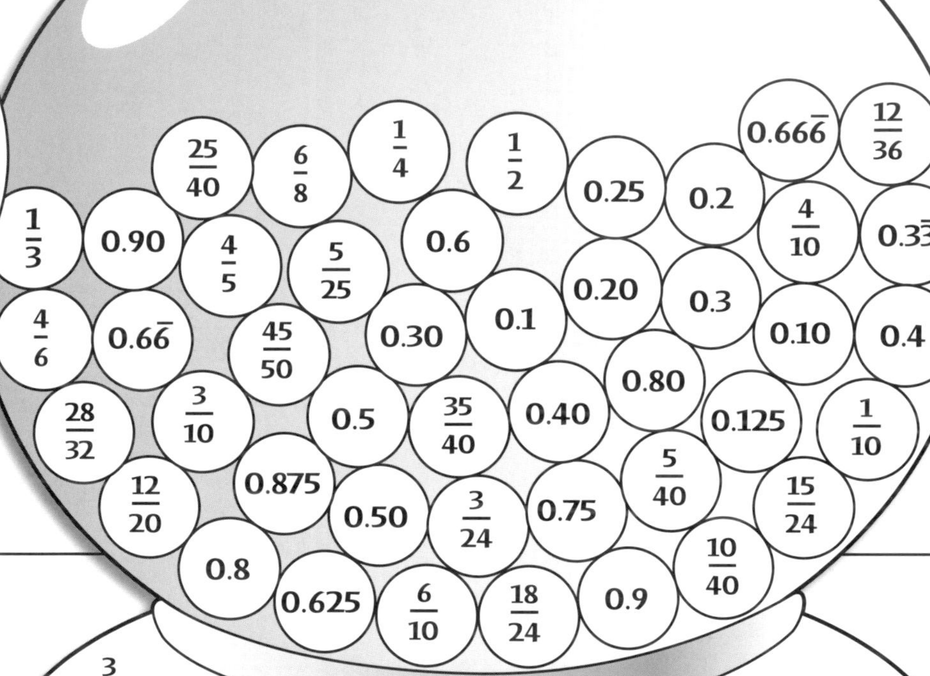

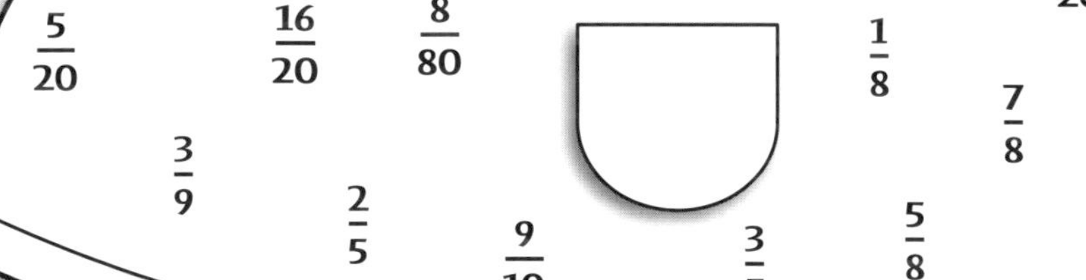

Answer Key for "Gumballs Galore!"

$\frac{8}{80} = 0.1, 0.10, \frac{1}{10}$	$\frac{5}{20} = 0.25, \frac{1}{4}, \frac{10}{40}$	$\frac{2}{5} = 0.4, 0.40, \frac{4}{10}$	$\frac{5}{8} = 0.625, \frac{25}{40}, \frac{15}{24}$	$\frac{16}{20} = 0.8, 0.80, \frac{4}{5}$
$\frac{1}{8} = 0.125, \frac{3}{24}, \frac{5}{40}$	$\frac{6}{20} = 0.3, 0.30, \frac{3}{10}$	$\frac{15}{30} = 0.5, 0.50, \frac{1}{2}$	$\frac{2}{3} = 0.6\overline{6}, \frac{4}{6}, 0.66\overline{6}$	$\frac{7}{8} = 0.875, \frac{28}{32}, \frac{35}{40}$
$\frac{1}{5} = 0.2, 0.20, \frac{5}{25}$	$\frac{3}{9} = 0.3\overline{3}, \frac{1}{3}, \frac{12}{36}$	$\frac{3}{5} = 0.6, \frac{6}{10}, \frac{12}{20}$	$\frac{3}{4} = 0.75, \frac{6}{8}, \frac{18}{24}$	$\frac{9}{10} = 0.9, 0.90, \frac{45}{50}$

How to use: Each pair needs a copy of the page, two different-colored pencils or crayons, and paper.

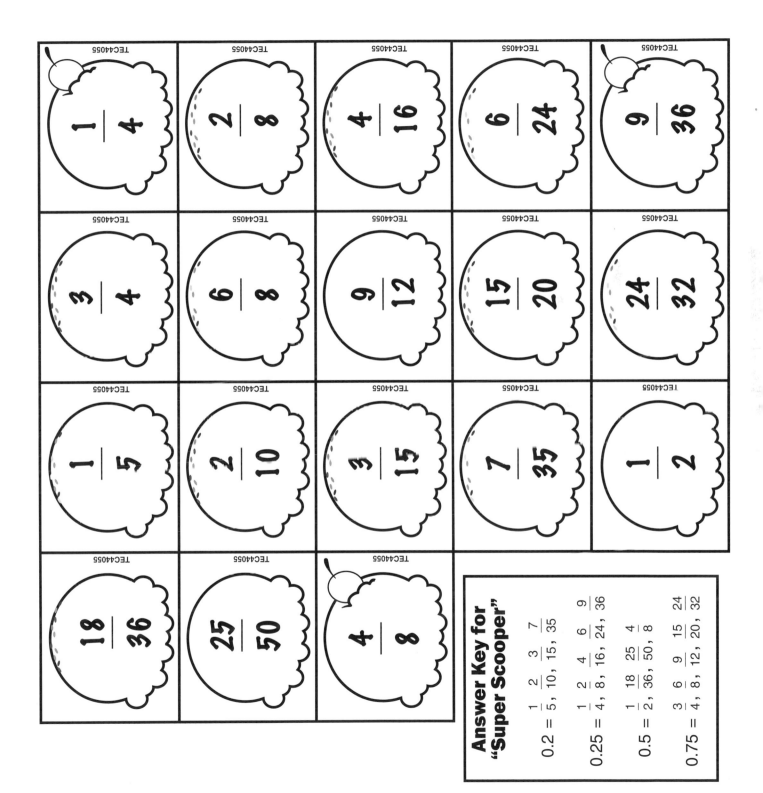

Center Cards and Answer Key

Use with "Super Scooper" on page 150.

$\frac{18}{36}$ $\frac{1}{5}$ $\frac{3}{4}$ $\frac{1}{4}$

$\frac{25}{50}$ $\frac{2}{10}$ $\frac{6}{8}$ $\frac{2}{8}$

$\frac{4}{8}$ $\frac{3}{15}$ $\frac{9}{12}$ $\frac{4}{16}$

$\frac{7}{35}$ $\frac{15}{20}$ $\frac{6}{24}$

$\frac{1}{2}$ $\frac{24}{32}$ $\frac{9}{36}$

Answer Key for "Super Scooper"

$0.2 = \frac{1}{5}, \frac{2}{10}, \frac{3}{15}, \frac{7}{35}$

$0.25 = \frac{1}{4}, \frac{2}{8}, \frac{4}{16}, \frac{6}{24}, \frac{9}{36}$

$0.5 = \frac{1}{2}, \frac{18}{36}, \frac{25}{50}, \frac{4}{8}$

$0.75 = \frac{3}{4}, \frac{6}{8}, \frac{9}{12}, \frac{15}{20}, \frac{24}{32}$

SUPER SCOOPER

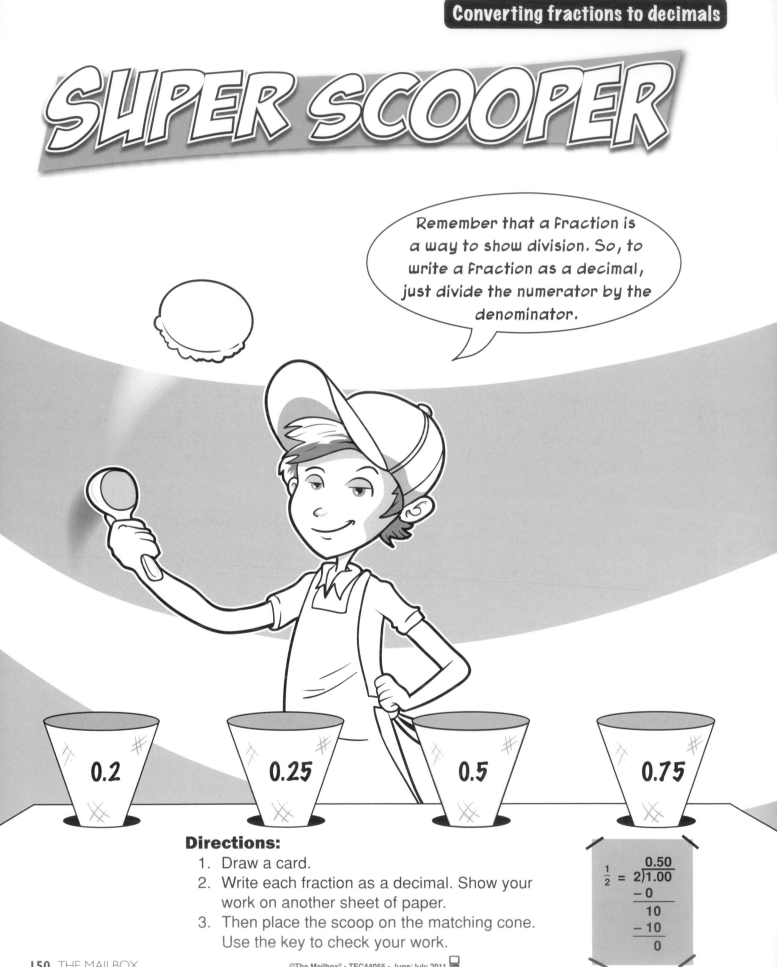

Remember that a fraction is a way to show division. So, to write a fraction as a decimal, just divide the numerator by the denominator.

0.2

0.25

0.5

0.75

Directions:

1. Draw a card.
2. Write each fraction as a decimal. Show your work on another sheet of paper.
3. Then place the scoop on the matching cone. Use the key to check your work.

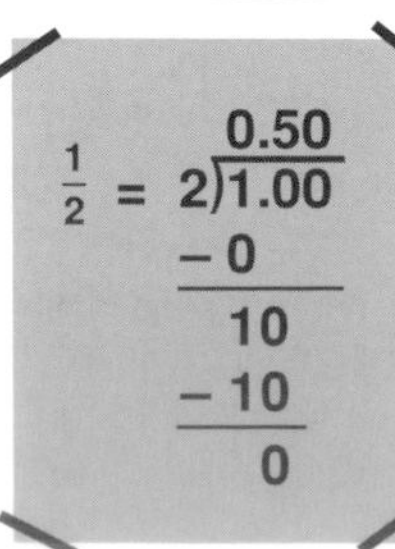

Name ____________________

Date ____________________

In a Cavern

Multiply. Write each product in simplest form. Then color each flashlight according to the code.

Code

orange = less than $\frac{1}{4}$

green = equal to or greater than $\frac{1}{4}$ but less than $\frac{1}{2}$

yellow = greater than $\frac{1}{2}$ but less than $\frac{3}{4}$

blue = greater than $\frac{3}{4}$

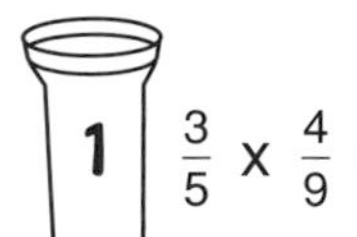
1. $\frac{3}{5} \times \frac{4}{9} =$

2. $\frac{8}{13} \times \frac{11}{12} =$

3. $\frac{7}{15} \times \frac{3}{10} =$

4. $\frac{24}{25} \times \frac{15}{18} =$

5. $\frac{14}{23} \times \frac{46}{49} =$

6. $\frac{13}{20} \times \frac{35}{39} =$

7. $\frac{28}{32} \times \frac{8}{21} =$

8. $\frac{9}{11} \times \frac{10}{54} =$

9. $\frac{11}{12} \times \frac{5}{7} =$

10. $\frac{12}{27} \times \frac{6}{16} =$

11. $\frac{8}{7} \times \frac{14}{16} =$

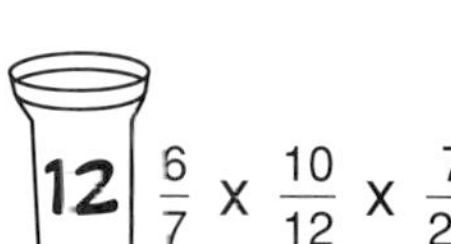
12. $\frac{6}{7} \times \frac{10}{12} \times \frac{7}{20} =$

13. $\frac{3}{4} \times \frac{24}{36} \times \frac{7}{8} =$

14. $\frac{2}{5} \times \frac{3}{8} \times \frac{4}{15} =$

15. $\frac{8}{21} \times \frac{7}{12} \times \frac{9}{11} =$

I get it! There's a c in stalactites, and they are on the ceiling. There's a g in stalagmites, and they are on the ground!

Bonus: The problem shown is incorrect. What mistake was made? Explain. $\frac{2}{9} \times \frac{3}{12} = \frac{24}{27} = \frac{8}{9}$

Name ______________________________

Date ____________________

Pick and Practice

Pick ______ activities to do.
When you finish an activity, color its number.

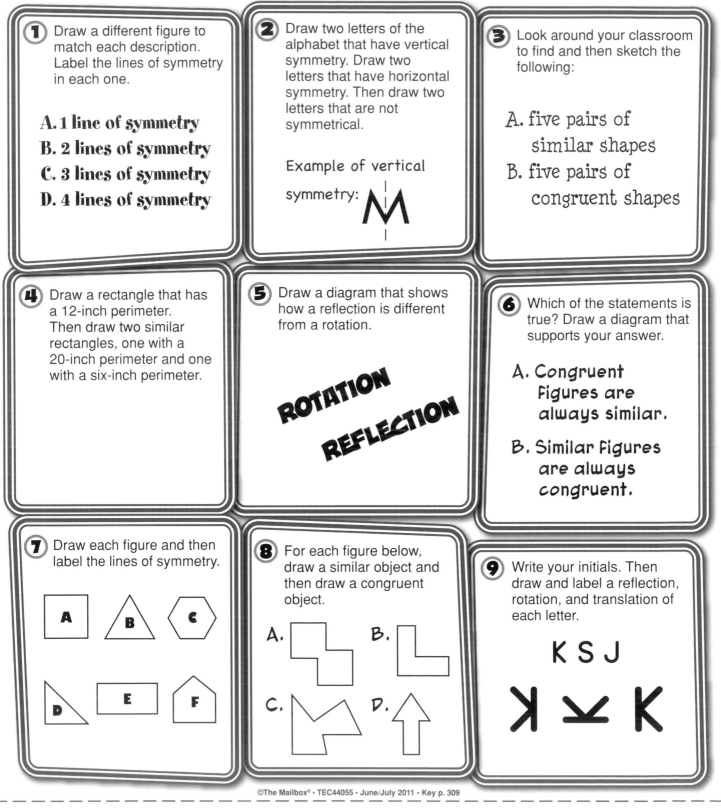

1 Draw a different figure to match each description. Label the lines of symmetry in each one.

A. 1 line of symmetry
B. 2 lines of symmetry
C. 3 lines of symmetry
D. 4 lines of symmetry

2 Draw two letters of the alphabet that have vertical symmetry. Draw two letters that have horizontal symmetry. Then draw two letters that are not symmetrical.

Example of vertical symmetry: M

3 Look around your classroom to find and then sketch the following:

A. five pairs of similar shapes
B. five pairs of congruent shapes

4 Draw a rectangle that has a 12-inch perimeter. Then draw two similar rectangles, one with a 20-inch perimeter and one with a six-inch perimeter.

5 Draw a diagram that shows how a reflection is different from a rotation.

ROTATION
REFLECTION

6 Which of the statements is true? Draw a diagram that supports your answer.

A. Congruent figures are always similar.
B. Similar figures are always congruent.

7 Draw each figure and then label the lines of symmetry.

F

8 For each figure below, draw a similar object and then draw a congruent object.

A.
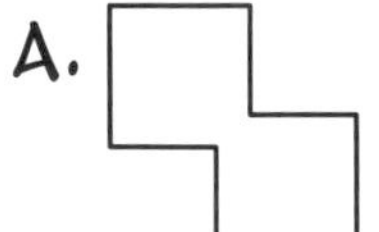
B.
C.

D.

9 Write your initials. Then draw and label a reflection, rotation, and translation of each letter.

K S J

K K K

Independent practice grid: Program the student directions on a copy of this page with the number of activities to be completed. Then copy the page for each student.

Name ______________________

Date ______________________

Forty Winks

Write each fraction in simplest form.

$\frac{2}{4}$ = ____ H	$\frac{4}{6}$ = ____ N	$\frac{25}{100}$ = ____ S	$\frac{10}{25}$ = ____ D
$\frac{3}{27}$ = ____ E	$\frac{10}{12}$ = ____ A	$\frac{6}{8}$ = ____ W	$\frac{20}{32}$ = ____ T
$\frac{8}{14}$ = ____ W	$\frac{12}{15}$ = ____ A	$\frac{20}{45}$ = ____ V	$\frac{8}{44}$ = ____ R
$\frac{3}{18}$ = ____ E	$\frac{22}{24}$ = ____ M	$\frac{21}{24}$ = ____ E	$\frac{12}{32}$ = ____ S
		$\frac{42}{49}$ = ____ O	$\frac{33}{77}$ = ____ D

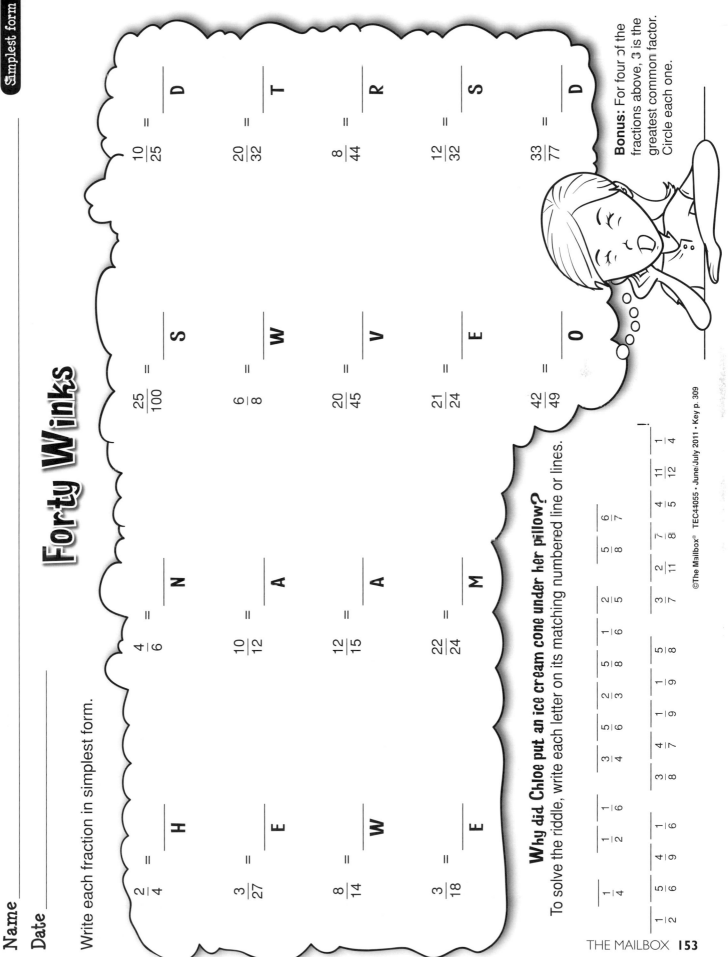

Why did Chloe put an ice cream cone under her pillow?

To solve the riddle, write each letter on its matching numbered line or lines.

___ $\frac{1}{4}$ ___ $\frac{1}{2}$ ___ $\frac{1}{6}$ ___ $\frac{3}{4}$ ___ $\frac{5}{6}$ ___ $\frac{2}{3}$ ___ $\frac{5}{8}$ ___ $\frac{1}{6}$ ___ $\frac{2}{5}$ ___ $\frac{5}{8}$ ___ $\frac{6}{7}$

___ $\frac{1}{2}$ ___ $\frac{5}{6}$ ___ $\frac{4}{9}$ ___ $\frac{1}{6}$ ___ $\frac{3}{8}$ ___ $\frac{4}{7}$ ___ $\frac{1}{9}$ ___ $\frac{1}{9}$ ___ $\frac{5}{8}$ ___ $\frac{3}{7}$ ___ $\frac{2}{11}$ ___ $\frac{7}{8}$ ___ $\frac{4}{5}$ ___ $\frac{11}{12}$ ___ $\frac{1}{4}$!

Bonus: For four of the fractions above, 3 is the greatest common factor. Circle each one.

Names ____________________

Date ____________________

On a Roll!

A Game for Two Players

Directions:

1. Fold the answer key behind the page. Then choose a crayon or colored pencil that is a different color than your partner's.
2. In turn, choose a box on the page. Write the matching probability in the ball. Have your partner check the key.
3. If you are incorrect, erase your answer. Your turn is over.
4. If you are correct, color the ball. Then roll the die or dice as described in your box. If your roll matches the description, take another turn. If your roll doesn't match, your turn is over.
5. Keep playing until all the balls are colored. The player who colors more balls wins.

1. If you roll one die, what is the probability of rolling a number 1? 	2. If you roll one die, what is the probability of not rolling a number 2? 	3. If you roll one die, what is the probability of rolling a number 3 or 6? 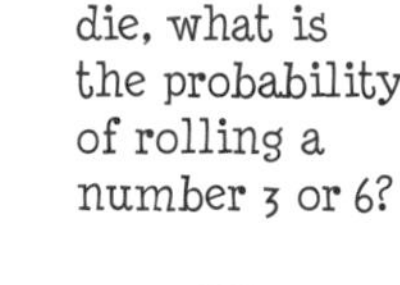	4. If you roll one die, what is the probability of rolling a number 1, 2, or 3? 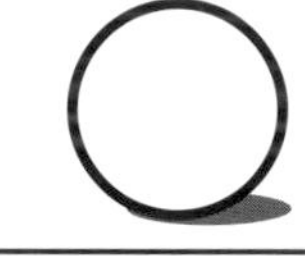	5. If you roll one die, what is the probability of rolling an even number? 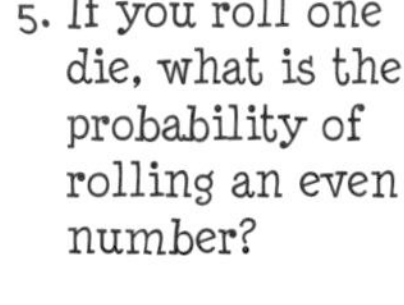	6. If you roll one die, what is the probability of rolling an odd number? 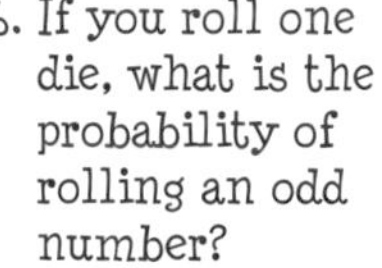 
7. If you roll one die, what is the probability of rolling a number less than five?	8. If you roll one die, what is the probability of rolling a number greater than two? 	9. If you roll two dice, what is the probability of rolling a number 1? 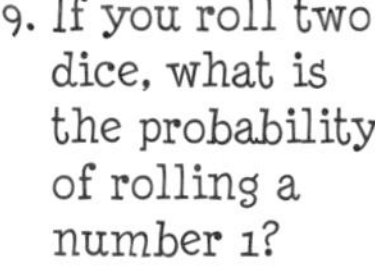	10. If you roll two dice, what is the probability of not rolling a number 2? 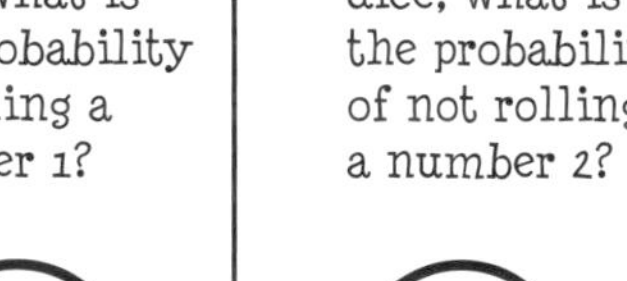	11. If you roll two dice, what is the probability of rolling a number 3 or 6? 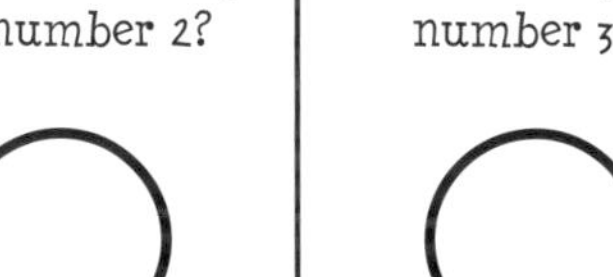	12. If you roll two dice, what is the probability of rolling a number 1, 2, 3, or 4? 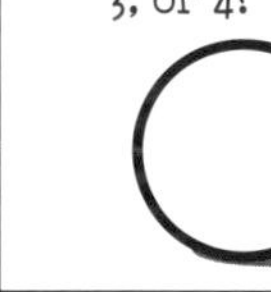
13. If you roll two dice, what is the probability of rolling an even number? 	14. If you roll two dice, what is the probability of rolling an odd number? 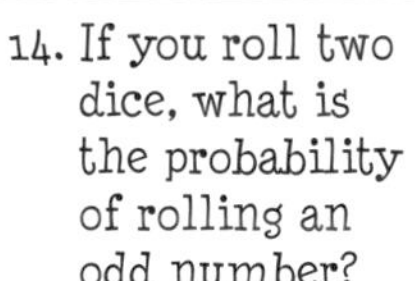 	15. If you roll two dice, what is the probability that their sum will be less than five? 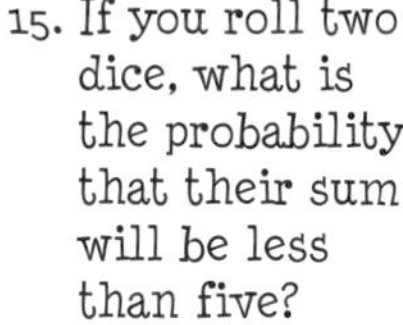 	16. If you roll two dice, what is the probability that their sum will be five or greater? 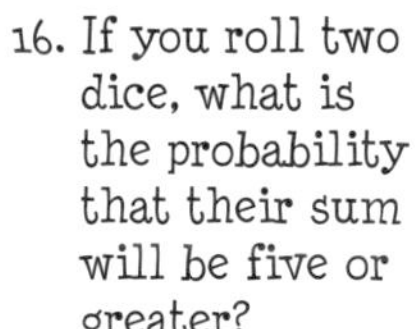 	17. If you roll two dice, what is the probability of rolling doubles? 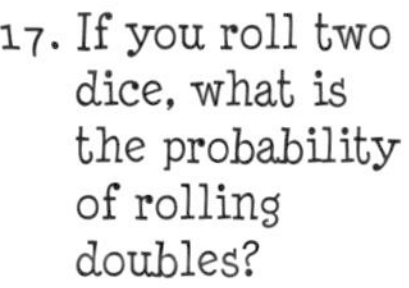 	18. If you roll two dice, what is the probability that their product will be six or less? 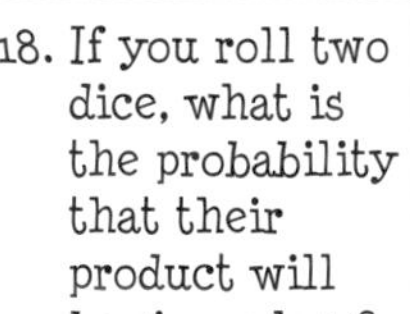

Answer Key for "On a Roll!"

1. $\frac{1}{6}$ 2. $\frac{5}{6}$ 3. $\frac{1}{3}$ 4. $\frac{1}{2}$ 5. $\frac{1}{2}$ 6. $\frac{1}{2}$ 7. $\frac{2}{3}$ 8. $\frac{2}{3}$ 9. $\frac{1}{6}$ 10. $\frac{5}{6}$ 11. $\frac{1}{3}$ 12. $\frac{3}{4}$ 13. $\frac{1}{2}$ 14. $\frac{1}{2}$ 15. $\frac{1}{6}$ 16. $\frac{5}{6}$ 17. $\frac{1}{6}$ 18. $\frac{7}{18}$

How to use: Each pair of students needs a copy of the page, two dice, and two different-color crayons or pencils.

Name ______________________

Level A

NUMBER AND OPERATIONS

1 An airplane carries 198 passengers. Each traveler's suitcase weighs about 50 pounds. About how much does the luggage weigh altogether? How did you find your answer?

NUMBER AND OPERATIONS

2 Patrick solved the problem below. Is his answer correct? Explain.

$$\begin{array}{r} 785 \\ +\ 491 \\ \hline 1{,}176 \end{array}$$

NUMBER AND OPERATIONS

3 Morgan's estimate for the problem below is 900. Macey thinks the best estimate is 1,000. Who is correct? How do you know?

389 + 615

MEASUREMENT

4 Trey's kite has 30 yards of kite string. Todd's kite has 100 feet of string. Whose kite can fly higher? How did you find your answer?

ALGEBRA

5 Micah created a pattern using the following rule: multiply by two; then subtract four. Can these patterns be Micah's? Why or why not?

7, 10, 16, 28,...

3, 2, 0,...

DATA ANALYSIS AND PROBABILITY

6 Which two graphs would fit the data given below? Explain your choices.

A. circle graph
B. bar graph
C. line graph

Girls' Favorite Sports
volleyball = 31%
basketball = 23%
tennis = 10%
soccer = 36%

Name ______________________

Level B

NUMBER AND OPERATIONS

1 Write the missing digit in the number below to make this statement true: the tenths and hundreds digits have the same sum as the tens and hundredths digits. Explain your answer.

9___5.28

NUMBER AND OPERATIONS

2 Which numbers below are even when rounded to the nearest whole number? How do you know?

721.9 375.4 868.1 954.5

NUMBER AND OPERATIONS

3 Which decimal is the best estimate for the dot's location? Why?

0.09 8.8 0.1 0.75

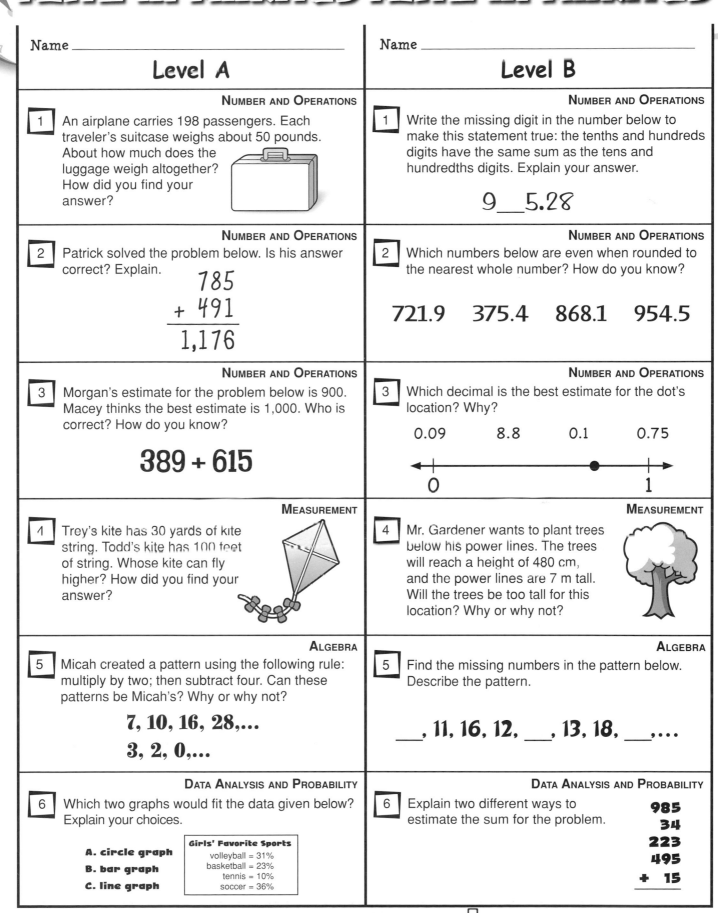

0 1

MEASUREMENT

4 Mr. Gardener wants to plant trees below his power lines. The trees will reach a height of 480 cm, and the power lines are 7 m tall. Will the trees be too tall for this location? Why or why not?

ALGEBRA

5 Find the missing numbers in the pattern below. Describe the pattern.

___, 11, 16, 12, ___, 13, 18, ___,...

DATA ANALYSIS AND PROBABILITY

6 Explain two different ways to estimate the sum for the problem.

$$\begin{array}{r} 985 \\ 34 \\ 223 \\ 495 \\ +\ 15 \\ \hline \end{array}$$

Note to the teacher: Copy the entire page, one level, or selected problems to distribute to students. When a student solves a problem, he checks its box. If desired, display the page and have students solve the problems on their own papers.

Name ______________________

Level A

NUMBER AND OPERATIONS

1 This box of dog treats can be divided equally among two, three, or five dogs. What is the smallest number of treats that can be inside the box? Explain your answer.

DOG TREATS

NUMBER AND OPERATIONS

2 What is the smallest number that rounds to one million? What is the largest number? How do you know?

1,000,000

NUMBER AND OPERATIONS

3 Arrange these numbers into three sets whose sums each equal 100. How did you find your answer?

8 20 35 48 63 9 25 40 52

DATA ANALYSIS AND PROBABILITY

4 Which outcome is more likely? Why?

A. The spinner will not land on soccer.
B. The spinner will land on either soccer or basketball.

soccer
kickball
basketball

MEASUREMENT

5 Justin's brother will be four feet tall when he grows two more inches. How many inches tall is Justin's brother now? How did you find your answer?

GEOMETRY

6 Which of the terms shown describe the figure below? Explain your answer.

quadrilateral trapezoid
pentagon polygon
closed figure diagonal

Name ______________________

Level B

NUMBER AND OPERATIONS

1 The median and the mode for this set of data are the same. Why?

52, 46, 20, 52, 15, 52, 84

NUMBER AND OPERATIONS

2 Which of these are equivalent to 0.3? How do you know?

thirty hundredths
three hundredths
thirty-three thousandths
three tenths

NUMBER AND OPERATIONS

3 Abby says the factors of 36 are 1, 2, 3, 4, 6, and 9. Is she correct? Why or why not?

?

GEOMETRY

4 Which of these coordinates matches a point on the *x*-axis? Explain your answer.

A. (0, 3)
B. (5, 1)
C. (4, 0)

y
x

DATA ANALYSIS AND PROBABILITY

5 The Fisher High students are choosing a new mascot and school color. How many possible combinations are there? How do you know?

Mascots: bear, eagle, jaguar, lion
Colors: red, blue, silver, gold

MEASUREMENT

6 Carter ran 800 yards in 360 seconds. Did he take more or less than five minutes? Explain.

001 23

How to use: Copy the entire page, one level, or selected problems to distribute to students. When a student solves a problem, he checks its box. If desired, display the page and have students solve the problems on their own papers.

MATH IN MINUTES MATH IN MINUTES

Name ______________________

Level A

NUMBER AND OPERATIONS

1 Brooke and Wesley both solved the problem below. Brooke says the answer is 22, but Wesley thinks it's 17. Who is correct? Explain.

$$5 + 6 \times 2$$

NUMBER AND OPERATIONS

2 Which fraction is not in its lowest terms? How do you know?

$\frac{9}{16}$ $\frac{10}{21}$ $\frac{7}{12}$ $\frac{2}{9}$ $\frac{9}{15}$ $\frac{4}{5}$

NUMBER AND OPERATIONS

3 Which is larger, the sum of these decimals or their product? Explain.

0.2 0.5

MEASUREMENT

4 Ms. Stevens has 20 small glue bottles. Each bottle holds 150 mL of glue. If she buys a 2L bottle of glue, will she be able to fill all 20 bottles? Why or why not?

GLUE

GEOMETRY

5 How many of the letters below consist of both parallel and perpendicular lines? Explain.

M A T H E M A T I C S

DATA ANALYSIS AND PROBABILITY

6 There are 5 red marbles, 3 yellow marbles, and 7 blue marbles in a bag. Which is more likely? Why?

A. You draw a red marble from the bag.
B. You draw a blue marble from the bag.

Name ______________________

Level B

NUMBER AND OPERATIONS

1 Grace biked 7 miles on Monday, 12 miles on Tuesday, 9 miles on Wednesday, 11 miles on Thursday, and 9 miles on Friday. Including Saturday, her average distance biked per day was 10 miles. How many miles did she ride on Saturday? How do you know?

NUMBER AND OPERATIONS

2 Choose the fraction that is equivalent to 0.2. How did you find your answer?

$\frac{3}{12}$ $\frac{4}{8}$ $\frac{5}{10}$ $\frac{2}{5}$ $\frac{3}{15}$ $\frac{1}{2}$

NUMBER AND OPERATIONS

3 Imagine that you round each factor in the problem shown to its largest place value. Then you multiply the rounded factors. Could the estimate be greater than 90,000? Why or why not?

□□□
x □□

MEASUREMENT

4 For spirit week, the student council is giving all 475 students a special ribbon. Each ribbon will be 10 cm long. How much ribbon should the council buy? Explain.

20 m 30 m 40 m 50 m

GEOMETRY

5 Principal Thompson wants to build a new playground. Which design will give students more room to play? How do you know?

60 ft. × 60 ft. 90 ft. × 40 ft.

DATA ANALYSIS AND PROBABILITY

6 There are 5 nickels, 3 dimes, 4 quarters, and 6 pennies in your pocket. If you draw two coins, which is more likely? How do you know?

A. You draw a nickel and a quarter.
B. You draw a quarter and a penny.

How to use: Copy the entire page, one level, or selected problems to distribute to students. When a student solves a problem, he checks its box. If desired, display the page and have students solve the problems on their own papers.

MATH IN MINUTES MATH IN MINUTES

Name ______________________

Level A

NUMBER AND OPERATIONS

1 Write the steps you would take to compare these numbers. Then put them in order.

35,212 35,321 35,012

NUMBER AND OPERATIONS

2 The Snyders (5 adults and 3 children) are going to the zoo. Should they buy the family pass or individual tickets? Explain.

Zoo Tickets	
Adult	$15.00
Child	$12.00
Family Pass	$150.00

NUMBER AND OPERATIONS

3 Bryce solved the problem below. Is his answer correct? Explain.

$$7\overline{)696} = 98\text{ R}1$$

MEASUREMENT

4 Adalyn is making 5 friendship bracelets. She needs 6 inches of elastic for each one. Adalyn has 1 yard of elastic. Does she have enough? How do you know?

DATA ANALYSIS AND PROBABILITY

5 If you spin each spinner, how many different combinations might you get? How did you find your answer?

R B G P

1 2 3

GEOMETRY

6 Which angle in this triangle measures 120 degrees? How do you know?

A B C

Name ______________________

Level B

NUMBER AND OPERATIONS

1 You have six pushpins and two staples. How many paper clips are they worth? How do you know?

3 paper clips = 1 staple
2 staples = 1 pushpin

NUMBER AND OPERATIONS

2 Each week for 12 weeks, Marshall buys 4 packs of baseball cards. Each pack costs $0.94. How many packs of cards does he buy? Will he spend over $55? Explain.

ALGEBRA

3 Hope wrote these fractions in order from least to greatest. Is she correct? How do you know?

$$1\frac{1}{2} \quad 1\frac{1}{3} \quad 1\frac{5}{6} \quad 1\frac{3}{4}$$

MEASUREMENT

4 Ms. Motley needs 6 gallons of juice. She buys 6 quarts of orange juice, 8 quarts of apple juice, and 4 quarts of grape juice. Does she have enough juice? Explain how you know.

DATA ANALYSIS AND PROBABILITY

5 What is the probability of getting a striped gumball? Write your answer as a fraction in simplest form. How did you find your answer?

GEOMETRY

6 Complete the inequality below with <, >, or =. Explain your answer.

the measure of one angle from a square ◯ the measure of one angle from an equilateral triangle

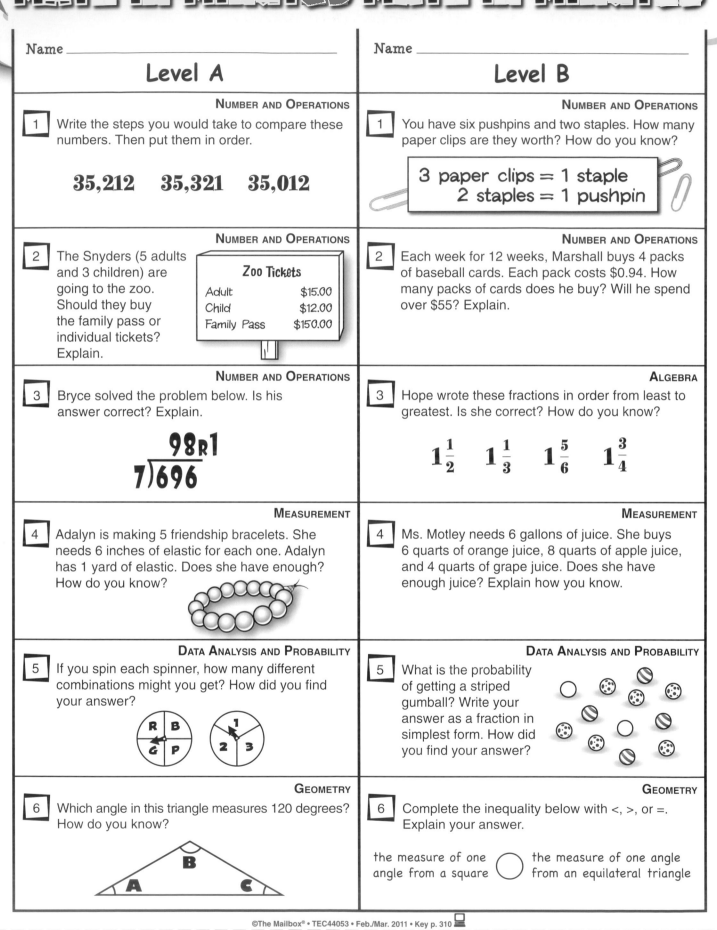

Note to the teacher: Copy the entire page, one level, or selected problems to distribute to students. When a student solves a problem, he checks its box. If desired, display the page and have students solve the problems on their own papers.

Math in Minutes Math in Minutes

Name ______________________________

LEVEL A

NUMBERS AND OPERATIONS

1 Which is the best estimate for the problem below? Explain your choice.

$$\frac{3}{10} + \frac{4}{9} = n$$

A. Greater than 1 B. Less than 1

NUMBERS AND OPERATIONS

2 Which fraction does not belong in each group? Explain how you know.

A. $\frac{4}{6}$, $\frac{7}{9}$, $\frac{2}{3}$, $\frac{8}{12}$

B. $\frac{1}{5}$, $\frac{5}{25}$, $\frac{3}{15}$, $\frac{4}{16}$

C. $\frac{3}{24}$, $\frac{5}{45}$, $\frac{1}{8}$, $\frac{7}{56}$

NUMBERS AND OPERATIONS

3 Bryce's band director wants him to practice four hours each week. Bryce has practiced for 45 minutes five different times this week. Does he still need to practice? Why or why not?

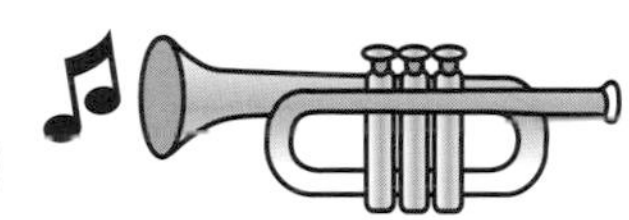

MEASUREMENT

4 Maggie wants to convert a measurement from cups to pints. Which operation should she use? How do you know?

multiplication addition

subtraction division

DATA ANALYSIS AND PROBABILITY

5 Karsen is ready to wrap her mom's present. How many possible combinations are there if she uses one type of paper and one color of ribbon? Explain.

wrapping paper: **flowers**, **hearts**, **polka dots**, **stripes**

ribbon: **pink**, **purple**, **blue**, **yellow**, **red**

ALGEBRA

6 Find the value of x and of y to make both equations true. Explain how you found your answers.

$$x + y = 20$$
$$y - x = 10$$

Name ______________________________

LEVEL B

NUMBERS AND OPERATIONS

1 Which number has the fewest prime factors? Explain your choice.

24 25 30

NUMBERS AND OPERATIONS

2 Is the sum of these numbers greater than or less than $\frac{1}{2}$? Explain how you know.

$$\frac{1}{4} + 0.3 = n$$

NUMBERS AND OPERATIONS

3 What percent of these are not round? How do you know?

MEASUREMENT

4 Ella needs two gallons of water to make lemonade. She only has an eight-ounce measuring cup. How many times will she have to fill the cup to make two gallons? How do you know?

DATA ANALYSIS AND PROBABILITY

5 Addison rolls a die 30 times. How many times do you think he will roll a four? Explain your answer.

GEOMETRY

6 Four quadrilaterals have the measurements shown. Which quadrilateral has both the smallest area and the greatest perimeter? How do you know?

A. 3" x 5" **C.** 1" x 10"

B. 4" x 4" **D.** 2" x 8"

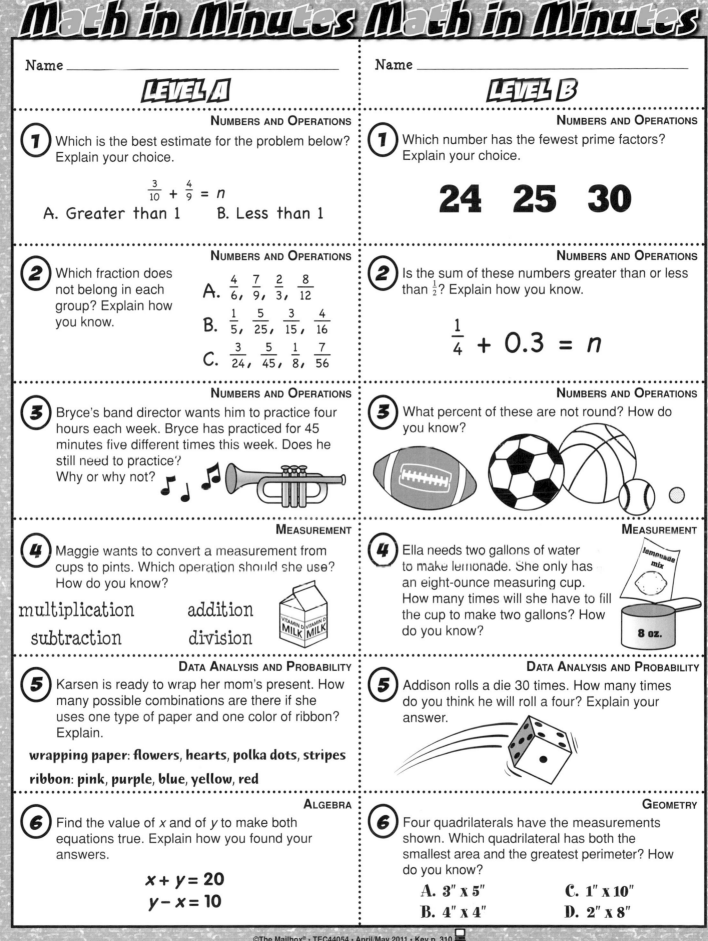

How to use: Copy the entire page, one level, or selected problems to distribute to students. When a student solves a problem, he shades its circle. If desired, display the page and have students solve the problems on their own papers.

Math in Minutes Math in Minutes

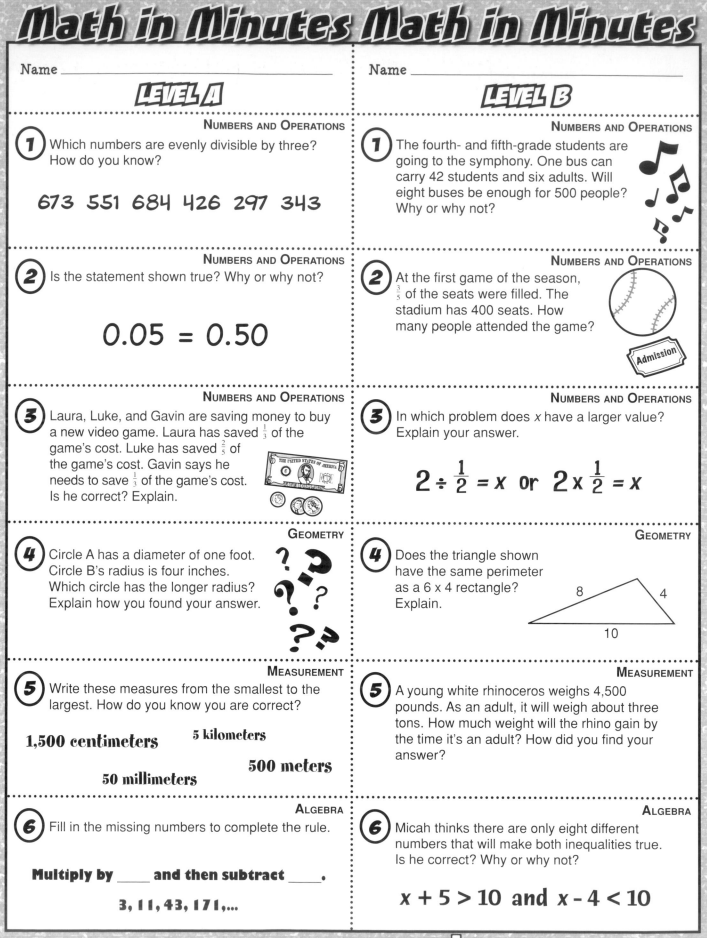

Name ____________________

LEVEL A

NUMBERS AND OPERATIONS

1 Which numbers are evenly divisible by three? How do you know?

673 551 684 426 297 343

NUMBERS AND OPERATIONS

2 Is the statement shown true? Why or why not?

$$0.05 = 0.50$$

NUMBERS AND OPERATIONS

3 Laura, Luke, and Gavin are saving money to buy a new video game. Laura has saved $\frac{1}{3}$ of the game's cost. Luke has saved $\frac{2}{5}$ of the game's cost. Gavin says he needs to save $\frac{1}{3}$ of the game's cost. Is he correct? Explain.

GEOMETRY

4 Circle A has a diameter of one foot. Circle B's radius is four inches. Which circle has the longer radius? Explain how you found your answer.

MEASUREMENT

5 Write these measures from the smallest to the largest. How do you know you are correct?

1,500 centimeters 5 kilometers

500 meters

50 millimeters

ALGEBRA

6 Fill in the missing numbers to complete the rule.

Multiply by ____ and then subtract ____.

3, 11, 43, 171,...

Name ____________________

LEVEL B

NUMBERS AND OPERATIONS

1 The fourth- and fifth-grade students are going to the symphony. One bus can carry 42 students and six adults. Will eight buses be enough for 500 people? Why or why not?

NUMBERS AND OPERATIONS

2 At the first game of the season, $\frac{3}{5}$ of the seats were filled. The stadium has 400 seats. How many people attended the game?

NUMBERS AND OPERATIONS

3 In which problem does x have a larger value? Explain your answer.

$$2 \div \frac{1}{2} = x \text{ or } 2 \times \frac{1}{2} = x$$

GEOMETRY

4 Does the triangle shown have the same perimeter as a 6 x 4 rectangle? Explain.

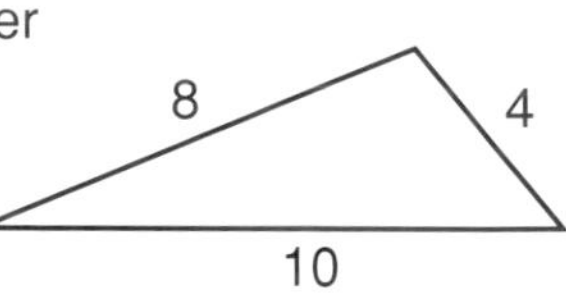

MEASUREMENT

5 A young white rhinoceros weighs 4,500 pounds. As an adult, it will weigh about three tons. How much weight will the rhino gain by the time it's an adult? How did you find your answer?

ALGEBRA

6 Micah thinks there are only eight different numbers that will make both inequalities true. Is he correct? Why or why not?

$$x + 5 > 10 \text{ and } x - 4 < 10$$

How to use: Copy the entire page, one level, or selected problems to distribute to students. When a student solves a problem, he shades its circle. If desired, display the page and have students solve the problems on their own papers.

MATH

MIND BUILDERS

MIND BUILDER 1

Draw a third arrow by adding only two straight lines.

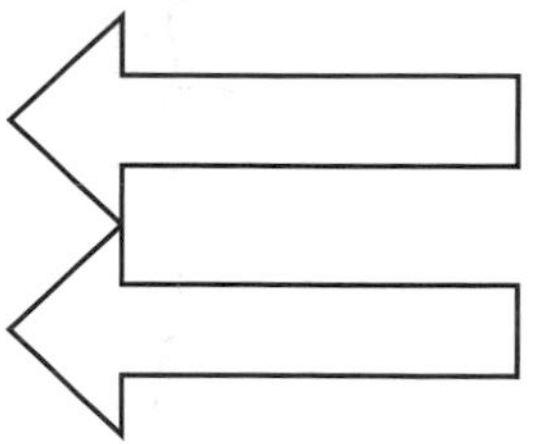

TEC44050

MIND BUILDER 2

Use each digit from 1 through 9 only once to write a problem with the sum of 99,999.

3 2 9 4 7 5 6 8 1

TEC44050

MIND BUILDER 3

How many cookies would you need to make a square that has four cookies on each side?

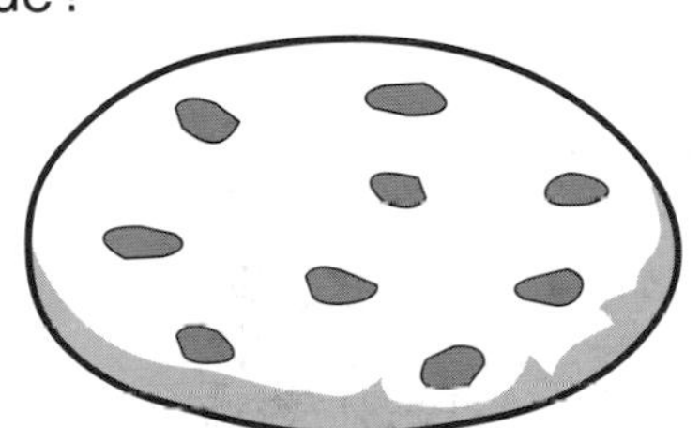

TEC44050

MIND BUILDER 4

Name two consecutive multiples of 3 whose sum is 45. Then list four more pairs of multiples of 3 whose sums are 45 but that are not consecutive.

? + ? = 45

TEC44050

MIND BUILDER 5

Draw a path from the left side of the maze to the right so that the numbers on each side of the line are prime numbers.

Start → (left) End (right)

6	2	21	14	8
5	3	13	15	29
7	9	19	11	17
20	10	23	7	25

TEC44050

MIND BUILDER 6

Complete each number pattern below and then describe it.

A. 14, 7, 10, 5, 8, ____, ____

B. 4, 12, 6, 18, 12, ____, ____

C. 5, 10, 20, 35, 55, ____, ____

TEC44050

MIND BUILDER 7

Using fractions, write an addition sentence to describe the shaded parts of this shape.

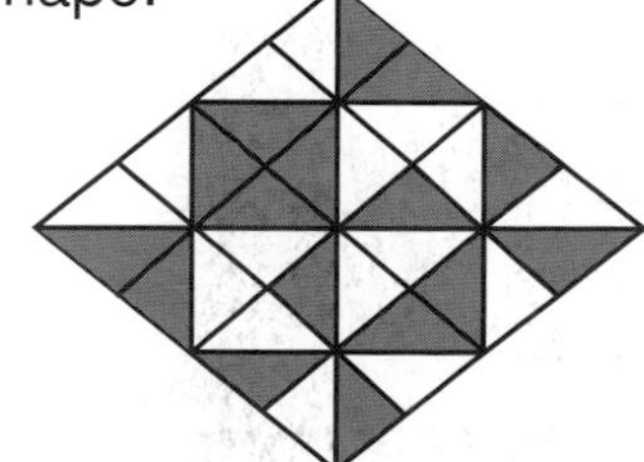

TEC44050

MIND BUILDER 8

If five follows eight and one follows nine, what follows seven? Hint: think about each number's word form.

8, 5
9, 1
7, ?

TEC44050

Note to the teacher: Give each student a copy of this page (or one card at a time) to work on during free time. Have the student solve the problems on a separate sheet of paper.

MATH

MIND BUILDERS

MIND BUILDER 1

Draw this diagram without lifting your pencil, crossing any lines, or tracing a line more than once.

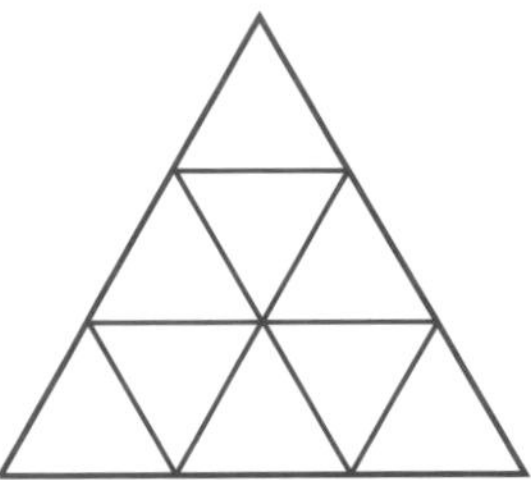

TEC44051

MIND BUILDER 2

How could you score 40 points on this dartboard with six darts? Seven darts? Eight darts? Nine darts?

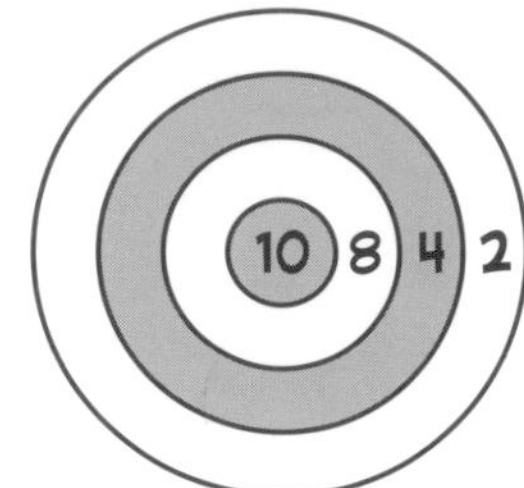

TEC44051

MIND BUILDER 3

Which of these will always result in an odd number?

A. odd number – odd number
B. even number – even number
C. odd number – even number
D. odd number × even number
E. odd number × odd number

TEC44051

MIND BUILDER 4

How many four-digit numbers can you make that fit this description?

The sum of all four digits is 8.
The tens digit is 2 more than the hundreds digit.

?, ? ? ?

TEC44051

MIND BUILDER 5

Imagine that an eight-ounce box of uncooked spaghetti has 270 pieces, and each piece is ten inches long. How many yards of spaghetti are in an eight-ounce box? How many yards are in a two-pound box?

TEC44051

MIND BUILDER 6

How many squares can you draw by connecting four dots at a time?

TEC44051

MIND BUILDER 7

Cory's crazy clock chimes once at 1:00 AM, twice at 2:00 AM, and so on. However, the clock chimes 13 times at 1:00 PM, 14 times at 2:00 PM, and so on. How many times will the clock chime in a 24-hour day?

TEC44051

MIND BUILDER 8

What is 3 times half the product of 6 and 12?

TEC44051

How to use: Give each student a copy of this page (or one card at a time) to work on during free time. Have the student solve the problems on a separate sheet of paper.

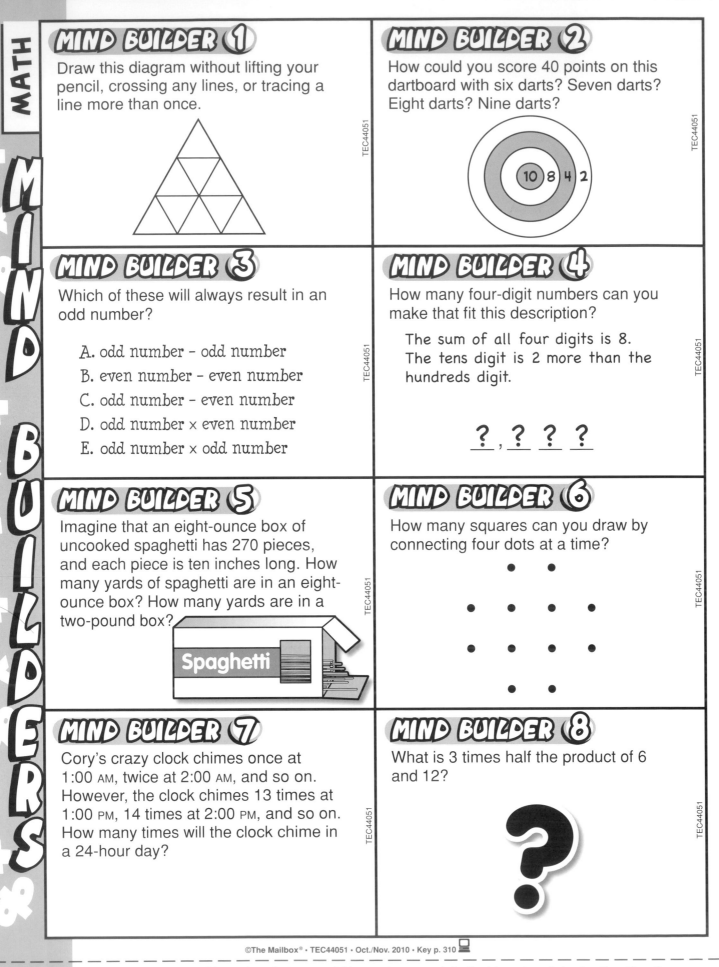

MIND BUILDERS

MIND BUILDER 1

The digit and comma sets below are part of a nine-digit number with a value less than 300,000,000. Arrange the sets to make the nine-digit number.

81, 9 **6, 8** **47** **29**

___ ___ ___, ___ ___ ___, ___ ___ ___

TEC44052

MIND BUILDER 2

The three glasses on the right are empty. The three glasses on the left are full. Imagine you can only touch one glass. How can you arrange the glasses so they alternate between full and empty? Explain.

TEC44052

MIND BUILDER 3

These math sentences are true. Which two-digit number can DC represent?

$$C + C + C + C + C + C = DC$$

$$C + D > 7$$

TEC44052

MIND BUILDER 4

One bottle of water costs $1.89. If the bottle costs $1.53, how much does the water cost? How much would the water to fill four bottles cost? How much would the four bottles cost without the water? How much would four bottles of water cost?

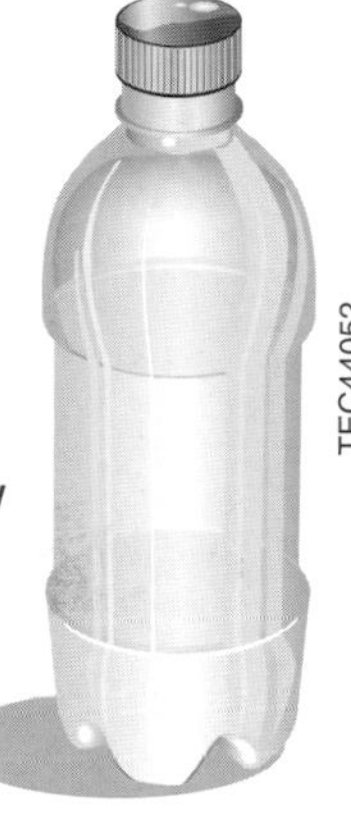

TEC44052

MIND BUILDER 5

Use the clues to find the value of the cash in my wallet.

Clue 1: I have 30 bills in my wallet. There are $1, $5, $10, and $20 dollar bills.
Clue 2: I have three more $1 bills than $5 dollar bills.
Clue 3: I have one more $10 bill than $20 dollar bills.
Clue 4: I have seven $20 bills.

How many $1, $5, $10, and $20 dollar bills do I have? What is the total value?

TEC44052

MIND BUILDER 6

Write your first and last name in block letters. Then draw lines of symmetry through the letters.

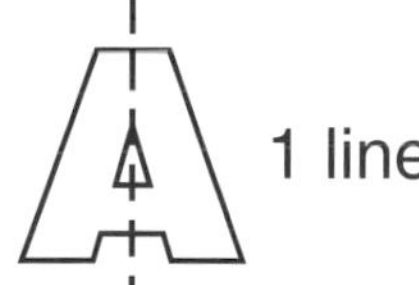

1 line

0 lines

TEC44052

MIND BUILDER 7

Write a fraction to represent each labeled section of the drawing.

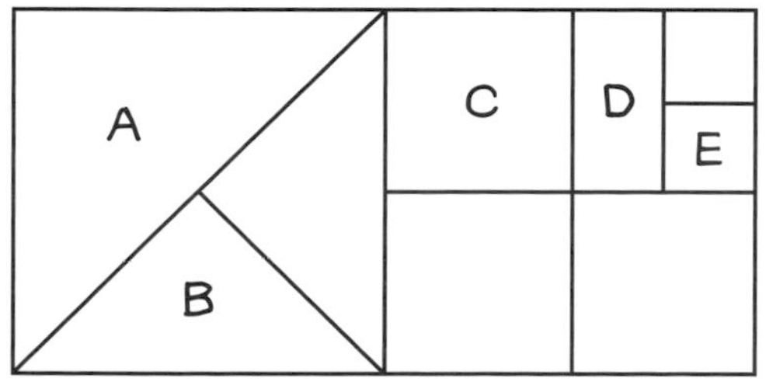

TEC44052

MIND BUILDER 8

A. If you cut two vertices off of a square, how many vertices will the shape have?
B. If you cut off each vertex of a triangle, how many vertices will the shape have?

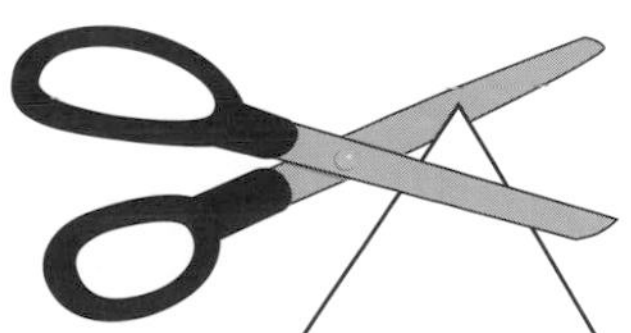

TEC44052

How to use: Give each student a copy of this page (or one card at a time) to work on during free time. Have the student solve the problems on a separate sheet of paper.

MIND BUILDERS

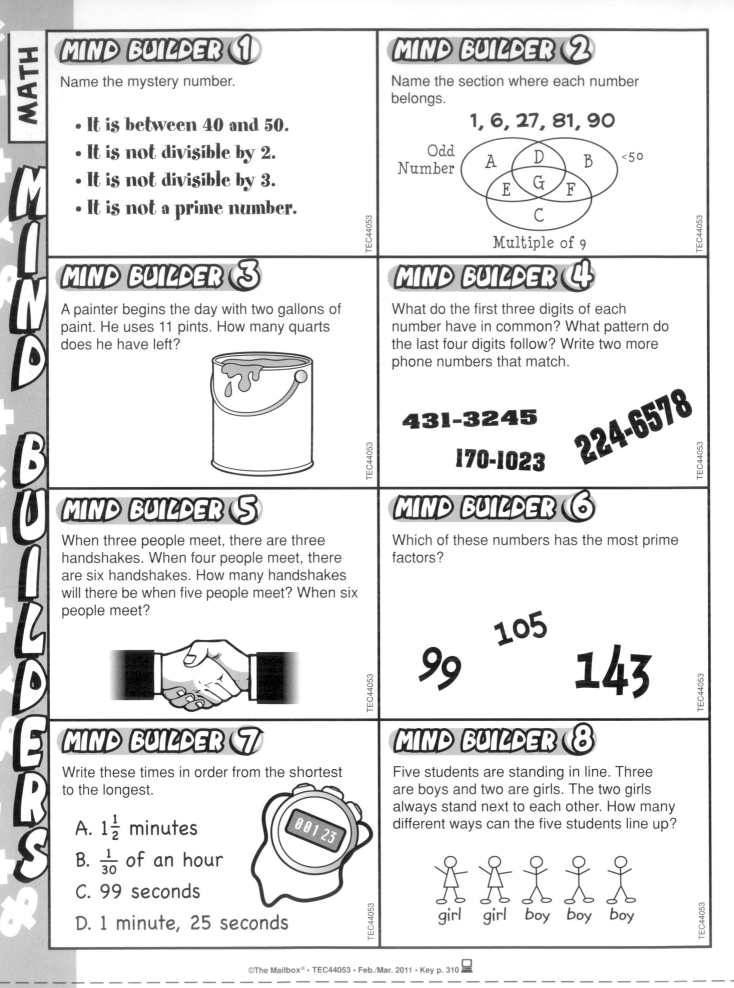

MIND BUILDER 1

Name the mystery number.

- It is between 40 and 50.
- It is not divisible by 2.
- It is not divisible by 3.
- It is not a prime number.

TEC44053

MIND BUILDER 2

Name the section where each number belongs.

1, 6, 27, 81, 90

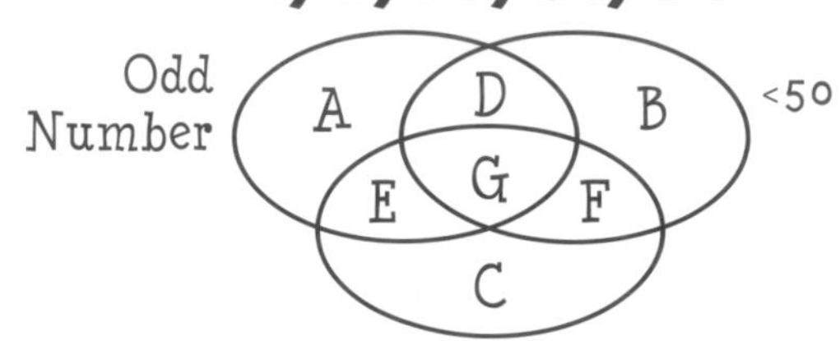

TEC44053

MIND BUILDER 3

A painter begins the day with two gallons of paint. He uses 11 pints. How many quarts does he have left?

TEC44053

MIND BUILDER 4

What do the first three digits of each number have in common? What pattern do the last four digits follow? Write two more phone numbers that match.

431-3245

170-1023

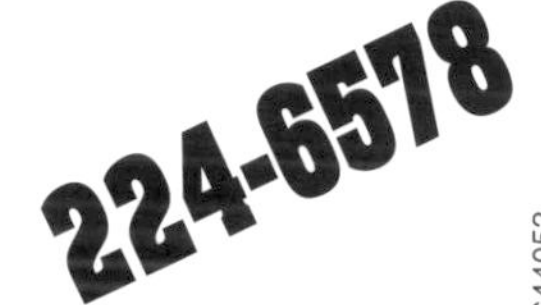

TEC44053

MIND BUILDER 5

When three people meet, there are three handshakes. When four people meet, there are six handshakes. How many handshakes will there be when five people meet? When six people meet?

TEC44053

MIND BUILDER 6

Which of these numbers has the most prime factors?

105

99 **143**

TEC44053

MIND BUILDER 7

Write these times in order from the shortest to the longest.

A. $1\frac{1}{2}$ minutes

B. $\frac{1}{30}$ of an hour

C. 99 seconds

D. 1 minute, 25 seconds

TEC44053

MIND BUILDER 8

Five students are standing in line. Three are boys and two are girls. The two girls always stand next to each other. How many different ways can the five students line up?

TEC44053

 How to use: Give each student a copy of this page (or one card at a time) to work on during free time.

MIND BUILDERS

MATH

MIND BUILDER 1

Which of these are true?

A. △△ = ○
B. □ = ○
C. ○○ = □
D. ○□ = △△△△△△

TEC44054

MIND BUILDER 2

On a map legend, a half inch represents 80 miles. The distance between two cities on the map is $2\frac{1}{4}$ inches. How many miles apart are the cities?

|——| = 80 miles

TEC44054

MIND BUILDER 3

Add +, –, x, ÷, or ( ) to make each sentence true.

A. 12 9 3 = 4
B. 4 5 3 6 = 2
C. 20 12 1 2 = 24

+ – × ( ) ÷

TEC44054

MIND BUILDER 4

Shape A is changed to shape B.

A. Does the perimeter change? Why or why not?
B. Does the area change? Why or why not?

A: 4 in. × 8 in.
B: 2 in. × 6 in.

TEC44054

MIND BUILDER 5

If you add the two digits of the mystery number and then multiply the sum by 7, the answer is the mystery number. Find three or more numbers that fit this pattern.

(? + ?) x 7 = ??

TEC44054

MIND BUILDER 6

How many phone calls are made when each of five friends shares one phone call with each of the others? Draw a diagram to find the answer. How many phone calls would be made with six friends? With seven friends?

TEC44054

MIND BUILDER 7

Anke and Amelia each have four coins. Altogether they have $1.06. Amelia's coins are worth $0.46 more than Anke's. What coins does each girl have?

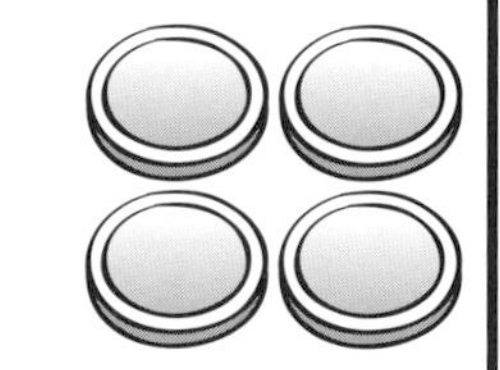

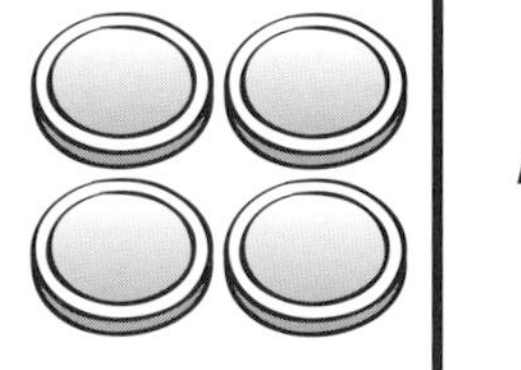
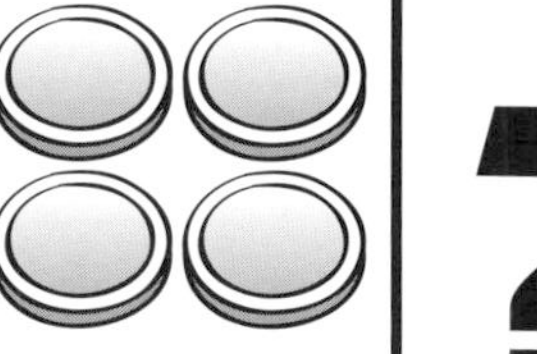

TEC44054

MIND BUILDER 8

Find five consecutive numbers that total 600. How did you find the numbers?

TEC44054

How to use: Display this page or give each student a copy of the page (or one card at a time) to work on during free time. Have the student solve the problems on a separate sheet of paper.

MIND BUILDERS

MATH

MIND BUILDER 1

Sue has a plan for every minute of the first day of summer vacation. She's going to spend exactly $\frac{1}{4}$ of the day at the pool, $\frac{1}{6}$ at the library, $\frac{1}{8}$ talking to her best friend, $\frac{1}{12}$ eating, and $\frac{1}{3}$ sleeping. Has Sue accounted for every minute of her first day? Why or why not?

TEC44054

MIND BUILDER 2

The sum of $1\frac{1}{5}$ and 6 has the same value as the product of $1\frac{1}{5}$ and 6. Find two more number pairs (whole numbers and mixed numbers) that follow the same pattern.

$$1\frac{1}{5} + 6 = 7\frac{1}{5}$$

$$1\frac{1}{5} \times 6 = 7\frac{1}{5}$$

TEC44054

MIND BUILDER 3

Find the sum of all the correctly spelled number words. Then subtract the total of all the incorrectly spelled words. What is the answer?

fourty
eighty
seventy
elevin
one hunderd
twelve
eighteen
fivteen
ninteen
twenty
forteen

TEC44054

MIND BUILDER 4

Tia's dog, Waggles, has ten puppies on June 1. Tia's mom says all the puppies must be sold by her father's birthday in 68 days. Tia's birthday is three months and six days prior to the puppies' birthday. Tia's mother celebrates her birthday fourteen weeks after Tia's. List the family's birthdays.

TEC44054

MIND BUILDER 5

This marble box has nine compartments. The center one is not used. Arrange marbles so there is at least one marble in each compartment and five marbles in each row.

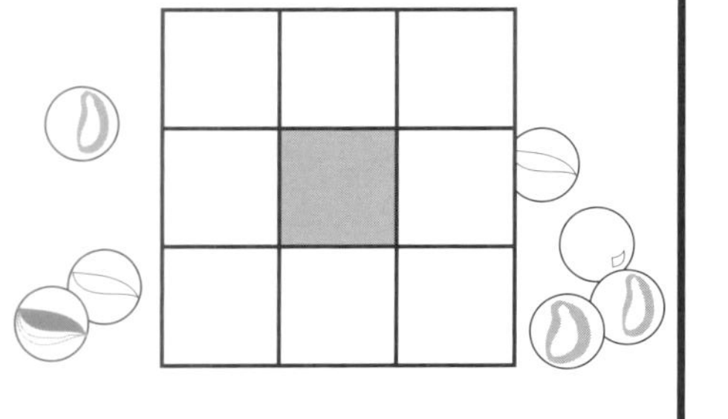

TEC44054

MIND BUILDER 6

Amy is 8 years younger than her sister Adalyn. Amy is 30 years older than her daughter Kelsie, who is 3 years older than her brother Kyle. If Kyle is 10, how old is Adalyn?

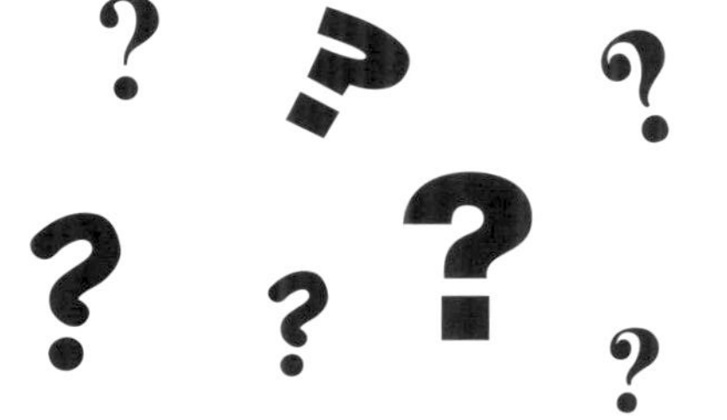

TEC44054

MIND BUILDER 7

Draw the next three shapes in this series.

TEC44054

MIND BUILDER 8

Eight woodchucks cleared a path in two days. The first day, they cleared 65,664 inches total. On the second day, they cleared another 51,456 inches. On average, how many feet did each woodchuck clear over the two days?

TEC44054

 Key p. 310

How to use: Display this page or give each student a copy of this page (or one card at a time) to work on during free time. Have the student solve the problems on a separate sheet of paper.

Seasonal

SKILLS FOR THE SEASON

Back to school

Name Kyle
Date 8-27

Sign Here, Please!

Find a different classmate to sign each square.
Each student may only sign your sheet twice.

I was born in a different state.
I am the oldest child in my family. Aiden
I can count to ten in a different language. Arianna
I can water-ski.
I can touch my tongue to my nose.
I do not like chocolate.
I know how to do martial arts.
I am an only child. Lila
I grew up in this town. Gavin
I can text really fast.
I can flip off the diving board.
My family has a wacky pet.
I play two different sports.
I have eaten sushi.
I am left-handed. Isiah
I have traveled to a different state.
I like broccoli.
I am double-jointed. Sophia
My birthday is in the summer.
I have a cool nickname.

Sign Here, Please!

Back-to-school icebreaker

Help your students get to know one another with a fresh take on this classic icebreaker. Give each child a copy of page 180. Then have students ask classmates to sign the squares that describe them. To be sure students interact with as many classmates as possible, stipulate that each child may sign only one or two spaces per sheet.

Ann Fisher, Toledo, OH

Math About Me

Mixed computation

Start the year off with mathematical thinking by having each student choose five numbers that tell something important about her. Next, guide the student to create a banner like the one shown. Have the child use each of her numbers as the solution to a math problem and then explain the number's significance. Encourage students to vary the operations to include addition, subtraction, multiplication, and division. Then post students' work on a board titled "Math About Us!"

Johanna Funke, Eden Elementary, Eden, NY

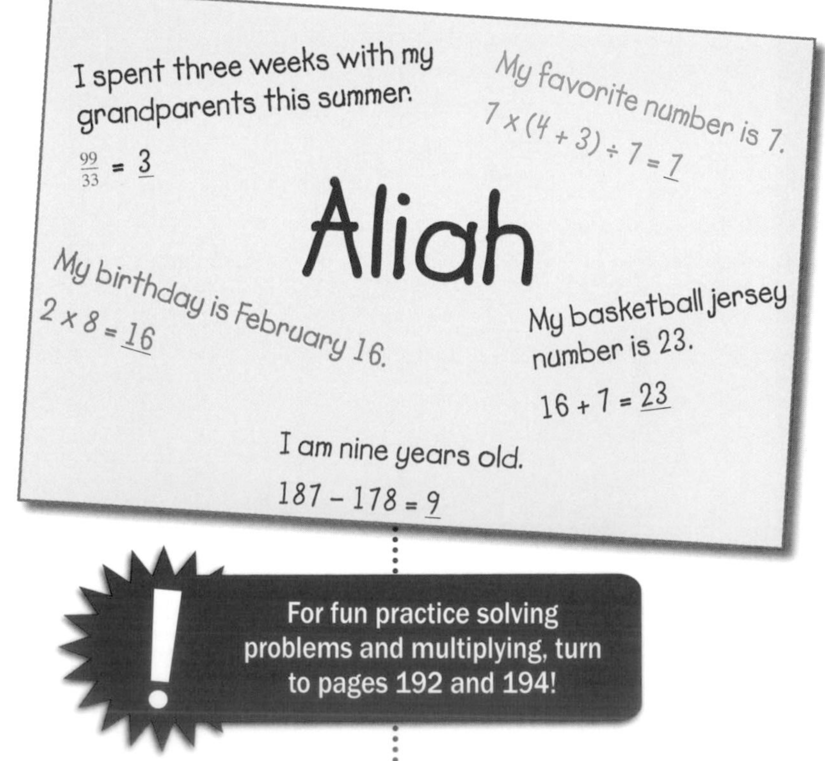

For fun practice solving problems and multiplying, turn to pages 192 and 194!

A Sneak Peek

Making predictions

Capitalize on students' curiosity about your life outside of school to build excitement for the new school year! In advance, post a list of questions about yourself, such as the ones shown. Next, challenge each child to guess and record the answer to each question. Then have students share several predictions before you reveal each answer. Your class will love learning all about you!

Who Is Ms. Jones?

1. What is my middle name?
2. Where was I born?
3. How many brothers and/or sisters do I have?
4. Do I have any children? If so, how old are they?
5. If I could only eat one food for a week, what would I choose?
6. What kind of music do I listen to when I'm driving?
7. Do I have a favorite sports team? If so, which team?
8. Do I have any pets at home? If so, what?
9. What is my favorite way to spend free time?
10. What do I love most about being a teacher?

How Time Flies!

Fractions

Here's a fun idea for reinforcing fraction skills in just minutes a day. Each morning, announce the number of days you've been in school. Then guide students to name the day as a fraction of the full school year, reducing it as necessary. If desired, celebrate certain fractions of the year, such as the half-year mark, by giving each student half a treat or cutting a homework assignment in half!

Mary Brenner, Oak Park Elementary, Ocean Springs, MS
Brooke Blake, Wentworth Elementary, Wentworth, NH

Centered on Amendments

Bill of Rights

Commemorate Constitution Week (September 17–23) with this Bill of Rights learning center. To prepare, copy and cut apart the cards and questions from page 181. Then fold the answer key section behind the questions as shown. At the center, a student matches each amendment card with its description. Next, he checks the key and reorders any matches as necessary. Then the child answers each question, citing specific amendments in his response.

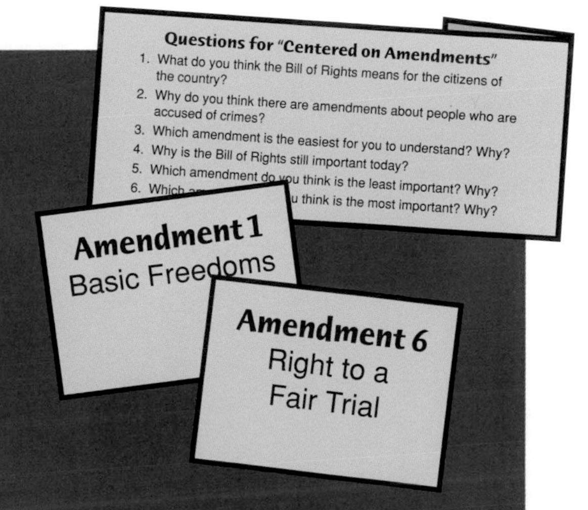

Questions for "Centered on Amendments"
1. What do you think the Bill of Rights means for the citizens of the country?
2. Why do you think there are amendments about people who are accused of crimes?
3. Which amendment is the easiest for you to understand? Why?
4. Why is the Bill of Rights still important today?
5. Which amendment do you think is the least important? Why?
6. Which
u think is the most important? Why?
Amendment 1
Basic Freedoms
Amendment 6
Right to a
Fair Trial

SKILLS FOR THE SEASON

Fall Banners

Measurement to ⅛-inch

Celebrate fall with this hands-on idea! Display the chart shown. Then guide each student to divide and illustrate a 4-inch x 20-inch strip of bulletin board paper according to the displayed directions. Finally, post students' work on a board titled "Fall Favorites."

Section Length	Illustration
1¼ in.	Write your name in fall colors.
3⅛ in.	Draw a colorful fall leaf.
1⅜ in.	Write about something you do with fall leaves.
½ in.	Color the space a solid fall color.
⅞ in.	Draw a design of red, orange, and yellow leaves.
1¼ in.	Write about something else you do with fall leaves.
¾ in.	Write the date fall begins *(September 22, 2010)*.
1⅞ in.	Draw a colorful fall leaf.
¼ in.	Color the space a solid fall color.
2⅝ in.	Draw a picture of your favorite fall holiday.
⅛ in.	Color the space a solid fall color.
1⅜ in.	Write about a person for whom you're thankful.
2⅝ in.	Draw a colorful fall leaf.
⅞ in.	Draw a thing for which you're thankful.
1¼ in.	Write "Autumn" in fall colors.

"Will You Walk Into My Parlor?"

Persuasive writing

To introduce this seasonal activity, read aloud the first few stanzas of the poem "The Spider and the Fly" by Mary Howitt. Next, challenge each student to write a letter from the spider to the fly that will convince the fly to land on the spider's sticky web. Have each student write her final copy on a spider-shaped cutout. Then post students' work on a bulletin board decorated with a yarn web and titled "A Web of Persuasion."

Annette Bright, Emerson School, Kansas City, KS

Count Angula
Measuring angles

For fun protractor practice, give each student a copy of page 182 and a protractor. Then guide the child to find at least 15 different angles on Count Angula. Have the student draw each angle's arc and record its measurement. When the child finishes, challenge her to draw another seasonal character with ten or more different angles. As time allows, have students trade drawings and measure the angles in each other's work.

Lora Earnest, Wapello, IA

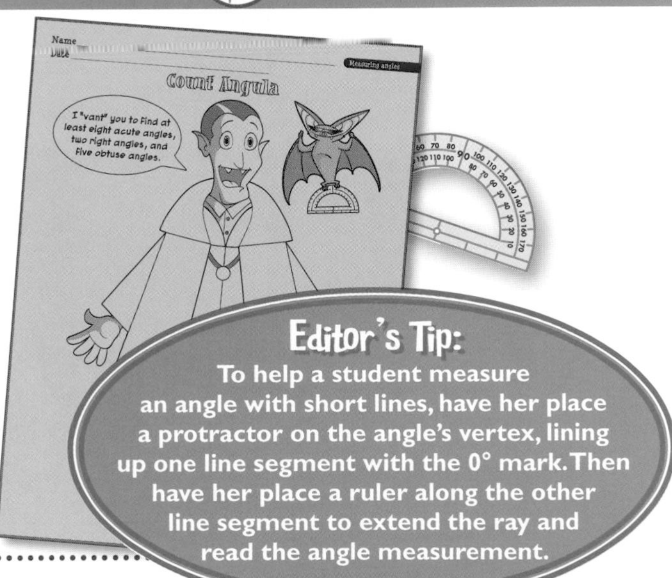

Editor's Tip: To help a student measure an angle with short lines, have her place a protractor on the angle's vertex, lining up one line segment with the 0° mark. Then have her place a ruler along the other line segment to extend the ray and read the angle measurement.

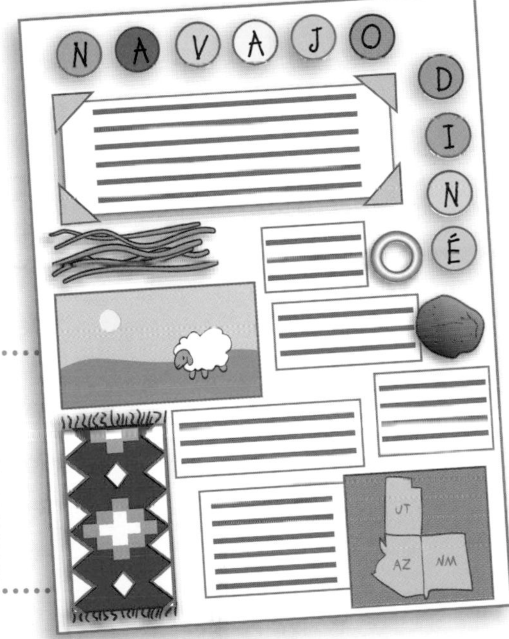

Bits and Pieces
Research

Research Topics	
homes	trade
tools	family life
food	hunting
clothing	farming
arts and crafts	

Commemorate National American Indian Heritage Month (November) with this partner project. First, assign each pair of students a Native American group that lives or lived in your state or region. Next, guide the duo to find information on three or more of the topics shown. Then have the twosome use scrapbooking techniques to create a page displaying its work. The partners might include a symbolic border or shapes, hand-drawn maps, student-made artifacts, or actual objects to give their report dimension. If desired, bind students' work in a class book titled "A Native American Scrapbook."

Marie E. Cecchini, West Dundee, IL

"Verb-ucopia"
Types of verbs

Give students artful parts-of-speech practice with this classic Thanksgiving symbol. Have each child cut out and color the cornucopia from a copy of page 183. Next, designate a different fall vegetable for each verb type. Have each child make matching vegetable-shaped cutouts and list verb examples on each one. Then have the student glue his vegetables onto his cornucopia. For a seasonal display, post students' work on a board titled "'Verb-ucopia'—An Abundance of Verbs."

Cathy Brajuha and Diane Meyer, Nathan Hale Middle School, Northvale, NJ

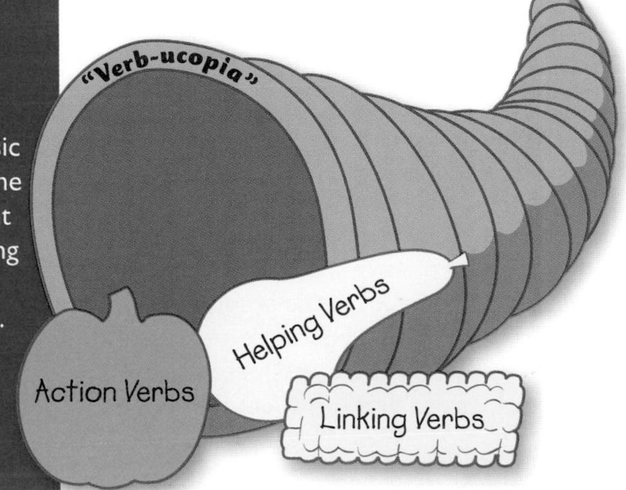

SKILLS FOR THE SEASON

"State-ly" Snowmen

State research

These cool decorations publicize resources and products found, grown, or made in your state. First, have each small group research your state's natural resources and products. Next, have the students make a paper snowman embellished with actual or paper versions of the resources and products from your state. Then have each group describe its creation from the snowman's point of view. If desired, display students' work on a board titled "'State-ly' Snowmen."

Julie Baker, West Boyd Elementary, Butte, NE

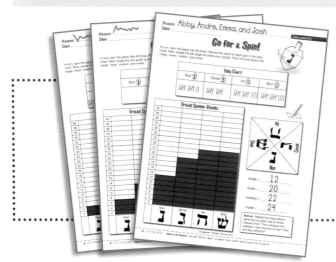

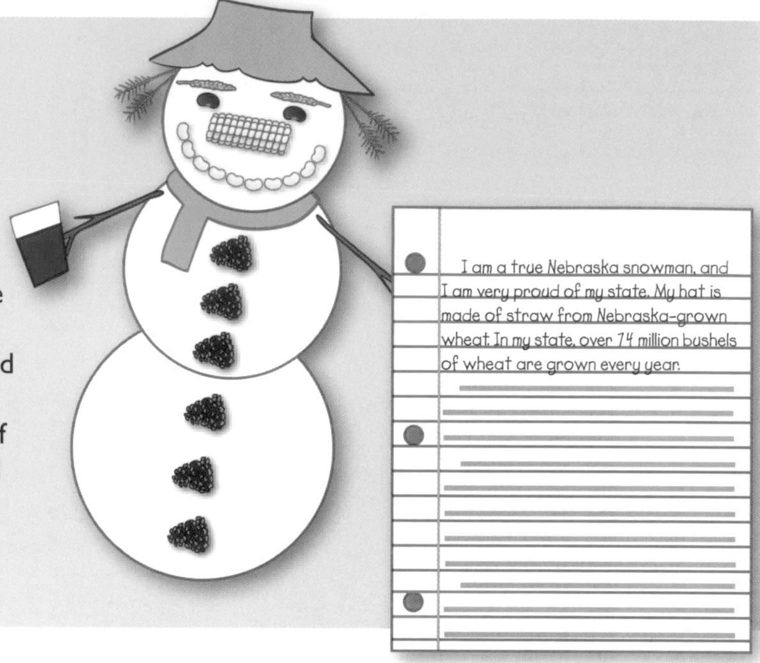

I am a true Nebraska snowman, and
I am very proud of my state. My hat is
made of straw from Nebraska-grown
wheat. In my state, over 74 million bushels
of wheat are grown every year.

Go for a Spin!

Making a bar graph, calculating statistics

Highlight data analysis with this Hanukkah-related activity. Guide each pair of students to follow the directions on a copy of page 184. Next, have each duo work with another twosome to combine their data and calculate the new range, mean, median, and mode on another copy of page 184. Then compare and discuss students' results.

Santa "Cause"

Cause and effect

Here's a quick idea that starts with brainstorming silly situations in which Santa might find himself. After coming up with several silly situations, have each child write four different cause-and-effect statements about Santa Claus, his North Pole toy shop, elves, reindeer, or other Christmas character. Next, have the student fold a sheet of paper into four sections and illustrate one statement in each box. Then have the child record the matching sentence, writing the cause in green and the effect in red.

Teresa Vilfer-Snyder, Fredericktown Intermediate, Fredericktown, OH

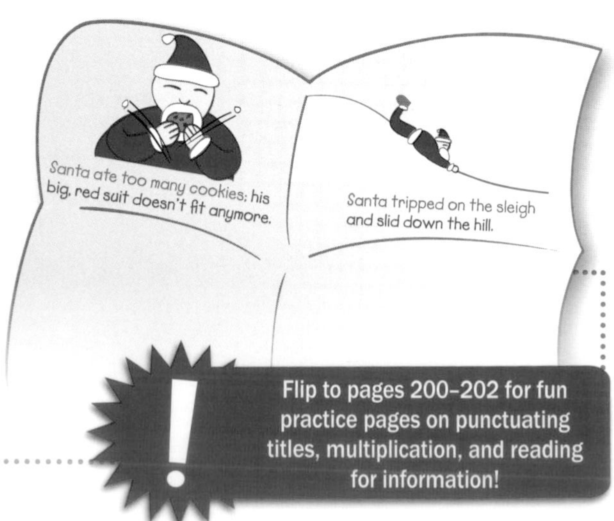

Santa ate too many cookies; his big, red suit doesn't fit anymore.
Santa tripped on the sleigh and slid down the hill.

Flip to pages 200–202 for fun practice pages on punctuating titles, multiplication, and reading for information!

Wintry Grids

Ordered pairs

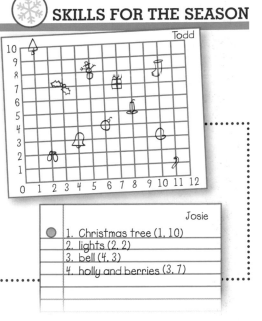

For seasonal math practice, give each student a sheet of graph paper. Guide the child to draw and label the *x*- and *y*-axes. Next, have the student draw 12 winter or holiday symbols she associates with the season at 12 different points. Then, on lined paper, have the child list each symbol and its coordinates. After each student finishes, she trades her graph with a partner and lists the name and coordinates for each of the symbols her partner drew. Finally, students return their papers and check each other's work.

Leigh Anne Newsom, Cedar Road Elementary, Chesapeake, VA

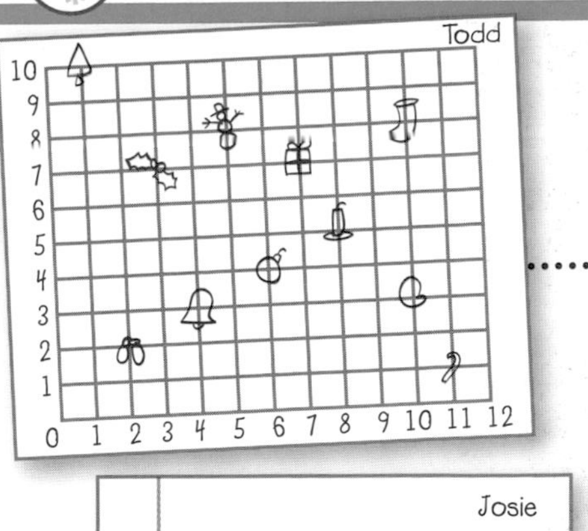

Kwanzaa Candles

Narrative writing

Highlight the principles of Kwanzaa with this thought-provoking idea. To begin, review the seven principles with students. Then guide each child to write a story in which the main character faces a problem and then solves it by demonstrating one or more of the principles. To publish his work, have the student follow the directions shown. Then have students set their candles on a table or shelf alongside a card titled "Lighting the Way With Kwanzaa's Principles."

Materials for each student: small, clean cardboard tube; cupcake liner; access to yellow, red, green, and black construction paper; lined paper; scissors; stapler; glue

Steps:

1. Cut the lined paper in half, making two 4" x 10½" pages. Write your story's final draft on the pages.
2. Staple the pages of your story together in the top left corner. Then make a yellow flame-shaped cutout and staple it to the upper left edge of your papers.
3. Cover a cardboard tube with red, black, or green construction paper. Then glue the bottom of your tube inside a cupcake liner.
4. Roll up your story and slide it into the tube so the flame shows at the top.

Amy Barsanti, Pines Elementary, Plymouth, NC

New Year—New Goals

Setting goals

Start off the New Year on a positive note with this idea! First, guide each student to set five goals for the rest of the school year. Next, use an overhead projector to project the silhouette of each student's head onto construction paper and trace it in pencil. Then have the child cut out her silhouette and write her goals on it. Post students' work on a board titled "New Year—New Goals."

Shanna Beber, Laplace Elementary, Laplace, LA

It's a Fact!

Research, problem solving

Commemorate National Black History Month with this whole-class activity. First, guide each student to research a famous African American and create a story problem about his subject. (Remind the child to include at least one distracter in his problem.) Have the student write his problem on one side of an index card and jot the answer on the other side. To check their work, have students trade cards with partners and solve each other's problems. Then collect the cards, punch holes in them, and slide them onto a loose-leaf ring. Keep the ring handy and start each February math session with an interesting story problem about a famous African American.

Leigh Anne Newsom, Chittum Elementary, Chesapeake, VA

Serena Williams was born in 1981. She won the U.S. Open in 1999. Since 1999, Serena has won 22 grand slam tennis matches. In 2002, Serena was ranked as the number one female tennis player in the world. What is the average number of grand slam tennis matches Serena has won each year since 1999?

Serena has won an average of 1.8 grand slam matches each year since 1999.

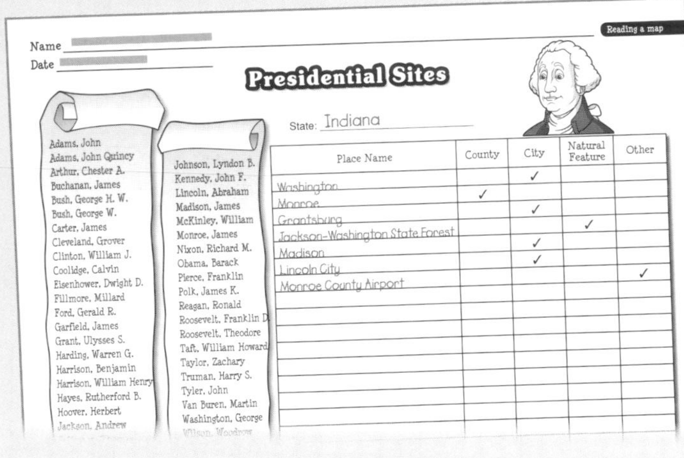

Name

Date

Reading a map

Presidential Sites

Adams, John
Adams, John Quincy
Arthur, Chester A.
Buchanan, James
Bush, George H. W.
Bush, George W.
Carter, James
Cleveland, Grover
Clinton, William J.
Coolidge, Calvin
Eisenhower, Dwight D.
Fillmore, Millard
Ford, Gerald R.
Garfield, James
Grant, Ulysses S.
Harding, Warren G.
Harrison, Benjamin
Harrison, William Henry
Hayes, Rutherford B.
Hoover, Herbert
Jackson, Andrew

Johnson, Lyndon B.
Kennedy, John F.
Lincoln, Abraham
Madison, James
McKinley, William
Monroe, James
Nixon, Richard M.
Obama, Barack
Pierce, Franklin
Polk, James K.
Reagan, Ronald
Roosevelt, Franklin D.
Roosevelt, Theodore
Taft, William Howard
Taylor, Zachary
Truman, Harry S.
Tyler, John
Van Buren, Martin
Washington, George
Wilson, Woodrow

State: Indiana

Place Name	County	City	Natural Feature	Other
Washington		✓		
Monroe	✓			
Grantsburg		✓		
Jackson-Washington State Forest			✓	
Madison		✓		
Lincoln City		✓		
Monroe County Airport				✓

Executive Sites

Reading a map

For this presidential celebration, stock a center with a United States atlas and 50 copies of page 185. Have each pair of students label a page with a state name. Then lead the partners to study the state's map. Each time they find a county, city, natural feature, or other place named after a president, they record the name and check the appropriate column. Extend the activity by challenging students to study inset city maps and find streets with presidential names.

Sweet Sums

Adding fractions, simplest form

Grab a bag of conversation-heart candy and give each child a handful for this fun idea! Have each student write a fraction to describe each color of her hearts. Then guide each student and a partner to add their fractions and write the sums in simplest form. Next, have students repeat the activity with a small group. Finally, guide students to add all the groups' fractions to describe the class's candy heart colors.

Rachel Pepe, River Place Elementary, Austin, TX

Palatable Produce

Plants, categorizing foods

Here's a science exploration that's perfect for National Nutrition Month (March). Copy and cut apart the food cards from page 186. Then list on the board the plant parts shown. Next, divide the class into two teams. In turn, have a student from each team draw a card and tape it under one of the categories. If the student is correct, the team earns a point. If she is incorrect, have her return the card to the pile. Repeat until all the cards have been correctly sorted. Then count up the points to see which team really knows its plants!

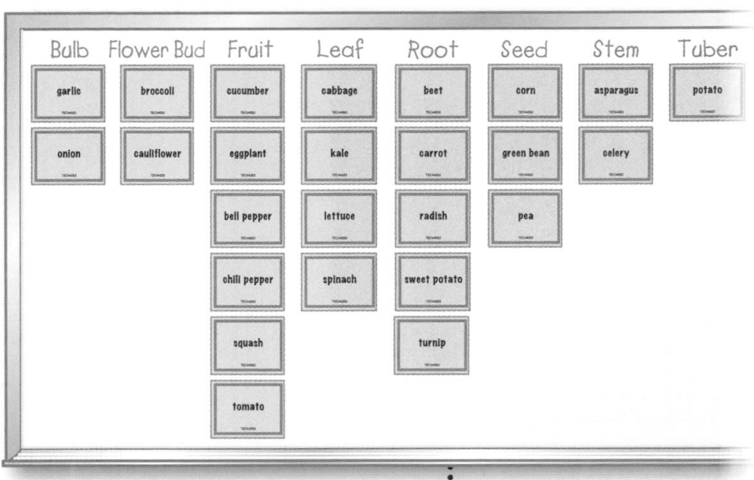

Bulb
garlic
onion
Flower Bud
broccoli
cauliflower
Fruit
cucumber
eggplant
bell pepper
chili pepper
squash
tomato
Leaf
cabbage
kale
lettuce
spinach
Root
beet
carrot
radish
sweet potato
turnip
Seed
corn
green bean
pea
Stem
asparagus
celery
Tuber
potato

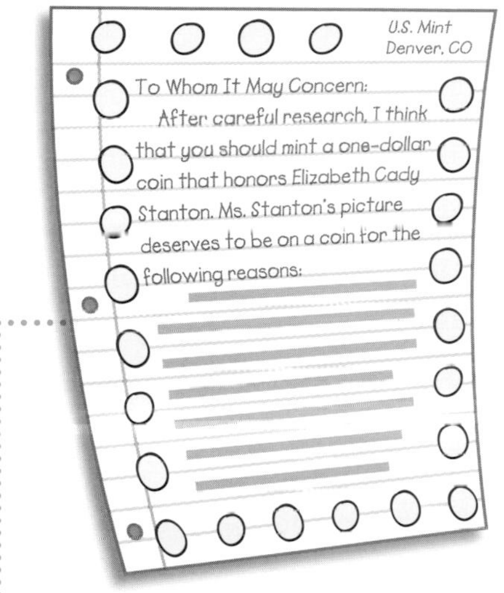

Heads—She Wins!

Writing a persuasive letter

For this Women's History Month activity, brainstorm with the class a list of important or famous women. Next, explain that Susan B. Anthony, an early leader of the women's rights movement, was the first woman to be pictured on a United States coin. Then have each student choose a woman from the brainstormed list and draft a letter that persuades a U.S. mint (in Denver, Colorado; Philadelphia, Pennsylvania; San Francisco, California; or West Point, New York) to create a coin that honors the woman.

Marie E. Cecchini, West Dundee, IL

Leprechaun Logic

Multiplying fractions, mixed numbers

Introduce this leprechaun-themed activity a few days before St. Patrick's Day. Display the recipe shown (without the items in parenthesis) and explain that it serves four leprechauns. Next, challenge each student to figure out how many batches a class of 15 leprechaun students would need. Then guide him to adjust the recipe accordingly. Repeat with several different-size classes. Finally, have students adjust the recipe for the number of students in your class. Then announce the items in parenthesis and have student volunteers bring in the ingredients for a fun St. Patrick's Day snack.

Idy Butz, Ruth Hoppin Elementary, Three Rivers, MI

Leprechaun Nibbles

$\frac{1}{3}$ cup good luck (cereal with shamrock shapes)
$\frac{1}{2}$ cup gold nuggets (popcorn)
$\frac{3}{4}$ cup gold coins (vanilla wafers)
$\frac{1}{4}$ cup rainbow wishes (jelly beans)
$\frac{1}{8}$ cup leprechaun potatoes (peanuts)
Mix together and enjoy.
Serves four leprechauns.

For super seasonal skill builders, flip to pages 204–206.

SKILLS FOR THE SEASON

Water Woes
Water pollution, inquiry

For this Earth Day exploration, display a clear cup of water. Then add a drop of food coloring (pollution) and discuss the results with students. *(The food coloring quickly tints, or pollutes, the clear water.)* Next, provide materials such as those shown and challenge each small group of students to invent a method for clearing the water of its pollution. Then give each group a clear cup of water and add a drop of food coloring. Have the students test their idea, record its results, and draw a conclusion. Follow up with a discussion about water pollution and the challenge of cleaning it up.

Heidi Kobs, Scales Technology Academy, Tempe, AZ

tissues
cotton balls
eyedroppers
spoons
scraps of fabric
hand sanitizer
paper towels
toothbrushes
felt
cardboard
yarn
foil
plastic wrap
clay
glue

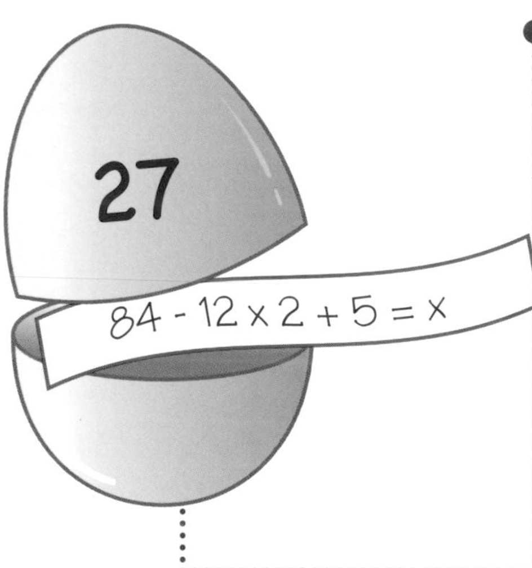

"Eggs-tra" Practice!
Mixed review

To prepare this springtime review, number a plastic egg for each student in your class. Next, program the same number of paper strips with questions from a current topic, math problems, or vocabulary words. Put each strip in a different plastic egg and tuck the eggs in classroom nooks. Then have each child number a sheet of paper to match the number of eggs and go on a hunt. When a student finds an egg, he opens it and solves the problem, answers the question, or defines the word on the appropriately numbered line. Then he puts the strip back in the egg, returns the egg to its niche, and hunts for another one.

Sherrie McWhorter, Hephzibah Elementary, Hephzibah, GA

A Lyrical Quest
Rhyme schemes

In honor of National Poetry Month (April), have students go on a rhyme scheme scavenger hunt. In advance, gather an assortment of poetry books. Then guide students to recite a nursery rhyme and identify its rhyming words. Next, name the rhyme scheme. *(Give each set of rhyming lines a different letter of the alphabet.)* Repeat with other nursery rhymes before challenging each student to find poems that match the rhyme schemes on a copy of page 187.

"Twinkle, Twinkle, Little Star"

Twinkle, twinkle, little star, ***a***
How I wonder what you are! ***a***
Up above the world, so high, ***b***
Like a diamond in the sky. ***b***

The rhyme scheme is *aabb*.

Going Buggy?

Conducting a survey, data analysis

There's a springtime "ewww!" factor built right into this activity! Have each student survey 12 people—not including her classmates—using a copy of page 188 to find out how they feel about certain bugs. Next, have the child analyze her results and create a graph as guided on the page. Then have each student add her results to a class tally chart. Finally, guide small groups of students to analyze the data and create a different type of graph.

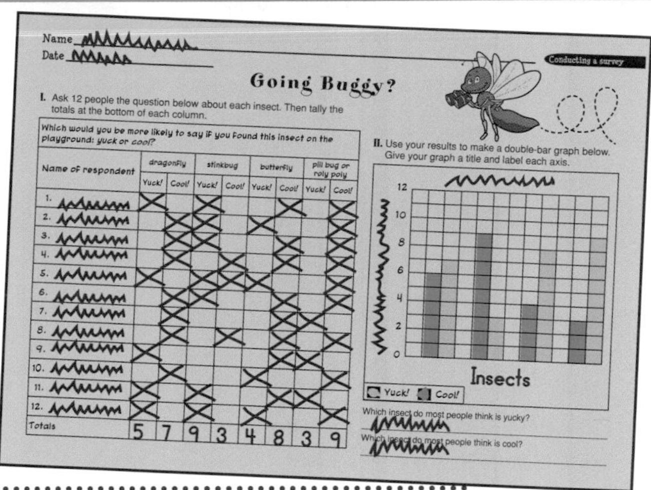

Name

Date

Conducting a survey

Going Buggy?

I. Ask 12 people the question below about each insect. Then tally the totals at the bottom of each column.

Which would you be more likely to say if you found this insect on the playground: yuck or cool?

Name of respondent	dragonfly		stinkbug		butterfly		pill bug or roly poly	
	Yuck!	Cool!	Yuck!	Cool!	Yuck!	Cool!	Yuck!	Cool!
1.								
2.								
3.								
4.								
5.								
6.								
7.								
8.								
9.								
10.								
11.								
12.								
Totals	5	7	9	3	4	8	3	9

II. Use your results to make a double-bar graph below. Give your graph a title and label each axis.

12
10
8
6
4
2
0
Insects
Yuck! Cool!

Which insect do most people think is yucky?

Which insect do most people think is cool?

Cinco de Mayo

Problem solving

To give students festive math practice, program numbered sombrero shapes with story problems. On matching numbered maraca shapes, jot the answers. Then put the shapes in two separate envelopes. A student draws a sombrero, solves the problem, and then finds the matching maraca to check his work. (For a fun display, post the sombreros and an envelope with the maracas on a board titled *¡Viva Matemáticas!*)

Lynn Barbieri, Center Elementary, Pittsburgh, PA

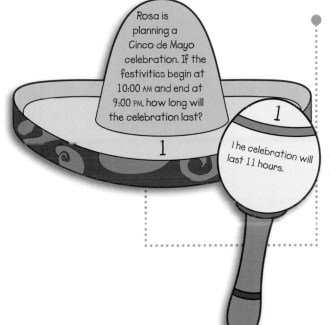

Rosa is planning a Cinco de Mayo celebration. If the festivities begin at 10:00 AM and end at 9:00 PM, how long will the celebration last?

1

1

The celebration will last 11 hours.

Memory Lane

Mother's Day

Here's a fun twist on the handprint cards young children often make for their moms. First, have each student trace her hand on a sheet of unlined paper and decorate the hand shape. Next, display the poem shown and read it aloud with students. Then have each child copy the poem beside her hand shape, roll up the page, tie it with a piece of string or ribbon, and take the scroll home for Mother's Day. What a fun surprise for moms or other important adults!

Drusilla Ferguson, Bluewell Elementary, Bluefield, WV

My Handprint

It seems like only yesterday
That I was starting school.
The thought of leaving home
Made me cry a pool.

Well, I'm growing older.
Tiny handprints are no more.
Instead of toy trucks and dolls,
It's time for friends, phones, and malls!

So here's another handprint.
Now, don't you shed a tear!
Happy Mother's Day 2010
From me in my fifth-grade year!

SKILLS FOR THE SEASON

On the Road to Success
End of the year

This end-of-the year activity turns into a fun back-to-school display! To begin, brainstorm with students a list of different road signs. Then have each child choose one and think about how it can be used to give next year's students advice. Next, have the student draw the sign on construction paper, add his suggestion, and then cut out the shape. Post the signs on a board titled "On the Road to Success." After the last day of school, cover the board for the summer. When you return to school in the fall, simply remove the cover. What a great way to welcome your new students!

Lisa Cullen, Parkview Elementary, Rosemount, MN

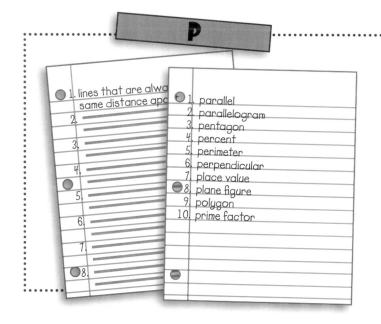

Famous Last Words
Vocabulary

Here's a great idea for reviewing the vocabulary from any subject. Write the letters of the alphabet except *J*, *K*, *Q*, *X*, *Y*, and *Z* on separate paper strips. Have each child draw a strip and then find ten important words in his textbook that begin with that letter. Next, guide the student to write the definition of each word without naming it and record the words on a separate paper to use as a key. Collect students' work and redistribute the papers, making sure each child has a list other than his own. Then have each student read the definitions and identify the words. Finally, have students return the papers to their originators and check each other's work.

Ending the Year on a Positive Note
End of the year, following directions

For this year-end project, display a copy of page 189 and guide each student to follow the directions on the page. Then have each child take her work home to share with her family.

adapted from an idea by Ann E. Fisher, Toledo, OH

Hip, Hop
Measurement

Celebrate Sports America Kids Month (June) with this active idea! Have each pair of students make a five-column chart labeled as shown. Next, give each duo a piece of chalk and a measuring tape, ruler, or yardstick. Then take students outside. Have each pair draw a chalk starting line. For each hopping event, have one student in each pair stand with his toes touching the line. The child takes one hop and his partner measures the distance from the starting line to the heel of the shoe closer to the line. The partner records the measurement and then takes a turn hopping. When everyone has completed all four events, have students share their measurements to see who hopped the greatest distance in each event.

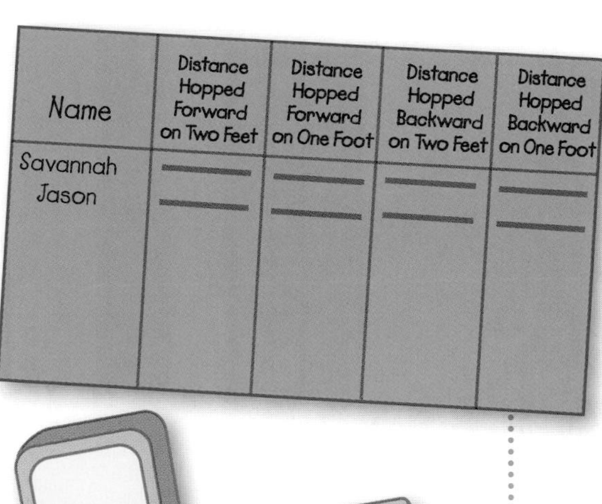

Name	Distance Hopped Forward on Two Feet	Distance Hopped Forward on One Foot	Distance Hopped Backward on Two Feet	Distance Hopped Backward on One Foot
Savannah				
Jason				

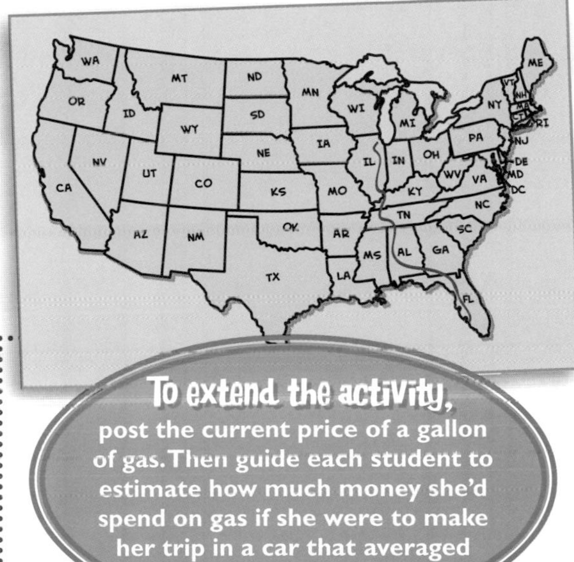

To extend the activity, post the current price of a gallon of gas. Then guide each student to estimate how much money she'd spend on gas if she were to make her trip in a car that averaged 25 miles per gallon.

Summer Agenda
Geography, using map scale

Capitalize on your students' excitement about summer vacation and stretch their map skills! Have each child choose a place in the country that she would love to visit. Then guide the student to plot her route on a map and use the scale to calculate the distance to her destination. Next, guide the child to choose three tourist attractions she could visit along the way. Finally, have the student create an itinerary that lists her destination, each sightseeing stop she would make, and the total miles she would travel. As time allows, display a map of the country and have each child share her fantasy trip.

Marie E. Cecchini, West Dundee, IL

Summer Science Challenge
Life science

Here's an idea that's sure to build students' awareness of the world around them. Give each child a copy of the grid on page 190 and challenge him to find everything listed on the page during his summer vacation. Each time the student observes or reads about an item, he checks and dates the appropriate box, trying to check all the spaces on the page. If desired, offer students small prizes for each completed grid they bring back and show you when school resumes!

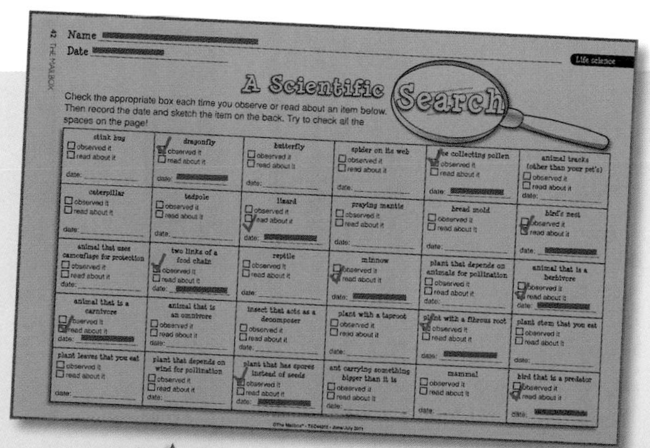

Flip to page 212 for a skill-building practice page on equivalent forms!

Name ______________________________

Date ______________________________

Sign Here, Please!

Find a different classmate to sign each square.
Each student may only sign your sheet twice.

 Note to the teacher: Use with "Sign Here, Please!" on page 168.

Bill of Rights Cards

Use with "Centered on Amendments" on page 169.

B The national government only has the powers listed in the Constitution. Other powers belong to the state governments or to the people.

TEC44050

D The government cannot make a law that limits citizens' freedom of religion, freedom of speech, freedom of the press, or right to assemble and ask the government to hear their complaints.

TEC44050

F People have the right to own weapons.

TEC44050

H The government cannot force citizens to keep soldiers in their houses.

TEC44050

J A person accused of a crime cannot be forced to pay too much bail or be subjected to cruel or unusual punishment.

TEC44050

A A person's home or property cannot be searched or taken away without a good reason.

TEC44050

C A person cannot be charged with the same crime twice. A person does not have to testify against herself.

TEC44050

E People have other rights not listed in the Constitution. These human rights include "Life, Liberty, and the pursuit of Happiness."

TEC44050

G A person accused of a crime is guaranteed a fair trial. The accused person has the right to have a lawyer defend him.

TEC44050

I If a person sues another for over $20, the case can be tried by a jury.

TEC44050

Amendment 1 Basic Freedoms TEC44050	**Amendment 2** Weapons TEC44050	**Amendment 3** Housing Soldiers TEC44050	**Amendment 4** Searches and Seizures TEC44050	**Amendment 5** Rights of Accused Persons TEC44050
Amendment 6 Right to a Fair Trial TEC44050	**Amendment 7** Jury Trial in Civil Cases TEC44050	**Amendment 8** Bail and Punishment TEC44050	**Amendment 9** Rights of the People TEC44050	**Amendment 10** Powers of the States and the People TEC44050

Questions for "Centered on Amendments"

1. What do you think the Bill of Rights means for the citizens of the country?
2. Why do you think there are amendments about people who are accused of crimes?
3. Which amendment is the easiest for you to understand? Why?
4. Why is the Bill of Rights still important today?
5. Which amendment do you think is the least important? Why?
6. Which amendment do you think is the most important? Why?

TEC44050

Fold.

Answer Key for "Centered on Amendments"

A. Amendment 4 F. Amendment 2
B. Amendment 10 G. Amendment 6
C. Amendment 5 H. Amendment 3
D. Amendment 1 I. Amendment 7
E. Amendment 9 J. Amendment 8

Name ____

Date ____________________________________

Count Angula

I "vant" you to find at least eight acute angles, two right angles, and five obtuse angles.

Cornucopia Pattern

Use with "'Verb-ucopia'" on page 171.

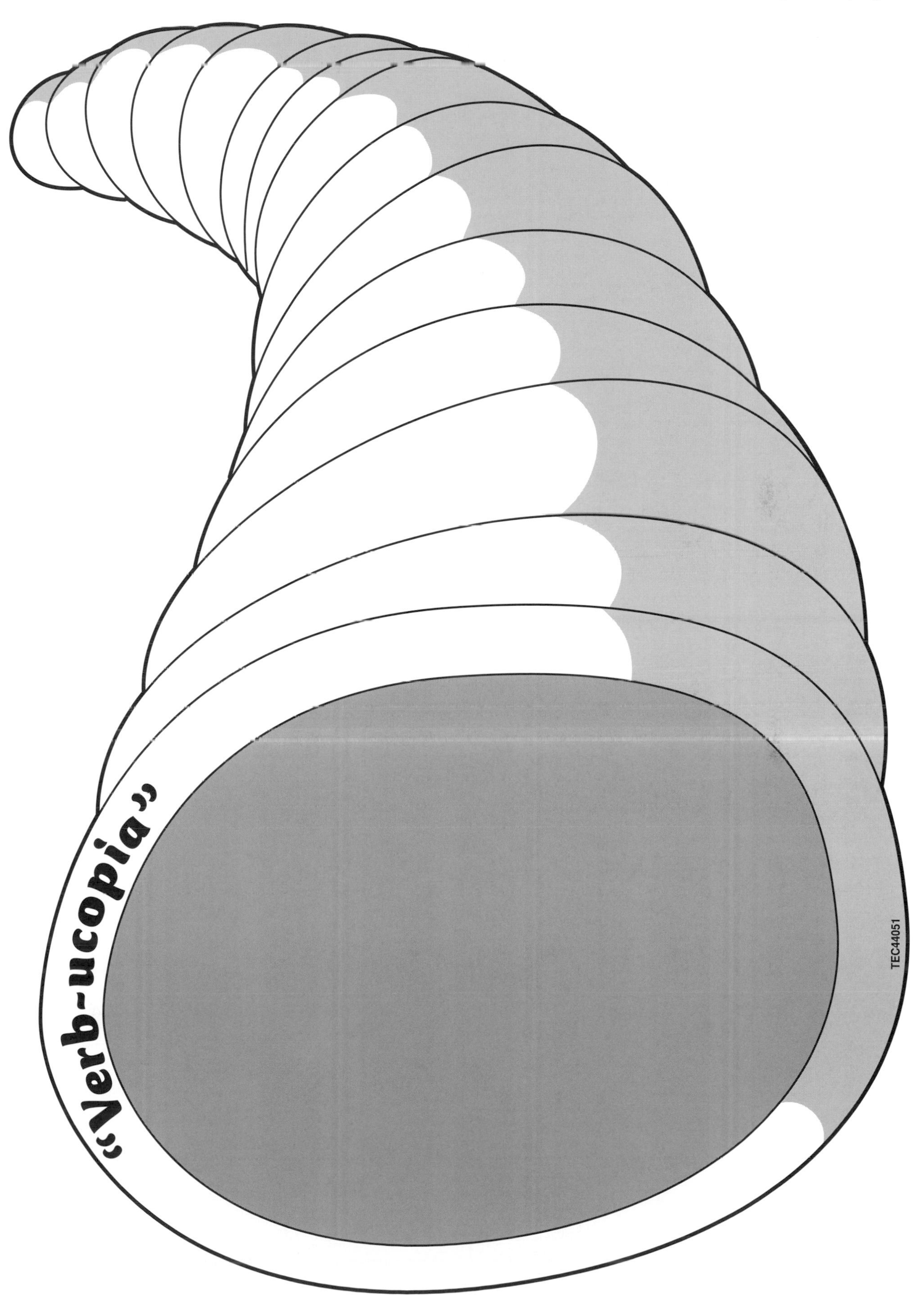

Names ______________________________ **Data analysis**

Date ______________________

Go for a Spin!

In turn, spin the paper clip 40 times. Record the result of each spin in the tally chart. Next, shade the bar graph to show your results. Then find and record the range, mean, median, and mode.

Tally Chart			
Nun נ	Gimel ג	He ה	Shin ש

Dreidel Spinner Results				
40				
38				
36				
34				
32				
30				
28				
26				
24				
22				
20				
18				
16				
14				
12				
10				
8				
6				
4				
2				
	Nun נ	Gimel ג	He ה	Shin ש

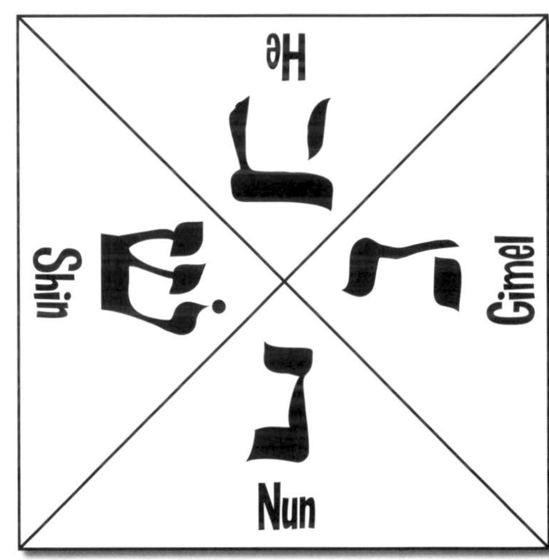

range = ______________

mean = ______________

median = ______________

mode = ______________

Bonus: Repeat the steps above, spinning the paper clip 20 times instead of 40. Then compare the statistics. How are they similar? How are they different?

 Note to the teacher: Use with "Go for a Spin!" on page 172. Each student needs a paper clip and pencil.

Name ______________________________

Date ______________________________

Presidential Sites

Adams, John
Adams, John Quincy
Arthur, Chester A.
Buchanan, James
Bush, George H. W.
Bush, George W.
Carter, James
Cleveland, Grover
Clinton, William J.
Coolidge, Calvin
Eisenhower, Dwight D.
Fillmore, Millard
Ford, Gerald R.
Garfield, James
Grant, Ulysses S.
Harding, Warren G.
Harrison, Benjamin
Harrison, William Henry
Hayes, Rutherford B.
Hoover, Herbert
Jackson, Andrew
Jefferson, Thomas
Johnson, Andrew
Johnson, Lyndon B.
Kennedy, John F.
Lincoln, Abraham
Madison, James
McKinley, William
Monroe, James
Nixon, Richard M.
Obama, Barack
Pierce, Franklin
Polk, James K.
Reagan, Ronald
Roosevelt, Franklin D.
Roosevelt, Theodore
Taft, William Howard
Taylor, Zachary
Truman, Harry S.
Tyler, John
Van Buren, Martin
Washington, George
Wilson, Woodrow

State: ______________________________

Place Name	County	City	Natural Feature	Other

Note to the teacher: Use with “Executive Sites” on page 174.

Food Cards

Use with "Palatable Produce" on page 175.

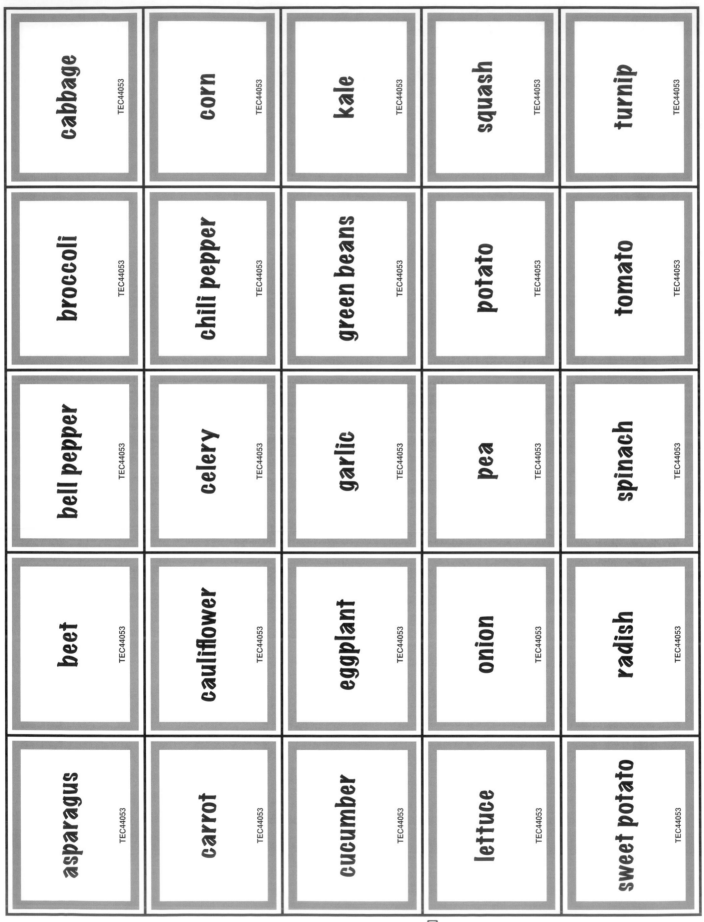

cabbage TEC44053	corn TEC44053	kale TEC44053	squash TEC44053	turnip TEC44053
broccoli TEC44053	chili pepper TEC44053	green beans TEC44053	potato TEC44053	tomato TEC44053
bell pepper TEC44053	celery TEC44053	garlic TEC44053	pea TEC44053	spinach TEC44053
beet TEC44053	cauliflower TEC44053	eggplant TEC44053	onion TEC44053	radish TEC44053
asparagus TEC44053	carrot TEC44053	cucumber TEC44053	lettuce TEC44053	sweet potato TEC44053

Name ______________________________

Date ______________________________

A Lyrical Quest

Write each poem title inside quotation marks. Underline the book's title.

Find poems with the rhyme schemes listed below. When you find one, color the matching shield. Then write the poem's title and author's name plus the title of the book and the page on which you found the poem.

abcb

poem ______________________________

poet ______________________________

book ______________________________ page ______

abab

poem ______________________________

poet ______________________________

book ______________________________ page ______

aabba

poem ______________________________

poet ______________________________

book ______________________________ page ______

abab cdcd...

poem ______________________________

poet ______________________________

book ______________________________ page ______

aa bb cc dd...

poem ______________________________

poet ______________________________

book ______________________________ page ______

other: ______________

poem ______________________________

poet ______________________________

book ______________________________ page ______

Note to the teacher: Use with "A Lyrical Quest" on page 176.

Name ____________________

Date ____________________

Going Buggy?

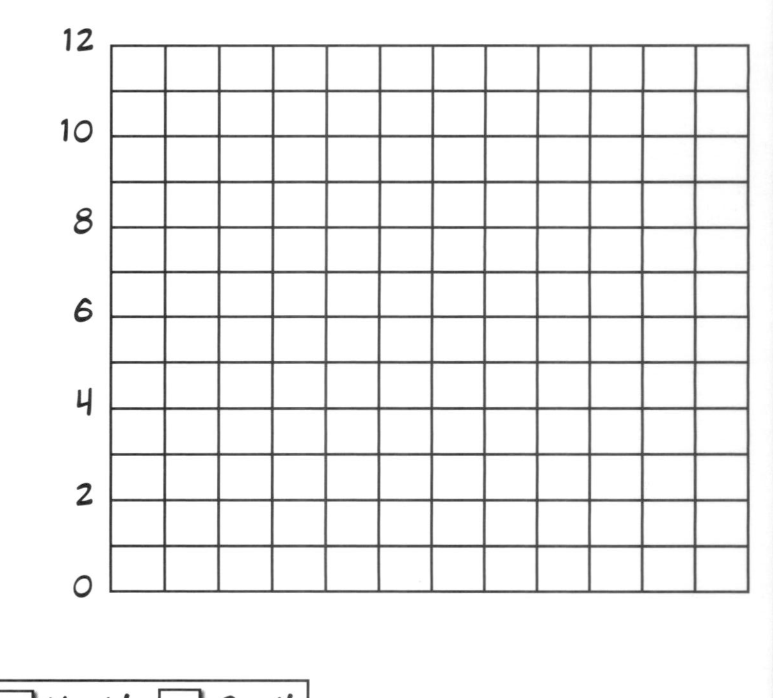

I. Ask 12 people the question below about each insect. Then tally the totals at the bottom of each column.

Which would you be more likely to say if you found this insect on the playground: yuck or cool?

Name of respondent	dragonfly		stinkbug		butterfly		pill bug or roly poly	
	Yuck!	Cool!	Yuck!	Cool!	Yuck!	Cool!	Yuck!	Cool!
1.								
2.								
3.								
4.								
5.								
6.								
7.								
8.								
9.								
10.								
11.								
12.								
Totals								

II. Use your results to make a double-bar graph below. Give your graph a title and label each axis.

12

10

8

6

4

2

0

☐ Yuck! ☐ Cool!

Which insect do most people think is yucky?

____

Which insect do most people think is cool?

____

Note to the teacher: Use with "Going Buggy?" on page 177.

Materials: 12" x 18" sheet of construction paper; scissors; markers, crayons, or colored pencils; tape; a good memory

Directions:

A. Fold the paper in half and cut it into two 6" x 18" strips. Then accordion-fold each strip two times.

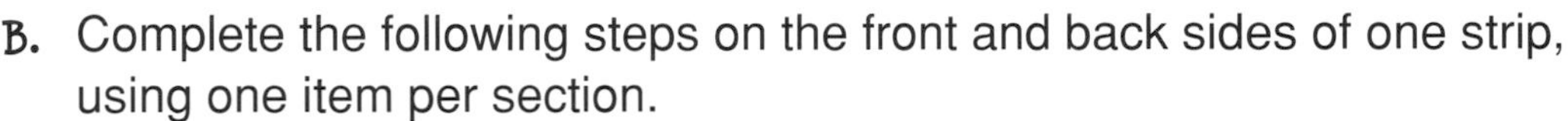

B. Complete the following steps on the front and back sides of one strip, using one item per section.
   1. Write "A Noteworthy Year" in big, fancy letters.
   2. Draw a self-portrait. Label it.
   3. Write "responsibility" in fancy letters. Then write about a time during this past year when you acted responsibly.
   4. Draw a picture of your teacher. Label it.
   5. Describe a time during this past year when you worked with others and had awesome results.
   6. Draw a picture about your favorite school subject. Label it.

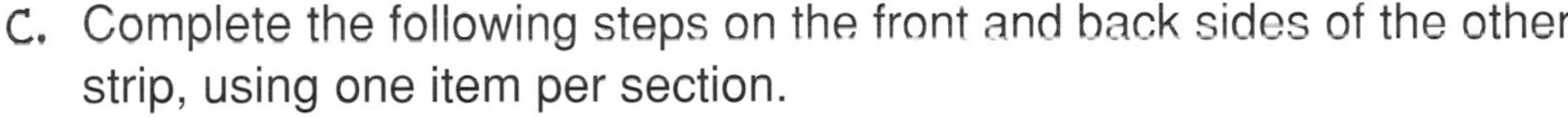

C. Complete the following steps on the front and back sides of the other strip, using one item per section.
   1. Write a paragraph about the most important thing you learned this year. Draw a neat border—such as flowers, stars, or squiggly lines—around the section.
   2. Illustrate the climax of the best book you read this year. Write the book's title and author's name.
   3. Illustrate an event from your favorite activity this year. Label it.
   4. Draw a picture of your favorite food to eat for lunch at school. Label it.
   5. What will you miss most about this year? Describe it.
   6. Draw a picture of your school with your school's name. Below the picture, write the phrase "Home of _____." Fill in the blank.

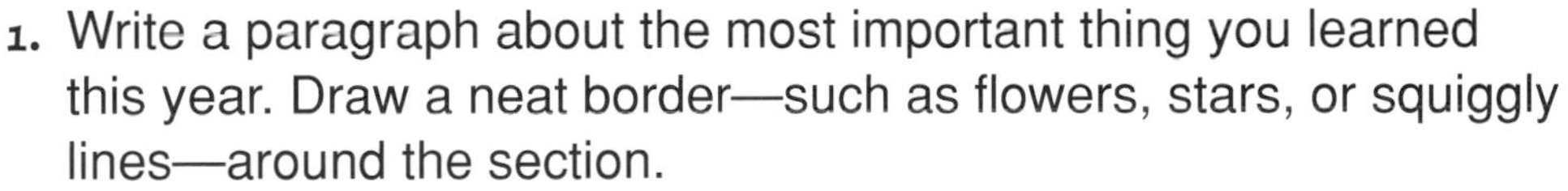

D. Tape the two strips together to make an accordion book about this noteworthy year!

Note to the teacher: Use with "Ending the Year on a Positive Note" on page 178.

Name ______________________________

Date ______________________

A Scientific Search

Check the appropriate box each time you observe or read about an item below. Then record the date and sketch the item on the back. Try to check all the spaces on the page!

stink bug ☐ observed it ☐ read about it date: ________	dragonfly ☐ observed it ☐ read about it date: ________	butterfly ☐ observed it ☐ read about it date: ________	spider on its web ☐ observed it ☐ read about it date: ________	bee collecting pollen ☐ observed it ☐ read about it date: ________	animal tracks (other than your pet's) ☐ observed it ☐ read about it date: ________
caterpillar ☐ observed it ☐ read about it date: ________	tadpole ☐ observed it ☐ read about it date: ________	lizard ☐ observed it ☐ read about it date: ________	praying mantis ☐ observed it ☐ read about it date: ________	bread mold ☐ observed it ☐ read about it date: ________	bird's nest ☐ observed it ☐ read about it date: ________
animal that uses camouflage for protection ☐ observed it ☐ read about it date: ________	two links of a food chain ☐ observed it ☐ read about it date: ________	reptile ☐ observed it ☐ read about it date: ________	minnow ☐ observed it ☐ read about it date: ________	plant that depends on animals for pollination ☐ observed it ☐ read about it date: ________	animal that is a herbivore ☐ observed it ☐ read about it date: ________
animal that is a carnivore ☐ observed it ☐ read about it date: ________	animal that is an omnivore ☐ observed it ☐ read about it date: ________	insect that acts as a decomposer ☐ observed it ☐ read about it date: ________	plant with a taproot ☐ observed it ☐ read about it date: ________	plant with a fibrous root ☐ observed it ☐ read about it date: ________	plant stem that you eat ☐ observed it ☐ read about it date: ________
plant leaves that you eat ☐ observed it ☐ read about it date: ________	plant that depends on wind for pollination ☐ observed it ☐ read about it date: ________	plant that has spores instead of seeds ☐ observed it ☐ read about it date: ________	ant carrying something bigger than it is ☐ observed it ☐ read about it date: ________	mammal ☐ observed it ☐ read about it date: ________	bird that is a predator ☐ observed it ☐ read about it date: ________

Note to the teacher: Use with "Summer Science Challenge" on page 179.

Name ____________________

Date ____________________

THE MYSTERY TEACHER

Use context clues to decide what the boldfaced words mean. Write each word's number next to the matching definition.

It's the first day of school, and I have no idea who my new teacher is. I know her name. It's Ms. Turner. But I don't know anything about her. No one does. She's an (1) **enigma.** So I'm standing here, (2) **loitering** outside the classroom, (3) **waffling** between excitement and fear. My friends and I are (4) **speculating.** We have so many questions. Even my favorite teacher, Ms. Brown, says she is (5) **unacquainted** with Ms. Turner. That's (6) **peculiar.** Ms. Brown knows everyone. All of a sudden, we hear the sound of shoes (7) **clattering** on the floor. Ms. Turner is coming.

The door to our classroom swings open, and all I see are two arms clinging to a (8) **cumbersome** load of textbooks. The books look as if they're about to (9) **topple,** so I reach out to help. Then I look up. I see Ms. Turner's kind (10) **countenance** and sunny smile. I recognize her (11) **luminous** (12) **cardigan**. Light dances off it, making me smile. I saw that crazy sweater all year last year. Ms. Turner, it turns out, is Ms. Brown. I'm (13) **flabbergasted.** Ms. Brown got married this summer and changed her name. My surprise (14) **transforms** into excitement. I already know my teacher!

_____ L. reflecting light

_____ Y. big and hard to carry

_____ R. fall over

_____ P. completely surprised

_____ I. sweater that opens in the front

_____ S. making a rattling noise

_____ A. does not know personally

_____ O. strange

_____ E. changing one's mind back and forth

_____ D. a mysterious person

_____ F. guessing

_____ T. changes

_____ C. face or expression

_____ H. standing around

Bonus Box: Rewrite the second paragraph, giving the story a different ending. Use the boldfaced words in your new ending.

WHY DID THE STUDENTS TIE THEIR SHOELACES TOGETHER?

To find out, write each letter from above on its matching numbered line or lines below.

They were getting ___ ___ ___ ___ ___ (9 3 5 1 8) ___ ___ ___ (4 6 9) ___ ___ ___ ___ ___ (14 2 3 12 9) ___ ___ ___ ___ ___ (10 11 5 7 7) ___ ___ ___ ___ (14 9 12 13)!

Name ____________________

Date ____________________

THINK IT OVER

Solve each problem.

1. Devin wants to make a supersize cupcake for each of his 24 classmates, three teachers, and principal. He can make nine supersize cupcakes with one cupcake mix. How many mixes will he need?

____

2. The temperature on the first day of school is 12° warmer than the average of the last five years' temperatures. Those temperatures were 76°F, 83°F, 69°F, 72°F, and 75°F. What is the temperature on the first day of school?

____

3. There is a penny drive at school. Amber collected 1,132 pennies in June and 639 in July. Devin collected 653 pennies in June and 1,057 in July. Who collected more pennies?

____

4. Devin gets on the bus at 7:32. He gets off at 8:07. How long is Devin on the bus?

____

5. Amber's bookbag costs $15.38. She pays for it with a twenty-dollar bill. What change should Amber get back?

____

6. Devin buys three boxes of pencils. He gets $3.25 in change from a ten-dollar bill. How much does each box of pencils cost?

____

7. Amber is decorating her book cover with stamps in the following pattern: butterfly, flower, butterfly, flower. Will the 15th stamp be a butterfly or a flower?

____

8. Devin's mom bought most of his school supplies at a sale eight weeks and four days ago. How many days ago was the sale?

____

9. One folder costs $0.79. Folders also come in packs of 2 for $1.50, 3 for $2.30, 4 for $3.12, and 5 for $3.75. Amber needs six folders. Which combination costs the least?

____

10. At Amber's school, 27 fewer students are enrolled this year than were enrolled last year. This year, 485 students are signed up. How many students were enrolled last year?

____

Bonus Box: Devin says the letter *e* is the most frequently used letter of our alphabet. Do you believe him? Why or why not?

Name ____________________

Date ____________________

Constitutional Autographs

Circle each word that should be capitalized.

Did you find the 39 words that should be capitalized?
We t

1. The Constitutional Convention began may 25, 1787.
2. delegates from 12 states worked on the Constitution for almost four months.
3. They finished on september 17, 1787.
4. On that day, 39 out of 55 delegates signed the United states Constitution.
5. james madison is called the "Father of the Constitution."
6. Madison earned that nickname because he was a powerful speaker and kept the best records of the debates.
7. the delegates often disagreed about the details of the constitution.
8. The first delegate who signed the Constitution was george washington.
9. george washington was one of only two men who signed the Constitution and later became a U.S. president.
10. james madison was the only other man who signed the Constitution and later became a U.S. president.
11. at age 81, benjamin franklin was the oldest person to sign the Constitution.
12. The delegates signed the constitution in geographical order, from north to south.
13. The delegate from new hampshire was followed by the delegates from massachusetts, connecticut, new york, new jersey, pennsylvania, delaware, maryland, virginia, north carolina, south carolina, and georgia.
14. The youngest delegate to sign the constitution was 26 years old.
15. the original constitution is on display in the National Archives Building in washington, DC.

Bonus Box: *Practice writing your signature (your full name in cursive) until it looks formal enough that you'd be proud to sign an important document like the U.S. Constitution.*

Name ____________________

Date ____________________

A GRAND EXPLORER

Multiply. Shade the box that matches each product.

1. 37 x 5
2. 24 x 7
3. 88 x 4
4. 96 x 8
5. 71 x 9
6. 308 x 5
7. 679 x 4
8. 277 x 6
9. 818 x 3
10. 667 x 5
11. 494 x 3
12. 239 x 9
13. 186 x 7
14. 730 x 2

4,000 C	185 L	765 O	352 E	1,204 R	1,302 G	2,151 P	748 O	168 T	2,716 K	3,335 S
1,540 B	1,460 H	286 N	639 U	515 A	768 G	1,482 J	2,039 D	2,454 M	776 O	1,662 Z

This Spanish explorer was looking for southwestern cities said to be rich in gold. Instead, he and his men discovered the Great Plains, Palo Duro Canyon, the Continental Divide, and the Grand Canyon.

To name the explorer, write the letters from the boxes you did not shade in order on the lines below.

FRANCISCO VÁSQUEZ DE ___ ___ ___ ___ ___ ___ ___ ___

Name ____________________

Date ____________________

GRAB AND GO!

Add or subtract to complete each problem.
Then shade the matching acorn.

1. 36.49 − 21.63 = [ ]

2. 41.23 + [ ] = 62.61

3. 27.86 + 1.33 = [ ]

4. [ ] − 2.45 = 11.17

5. 13.39 + [ ] = 29.79

6. [ ] + 6.12 = 10.00

7. 67.44 + [ ] = 89.99

8. [ ] − 8.71 = 6.31

9. 18.04 − 5.31 = [ ]

10. 86.63 + 72.51 = [ ]

11. 76.59 + [ ] = 80.97

12. 71.16 − 19.48 = [ ]

13. 40.73 + [ ] = 57.99

14. [ ] − 27.61 = 36.61

15. 32.47 + 28.55 = [ ]

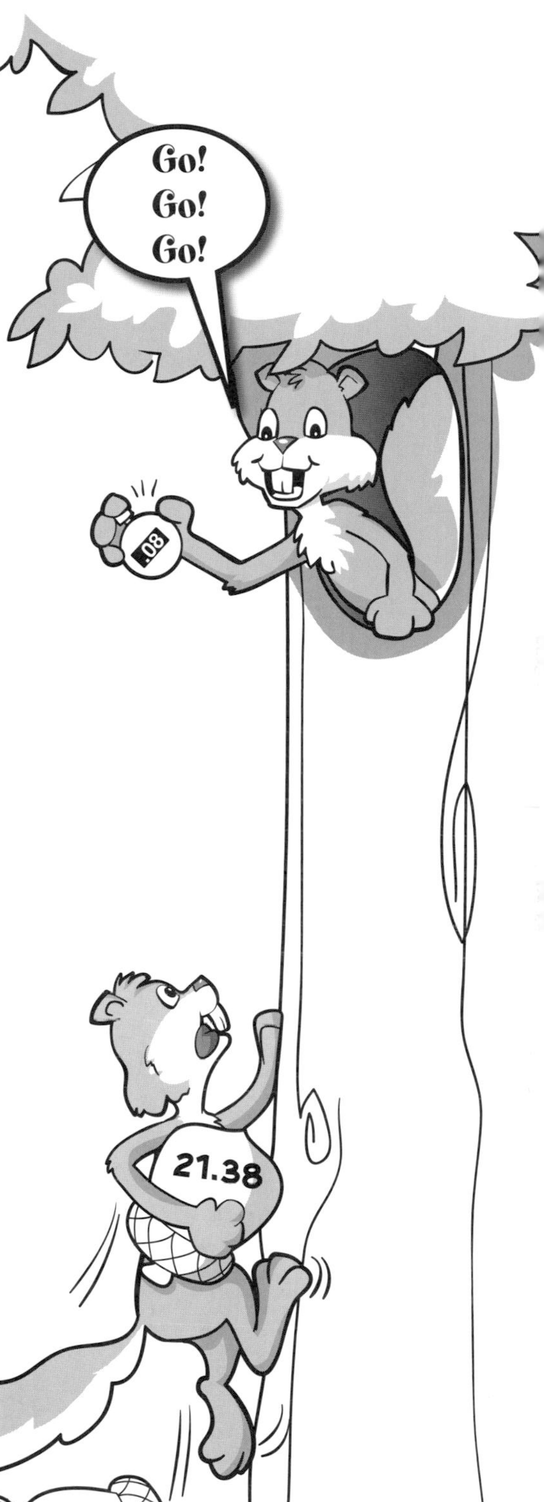

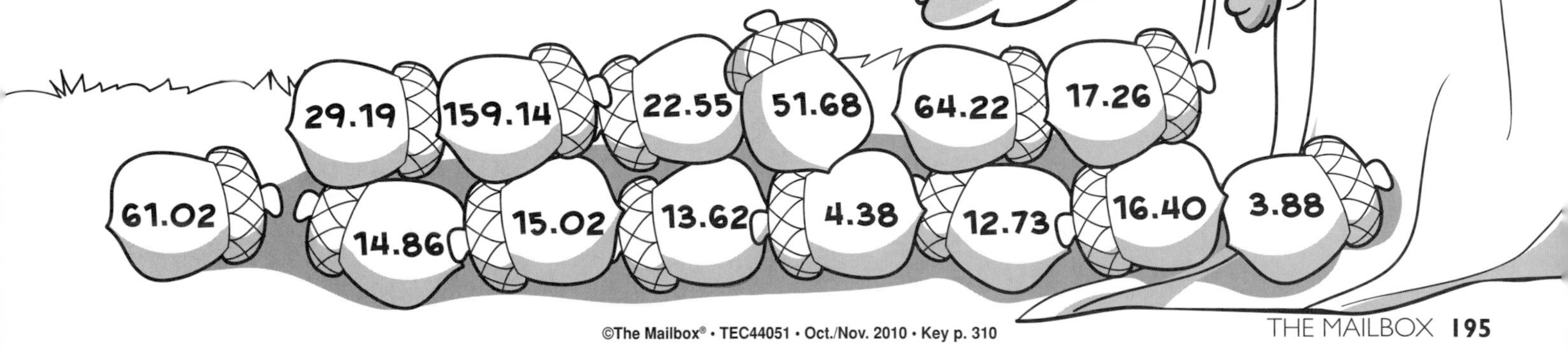

Name ____________________

Date ____________________

BARE BONES

Write a one-sentence summary of each paragraph on the lines below.

What should I wear to the party this year? I'm tired of always being the skeleton!

It would be hard to imagine your body without a skeleton. Your skeleton is your body's framework. Made of a network of bones, your skeleton holds everything together. It protects your organs and is an anchor for your muscles.

Have you ever wondered how many bones you have in different parts of your body? You have 29 bones in your skull alone! There are 25 bones in your chest and 26 in your spine. Each of your arms has 32 bones, while each leg has 31. Altogether, there are 206 bones in the human skeleton.

The bones in your skeleton are connected at joints. Fixed joints, like the ones in your skull, cannot move. A hinge joint, such as your elbow, can move only in one direction. Your shoulders and hips are ball-and-socket joints. They can swing in two directions and also twist. Ball-and-socket joints allow the most movement.

Did you know that your bones are alive? Living bones are not white and brittle. They are tough and somewhat elastic. Blood vessels continually carry blood to your bones. The vessels pass through small holes in the surface of the bones, keeping them alive.

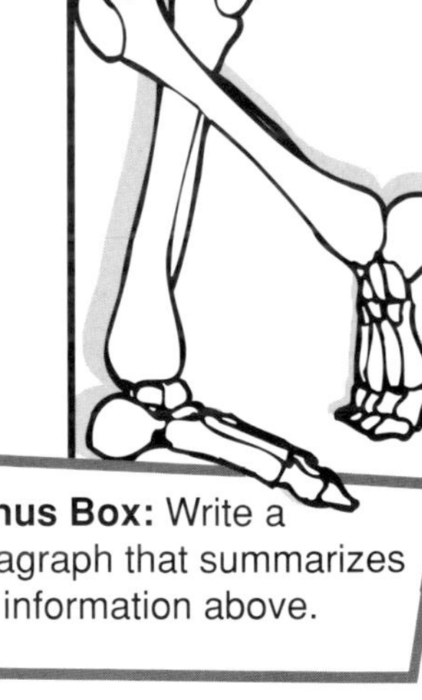

5

Your spine is made of a flexible row of bones called vertebrae. The bones in your spine protect your spinal cord. Each vertebra can move a little against the next one. Because of this, you can flex your spine. This means you can bend over, sit down, and even do the twist!

Bonus Box: Write a paragraph that summarizes the information above.

Summary sentence for paragraph 1: ____________________

Summary sentence for paragraph 2: ____________________

Summary sentence for paragraph 3: ____________________

Summary sentence for paragraph 4: ____________________

Summary sentence for paragraph 5: ____________________

Name ____________________

Date ____________________

In Honor

Write the letter for each ordered pair below to complete the Veterans Day poem.

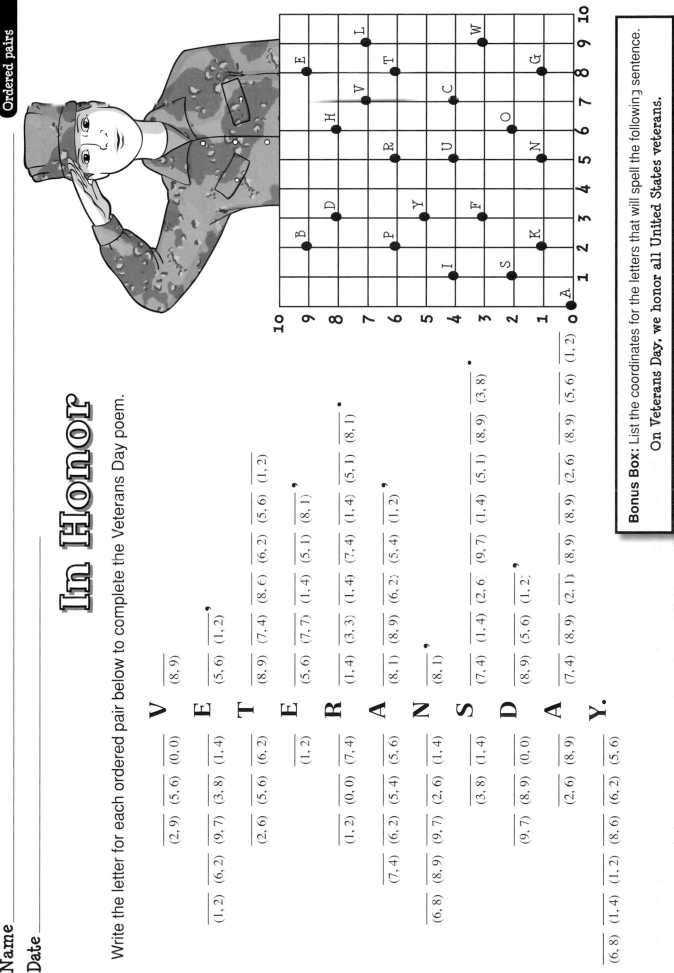

___ ___ ___ **V** ___
(2, 9) (5, 6) (0, 0) (8, 9)

___ ___ ___ ___ ___ **E** ___ ___,
(1, 2) (6, 2) (9, 7) (3, 8) (1, 4) (5, 6) (1, 2)

___ ___ ___ **T** ___ ___ ___ ___ ___ ___
(2, 6) (5, 6) (6, 2) (8, 9) (7, 4) (8, 6) (6, 2) (5, 6) (1, 2)

___ **E** ___ ___ ___ ___ ___,
(1, 2) (5, 6) (7, 7) (1, 4) (5, 1) (8, 1)

___ ___ ___ **R** ___ ___ ___ ___ ___ ___ ___.
(1, 2) (0, 0) (7, 4) (1, 4) (3, 3) (1, 4) (7, 4) (1, 4) (5, 1) (8, 1)

___ ___ ___ ___ **A** ___ ___ ___ ___ ___,
(7, 4) (6, 2) (5, 4) (5, 6) (8, 1) (8, 9) (6, 2) (5, 4) (1, 2)

___ ___ ___ ___ ___ **N** ___,
(6, 8) (8, 9) (9, 7) (2, 6) (1, 4) (8, 1)

___ ___ **S** ___ ___ ___ ___ ___ ___ ___ ___.
(3, 8) (1, 4) (7, 4) (1, 4) (2, 6) (9, 7) (1, 4) (5, 1) (8, 9) (3, 8)

___ ___ ___ **D** ___ ___ ___,
(9, 7) (8, 9) (0, 0) (8, 9) (5, 6) (1, 2)

___ ___ **A** ___ ___ ___ ___ ___ ___ ___ ___ ___
(2, 6) (8, 9) (7, 4) (8, 9) (2, 1) (8, 9) (8, 9) (2, 6) (8, 9) (5, 6) (1, 2)

___ ___ ___ ___ ___ ___ **Y.**
(6, 8) (1, 4) (1, 2) (8, 6) (6, 2) (5, 6)

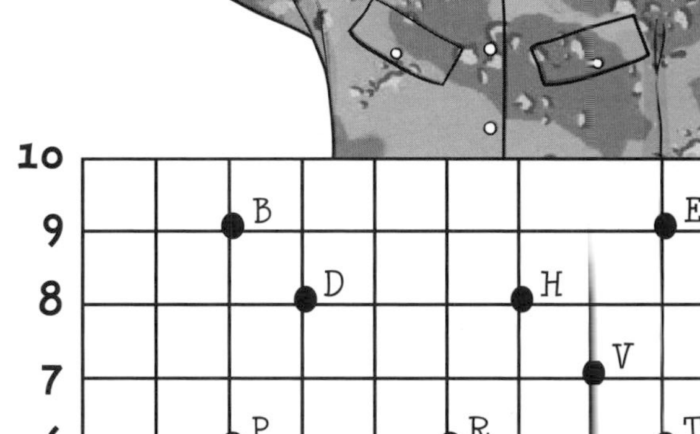

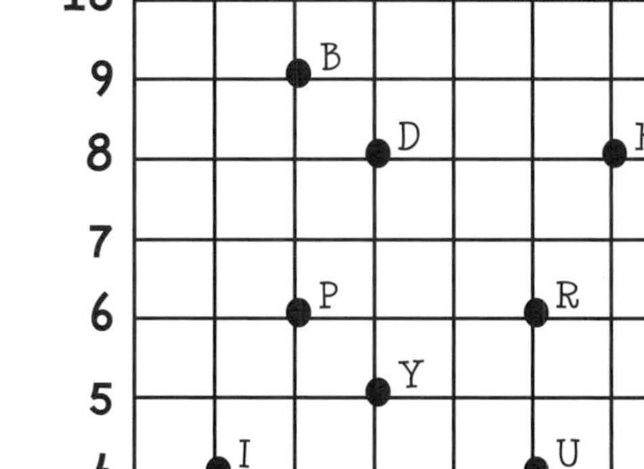
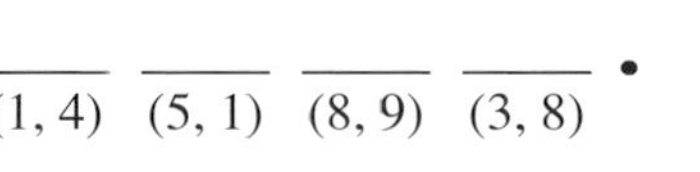
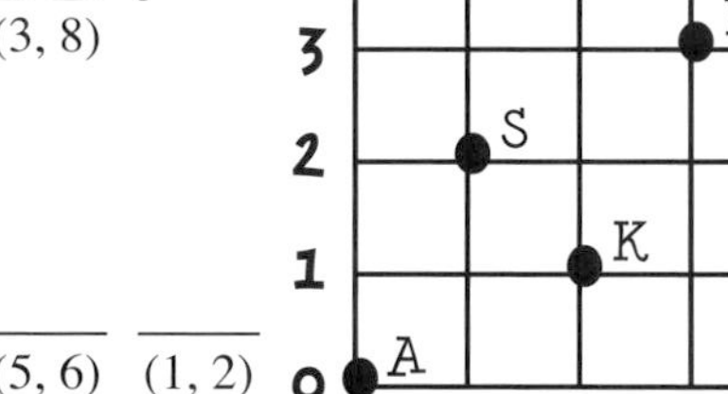

Bonus Box: List the coordinates for the letters that will spell the following sentence.

On Veterans Day, we honor all United States veterans.

Name ______________________________ **Dictionary skills**

Date ______________________________

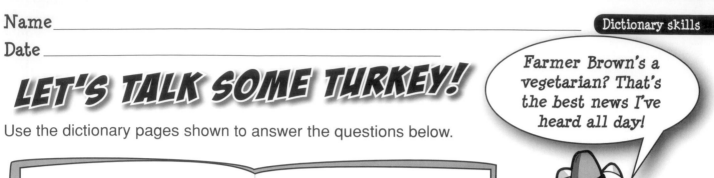

LET'S TALK SOME TURKEY!

Use the dictionary pages shown to answer the questions below.

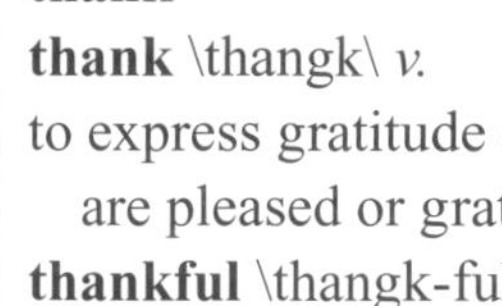

thank **time**

thank \thangk\ *v.*
to express gratitude or say that you are pleased or grateful

thankful \thangk-fuhl\ *adj.*
feeling or expressing thanks
syn. see *grateful*

Thanksgiving Day \thangks-gihv-ihng day\ *n.*
a special day set aside for giving thanks

that \that\ *pron.*
the person or thing being mentioned

tom **twist**

tom \tom\ *n.*
a male turkey

trim \trihm\ *v.* **trims, trimmed, trimming**
to remove or cut away parts that are not needed

trimming \trihm-ing\ *n.*
something that is used to decorate something else
something that goes along with a main dish

turkey \tur-kee\ *n.*
a large North American bird with brown feathers

Farmer Brown's a vegetarian? That's the best news I've heard all day!

1. What are the guide words on the page with *turkey?* ______________________________
2. Which of the words are nouns? ______________________________
____
3. Where would you divide *thankful?* ______________________________
4. What is the past tense form of *trim?* ______________________________
5. In the following sentence, what does the underlined word mean?

   It took Mom all day to prepare the turkey and all the <u>trimmings</u>.

   ____
6. A hen is a female turkey. What is the name for a male turkey? ______________________________

Read each pair of guide words. Then circle the words you would find on each page.

7. **bacon–book**	8. **fact–food**	9. **salt–stir**	10. **pepper–place**
bowl	feast	sweet	pie
berries	family	spoon	potatoes
bake	fall	serve	pass
burn	football	stuffing	pumpkin
boil	favorite	serving	piece

Bonus Box: Pretend you are teaching someone how to use a dictionary. Write an explanation that tells how to find the word *dessert*.

Name ______________________________ Date ______________________

An Amazing Feat

If the fractions in a box are equivalent, lightly shade the oval.

$\frac{2}{4}, \frac{1}{2}$ Arctic	$\frac{1}{3}, \frac{3}{9}$ Alaskan	$\frac{1}{5}, \frac{10}{20}$ They	$\frac{5}{20}, \frac{1}{4}$ Polar	$\frac{9}{24}, \frac{3}{8}$ They
$\frac{1}{3}, \frac{2}{6}$ some	$\frac{2}{5}, \frac{15}{30}$ all	$\frac{2}{3}, \frac{12}{18}$ do	$\frac{1}{3}, \frac{9}{18}$ can	$\frac{1}{2}, \frac{4}{8}$ jump
$\frac{10}{12}, \frac{5}{6}$ when	$\frac{2}{16}, \frac{1}{8}$ for	$\frac{1}{3}, \frac{2}{18}$ because	$\frac{6}{15}, \frac{2}{5}$ especially	$\frac{2}{6}, \frac{4}{8}$ a
$\frac{8}{12}, \frac{4}{8}$ house	$\frac{2}{3}, \frac{4}{6}$ hooves	$\frac{10}{16}, \frac{5}{8}$ won't	$\frac{4}{5}, \frac{12}{20}$ can't	$\frac{3}{4}, \frac{12}{16}$ can
$\frac{1}{2}, \frac{5}{10}$ lower	$\frac{9}{15}, \frac{3}{5}$ almost	$\frac{1}{2}, \frac{6}{8}$ jump	$\frac{7}{8}, \frac{14}{16}$ move	$\frac{1}{3}, \frac{5}{15}$ house

Which reindeer can jump higher than a house?

To find out, write the words from the unshaded ovals in order on the lines.

__________ __________ __________ __________

__________ __________ __________ __________!

Bonus: Correct one fraction in each unshaded box to make the fractions equivalent.

Name ______________________________
Date ______________

Snow E. Day

Find the title or titles in each sentence. Draw ≡ under each letter that should be capitalized. Then underline the title or add quotation marks as appropriate.

Rules to Remember

- Underline titles of books, newspapers, movies, CDs, and magazines.
- Use quotation marks around titles of articles, songs, poems, and book chapters.
- In titles, capitalize the first word and last word. Capitalize every word in between except for *a, an, the, by, for, with, in, of, and, or,* and *but.*

1. I'm reading a book titled the bitter cold by Ben N. Snow.

2. I read a funny article in skating world magazine.

3. The article was figure eights written by S. Kate Ting.

4. Do you have the book frostbite written by Mr. Art Tic?

5. Have you heard the song logs in the fireplace by R. U. Warm?

6. I memorized the poem snowflakes for class.

7. The book I'm reading now is it's tough being a snowman.

8. The first chapter is titled I have a nose for carrots.

9. I checked out how to build a snow fort by Kenny Doit from the library.

10. I want to read the article bundle up by Mitt N. Boots.

11. I found the article in winter care magazine.

12. I've wanted to visit Alaska ever since I read Julie of the wolves.

13. The picture of us sledding is in today's edition of the icicle news.

14. At the Snowball Dance, the band played wintertime waltz.

15. I think I'll read skiing safely, the article in the downhill fun magazine, again.

Whoa! These things have minds of their own!

Bonus: Using correct capitalization and punctuation, write the titles of a book, a song, and a magazine that all begin with *s.*

Name ____________________

Date ____________________

Give It a Spin!

Multiply. Then shade the matching answer on the dreidel. The unshaded number is the product for number 20. Use the product to find the missing digits.

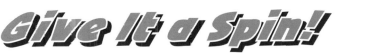

1. 248 × 73

2. 309 × 25

3. 445 × 31

4. 200 × 60

5. 196 × 57

6. 882 × 46

7. 626 × 19

8. 115 × 18

9. 505 × 82

10. 733 × 39

11. 914 × 45

12. 566 × 89

13. 428 × 24

14. 351 × 77

15. 196 × 45

16. 976 × 78

17. 683 × 56

18. 218 × 19

19. 107 × 81

20.

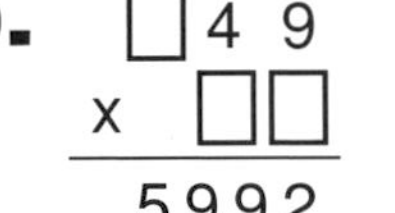

```
   □4 9
 x  □□
  5992
+22470
 ─────
  □
```

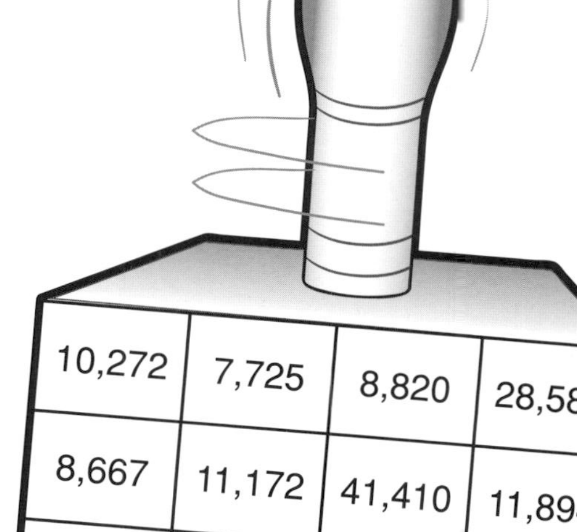

10,272	7,725	8,820	28,587
8,667	11,172	41,410	11,894
50,374	38,248	12,000	28,462
18,104	41,130	27,027	4,142
2,070	13,795	76,128	40,572

Bonus: Sophie says 896 × 72 = 8,064. Is she correct? If not, explain where she made her mistake.

Name ______________________________ Reading for information
Date ______________________

A Peaceful Man

Use these facts to fill in the missing information in the notes below.

- Martin Luther King Jr. was born in Atlanta, Georgia, on January 15, 1929.
- A great student, Martin skipped both the ninth and twelfth grades.
- Martin was just 15 when he entered college in 1944.
- Martin graduated from college in 1948 and immediately entered seminary school.
- Martin and Coretta Scott were married in 1953.
- In 1955, Martin earned a PhD from Boston University.
- The Kings had two sons and two daughters.
- Dr. King's first civil rights action was to lead the bus boycott in Montgomery, Alabama, in 1955.
- On August 28, 1963, King gave his "I have a dream" speech in Washington, DC.
- In 1964, when he was just 35, Dr. King was awarded the Nobel Peace Prize.
- Martin Luther King Jr. was shot on April 4, 1968.

Notes on Dr. King

1. was born on January _____, 1929
2. skipped grades 9 and _____
3. had _____ sons
4. graduated from college in 19_____
5. led Montgomery bus boycott in 19_____
6. gave his "I have a dream" speech on August 28, 19_____
7. was _____ when he received the Nobel Peace Prize
8. had _____ daughters
9. was _____ years old when he started college
10. received the Nobel Peace Prize in 19_____
11. shot on April 4, 19_____
12. entered seminary school in 19_____

To finish the drawing below, connect the numbers from your answers in order.

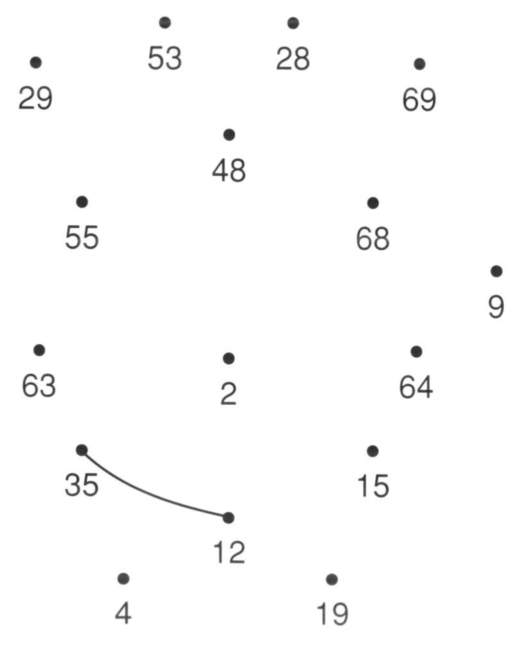

Bonus: Rewrite notes 1–12 so their order matches the facts above.

Name ____________________ **Using commas**

Date ____________________

Difference Makers

Editing Marks
Delete. ℘
Add a comma. ^

If commas are used correctly in the sentence, circle the letter in the "Correct" column.
If commas are not used correctly, circle the letter in the "Incorrect" column.
Then use the editing marks shown to correct the sentence.

	Sentence	Correct	Incorrect
1.	As a leader of the Underground Railroad, Harriet Tubman made 19 trips into slave-holding states to help slaves escape to freedom.	C	M
2.	Rosa Parks, a civil rights activist, refused to give up her bus seat in Montgomery, Alabama.	A	T
3.	"I want to be the president of a bank like Maggie Walker was" Kayla said.	P	R
4.	Duke Ellington, and Louis Armstrong were leading jazz bandleaders.	A	T
5.	In the 1920s, Langston Hughes was one of many famous African American writers.	E	S
6.	Alice Walker Maya Angelou and Toni Morrison are famous authors now.	I	R
7.	Thurgood Marshall, the first African American Supreme Court Justice, served from 1967 until 1991.	G	B
8.	Nikki Giovanni is a professor at Virginia Tech in Blacksburg Virginia and she's written more than 30 children's and adult books.	T	W
9.	Marcus explained, "Jackie Robinson was the first African American player in major league baseball."	O	L
10.	On August 28 1963, Dr. Martin Luther King Jr. gave one of his most famous speeches.	C	O
11.	George Washington, Carver created more than 475 products from peanuts sweet potatoes pecans and wood shavings.	S	D
12.	In 2001, Colin Powell became the first African American secretary of state.	S	P
13.	Douglas Wilder, the first African American governor, was the mayor of Richmond Virginia from 2005 until 2009.	M	O
14.	On August 10, 1983, Guion Stewart Bluford Jr. became the first African American to travel into space.	N	A

Considered the Father of Black History, I was one of the people who proposed Negro History Week in 1926. That week became Black History Week in the 1970s. Then, in 1976, Black History Month was established. What was my name?

To find out, write each circled letter from above in order on the lines below.

__ __ __ __ __ __   __.   __ __ __ __ __ __ __

Bonus: Which of the famous people above would you most like to meet? Explain.

Name ______________________________ Computation review
Date ______________________

Fast Flowers

Solve each problem. Cross out the matching answer on the grid below.

A. 478 + 123

B. 384 − 265

C. 3)549

D. 25 x 15

E. 132 x 14

F. 507 − 364

G. 9)801

H. 293 + 438

I. 587 − 428

J. 9)315

K. 165 + 296

L. 23 x 11

M. 3,174 + 5,877

N. 7,816 − 1,609

O. 8)704

P. 96 x 29

Q. 5,287 − 3,159

R. 7)154

S. 1,214 + 1,977

T. 426 x 15

U. 7)441

V. 2,703 + 3,425

W. 3,986 − 1,499

X. 197 x 23

Y. 6,381 − 2,652

Which flowers are the most popular for Valentine's Day?

Find the row in which all the numbers are crossed out.

red roses	3,729	3,191	183	461	88	35	143
white roses	159	184	6,207	22	6,390	2,128	63
daisies	731	2,784	3,728	34	120	1,848	9,051
lilies	2,028	145	20	6,128	89	601	85
carnations	119	375	4,531	90	2,487	253	158

Bonus: One customer orders a bouquet with 80 flowers. He wants an equal number of red roses, white roses, daisies, lilies, and carnations. How many carnations will be in the bouquet? How did you find your answer?

Name ______________________________

Date ______________________

Powerful Presidents

Draw a line from each weak verb to a synonym that is a strong verb.

As the first president, I **did** a lot.

It would sound better if you said, "As the first president, I **accomplished** a lot!"

Weak Verbs	Strong Verbs
laugh	observe
get	own
run	bellow
make	clutch
wash	create
yell	acquire
have	stroll
eat	guzzle
sleep	crave
tell	chuckle
drink	snooze
hold	dash
see	devour
walk	scrub
want	advise

Complete each sentence with a strong verb. (Use a stronger verb than the word in parentheses.)

1. "Welcome to Washington, DC," our tour guide __________ (yells).
2. We __________ (walk) around the city.
3. I __________ (laugh) when I think about George Washington's false teeth.
4. Apparently, some of Washington's dentures were __________ (made) of ivory.
5. We __________ (see) more monuments than I can count.
6. At noon, everyone __________ (eats) their lunches.
7. I __________ (tell) the bus driver I'm carsick.
8. After we tour the White House, I am so thirsty that I __________ (drink) two bottles of water.
9. I wonder which president __________ (had) the wackiest pet.
10. I stop and __________ (get) a T-shirt for a souvenir.
11. Then I __________ (run) from the hotel to the bus.
12. I am so tired that I __________ (sleep) the whole bus ride home.

Bonus: Skim three pages of a book you are reading or a textbook. Make a list of the verbs you read. Then highlight the strong ones.

Name ______________________________

Date ______________________

Multistep problem solving with money

Lucky Leaves?

Solve on another sheet of paper. Then shade the clover with the matching solution.

1. Liam spends $8.79 for a new hat and $11.46 for new boots. Liam had $25.00. How much money does he have left?	2. Liam takes $200.00 to the store to buy unicorn food. Each bag costs $14.00. Liam buys the most bags he can. How many bags does he buy?	3. Liam loses eight shamrock coins and 11 moon coins. Each shamrock coin is worth $45.75. Each moon coin is worth $63.25. What is the total value of the missing coins?
4. Liam has $500.00 He buys eight large pots for gold and four small pots for gold. Liam spends all $500.00 If the large pots each cost $50.00, how much does each small pot cost?	5. Rainbow paint costs $136.96 per can. Liam can paint eight rainbows with just one can. How much would it cost to paint two rainbows?	6. The unicorns get into the rainbow paint again! Each day of the week, they spill two cans. Each can costs $136.96. How much will it cost to replace the paint?
7. Liam is building a fence to keep the unicorns out of the clover patch. He bought 96 boards for $2.45 each and 24 posts for $5.88 each. How much did he spend on the fence?	8. Liam stocks the pots of gold at the ends of three rainbows. He puts $645.25 in each pot. Liam started out with $2,000.00 How much money does he have left?	9. Ten new shamrock plants cost $1.20. Liam needs to plant a field of 3,000 shamrocks. How much will he spend?
10. This week's feed-store special is four unicorn treats for $1.00. If Liam has $45.75, how many treats can he buy?		

Uh-oh! This isn't a four-leaf clover!

What happened when Liam found poison ivy in the clover patch?

To find out, write the unshaded words in order from left to right.

__________ __________

__________ __________

of __________

__________!

He $273.92

had $1,016.00

changed $1,061.75

His $34.24

luck $360.00

good $1,917.44

some $64.25

gold 14

a $235.20

rash $17.12

rubbed $376.32

is $4.75

bad $375.00

of 183

ivy $25.00

luck 207

Bonus: Next week's special at the feed store is ten unicorn treats for $2.00. If Liam has $60.00, how many treats can he buy?

Name ____________________________________

Date ____________________________

One Plucked Peacock

Find the diagram that matches each description. Write the letter on the line. Hint: some pictures will be used more than once.

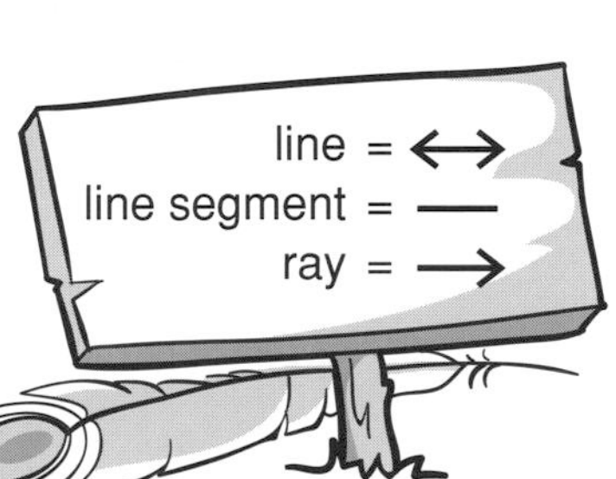

_______ 1. $\overleftrightarrow{AC}$ intersects $\overleftrightarrow{BC}$

_______ 2. $\overline{DC}$ is parallel to $\overline{AB}$

_______ 3. $\overleftrightarrow{AB}$ and $\overleftrightarrow{CD}$ are parallel

_______ 4. $\overline{AB}$ is perpendicular to $\overrightarrow{BC}$

_______ 5. $\overleftrightarrow{AD}$ intersects $\overleftrightarrow{BC}$

_______ 6. Point C is on ray $\overrightarrow{AB}$

_______ 7. $\overrightarrow{AB}$ intersects $\overrightarrow{AC}$ at point A

_______ 8. $\overleftrightarrow{AB}$ is perpendicular to $\overleftrightarrow{CD}$

_______ 9. C is the midpoint of $\overline{BD}$

_______ 10. $\overrightarrow{EF}$ intersects $\overleftrightarrow{AD}$

_______ 11. $\overline{AB}$ intersects $\overline{BC}$

_______ 12. $\overrightarrow{CA}$ intersects $\overleftrightarrow{DC}$

_______ 13. $\overleftrightarrow{AC}$ and $\overleftrightarrow{DB}$ are parallel

_______ 14. $\overline{CA}$ is perpendicular to $\overleftrightarrow{AB}$

_______ 15. $\overleftrightarrow{CD}$ intersects $\overline{DB}$

Did you hear the story about the peacock that lost its feathers?

To answer the riddle, write each letter on its matching numbered line or lines.

___ ___   ___ ___ ___   ___
7 8   5 2 6   11

___ ___ ___ ___ ___ ___ ___ ___ ___
3 9 2 13 8 7 4 1 12

"___ ___ ___ ___"!
8 11 7 12

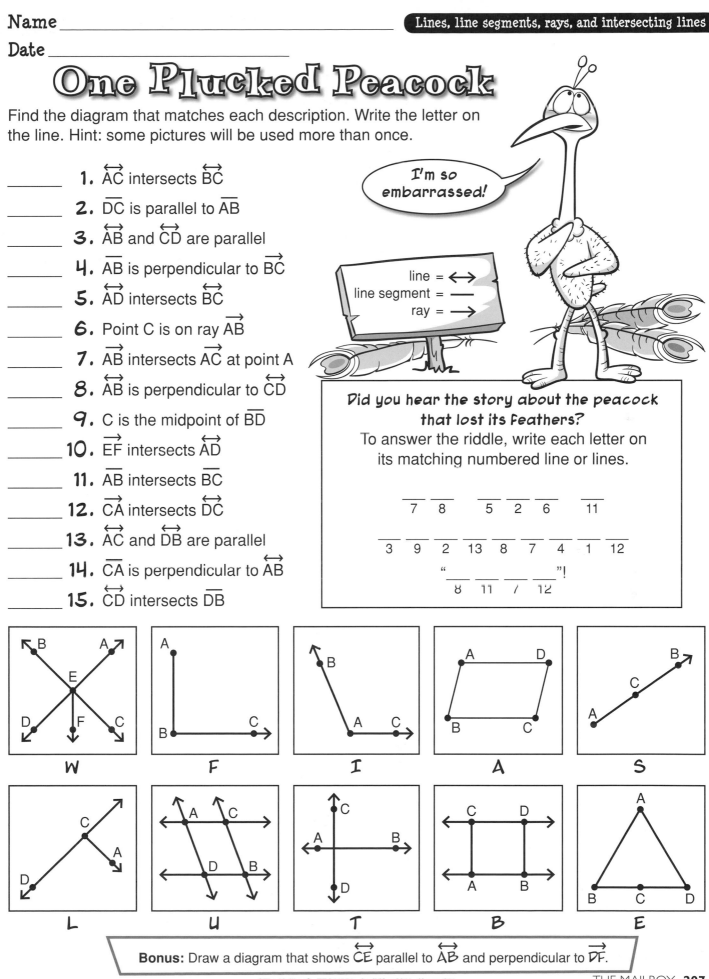

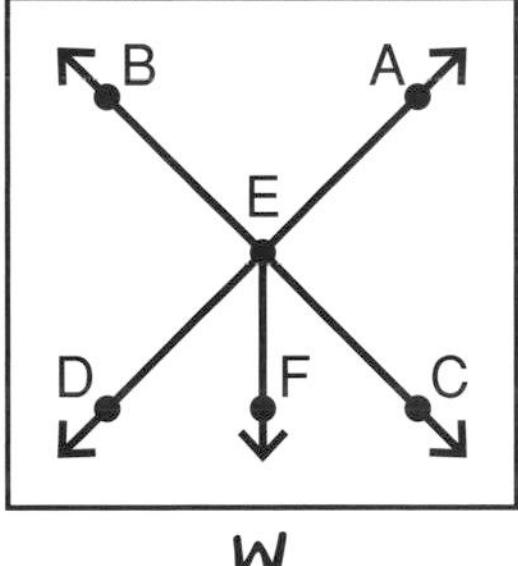

W

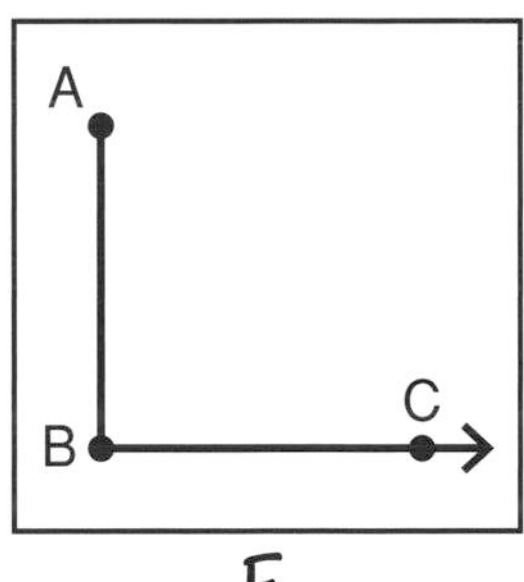

F

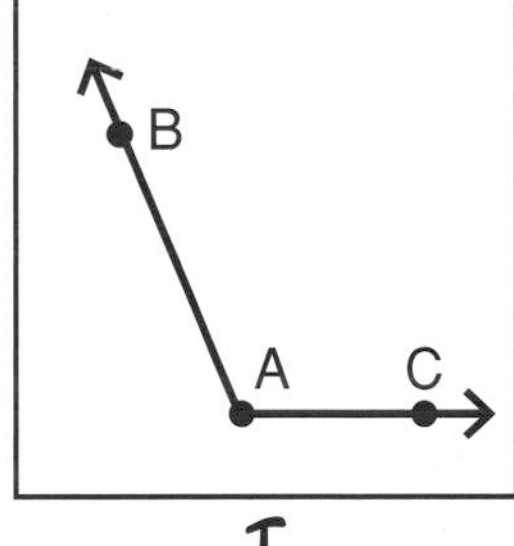

I

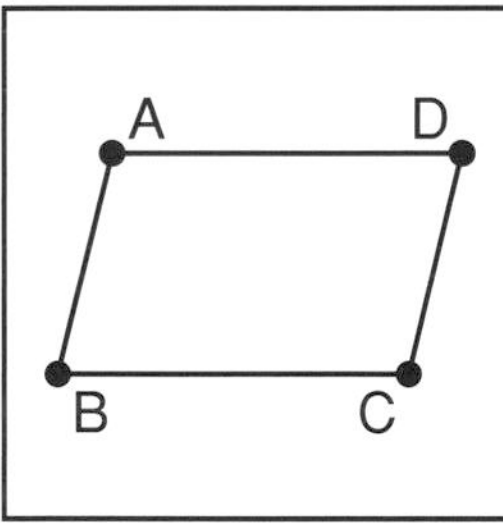

A

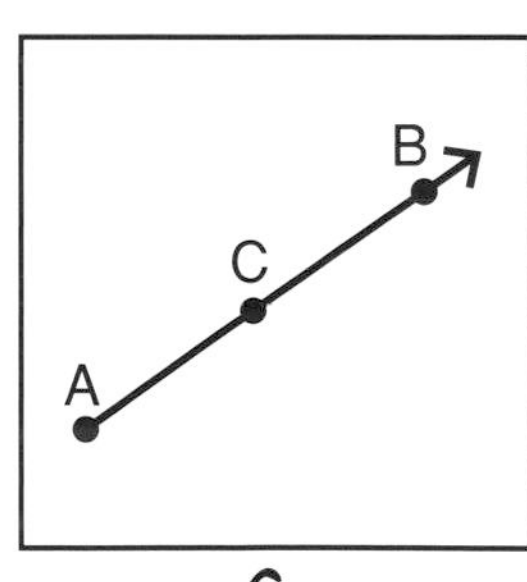

S

L

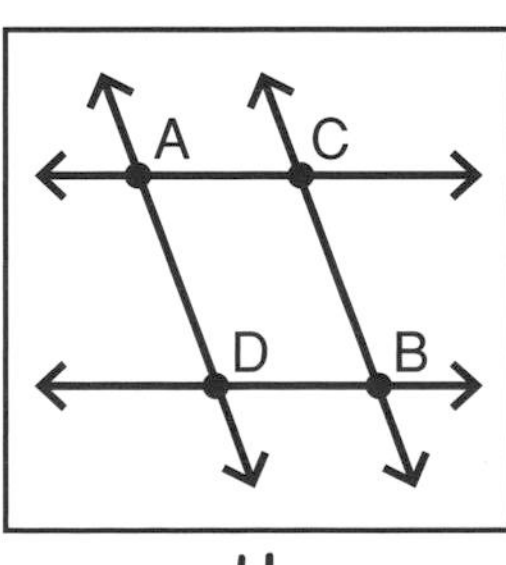

U

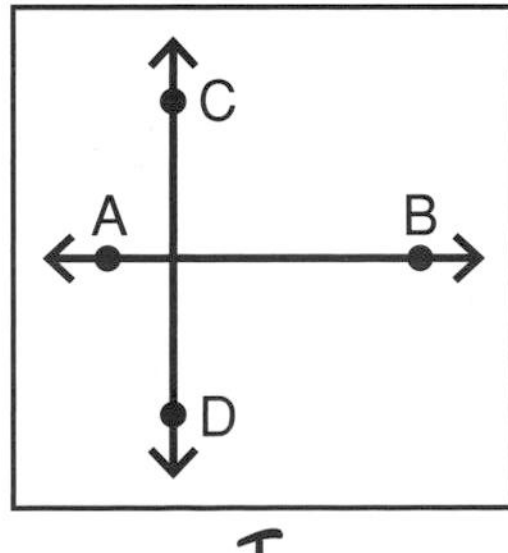

T

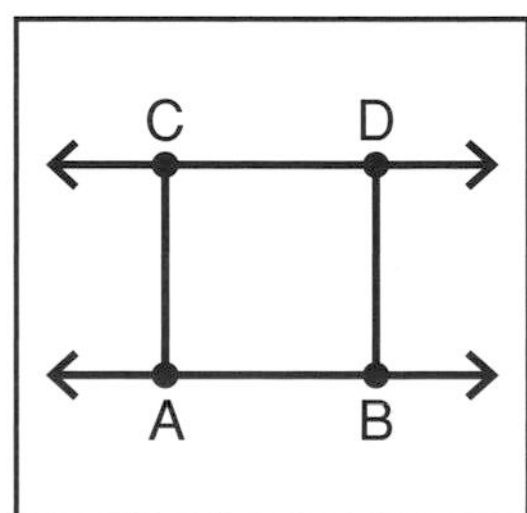

B

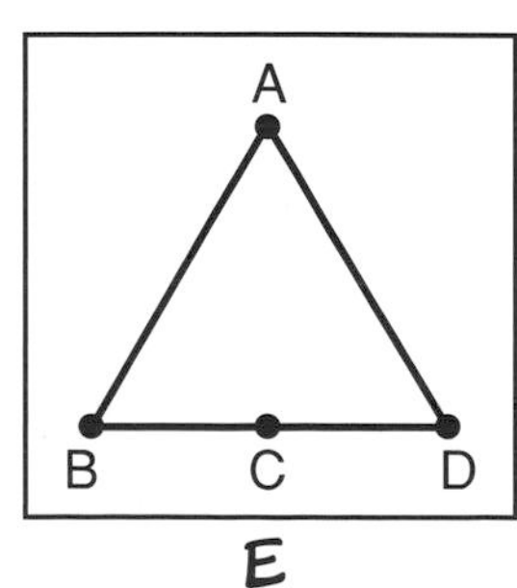

E

Bonus: Draw a diagram that shows $\overleftrightarrow{CE}$ parallel to $\overleftrightarrow{AB}$ and perpendicular to $\overrightarrow{DF}$.

Name ______________________

Date ______________

Some Pun!

On another sheet of paper, rewrite each statement so that it is a riddle. Make sure the question and the answer are complete sentences.

Example: A car is not a car when it turns into a garage.
When isn't a car a car?
A car isn't a car when it turns into a garage!

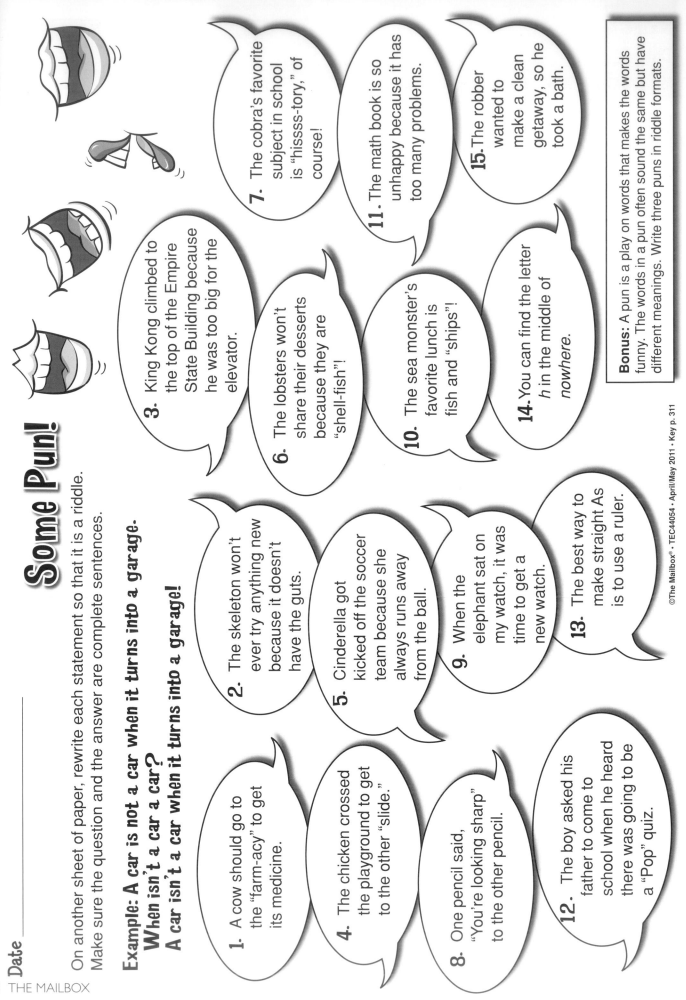

1. A cow should go to the "farm-acy" to get its medicine.
2. The skeleton won't ever try anything new because it doesn't have the guts.
3. King Kong climbed to the top of the Empire State Building because he was too big for the elevator.
4. The chicken crossed the playground to get to the other "slide."
5. Cinderella got kicked off the soccer team because she always runs away from the ball.
6. The lobsters won't share their desserts because they are "shell-fish"!
7. The cobra's favorite subject in school is "hissss-tory," of course!
8. One pencil said, "You're looking sharp" to the other pencil.
9. When the elephant sat on my watch, it was time to get a new watch.
10. The sea monster's favorite lunch is fish and "ships"!
11. The math book is so unhappy because it has too many problems.
12. The boy asked his father to come to school when he heard there was going to be a "Pop" quiz.
13. The best way to make straight As is to use a ruler.
14. You can find the letter *h* in the middle of *nowhere*.
15. The robber wanted to make a clean getaway, so he took a bath.

Bonus: A pun is a play on words that makes the words funny. The words in a pun often sound the same but have different meanings. Write three puns in riddle formats.

Name ____________________

Date ____________________

PARK PICKUP

Write either *good* or *well* to complete each sentence. Then circle the noun or verb being described. Shade each piece of trash as you circle its word.

Hint: *Good* is an adjective that can describe a noun. *Well* is an adverb that can describe a verb, an adverb, or an adjective.

Litterbugs sure did a *good* job of creating a mess!

Thanks to this pollution, I'm not feeling very *well*.

CLANCY PARK

1. I asked my parents, "How __________ do you remember Clancy Park?"
2. I gave them __________ reasons why we needed to make it clean and safe.
3. My mom is __________ at calling and asking for volunteers.
4. Dad's colorful flyers were __________-placed around town.
5. We had a __________ turnout for the cleanup.
6. I knew most of the people who came to help very __________.
7. Molly did a __________ job looking under all the bushes to find trash.
8. Joel is a __________ painter; he made the swings look new again.
9. Jeff finished __________ ahead of the rest of us and did __________ work.
10. Teresa was __________ at collecting cans and bottles to recycle.
11. We all worked __________ past noon.
12. Many of the plants could not grow __________ because of the trash.
13. The bags held up __________ with all the trash we stuffed in them.
14. The park is now a __________ place for children to play safely.
15. We cleaned the park so __________ it didn't even look like the same place.

Bonus: Write two sentences about Earth Day using *good* and *well* in each one. Then circle the words that are being described.

held Teresa turnout reasons grow knew work place cleaned mom placed ahead painter remember job past

Name ______________________________

Date ______________________________

Vacation Bound

Add or subtract. Write each answer in simplest form.

1. $5\frac{2}{8} + 6\frac{3}{8}$ — S 

2. $7\frac{3}{5} - 2\frac{1}{5}$ — I 

3. $\frac{3}{7} + \frac{1}{2}$ — T 

4. $\frac{7}{9} - \frac{2}{3}$ — E

5. $\frac{7}{8} + \frac{3}{12}$ — I 

6. $12\frac{13}{15} - 6\frac{11}{15}$ — N 

7. $3\frac{1}{4} + 1\frac{3}{8}$ — O 

8. $\frac{3}{4} - \frac{5}{16}$ — I 

9. $\frac{9}{12} + \frac{5}{6}$ — T

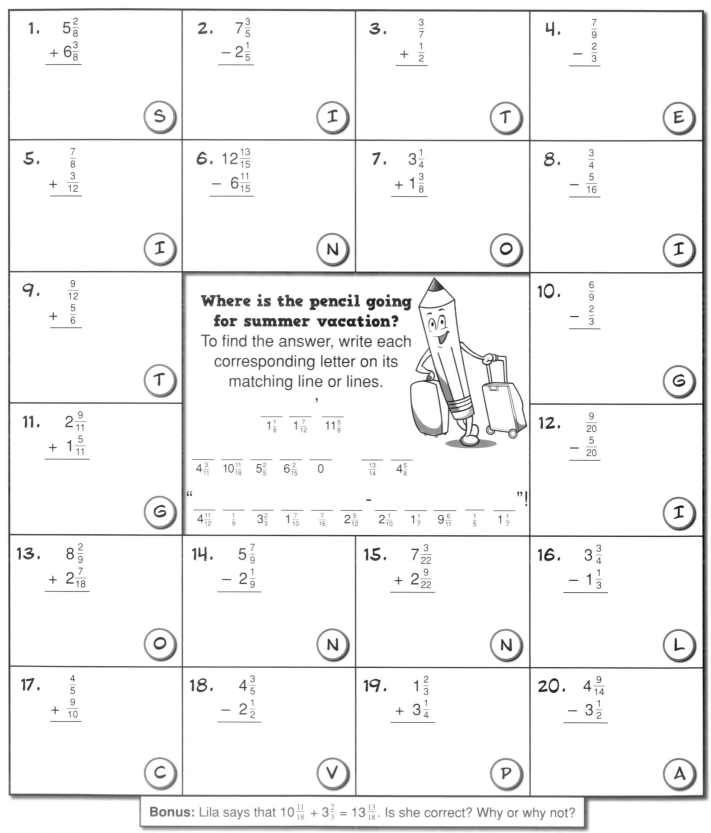

Where is the pencil going for summer vacation?

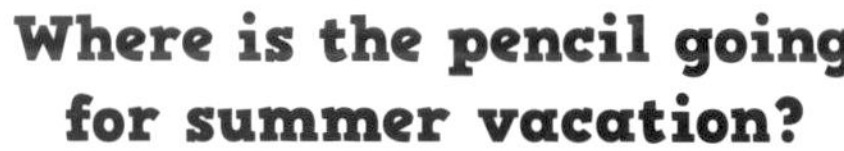

To find the answer, write each corresponding letter on its matching line or lines.

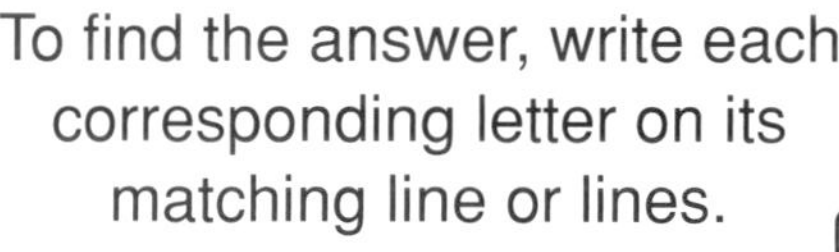

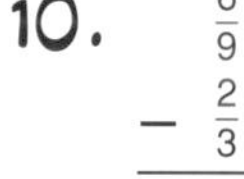

___ ___ ’ ___
$1\frac{1}{8}$ $1\frac{7}{12}$ $11\frac{5}{8}$

___ ___ ___ ___ ___   ___ ___
$4\frac{3}{11}$ $10\frac{11}{18}$ $5\frac{2}{5}$ $6\frac{2}{15}$ 0 $\frac{13}{14}$ $4\frac{5}{8}$

“___ ___ ___ ___ ___ ___ - ___ ___ ___ ___ ___”!
$4\frac{11}{12}$ $\frac{1}{9}$ $3\frac{2}{3}$ $1\frac{7}{10}$ $\frac{7}{16}$ $2\frac{5}{12}$ $2\frac{1}{10}$ $1\frac{1}{7}$ $9\frac{6}{11}$ $\frac{1}{5}$ $1\frac{1}{7}$

10. $\frac{6}{9} - \frac{2}{3}$ — G

11. $2\frac{9}{11} + 1\frac{5}{11}$ — G 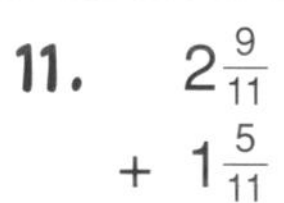

12. $\frac{9}{20} - \frac{5}{20}$ — I

13. $8\frac{2}{9} + 2\frac{7}{18}$ — O 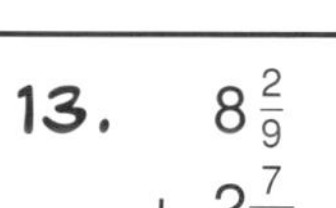 

14. $5\frac{7}{9} - 2\frac{1}{9}$ — N

15. $7\frac{3}{22} + 2\frac{9}{22}$ — N

16. $3\frac{3}{4} - 1\frac{1}{3}$ — L 

17. $\frac{4}{5} + \frac{9}{10}$ — C 

18. $4\frac{3}{5} - 2\frac{1}{2}$ — V 

19. $1\frac{2}{3} + 3\frac{1}{4}$ — P

20. $4\frac{9}{14} - 3\frac{1}{2}$ — A

Bonus: Lila says that $10\frac{11}{18} + 3\frac{2}{3} = 13\frac{13}{18}$. Is she correct? Why or why not?

Name ______________________________

Date ______________________

Jump In!

Write a word or words from below to complete each metaphor.
Then circle the noun or nouns that are being described.

1. The clouds in the summer sky were ____________________.
2. The water was a sparkling ____________________.
3. The warm water made the pond a ____________________ waiting for bathers.
4. Two turtles, ____________________ soaking up the sun's rays, rested on a log.
5. Adam, Marissa, and Tyler were ____________________ hitting the water.
6. Each splash was a ____________________.
7. Sierra, a ____________________ on the shore, was the last one to jump in.
8. The kids were ____________________ darting through the pond.
9. Adam was a ____________________ diving to the bottom of the pond.
10. The bottom of the pond was a sandy ____________________.
11. A catfish was a ____________________ peeking out from the bank.
12. Sierra and Marissa, ____________________ cutting through the water, raced across the pond.
13. Adam and Tyler were ____________________, splashing and playing in the water.

nosy neighbor	carpet
otter	cotton candy
sloth	field of diamonds
tadpoles	submarine
water balloons	watery firework
bathtub	sunbathers
swordfish	dolphins
statue	cannonballs

14. After an hour of energetic swimming, Adam was a ____________________ crawling from the water onto the beach.
15. Sierra was an ____________________, floating easily on the water.
16. The afternoon ended when dark clouds, ____________________ ready to burst, gathered on the horizon.

Bonus: Choose five sentences above. Then draw a sketch to show what each one's metaphor describes.

Name ______________________________

Date ______________________

Gotcha?

In each row, shade the boxes with equivalent forms.

1. $\frac{4}{10}$	0.4 **S**	0.2 **W**	$\frac{2}{5}$ **T**	$\frac{12}{30}$ **R**
2. 0.05	$\frac{5}{100}$ **E**	$\frac{1}{10}$ **F**	$\frac{1}{20}$ **N**	0.050 **M**
3. $\frac{7}{100}$	$\frac{35}{500}$ **O**	0.07 **P**	$\frac{14}{200}$ **I**	0.7 **H**
4. 0.9	0.90 **E**	0.090 **Y**	$\frac{27}{30}$ **D**	$\frac{9}{10}$ **K**
5. 0.5	$\frac{5}{10}$ **I**	$\frac{50}{100}$ **N**	0.05 **R**	$\frac{1}{2}$ **T**
6. $\frac{8}{10}$	$\frac{4}{5}$ **A**	0.8 **S**	0.08 **O**	$\frac{32}{40}$ **W**
7. 0.25	$\frac{2}{8}$ **H**	0.025 **A**	$\frac{25}{100}$ **Q**	$\frac{1}{4}$ **N**
8. $\frac{3}{4}$	$\frac{9}{12}$ **E**	$\frac{15}{20}$ **O**	0.75 **F**	0.34 **E**
9. 0.1	$\frac{1}{100}$ **K**	$\frac{1}{10}$ **G**	$\frac{6}{60}$ **I**	0.10 **E**
10. $\frac{60}{100}$	$\frac{2}{5}$ **I**	0.6 **N**	$\frac{6}{10}$ **L**	0.60 **H**
11. $\frac{12}{15}$	$\frac{4}{5}$ **X**	0.8 **Y**	$\frac{8}{10}$ **D**	$\frac{3}{5}$ **S**
12. 0.01	0.010 **C**	$\frac{5}{500}$ **H**	0.1 **D**	$\frac{1}{100}$ **E**
13. $\frac{6}{20}$	0.03 **L**	$\frac{3}{10}$ **B**	0.3 **A**	$\frac{12}{40}$ **K**
14. 0.2	0.20 **R**	$\frac{1}{5}$ **C**	$\frac{4}{20}$ **H**	$\frac{2}{20}$ **P**
15. $\frac{3}{8}$	$\frac{12}{32}$ **N**	0.375 **G**	$\frac{6}{16}$ **E**	0.35 **T**

Bonus: Write an equivalent fraction or decimal for each unshaded number in the chart above.

Which sea animal was voted best dressed?

To find the answer, write the letters from the unshaded boxes on the matching numbered line or lines.

___ ___ ___   ___ W ___ ___ ___ ___ ___ ___ ___ – ___ ___
15 3 8   11 1 6 5 12 2 10 11 3   10 15

___ ___ W ___ ___ ___   ___ ___ ___ ___ ___   ___ ___ ___ ___ ___!
7 13 1 7 4 11   13 6 6 9 11   11 3 7 5 14

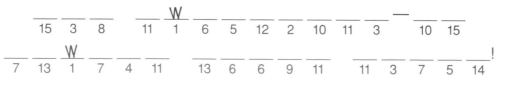

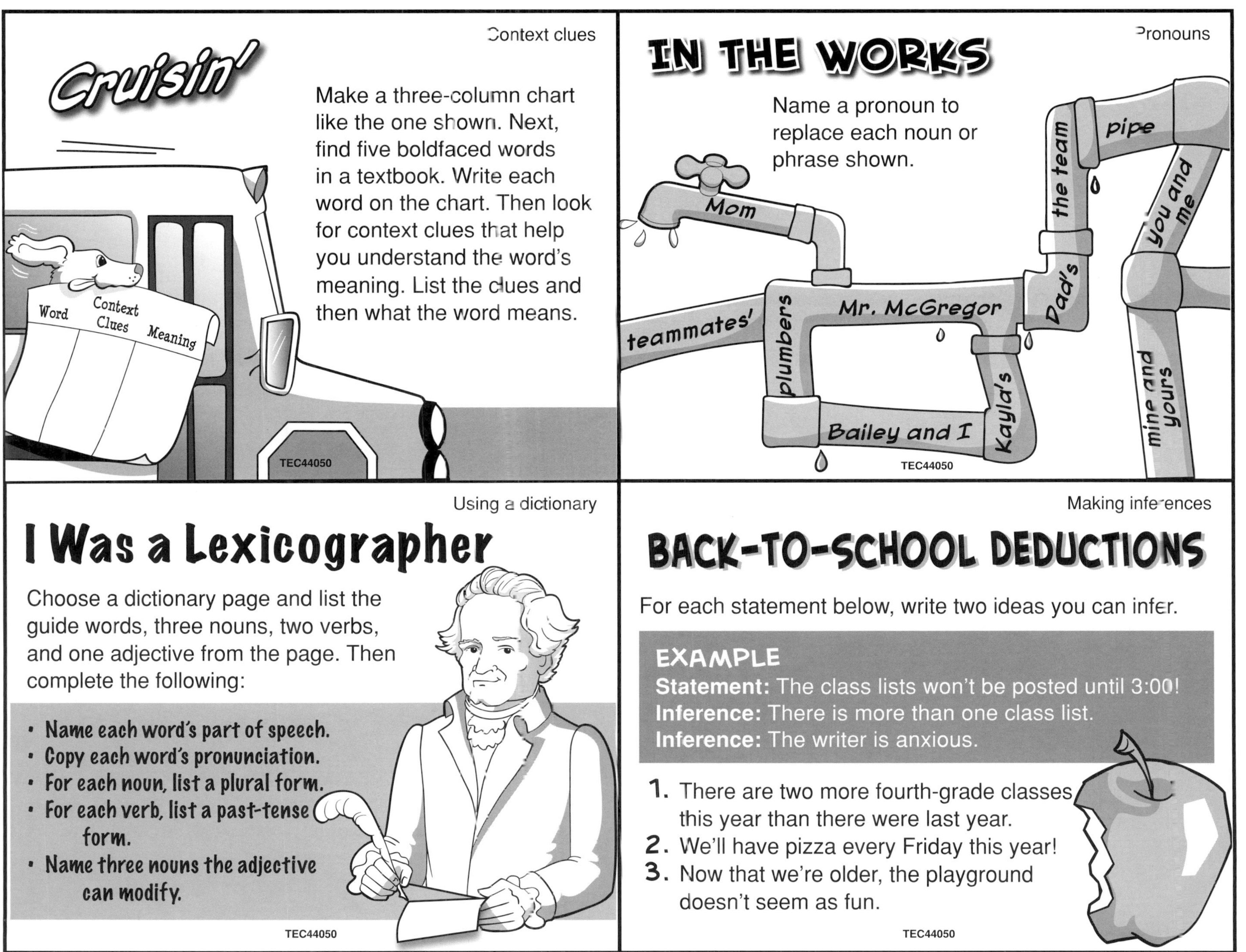

Context clues

Cruisin'

Make a three-column chart like the one shown. Next, find five boldfaced words in a textbook. Write each word on the chart. Then look for context clues that help you understand the word's meaning. List the clues and then what the word means.

TEC44050

Pronouns

IN THE WORKS

Name a pronoun to replace each noun or phrase shown.

TEC44050

Using a dictionary

I Was a Lexicographer

Choose a dictionary page and list the guide words, three nouns, two verbs, and one adjective from the page. Then complete the following:

- Name each word's part of speech.
- Copy each word's pronunciation.
- For each noun, list a plural form.
- For each verb, list a past-tense form.
- Name three nouns the adjective can modify.

TEC44050

Making inferences

BACK-TO-SCHOOL DEDUCTIONS

For each statement below, write two ideas you can infer.

EXAMPLE
Statement: The class lists won't be posted until 3:00!
Inference: There is more than one class list.
Inference: The writer is anxious.

1. There are two more fourth-grade classes this year than there were last year.
2. We'll have pizza every Friday this year!
3. Now that we're older, the playground doesn't seem as fun.

TEC44050

Use as center or free-time activities.

Expanded form

Everybody, Stretch!

Copy each number below. Then write the number's expanded form inside a stretched-out snake shape.

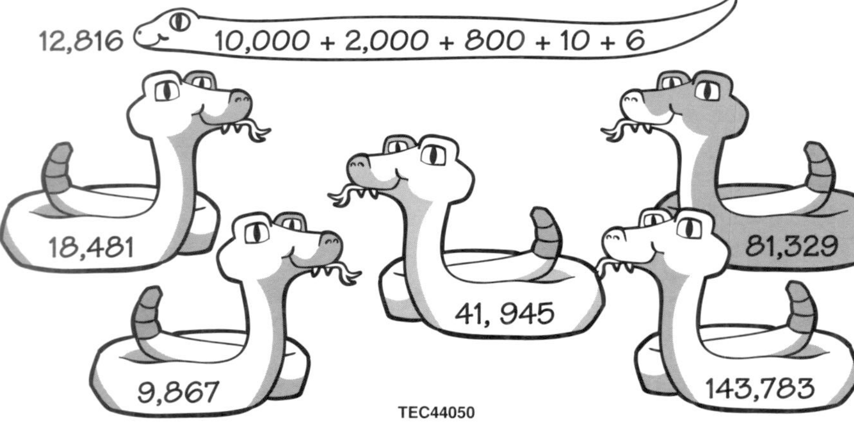

TEC44050

Coordinate pairs

Bumper Crop

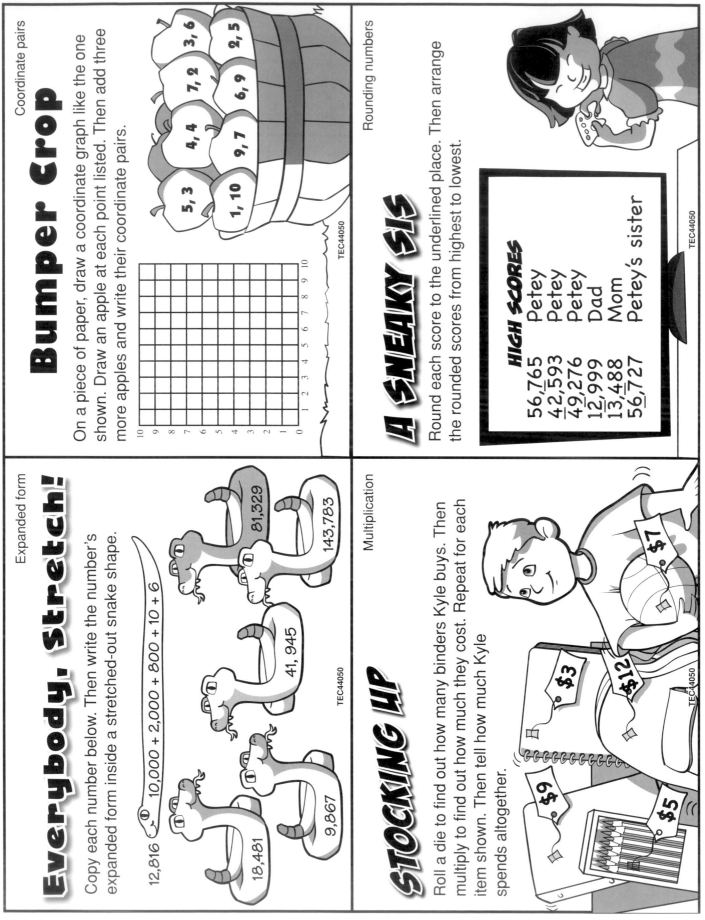

On a piece of paper, draw a coordinate graph like the one shown. Draw an apple at each point listed. Then add three more apples and write their coordinate pairs.

5, 3 · 4, 4 · 7, 2 · 3, 6 · 1, 10 · 9, 7 · 6, 9 · 2, 5

TEC44050

Multiplication

STOCKING UP

Roll a die to find out how many binders Kyle buys. Then multiply to find out how much they cost. Repeat for each item shown. Then tell how much Kyle spends altogether.

TEC44050

Rounding numbers

A SNEAKY SIS

Round each score to the underlined place. Then arrange the rounded scores from highest to lowest.

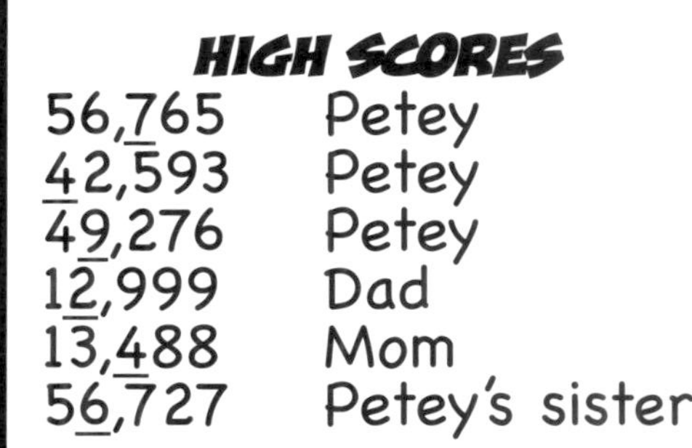

HIGH SCORES
56,765 Petey
42,593 Petey
49,276 Petey
12,999 Dad
13,488 Mom
56,727 Petey's sister

TEC44050

Language Arts Activity Cards

Use as center or free-time activities.

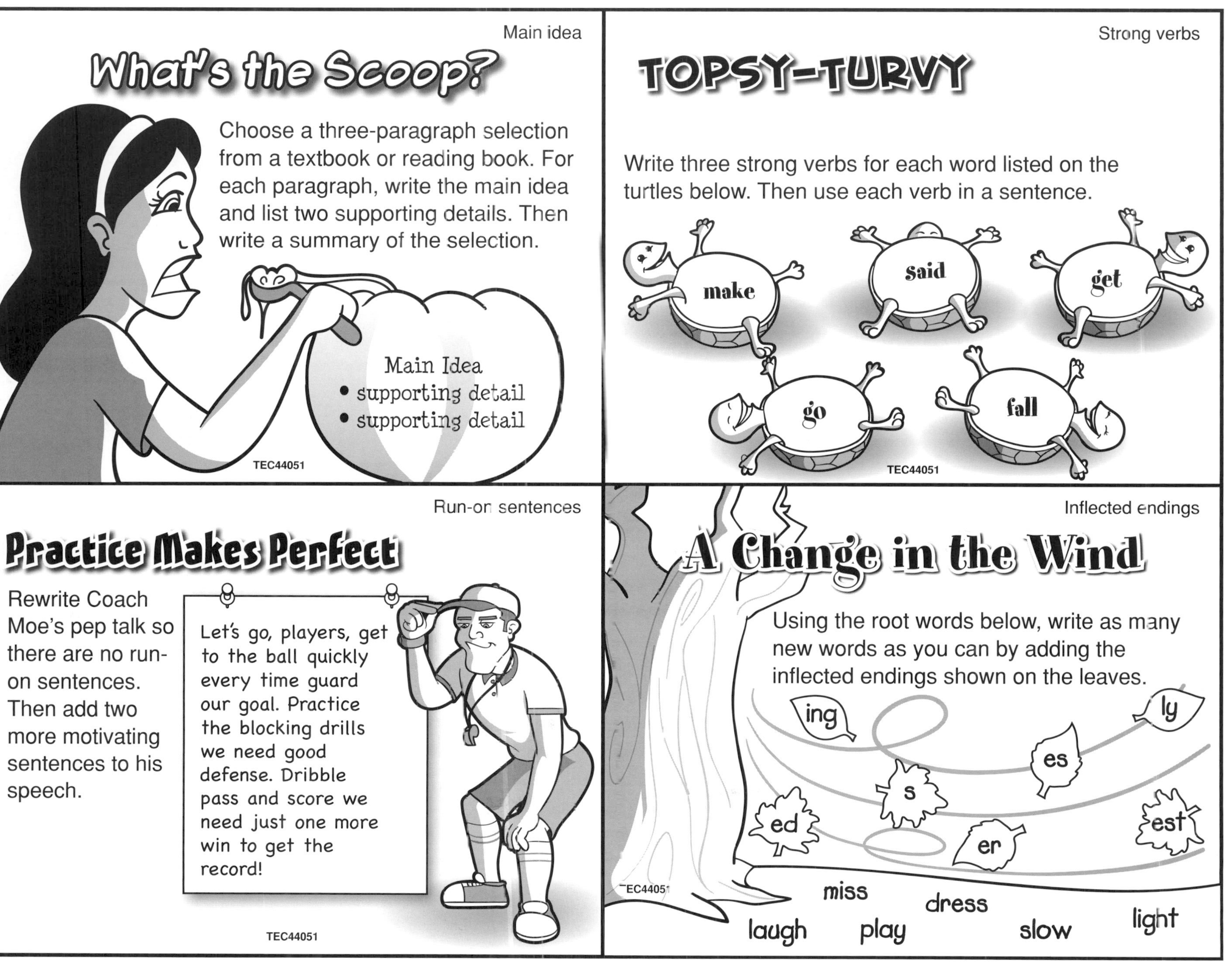

Main idea

What's the Scoop?

Choose a three-paragraph selection from a textbook or reading book. For each paragraph, write the main idea and list two supporting details. Then write a summary of the selection.

TEC44051

Strong verbs

TOPSY-TURVY

Write three strong verbs for each word listed on the turtles below. Then use each verb in a sentence.

TEC44051

Run-on sentences

Practice Makes Perfect

Rewrite Coach Moe's pep talk so there are no run-on sentences. Then add two more motivating sentences to his speech.

Let's go, players, get to the ball quickly every time guard our goal. Practice the blocking drills we need good defense. Dribble pass and score we need just one more win to get the record!

TEC44051

Inflected endings

A Change in the Wind

Using the root words below, write as many new words as you can by adding the inflected endings shown on the leaves.

laugh miss play dress slow light

TEC44051

Math Activity Cards

Use as center or free-time activities.

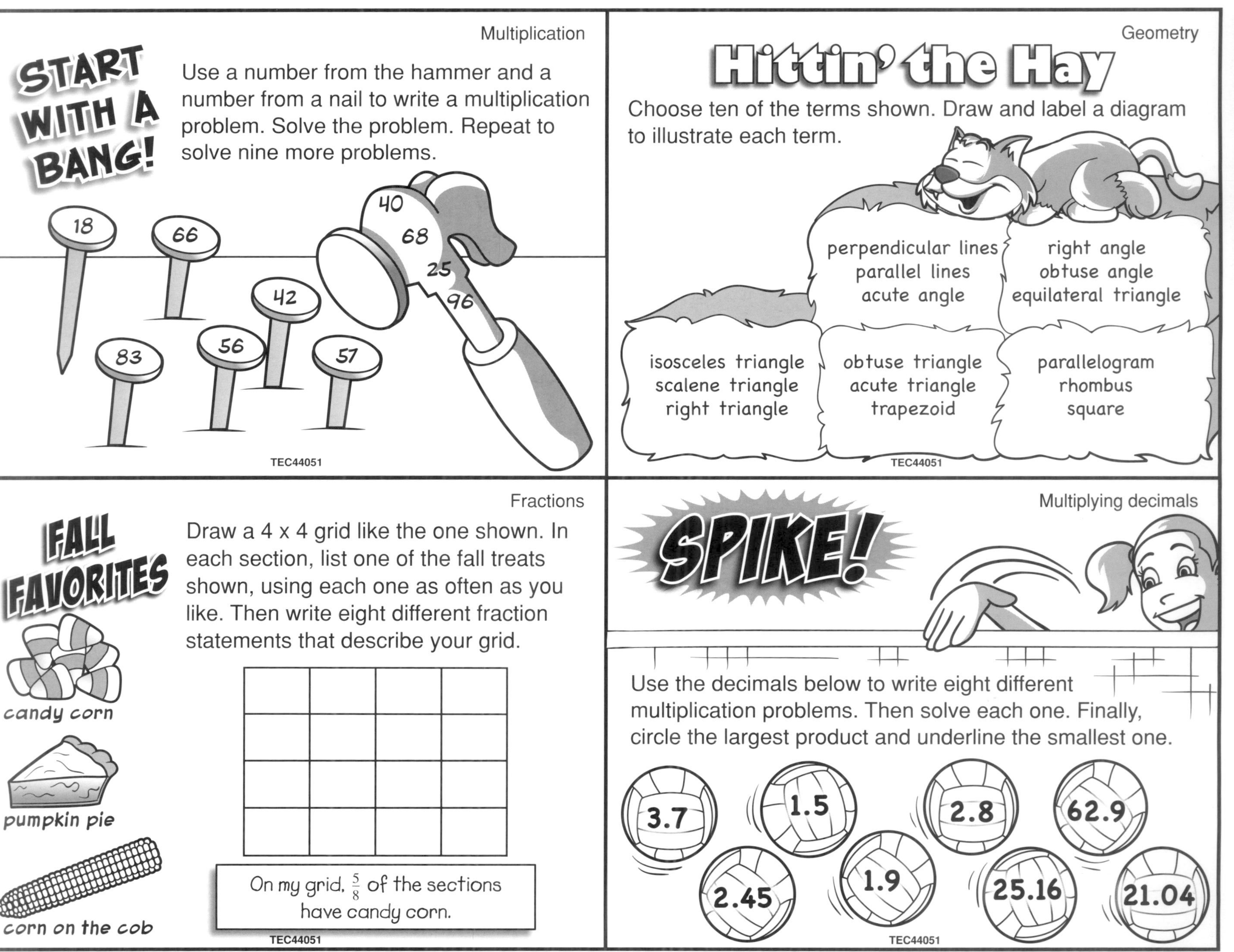

Multiplication

START WITH A BANG!

Use a number from the hammer and a number from a nail to write a multiplication problem. Solve the problem. Repeat to solve nine more problems.

TEC44051

Geometry

Hittin' the Hay

Choose ten of the terms shown. Draw and label a diagram to illustrate each term.

perpendicular lines
parallel lines
acute angle

right angle
obtuse angle
equilateral triangle

isosceles triangle
scalene triangle
right triangle

obtuse triangle
acute triangle
trapezoid

parallelogram
rhombus
square

TEC44051

Fractions

FALL FAVORITES

Draw a 4 x 4 grid like the one shown. In each section, list one of the fall treats shown, using each one as often as you like. Then write eight different fraction statements that describe your grid.

On my grid, $\frac{5}{8}$ of the sections have candy corn.

TEC44051

Multiplying decimals

SPIKE!

Use the decimals below to write eight different multiplication problems. Then solve each one. Finally, circle the largest product and underline the smallest one.

TEC44051

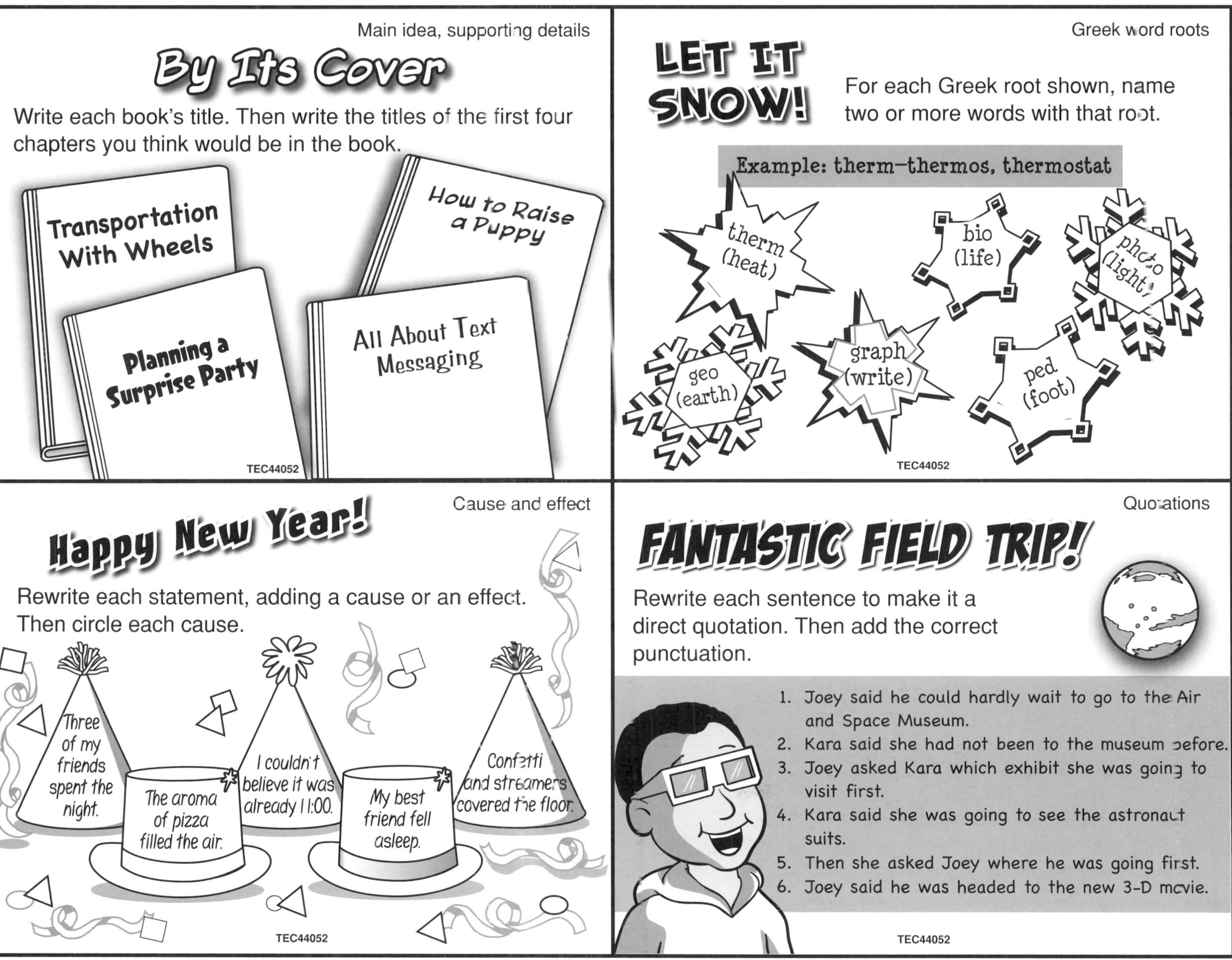

Transportation With Wheels
Planning a Surprise Party
How to Raise a Puppy
All About Text Messaging
therm (heat)
bio (life)
photo (light)
geo (earth)
graph (write)
ped (foot)
Three of my friends spent the night.
The aroma of pizza filled the air.
I couldn't believe it was already 11:00.
My best friend fell asleep.
Confetti and streamers covered the floor.

Main idea, supporting details

By Its Cover

Write each book's title. Then write the titles of the first four chapters you think would be in the book.

TEC44052

Greek word roots

LET IT SNOW!

For each Greek root shown, name two or more words with that root.

Example: therm–thermos, thermostat

TEC44052

Cause and effect

Happy New Year!

Rewrite each statement, adding a cause or an effect. Then circle each cause.

TEC44052

Quotations

FANTASTIC FIELD TRIP!

Rewrite each sentence to make it a direct quotation. Then add the correct punctuation.

1. Joey said he could hardly wait to go to the Air and Space Museum.
2. Kara said she had not been to the museum before.
3. Joey asked Kara which exhibit she was going to visit first.
4. Kara said she was going to see the astronaut suits.
5. Then she asked Joey where he was going first.
6. Joey said he was headed to the new 3-D movie.

TEC44052

Math Activity Cards

Use as center or free-time activities.

Multiplication

GOING, GOING, GONE!

Use the code to write each problem. Then multiply.

Code			
A = 1	B = 2	F = 3	H = 4
I = 5	L = 6	M = 7	N = 8
O = 9	R = 1	T = 2	U = 3

① BAT x AT

② RUN x TO

③ OUT x OH

④ HIT x TO

⑤ MLB x ON

⑥ FAN x IN

TEC44052

Area

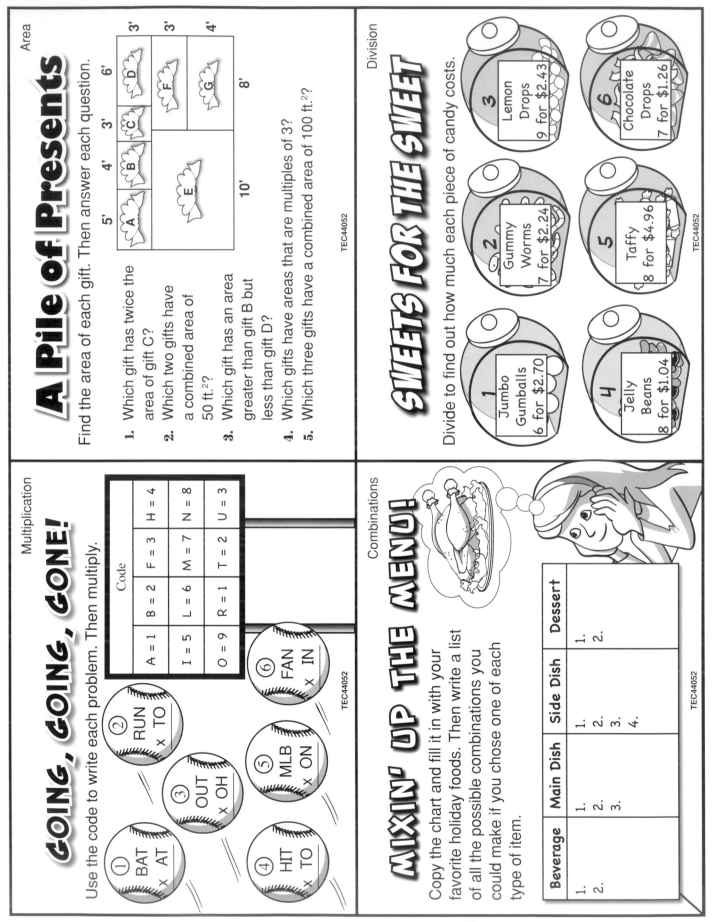

A Pile of Presents

Find the area of each gift. Then answer each question.

A (5' × 3')	B (4' × 3')	C (3' × 3')	D (6' × 3')
E (10' × 7')		F (8' × 3')	
		G (8' × 4')	

1. Which gift has twice the area of gift C?
2. Which two gifts have a combined area of 50 ft.^{2}?
3. Which gift has an area greater than gift B but less than gift D?
4. Which gifts have areas that are multiples of 3?
5. Which three gifts have a combined area of 100 ft.^{2}?

TEC44052

Combinations

MIXIN' UP THE MENU!

Copy the chart and fill it in with your favorite holiday foods. Then write a list of all the possible combinations you could make if you chose one of each type of item.

Beverage	Main Dish	Side Dish	Dessert
1. 2.	1. 2. 3.	1. 2. 3. 4.	1. 2.

TEC44052

Division

SWEETS FOR THE SWEET

Divide to find out how much each piece of candy costs.

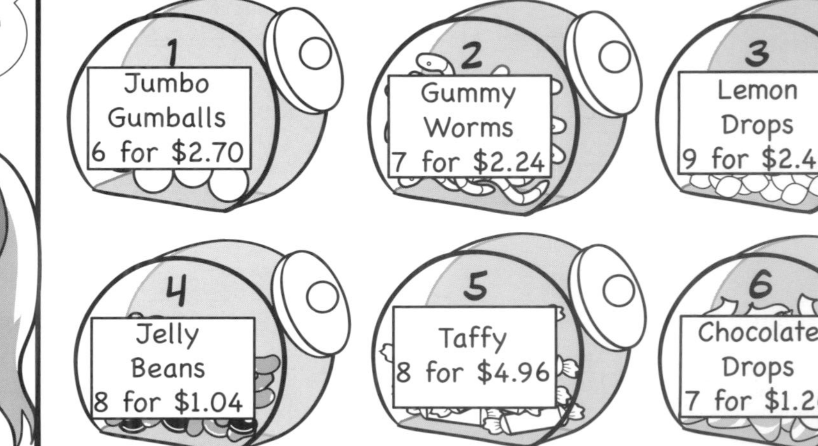

TEC44052

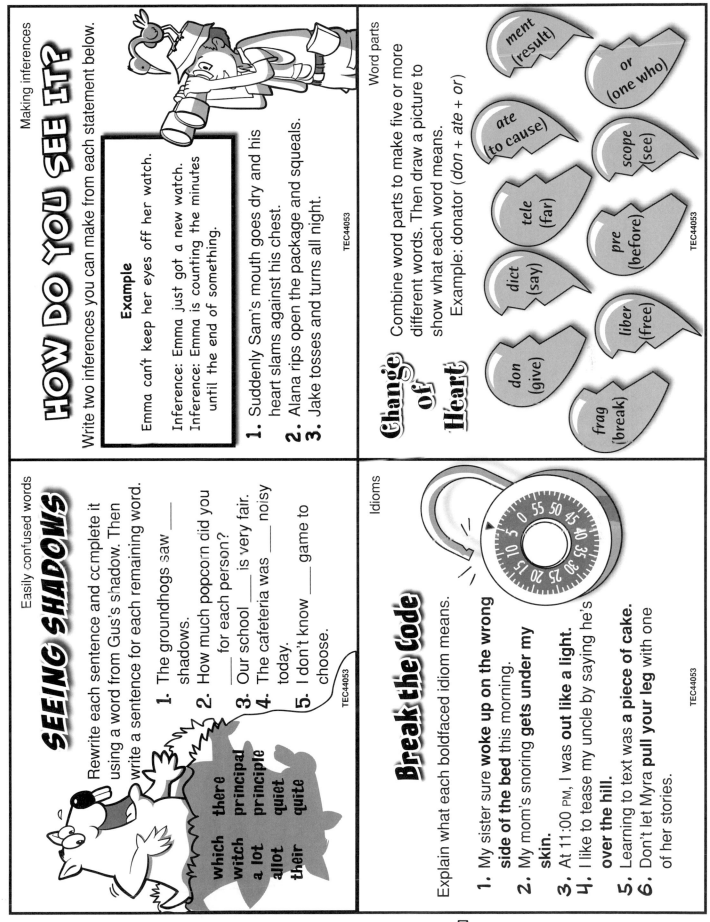

Language Arts Activity Cards

Use as center or free-time activities.

Easily confused words

SEEING SHADOWS

Rewrite each sentence and complete it using a word from Gus's shadow. Then write a sentence for each remaining word.

which
witch
a lot
allot
their
there
principal
principle
quiet
quite

1. The groundhogs saw ___ shadows.
2. How much popcorn did you ___ for each person?
3. Our school ___ is very fair.
4. The cafeteria was ___ noisy today.
5. I don't know ___ game to choose.

TEC44053

Making inferences

HOW DO YOU SEE IT?

Write two inferences you can make from each statement below.

> **Example**
> Emma can't keep her eyes off her watch.
>
> Inference: Emma just got a new watch.
> Inference: Emma is counting the minutes until the end of something.

1. Suddenly Sam's mouth goes dry and his heart slams against his chest.
2. Alana rips open the package and squeals.
3. Jake tosses and turns all night.

TEC44053

Idioms

Break the Code

Explain what each boldfaced idiom means.

1. My sister sure **woke up on the wrong side of the bed** this morning.
2. My mom's snoring **gets under my skin.**
3. At 11:00 PM, I was **out like a light.**
4. I like to tease my uncle by saying he's **over the hill.**
5. Learning to text was **a piece of cake.**
6. Don't let Myra **pull your leg** with one of her stories.

TEC44053

Word parts

Change of Heart

Combine word parts to make five or more different words. Then draw a picture to show what each word means.

Example: donator (*don* + *ate* + *or*)

don (give) | *dict* (say) | *tele* (far) | *ate* (to cause) | *ment* (result) | *frag* (break) | *liber* (free) | *pre* (before) | *scope* (see) | *or* (one who)

TEC44053

Math Activity Cards

Use as center or free-time activities.

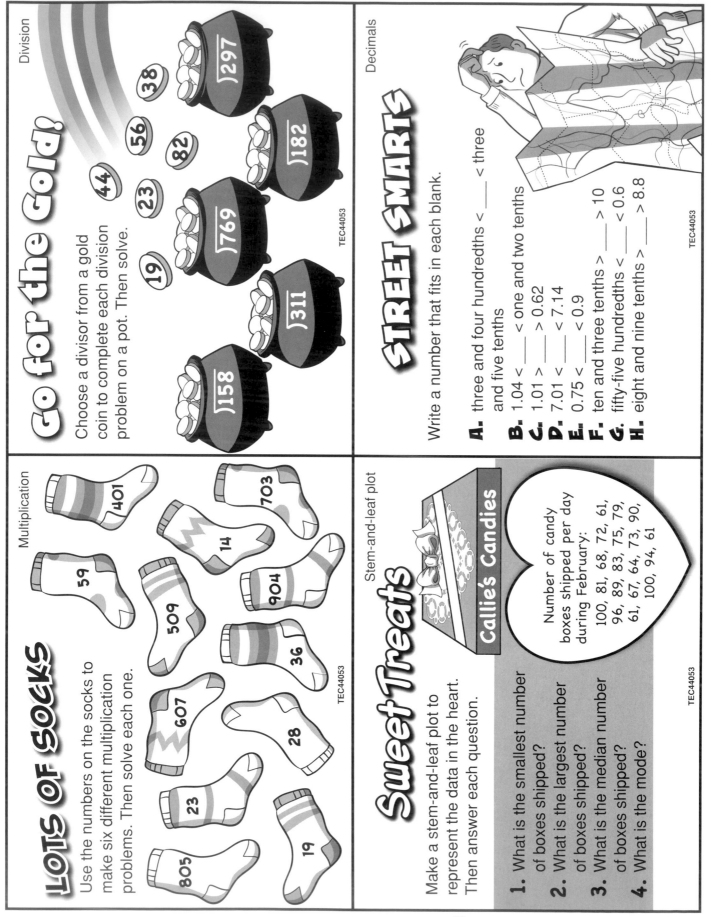

Multiplication

LOTS OF SOCKS

Use the numbers on the socks to make six different multiplication problems. Then solve each one.

TEC44053

Division

Go for the Gold!

Choose a divisor from a gold coin to complete each division problem on a pot. Then solve.

TEC44053

Stem-and-leaf plot

Sweet Treats

Make a stem-and-leaf plot to represent the data in the heart. Then answer each question.

Callie's Candies

Number of candy boxes shipped per day during February:

100, 81, 68, 72, 61, 96, 89, 83, 75, 79, 61, 67, 64, 73, 90, 100, 94, 61

1. What is the smallest number of boxes shipped?
2. What is the largest number of boxes shipped?
3. What is the median number of boxes shipped?
4. What is the mode?

TEC44053

Decimals

STREET SMARTS

Write a number that fits in each blank.

A. three and four hundredths < ___ < three and five tenths
B. 1.04 < ___ < one and two tenths
C. 1.01 > ___ > 0.62
D. 7.01 < ___ < 7.14
E. 0.75 < ___ < 0.9
F. ten and three tenths > ___ > 10
G. fifty-five hundredths < ___ < 0.6
H. eight and nine tenths > ___ > 8.8

TEC44053

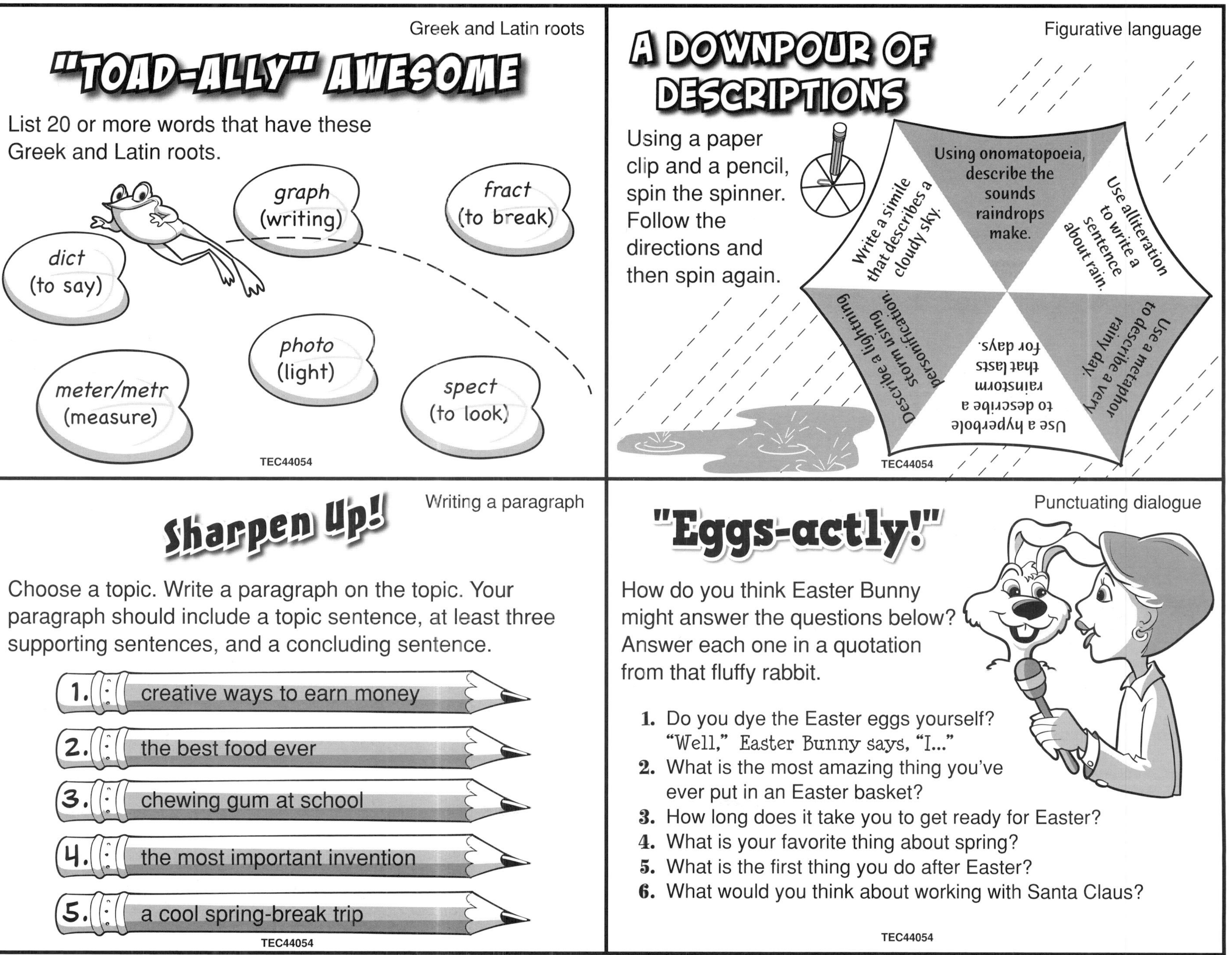
Greek and Latin roots
"TOAD-ALLY" AWESOME
List 20 or more words that have these Greek and Latin roots.
dict (to say)
graph (writing)
fract (to break)
photo (light)
meter/metr (measure)
spect (to look)
TEC44054
Figurative language
A DOWNPOUR OF DESCRIPTIONS
Using a paper clip and a pencil, spin the spinner. Follow the directions and then spin again.
Using onomatopoeia, describe the sounds raindrops make.
Use alliteration to write a sentence about rain.
Use a metaphor to describe a very rainy day.
Use a hyperbole to describe a rainstorm that lasts for days.
Describe a lightning storm using personification.
Write a simile that describes a cloudy sky.
TEC44054
Writing a paragraph
Sharpen Up!
Choose a topic. Write a paragraph on the topic. Your paragraph should include a topic sentence, at least three supporting sentences, and a concluding sentence.
1. creative ways to earn money
2. the best food ever
3. chewing gum at school
4. the most important invention
5. a cool spring-break trip
TEC44054
Punctuating dialogue
"Eggs-actly!"
How do you think Easter Bunny might answer the questions below? Answer each one in a quotation from that fluffy rabbit.
1. Do you dye the Easter eggs yourself?
"Well," Easter Bunny says, "I..."
2. What is the most amazing thing you've ever put in an Easter basket?
3. How long does it take you to get ready for Easter?
4. What is your favorite thing about spring?
5. What is the first thing you do after Easter?
6. What would you think about working with Santa Claus?
TEC44054

Math Activity Cards

Use as center or free-time activities.

Area

READY TO WRAP

Find the missing measurement for each sheet of wrapping paper.

TEC44054

Division

Surf's Up!

Use the numbers on the surfboards to write six different division problems. Use the numbers in the circles as the divisors. Solve each problem.

TEC44054

Greater multiplication

TOO COOL

Use the numbers on the ice cream scoops to write and solve six different multiplication problems.

TEC44054

Range, median, mode, and mean

A "Buzz-y" Time of Year

Find the range, median, mode, and mean for each set of test scores.

Who has the highest mean test score?

TEC44054

Descriptive writing

I Scream! You Scream!

Using your five senses, write a paragraph that describes your favorite summer treat.

What does it smell like?

How does it taste?

What is its texture like?

When you look at it, what do you see?

Does it make any sound?

Do you make any sounds when you eat it?

TEC44055

Idioms

IT'S A PIECE OF CAKE!

Write a dialogue between you and your best friend. Use four of the idioms below in your dialogue.

Actions speak louder than words.
Hold your horses.
Leopards don't change their spots.
Keep your chin up.
Hit the books.
Let the cat out of the bag.
Every cloud has a silver lining.
They are a dime a dozen.

TEC44055

Character analysis

CATCH A WAVE!

Choose an important character from a recently read story. Draw a five-column chart labeled as shown. Next, make notes in each column about the character. Then use your notes to describe the character.

Things the character does	Things the character thinks	Main problem the character faces	The character's strengths	The character's weaknesses

TEC44055

Compound subjects and predicates

PET PROJECT

For each sentence on a bone, roll a die.

- If you roll 2 or 3, revise the sentence so it has a compound subject.
- If you roll 4 or 5, revise the sentence so it has a compound predicate.
- If you roll 1 or 6, revise the sentence so it has a compound subject and a compound predicate.

Canaries make fun pets.

If you give hamsters paper, they will chew it up.

Puppies will play for hours.

Kittens have very sharp claws.

Some snakes need warming stones.

TEC44055

Math Activity Cards

Use as center or free-time activities.

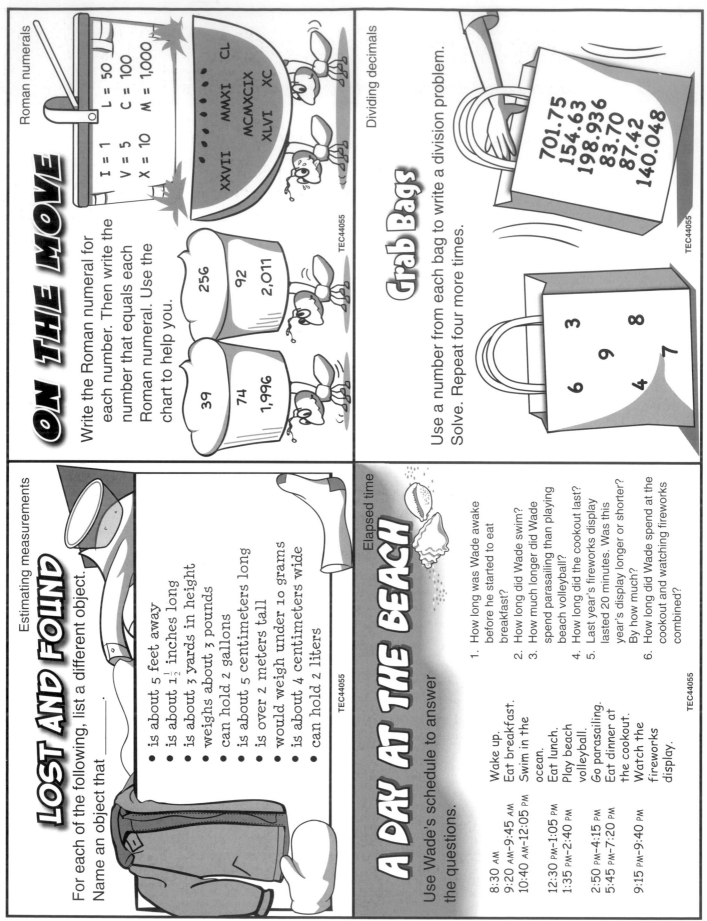

Estimating measurements

LOST AND FOUND

For each of the following, list a different object. Name an object that ______.

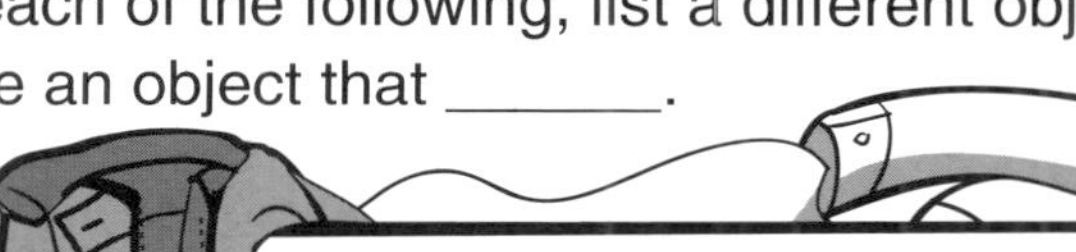

- is about 5 feet away
- is about $1\frac{1}{2}$ inches long
- is about 3 yards in height
- weighs about 3 pounds
- can hold 2 gallons
- is about 5 centimeters long
- is over 2 meters tall
- would weigh under 10 grams
- is about 4 centimeters wide
- can hold 2 liters

TEC44055

Roman numerals

ON THE MOVE

Write the Roman numeral for each number. Then write the number that equals each Roman numeral. Use the chart to help you.

I = 1	L = 50
V = 5	C = 100
X = 10	M = 1,000

39, 74, 1,996

256, 92, 2,011

XXVII, MMXI, CL, MCMXCIX, XLVI, XC

TEC44055

Elapsed time

A DAY AT THE BEACH

Use Wade's schedule to answer the questions.

8:30 AM	Wake up.
9:20 AM–9:45 AM	Eat breakfast.
10:40 AM–12:05 PM	Swim in the ocean.
12:30 PM–1:05 PM	Eat lunch.
1:35 PM–2:40 PM	Play beach volleyball.
2:50 PM–4:15 PM	Go parasailing.
5:45 PM–7:20 PM	Eat dinner at the cookout.
9:15 PM–9:40 PM	Watch the fireworks display.

1. How long was Wade awake before he started to eat breakfast?
2. How long did Wade swim?
3. How much longer did Wade spend parasailing than playing beach volleyball?
4. How long did the cookout last?
5. Last year's fireworks display lasted 20 minutes. Was this year's display longer or shorter? By how much?
6. How long did Wade spend at the cookout and watching fireworks combined?

TEC44055

Dividing decimals

Grab Bags

Use a number from each bag to write a division problem. Solve. Repeat four more times.

6, 3, 9, 4, 8, 7

TEC44055

Science

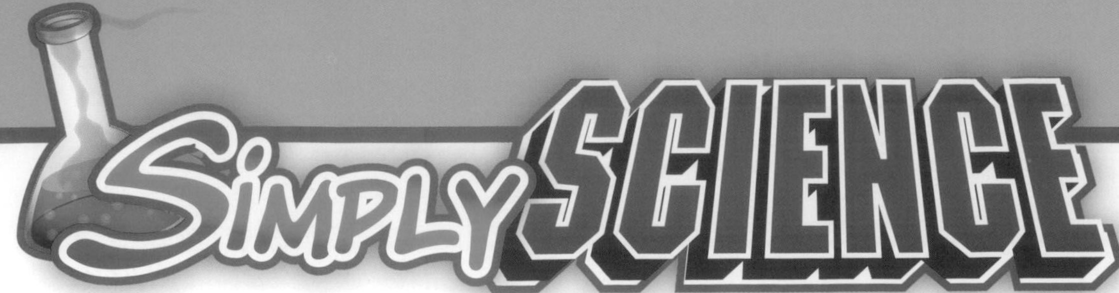

I Wonder...

Investigating scientific developments

Put your students' curiosity to work with this inquiry-based center. In advance, copy and cut apart the invention cards and questions on page 234. Then stock a center with research materials and the cards and questions. A student chooses a card, thinks about the invention, and then answers each question on his own paper. Next, he researches the invention and compares his ideas with the facts that answer each question.

Ann Fisher, Toledo, OH

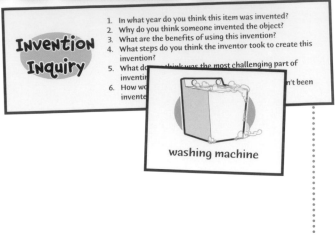

Invention Inquiry

1. In what year do you think this item was invented?
2. Why do you think someone invented the object?
3. What are the benefits of using this invention?
4. What steps do you think the inventor took to create this invention?
5. What d... the most challenging part of inventi...
6. How w... n't been invente...

washing machine

Head and Thorax

(sung to the tune of "Head and Shoulders")

Head and thorax, abdomen, abdomen,
Head and thorax, abdomen, abdomen,
Exoskeleton, compound eyes,
Wings, antennae, mouthparts, and six legs!

Put It to Music

Animal features

Teach your class this catchy tune about the important parts of an insect. Then add some fun by having students sing it faster and faster or in rounds. Next, challenge each pair of students to create a similar song that describes the important features of an arachnid, a reptile, an amphibian, or a mammal. Then have each duo teach the class its ditty.

Rebecca Juneau, Highland Elementary, Lake Stevens, WA

It's All About the Tilt!

Weather

Use this activity to help students identify the reasons seasons change. To begin, have each child fold a sheet of paper in half vertically and then fold the paper in half two more times horizontally. Next, guide the student to unfold the last two folds and cut the top flap at each fold to create four flaps, as shown. Then have her illustrate the positions of the sun and Earth during each season in the Northern Hemisphere. After she finishes, she lifts the flap and describes the connections between the position of the sun and Earth and each season's weather patterns.

Karren Sewell, Russellville, AL

Winter
Equator
North
South
Spring
North
South
We have summer when the North Pole is tilted toward the sun. We get more than 12 hours of sunlight and it is warmer. The South Pole is tipped away from the sun, and the Southern Hemisphere has winter. It has less than 12 hours of sunlight and it is colder there.
Fall
North
South

Stars in the Sky

Constellations

For this cross-curricular idea, have each child number a 10 x 10 grid as shown. Next, read aloud the Big Dipper coordinate pairs shown, guiding each student to plot and connect the points to draw the constellation. Then have each child choose a different constellation and plot its main stars on a 10 x 10 grid. After that, guide the student to record the constellation's name and matching coordinate pairs on an index card. As time allows, have students trade cards and then draw and name different constellations.

adapted from an idea from Marie E. Cecchini, West Dundee, IL

Big Dipper Coordinate Pairs

(10, 1), (9, 1), (7, 2), (6, 3), (6, 5), (2, 5), (1, 3), (6, 3)

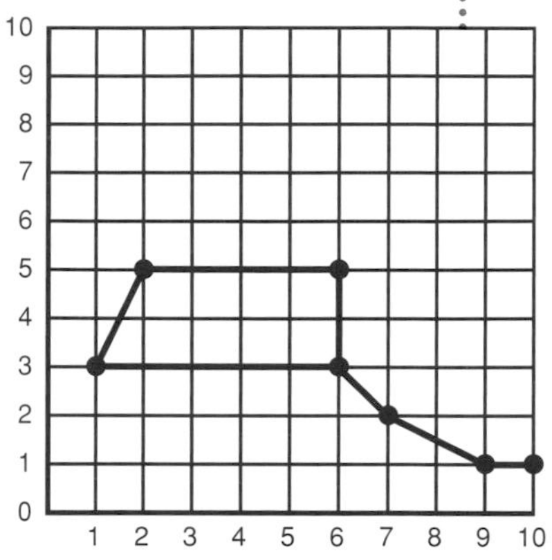

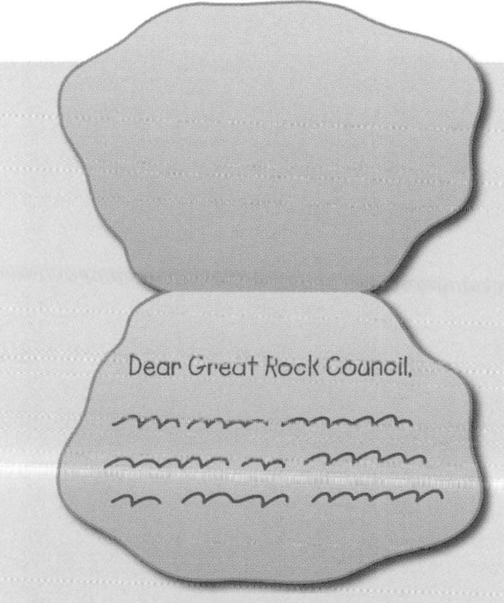

A Rocky Road

Erosion, weathering

To get this activity started, have each student pretend to be a rock that is tired of weathering and erosion. Next, guide the rock to draft a letter of complaint to the Great Rock Council. In her letter, have each rock describe the processes and explain why they upset her. If desired, have each child fold a light-colored sheet of construction paper in half, trim the paper to resemble a rock, and write her final copy inside. Then post students' work on a board titled "Erosion—It's a Rocky Road!"

Karen Kuo, Glenn C. Hardin Intermediate, Duncanville, TX

Decisions, Decisions

Animal classification

Introduce this idea by first displaying a copy of page 235. Jot "our class" in the top box and then divide students into two groups: boys and girls. Fill these designations in the next two boxes on the page. Then name two more subcategories and have students divide themselves accordingly. Repeat with two more subcategories, filling in the boxes as you go. After filling in all the boxes, discuss the final groupings. Next, have each pair of students label a copy of page 235 with a broad animal category, such as cats or dogs. Then guide the twosome to fill in the boxes with categories and subcategories that would help classify those animals.

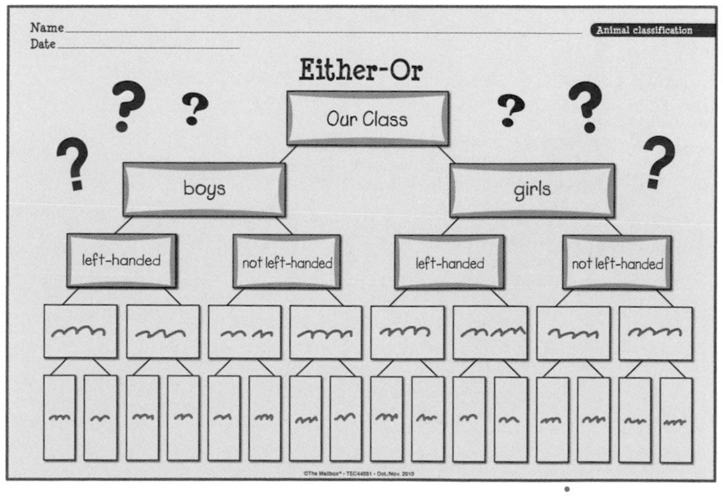

Layers of Learning

Types of clouds

For these 3-D booklets, guide each child to stack three sheets of unlined paper 1½-inches apart. Have each student fold the pages down and then staple them together as shown. Next, the student rotates the book so the stapled edge is at the bottom. Then she draws the ground on the first flap and labels the flaps with types of clouds and their heights. After that, the child describes each cloud type inside its flap. Finally, she glues bits of a cotton ball on the flaps to represent the clouds.

Emily Clark, Vernal, UT

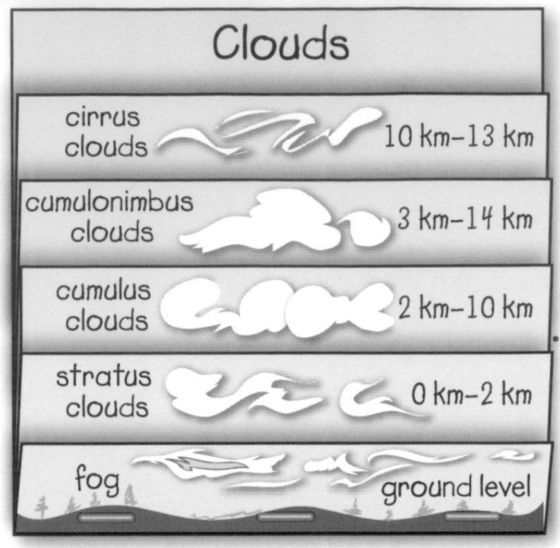

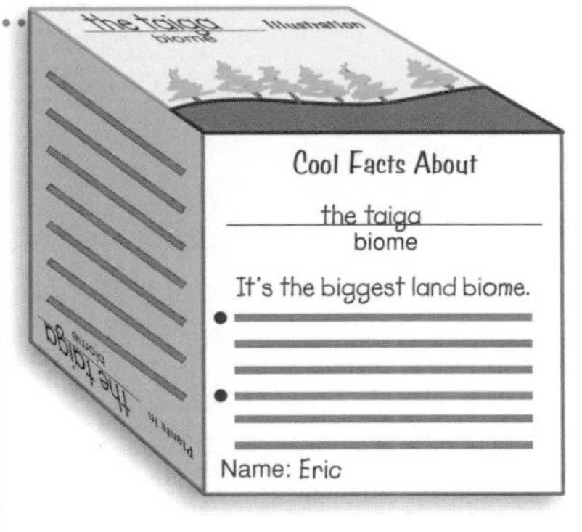

Definition
Location
Plants
Animals
Climate
Cool Facts

Rock-and-Roll Research

Biomes

To start this simple project, assign each student a biome. Next, post the categories shown and provide access to research materials. Guide each child to research his biome. Then have him fill out each side of the cube pattern from page 236. To follow up, group students so that different biomes are represented in each group. Then have the students take turns rolling their cubes and sharing the information that lands on top.

The Pluses and Minuses

Static electricity

Here's an activity that shows students how electrical charges can move. Begin by having each child draw three positive and three negative signs on a sheet of paper. Then have the student inflate a balloon and draw three positive and three negative signs on it. Explain that the paper and balloon have equal numbers of positive and negative signs, or charges, and that rubbing can cause negative charges to move from one object to another. Next, have each student cut out her paper negative signs and set them back on the paper. Then have the child rub her balloon over the paper until the balloon starts picking up negative signs. Finally, guide the student to sketch and describe her results before drawing a conclusion about the objects' charges. *(The balloon picks up negative charges from the paper, so it has a negative charge. Since the paper now has more positive charges, it has a positive charge.)*

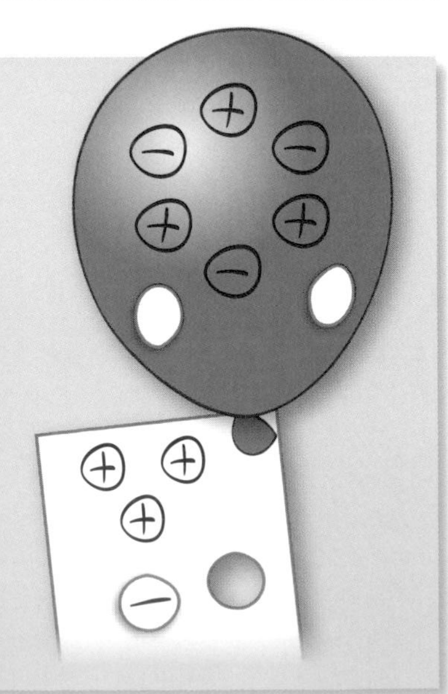

Five Questions

Vocabulary review

For this whole-class game, jot important science terms on index cards. Next, have a student come to the front of the room. Secretly show the card to the class and then tape it to the child's back. Explain that the student can ask five questions to figure out the mystery term; however, the class can only answer yes or no. After five questions, have the student guess the word. If he's correct, award a point toward a class reward. If he's not correct, show him the card and keep playing as time allows.

Chaya Honigwachs, Bnos Rivka, Lakewood, NJ

hypothesis

Does this word have anything to do with animals?

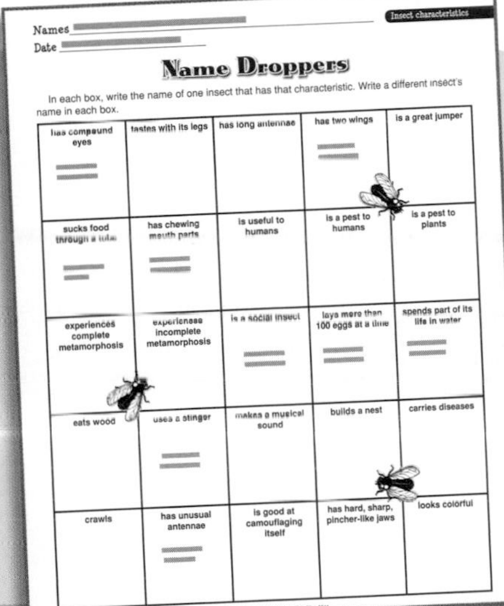

Names

Date

Insect characteristics

Name Droppers

In each box, write the name of one insect that has that characteristic. Write a different insect's name in each box.

has compound eyes	tastes with its legs	has long antennae	has two wings	is a great jumper
sucks food through a tube	has chewing mouth parts	is useful to humans	is a pest to humans	is a pest to plants
experiences complete metamorphosis	experiences incomplete metamorphosis	is a social insect	lays more than 100 eggs at a time	spends part of its life in water
eats wood	uses a stinger	makes a musical sound	builds a nest	carries diseases
crawls	has unusual antennae	is good at camouflaging itself	has hard, sharp, pincher-like jaws	looks colorful

Name Droppers

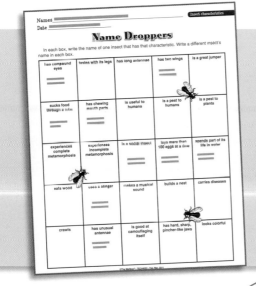

Animal adaptations, insects

Here's a supersimple idea for investigating insect characteristics. Just provide research materials and copies of page 237. Then challenge each pair of students to name a different insect for each characteristic listed on the page. When a duo finishes, have the partners trade papers with another pair and check each other's work.

That's Cool!

Heat transfer

With this small-group contest, students explore the transference of heat. To begin, present the rules shown and give each small group a plastic cup with an equal-size ice cube. Then challenge each group to melt its ice the fastest. When one group's ice is melted, congratulate the winning group and then have each student write about the contest. Guide the child to describe her group's plans, methods, and results using terms like *conduction, transfer, radiation,* and *thermal energy.*

Rules of the Ice Cube Challenge

1. You may not use any artificial or mechanical heat source, such as lightbulbs, heaters, or the heat that comes off a computer.
2. You may not put the ice in anyone's mouth.
3. You may not break, cut, or crush the ice.
4. You may use body heat.
5. You may use solar heat.

All About Digestion

Human systems

This bingo game will help students get on track with the digestive tract! To prepare, cut apart a copy of the definition cards at the bottom of page 231 and put the cards in a bag. Then have each child cut out the grid and cards from a copy of page 238 and glue the cards on the grid in random order. Next, give each student 16 game markers. Draw a definition card and read aloud the definition. Have each child find the matching term on her grid and put a marker on it. When a student covers four spaces in a row, she calls out, "Digested!" Award a small prize to the winner; then have students clear their grids and play again!

Emily Clark, Vernal, UT

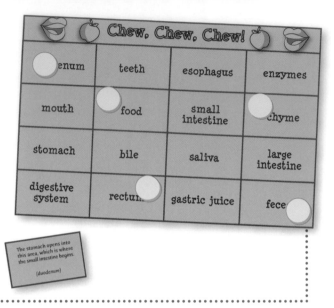

Chew, Chew, Chew!

enum	teeth	esophagus	enzymes
mouth	food	small intestine	chyme
stomach	bile	saliva	large intestine
digestive system	rectu	gastric juice	fece

The stomach opens into this area, which is where the small intestine begins.

(duodenum)

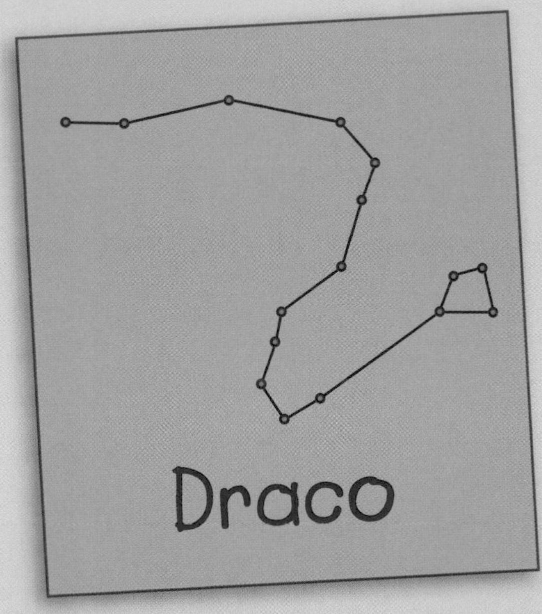

Seeing Stars

Constellations

Bring constellations down to Earth with this hands-on activity. To begin, display a constellation map and the mystery constellations on page 239. Then have each student choose a constellation and follow the directions shown to plot and identify the group of stars. As time allows, repeat the activity and then post students' work on a board titled "Seeing Stars!"

Melissa Tilton, Lakes Region Christian School, Laconia, NH

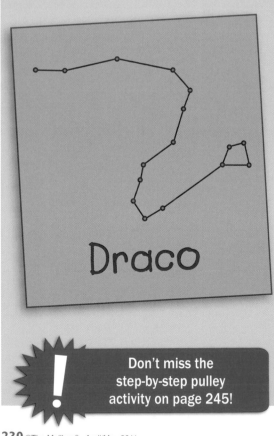

Materials for each student: small piece of cardboard, sheet of construction paper, pushpin

Directions:

1. Place the construction paper on the cardboard. Using a pushpin, plot the stars that make up the constellation. Then set the cardboard and pushpin aside.
2. Draw straight lines to connect the stars.
3. Find the constellation on the map and then label your work.

Don't miss the step-by-step pulley activity on page 245!

Grounded?

Plant growth, inquiry

For this exploration, post the question "How does gravity affect the way plants grow?" Next, have each child set up a recording sheet, record the question, and hypothesize an answer. Then guide each small group of students to set up the experiment by following the directions shown.

When the plants sprout, have each group turn its bottle on its side, record the step, and make a hypothesis about how the tilted plant and its roots will grow. After a week, have students record their observations and draw conclusions about gravity's effect on the way plants grow. *(The roots respond positively to gravity by growing down. The sprouts respond negatively by growing up.)* Finally, challenge students to find out what *geotropism* means and explain how it applies to the exploration.

Materials for each small group: plastic water bottle, permanent marker, gravel, soil, 2 uncooked beans (pinto, lima, or kidney), construction paper, water

Directions:

1. Write your names on the bottle. Next, roll up a piece of construction paper to make a funnel. Use the funnel to pour an inch of gravel into the bottle. Then pour soil to within an inch of the top.
2. Add water until it drips into the gravel. Then drop two beans in the bottle. Use a pencil to gently poke the beans into the soil.
3. Set the bottle in a sunny place. Record your steps.

Dr. Barbara Leonard, Winston-Salem, NC

Definition Cards

Use with "All About Digestion" on page 230.

The stomach opens into this area, which is where the small intestine begins. *(duodenum)* TEC44054	This ten-inch-long muscular tube moves food from the mouth to the stomach. *(esophagus)* TEC44054	This baglike organ is used to store and digest food. *(stomach)* TEC44054	This is the part of the body where digestion begins. *(mouth)* TEC44054
These molecules speed up chemical reactions, such as breaking down food during digestion. *(enzymes)* TEC44054	This is found in the stomach and helps break down proteins. *(gastric juice)* TEC44054	This sticky fluid moistens and softens foods that enter the mouth. *(saliva)* TEC44054	Most of digestion occurs in this long, narrow tube. *(small intestine)* TEC44054
Shorter than the small intestine, this tube absorbs water from undigested food. *(large intestine)* TEC44054	This fluid is sent from the liver to the small intestine. It helps break down fat. *(bile)* TEC44054	The last part of the large intestine, this is where waste passes out of the body. *(rectum)* TEC44054	This group of organs works together to break food into smaller parts. *(digestive system)* TEC44054
This is the name for waste eliminated from the body. *(feces)* TEC44054	Found in the mouth, these bonelike structures grind and crush food. *(teeth)* TEC44054	This provides energy and nutrients for the human body. *(food)* TEC44054	This is the name for food that is partly digested when it leaves the stomach. *(chyme)* TEC44054

Poetic Research

Solar system

Engage students in stellar research with this fact-filled rhyme. Display the poem from the bottom half of page 233 and lead students to choral-read it. Then challenge each pair of students to research a planet and write rhyming couplets that describe its important features.

To travel our system,
start at the sun.
In the center of it all, our
voyage has begun.

Marilyn Marszalek, Edinboro Elementary, Edinboro, PA

Living Things

Animal kingdom

Post a list of activities such as those shown. Then, when a student finishes an assignment early, she chooses an activity from the list and completes it independently. When a child finishes a task, she shares her work with the class.

- Create a new way of classifying mammals, insects, and reptiles. Explain your method in a chart, poster, or written report.
- **Illustrate the meaning of food chain.**
- Graph the life expectancies of ten vertebrates. Include at least one example from each of the five classes of vertebrates.
- **Make a chart which lists ten animals and how they defend themselves from their enemies.**
- Investigate an endangered animal. Develop a plan to help preserve this animal.
- **Make a word search puzzle of 25 vertebrates. Provide a word bank.**
- On five index cards, describe five different invertebrates. Draw the animals on the cards' flip sides.
- **Make a poster that shows an animal's life cycle.**

Mystery Minerals

Rock and mineral attributes

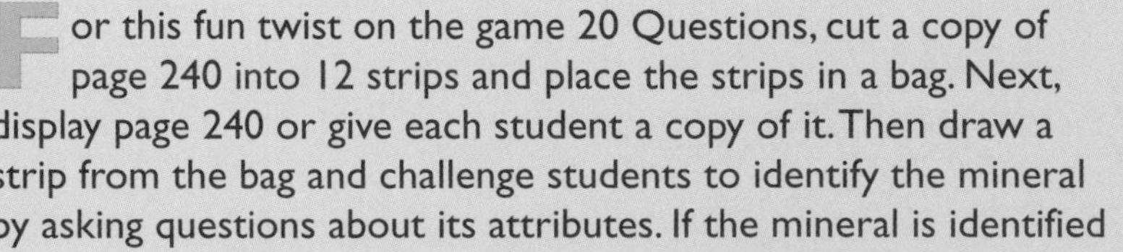

For this fun twist on the game 20 Questions, cut a copy of page 240 into 12 strips and place the strips in a bag. Next, display page 240 or give each student a copy of it. Then draw a strip from the bag and challenge students to identify the mineral by asking questions about its attributes. If the mineral is identified in ten or fewer questions, draw a new slip and play another round. If not, read aloud the mineral's attributes one at a time until the class identifies the mystery mineral.

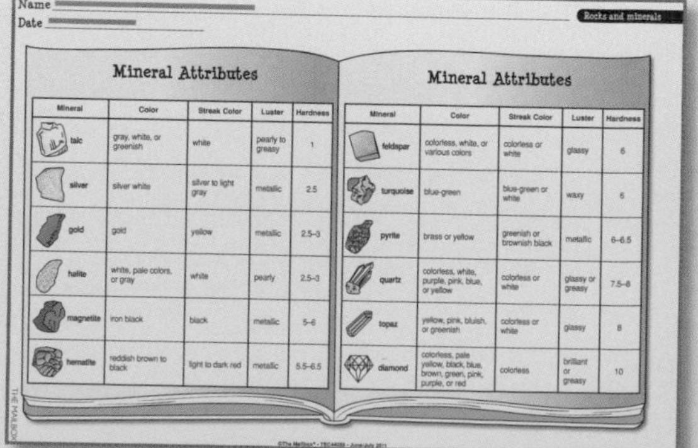

Name
Date

Rocks and minerals

Mineral Attributes

Mineral	Color	Streak Color	Luster	Hardness
talc	gray, white, or greenish	white	pearly to greasy	1
silver	silver white	silver to light gray	metallic	2.5
gold	gold	yellow	metallic	2.5–3
halite	white, pale colors, or gray	white	pearly	2.5–3
magnetite	iron black	black	metallic	5–6
hematite	reddish brown to black	light to dark red	metallic	5.5–6.5

Mineral Attributes

Mineral	Color	Streak Color	Luster	Hardness
feldspar	colorless, white, or various colors	colorless or white	glassy	6
turquoise	blue-green	blue-green or white	waxy	6
pyrite	brass or yellow	greenish or brownish black	metallic	6–6.5
quartz	colorless, white, purple, pink, blue, or yellow	colorless or white	glassy or greasy	7.5–8
topaz	yellow, pink, bluish, or greenish	colorless or white	glassy	8
diamond	colorless, pale yellow, black, blue, brown, green, pink, purple, or red	colorless	brilliant or greasy	10

Visual High Jinks

Inquiry, sight

Pique students' interest with these quick investigations. For each one, have students follow the directions as you read them aloud. Next, guide students to describe in their journals what they did and what they saw. Then have each child postulate the phenomenon's explanation. Follow up with a class discussion.

The Shifting Pencil

Hold a pencil about one foot in front of your face. Next, close your left eye. Line up the pencil with an object in the distance, such as a door or window frame. Without moving your head or the pencil, open your left eye and close your right eye. *(The pencil will seem to move to the right.)*

Another Pencil?

Hold a pencil about one foot in front of your face. Focus both eyes on an object in the background behind the pencil. *(It will seem as though there are two pencils.)* Next, focus on the pencil. *(It will seem as though there are two of the object.)*

A Hole in One

Roll a piece of paper into a tube that is about one inch wide. Hold the tube in your right hand and look through the tube with your right eye, keeping your left eye open. While you're looking through the tube, hold your left hand next to the tube's left side with your palm facing yourself. *(It will seem as though there is a hole in your left hand.)*

Sightseeing in the Solar System

To travel our system, start at the sun.
In the center of it all, our voyage has begun.

Zip to Mercury! It's first; you'll get there soon.
It's the closest to the sun and has craters like our moon.

Venus is called Earth's twin 'cause they're nearly the same size.
On this planet, it's 117 days from sunrise to sunrise!

Next is Earth with a majestic sky of blue.
Its oxygen and water make it just right for me and you!

The fourth planet, Mars, looks as though it's covered in rust.
Mars has two moons, so stopping there is a must.

On to Jupiter, the planet with the greatest girth—
Its Great Red Spot is wider than the Earth!

Saturn's icy rings are its claim to fame,
But its many moons and satellites also deserve acclaim!

Uranus is a puzzle! Does it have something to hide?
Its axis tilts so far that it rotates on its side!

Our last stop is Neptune, farthest planet from the sun:
It's surrounded by clouds of frozen gas. And now our trip is done!

Note to the teacher: Use with "Poetic Research" on page 232.

Invention Cards

Use with "I Wonder…" on page 226.

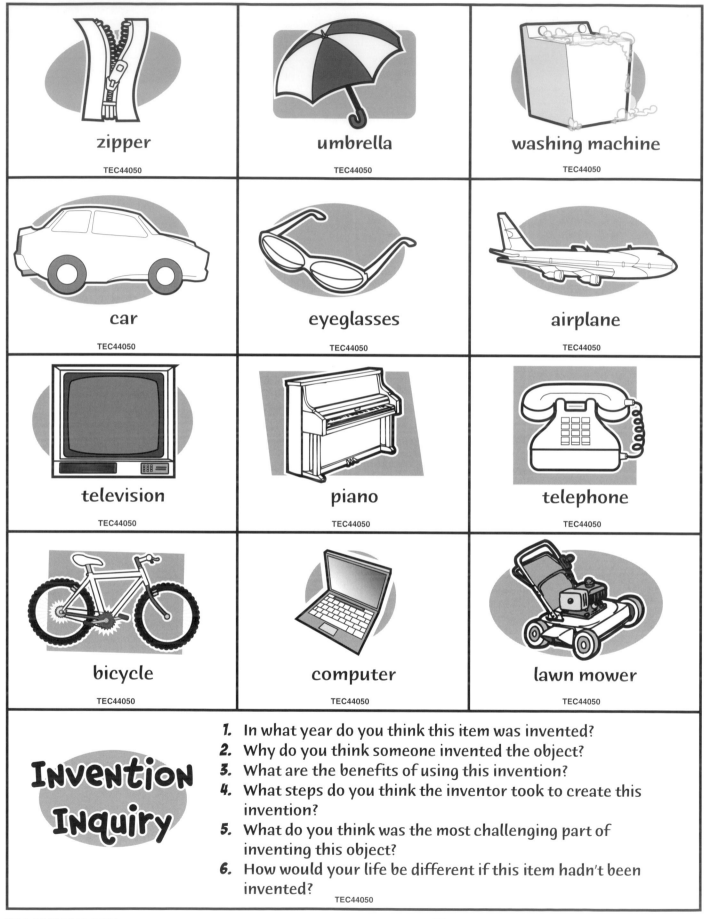

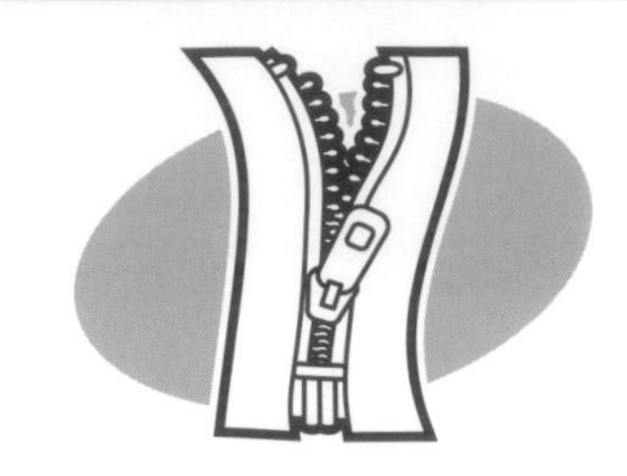

zipper

TEC44050

umbrella

TEC44050

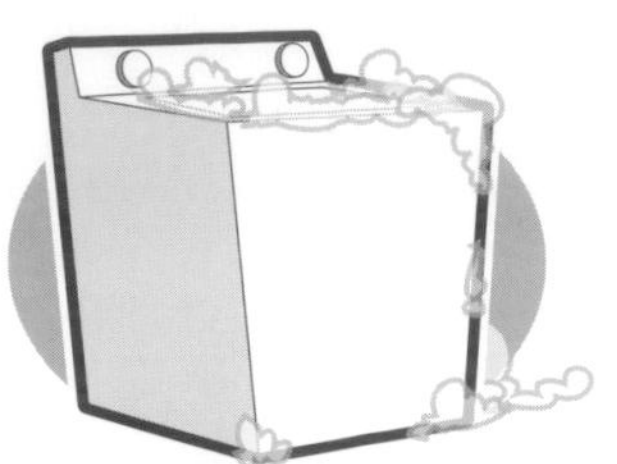

washing machine

TEC44050

car

TEC44050

eyeglasses

TEC44050

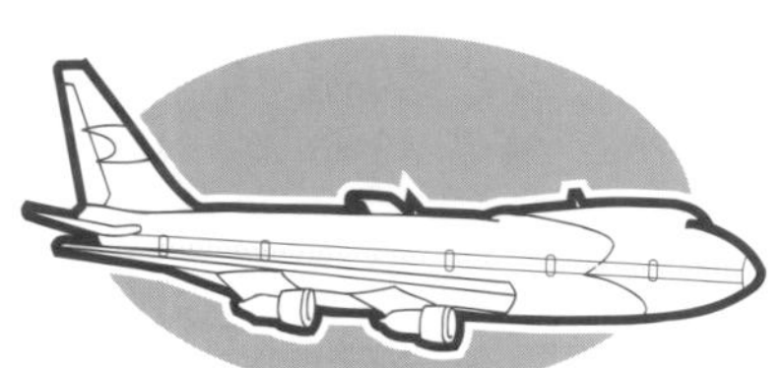

airplane

TEC44050

television

TEC44050

piano

TEC44050

telephone

TEC44050

bicycle

TEC44050

computer

TEC44050

lawn mower

TEC44050

1. In what year do you think this item was invented?
2. Why do you think someone invented the object?
3. What are the benefits of using this invention?
4. What steps do you think the inventor took to create this invention?
5. What do you think was the most challenging part of inventing this object?
6. How would your life be different if this item hadn't been invented?

TEC44050

Name______________________________

Date__________________

Either-Or

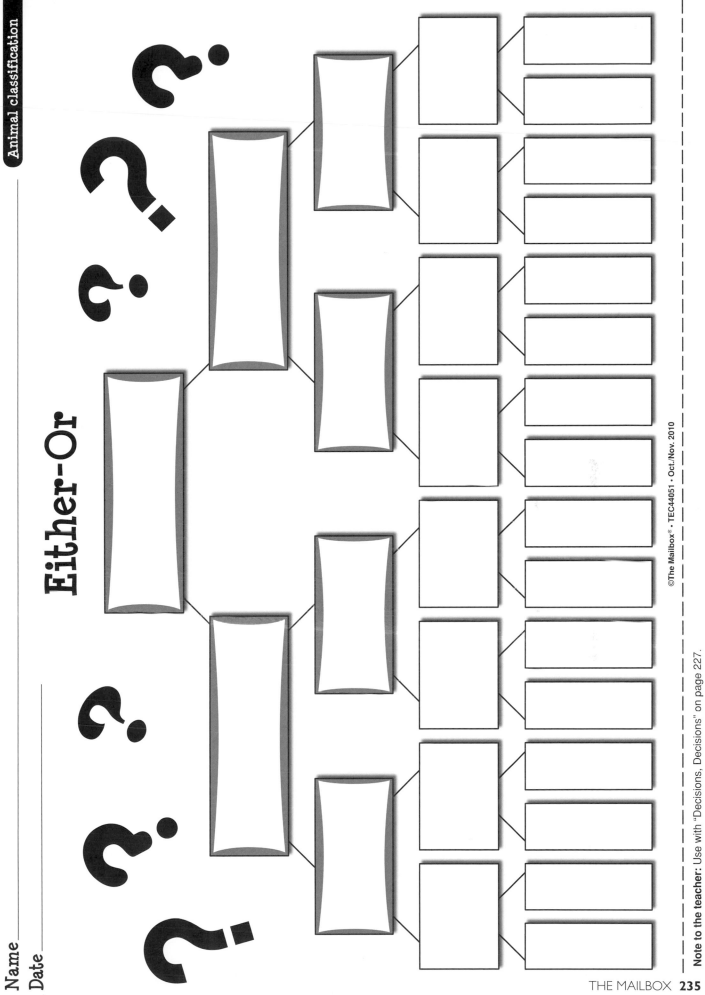

Note to the teacher: Use with “Decisions, Decisions” on page 227.

Cube Pattern

Use with "Rock-and-Roll Research" on page 228.

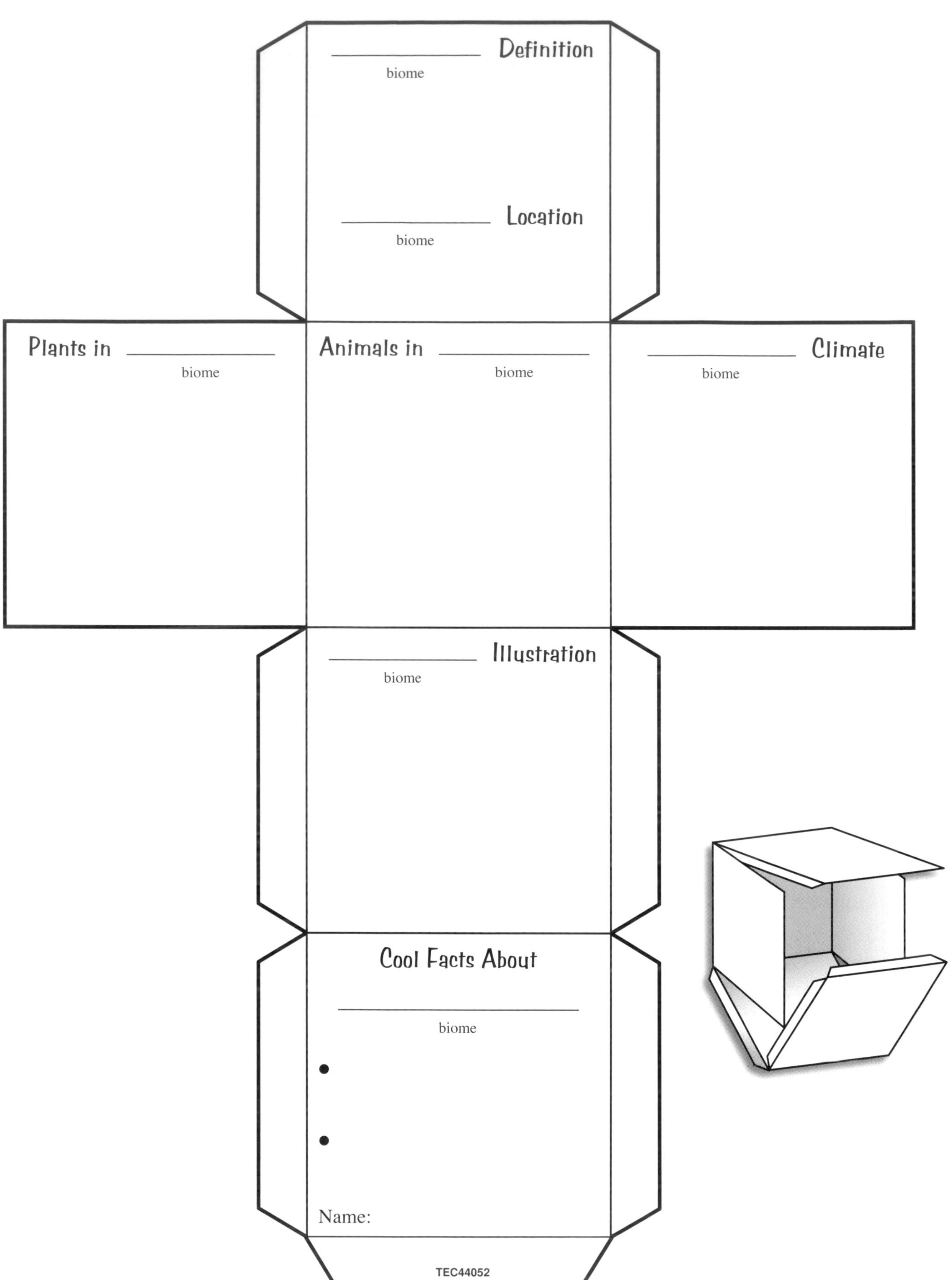

Names ______________________________

Date ______________

Name Droppers

In each box, write the name of one insect that has that characteristic. Write a different insect's name in each box.

has compound eyes	tastes with its legs	has long antennae	has two wings	is a great jumper
sucks food through a tube	has chewing mouth parts	is useful to humans	is a pest to humans	is a pest to plants
experiences complete metamorphosis	experiences incomplete metamorphosis	is a social insect	lays more than 100 eggs at a time	spends part of its life in water
eats wood	uses a stinger	makes a musical sound	builds a nest	carries diseases
crawls	has unusual antennae	is good at camouflaging itself	has hard, sharp, pincher-like jaws	looks colorful

Note to the teacher: Use with "Name Droppers" on page 229.

Digestion Cards and Grid

Use with "All About Digestion" on page 230.

bile	chyme	digestive system	duodenum
esophagus	enzymes	feces	food
gastric juice	large intestine	mouth	rectum
saliva	small intestine	stomach	teeth

Chew, Chew, Chew!

Mystery Constellations

C

D

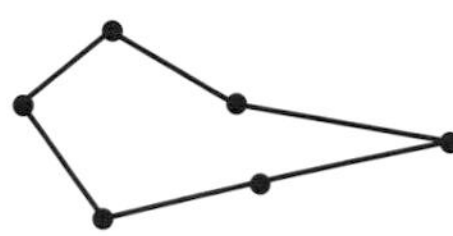

E

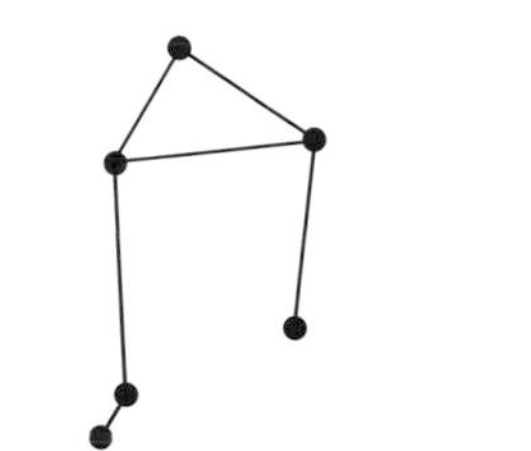

F

G

H

I

J

Note to the teacher: Use with "Seeing Stars" on page 230.

Name ______________________

Date ______________________

Mineral Attributes

Mineral	Color	Streak Color	Luster	Hardness
talc	gray, white, or greenish	white	pearly to greasy	1
silver	silver white	silver to light gray	metallic	2.5
gold	gold	yellow	metallic	2.5–3
halite	white, pale colors, or gray	white	pearly	2.5–3
magnetite	iron black	black	metallic	5–6
hematite	reddish brown to black	light to dark red	metallic	5.5–6.5

Mineral Attributes

Mineral	Color	Streak Color	Luster	Hardness
feldspar	colorless, white, or various colors	colorless or white	glassy	6
turquoise	blue-green	blue-green or white	waxy	6
pyrite	brass or yellow	greenish or brownish black	metallic	6–6.5
quartz	colorless, white, purple, pink, blue, or yellow	colorless or white	glassy or greasy	7.5–8
topaz	yellow, pink, bluish, or greenish	colorless or white	glassy	8
diamond	colorless, pale yellow, black, blue, brown, green, pink, purple, or red	colorless	brilliant or greasy	10

Note to the teacher: Use with "Mystery Minerals" on page 232.

Name ____________________

Date ____________________

Go for the Gold!

An astronaut's visor has a superthin coating of gold to reflect heat and light!

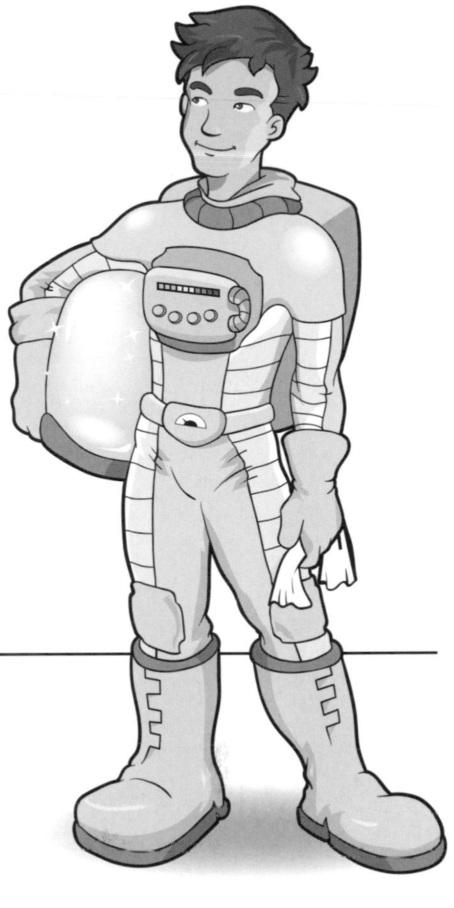

Where Can You Find Gold?

Gold can be found in almost all kinds of rocks and soils. In fact, even oceans contain a huge amount of gold. Most of the gold is not found in one place though. The ocean's gold is dissolved in the water. Mining the ocean gold is not practical. It would cost more to extract the gold than it would be worth. The massive deposits of gold in South Africa make gold easier to mine there. South Africa is the world's top gold producer. Australia is the second largest producer. The third largest gold-producing country is the United States.

Golden Facts

No one really knows when gold was first discovered. We do know it has been used for money and jewelry for thousands of years. When it's used, gold is most often mixed with one or more other metals to make a gold *alloy*. Because they cost less, gold alloys are used much more often than pure gold. Gold alloys are described in karats. Each alloy is made up of 24 parts. One karat is equal to $\frac{1}{24}$ of the alloy. So pure gold is 24-karat gold, and 14-karat gold is made up of 14 parts gold. The other ten parts are a metal or metals other than gold.

What's All the Fuss About?

Gold is one of the shiniest, or most *lustrous*, metals. It reflects heat rays better than any other metal, and gold does not rust. This soft metal can also be pounded thinner than any other metal. An amount of gold about the size of a coin can be pulled into a wire over 50 miles long!

Bonus Box: Gold conducts electricity better than most metals. So it is often used in computers. On another sheet of paper, list other uses for gold. For each item you list, tell why gold is the best metal for the job.

Answer each question.

1. Gold should be mined from the ocean. Do you agree with this statement? Explain. ____________________
2. In the article, what does the word *alloy* mean? ____________________
3. Write the fraction that describes the amount of gold in an 18-karat gold ring. ____________________
4. Why is there a thin layer of gold on astronauts' helmet visors? ____________________
5. What do you think is the most important feature of gold? Why? ____________________

Name ______________________________

Date ______________________________

Ooh, That Smell!

The aroma of a *Rafflesia* flower was once described as "a penetrating smell more repulsive than any buffalo carcass in an advanced stage of decomposition."

There is a rare but famous plant hiding in the jungles of Southeast Asia. The giant *Rafflesia* is a parasite, a plant that gets the nutrients it needs from a host plant. Living quietly inside its host, a *Rafflesia* is an odd plant. It has no chlorophyll. It doesn't have stems or leaves either. The *Rafflesia*'s claim to fame is its flower.

When a *Rafflesia* bud bursts from its host vine, it looks like a cabbage. The bud slowly opens into a bright red flower that has sagging, speckled petals. A single flower can be three feet wide and weigh over 20 pounds! That makes the *Rafflesia* bloom famous. It is the world's largest flower.

The *Rafflesia* is also well-known for its scent. This giant flower smells like rotting meat. The putrid odor attracts flies and beetles. To these insects, a dead animal means food. So flies and beetles come to the flower looking for rotten meat. The stink, however, is just a trick. It draws in the bugs, which land on the flower, pick up the pollen, and carry it to another foul-smelling *Rafflesia* flower.

Bonus Box: Research Venus flytraps. Draw a Venn diagram to show how *Rafflesia* plants and Venus flytraps are the same and how they are different.

Cross out the incorrect word or words in each sentence. Then write the correct word or words on the lines.

1. *Rafflesia* flowers grow in the deserts of Southeast Asia. ______________
2. Like most plants, the *Rafflesia* has no chlorophyll. ______________
3. A parasite gets its nutrients from soil. ______________
4. The bud of the *Rafflesia* can be three feet wide. ______________
5. The flower's delightful smell attracts flies and beetles. ______________
6. When a fly lands on a *Rafflesia* flower, it is looking for rotten fruit. ______________
7. Flies and beetles carry seeds from one *Rafflesia* flower to another. ______________
8. The *Rafflesia* plant depends on tourists for pollination. ______________

Name ________________________________

Date ________________________

Think Pink!

Some river dolphins aren't gray at all; they're pink!

What do you picture when you think of a dolphin? Do you see a shiny, gray mammal darting in and out of waves? If you do, you're probably thinking of a marine dolphin. Most marine dolphins are sleek, gray creatures that frolic in the ocean. There is another group of dolphins to add to the picture. These dolphins, river dolphins, don't live in oceans. Most of them live in fresh water instead.

River dolphins can be found in Asia and in South America. They live in warm rivers and lakes. Shallow, murky waters mean river dolphins don't dart around like their marine cousins. They move slower.

The Amazon River dolphin, or *boto,* has adapted well to its dark and muddy home. A boto's flippers are big and wide. They act almost like paddles, helping the dolphin make its way through shallow waters.

With a snout four times as long as a marine dolphin's, the boto is an efficient hunter. Stiff hairs at the end of the boto's snout help it feel around for food in the mud. The boto's front cone-shaped teeth help it grab its prey. Its back teeth are flat like our molars. With its back teeth, the boto cracks open shells and chews its prey: crabs, river turtles, armored catfish, piranha, and other small fish.

Shade the circle next to the best answer for questions 1–5. Then answer questions 6–8 on another sheet of paper.

1. According to the selection, why don't river dolphins move as quickly as marine dolphins?
   - Ⓐ Their flippers are so big that they slow them down.
   - Ⓑ It's hard to see in the dark, muddy rivers.
2. What is the author's purpose for writing this selection?
   - Ⓐ to inform
   - Ⓑ to persuade
3. What does *murky* mean in paragraph 2?
   - Ⓐ sleek and gray
   - Ⓑ dark and muddy
   - Ⓒ big and wide
4. Which part of a river dolphin is four times longer than that of a marine dolphin?
   - Ⓐ its flippers
   - Ⓑ its teeth
   - Ⓒ its snout
5. Which word best shows what *frolic* means in the first paragraph?
   - Ⓐ play Ⓑ merry
6. Which part of the dolphin is the snout? How do you know?
7. Why do you think the author compares the bota's back teeth to our molars?
8. Underline the main idea in each paragraph. Then write a paragraph in your own words that summarizes the selection.

Bonus: Circle three facts in the selection. Then use your own words to paraphrase each one.

Name ______________________________

Date ______________________

A "CELL-EBRATION"

There are more than ten trillion (10,000,000,000,000) cells in the human body!

All plants and animals are made up of cells—the tiny building blocks of every living thing. Most cells are $\frac{1}{1,000}$ of an inch wide, too small to see without a microscope. If you could see them, you could fit about 500 of those cells in a period. There are cells you can see, though. The biggest cells are the yolks in birds' eggs. Each yolk is a single cell.

No matter its size, each type of cell has a special job. Every cell is alive and breathing. Cells absorb food, and they eliminate waste. Cells grow. They reproduce, and they die.

While most plant cells look like cubes or boxes, animal cells take many different shapes. Those shapes are connected to the jobs the cells do. Some muscle cells are long and thin so they can contract when they work. Nerve cells have long branches and may resemble trees. The branches of a nerve's cell help it send messages all over the body. Red blood cells are specially shaped, almost like rubber rafts, to float in an animal's bloodstream.

Draw a line to connect each cell to its name. Then complete items 2–6 on another sheet of paper.

1.

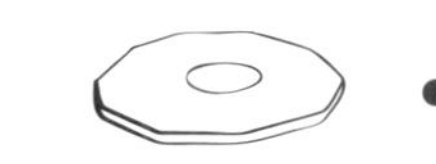

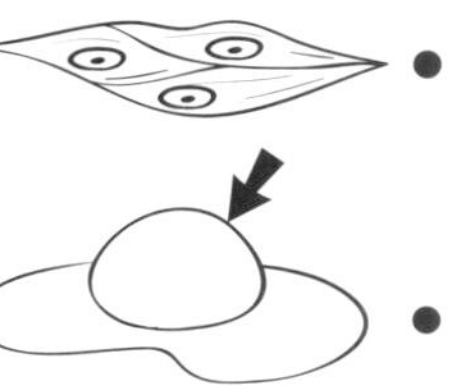

A. nerve cell

B. muscle cell

C. red blood cell

D. yolk cell

E. skin cell

2. Skin cells are flat. Why do you think skin cells are flat? Use evidence from the paragraph to support your answer.

3. Since a bird's egg yolk is the largest type of cell, which bird's egg yolk do you think is the largest of all cells? Why?

4. What do you think happens when a cell dies? Explain.

5. Why do you think the author wrote that cells "absorb food" instead of "eat"?

6. Write two questions about this selection.

Heave-Ho!

What You Need

empty thread spool

3-foot length of string or ribbon

shoe (or another heavy object)

pencil

paper (one sheet for each student)

Key Vocabulary	
force	pulley
motion	work

What You Do

1. Tie one end of the string around the heavy object. Take turns lifting the object six inches off the floor.

2. Observe. Then sketch the action and label the directions of force and motion. Explain what happened when you pulled the string.

3. Put the spool on a pencil and hold the pencil level.

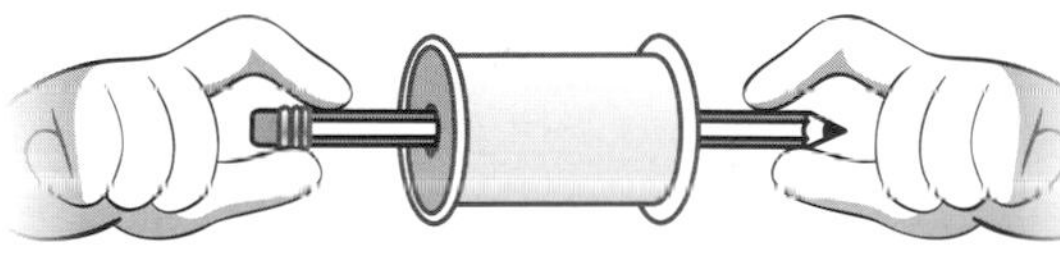

4. Have your partner slide the free end of the string over the spool. Take turns slowly pulling down the string, lifting the object six inches off the floor.

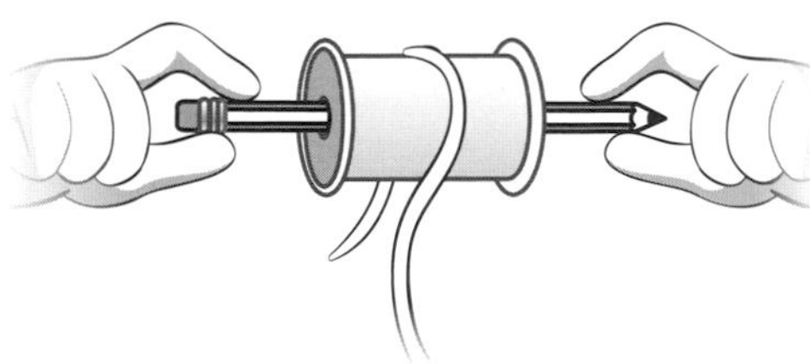

5. Observe. Then sketch the action. Label the directions of force and motion. Explain what happened when you pulled the string.

6. Compare the actions. How might you use a pulley?

Step-by-step partner activity: Copy this card and put it in a plastic page protector for durability. Then put the card and the needed materials at a center.

Rain Check

What You Need

3 kinds of rocks (two of each kind)
6 clear plastic cups
vinegar (or another acidic liquid)
water

Key Vocabulary

acidic
damage
precipitation
pollution

What You Do

1. Pour $\frac{1}{2}$ cup of vinegar in each of three cups. Then pour $\frac{1}{2}$ cup of water in each of the three remaining cups.
2. For each rock pair, place one rock in a cup of vinegar and one in a cup of water. Label each cup.
3. Make a chart like the one shown. Observe and describe each rock. Then on the back of your chart, write about what you think will happen in the next 24 hours.

Rock Description	In Water			In Vinegar		
	Initial observation	After 24 hours	After 7 days	Initial observation	After 24 hours	After 7 days

4. Observe the rocks after 24 hours. Describe any changes in the rocks or the liquids.
5. Observe the rocks after seven days. Describe any changes in the rocks or the liquids.
6. What did you learn about the effect of water and acid rain (vinegar) on rocks? What do you think will happen if the rocks are left in the vinegar and water for 14 days? For one month? For one year? Write your conclusions on the back of your chart.

Step-by-step partner activity: Copy this card and put it in a plastic page protector for durability. Then put the card and the needed materials at a center.

Social Studies

EXPLORING Social Studies

Seek and Find

Geography, natural features

Help students get acquainted with their social studies textbooks and identify important natural features with this fun scavenger hunt! To begin, display a list of questions about important landforms and bodies of water such as those shown, making sure the feature's name isn't mentioned. Next, challenge each pair of students to use a social studies textbook to find and name each feature. When time is up, announce the answers and then declare the students who find the most features your class's geography champions!

Marie E. Cecchini, West Dundee, IL

What is the world's longest river? *(Nile River)*
What is the world's smallest ocean? *(Arctic Ocean)*
Which ocean is the largest? *(Pacific Ocean)*
What is the world's longest mountain range? *(Andes Mountains)*
What is the highest mountain in the world? *(Mount Everest)*
What is the world's highest mountain range? *(Himalayas)*
What is the world's largest desert? *(Sahara)*
What are the oldest mountains in North America? *(Appalachians)*

On the Cover

State research

Here's a cool idea for state reports that are going places! When a student is ready to publish his state report, have him find out what the state's license plate looks like. Next, have the child fold a sheet of paper in half to make a cover. Then have him draw the license plate on the front, writing his name as the plate's letters, as shown. Finally, have the child write his report on half sheets of paper and staple them inside the license plate cover.

Marie E. Cecchini

State Short Forms

Geography, state abbreviations

For this fast-paced partner game, each pair of students cuts apart the cards from a copy of page 254. The partners shuffle the cards. Then, in turn, one partner draws a card and reads a state's postal abbreviation. The student's partner names the state. If she's correct, she gets the card. If she's not correct, the card is returned to the pile. When all the cards have been played, the student with the most cards wins the game.

Marie E. Cecchini

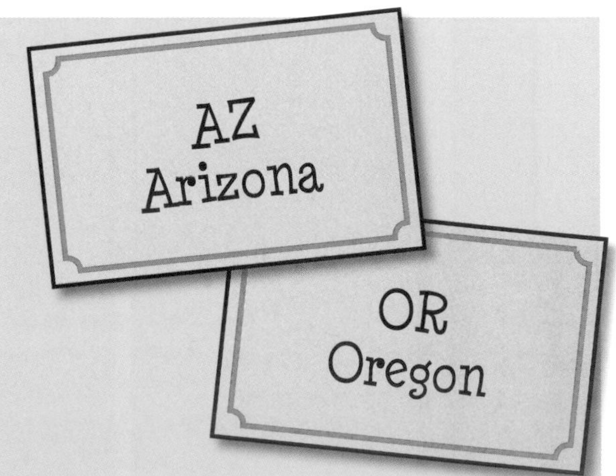

EXPLORING Social Studies

A Walk Through Time

Creating a timeline

For this idea, have each student make two construction paper cutouts shaped like feet. Next, assign each child an important event in your state's or the country's history. Have the student summarize the event on one foot cutout and record the event's date on the other one. Guide students to arrange their cutouts in chronological order and tape them in a sequential path on the walls of your room. For a great hall display, have students tape their cutouts to form a trail in the hall and add the title "In Step With History."

Melody Mattox, Grenada Upper Elementary, Grenada, MS

What colors are in the state flag?
New Mexico's state flag is yellow and red.

State Studies

Research

Looking for an independent state research activity? Try this! Make a class supply of page 255 and provide access to research materials. Then challenge each student to find the answer to every question on the page (and, in the process, learn a lot about your state). Finally, have students cut apart the boxes on the finished page and staple them together to make a minibooklet full of interesting and important facts about your state.

Name That Shape!

Geography

Here's a fun class game that helps students learn the states. Before playing, have each child study a U.S. map. Also program paper strips with the names of the states. To play, have a student volunteer take a strip and draw on the board the outline of the listed state. Give students three guesses to name the state. If the first guess is correct, the class earns three points. If the second guess is correct, award two points. If the third guess is correct, award one point. Award an extra point if students can name the state's capital. This game can be stopped and then continued anytime. Just keep track of the class's points and award a small prize when students earn a predetermined score.

Julie Gose, Hagerstown Elementary, Hagerstown, IN

EXPLORING Social Studies

City Sleuths

Geography

Engage students in map study with this fun challenge. Have each student study a political map of the country. Then secretly choose a state. Name the state's capital and challenge students to find the state. After ten seconds, ask students to point on their maps to the state they think you've picked. Then name one of the state's major cities and repeat the challenge. Repeat with one more city if desired. Then announce the state and start over! For variety, focus on your state, naming cities within a specific county, parish, or borough.

Ann Fisher, Toledo, OH

This state's capital is Montgomery.

One of its major cities is Mobile.

Keeping Up With the Times

Current events

Have each small group choose an article from a current newspaper. Next, have the students in the group read and discuss the article. Then have the group choose one of the options shown to summarize its reading. Set aside time for each small group to share its work.

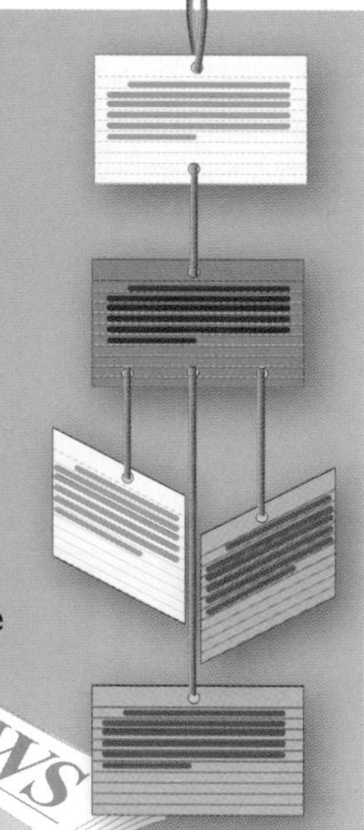

Current Events Tasks

- Using five index cards, make a mobile about the article.
  - Card 1: Write the article's title, author's name, newspaper's name, and its date.
  - Card 2: Describe the article's main idea.
  - Cards 3–5: Describe three important supporting details.
- Identify the five Ws of the article (who, what, when, where, and why).
- What do you think? Write a group opinion about the article. List evidence from the article to support your opinion.
- Create a picture that shows the article's main idea. Write a caption that explains what the picture has to do with the event.
- Write and answer five questions about the article.
- Draw a cartoon with five panels that summarizes the article.

Colonial Travel Expo

American history, research

Here's an idea for helping students connect with colonial life. Have each student choose one of the original 13 colonies and pretend to be a travel agent responsible for drawing visitors to the colony. Guide each student to create a pamphlet about the colony complete with tours, special events, and driving directions. Also have the child write a promotional speech sure to attract attention. When students finish, have them rearrange their desks like booths at a travel fair, take turns giving their speeches, and then spend a few minutes walking around and reading each other's pamphlets.

Virginia
Get Captain John Smith's autograph!
Daily tours of Jamestown!

Katie Kolowski
Bolin School
East Peoria, IL

EXPLORING Social Studies

Name That Person

Research, history

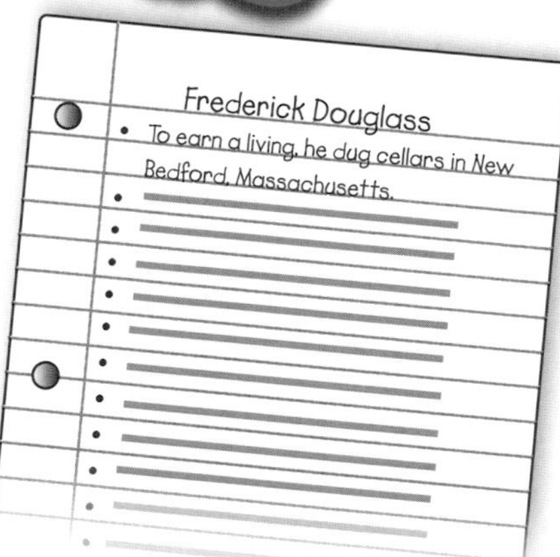

Frederick Douglass
To earn a living, he dug cellars in New Bedford, Massachusetts.

To put the focus on people who make history, have each student choose an important historic figure you've studied. Guide the child to research the person, identifying and recording six interesting details and six important details about him or her. Next, have the student arrange the details in a bulleted list starting with the least-known fact and ending with the most well-known fact. For a fun follow-up, collect students' work. Then choose one list and read the first fact. Challenge students to name the individual. If they can't, read the next fact, continuing until the correct historic figure is named. Once the person is named, read any remaining facts and post students' work on a board titled "Fascinating Historic Figures."

Vicki Vander Lugt, Boyden-Hull Elementary, Boyden, IA

Pen to Paper

Critical thinking

This minijournal is a win-win way to start social studies sessions! To begin, have each child fold a sheet of paper in fourths, cut apart the sections, staple them together, and jot his name at the top. Next, display a prompt from page 256 and challenge the student to write a thoughtful response that fits on one page of his pad. (The small page forces students who ramble to get to the point and is less intimidating for your struggling students!) Then, to check students' work, simply collect the notepads each day or at the end of the week—no heavy notebooks to lug home!

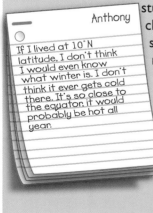

Anthony

If I lived at 10°N latitude, I don't think I would even know what winter is. I don't think it ever gets cold there. It's so close to the equator, it would probably be hot all year.

Where the Rivers Run

Geography

Splash into this natural-features exploration! First, have each pair of students research a major river, such as one of those listed. Next, have the pair glue yarn on a large sheet of construction paper to show the river's path, tributaries, and mouth. Then have the pair name each tributary, the country or countries through which the river runs, and five important facts about the river. Share students' work by posting it on a board titled "Where the Rivers Run."

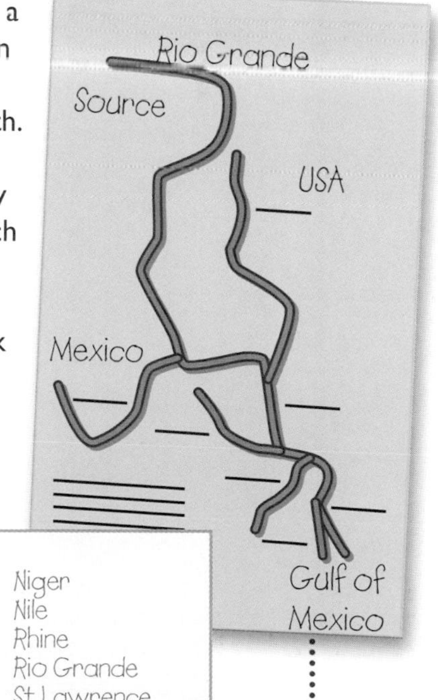

Major Rivers

Amazon	Indus	Niger
Colorado	Jordan	Nile
Columbia	Mekong	Rhine
Congo	Mississippi	Rio Grande
Danube	Missouri	St. Lawrence
Ganges	Nelson-Saskatchewan	Tigris-Euphrates
		Yangtze

EXPLORING Social Studies

Capital Mash-Ups

Geography, states, state capitals

To introduce this thought-provoking game, post the intertwined names of your state and state capital (see example). Challenge students to figure out the mystery names. Then divide students into small groups, post another entangled pair of state and capital names, and award one point to the first group to identify the names. Repeat with other mashed-up state and capital names as time allows.

Ann E. Fisher, Toledo, OH

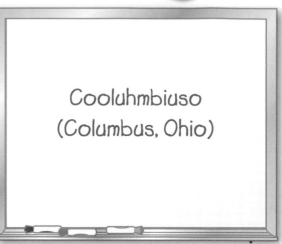

Cooluhmbiuso
(Columbus, Ohio)

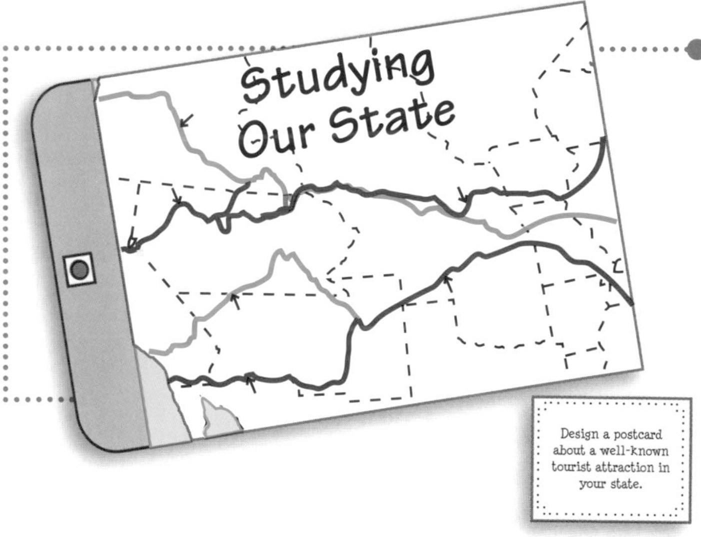

Studying Our State
Design a postcard about a well-known tourist attraction in your state.

Stately Research

State studies

Here's a social studies solution to keep early finishers on task! Copy and cut apart the cards from page 257 and put them in an envelope. (If desired, cover the envelope with part of an old state map.) When a student finishes an assignment early, she draws a card from the envelope and goes to work on the activity. After she finishes, she returns the card to the envelope and posts her work on a board titled "Studying Our State."

Revolutionary Concentration

US history

For this Revolutionary review, have each pair of students cut out the name and biography cards from a copy of page 258. Then have the pair spread the cards facedown in two separate piles. Each partner takes turns flipping one card in each pile. If the name and biography cards match, the player keeps the cards. If the cards don't match, the player turns them back over. When all the matches have been made, the player with the most matches wins.

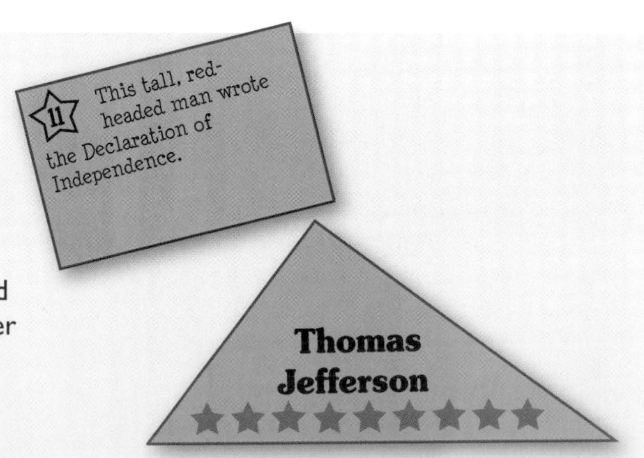

11
This tall, red-headed man wrote the Declaration of Independence.
Thomas Jefferson

EXPLORING Social Studies

Fold and Flip Timeline

History

Have your students make flipbook study guides to help them remember the sequence of important historical events. First, have each child fold a sheet of construction paper in half. Next, have her fold the top half back one inch to make a crease and then write the name of the important event in that space. After that, guide the child to identify five to ten important happenings and cut the top half of her paper into the same number of strips. Have the student label each strip with a date, location, or key phrase. Finally, have the student fold each strip back and summarize the event underneath.

The Civil War
Confederate troops attacked Fort Sumter.
July 21, 1861
March 9, 1862
June 25–July 1, 1862
December 13, 1862
January 1, 1863
July 1–3, 1863
November 19, 1863
November 15, 1864
May 26, 1865

Amber Barbee, Wharton, TX

Where in the World?

Geography

For this ongoing idea, post a world map on a bulletin board. Then have each student read the label of his shoes, jacket, snack, or a classroom object to find out where it was made. Direct the child to draw and cut out a small picture of the item and then find the article's country or state of origin on the map. Next, have the student tack one end of a length of yarn to the location, extend the yarn past the map, and staple it and the child's drawing to the board. Encourage students to add other items to the board as they notice where the things they use are made.

Colleen Dabney, Williamsburg, VA

Sudoku-Style Reporting

State research

Make a game of sharing state research! After a child researches a state, have him identify the five most important facts about the state and then describe each fact on a different index card. Next, have the student flip each card and draw a symbol that represents its fact on the back. Then give each child a copy of the mat and card patterns on page 259 and guide him to follow the steps shown to create a sudoku-style puzzle. Finally, have each student read his facts aloud and set his puzzle on his desk. As time allows, have students visit each other's desks, solve their classmates' puzzles, and review important state facts as they go!

Karen Pickett, Collegiate School, Richmond, VA

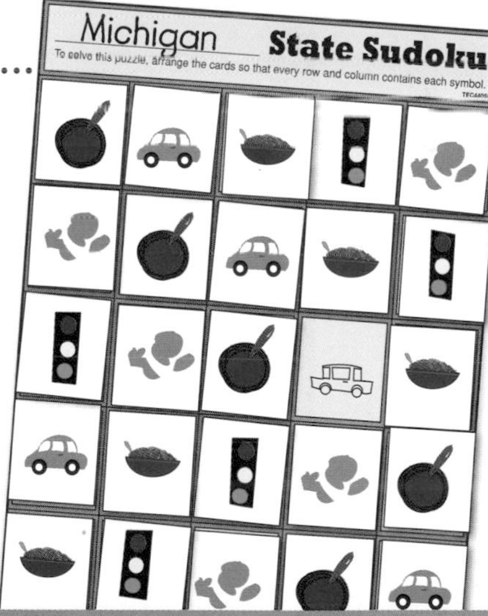

Michigan
State Sudoku
To solve this puzzle, arrange the cards so that every row and column contains each symbol.

Directions:

1. To create your puzzle, draw one symbol in one space on the grid. Then draw that symbol on four cards.
2. Draw each of the other symbols on five different cards, so that there are symbols on all of the 24 cards.
3. Cut apart the cards and the grid. Put your cards in a bag until it's time to play.

State Postal Code Cards

Use with "State Short Forms" on page 248.

AK Alaska TEC44050	AL Alabama TEC44050	AR Arkansas TEC44050	AZ Arizona TEC44050	CA California TEC44050
CO Colorado TEC44050	CT Connecticut TEC44050	DE Delaware TEC44050	FL Florida TEC44050	GA Georgia TEC44050
HI Hawaii TEC44050	IA Iowa TEC44050	ID Idaho TEC44050	IL Illinois TEC44050	IN Indiana TEC44050
KS Kansas TEC44050	KY Kentucky TEC44050	LA Louisiana TEC44050	MA Massachusetts TEC44050	MD Maryland TEC44050
ME Maine TEC44050	MI Michigan TEC44050	MN Minnesota TEC44050	MO Missouri TEC44050	MS Mississippi TEC44050
MT Montana TEC44050	NC North Carolina TEC44050	ND North Dakota TEC44050	NE Nebraska TEC44050	NH New Hampshire TEC44050
NJ New Jersey TEC44050	NM New Mexico TEC44050	NV Nevada TEC44050	NY New York TEC44050	OH Ohio TEC44050
OK Oklahoma TEC44050	OR Oregon TEC44050	PA Pennsylvania TEC44050	RI Rhode Island TEC44050	SC South Carolina TEC44050
SD South Dakota TEC44050	TN Tennessee TEC44050	TX Texas TEC44050	UT Utah TEC44050	VA Virginia TEC44050
VT Vermont TEC44050	WA Washington TEC44050	WI Wisconsin TEC44050	WV West Virginia TEC44050	WY Wyoming TEC44050

Name ______________________________
Date ______________________________

State Questions and Answers

What colors are in the state flag?	What is the state's nickname?	What are two important natural resources in the state?	What is the largest city in the state?
What is a famous state landmark?	What is the state tree?	What is the state's average temperature?	What is the state motto?
What is the state capital?	Who is the state's governor?	How many regions are in the state?	What is the state flower?
What is the state's average yearly rainfall?	What is the biggest lake in the state?	What is a food for which the state is famous?	What is a plant that is grown in the state?
How many miles wide is the state?	What is a river that flows through the state?	How many people live in the state?	What is the most famous spot in the state?

WOW!

Note to the teacher: Use with "State Studies" on page 249.

Name ____________________

Date ____________________

Pen-to-Paper Prompts

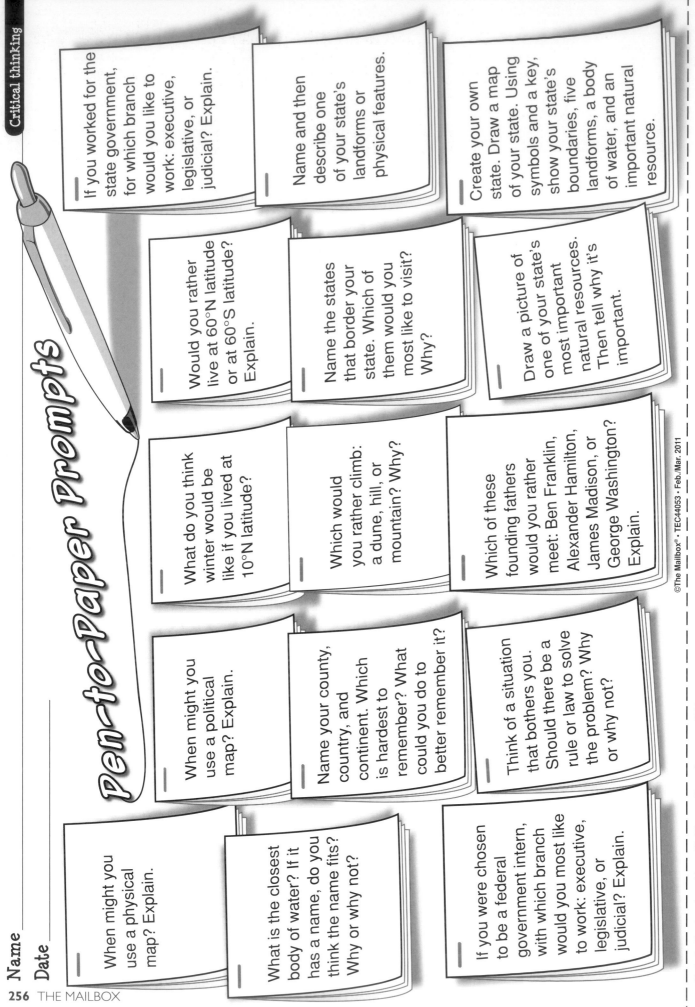

- When might you use a physical map? Explain.
- When might you use a political map? Explain.
- What do you think winter would be like if you lived at 10°N latitude?
- Would you rather live at 60°N latitude or at 60°S latitude? Explain.
- If you worked for the state government, for which branch would you like to work: executive, legislative, or judicial? Explain.
- What is the closest body of water? If it has a name, do you think the name fits? Why or why not?
- Name your county, country, and continent. Which is hardest to remember? What could you do to better remember it?
- Which would you rather climb: a dune, hill, or mountain? Why?
- Name the states that border your state. Which of them would you most like to visit? Why?
- Name and then describe one of your state's landforms or physical features.
- If you were chosen to be a federal government intern, with which branch would you most like to work: executive, legislative, or judicial? Explain.
- Think of a situation that bothers you. Should there be a rule or law to solve the problem? Why or why not?
- Which of these founding fathers would you rather meet: Ben Franklin, Alexander Hamilton, James Madison, or George Washington? Explain.
- Draw a picture of one of your state's most important natural resources. Then tell why it's important.
- Create your own state. Draw a map of your state. Using symbols and a key, show your state's boundaries, five landforms, a body of water, and an important natural resource.

Note to the teacher: Use with "Pen to Paper" on page 251.

Social Studies Early Finisher Task Cards

Use with "Stately Research" on page 252.

Create a magazine advertisement that will encourage tourists to visit your state. TEC44054	Research a business that is important in your state. Write an article about it. TEC44054	Design a plaque for the state capitol that tells about the governor. TEC44054
Make a list of all the universities and colleges in your state. TEC44054	Create a flag for your county. TEC44054	Draw a timeline with ten or more important events from your state's history. TEC44054
Design a postcard about a well-known tourist attraction in your state. TEC44054	Make a collage showing pictures of products that are made in your state. TEC44054	Choose a new nickname for your state. Explain your choice. TEC44054
Create a poster about your state's most important natural resources. TEC44054	Write ten trivia questions about your state on index cards. Write the answers on the cards' backs. TEC44054	Design a stamp that celebrates the date your state became part of the United States. TEC44054
Design a toy that is based on an animal from your state. TEC44054	Draw an outline of your state. Show your state's main rivers and lakes. TEC44054	Make a list of the six most populated cities in your state. TEC44054

Name and Biography Cards

Use with "Revolutionary Concentration" on page 252.

1 This American naval captain captured 16 ships on his first cruise aboard the *Providence*. TEC44054	2 He was the first man killed in the Boston Massacre. TEC44054	3 This revolutionary soldier was responsible for southern victories over the British. TEC44054	4 She influenced her husband, John, to think about women's rights. TEC44054
5 He is famous for saying, "Give me liberty or give me death!" TEC44054	6 She was a slave who wrote a poem about America's struggle for freedom. TEC44054	7 He persuaded the French to help the colonists during the war. TEC44054	8 He rode with Samuel Prescott and William Dawes to warn Concord colonists that the British were coming. TEC44054
9 He became a hero when he volunteered to spy on the British for George Washington. TEC44054	10 He led Americans in their fight for independence. TEC44054	11 This tall, red-headed man wrote the Declaration of Independence. TEC44054	12 This woman took her husband's place when he was killed during a battle. She kept fighting until she was seriously wounded. TEC44054
13 This Prussian-American general reformed the army to make it more disciplined and efficient. TEC44054	14 He was one of the first people to propose independence. He also helped write the Declaration of Independence. TEC44054	15 She carried pitchers of water to her husband and other soldiers as they fought in the Battle of Monmouth. TEC44054	16 He was a French military leader who served as a major general in the Continental Army. TEC44054
John Adams / Abigail Adams TEC44054	Margaret Corbin / Crispus Attucks TEC44054	Benjamin Franklin / Marquis de Lafayette TEC44054	Nathan Hale / Nathanael Greene TEC44054
Patrick Henry / Mary "Molly Pitcher" Hays TEC44054	John Paul Jones / Thomas Jefferson TEC44054	Friedrich von Steuben / Paul Revere TEC44054	Phillis Wheatley / George Washington TEC44054

State Sudoku Grid and Cards

Use with "Sudoku-Style Reporting" on page 253.

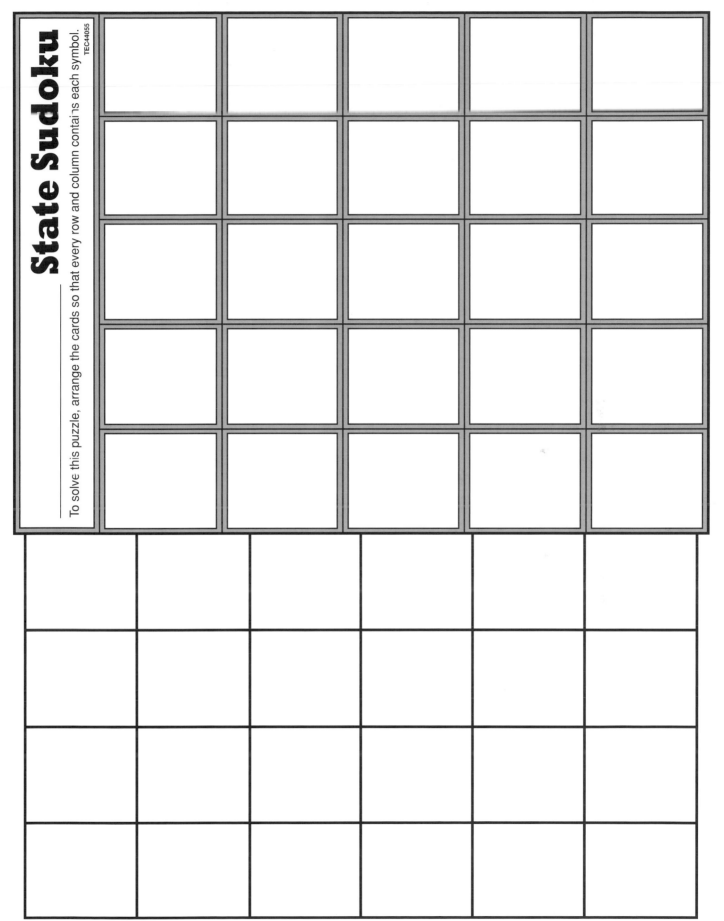

State Sudoku

To solve this puzzle, arrange the cards so that every row and column contains each symbol.

TEC44055

Name ______________________________

Date ______________________________

Where in the World?

country name

What's the official language?

What's the country's capital?

What's the country's population?

How much land does the country cover?

What type of government does the country have?

Does the country have a motto?
If so, what is it?

Draw the national flag in the space below. Then color it.

What does the flag represent?

Describe three fascinating facts about the country.

-
-
-

Bonus: Using the information above, write a report about the country you studied.

 How to use: Provide research materials and have each student use the page to research a country other than his own.

Name ____________________

Date ____________________

In Honor of Working People

In Nome, Alaska, some people celebrate Labor Day with a bathtub race—they push each other in bathtubs full of water!

In the late 1800s, Americans worked hard! The average worker worked 12-hour days, seven days a week. Working conditions were not good. Many of the workers were children. At the time, laws to protect children were not strongly enforced. That meant children worked long hours too.

Workers were unhappy. They wanted to let their employers know how they felt. So they began to join other workers by forming groups called unions. Then, on September 5, 1882, 10,000 people took a half day off from work. They marched from New York's city hall to Union Square. The march, held in honor of American workers, was the first Labor Day march. Each of those marchers gave up a half-day's pay, but they let their employers know they wanted change.

Marches, or parades, were held in more and more states after that. In 1894, Congress declared Labor Day a legal holiday. Labor Day, a holiday for workers, is now observed yearly on the first Monday in September.

Draw a line to match each question to its best answer. Not all answers will be used.

1. In what year did Labor Day become a legal holiday? •
2. What is the author's purpose for writing the selection? •
3. According to the selection, why is Labor Day observed? •
4. According to the selection, why did children work long hours? •
5. Why does the author state, "Each of those marchers gave up a half-day's pay..."? •

- to show that the workers made a sacrifice
- to honor working people
- There were no laws to protect children at the time.
- to show that the workers earned a half-day's pay
- to persuade
- It was the first day unions were organized.
- 1882
- to inform
- 1894
- to entertain
- Laws to protect children were not strongly enforced.
- Children had to work to help their families.

6. On another sheet of paper, write a summary of the selection. Include **three** important ideas in your summary.

Name ____________________

Date ____________________

Our American Giants

The tallest peak in the Rockies is 7,749 feet taller than the highest peak in the Appalachians.

The Appalachian Mountains and the Rocky Mountains are the two largest mountain systems in North America. The Appalachian Mountains stretch 1,500 miles from Quebec, Canada, to Alabama. The Rocky Mountains, twice as long as the Appalachians, reach from the Yukon of Canada into New Mexico.

The oldest mountains in America, the Appalachians, began forming about 435 million years ago. The Rockies are much younger. They started taking shape around 170 million years ago.

Both mountain systems are rich in mineral resources. With deposits that include gold, lead, silver, copper, zinc, coal, natural gas, and uranium, mining is a chief industry in the Rockies. Fifty thousand square miles of coal deposits make mining a major industry in the Appalachians also.

Farming is important to the people who live in both mountain systems. Farm products from the Appalachians include poultry, apples, dairy foods, hay, potatoes, and wheat. In the Rockies, raising cattle or sheep are important types of farming.

Mount Mitchell, at 6,684 feet, is the highest peak in the Appalachian Mountains.

Mount Elbert, at 14,433 feet, is the tallest peak in the Rocky Mountains.

Use facts from the selection to complete the Venn diagram below.

Rocky Mountains | **Appalachian Mountains**

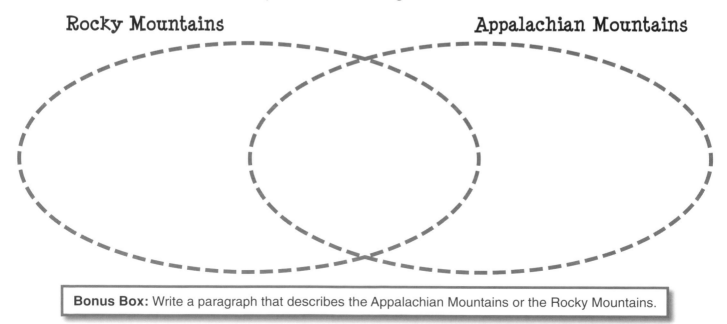

Bonus Box: Write a paragraph that describes the Appalachian Mountains or the Rocky Mountains.

Name ______________________________

Date ______________________________

HELP WANTED: JOBS IN COLONIAL AMERICA

During the 1600s, a town crier's job was to stand on the street and call out the news.

What kind of job would you have had if you were a colonist? At first, you would have probably been a farmer. Farming was the most common job in the colonies. Farmers raised cash crops such as corn, wheat, rice, and tobacco. Then they sold their crops to England and to other colonies.

As the colonies grew, trades grew too. You could have tried your hand at fishing or whaling, especially if you lived in Massachusetts. The waters there were rich with fish and whales. That's where the colonies' most important fishing ports were.

Forests supplied a lot of wood in colonial times. Lumbering became an important industry. As you considered ways to make a living, you might have chosen to be a logger.

Or you might have become a shipbuilder. At the time, ships were made of wood. The wood in the colonies was good for building ships, and there was a shortage of good shipbuilding wood in England. So shipbuilding became an important business in the colonies.

If you weren't a farmer, a fisherman, a logger, or a shipbuilder, you might have been a miner. In most colonies, there was an iron ore mine. The colonists sent some crude iron back to England to be finished, but they kept a lot of the iron. So you might have found yourself employed in the ironworks, turning the metal into kettles, pots, or wire. Then again, you might have been a blacksmith who hammered out nails, hinges, and tools from hot iron.

Bonus: Circle five important terms in the article. Tell why you chose each one.

Complete each item.

1. Underline the term *cash crops* in the fourth sentence. What do you think the term means?
____
2. Draw a box around each colonial job mentioned in the article. Then list them. ______________________________
____
3. Why did shipbuilding become an important business in the colonies? ______________________________
____
____
4. Why were the colonies' most important ports in Massachusetts? ______________________________
____
____
5. Underline the term *crude iron* in the fifth paragraph. What do you think the term means?
____
6. Which one of these colonial jobs would you have chosen? Why? ______________________________
____
____
____

Name ______________________________

Date ____________________

A Need to Read

The first thing Booker T. Washington learned to read was the number 18, which was written on the salt barrels he worked to fill each day.

Booker T. Washington was born into slavery on April 5, 1856, in Virginia. He was nine years old when all slaves in the United States were freed. His stepfather found work in West Virginia, and his family had to move. Their new home was 200 miles away. Booker, his brother, and his sister walked much of the way.

In West Virginia, Booker and his brother went to work with their stepfather. He was a salt packer, and the boys had to help him. The work was hard. They went to work as early as 4:00 AM. Their work day lasted until dark. Once Booker taught himself to read the number 18, he decided he would learn to read and write.

Booker was allowed to go to school only after he worked in the morning. When Booker was 16, he left his home in West Virginia. He enrolled in the Hampton Institute in Virginia and worked as a janitor to pay his way through school. Booker graduated in 1875 and became a teacher at the school in 1879.

In 1881, Booker founded the Tuskegee Normal and Industrial Institute. Booker started his school with a one-room shack and 30 students. He became the school's first teacher and principal. Booker believed that learning a trade was the only way people who had been slaves could escape poverty. The institute, now known as Tuskegee University, ranks as one of the nation's top universities.

Bonus: Why do you think Booker T. Washington's story is important?

Add the correct dates to the timeline below.

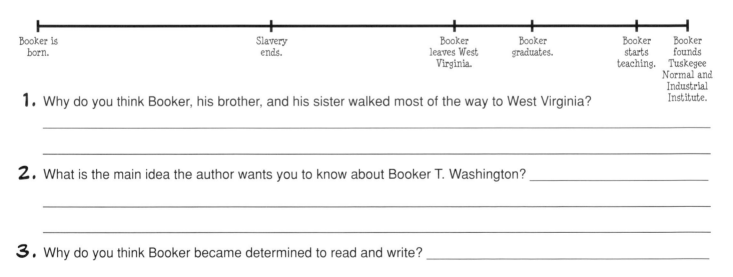

Booker is born. — Slavery ends. — Booker leaves West Virginia. — Booker graduates. — Booker starts teaching. — Booker founds Tuskegee Normal and Industrial Institute.

1. Why do you think Booker, his brother, and his sister walked most of the way to West Virginia?

2. What is the main idea the author wants you to know about Booker T. Washington? ______________

3. Why do you think Booker became determined to read and write? ______________

4. Why do you think Booker became a teacher? ______________

5. If he gave a speech to today's Tuskegee University students, what do you think Booker T. Washington would say?

Name ____

Date ____________________

Sacagawea Comes Home

When she was about 12 years old, Sacagawea was captured and taken from her Shoshone home to a village about 500 miles away.

Sacagawea's husband was hired by Meriwether Lewis and William Clark in the winter of 1804. Her husband's job was to help interpret Native American languages as Lewis and Clark made their journey west. The explorers hoped Sacagawea might also help them communicate with the Shoshone when they reached the Rocky Mountains.

Sacagawea and her husband joined Lewis and Clark at their winter camp in North Dakota. When the explorers set out in April 1805, 33 people made up the permanent party. The party—including Sacagawea, her husband, and their baby—set out in eight canoes.

When the party reached the Great Falls of the Missouri River, Lewis and Clark realized they could not keep going by water. So, in the middle of June, the party set out on foot. They carried their canoes and supplies over rough, rocky trails. It was hot and humid. The party was harassed by hailstorms, sharp cactus spines, rattlesnakes, and grizzly bears.

Lewis and Clark hoped to get horses from a friendly group of Native Americans. In mid-August, the party met a band of Shoshone Indians. Sacagawea was asked to interpret. She knew the chief—he was part of her long lost family. Sacagawea helped Lewis and Clark trade for horses and supplies. They were also given a guide who helped them get through the Rocky Mountains.

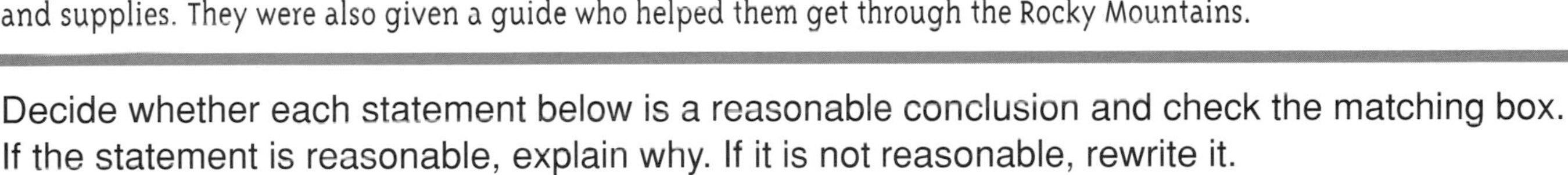

Decide whether each statement below is a reasonable conclusion and check the matching box. If the statement is reasonable, explain why. If it is not reasonable, rewrite it.

Reasonable	Not Reasonable	
		1. Lewis and Clark knew that Sacagawea was part of a Shoshone tribe. ____________
		2. Lewis and Clark spoke many Native American languages. ____________
		3. While Lewis and Clark were in their winter camp, they were not exploring. ____________
		4. Sacagawea was in Lewis and Clark's winter camp for only one month. ____________
		5. There were at least six people in each of the permanent party's canoes. ____________
		6. It took the exploration party almost two months to get to the Great Falls. ____________

Bonus: How do you think Sacagawea felt when she realized the chief of the Shoshone tribe was part of her long lost family? Explain.

Name ______________________________

Date ____________________

"When in the Course..."

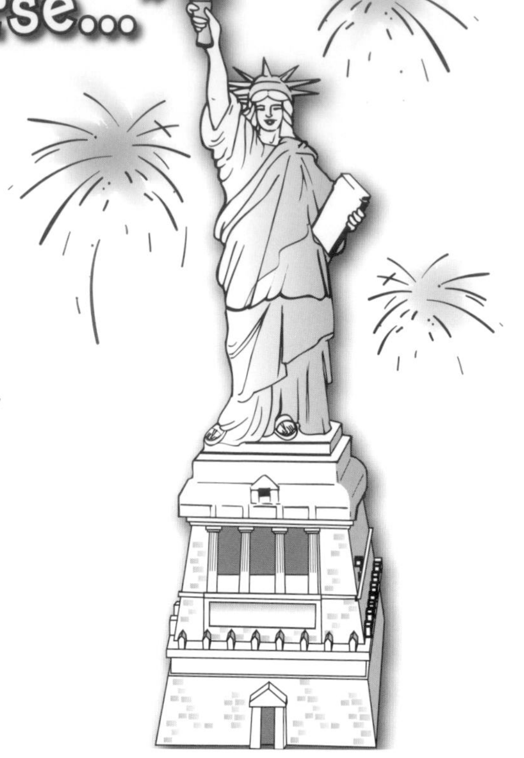

In the country's largest fireworks display, 40,000 fireworks shells were launched from barges in the Hudson River in New York City. (July 4, 2010)

On July 4, 1776, the Second Continental Congress officially accepted the Declaration of Independence. The American colonies were now free and independent states. One year later, the town of Philadelphia marked the declaration's anniversary with bonfires, bells, and fireworks.

As time passed, other towns began celebrating the Fourth of July too. They observed the date with speeches, processions or marches, contests, picnics, military displays, and fireworks. Independence Day became a formal holiday in 1870.

Today, the Fourth of July is celebrated across the country. Though technology and times have changed, our celebrations are not unlike those of the past. People often celebrate with picnics and barbecues. Many cities hold parades, concerts, speeches, and—best of all—fireworks displays.

---

1. On what date was the first Independence Day celebration held? ______________________
2. In which year did the Fourth of July became an official US holiday? ______________________
3. For how long has America's independence been celebrated with fireworks? ______________________
4. Why do you think we celebrate the Fourth of July with fireworks? ______________________
5. Write the statement from above that contains an opinion. Circle the opinion. ______________________
6. Summarize the selection. ______________________

Bonus: Draw a Venn diagram labeled as shown. Then complete the diagram with facts from the selection.

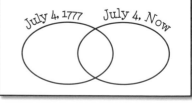

July 4, 1777 | July 4, Now

Classroom Displays

CLASSROOM DISPLAYS

Welcome your students back to school with a sweet display! Write each student's name on a separate construction paper cutout of your favorite candy. Then post an empty bag of the candy along with the cutouts on a board decorated as shown.

Heather Kime Markland, Chatham Park Elementary, Haverford, PA

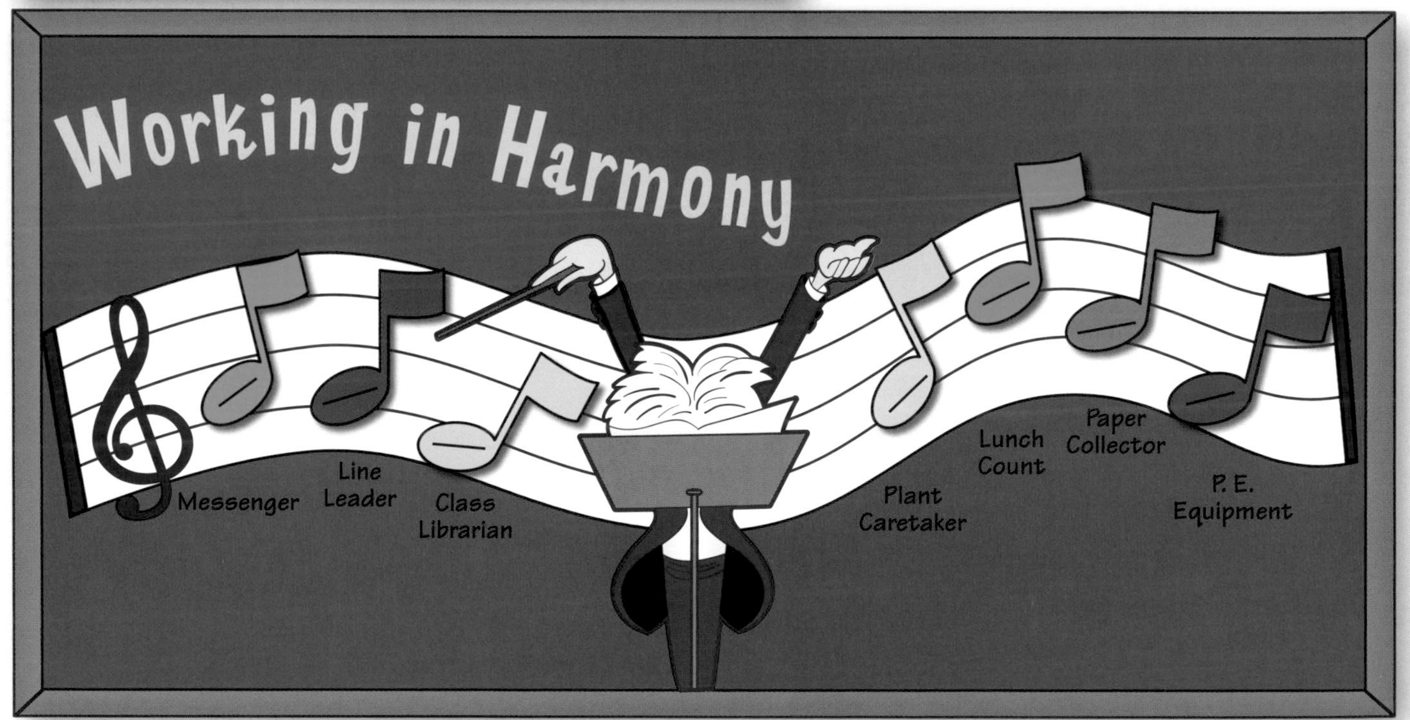

For this classroom helper board, draw a music staff and clef on the board and list classroom jobs as shown. Next, post an enlarged copy of the conductor pattern from page 278. Then program copies of the note pattern on page 278 with students' names. Pin one note on the staff above each job and then rotate notes each week so a different melody will always be playing!

Have each student choose an example of his best work and explain his selection on a copy of the hand pattern from page 279. Then display students' work and explanations along with an enlarged copy of the hand pattern and the title shown.

To highlight problem-solving strategies, program several bone-shaped cutouts with different strategies. Then post them on a board along with an enlarged copy of the dog pattern from page 279.

CLASSROOM DISPLAYS

For this good-work display, post an enlarged copy of the crow from page 271 on a board with the title shown. Then have each child choose an example of her best work and tell why she chose it on her own copy of the crow.

Jodi G. Zeis, Elgin, SC

To make your good-work display easy to refresh, use Velcro fasteners to mount a clear page protector on the wall for each student. When a student completes an assignment you're both proud of, she just slips the paper into her protector and adds a seasonal pattern such as the crow.

Want your young writers to pen strong leads? Try this! Post different types of leads on large pencil or pen shapes. Then guide students to record the excellent introductions they hear or read on index cards and add the cards to the display under the appropriate headings. When it's time to write, have each child use the models as inspiration for his own great beginning!

Amy Kotara, Lamar Elementary, Pampa, TX

Keep important math vocabulary top of mind with this fun display. Have each student write an important math term on a copy of the cow pattern on page 280. Then have the child define and/or illustrate the term on a copy of the hay bale pattern. Post students' work as shown.

Crow Pattern

Use with "Work Worth Crowing About" on page 270.

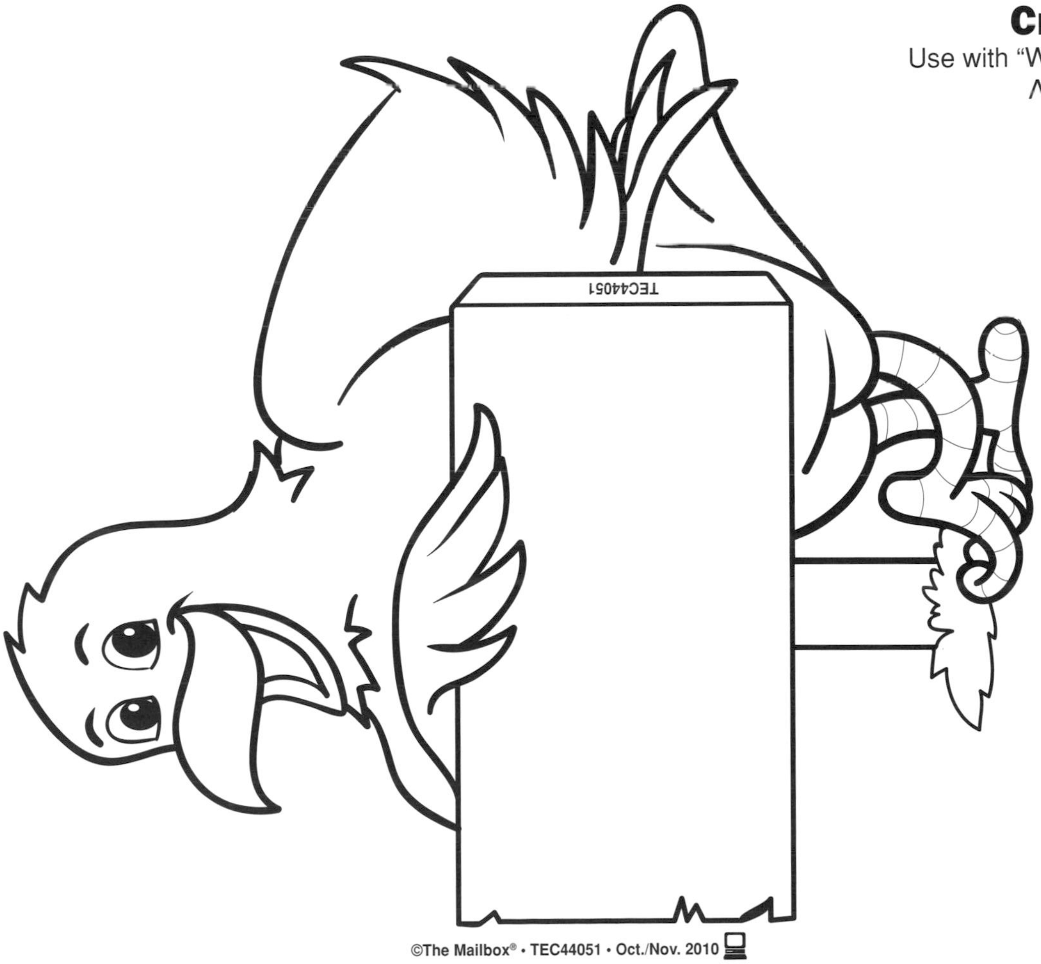

CLASSROOM DISPLAYS

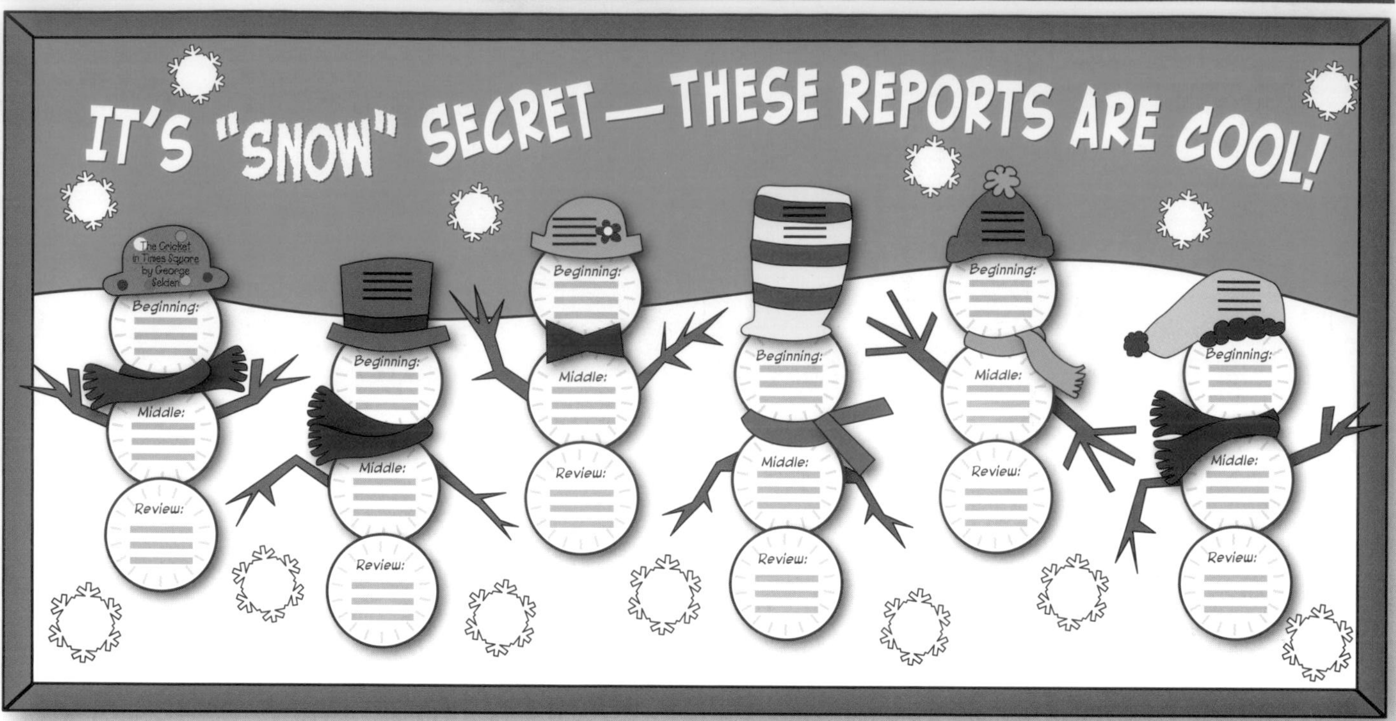

For this reading display, have each student summarize the beginning and middle of her book on two six-inch paper plates. On a third plate, guide the child to write a review of the book without giving away its ending. Next, have the child staple the plates together to make a snowman, list the book's title and author on a construction paper hat, and add details to personalize her snowman. Then display students' work as shown.

Ruth Albert, Whispering Pines Elementary, Boca Raton, FL

Want to give your good-work display a fresh look? Have each student choose a sample of his best work and cut out a pair of construction paper pawprints. Then post students' work and pawprint cutouts, along with an enlarged copy of the dog pattern on page 273, and title the board as shown.

Colleen Dabney, Williamsburg, VA

Here's a great idea for reinforcing place value! Staple black paper across the bottom of a board to create a street. Next, staple white paper strips down the middle for the dividing line. Then program four copies of the house pattern on page 281 as shown. Finally, arrange and number cards in the columns to review place value and rounding skills.

Dog Pattern

Use with "'Paws-itively' Great Work!" on page 272.

CLASSROOM DISPLAYS

For this seasonal display, each student draws and cuts out a large construction paper kite. Then he decorates the kite to show his hopes and dreams for the future. Next, the child traces the kite onto lined paper, cuts it out, and writes about those dreams. The student staples one edge of the kites together and tapes a length of yarn to the back of the lined paper. Then, on each bow from a copy of page 275, he lists a different character trait that will help him achieve his dreams. To finish his kite, the child cuts out the bows and tapes them to the string.

Geraldine Gramil, St. John Regional Catholic School, Frederick, MD

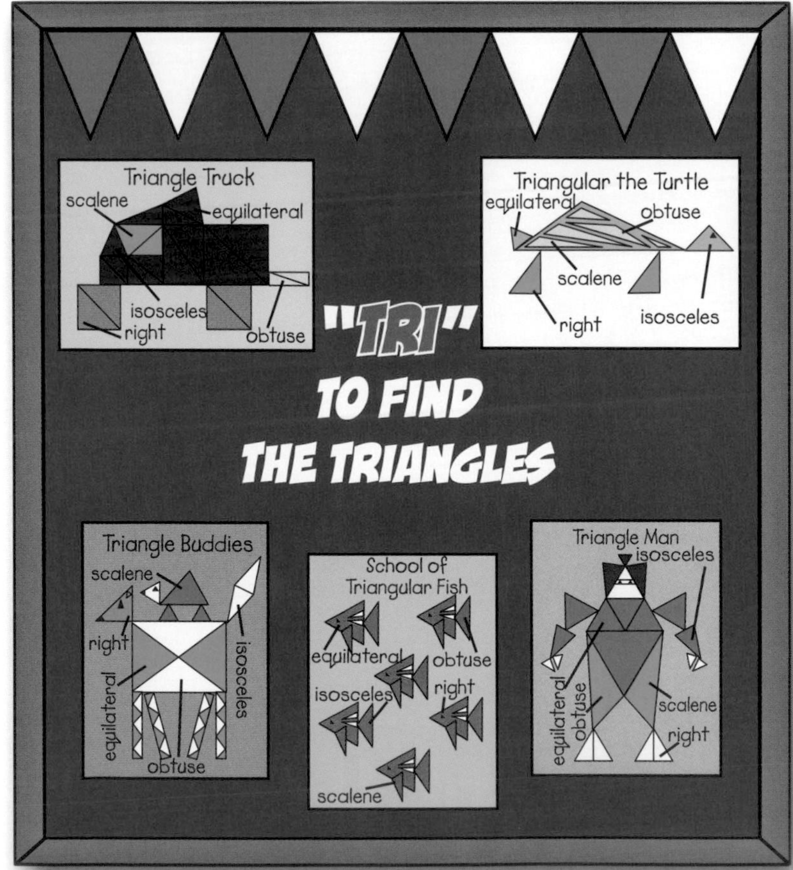

To highlight triangle concepts, challenge each student to draw a picture that includes each type of triangle you've studied. Have the child label one example of each triangle and title his drawing. Then post students' work on a board titled as shown.

Geraldine Gramil

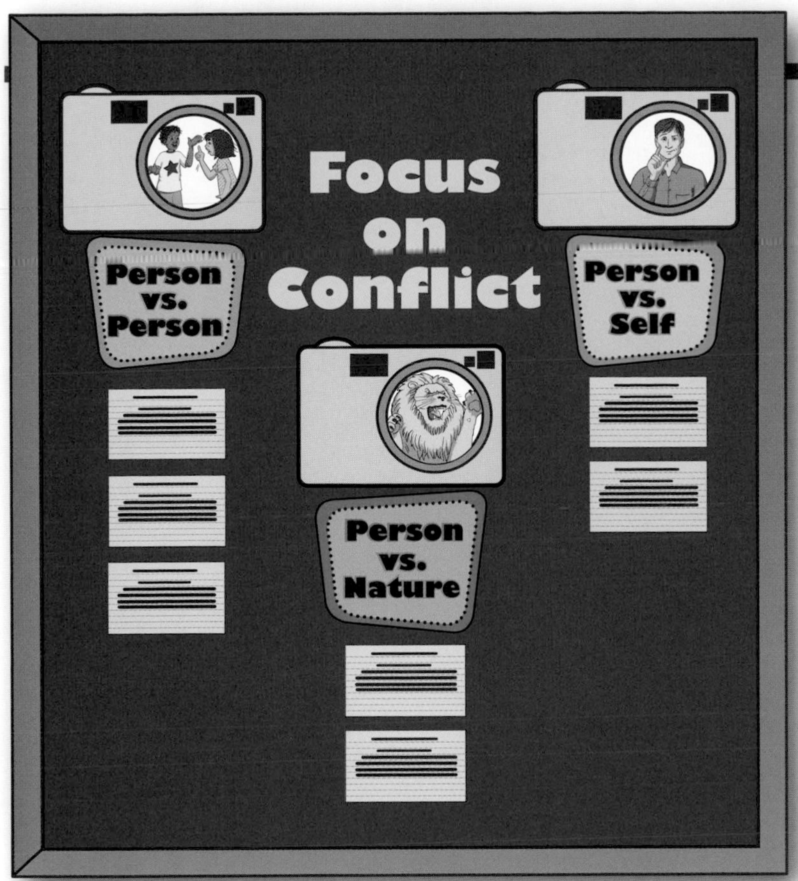

To set up this interactive reading display, draw three camera shapes. Next, cut out the conflict circles and labels from a copy of page 282. Post all the pieces on a board as shown. As a student reads a story, she identifies each conflict. On an index card, the student records the story's title, author, and a summary of the conflict. Then the child posts her card under the appropriate camera.

Colleen Dabney, Williamsburg, VA

Bow Patterns

Use with "Touch the Sky!" on page 274.

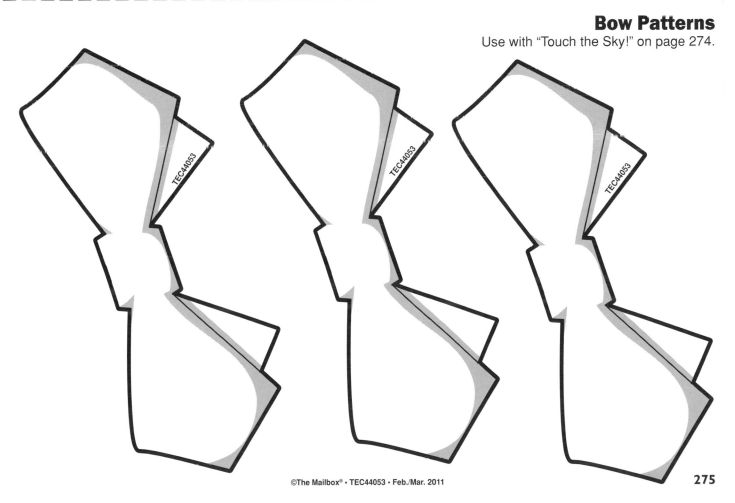

TEC44053

TEC44053

TEC44053

CLASSROOM DISPLAYS

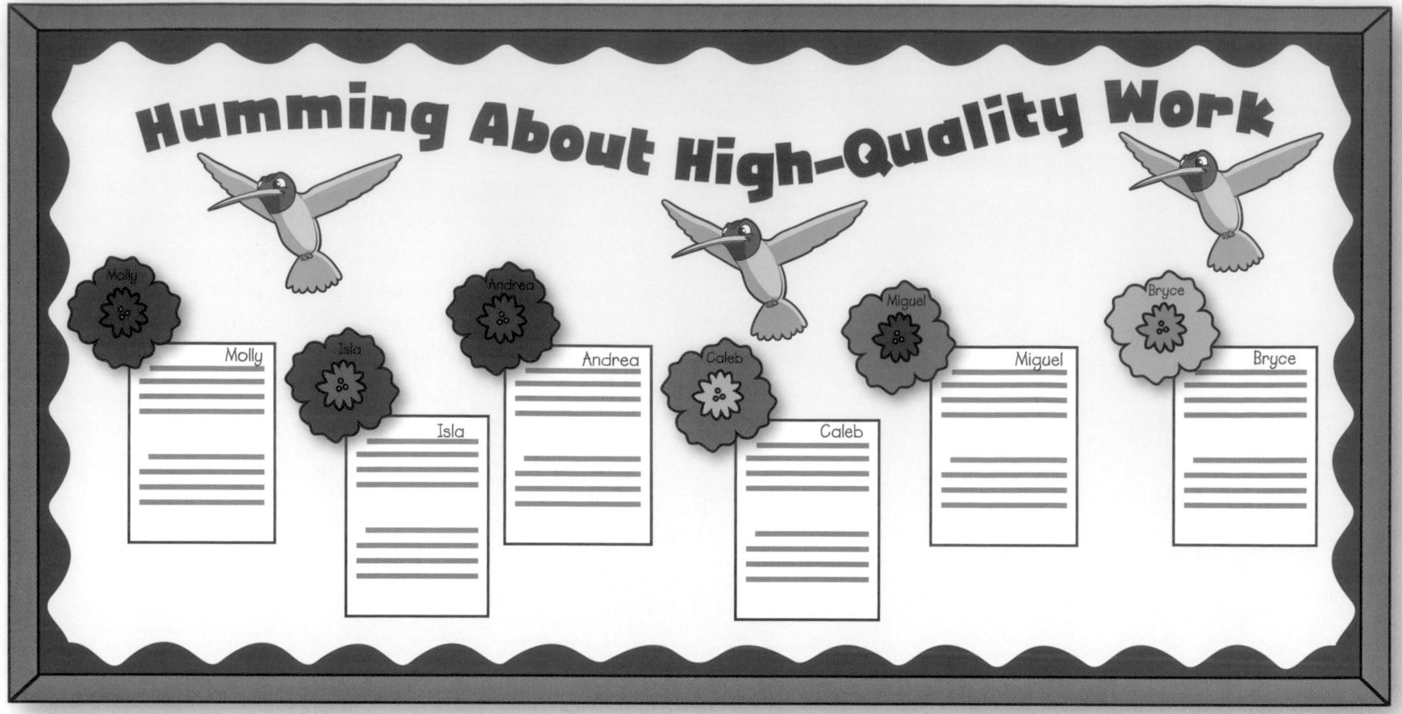

Celebrate spring with this bright display of excellent work! Have each student create a construction paper flower and write her name on it. Post each flower beside an example of the child's best work and add colorful hummingbirds.

Colleen Dabney, Williamsburg, VA

DOWN-TO-EARTH HAIKU
A healthy planet
Clean earth, clean water, clean air
Earth, dirt, soil, planet
Ben
*A haiku is a 17-syllable unrhymed poem written in three lines. The first and third lines each have five syllables. The second has seven syllables.

Combine National Poetry Month and Earth Day with this earthy display. First, guide each student to write a haiku* about the environment. Have the child write his poem on recycled paper and embellish it with construction paper scraps; then post students' work as shown.

Colleen Dabney

CLASSROOM DISPLAYS

Motivate students to read this summer with book recommendations from their classmates! Have each student summarize on a surfboard shape a favorite book she read this year. Then have her read her summary aloud before adding it to this splashing display!

Colleen Dabney, Williamsburg, VA

For this year-end display, trim bulletin board paper in the shape of a giant autograph book. Have each child write a sentence or two on it about his most memorable moment this year and then autograph it with flourish.

Conductor and Note Patterns

Use with "Working in Harmony" on page 268.

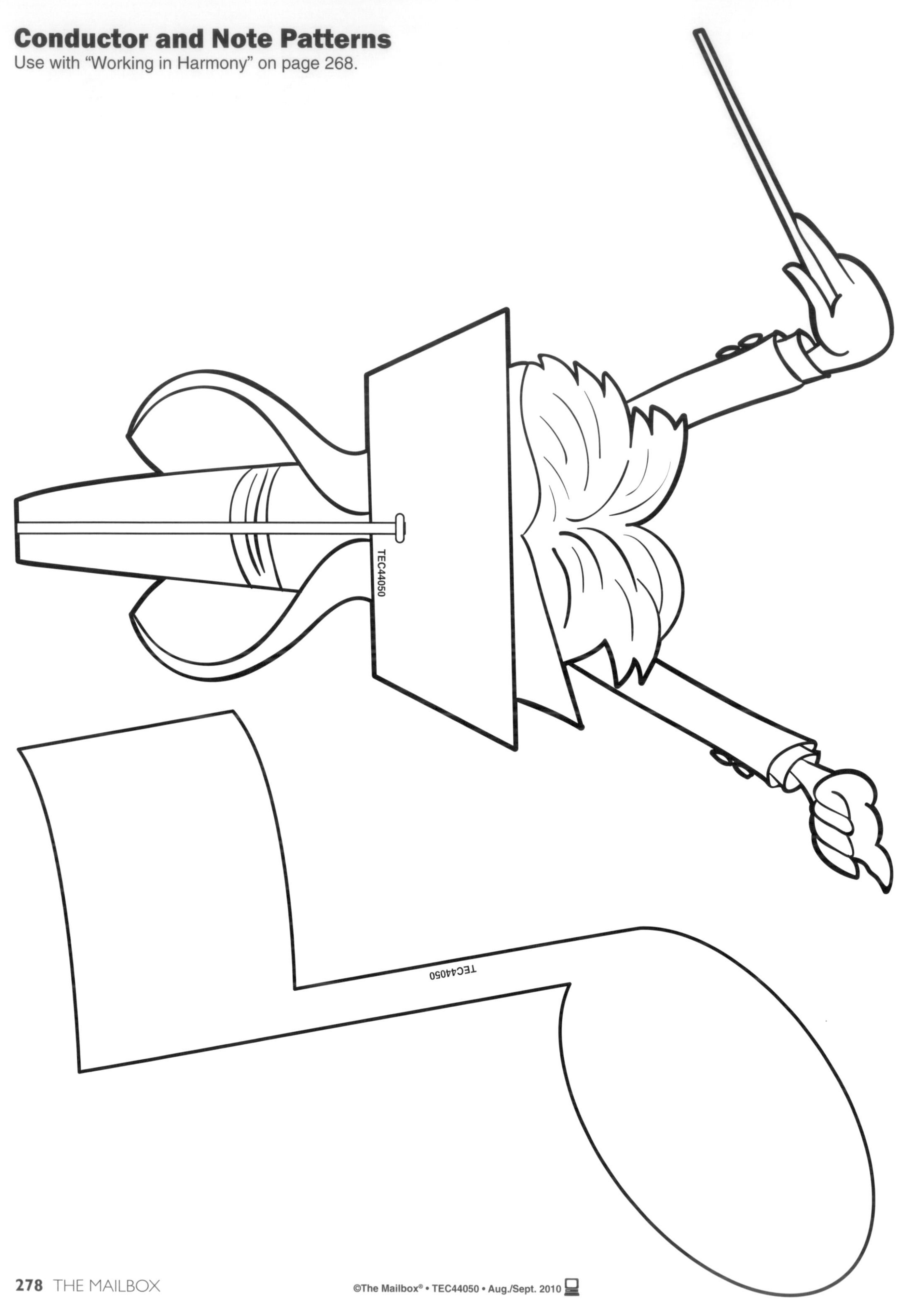

Hand Pattern

Use with "Pointing Out Great Work!" on page 269.

Dog Pattern

Use with "Digging In to Problem Solving" on page 269.

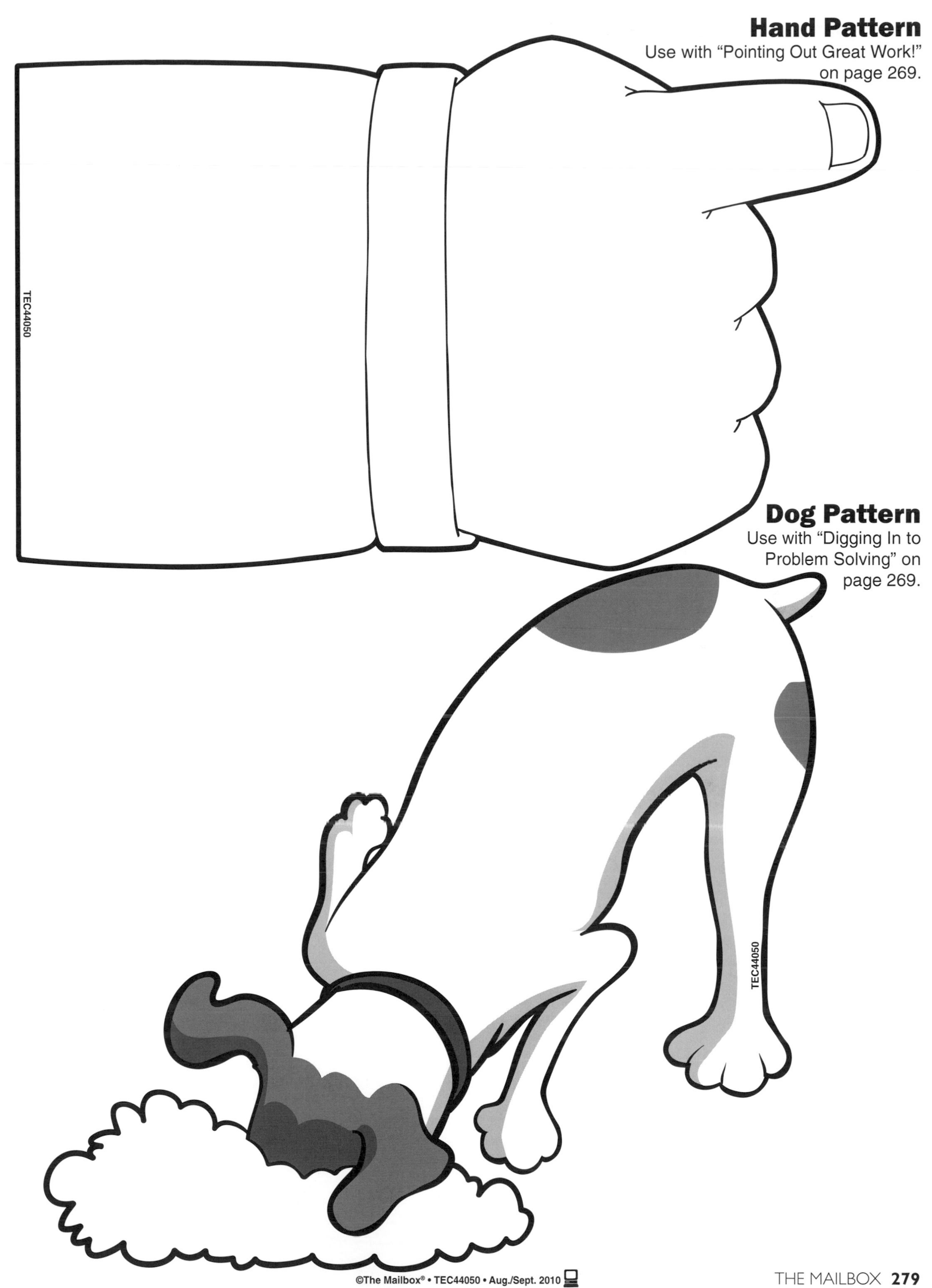

Cow and Hay Bale Patterns

Use with "In the 'Mooood' for Math" on page 271.

House Pattern

Use with "Numeration Street" on page 273.

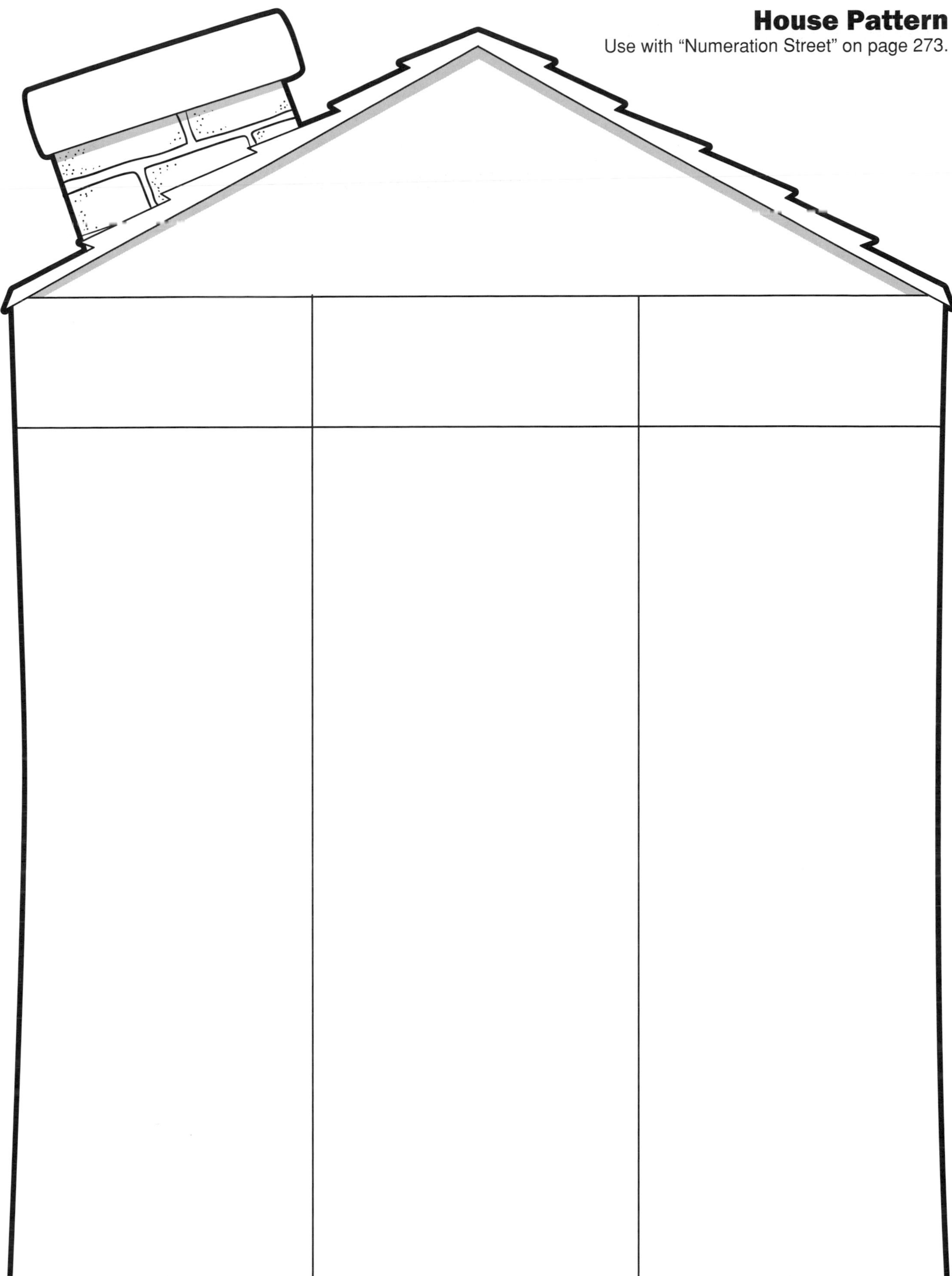

Conflict Circles

Use with "Focus on Conflict" on page 275.

Person
vs.
Nature

TEC44053

Management Tips & Timesavers

Management Tips and Timesavers

Ready Records

For **on-the-spot record keeping,** stack several copies of your class list on a handy clipboard. Any time you're collecting materials or paperwork, grab the clipboard. Write the name of the item you're collecting at the top of a fresh class list and then highlight each student's name as he turns in his form, supply, or money—no more wondering who turned in what!

Nicole Hillegas, Everett Elementary, Everett, PA

Name-Dropper

Reuse **students' nameplates** instead of tossing them once you've learned your children's names. Just have each student tuck her nameplate into the pocket of her binder. When the principal, a guest, or a parent volunteer visits your class, have each child pull out her nameplate and place it on her desk. With just a glance, your visitor will be able to call on or respond to any student by name!

Joyce Hovanec, Glassport Elementary, Glassport, PA

Beat the Clock!

Here's a clever idea that's sure to speed up **classroom cleanup!** First, make two copies of page 290. Glue one grid onto a large envelope and cut apart the other one to create task cards. At the end of the day, set out the grid and give each student a card. Next, announce that students have one minute to complete their tasks and place their cards on the grid's matching sections. If all the tasks are completed (and cards are returned) before time is up, award a point toward a class reward. Then tuck the cards into the envelope, and you're ready for tomorrow's cleanup!

Cheryl Zellhoefer, Tecopa, CA

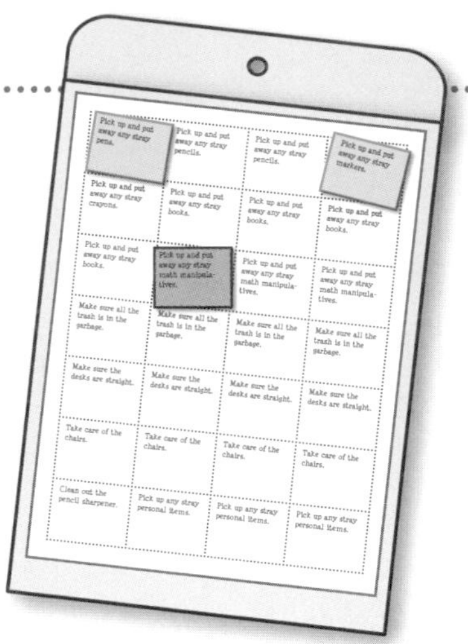

Wish Cards

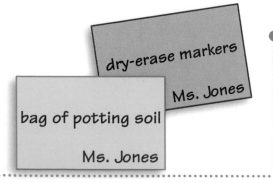

Instead of sending around a sheet asking for **classroom donations,** list each item you need on separate index cards along with your name. Then spread out the cards near your sign-in sheet at open house. Each parent who spots an item she'd like to share simply picks up the card and takes it with her. The sturdy card makes a great reminder!

dry-erase markers
Ms. Jones

bag of potting soil
Ms. Jones

Management Tips and Timesavers

Gold-Star Club

Motivate students to turn in their **homework assignments** on time with this tip! Program a copy of the Gold-Star Club membership cards on page 291 with expiration dates. Then copy and cut apart a class supply. Have each child jot his name on a card and keep it handy. Each time the student turns in his homework on time, initial a box on his card. After you initial the card ten times, it becomes a homework pass!

Kim Tenney, St. Luke's Lutheran School, Oviedo, FL

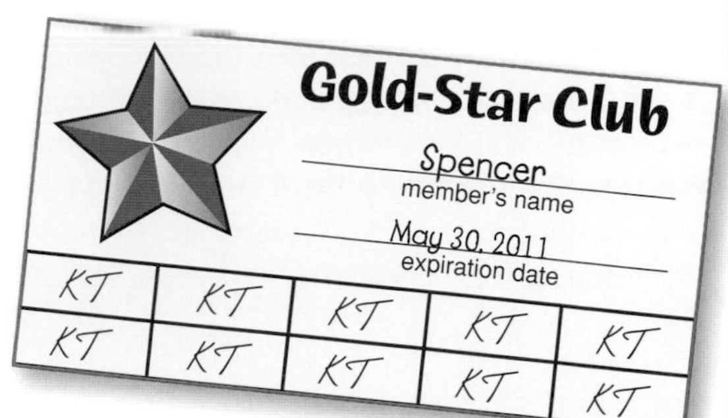

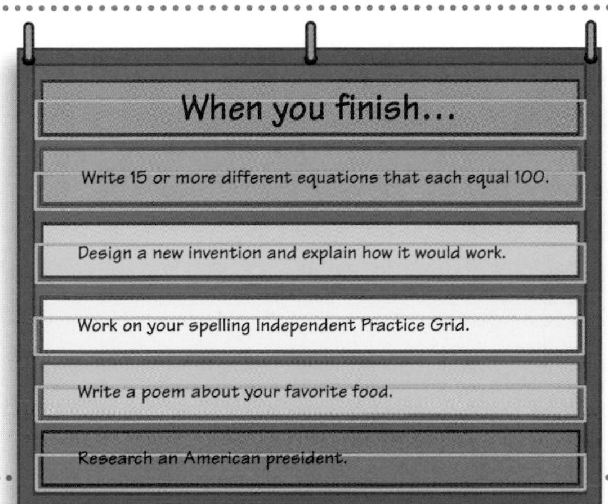

When you finish...
Write 15 or more different equations that each equal 100.
Design a new invention and explain how it would work.
Work on your spelling Independent Practice Grid.
Write a poem about your favorite food.
Research an American president.

When You Finish...

Keep **early finishers** engaged with this quick tip. Laminate several sentence strips and program each one with a skill-building task. Then display the strips in a pocket chart. When a student finishes, she chooses a task and gets to work! Keep the tasks fresh by periodically wiping off the strips and replacing the tasks.

Colleen Hoover, Juniper Elementary, Hesperia, CA

Work While You Wait

Ever look up from your desk to find a line of chattering **students waiting for your attention**? Try this! Keep decks of multiplication and division cards on the corner of your desk. Then have any student waiting for your attention pick up a handful of cards and review his facts.

Jeannie Pavlik, Pittsville Elementary, Pittsville, WI

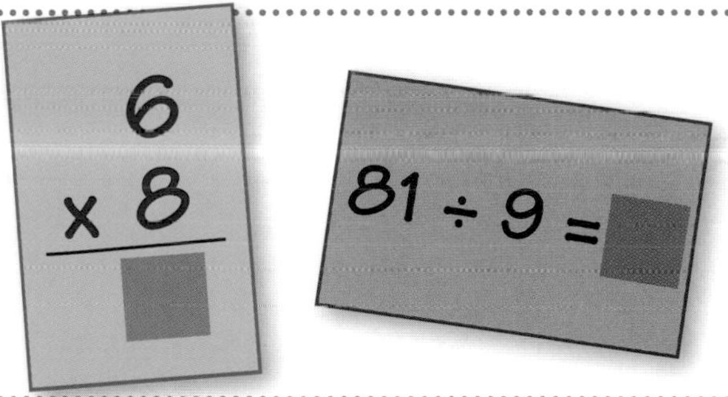

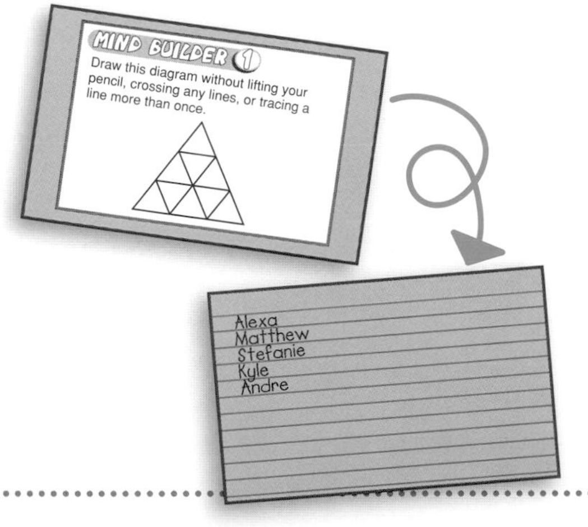

Keep Them Challenged!

To **differentiate instruction** and keep students on task while you work with small groups, glue independent activity cards onto index cards. Then, after a student completes the card's task, she flips the card and signs the back. With just a glance, she'll know whether she has completed the activity and won't waste any time getting to work on a different card!

Shauna Mayo, Robert E. Lee Elementary, Petersburg, VA

Management Tips and Timesavers

I'm Done! Now What?

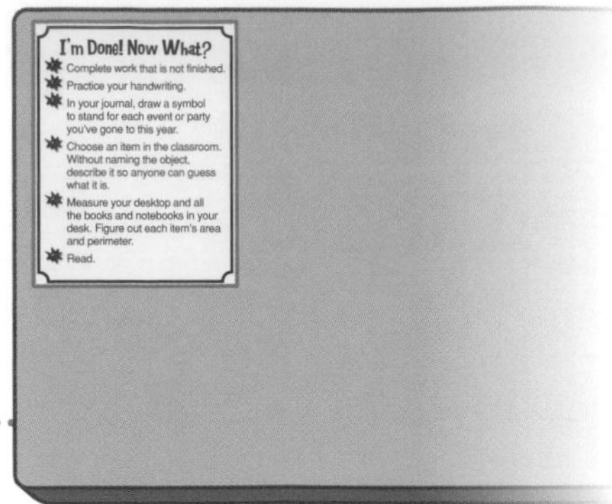

Here's a trouble-free idea for managing your **early finishers.** Copy and cut apart the cards on page 292 and tape one to each student's desk. When a student finishes his work early, have him choose an activity from the list and keep on working.

Michelle Yelton, Saints Peter and Paul School, California, KY

Smile All the While

This clever tip is sure to keep **inattentive or struggling students** on track! Break the child's assignments into manageable sections by drawing a colorful smiley face partway down the page. When the child comes to the smiley face, she brings her paper to you for a quick check. Then she returns to work. If there's still a lot of work on the page, draw a second smiley face further down before sending the student back to work.

Rose Degregorio, Ben Franklin Elementary, Bethel Park, PA

Face the Music

To signal that it's **time to clean up** one activity and move on to the next, play a 15- to 30-second clip of music. Challenge each student to have his desk ready for the next lesson by the time the clip ends. If desired, divide students into teams and award points to the teams that are ready on cue.

Therese Durhman, Mountain View School, Hickory, NC

Simple Storage

Want to keep those unruly **bulletin board borders** in order? Try this! Roll up each border and put it inside an empty frosting container. Then tape a piece of the border to the tub and stack the tubs so each border shows.

Kathy Goebel, George Washington Elementary, Eastlake, OH

Need to Know

Instead of saving the review game until you've finished a unit, use it as a playful **pretest!** By playing the game before teaching the unit, you can encourage students' interest in the topic, access prior knowledge, and build background knowledge. Then you can focus your attention on teaching what your students don't know!

Michelle Bayless, Zushi, Japan

Management Tips and Timesavers

Minds at Work!

Want your students to **walk quietly through the halls** on their way to another class or the lunchroom? Challenge them to find something related to a current topic—such as a prime number, a word with a specific prefix, or even an example of a simple machine—as they walk. Then, when students return to class, take a few minutes to have them share their examples.

Terry Healy
Marlatt Elementary
Manhattan, KS

Be on the lookout for an adverb with the suffix that means "in a certain way."

That's the Ticket!

Instead of taking the time to grade every student's **practice pages,** randomly pick three or four pages from each assignment. Give the pages a quick check and staple a ticket worth five points to each paper that's been appropriately completed. Each child saves her ticket and then attaches it to a future assignment to earn five extra points on her grade!

Vicki Bailey, Sumrall Elementary, Sumrall, MS

Clearly Organized

To keep the **pages students turn in** organized, tape page protectors to the fronts of several folders. When it's time for students to turn in their work, slide a copy of the assignment into the page protector and set out the folder. For an assignment that students complete on their own paper, jot the task information on a paper slip and slide it into the page protector. Your students will know exactly where to place each assignment, and you won't have to spend time sorting papers before you start grading them!

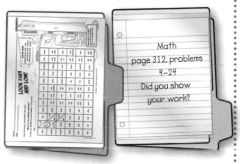

Math
page 312, problems
4–24
Did you show
your work?

Patty Slagel, Ashburn Elementary, Ashburn, VA

Fourth Grade at a Glance

In the Learning Loop

Help your students **let their parents know what they're learning.** From time to time, guide each child to describe on a copy of page 293 a class experiment, activity, or topic of study. Next, have the student take the page home and share it with his parent or guardian, who then jots a quick note at the bottom of the page. If desired, give a small reward to each child who returns his completed page. Then save each student's pages and compile them to make a booklet that's full of the year's memories.

Jeannie Pavlik, Pittsville Elementary, Pittsville, WI

Salutations!

To help your **substitute teacher feel welcome,** keep water bottles, mints, and pieces of chocolate handy. Then, when you set out your plans for the substitute teacher, add a bottle of water along with a few mints or some chocolate and a simple note.

Karen Guess, St. Richard's School, Indianapolis, IN

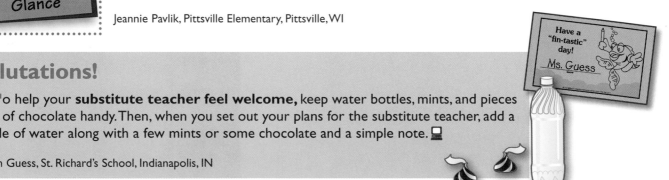

Have a "fin-tastic" day!
Ms. Guess

Management Tips and Timesavers

Mobile Mufflers

Recycle headphones into **noise blockers** for students who are easily distracted. Simply snip the cord off computer headphones that no longer work. The headphones' thick padding muffles sounds in the classroom and helps children focus on their work.

Jeannie Pavlik, Pittsville Elementary, Pittsville, WI

"Egg-cessible" Supplies

Keep extra **sharpened pencils** handy with this "egg-cellent" idea. Turn a sanitized egg carton upside down and poke a narrow hole in each cup. Place a sharpened pencil in each hole. When a child needs a pencil, he takes one from the carton; then he returns it at the end of the day. Task a student helper with sharpening the supply for the next day.

Kim Brown, Greenfield, IN

Make Time for Everyone

If a child has a **question about how to complete a task**, have her write it on a sticky note and place it on the corner of her desk. Circulate the room to address individual questions. If a student generates a critical-thinking question about the content of the activity, have her write the question on a sticky note and place it in a designated spot on the board. When the activity is complete, refer to the questions on the board to lead a follow-up discussion.

Do I need to write my answers in complete sentences?

Terry Healy, Marlatt Elementary, Manhattan, KS

Functional Freebies

Repurpose unneeded bill payment **envelopes**. Save them for sending home change from a class trip, project, or book order or for when you want to send a note home.

Beth Hagel, Paul V. Fly Elementary, East Norristown, PA

Storage Solution

Here's an easy way to keep **file folder activities** contained when they're not in use. Stick self-adhesive Velcro dots inside the corners of the folder. (If you store the accompanying cards inside the folder too, add a few more dots along the inside edges.)

Mary Samson, Rockfish-Hoke Elementary, Raeford, NC

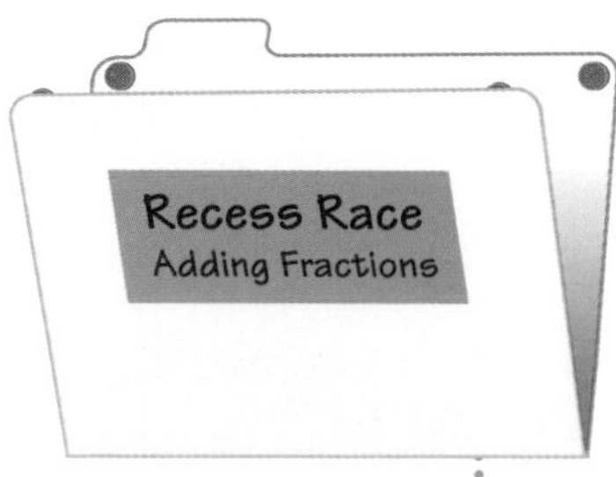

Management Tips and Timesavers

Strive for Five!

Next time you have a few minutes between lessons, try this **quick review.** Draw your handprint on the board and write a topic on the palm. Then call on different students to give separate responses on the topic and jot each correct response on a different digit. Repeat with another topic if you have a minute or two more!

Isobel Livingston, Rahway, NJ

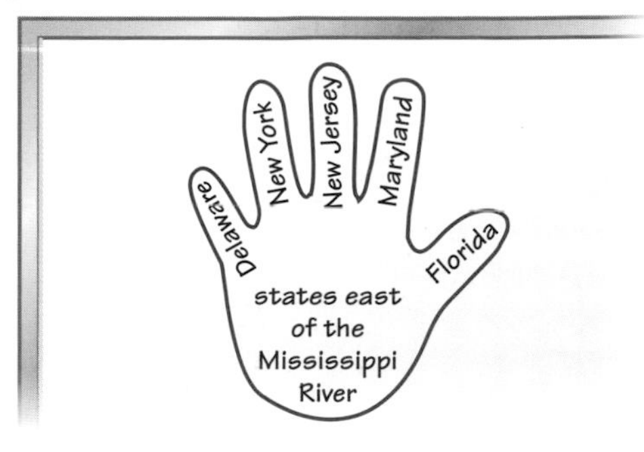

Ready to Respond

Prompt students to take **think time** and encourage them to contribute to class discussions with this handy sign. To make the sign, cut out a copy of the top of page 294. Fold the cutout in half, tape a craft stick between the halves, and then glue the halves together. When you want students to think about a question or topic, raise the sign, showing the "Think!" side. Once you feel students have had time to process, flip the sign to signal that it's time to share.

Saba Malik, Islamic Day School, East Orange, NJ

Groups at a Glance

Help parent volunteers keep track of their **field trip groups** with this simple solution. Before leaving school, give each chaperone a colored sheet of paper with a list of the students in her group. Also have each student pin a paper circle in the matching color to his shirt. Then each volunteer can quickly gather her group by calling out its color.

Renee Silliman, Spring Shadows Elementary, Houston, TX

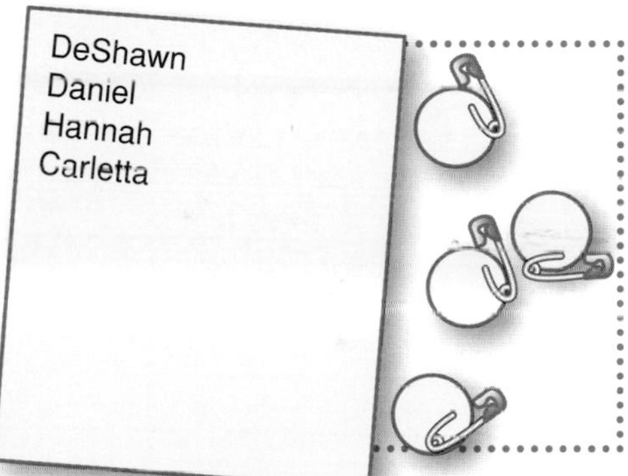

Delegating Duties

Here's a great tip for carving out a little extra **one-on-one time**! Put your class helpers or officers in charge of supervising the end-of-the-day cleanup. Then you can quickly check in with individual students before they head home!

Merrill Watrous, Fox Hollow French Immersion School, Eugene, OR

Clean and orderly can't be beat.
To show my thanks, you get a
NEAT TREAT!
Ms. Langland

Neat Treat

Want to **reward neatness?** Try this! Each time a child neatly completes an assignment or keeps his desk organized and tidy, give him a copy of a coupon from the bottom of page 294. Then periodically let students redeem their coupons for small prizes or free time.

Beverly Langland, Trinity Christian Academy, Jacksonville, FL

Pick up and put away any stray pens.	Pick up and put away any stray pencils.	Pick up and put away any stray pencils.	Pick up and put away any stray markers.
Pick up and put away any stray crayons.	Pick up and put away any stray books.	Pick up and put away any stray books.	Pick up and put away any stray books.
Pick up and put away any stray books.	Pick up and put away any stray math manipulatives.	Pick up and put away any stray math manipulatives.	Pick up and put away any stray math manipulatives.
Make sure all the trash is in the garbage.	Make sure all the trash is in the garbage.	Make sure all the trash is in the garbage.	Make sure all the trash is in the garbage.
Make sure the desks are straight.	Make sure the desks are straight.	Make sure the desks are straight.	Make sure the desks are straight.
Take care of the chairs.	Take care of the chairs.	Take care of the chairs.	Take care of the chairs.
Clean out the pencil sharpener.	Pick up any stray personal items.	Pick up any stray personal items.	Pick up any stray personal items.

 Note to the teacher: Use with "Beat the Clock!" on page 284.

Gold-Star Club Membership Cards

Use with "Gold-Star Club" on page 285.

Gold-Star Club

member's name

expiration date

TEC44051

Gold-Star Club

member's name

expiration date

TEC44051

Gold-Star Club

member's name

expiration date

TEC44051

Gold-Star Club

member's name

expiration date

TEC44051

Gold-Star Club

member's name

expiration date

TEC44051

Gold-Star Club

member's name

expiration date

TEC44051

Gold-Star Club

member's name

expiration date

TEC44051

Gold-Star Club

member's name

expiration date

TEC44051

Gold-Star Club

member's name

expiration date

TEC44051

Gold-Star Club

member's name

expiration date

TEC44051

Desk Task Cards

Use with "I'm Done! Now What?" on page 286.

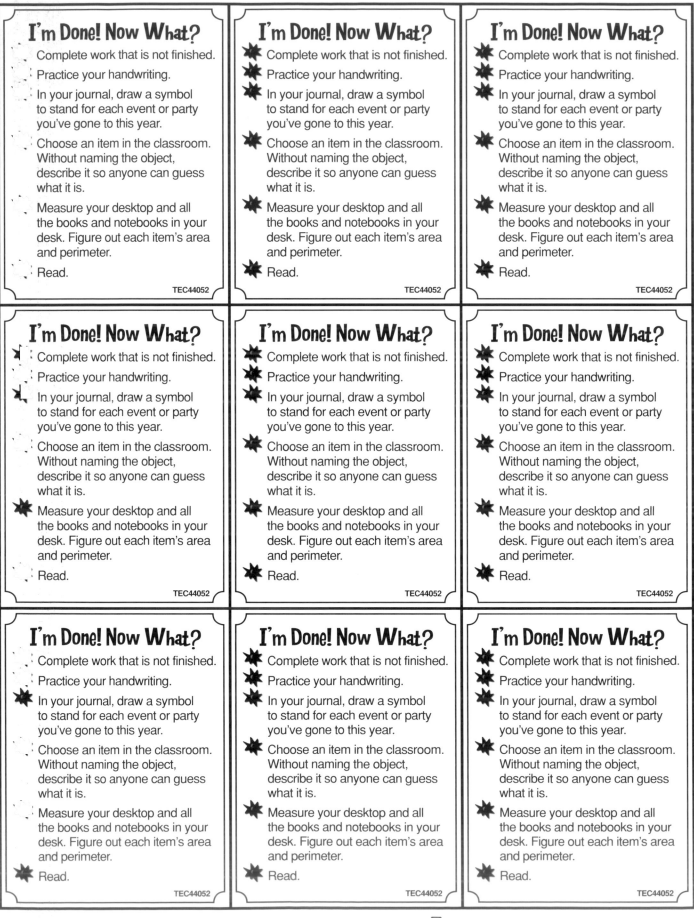

I'm Done! Now What?

- Complete work that is not finished.
- Practice your handwriting.
- In your journal, draw a symbol to stand for each event or party you've gone to this year.
- Choose an item in the classroom. Without naming the object, describe it so anyone can guess what it is.
- Measure your desktop and all the books and notebooks in your desk. Figure out each item's area and perimeter.
- Read.

TEC44052

I'm Done! Now What?

- Complete work that is not finished.
- Practice your handwriting.
- In your journal, draw a symbol to stand for each event or party you've gone to this year.
- Choose an item in the classroom. Without naming the object, describe it so anyone can guess what it is.
- Measure your desktop and all the books and notebooks in your desk. Figure out each item's area and perimeter.
- Read.

TEC44052

I'm Done! Now What?

- Complete work that is not finished.
- Practice your handwriting.
- In your journal, draw a symbol to stand for each event or party you've gone to this year.
- Choose an item in the classroom. Without naming the object, describe it so anyone can guess what it is.
- Measure your desktop and all the books and notebooks in your desk. Figure out each item's area and perimeter.
- Read.

TEC44052

I'm Done! Now What?

- Complete work that is not finished.
- Practice your handwriting.
- In your journal, draw a symbol to stand for each event or party you've gone to this year.
- Choose an item in the classroom. Without naming the object, describe it so anyone can guess what it is.
- Measure your desktop and all the books and notebooks in your desk. Figure out each item's area and perimeter.
- Read.

TEC44052

I'm Done! Now What?

- Complete work that is not finished.
- Practice your handwriting.
- In your journal, draw a symbol to stand for each event or party you've gone to this year.
- Choose an item in the classroom. Without naming the object, describe it so anyone can guess what it is.
- Measure your desktop and all the books and notebooks in your desk. Figure out each item's area and perimeter.
- Read.

TEC44052

I'm Done! Now What?

- Complete work that is not finished.
- Practice your handwriting.
- In your journal, draw a symbol to stand for each event or party you've gone to this year.
- Choose an item in the classroom. Without naming the object, describe it so anyone can guess what it is.
- Measure your desktop and all the books and notebooks in your desk. Figure out each item's area and perimeter.
- Read.

TEC44052

I'm Done! Now What?

- Complete work that is not finished.
- Practice your handwriting.
- In your journal, draw a symbol to stand for each event or party you've gone to this year.
- Choose an item in the classroom. Without naming the object, describe it so anyone can guess what it is.
- Measure your desktop and all the books and notebooks in your desk. Figure out each item's area and perimeter.
- Read.

TEC44052

I'm Done! Now What?

- Complete work that is not finished.
- Practice your handwriting.
- In your journal, draw a symbol to stand for each event or party you've gone to this year.
- Choose an item in the classroom. Without naming the object, describe it so anyone can guess what it is.
- Measure your desktop and all the books and notebooks in your desk. Figure out each item's area and perimeter.
- Read.

TEC44052

I'm Done! Now What?

- Complete work that is not finished.
- Practice your handwriting.
- In your journal, draw a symbol to stand for each event or party you've gone to this year.
- Choose an item in the classroom. Without naming the object, describe it so anyone can guess what it is.
- Measure your desktop and all the books and notebooks in your desk. Figure out each item's area and perimeter.
- Read.

TEC44052

Name ______________________
Date ______________________

In the Learning Loop

This is the latest in my learning loop:
What do you think, ____________?
parent/guardian
parent/guardian's signature

How to use: Use with "In the Learning Loop" on page 287.

Think Time Pattern

Use with "Ready to Respond" on page 289.

Think!

TEC44055

Coupons

Use with "Neat Treat" on page 289.

Clean and orderly can't be beat.
To show my thanks, you get a

TEC44055

Clean and orderly can't be beat.
To show my thanks, you get a

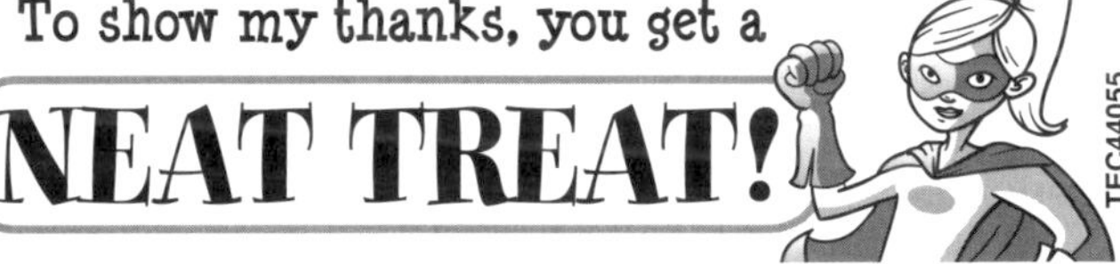

TEC44055

Clean and orderly can't be beat.
To show my thanks, you get a

TEC44055

Clean and orderly can't be beat.
To show my thanks, you get a

TEC44055

Clean and orderly can't be beat.
To show my thanks, you get a

TEC44055

Clean and orderly can't be beat.
To show my thanks, you get a

NEAT TREAT!

TEC44055

Our Readers Write

School-Year Speculations

To **spark my students' curiosity** on the first day of school, I label large sheets of construction paper with different topics we'll cover during the year. Then I guide students to generate questions about the topics, recording each question under the matching topic. I post the pages on a board titled "I Wonder…" When I introduce each new topic, we review the questions and try to find the answers as we study. At the end of the year, we review all the pages to celebrate a year full of learning!

Emily Dearstyne, Pleasant Valley Elementary, Schenectady, NY

Electricity

Why do I get shocked when I walk across carpet and then touch something?

Story Slides

To give my students practice describing **story elements,** I have them make PowerPoint presentations. After reading a story, I guide each child to create one slide about each of the story's elements. The students add graphics, sounds, and pictures to create slides that show they really understand each element.

Susan Appleton
Meadville Elementary
Nathalie, VA

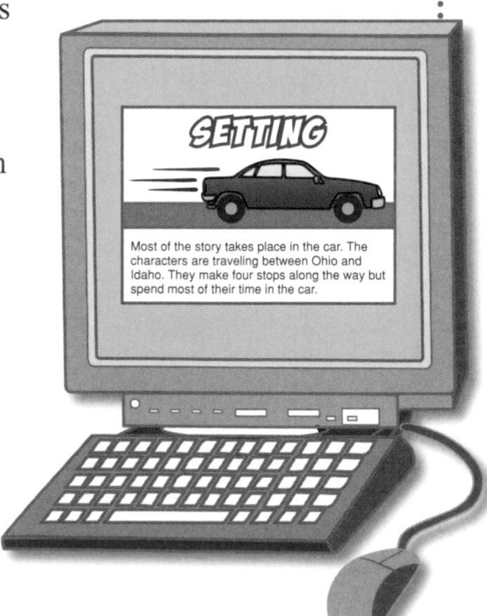

SETTING
Most of the story takes place in the car. The characters are traveling between Ohio and Idaho. They make four stops along the way but spend most of their time in the car.

Believing Is Achieving

To **motivate my students,** I have them "bury" things they think they can't do. First, I ask each student to list anything about the upcoming school year that worries him. Then I make a big deal of burying students' worries. I collect their lists, place the lists inside a shoebox labeled "RIP, Worries," and bury the box at the back of a closet. Then I dare students to believe in themselves now that we've buried their worries. I leave the box buried until the end of the year when I "dig" it up and have each student revise his list to reflect his accomplishments.

Ileana Rios, Christ the King School, Norfolk, VA

Spelling Address Book

I give each of my students an inexpensive address book to keep track of **commonly misspelled and challenging words.** When a student identifies a problematic word, he writes the word correctly in his address book, creating a quick and easy reference to use anytime he writes.

Tammy Walker, Whitesburg Christian Academy, Huntsville, AL

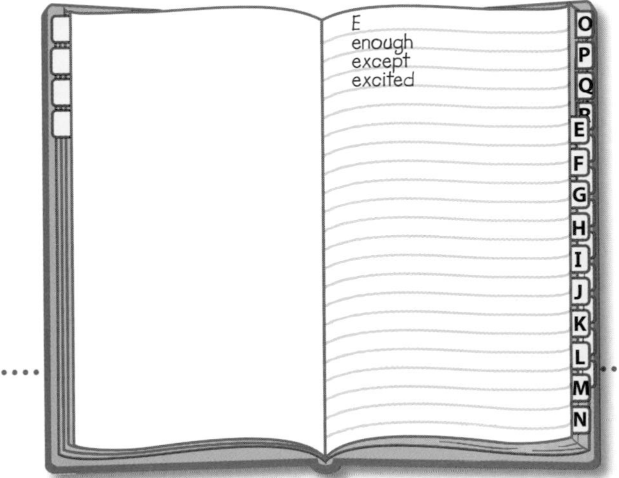

Unique Desk Tags

For a fun **open house** challenge, I have each student create anagrams of his first and last names. Then I have him transfer his anagrams to an index card, decorate the card, and tape it to his desk. When parents arrive, they happily solve the puzzles to find their children's desks. This icebreaker sets the tone for a great evening.

Chris Hunger, Maddock Elementary, Burbank, IL

Math Bee

Instead of a traditional spelling bee, I hold a **place value bee** when we have a few extra minutes! I have students grab scrap paper and pencils and line up. Then I call out a string of digits, and each student records the number, adding commas as appropriate. Next, I ask the child at the front of the line to read the number aloud. If the student answers correctly, she moves to the back of the line. If she is incorrect, she takes a seat and continues recording each number as my backup checker. We play until time is up or only one student is left standing.

Jennifer Otter, Oak Ridge, NC

FOUR, FIVE, SIX, SEVEN.

FOUR THOUSAND, FIVE HUNDRED SIXTY-SEVEN.

Prizewinning Words

Motivating my students to use new **vocabulary** words in their writing was a challenge until I started using raffle tickets! Now, each time I notice that a student has correctly used a vocabulary word in her writing, I give her a ticket. She writes her name on the back of the ticket and drops it in my "Prizewinning Words" jar. Each week, I draw one ticket from the jar and award the winner a homework pass.

Kristine Toland
Bayview Elementary
Belford, NJ

Kylynn

Our Readers Write

Bull's-Eye!

For quick and easy **morning work,** I display a laminated bull's-eye. Each day, I write a number in the center using a wipe-off marker. Then I have each student write at least ten equations that equal the targeted number. Depending on the time of year, I specify the operations students should use.

Leigh Newsom, Cedar Road Elementary, Chesapeake, VA

Just Picture It!

To **review science vocabulary,** I write key terms on index cards and divide the class into two teams. In turn, each team chooses an artist who takes a card and draws a picture on the board to represent the word. If the artist's team members guess correctly, the team earns a point. If they don't, the other team gets a chance to guess and steal the point. Each team picks a new artist after every round. Once all the terms have been drawn, the team with more points wins.

Rebecca Juneau, Highland Elementary, Lake Stevens, WA

Birthday Bags

Intermediate students still like to celebrate their **birthdays,** but they don't want cute little trinkets. So I make inexpensive treat bags. I fill each bag with a homework pass, a mechanical pencil, and one or two other small items that I've found at discount stores. Then, on the morning of a student's birthday, I set a treat bag on her desk so it's there at the start of her special day.

Christy Matthes, Stingel Intermediate, Mansfield, OH

Word List With a Twist

Looking for a **vocabulary skill builder** you can use anytime? I challenge my students to list all the words they can think of that fit a certain category. For example, I might have students list words that begin and end with the same letter. Then, after one minute, I have students share words from their lists, and I add a point toward a class reward for every word that meets the criteria. To keep my students on their toes, I change the category every time we play.

Isobel Livingstone, Rahway, NJ

WORD LIST CATEGORIES

- words that have two *a*'s
- words that have double consonants
- words that contain the letter *x*
- words that are synonyms for common words such as *good, big, small, say,* or *go*
- words we use that came from other languages

Place Value Deposits

To teach my students how to keep their **decimal points** lined up, I have them add and subtract on deposit slips. I created a simple bank deposit slip. Then I made copies, which I give students when I introduce decimals. Not only do these forms help my students master adding and subtracting with decimals, but they also introduce them to the world of banking!

Melissa Tilton, Lakes Region Christian School, Laconia, NH

CHECKING/SAVINGS DEPOSIT

Maria
Name

Date October 18, 2010

		50.	36
	+	95.	55
Subtotal		144	91
Less cash received	–	96.	73
Total		48.	18

A Time Zone Wall

To teach my students about **time zones**, I bought four inexpensive clocks: three that were the same and one that was different. I set the different clock to show our time (eastern standard time) and set the other clocks to show central, mountain, and Pacific standard times. Then I labeled the clocks and hung them in order above a U.S. time zone map.

Lynn Powell, McArthur Elementary, Pensacola, FL

Eastern Standard Time

Essay Countdown

I teach my students this little ditty about the important **components of a good essay.** Then, when they are writing, they can hum it to themselves and remember what to include!

Linda Weaver, Roosevelt Elementary, Worcester, MA

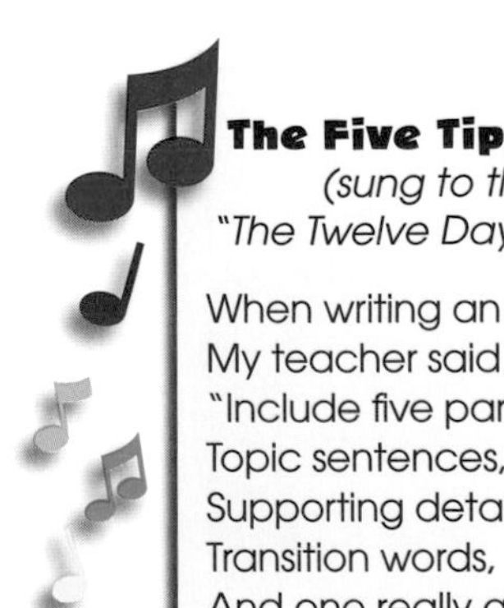

The Five Tips of Writing
(sung to the tune of "The Twelve Days of Christmas")

When writing an essay,
My teacher said to me,
"Include five paragraphs,
Topic sentences,
Supporting details,
Transition words,
And one really great beginning."

Perimeter Hunt

For a fun **measurement challenge,** I have students use perimeter clues to find objects in the classroom. First, I measure the tops or sides of ten square or rectangular classroom items. Next, I list the measurements on the board. Then I give each small group a measuring tape and a recording sheet and send my students on a hunt!

Christina Scannell, San Jose, CA

			Group 2
	Measurements	Perimeter	Object
1.			
2.			

Meet the Mark Brothers

Do your students have trouble using **quotation marks** correctly? Mine did. So I made large construction paper quotation marks. Then I glued wiggle eyes onto each one and introduced my class to the Mark brothers—Quo Mark and Tation Mark. I explained that the brothers always stay together and then showed students how they capture spoken words, certain titles, and ending punctuation. After that, I posted the Mark brothers as a fun reminder.

Emily Dause, South Mountain Elementary, Dillsburg, PA

Dear Marvin,

To address **character education,** I write weekly letters to our classroom advice columnist (a stuffed dog named Marvin). I write about problems I've seen in our classroom or situations outside school that I think students need help addressing. Then I read the letter aloud and ask students to help Marvin respond. I guide each small group of students to discuss the issue, come up with a solution, and write a responding letter, as Marvin. If we don't have time to discuss their responses, I post them along with my original letter for a thought-provoking display.

Karen Slattery, Dunrankin Drive Public School
Mississauga, Ontario, Canada

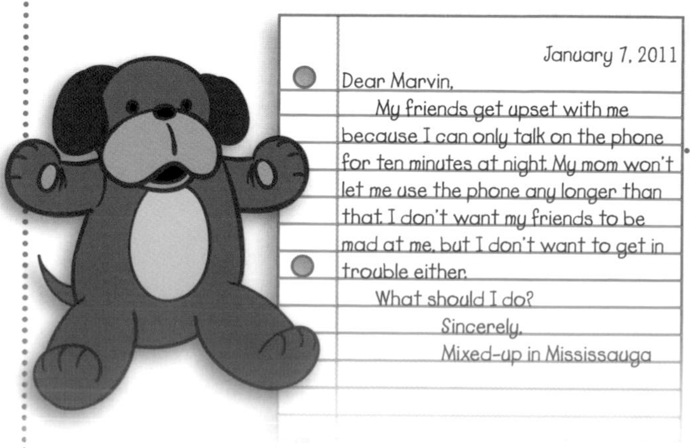

January 7, 2011

Dear Marvin,

My friends get upset with me because I can only talk on the phone for ten minutes at night. My mom won't let me use the phone any longer than that. I don't want my friends to be mad at me, but I don't want to get in trouble either.

What should I do?

Sincerely,
Mixed-up in Mississauga

Around and Around

I give each student a free or discarded CD to explore **circle attributes.** I have the student trace the CD's circumference with his finger to get the idea that this term describes the distance around a circle. Then I have him wrap rubber bands around the CD to find the center and explore chords, diameter, and even fractional parts.

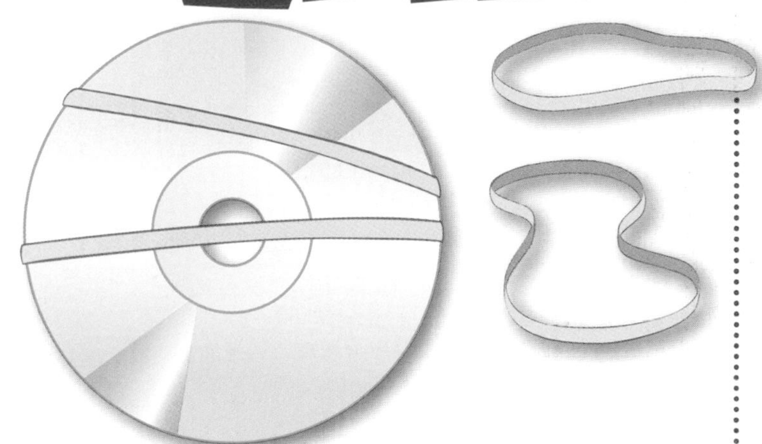

Theresa Cress, Bellingrath Hills Elementary
Greenwell Springs, LA

Very Van Gogh

To encourage my students to **use colorful words** when they write, I display a print of Vincent van Gogh's "The Starry Night." We talk about the painting and its vivid images. Next, I tell students that their writing can be just as vivid. I write Van Gogh's name vertically and turn it into a fun acrostic reminder that I post next to the painting.

Colleen Dabney, Williamsburg, VA

Vary your vocabulary.

Always choose strong verbs—show action!

Nouns, are they specific?

Go for sensory words!

Overused words should be eliminated.

Grab a thesaurus if you need one.

Have fun writing!

Under Construction

To help my students understand that pressure can form **metamorphic rock,** I use bread! I give each student a plastic bag with a half slice of wheat bread and a half slice of white bread to represent the sedimentary, or parent, rock. Then I have the child press down on the bread to change its form.

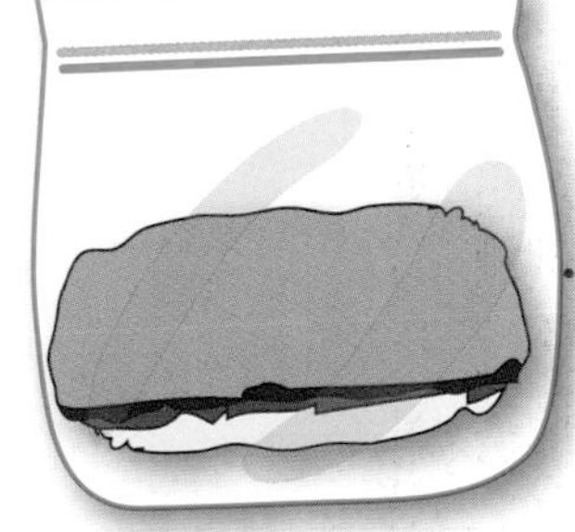

Karen Slattery
Dunrankin Drive Public School
Mississauga, Ontario, Canada

Editor's Tip:

- To model heat metamorphosis, place a slice of bread (parent rock) for every five students on a heated griddle and toast the bread. Then have each small group of students compare a cooled slice of toast (metamorphic rock) with a slice of bread (parent rock).
- To model heat and pressure metamorphosis, place a slice of bread (parent rock) for every five students on a heated griddle and then put a baking sheet and a heavy heat-proof object on top. Flip the bread and repeat. Then have each small group compare a cooled slice of toast with the other models.

Patriotic Reminder

To keep my students from confusing **the U.S. Constitution and the Declaration of Independence,** I created this action-rhyme reminder. I post the poem and guide students to perform actions to engage them mentally, verbally, and physically as we read the poem aloud.

Barbara Majoy, Meadowlawn Intermediate, Sandusky, OH

The declaration freed us	*Act out signing a name.*
From England and its king.	*Point east.*
The Constitution was the plan	*Put hands together to form a book.*
To let our freedom ring.	*Extend arms to represent being free.*

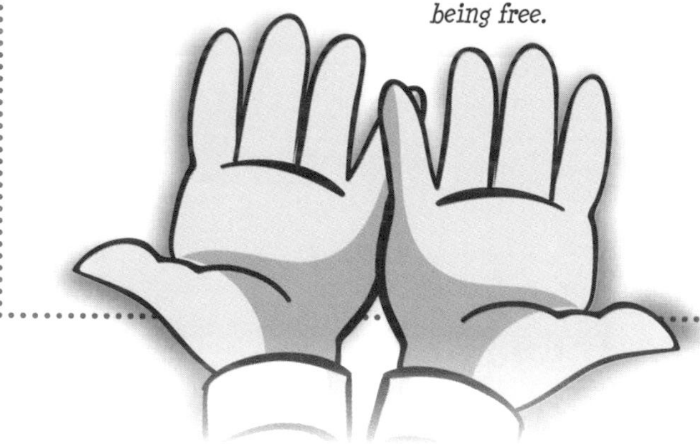

Bloomin' Math

Three-digit by two-digit multiplication can be quite challenging, so I have my students think of tulips! I write a sample problem, leaving extra space between the factors, and complete the first step (multiplying the digits in the top factor by the ones digit). Next, I draw a tulip above the second factor so the leaves and flower point from the digit in the tens place to each digit in the top factor. Then I complete the problem. While a student is learning the process, I have him leave extra space in each problem and draw the tulip reminder.

Jo Young, Margaretta Carey Elementary, Waverly, IA

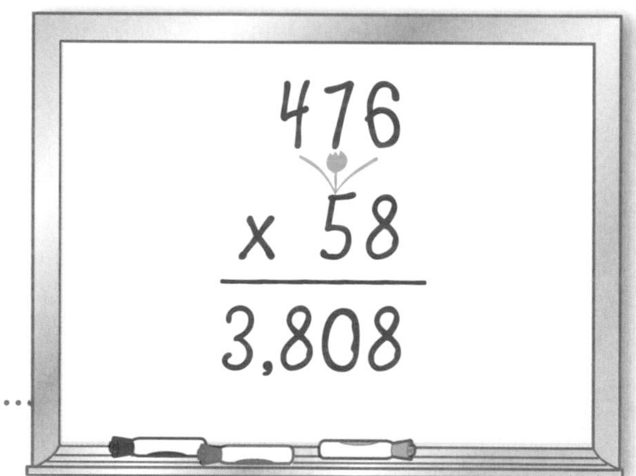

Spelling Parts

As part of their weekly **spelling practice,** I have my students turn their spelling words into fractions. For each word, a student writes a fraction in simplest form to describe the part of the word that is vowels. Then she writes a fraction to describe the part of the word that is consonants.

Leigh Newsom, Cedar Road Elementary, Chesapeake, VA

brightness

vowels: $\frac{1}{5}$ of brightness
consonants: $\frac{4}{5}$ of brightness

Reuse—Recycle

I bring used dryer sheets to school and reuse them as handy and disposable whiteboard erasers!

April LeFevers,
Horace Maynard Middle, Maynardville, TN

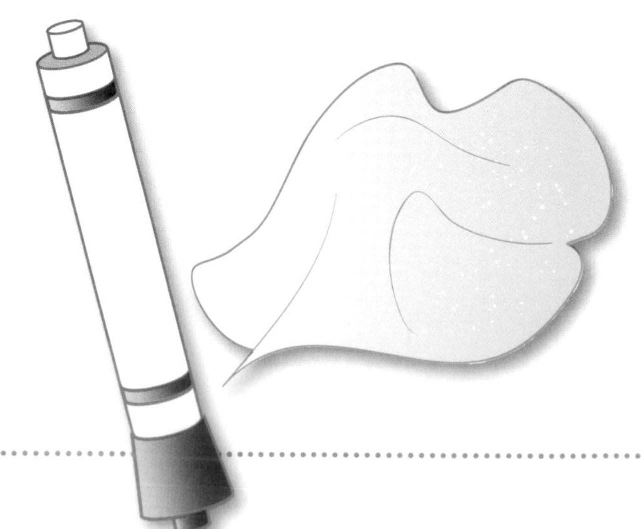

Wacky Writing Helpers

I make **editing** more fun with Eye-Popping Pete pencils. For each one, I wrap the middle of a pipe cleaner around the end of a colored pencil. Then I make a small coil at each pipe cleaner end and glue a wiggle eye on each coil. I keep several of the pencils at our writing center. When it's time for a student to edit her writing, she uses an Eye-Popping Pete pencil to help find and then correct mistakes.

Tina Alvear, Winston-Salem, NC

Answer Indicators

Fun is the name of the game with these simple **game buzzers**! Before my students play a class game, I set out an empty stapler for each team. To answer a question or take a turn, a contestant just taps the end of his team's stapler. Click!

Annmarie Cullen, Boston, MA

Holes in One

My students love this spin on **multiple-choice practice**! I make a narrow answer strip that has a column for each choice of a multiple-choice practice page. Then I put copies of the page and answer strip at a center along with several hole punchers. A student determines each item's answer and then punches a hole in the strip's matching space. This makes it fun for the kids and easy for me to grade!

Joyce Hovanec
South Allegheny Elementary
Port Vue, PA

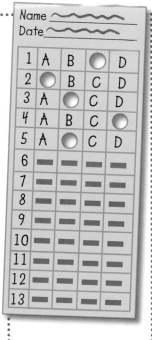

Soup's On!

Nothing beats having a **ready-to-eat meal** when I get home during this hectic time of year! I start this simple dish before school and, by the time I get home, it's ready to serve.

Robin Kralemann, Clippard Elementary, Cape Girardeau, MO

No-Peek Stew

Ingredients:

one 10.75-ounce can golden mushroom soup
one 10.75-ounce can French onion soup
¼ – ½ soup can of water, beef broth, or chicken broth
1 pound stew meat

Directions:

Place the ingredients in a slow cooker. Cook on low all day. Serve over egg noodles or rice.

Firsthand Accounts

To make my fifth graders' **transition to middle school** a bit easier, I set up a peer panel. I invite students from the past two years as speakers on the panel. Then I have my current students write their questions about middle school on index cards and put their cards in a basket. On the day of the panel, my former students sit at the front of the room and take turns drawing questions and answering them. Not only do my current students get firsthand information, but they also head to middle school with a few more familiar faces to find!

Rebecca Juneau, Highland Elementary, Lake Stevens, WA

Ideas in One Place

Even before the school year winds down, I start **planning for next year**. As I think of supplies next year's students will need, I list them on the May page of my desk calendar. Then, when it's time to prepare the coming year's supply list, I already have a head start. I also jot notes on my June page about ideas I'd like to try next year. When the school year is over, I rip off the June page and take it home with me to think about ideas over the summer.

Missy Goldenberg
Leawood, KS

May 2011

S	M	T	W	T	F	S
1	2	3	4	5	6	7
8	9	10	11	12	13	14
15	16	17	18	19	20	21
22	23	24	25	26	27	28
29	30	31	Supplies			

Working Hand in Hand

This action rhyme helps my students remember the **branches of government**.

Barbara Majoy, Meadowlawn Intermediate, Sandusky, OH

The legislators write our laws.	*Pretend to write on hand.*
The executive is the boss.	*Salute with right hand.*
The judges will preside	*Hold index finger in air.*
In cases won or lost.	*Form a* W *and then an* L *with one hand.*

Book a Trip

I've found that a field trip to our local library encourages my students to keep **reading all summer long**. Prior to the trip, I have students fill out library card applications and I submit them. When we arrive at the library, the students take a tour, learn about the summer reading program, and get their library cards. By the time we leave, students have books they're eager to read and they're more comfortable with visiting the library!

Sarah Watson, Clio, MI

Secondhand Storage

I reuse disposable wipe containers as **handy storage** for keeping extra supplies organized! I use them to store markers, sharpened pencils, sticky note pads, and erasers. I just tape a note to the front of each container so I don't forget what's inside. Then I keep the containers neatly stacked in my small classroom.

Valarie Dillard
Friendship Elementary
Winston-Salem, NC

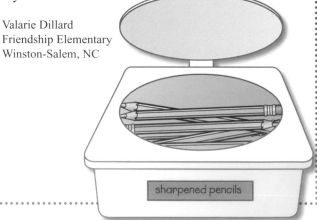

sharpened pencils

Our Readers Write

Online Preview

The end of the year may seem like a good time to clear out your **classroom website,** but wait a bit longer—its content can help your incoming students too! I leave my classroom website as is until school starts in the fall. That way, students who are headed to my grade can visit the site over the summer and get a better idea of what learning projects might be ahead for them!

Jennifer Waggoner, Murphy Ranch Elementary, Whittier, CA

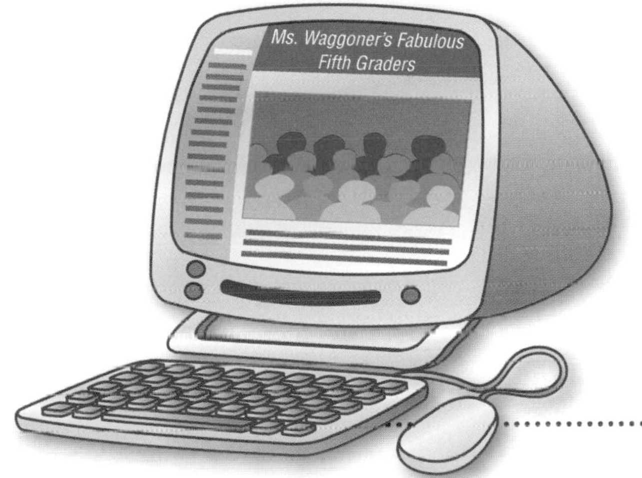

Tagged With Standards

Printer labels not only make my ready-to-use centers and games easy to file, but they alert visitors to my room of the standards my students are working on. As I plan, I simply key in the standard, print out the label, and attach it to the activity. When I'm ready to put the activity away, I know just where to file it!

Deborah Hoyle, Village Meadows Elementary, Phoenix, AZ

Locating decimals, fractions, and mixed numbers on a number line
HANGING AROUND
0
0.1
0.8
1
2
2.5
3
Directions:
1. Shuffle the cards and then draw one.
2. Read the fraction, mixed number, or decimal. Decide whether the card belongs on one of the laundry lines. If it does, place the card on the line. If it doesn't, set it next to the mat. (Not all the cards belong on a laundry line.)
3. As you sort the cards, put them in order. Use the key to check your work.
4. Record the fractions, mixed numbers, and decimals in order, including the unused cards. Use the key to check your work.
Express fractions as fair sharing, parts of a whole, parts of a set, and locations on a real number line.

Over and Over

Instead of drawing a **commonly used table or chart** on my whiteboard again and again, I've found this trick to be a real timesaver! I draw the chart on a section of my board using an overhead pen. Then I complete the chart using a dry-erase marker. When I need to update the chart, I erase the words with a whiteboard eraser, leaving the chart behind. When I'm ready to replace the chart, I wipe it away with a damp paper towel!

Julie Peterson, Olive C. Martin Elementary, Lake Villa, IL

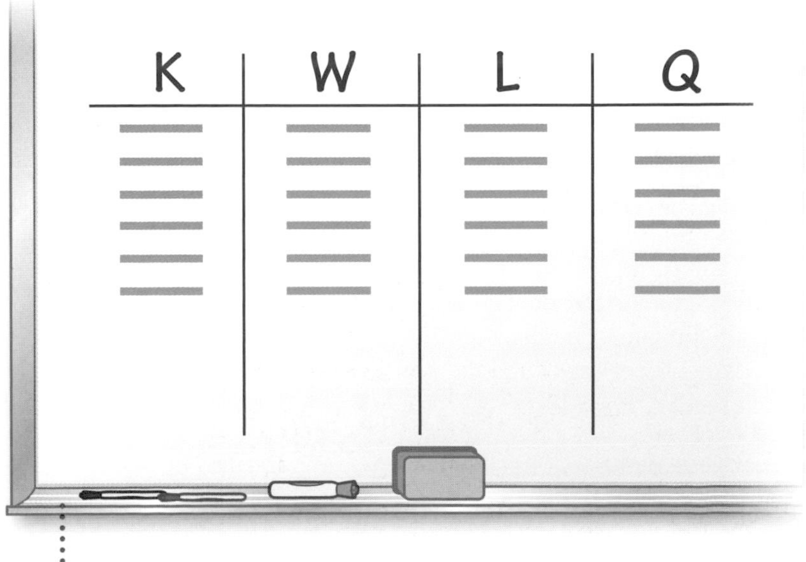

Show of Support

I love to energize my coworkers with fun **year-end pick-me-ups**. Before school, I slip anonymous thank-you cards in the mailboxes of fellow teachers, including a piece of candy with each note. On another day, I leave a daisy in each staff member's mailbox. These pick-me-ups just take a few minutes to deliver, but they certainly help us tackle the end of the year with smiles!

Shawna Whartenby, South Pasadena, CA

Measurement Jingle

Sing a few rounds of this song and students are sure to remember how to solve for **area.**

(sung to the tune of "The Mulberry Bush")

Area equals length times width,
Length times width, length times width.
Area equals length times width.
It's labeled in square units.

Teresa Vilfer-Snyder, Fredericktown Intermediate, Fredericktown, OH

Different Kind of Word Wall

I turn a small display space into a fun **vocabulary-building** activity. First, I arrange colored construction paper squares in a 5 x 5 grid. Next, I randomly place black die-cut letters on each paper square. After I do a quick check to make sure the letters make student-friendly words, I have students use free time to make as many words as they can from adjacent letters. Each child writes his list on an index card and then posts the card along the perimeter of the board as part of a border. When the border is complete, I change the letters on the grid and we start over!

Kara Montgomery, Central Elementary, Plainfield, IN

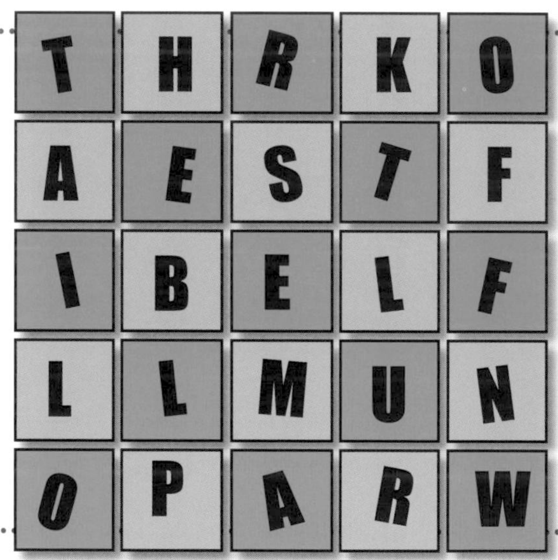

Clearly Fun

This simple idea is all about **saving copies!** When a child wants to complete a puzzle page in a student magazine, I have her clip a transparent sheet on top of the page and use an overhead pen to solve the puzzle. After the student completes and checks the puzzle, she wipes the transparency clean with a damp paper towel and the puzzle's ready for the next reader.

Tami Jardinella, Mt. Tabor School, Mt. Tabor, NJ

Geometric Exercises

I use kinesthetic warm-ups to get my students moving and give them practice with **transformations.** For rotations, each child keeps one toe in place on the floor and then steps with her other foot to rotate her body around it. For reflections, each student faces a spot on the floor and then steps to the opposite side of the spot as she does an about-face. For translations, each child chooses a spot on the floor and slides past the spot while facing it.

Melissa Barbay, Hull-Daisetta Elementary, Hull, TX

Answer Keys

Page 19

Order may vary.

The plural forms of some nouns are irregular.

goose, geese
mouse, mice
tooth, teeth
woman, women

If the noun ends in a consonant and then *y*, change the *y* to *i* and add *es*.

activity, activities
battery, batteries
century, centuries
company, companies
property, properties
strategy, strategies

If the noun ends in a vowel and then *y*, add *s*.

alley, alleys
birthday, birthdays
highway, highways
holiday, holidays
journey, journeys
valley, valleys

If the noun ends in *sh, ch, x, s,* or *z*, add *es*.

brush, brushes
bus, buses
buzz, buzzes
equinox, equinoxes
fax, faxes
lunch, lunches
recess, recesses
toolbox, toolboxes
wrench, wrenches

Page 26

When: always, before, early, eventually, finally, first, forever, late, never, now, often, sometimes, soon, then, tomorrow, tonight, usually, yesterday

Where: above, anywhere, away, backward, before, down, everywhere, here, inside, near, outside, there, underneath

How: clumsily, fast, gracefully, happily, hard, loudly, perfectly, quickly, quietly, shyly, skillfully, slowly, together, too, well

Page 35

1. green
2. yellow
3. yellow
4. green
5. yellow
6. green
7. green
8. yellow
9. yellow
10. yellow
11. green
12. yellow
13. green
14. yellow

It should go to a "RE-TAIL" STORE!

Bonus Box: Answers may vary.

Page 38

1. players'
2. referee's
3. ball's
4. fans'
5. seats'
6. court's
7. goal's
8. backboard's
9. teams'
10. shoe's
11. clock's
12. coach's
13. trainer's
14. mascots'

Bonus Box: Answers may vary.

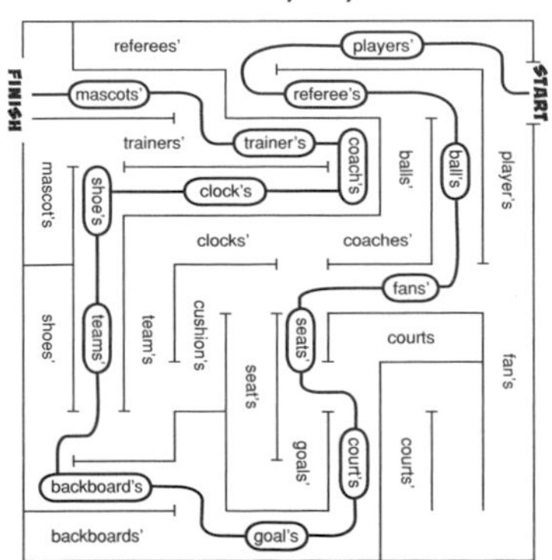

Page 39

1. The cookie jar was empty, so Mom decided to make cookies.
2. Due to an interruption, Mom burned the first batch.
3. She left the next batch of cookies on the table because they were hot.
4. Maddy grabbed a cookie right from the pan; consequently, she burned her fingers.
5. Then a mouse got a snack because Maddy dropped her cookie on the floor.
6. The cat almost caught the mouse since it stopped to nibble the cookie.
7. The mouse scurried past the dog, which caused the dog to jump onto the kitchen table.
8. The cookies flew onto the floor as a result of the dog's jump.
9. Since the cat slid through the cookies, there were crumbs all over the floor.
10. The dog got blamed for the mess because it was eating a cookie when Mom came in.
11. Mom was furious about the mess; therefore, the dog was sent outside.
12. As a result of the disaster, the cookie jar was still empty.
13. Since we didn't get any of the cookies, our stomachs started growling.
14. To solve the problem of the growling stomachs, Mom started mixing a fresh batch of cookies.

The cookie went to the doctor because it felt crummy!

Page 41

1. B
2. C
3. A
4. B
5. C

6–10. Answers may vary.

Bonus: Summaries will vary.

Page 42

Answers for 1–3, 8, and 9 may vary.

4. *aqua:* aquarium, aquifer
   mob, mot, mov: remove, promote
   port: export, portable
   terr: extraterrestrial, territory
   vac: vacuum, evacuate
   vid, vis: invisible, evidence
6. see ⟶ *vid, vis*
   water ⟶ *aqua*
   time ⟶ *chron*
   move ⟶ *mob, mot, mov*
   measure ⟶ *meter*
   star ⟶ *ast*
   empty ⟶ *vac*
   earth ⟶ *geo*
   carry ⟶ *port*
   life ⟶ *bio*
   write ⟶ *graph*
   land ⟶ *terr*
7. Definitions may vary.
   A. aquamarine, greenish blue
   B. asteroid, small rocky bodies found in space
   C. biology, the study of living things
   D. chronicle, events arranged in order by time
   E. geology, the study of the history of Earth
   F. graphite, carbon used in lead pencils
   G. kilometer, a metric unit of length equal to 1,000 meters
   H. mobilize, to put into movement
   I. transport, to carry from one place to another
   J. terrain, a piece of land
   K. vacation, a time spent away from home
   L. videophone, a phone with which users can see each other

Page 45

1. come
2. fills
3. like
4. say
5. are
6. go
7. begins
8. is
9. are
10. seem
11. are
12. enters
13. is
14. are
15. watch
16. race
17. paddle
18. hit
19. compete
20. are
21. earn
22. gets
23. wins
24. raise

Page 46

December 7, 2010

1234 Mystery Lane
Somewhere, NY 56789

Dear Ms. Watson,

I hear that you've enrolled in my old supersecret spy academy. Wat wonderful news! I woud like to offer my support and best wishes. If you happin to meet Samantha Spade, please give her my best. We took beginning code-breaking together. Ms. Spade used to be a supersecret agent but now she might soon be one of youre teachers. She teaches advanced code-breaking at your scool.

I still remember my first day at the academy. I took a nine-hour buse ride to get there. It was a long trip from my hoem. During the first day, the chief of polic came to welcome us. Woulde you believe I was one of only 20 students? There must be hundreds of students there now.

Have you learned how to makke invisible ink yet? I think that was my favorite lesson. Old Professor Hardy had each of us brind a lemon to class. Then we used the lemon juice to write secret messages. After we heated the lemon juice, we could read each other's messages and then write badk. This reminds me; there's a secret message in this letter. I wish you good luck finding the message and even better luck at the supersecret spy academy.

Sincerely,

Herlock Sholmes

What would happen if you took your school bus home? The police would make you bring it back.

Bonus: Letters will vary.

Page 47

1. go
2. buy
3. tear
4. bring
5. hear
6. take
7. write
8. think
9. grow
10. catch
11. begin
12. break
13. choose
14. draw
15. drive
16. freeze
17. slide
18. sting
19. swim
20. teach
21. tell
22. burst
23. cling
24. drink
25. wear
26. beat
27. forgive
28. hide
29. keep
30. bite

It never got sick because it was full OF "ANT-IBODIES!"

Bonus: torn, taken , begun, broken, drawn, frozen, swum, worn, forgiven, bitten

Page 48

Answers for 1–6, 8, and 9 will vary.

7. draft, fast, judge, mind, patch, quarter, shake, ship, skirt, tape

Page 49

Prepositional Phrase	Preposition	Object of the Preposition
1. for three hours	for	hours
2. to the building	to	building
3. for the crane	for	crane
4. After all this hard work	After	work
5. until midnight	until	midnight
6. on time	on	time
7. behind schedule	behind	schedule
8. before lunch	before	lunch
9. By the way	By	way
10. inside the crane's cab	inside	cab
11. underneath the seat	underneath	seat
12. beside your lunchbox	beside	lunchbox
13. for our lunch break	for	break
14. Since breakfast	Since	breakfast
15. at ten o'clock break	at	break
16. over that delivery van	over	van
17. With your careful guidance	With	guidance
18. in the far corner	in	corner
19. onto the crane	onto	crane
20. to the roof	to	roof
21. on the ground	on	ground
22. for us	for	us
23. After lunch	After	lunch
24. on our next job	on	job

Page 50

1. earlier	6. longer	11. younger	16. more
2. latest	7. less	12. most	17. best
3. faster	8. worst	13. better	18. better
4. biggest	9. more quietly	14. faster	19. luckier
5. fresher	10. noisiest	15. least	20. more seriously

<u>NOTHING—A FISH CAN'T TALK!</u>

Bonus: Answers will vary.

Page 51

Answers for 5 and 6 will vary.

1. Voice One is a grandchild. Voice Two is a grandfather.
2. "Grandpa's girl" is the grandfather's old car.
3. In the poem, the grandfather is giving his old car to his grandchild.
4. a teenager buying his or her first car

Bonus:

"Precious Girl"
for two voices
Grandfather is excited.
Grandchild isn't very excited.
The car is a gift.

(both)
teenagers
first cars
used cars

"Finally!"
one voice
Teenager is excited.
worked hard and saved money
buying own car

Page 53

1. compound
2. complex, because they can make loud noises slapping their chests
3. compound
4. complex, Although zebras mainly eat grass
5. complex, before you plan a safari
6. compound
7. complex, If you want to go to a jungle
8. compound
9. compound
10. complex, When it stands up
11. complex, Before you sleep in a jungle
12. compound
13. complex, Because elephants have no sweat glands
14. compound
15. complex, although it spends most of its time in the water
16. compound
17. compound
18. complex, Because cheetahs run so fast
19. compound
20. complex, Since cheetah populations have rapidly declined
21. complex, Even though they are fascinating
22. compound
23. compound
24. complex, If you are afraid of snakes

Page 56

Answers will vary. Possible answers include the following:

1. has a skeleton made of cartilage
2. is 22 feet wide
3. can jump out of the water
4. is a filter feeder
5. it filters plankton from the water through its huge, open mouth
6. a bird flying through the water
7. has a mouth at the front of its head
8. is tiny plankton
9. Answers will vary.
10. to inform

Bonus: Answers will vary.

Page 57

1. is all ears
2. out of the blue
3. butterflies in his stomach
4. takes him under her wing
5. shows him the ropes
6. bites the bullet
7. walking on air
8. icing on the cake
9. like wildfire
10. hit the road
11. a walk in the park
12. the sky's the limit

Bonus: Answers will vary.

Page 58

Answers will vary.

1. canned soup
2. jelly
3. toothpaste
4. laundry detergent
5. window cleaner
6. frozen pizza
7. pancake batter
8. cereal
9. shampoo
10. ketchup
11. milk
12. popcorn
13. orange juice
14. eggs
15. adhesive bandages
16. cheese crackers

Bonus: Answers will vary.

Page 59

Responses will vary. Possible four-letter words include the following: *arts, bail, bait, bare, bear, bite, boat, cars, eats, item, lair, lame, late, mail, male, mare, mate, meal, meat, melt, mole, orbs, rail, rate, real, robe, role, rose, rows, sail, sale, salt, same, save, silo, site, soil, sole, some, swim, tail, tale, tame, tare, tear, tile, toil, vats, veal, veto, vets, vibe, vole, vote, wail, wait, warm, wave, wise, wilt,* and *wore.*

Page 60

nouns: contestant, day, dollars, encyclopedia, game, game show, laptop, opponent, question, questions, response, responses, prize, surprise, time, Otto Winn, Anita Wynn, years
adjectives: calm, consolation, correct, different, every, final, first, five, jumpy, nervous, new, next, right, ten, this, thousand, two, youngest
pronouns: he, her, his, it, no one, she, this, who
action verbs: answers, buy, buzzes, comes, get, gets, gives, hopes, knows, practicing, reads, says, tied, win, wins, won
linking verbs: are, is, seems
helping verbs: been, does, has, have, will
prepositions: before, for, on, over, to
adverbs: already, correctly, not, right, then, today, very

Page 61

1. A. ten; Writing "nine" in the blank adds another *e*.
   B. four; Writing "three" in the blank adds another *r*.
2. TOOTHPASTE
3. Answers may vary. Possible answers include cello, clarinet, fife, flute, harp, lute, oboe, organ, piano, tuba, viola, and violin.
4. Answers may vary.
5. tommorrow
   definitie
   occassion
   writting
   arithametic
   trackking
   truely
   <u>mistake</u>
6. A. SHIP
   B. TAXI
   C. TRAIN
   D. BIKE
7. Answers may vary. Possible answers include pencil, crayon, folder, marker, binder, and eraser.
8. A. mama
   B. potato
   C. banana

Page 62

1. Answers may vary. Possible answers include *bet, boot, bore, cob, coot, core, cot, oboe, ore, robe, robot, root,* and *toe*.
2. Answers may vary.
   A. deer B. bear C. cat D. hen E. hare
3. Answers may vary.
   A. orchestra conductor B. meteorologist C. carpenter
4. Answers may vary. Possible answers include pears, peaches, papayas, pineapple, plums, pomegranates, popcorn, peanuts, pecans, potato chips, punch, pizza, and pretzels.
5. a. It is easier to make **money** than to **keep** it.
   b. If you don't scale the **mountain,** you can't view the **plain.**
   c. Dig a **well** before you are **thirsty.**
6. Presidents' Day, Memorial Day, Independence Day, Labor Day, Columbus Day, Veterans Day, Thanksgiving Day
7. Answers may vary.
8. motel, melt

Page 63

1. Answers may vary. Possible answers include *aisle, I'll, isle; aye, eye, I; buy, by, bye; cents, sense, scents; cite, sight, site;* and *dew, do, due.*
2.

R	A	D	A	R
A	A		A	A
D		D		D
A	A		A	A
R	A	D	A	R

3. bad luck, real fake, same difference, jumbo shrimp, climb down
4. A. Rudolph
   B. Scrooge
   C. Tiny Tim
   D. Blitzen
5. Answers may vary.
6. Answers may vary. Possible answers include *are, earn, eye, near, ran, renew, wane, warn, wean, wear, were, yawn,* and *yearn*.
7. A. HOCANDLELIDAY
   B. CANEIAY
   C. CANEZAY
   D. CANEZAA
   E. CANZAA
   F. KWANZAA
8. A. head B. over C. wind

Page 64

Answers for 1, 2, 4, 5, and 6 will vary.

1. A. him; The other pronouns are plural.
   B. are; The other verbs are past tense.
   C. came; The other words are modifiers.
2. St. Paul, squirrel; Atlanta, gorilla; Indianapolis, hippopotamus; Frankfort, elephant.
3. A. atlas
   B. board
   C. pebble
   D. vertical
6. MOAT, MEAT, SEAT, SWAT
7. A. see
   B. dead
   C. rain
8. Remove "ALL EXTRA LETTERS," leaving "THIS IS A SILLY SENTENCE."

Page 65

Answers for 3, 5, and 7 will vary.

1. thought
2. A. DOCTORS
   B. PENCILS
   C. AIRFARE
   D. SHAMPOO
4. Tom <u>said</u> the <u>brakes</u> on <u>his</u> <u>truck</u> need to be <u>replaced</u> before he <u>drives</u> it to <u>work</u>. Otherwise, it may be <u>hard</u> for him to <u>stop</u> on <u>time</u>. <u>That's</u> why Tom is <u>going</u> to <u>the</u> <u>repair</u> <u>shop</u>.
6. A. boast, coast
   B. under, wonder
   C. threat, jet
   D. boulder, folder
   E. brief, grief
8. Possible answers include the following: *field, healed, kneeled, peeled, sealed, squealed, wield,* and *yield.*

Page 66

1. environment
2. A HANDFUL OF PATIENCE IS WORTH MORE THAN A BUSHEL OF BRAINS.
3. Answers will vary.
4. Answers will vary.
5. a. liquid
   b. adjective
   c. hiss
   d. eaten
6. Answers will vary. Possible answers include *aches, amuse, ashes, asset, cases, caste, casts, cause, chase, chasm, cheat, chess, haste, masts, mates, meats, mutes, mutts, sauce, scams, seams, shame, shuts, smash, stash, steam, tames, taste, teach, teams,* and *tests.*
7. a. state
   b. street
   c. strange
   d. stripe
   e. stocks
8. March; They are in reverse alphabetical order.

Page 80

1. fragment	2. fragment	3. run-on sentence
4. fragment	5. run-on sentence	6. run-on sentence
7. run-on sentence	8. fragment	9. run-on sentence
10. fragment	11. fragment	12. run-on sentence
13. fragment	14. run-on sentence	15. fragment

Page 115

A. 36 units^3	G. 36 units^3	M. 24 units^3
B. 24 units^3	H. 60 units^3	N. 24 units^3
C. 60 units^3	I. 36 units^3	O. 60 units^3
D. 40 units^3	J. 40 units^3	P. 36 units^3
E. 60 units^3	K. 24 units^3	
F. 40 units^3	L. 40 units^3	

Page 120

A. triangular pyramid
B. pentagon
C. cube
D. cylinder
E. cone net
F. hexagon
G. triangular pyramid net
H. rectangle
I. square pyramid net
J. cube net
K. octagon
L. cone
M. rectangular pyramid
N. trapezoid
O. cylinder net
P. rhombus
Q. rectangular prism net
R. square pyramid
S. triangular prism
T. sphere
U. triangular prism net
V. rectangular pyramid net
W. rectangular prism
X. parallelogram

Page 121

8 ounces = 1 cup, $\frac{1}{2}$ pint, $\frac{1}{4}$ quart, $\frac{1}{16}$ gallon
9 ounces = $1\frac{1}{8}$ cup, $\frac{9}{16}$ pint, $\frac{9}{32}$ quart, $\frac{9}{128}$ gallon
12 ounces = $1\frac{1}{2}$ cups, $\frac{3}{4}$ pint, $\frac{3}{8}$ quart, $\frac{3}{32}$ gallon
16 ounces = 2 cups, 1 pint, $\frac{1}{2}$ quart, $\frac{1}{8}$ gallon
32 ounces = 4 cups, 2 pints, 1 quart, $\frac{1}{4}$ gallon
44 ounces = $5\frac{1}{2}$ cups, $2\frac{3}{4}$ pints, $1\frac{3}{8}$ quarts, $\frac{11}{32}$ gallon

Page 122

Answers for 3–5 may vary.

1. plane figures: circle, hexagon, parallelogram, pentagon, rhombus, square, trapezoid, triangle; solid figures: cone, cube, cylinder, prism, pyramid, sphere
2. yes
6. Answers may vary. Possible answers include triangle IFJ, rectangle EGHF, parallelogram EGLI, hexagon BCGLJE, trapezoid BCGE, octagon BCGHLJFE, and pentagon EBCLJ.
7. no
8. Figure A is a cube. It has eight vertices, six faces, and equal sides. Figure B is a rhombus. It has two pairs of parallel sides, four vertices, and no right angles. Figure C is a hexagon. It has six vertices, three pairs of parallel sides, and no right angles. Figure D is a cone. It has a circular base, one vertex, and is three-dimensional.
9. no

Page 124

I.
1. <
2. >
3. >
4. <
5. >
6. =
7. >
8. =
9. >
10. <
11. <
12. <
13. >
14. =
15. >
16. <

II. 735; 1,230; 2,989; 2,998; 5,926; 7,146; 7,429; 9,905; 9,950; 22,605; 22,650; 37,005; 37,050; 49,202; 49,212; 82,466; 82,640; 126,400; 126,404; 307,806; 345,812; 370,608; 421,210; 600,148; 1,978,243; 1,987,234; 6,000,148; 6,643,932; 6,957,349

Page 125

1. 400
2. 2,000
3. 3,600
4. 6,000
5. 10,000
6. 24,000
7. 2,000
8. 6,000
9. 49,000
10. 60,000
11. 80,000
12. 180,000
13. 320,000
14. 120,000
15. 560,000
16. 160,000
17. 360,000
18. 150,000
19. 60,000
20. 720,000

Bonus Box:
1. 385
2. 2,328
3. 3,096
4. 5,149
5. 8,510
6. 22,253
7. 2,250
8. 6,136
9. 51,134
10. 53,300
11. 71,064
12. 177,940
13. 346,185
14. 125,257
15. 527,068
16. 169,560
17. 380,142
18. 158,184
19. 87,216
20. 652,210

Page 126

1. 7 (yellow)
2. 11 (blue)
3. 4 (green)
4. 2 (blue)
5. 28 (yellow)
6. 7 (green)
7. 8 (blue)
8. 7 (green)
9. 18 (yellow)
10. 9 (green)
11. 2 (blue)
12. 8 (yellow)
13. 1,206 (yellow)
14. 12 (green)
15. 10 (green)
16. 4 (blue)
17. 76 (yellow)
18. 100 (green)

Page 127

Answers for 1, 4, 6, 7, and 9 may vary.
2. Answers should be from 18 to 28.
3. Problem A requires regrouping and problem B does not.
5. 78 x 87 = 6,786; 96 x 69 = 6,624; 84 x 48 = 4,032; 62 x 26 = 1,612; 39 x 93 = 3,627; 56 x 65 = 3,640
8. A. 8
   B. 6
   C. 4

Page 128

1. A.

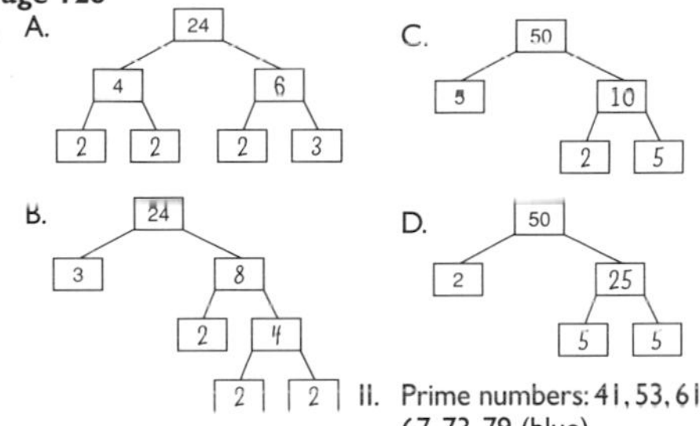

11. Prime numbers: 41, 53, 61, 67, 73, 79 (blue)
    Composite numbers: 27, 34, 39, 49, 58, 64, 70, 78, 81, 82, 87, 92 (orange)

Bonus Box: Answers may vary.

Page 129

A. 108 ft., 288 ft.^{2}
E. 96 ft., 252 ft.^{2}
H. 6' x 12', 36 ft., 72 ft.^{2}
N. 18' x 18', 72 ft., 324 ft.^{2}
B. 10' x 12', 44 ft., 120 ft.^{2}
L. 40 ft., 96 ft.^{2}
D. 60 ft., 144 ft.^{2}
I. 48 ft., 108 ft.^{2}
Y. 36' x 6', 84 ft., 216 ft.^{2}
R. 24' x 18', 84 ft., 432 ft.^{2}
G. 60 ft., 216 ft.^{2}
S. 6' x 6', 24 ft., 36 ft.^{2}

REALLY BIG HANDS!

Bonus Box: P = 192 ft.; A = 2,304 ft.^{2}

Page 130

1. day 2
2. zebra
3. lion
4. giraffe
5. lion
6. day 1
7. 19
8. 47
9. 39
10. 38.5

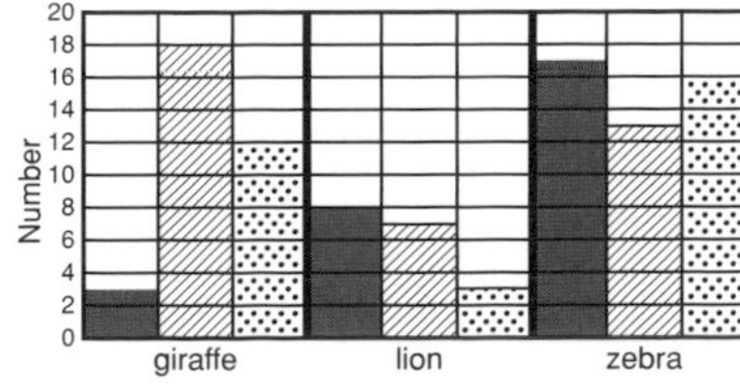

Number of Animal Pictures

2	8
3	0, 1, 5, 6, 8, 8, 9
4	2, 3, 5, 7, 7, 7

Page 134

Answers for 2, 3, and 8 may vary.
1. 91 ÷ 6 = 15 R1 or 97 ÷ 6 = 16 R1; 85 ÷ 7 = 12 R1; 425 ÷ 8 = 53 R1; 613 ÷ 9 = 68 R1
4. 329 ÷ 5 = 65 R4; 326 ÷ 5 = 65 R1; 327 ÷ 5 = 65 R2; 328 ÷ 5 = 65 R3
5. A. no, 244
   B. yes, 81 R2
   C. no, 357
   D. yes, 80 R2
6. 97 ÷ 8 = 12 R1; 63 ÷ 7 = 9; 408 ÷ 9 = 45 R3
7. A. 97 cows
   B. 38 cows
   C. 74 cows
   D. 216 cows
9. 123 ÷ 14 = 8 R11
   123 ÷ 25 = 4 R23
   123 ÷ 36 = 3 R15
   456 ÷ 14 = 32 R8
   456 ÷ 25 = 18 R6
   456 ÷ 36 = 12 R24

Page 135

1. 156 ounces
2. 44 goals
3. 96 jerseys
4. 352 miles
5. 551 tickets
6. 2,025 minutes
7. 111 autographs
8. 115 stitches
9. 432 bandages
10. 1,518 bandages
11. 270 minutes
12. 3,325 minutes

The Woodchucks score the most goals.

Bonus: Beavers, 24 x 4 = 96 goals; Woodchucks, 24 x 6 = 144 goals; 144 – 96 = 48 goals; The Woodchucks score 48 more goals than the Beavers.

Page 136

Answers may vary.
A. 16,000 (yellow)
B. 400 (blue)
C. 10,000 (yellow)
D. 900 (blue)
E. 4,100 (yellow)
F. 700 (blue)
G. 20 (blue)
H. 4,000 (yellow)
I. 660 (blue)
J. 6,300 (yellow)
K. 100 (blue)
L. 63,000 (yellow)
M. 150,000 (yellow)
N. 500 (blue)
O. 145,000 (yellow)
P. 20 (blue)
Q. 190,000 (yellow)
R. 400 (blue)
S. 250 (blue)
T. 5,600 (yellow)
U. 200 (blue)
V. 1,700 (yellow)
W. 100 (blue)
X. 2,500 (yellow)

Bonus: Answers may vary.

Page 137

A. 12
B. 21
C. 6
D. 20
E. 12
F. 20
G. 30
H. 15
I. 20
J. 12
K. 6
L. 10
M. 4
N. 24
O. 14
P. 9
Q. 35
R. 24
S. 36
T. 18

Bryce's smoothie is Blueberry Blitz.

Bonus: D

Page 138

Player 1		Player 2	
1.	T	1.	F
2.	T	2.	T
3.	F	3.	T
4.	F	4.	F
5.	T	5.	F
6.	T	6.	F
7.	F	7.	T
8.	T	8.	F
9.	T	9.	T
10.	F	10.	T
11.	F	11.	F
12.	T	12.	T

Page 139

Answers for 1–3, 5, and 6 will vary.
4. A. mean = 7, median = 8
   B. mean = 12, median = 11
   C. mean = 19, median = 21
7. 95
8. mode
9. A. mean = 6
   B. mean = 21, range = 13

Page 140

1. 46 R47
2. 226 R1
3. 271
4. 316
5. 442
6. 46 R21
7. 198 R13
8. 527
9. 583
10. 145 R9
11. 91 R3
12. 82 R33
13. 61 R33
14. 66 R55

remainder < 20: 2, 7, 10, 11
remainder > 20: 1, 6, 12, 13, 14
no remainder: 3, 4, 5, 8, 9

Bonus: no; The answer should be 59 R39.

Page 141

1. 43 minutes
2. 50 minutes
3. 20 minutes
4. 53 minutes
5. 1 hour, 29 minutes
6. 1 hour, 5 minutes
7. 2 hours, 35 minutes
8. 30 minutes
9. 19 minutes
10. 1 hour, 10 minutes

1. 12:15 PM
2. 11:45 AM
3. 12:35 PM
4. no

Bonus: yes; Explanations will vary.

Page 142

1. 12.34 (brown)
2. 17.27 (green)
3. 17.559 (purple)
4. 14.54 (blue)
5. 21.245 (orange)
6. 16.606 (yellow)
7. 14.27 (pink)
8. 12.34 (brown)
9. 21.245 (orange)
10. 9.655 (red)
11. 14.54 (blue)
12. 9.655 (red)
13. 16.606 (yellow)
14. 17.27 (green)
15. 17.559 (purple)
16. 14.27 (pink)

Bonus: Answers will vary.

Page 145

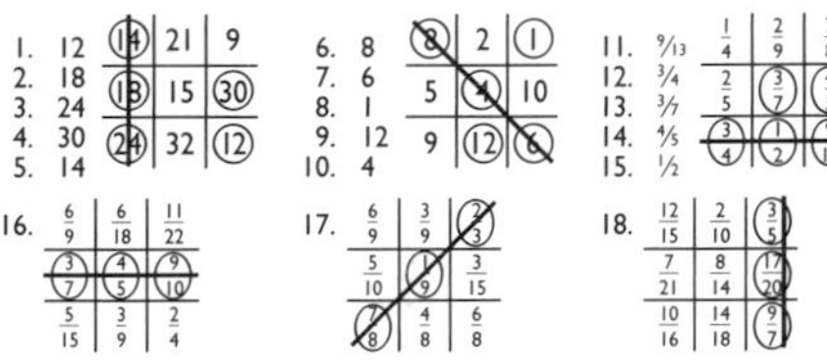

Bonus: $\frac{10}{32}$

Page 146

1. 9:30 PM
2. 125 tickets
3. 12:15 PM and 5:00 PM
4. between 10:00 AM and 12:15 PM
5. $1,350.00
6. Answers will vary.
7. popcorn and candy
8. soft pretzel
9. snacks that are not sweet
10. 15
11. 65
12. popcorn: $\frac{35}{100}$, or $\frac{7}{20}$; candy: $\frac{30}{100}$, or $\frac{3}{10}$ nachos; $\frac{15}{100}$, or $\frac{3}{20}$

Bonus: Answers will vary.

Page 147

Answers for 1, 3–5, and 7 will vary.
2.

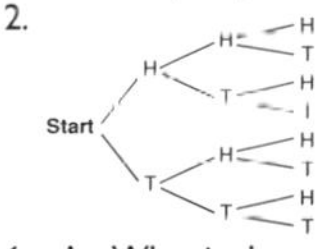

6. A. What is the probability of drawing a blue marble?
   B. What is the probability of drawing a green marble?
   C. What is the probability of drawing a yellow marble?
   D. What is the probability of drawing a red marble?
8.

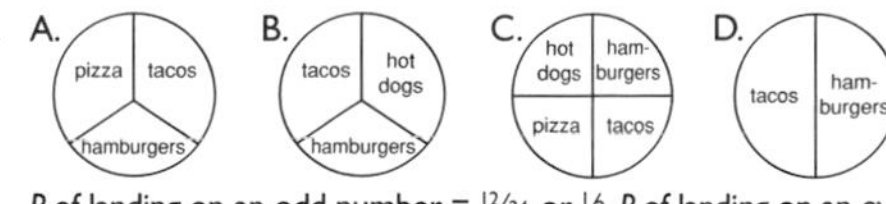

9. P of landing on an odd number = $\frac{12}{24}$, or $\frac{1}{2}$, P of landing on an even number = $\frac{12}{24}$, or $\frac{1}{2}$; P of landing on a prime number = $\frac{9}{24}$, or $\frac{3}{8}$

Page 151

1. $\frac{4}{15}$ (green)
2. $\frac{22}{39}$ (yellow)
3. $\frac{7}{50}$ (orange)
4. $\frac{4}{5}$ (blue)
5. $\frac{4}{7}$ (yellow)
6. $\frac{7}{12}$ (yellow)
7. $\frac{1}{3}$ (green)
8. $\frac{5}{33}$ (orange)
9. $\frac{55}{84}$ (yellow)
10. $\frac{1}{6}$ (orange)
11. 1 (blue)
12. $\frac{1}{4}$ (green)
13. $\frac{7}{16}$ (green)
14. $\frac{1}{25}$ (orange)
15. $\frac{2}{11}$ (orange)

Bonus: The second fraction was flipped before the numerators and denominators were multiplied.

Page 152

Answers for 1, 3, 5, 8, and 9 will vary.
2. Letters with vertical symmetry: A, H, I, M, O, T, U, V, W, X, and Y. Letters with horizontal symmetry: B, C, D, E, H, I, K, O, and X. Letters that are not symmetrical: F, G, J, L, N, P, Q, R, S, and Z.
4. p = 12 inches: l = 4 inches, w = 2 inches
   p = 20 inches: l = 6 inches, w = 4 inches
   p = 6 inches: l = 2 inches, w = 1 inch
6. Statement A is true.
7.

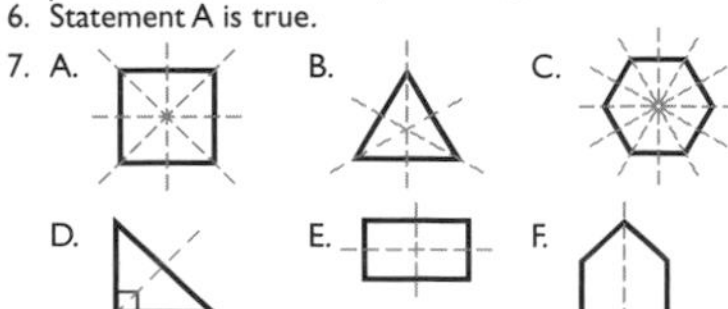

Page 153

$\frac{2}{4} = \frac{1}{2}$ $\frac{10}{25} = \frac{2}{5}$ $\frac{6}{8} = \frac{3}{4}$ $\frac{12}{15} = \frac{4}{5}$ $\frac{3}{18} = \frac{1}{6}$ $\frac{12}{32} = \frac{3}{8}$
$\frac{4}{6} = \frac{2}{3}$ $\frac{3}{27} = \frac{1}{9}$ $\frac{20}{32} = \frac{5}{8}$ $\frac{20}{45} = \frac{4}{9}$ $\frac{22}{24} = \frac{11}{12}$ $\frac{42}{49} = \frac{6}{7}$
$\frac{25}{100} = \frac{1}{4}$ $\frac{10}{12} = \frac{5}{6}$ $\frac{8}{14} = \frac{4}{7}$ $\frac{8}{44} = \frac{2}{11}$ $\frac{21}{24} = \frac{7}{8}$ $\frac{33}{77} = \frac{3}{7}$

SHE WANTED TO HAVE SWEET DREAMS!

Bonus: $\frac{3}{27}$, $\frac{12}{15}$, $\frac{3}{18}$, $\frac{21}{24}$

Page 155

Level A

1. about 10,000 pounds
2. no
3. Macey
4. Todd's kite, 30 yd = 90 feet
5. yes
6. A and B

Level B

1. 3
2. 721.9; 868.1
3. 0.75
4. no
5. **15**, 11, 16, 12, **17**, 13, 18, **14**; subtract 4, add 5
6. Answers may vary.
   rounding, 1,000 + 30 + 200 + 500 + 20 = 1,750; front-end estimating (900 + 30 + 200 + 400 + 10 = 1,540) and adjusting the remaining numbers (90 + 20 + 100 + 20 = 210), 1,540 + 210 = 1,750

Page 156

Level A

1. 30
2. 500,000; 1,499,999
3. Order may vary; 8 + 9 + 20 + 63 = 100, 48 + 52 = 100, 25 + 35 + 40 = 100
4. A
5. 46 inches
6. polygon, closed figure, pentagon

Level B

1. Answers may vary.
2. thirty hundredths, three tenths
3. no
4. C
5. 16
6. more than

Page 157

Level A

1. Wesley
2. $\frac{9}{15}$ reduces to $\frac{3}{5}$
3. the sum
4. No. She has 2,000 mL of glue and needs 3,000 mL.
5. two, H and E
6. B

Level B

1. 12 miles
2. $\frac{3}{15}$
3. Yes. 999 x 99 rounds to 1,000 x 100 = 100,000
4. 50 m
5. Both designs have the same area: 3,600 ft^2
6. B

Page 158

Explanations will vary.

Level A

1. 35,012 < 35,212 < 35,321
2. individual tickets
3. no
4. yes
5. 12
6. B

Level B

1. 42 paper clips
2. 48 packs, no
3. no
4. no
5. $\frac{1}{3}$
6. >

Page 159

Level A

1. B
2. A. $\frac{7}{9}$ B. $\frac{4}{16}$ C. $\frac{5}{45}$
3. yes
4. division
5. 20
6. $x = 5, y = 15$

Level B

1. 25
2. greater than $\frac{1}{2}$
3. 20 percent
4. 32
5. 5
6. Quadrilateral C

Page 160

Level A

1. 684, 426, 297
2. no
3. no
4. circle A
5. 50 mm < 1,500 cm < 500 m < 5 km
6. Multiply by 4 and then subtract 1.

Level B

1. no
2. 240 people
3. $2 \div \frac{1}{2} = x$
4. no
5. 1,500 lb.
6. yes

Page 161

1.
2. Answers may vary. 98,765 + 1,234 = 99,999
3. 12
4. 21 and 24; Nonconsecutive multiples are 18 and 27, 15 and 30, 12 and 33, 9 and 36, 6 and 39, and 3 and 42.
5.

6	2	21	14	8
5	3	13	15	29
7	9	19	11	17
20	10	23	7	25

6. A. 4, 7; Divide by 2 and then add 3.
   B. 36, 30; Multiply by 3 and then subtract 6.
   C. 80, 110; Add 5, then add 10, then add 15, then add 20, and so on.
7. Answers may vary. $\frac{4}{8} + \frac{8}{16}$
8. six; The number words for one through ten are listed alphabetically: eight, five, four, nine, one, seven, six, ten, three, two.

Page 162

1. Answers may vary.
2. Answers may vary.
   six darts: 10, 10, 8, 8, 2, 2
   seven darts: 10, 8, 8, 8, 2, 2, 2
   eight darts: 8, 8, 8, 8, 2, 2, 2, 2
   nine darts: 8, 4, 4, 4, 4, 4, 4, 4, 4
3. C, E
4. Answers may vary. Possible answers include 1,025; 1,133; 1,241; 2,024; 2,132; 2,240; 3,023; 3,131; 4,022; and 4,130.
5. 75 yards of spaghetti, 300 yards of spaghetti
6. 11 squares
7. 300 times
8. 108

Page 163

1. 296,881,947
2. Pick up the glass that is second from the left and pour the water into the fifth glass. Then return the second glass to its original position.
3. C = 6 and D = 3 or C = 8 and D = 4
4. The water costs $0.36. The water to fill four bottles cost $1.44. Four empty bottles cost $6.12. Four bottles of water cost $7.56.
5. There are seven $20 bills, eight $10 bills, six $5 bills, and nine $1 bills. The total value is $259.
6. Answers may vary.
7. A = $\frac{1}{4}$, B = $\frac{1}{8}$, C = $\frac{1}{8}$, D = $\frac{1}{16}$, E = $\frac{1}{32}$
8. A. 6 B. 6

Page 164

1. 49
2. 1, D
   6, B
   27, G
   81, E
   90, C
3. $2\frac{1}{2}$ quarts
4. The first three digits in each number add up to 8. The pattern for the last four digits is x, – 1, + 2, + 1. Phone numbers will vary.
5. five people, ten handshakes; six people, 15 handshakes
6. 105
7. D, A, C, B
8. four: GGBBB, BBBGG, BBGGB, BGGBB

Page 165

1. A, C, and D are true.
2. 360 miles
3. Possible answers include the following:
   A. 12 ÷ (9 ÷ 3) = 4
   B. (4 x 5) – (3 x 6) = 2
   C. (20 – 12) x (1 + 2) = 24
4. A. no B. yes
5. 21, 42, 63, 84
6. 10, 15, 21
7. Amelia has three quarters and one penny, and Anke has two dimes and two nickels.
8. 118, 119, 120, 121, 122

Page 166

1. no; She only planned for 23 of the day's 24 hours.
2. Answers will vary. Possible answers include $1\frac{1}{2}$ + 3 and $1\frac{1}{2}$ x 3, $1\frac{1}{3}$ + 4 and $1\frac{1}{3}$ x 4, $1\frac{1}{4}$ + 5 and $1\frac{1}{4}$ x 5, $1\frac{1}{6}$ + 7 and $1\frac{1}{6}$ x 7, $1\frac{1}{7}$ + 8 and $1\frac{1}{7}$ x 8, $1\frac{1}{8}$ + 9 and $1\frac{1}{8}$ x 9.
3. 201
4. Tia's birthday is February 23, Tia's mom's birthday is June 1, and Tia's dad's birthday is August 7.
5.
6. 51
7.
8. 1,220 feet

Page 191

1. D
2. H
3. E
4. F
5. A
6. O
7. S
8. Y
9. R
10. C
11. L
12. I
13. P
14. T

They were getting <u>READY FOR THEIR CLASS TRIP!</u>

Page 192

1. 4
2. 87°F
3. Amber
4. 35 minutes
5. $4.62
6. $2.25
7. butterfly
8. 60 days
9. 3 packs of 2 folders
10. 512

Bonus Box: Answers may vary.

Page 193

1. The Constitutional Convention began (may) 25, 1787.
2. (delegates) from 12 states worked on the Constitution for almost four months.
3. They finished on (september) 17, 1787.
4. On that day, 39 out of 55 delegates signed the United (states) Constitution.
5. (james) (madison) is called the "Father of the Constitution."
6. Madison earned that nickname because he was a powerful speaker and kept the best records of the debates.
7. (the) delegates often disagreed about the details of the (constitution)
8. The first delegate who signed the Constitution was (george) (washington)
9. (george) (washington) was one of only two men who signed the Constitution and later became a U.S. president.
10. (james) (madison) was the only other man who signed the Constitution and later became a U.S. president.
11. (at) age 81, (benjamin) (franklin) was the oldest person to sign the Constitution.
12. The delegates signed the (constitution) in geographical order, from north to south.
13. The delegate from (new) (hampshire) was followed by the delegates from (massachusetts), (connecticut), (new) (york), (new) (jersey), (pennsylvania), (delaware), (maryland), (virginia), (north) (carolina), (south) (carolina), and (georgia)
14. The youngest delegate to sign the (constitution) was 26 years old.
15. (the) original (constitution) is on display in the National Archives Building in (washington) DC.

Page 194

1. 185
2. 168
3. 352
4. 768
5. 639
6. 1,540
7. 2,716
8. 1,662
9. 2,454
10. 3,335
11. 1,482
12. 2,151
13. 1,302
14. 1,460

FRANCISCO VÁSQUEZ DE <u>CORONADO</u>

Page 195

1 14.86	6. 3.88	11. 4.38
2. 21.38	7. 22.55	12. 51.68
3. 29.19	8. 15.02	13. 17.26
4. 13.62	9. 12.73	14. 64.22
5. 16.40	10. 159.14	15. 61.02

Page 197

BRA**V**E	Bonus Box: On (6, 2) (5, 1)
SOLDI**E**RS,	Veterans (7, 7) (8, 9) (8, 6) (8, 9)
PRO**T**ECTORS	(5, 6) (0, 0) (5, 1) (1, 2) Day (3, 8)
S**E**RVING,	(0, 0) (3, 5), we (9, 3) (8, 9) honor
SAC**R**IFICING.	(6, 8) (6, 2) (5, 1) (6, 2) (5, 6) all
COUR**A**GEOUS,	(0, 0) (9, 7) (9, 7) United (5, 4)
HELPI**N**G,	(5, 1) (1, 4) (8, 6) (8, 9) (3, 8)
DI**S**CIPLINED.	States (1, 2) (8, 6) (0, 0) (8, 6)
LEA**D**ERS,	(8, 9) (1, 2) veterans (7, 7) (8, 9)
PE**A**CEKEEPERS.	(8, 6) (8, 9) (5, 6) (0, 0) (5, 1)
HISTOR**Y**.	(1, 2).

Page 198

1. tom, twist
2. Thanksgiving Day, tom, trimming, turkey
3. thank-ful
4. trimmed
5. something that goes along with a main dish
6. tom
7. berries, bake, boil
8. feast, family, fall, favorite
9. spoon, serve, serving
10. pie, piece

Bonus Box: Answers may vary.

Page 199

$\frac{2}{4}, \frac{1}{2}$ Arctic	$\frac{1}{3}, \frac{3}{9}$ Alaskan	$\frac{1}{5}, \frac{10}{20}$ They	$\frac{5}{20}, \frac{1}{4}$ Polar	$\frac{9}{24}, \frac{3}{8}$ They
$\frac{1}{3}, \frac{2}{6}$ some	$\frac{2}{5}, \frac{15}{30}$ all	$\frac{2}{3}, \frac{12}{18}$ do	$\frac{1}{3}, \frac{9}{18}$ can	$\frac{1}{2}, \frac{4}{8}$ jump
$\frac{10}{12}, \frac{5}{6}$ when	$\frac{2}{16}, \frac{1}{8}$ for	$\frac{1}{3}, \frac{2}{18}$ because	$\frac{6}{15}, \frac{2}{5}$ especially	$\frac{2}{6}, \frac{4}{8}$ a
$\frac{8}{12}, \frac{4}{8}$ house	$\frac{2}{3}, \frac{4}{6}$ hooves	$\frac{10}{16}, \frac{5}{8}$ won't	$\frac{4}{5}, \frac{12}{20}$ can't	$\frac{3}{4}, \frac{12}{16}$ can
$\frac{1}{2}, \frac{5}{10}$ lower	$\frac{9}{15}, \frac{3}{5}$ almost	$\frac{1}{2}, \frac{6}{8}$ jump	$\frac{7}{8}, \frac{14}{16}$ move	$\frac{1}{3}, \frac{5}{15}$ house

They all can because a house can't jump!

Bonus: Answers may vary.

Page 200

1. I'm reading a book titled the bitter cold by Ben N. Snow.
2. I read a funny article in skating world magazine.
3. The article was"figure eights"written by S. Kate Ting.
4. Do you have the book frostbite written by Mr. Art Tic?
5. Have you heard the song"logs in the fireplace"by R. U. Warm?
6. I memorized the poem"snowflakes"for class.
7. The book I'm reading now is it's tough being a snowman.
8. The first chapter is titled"I have a nose for carrots."
9. I checked out how to build a snow fort by Kenny Doit from the library.
10. I want to read the article"bundle up"by Mitt N. Boots.
11. I found the article in winter care magazine.
12. I've wanted to visit Alaska ever since I read Julie of the wolves.
13. The picture of us sledding is in today's edition of the icicle news.
14. At the Snowball Dance, the band played"wintertime waltz."
15. I think I'll read"skiing safely,"the article in the downhill fun magazine, again.

Bonus: Answers may vary.

Page 201

1. 18,104
2. 7,725
3. 13,795
4. 12,000
5. 11,172
6. 40,572
7. 11,894
8. 2,070
9. 41,410
10. 28,587
11. 41,130
12. 50,374
13. 10,272
14. 27,027
15. 8,820
16. 76,128
17. 38,248
18. 4,142
19. 8,667
20. 749 x 38 = 28,462

Bonus: Answers may vary

No; Sophie forgot to use a placeholder when she multiplied 896 by 70. 896 x 72 = 64,512

Page 202

1. 15
2. 12
3. 2
4. 48
5. 55
6. 63
7. 35
8. 2
9. 15
10. 64
11. 68
12. 48

Bonus: Order may vary. 1, 2, 9, 4, 12, 3, 8, 5, 6, 7, 10, 11

Page 203

		Correct	Incorrect
1.	As a leader of the Underground Railroad, Harriet Tubman made 19 trips into slave-holding states to help slaves escape to freedom.	Ⓒ	M
2.	Rosa Parks, a civil rights activist, refused to give up her bus seat in Montgomery, Alabama.	Ⓐ	T
3.	"I want to be the president of a bank like Maggie Walker was," Kayla said.	P	Ⓡ
4.	Duke Ellington and Louis Armstrong were leading jazz bandleaders.	A	Ⓣ
5.	In the 1920s, Langston Hughes was one of many famous African American writers.	Ⓔ	S
6.	Alice Walker, Maya Angelou, and Toni Morrison are famous authors now.	I	Ⓡ
7.	Thurgood Marshall, the first African American Supreme Court Justice, served from 1967 until 1991.	Ⓖ	B
8.	Nikki Giovanni is a professor at Virginia Tech in Blacksburg, Virginia, and she's written more than 30 children's and adult books.	T	Ⓦ
9.	Marcus explained, "Jackie Robinson was the first African American player in major league baseball."	Ⓞ	L
10.	On August 28, 1963, Dr. Martin Luther King Jr. gave one of his most famous speeches.	C	Ⓞ
11.	George Washington Carver created more than 475 products from peanuts, sweet potatoes, pecans, and wood shavings.	S	Ⓓ
12.	In 2001, Colin Powell became the first African American secretary of state.	Ⓢ	P
13.	Douglas Wilder, the first African American governor, was the mayor of Richmond, Virginia, from 2005 until 2009.	M	Ⓞ
14.	On August 10, 1983, Guion Stewart Bluford Jr. became the first African American to travel into space.	Ⓝ	A

CARTER G. WOODSON

Bonus: Answers will vary.

Page 204

A. 601
B. 119
C. 183
D. 375
E. 1,848
F. 143
G. 89
H. 731
I. 159
J. 35
K. 461
L. 253
M. 9,051
N. 6,207
O. 88
P. 2,784
Q. 2,128
R. 22
S. 3,191
T. 6,390
U. 63
V. 6,128
W. 2,487
X. 4,531
Y. 3,729

red roses

Bonus Box: 16; Explanation will vary.

Page 205

Weak Verbs **Strong Verbs**

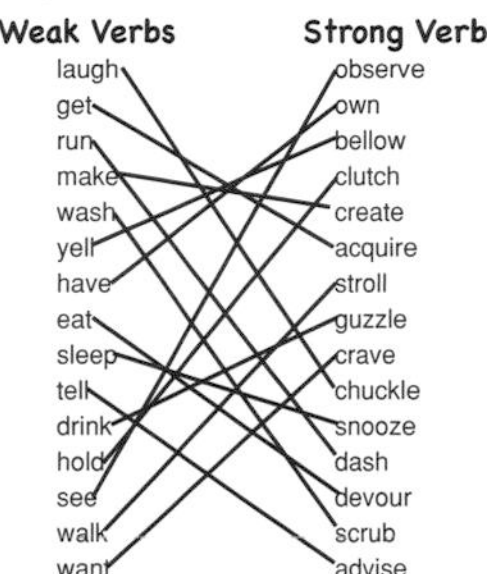

Verbs will vary.

Bonus: Answers will vary.

Page 206

1. $4.75
2. 14
3. $1,061.75
4. $25.00
5. $34.24
6. $1,917.44
7. $376.32
8. $64.25
9. $360.00
10. 183

He had a rash of bad luck!

Bonus: 300

Page 207

1. U
2. A
3. B
4. F
5. W
6. S
7. I
8. T
9. E
10. W
11. A
12. L
13. U
14. B
15. B

IT WAS A BEAUTIFUL "TAIL"!

Bonus: Diagrams will vary.

Page 208

1. Where should a cow go to get its medicine? It should go to the "farm-acy."
2. Why won't the skeleton ever try anything new? It doesn't have the guts.
3. Why did King Kong climb to the top of the Empire State Building? He was too big for the elevator.
4. Why did the chicken cross the playground? It wanted to get to the other "slide."
5. Why did Cinderella get kicked off the soccer team? She always runs away from the ball.
6. Why won't the lobsters share their desserts? They're "shell-fish"!
7. What is the cobra's favorite subject in school? It's "hissss-tory," of course!
8. What did one pencil say to the other pencil? "You're looking sharp."
9. What time was it when the elephant sat on my watch? It was time to get a new watch.
10. What is the sea monster's favorite lunch? It's fish and "ships"!
11. Why is the math book so unhappy? It has too many problems.
12. Why did the boy ask his father to come to school? He heard there was going to be a "Pop" quiz.
13. What's the best way to make straight As? Use a ruler.
14. What can you find in the middle of nowhere? You can find the letter *h*.
15. Why did the robber take a bath? He wanted to make a clean getaway.

Bonus: Answers will vary.

Page 209

1. well, remember
2. good, reasons
3. good, mom
4. well, pleased
5. good, turnout
6. well, knew
7. good, job
8. good, painter
9. well, ahead; good, work
10. good, Teresa
11. well, past
12. well, grow
13. well, held
14. good, place
15. well, cleaned

Bonus: Sentences will vary.

Page 210

1. $11\frac{5}{8}$
2. $5\frac{2}{5}$
3. $\frac{13}{14}$
4. $\frac{1}{9}$
5. $1\frac{1}{8}$
6. $6\frac{2}{15}$
7. $4\frac{5}{8}$
8. $\frac{7}{16}$
9. $1\frac{7}{12}$
10. 0
11. $4\frac{3}{11}$
12. $\frac{1}{5}$
13. $10\frac{11}{18}$
14. $3\frac{2}{3}$
15. $9\frac{6}{11}$
16. $2\frac{5}{12}$
17. $1\frac{7}{10}$
18. $2\frac{1}{10}$
19. $4\frac{11}{12}$
20. $1\frac{1}{7}$

IT'S GOING TO "PENCIL-VANIA"!

Bonus: No, the correct answer is $14\frac{5}{18}$.

Page 211

1. cotton candy; clouds
2. fields of diamonds; water
3. bathtub; pond
4. sunbathers; turtles
5. cannonballs; Adam, Marissa, Tyler
6. watery firework; splash
7. statue; Sierra
8. tadpoles; kids
9. submarine; Adam
10. carpet; bottom
11. nosy neighbor; catfish
12. swordfish; Sierra and Marissa
13. dolphins; Adam and Tyler
14. sloth; Adam
15. otter; Sierra
16. water balloons; clouds

Bonus: Sketches will vary.

Page 212

0.4 S	0.2 W	$\frac{2}{5}$ T	$\frac{12}{30}$ R
$\frac{5}{100}$ E	$\frac{1}{10}$ F	$\frac{1}{20}$ N	0.050 M
$\frac{35}{500}$ O	0.07 P	$\frac{14}{200}$ I	0.7 H
0.90 E	0.090 Y	$\frac{27}{30}$ D	$\frac{9}{10}$ K
$\frac{5}{10}$ I	$\frac{50}{100}$ N	0.05 R	$\frac{1}{2}$ T
$\frac{4}{5}$ A	0.8 S	0.08 O	$\frac{32}{40}$ W
$\frac{2}{8}$ H	0.025 A	$\frac{25}{100}$ Q	$\frac{1}{4}$ N
$\frac{9}{12}$ E	$\frac{15}{20}$ O	0.75 F	0.34 E
$\frac{1}{100}$ K	$\frac{1}{10}$ G	$\frac{6}{60}$ I	0.10 E
$\frac{2}{5}$ I	0.6 N	$\frac{6}{10}$ L	0.60 H
$\frac{4}{5}$ Y	0.8 Y	$\frac{8}{10}$ D	$\frac{3}{5}$ S
0.010 C	$\frac{5}{500}$ H	0.1 D	$\frac{1}{100}$ E
0.03 L	$\frac{3}{10}$ B	0.3 A	$\frac{12}{40}$ K
0.20 R	$\frac{1}{5}$ C	$\frac{4}{20}$ H	$\frac{2}{20}$ P
$\frac{12}{32}$ N	0.375 G	$\frac{6}{16}$ E	0.35 T

THE SWORDFISH—IT ALWAYS LOOKS SHARP!

Bonus: Answers will vary.

Page 213

"In the Works"

Answers may vary.

Mom: her, she

the team: it

plumbers: them, they

Bailey and I: we

Dad's: his

pipe: it

teammates': their

Kayla's: hers, her

Mr. McGregor: him, he

mine and yours: ours

you and me: us

Page 214

"Bumper Crop"

Students' apples and coordinate pairs will vary.

"Everybody Stretch!"

18,481 = 10,000 + 8,000 + 400 + 80 + 1

41,945 = 40,000 + 1,000 + 900 + 40 + 5

81,329 = 80,000 + 1,000 + 300 + 20 + 9

9,867 = 9,000 + 800 + 60 + 7

143,783 = 100,000 + 40,000 + 3,000 + 700 + 80 + 3

"A Sneaky Sis"

56,727 rounds to 57,000, Petey's sister

56,765 rounds to 56,800, Petey

49,276 rounds to 49,000, Petey

42,593 rounds to 40,000, Petey

13,488 rounds to 13,500, Mom

12,999 rounds to 13,000, Dad

Page 215

"Practice Makes Perfect"

Answers may vary.

Let's go, players! Get to the ball quickly every time. Guard our goal! Practice the blocking drills. We need good defense. Dribble, pass, and score. We need just one more win to get the record!

Sentences will vary.

"A Change in the Wind"

Order may vary.

laughs, laughing, laughed, laugher

dresses, dressing, dresser, dressed

plays, playing, player, played

misses, missed, missing

slows, slower, slowest, slowing, slowly, slowed

lights, lighting, lightest, lighter, lightly, lighted

Page 216
"Hittin' the Hay"
Order may vary.

perpendicular lines ✣
parallel lines
acute angle
right angle
obtuse angle
equilateral triangle △
isosceles triangle △
scalene triangle
right triangle
obtuse triangle
acute triangle
trapezoid
parallelogram
rhombus
square

Page 217
"Fantastic Field Trip!"
1. "I can't wait to go to the Air and Space Museum!" Joey said.
2. "Me either," Kara answered. "I've never been before."
3. "Which exhibit do you want to see first?" Joey asked.
4. "I want to see the astronauts' suits," Kara said.
5. "What about you?" Kara asked.
6. Joey said, "The 3-D show, of course."

Page 218
"Going, Going, Gone!"
1. 2,544
2. 4,002
3. 87,608
4. 13,108
5. 74,676
6. 18,444

"A Pile of Presents"
gift A = 15 ft.^{2}, gift B = 12 ft.^{2}, gift C = 9 ft.^{2}, gift D = 18 ft.^{2}, gift E = 70 ft.^{2}, gift F = 24 ft.^{2}, gift G = 32 ft.^{2}
1. gift D
2. gifts D and G
3. gift A
4. gifts A, B, C, D, and F
5. gifts B, D, and E

"Sweets for the Sweet"
1. \$0.45 per jumbo gumball
2. \$0.32 per gummy worm
3. \$0.27 per lemon drop
4. \$0.13 per jelly bean
5. \$0.62 per piece of taffy
6. \$0.18 per chocolate drop

Page 219
"Seeing Shadows"
1. their
2. allot
3. principal
4. quite
5. which

Sentences will vary but should include *witch, a lot, there, principle,* and *quiet.*

"Change of Heart"
dictate
donate
donator
donor
fragment
liberate
liberator
predict
predictor
telescope

Page 220
"Sweet Treats"

Stem	Leaf
6	1, 1, 1, 4, 7, 8
7	2, 3, 5, 9
8	1, 3, 9
9	0, 4, 6
10	0, 0

1. 61
2. 100
3. 77
4. 61

Page 222
"Ready to Wrap"
A. 14.5 cm
B. 13.6 cm
C. 8.3 cm
D. 6 cm
E. 12.5 cm

"A 'Buzz-y' Time of Year"
Biff Buzby: range = 22, median = 96, mode = 96, mean = 92
Bea Minor: range = 40, median = 95, mode = 100, mean = 90
Sophie Stinger: range = 4; median = 92.5; mode = 92, 95; mean = 93
Sophie Stinger has the highest mean test score.

Page 224
"On the Move"
39 = XXXIX
256 = CCLVI
74 = LXXIV
92 = XCII
1,996 = MCMXCVI
2,011 = MMXI
XXVII = 27
MMXI = 2,011
CL = 150
MCMXCIX = 1,999
XLVI = 46
XC = 90

"A Day at the Beach"
1. 50 minutes
2. 1 hour 25 minutes
3. 20 minutes
4. 1 hour 35 minutes
5. longer, 5 minutes
6. 2 hours

Page 239
A. Cassiopeia
B. Serpens
C. Ursa Major
D. Bootes
E. Libra
F. Corona Borealis
G. Perseus
H. Ursa Minor
I. Draco
J. Cepheus

Page 241
1. Answers may vary.
2. An alloy is a mixture of gold and one or more other metals.
3. $\frac{18}{24}$, or $\frac{3}{4}$
4. Gold reflects heat rays better than any other metal. It protects the astronaut from the sun's rays in space.
5. Answers may vary.
   Bonus Box: Answers will vary but may include the following:
   Gold film on office windows helps keep buildings cool because it reflects heat.
   Some dentists use gold for crowns because it is easy to shape and does not decay in the mouth.
   Artists can use thin sheets of gold, called gold leaf.
   Because it conducts electricity well, gold is used in radios, televisions, cell phones, calculators, global positioning systems, and personal digital assistants.

Page 242
Answers may vary.
1. *Rafflesia* flowers grow in the ~~deserts~~ of Southeast Asia. jungles
2. ~~Like~~ most plants, the *Rafflesia* has no chlorophyll. Unlike
3. A parasite gets its nutrients from ~~soil~~. its host.
4. The ~~bud~~ of the *Rafflesia* can be three feet wide. flower
5. The flower's ~~delightful~~ smell attracts flies and beetles. putrid
6. When a fly lands on a *Rafflesia* flower, it is looking for rotten ~~fruit~~. meat
7. Flies and beetles carry ~~seeds~~ from one *Rafflesia* flower to another. pollen
8. The *Rafflesia* plant depends on ~~tourists~~ for pollination. flies and beetles

Bonus Box: Answers may vary.

Page 243
1. B
2. A
3. B
4. C
5. A
6. The snout is the dolphin's beak or mouth.

7, 8. Answers may vary.

Bonus: Answers may vary.

Page 244

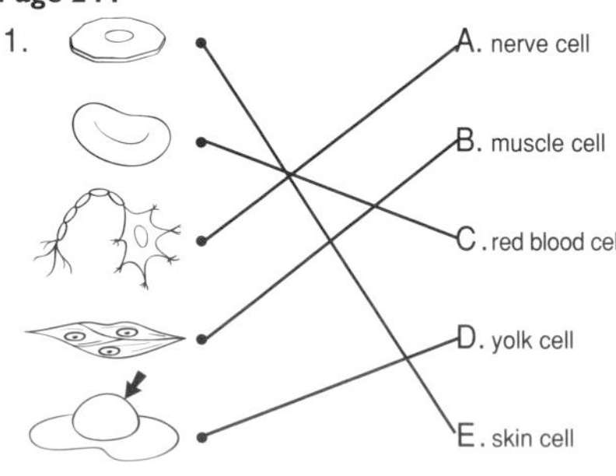
1.
A. nerve cell
B. muscle cell
C. red blood cell
D. yolk cell
E. skin cell

2–6. Answers will vary.

Page 258
1. John Paul Jones
2. Crispus Attucks
3. Nathanael Greene
4. Abigail Adams
5. Patrick Henry
6. Phillis Wheatley
7. Benjamin Franklin
8. Paul Revere
9. Nathan Hale
10. George Washington
11. Thomas Jefferson
12. Margaret Corbin
13. Friedrich von Steuben
14. John Adams
15. Mary "Molly Pitcher" Hays
16. Marquis de Lafayette

Page 261
1. 1894
2. to inform
3. to honor working people
4. Laws to protect children were not strongly enforced.
5. to show that the workers made a sacrifice
6. Summaries will vary.

Page 262
Rocky Mountains
largest mountain system in North America
3,000 miles long
stretch from the Yukon of Canada through New Mexico
began forming around 170 million years ago
mine gold, lead, silver, copper, zinc, coal, natural gas, and uranium
farm cattle and sheep
highest peak, Mount Elbert, 14,433 feet

Both
largest mountain systems in North America
formed hundreds of million years ago
rich in mineral resources
farming

Appalachian Mountains
second largest mountain system in North America
1,500 miles long
from Quebec, Canada, to Alabama
oldest mountain system in America
began forming about 435 million years ago
mine coal
farm poultry, apples, dairy foods, hay, potatoes, and wheat
highest peak, Mount Mitchell; 6,684 feet

Bonus Box: Paragraphs may vary.

Page 263
Answers for 1, 5, and 6 may vary.
2. town crier, farmer, fisherman, whaler, logger, shipbuilder, miner, ironworker, blacksmith
3. The wood in the colonies was good for building ships. There was a shortage of good shipbuilding wood in England.
4. The waters were rich with fish and whales.

Page 264

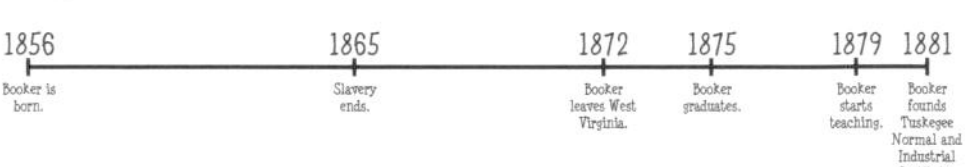
1856
Booker is born.
1865
Slavery ends.
1872
Booker leaves West Virginia.
1875
Booker graduates.
1879
Booker starts teaching.
1881
Booker founds Tuskegee Normal and Industrial Institute.

Answers for 1 and 3–5 will vary.

2. The author shows Booker T. Washington's early life and why he was determined to learn to read and later become an educator.

Bonus: Answers will vary.

Page 265
1. reasonable; Since Lewis and Clark hoped Sacagawea would help them communicate with the Shoshone, it's reasonable to assume they knew of her Shoshone heritage.
2. not reasonable; Lewis and Clark needed interpreters because they could not speak Native American languages.
3. reasonable; Lewis and Clark did not leave camp until April. It's reasonable to assume they were not exploring during the winter.
4. not reasonable; Sacagawea and her husband were at the winter camp for at least four months.
5. not reasonable; There could not have been six or more people in each canoe because there were eight canoes and only 33 people in the explorers' party.
6. reasonable; The explorers set out in canoes in April. They set out on foot in June, once they had reached the Great Falls, which was about two months later.

Bonus: Answers will vary.

Page 266
1. July 4, 1777
2. 1870
3. 234 years as of 2011
4. Answers will vary.
5. Many cities hold parades, concerts, speeches, and—best of all—fireworks displays.
6. Summaries will vary.

Bonus:

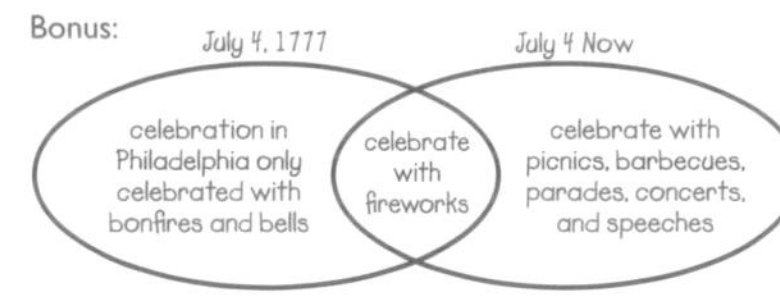
July 4, 1777
July 4 Now
celebration in Philadelphia only celebrated with bonfires and bells
celebrate with fireworks
celebrate with picnics, barbecues, parades, concerts, and speeches

INDEX

ISBN 978-161276141-1